beyond
integrity

A Judeo-Christian Approach to Business Ethics

beyond
integrity

third edition

Scott B. Rae and Kenman L. Wong

ZONDERVAN®

We want to hear from you. Please send your comments about this book to us in care of zreview@zondervan.com. Thank you.

ZONDERVAN

Beyond Integrity
Copyright © 1996, 2004, 2012 by Scott B. Rae and Kenman L. Wong

This title is also available as a Zondervan ebook.
Visit www.zondervan.com/ebooks.

Requests for information should be addressed to:

Zondervan, *Grand Rapids, Michigan 49530*

Library of Congress Cataloging-in-Publication Data

Beyond integrity : a Judeo-Christian approach to business ethics / [edited by] Scott B. Rae and
    Kenman L. Wong. — 3rd ed.
        p. cm.
    Includes bibliographical references and index.
    ISBN 978-0-310-29110-7 (hardcover)
    1. Business ethics. 2. Business — Religious aspects — Christianity. 3. Business — Religious
aspects — Judaism. I. Rae, Scott B. II. Wong, Kenman L., 1964 -
    HF5387.B49 2011
    174'.4 — dc23   2011030582

Cover design: Lucas Art and Design
Cover photos: Masterfile
Interior design: Matthew Van Zomeren

Printed in the United States of America

17 18 19 20 /DCI/ 22 21 20 19 18 17 16 15 14 13 12 11 10 9 8 7

Contents in Brief

Contents

Acknowledgments

We are very pleased to see the publication of the third edition of this book. When we began partnering on the first (released in 1996), we had little expectation that there would be demand for a second, much less a third edition. Similar to the first two efforts, there are many people who played important supportive roles. First, we would like to thank Katya Covrett and Jim Ruark at Zondervan for their fine editorial guidance, and Gail Neal for her patience and organization in handling many of the administrative details related to securing permission to reprint the articles included in the book. We also appreciate the efforts made by faculty members at other institutions who have adopted the book for classroom use and have taken time to reach out and share their insights about improving its contents.

We would also like to thank our colleagues (Scott's at Talbot School of Theology and Kenman's at Seattle Pacific University's School of Business & Economics) and friends in the business community. They have engaged us in many rich conversations about the intersections of business, economics, theology, and ethics and have often directed us to good resources. Several of them (Al Erisman, Jeff Van Duzer, Bill West, and Jim Harrington) also provided thoughtful feedback on an earlier edition of the book. We would like to acknowledge as well the contributions of many former students who have served (sometimes unwittingly) as "test audiences" for some of book's materials. A few even contributed case studies and/or ideas for them. Most of all, we want to express our deep gratitude to our families, who often have to tolerate (with grace) our physical, but more often mental absences when we are locked away in our studies working on writing projects.

Introduction

This is the third edition of a book that explores moral issues in business through the lens of Christian values. In the past decade, many headlines have alerted the business community and general public about the need for renewed efforts to connect business with deeper convictions about right and wrong and with a more compelling purpose than just "making money." While many people who got into deep trouble in recent years were senior executives, the study of ethics is critically important for people involved at all levels of business and for students about to enter the workforce.

A few years ago, the university at which I (Kenman) serve as a professor invited a successful graduate from a decade prior to speak at a dessert held to welcome newly accepted student majors into our department. Several speakers (all successful alumni) in the past at this annual event basically extolled the virtues of hard work and encouraged students to make the most of their current opportunities to learn and "network" with others. Because I had the sense that I had heard this all before, and because I had just hurried from helping coach my son's baseball team to make the event, I was listening with far less than rapt attention (my apologies to several former students). Suddenly I was jarred awake at the mention of my name.

The speaker confessed to not paying much attention when he was a student in the business ethics course I taught during his senior year. Setting my deflated ego aside for the moment, I listened as he described how he thought the need to study ethics was for other people. He shared how he figured he was a good person, had a deep commitment to his faith, and assumed much of what was covered in class would only apply much later in his career (if he reached the senior executive level). He then went on to describe his career path: auditor for a prestigious Big 4 accounting firm upon graduation and then a shift into mortgage banking a few years later. After joking that no one in the audience should follow him into the next industry he was going to enter (accounting and then mortgage banking have been under the spotlight for playing pivotal roles in triggering separate economic near-meltdowns during the past decade), he described what had surprised him most. The number of ethical questions he had to face right away, their level of complexity, and pressure to make choices he would not be proud of were things he said he was profoundly unprepared to face.

Now, he did happen to have the misfortune of entering fields that had lapses during the exact periods in which he worked in them, but we believe his story is worth sharing because of its broader applicability. Although most students may not face something as dramatic as accounting fraud or the subprime mortgage scandal upon graduation, ethical challenges are present in every profession, including business, health care, education, engineering, social work, law, and other areas, and at every level within them. According to the 2009 National Business Ethics Survey conducted by the Ethics Resources Center, just about half (49 percent) of employees surveyed reported witnessing unethical activity at work.[1]

Simply having "integrity," though helpful, is often insufficient for finding and enacting effective resolutions to ethical problems in the workplace. Our very sense of right and wrong is also often socially influenced by our peers and leaders. We may also be faced with competing obligations and pressures; and others with whom we work and must decide things may have different ideas about what they see as the correct course of action. Thus, if we simply count on our perceptions (which themselves may or may not be accurate, since we also tend to make errors, such as overrating ourselves — "self-serving bias") to navigate our way, we may quickly find ourselves on the wrong side of a decision.

This is where the formal study of ethics as applied to the professions can make an important contribution. Business ethics is both an academic discipline (a growing one at that) and an area of practice. It is a field that studies, develops, and applies standards of right and wrong to the workplace. Business ethics is concerned with avoiding wrongdoing (malevolence), but increasingly also with doing right (benevolence). As a discipline, it asks both critical ("What's *wrong* with a value or decision?") and constructive ("How can something be done in a way that honors good values?") questions and attempts to offer practical guidance based on the answers.

The field is a "normative" one that seeks to develop appropriate standards for what we "ought" to value and do, but it also has a strong descriptive dimension in trying to explain "why" we do things, such as understanding the key factors that "encourage" people to make ethical (and unethical) choices. In addition to focusing on individuals and who they are, how they make decisions, and how they should act, business ethics is also very much concerned with the dynamics, purposes, and values (and practices) imbedded in organizations and economic systems.

To be certain, the discipline is limited in what it can accomplish. Simply studying business ethics cannot make someone ethically "bulletproof" or guarantee perfect resolution to complex issues. However, undertaking the formal study of business ethics can help you make more intentional, reflec-

[1] See 2009 Ethics Resource Center, National Business Ethics Survey, http://www.ethics.org/nbes/. This figure (49 percent) is actually a slight improvement over the 2007 figure, which was 56 percent. A somewhat surprising finding of this survey is that a fairly low number of employees (only 8 percent; down from 10 percent in 2007) perceived pressure to commit an ethics violation. We would caution, however, that "perception" is highly dependent on awareness and sensitivity to what may be unethical or not. According to a Hudson survey, about one-third of employees say they have witnessed "unethical activity" at work. (http://www.marketwatch.com/story/one-third-of-us-workers-witness-unethical-behavior). According to an LRN survey, the figure is 25 percent (in the past six months); see http://www.lrn.com/lrn-ethics-study-ethics-impact-on-employee-engagement.html.

tive, and informed ethical decisions. Additionally, your awareness of the ethical implications of your actions and the influences exercised by your social environment (moral sensitivity), ability to evaluate choices through a refined framework (take a moral point of view), and ability to conceive of solutions that reflect appropriate and defensible values (moral imagination) can be improved.

Christian Ethics and Business

The underlying premise of this book is that ethics derived from Christian theology has much to contribute to improved individual decision making and to changing the climate of organizations and the systems and structures of business. As the field of business ethics has developed, however, it has primarily done so on a secular (devoid of religion) basis. Many good courses are offered, studies undertaken, and books written that rely on human reason alone (i.e., philosophy and social-scientific research methods), so what contribution might a book that takes a Judeo-Christian approach make?

At a minimum, the Christian tradition can be seen as a source of time- and circumstance-tested "Wisdom Literature," providing people from many backgrounds with meaning, inspiration, and moral guidance for thousands of years. For practicing Christians, the "worldview" or "story"/"narrative" of their faith also offers a "way of seeing," a lens from which to interpret, critique, and construct values and actions. Ethics that emanate from a divine source may also enhance moral commitment, contribute to a deeper sense of moral identity, and address the "moral motivation" (why be good?) question in a more compelling fashion. Moreover, faith traditions offer a vocabulary and, at their best, a supportive context in which "wrestling" with questions of right and wrong can be undertaken.

It is important to recognize, of course, that any attempt at deriving ethics from a transcendent/divine source must be made with great humility. Many grave errors have been made and harm done in the name of having a clear and certain mandate from "God." Christians also are hardly of one voice in their answers to moral questions, largely because the primary book (the Bible) that helps shape their moral identity has to be interpreted. This is a task that is complicated because of the distance between the context and culture in which it was written and the experiences, assumptions, and traditions of today's readers.

Christian theology also contributes some distinctive content to the development of norms (e.g., loving our enemies comes to mind). However, many Christian ethical standards resonate with those derived from other faith traditions and/or from "reason."[2] For some observers, this fact provides

[2] One debate within Christian theology/ethics is over the distinctiveness of Christian ethics. Different subtraditions hold various perspectives on this question. Some hold to natural law, so reason is all that is needed to discern divine law. Others would point to the fallen nature of reason and the need for Scripture.

evidence that "all religions are really the same." From a Christian perspective, however, we would expect to find similarities. Whether called "Christian" or not, the same God is the creator of all, and his image is at least partially reflected therein. So, whether a matter of "natural law" or "common grace," it is no accident that we find some shared ethical standards across religions, cultures, and historical time periods (though of course there are differences too).[3]

Our aim is to provide a helpful text for two primary audiences: (1) people who identify themselves as followers of Christ (from many denominations/subtraditions) and who seek guidance for how to live and act from their faith tradition, and (2) those of different faiths (including those who have faith that business can change for the better) who are interested in how ethics derived from one of the major traditions might critically and constructively engage with one of the most powerful existing cultural institutions and with the day-to-day work of many people around the globe.

Studying *Christian* ethics can strike some as (or even turn into) an exercise in judging others or pointing out how they don't measure up. We want to be clear that we are not claiming that Christians are more ethical than people from other (or no) faith traditions. If the New Testament gospel accounts are to be taken seriously, Jesus came to set us all on equal ground, largely by humbling the religiously proud. And the fact that some high-profile businesspeople who by many accounts were faithful church members (executives from Enron and WorldCom come to mind) have found themselves in unfortunate circumstances in recent years should remind us that we all are capable of wrongdoing. The Christian faith is not primarily about morals, though a response to grace would logically lead to efforts at living a life that is pleasing to God. Nor, worse yet, is the Christian faith about "moralizing," as in using ethical standards to point out flaws in others and make ourselves feel as if we are better than them.

And as you will see in later sections of this book, ethics derived from the Christian tradition most often do not arrive in the form of easy answers or formulas to solve all the problems we may encounter. In fact, the dearth of straightforward commands and/or casuistic rules ("if, then" type guidance) given the volume of the Bible is notable.[4] As N. T. Wright observes, those looking to the Bible are going to find few "thou shalts" and more guidance in the form of "once upon a time."[5] Although some direct commands can be found, the Bible mainly provides a larger narrative, many stories and principles among other forms of guidance (i.e., paradigms) that work to provide us with both a moral orientation and a framework or "fence posts." Ethical decision making (covered in more depth in chapter 1), must be undertaken through multiple forms of guidance: Looking "through" the Bible (as a lens

[3] John P. Fraedrich, "Philosophy Type Interaction in the Ethical Decision-Making Process of Retailers" (Ph.D. diss., Texas A&M University, College Station, Tex., 1988).

[4] See Dennis Hollinger, *Choosing the Good: Christian Ethics in a Complex World* (Grand Rapids: Baker Academic, 2002).

[5] N. T. Wright, "How Can the Bible be Authoritative?" *Vox Evangelica* 21 (1991): 7–32.

or way of seeing), and appropriately looking "to" it (for more specific guidance), in conjunction with reason (to understand the issues, gather facts, and interpret the Bible, etc.) and prayerful discernment within a faithful listening community (with different subtraditions differing in their weighting of one over the other). It is important to remember that even faithfully and diligently using these forms of guidance may still leave us with less than perfect or ideal choices. In a broken world, we are sometimes faced with making wise (versus perfect) decisions (in part, the subject of chapter 2).

If the Bible is inspired, one might wonder if God couldn't have made things easier for us by providing us with simple-to-use commands (a so-called "user's manual") for every life decision. He could have, we suppose, but in his infinite wisdom and love, he seems to have chosen not to do so. Without the need to wrestle with complexity and uncertainty, we would remain as children and would never develop into the people that a vision of a loving God would suggest. And if we had a complete manual, we would have much less need to rely on God or others (think of how often user manuals collect dust). Besides, given how clever we are at finding loopholes, can you imagine how big the rule book would need to be or how frequently it would need to be rewritten?

The Current Climate of Business

As noted earlier, business takes place in a very real social context, so an important issue that needs to be addressed is about the possibility of actual change that can take place. Can living according to Christian ethics really work to improve business, or is this just false hope given how bad things seem to be? This question seems especially pertinent given how many headlining scandals there have been during the past several decades. Much of what has occurred actually seems to be pulling the moral climate of business in opposite directions. Many of these unfortunate events make the need for better ethics much more apparent and, quite unintentionally, seem to serve to welcome attempts to establish them. However, other developments make the study and actual practice of sound behavior in business much more complex.

When we first started teaching university students and addressing business audiences on ethics-related topics, we spent a lot of time trying to convince people why ethics was important to their own well-being, their careers, and their organizations, and to the health of the broader economy. Due to recent events, few businesspeople (and students) now have to be convinced about the need for better ethics in business. Many people are out of work and businesses have been closed in what has been dubbed "The Great Recession."

Due in part to irrational exuberance of a housing bubble pumped up by unscrupulous dealing by many players within the financial system and perhaps lax government oversight influenced by corporate lobbying, many people have been hurt. Just a few years earlier, financial markets (and many individual retirement and investment accounts) lost much ground as a direct result of misleading statements by analysts employed by highly respected investment firms, and by corporate bankruptcies (such as Enron and World-Com) precipitated by fraudulent accounting statements.

These events, and ensuing media images of executives being led away in handcuffs, have helped teach hard but important lessons, that a solid moral foundation is necessary to our well-being, both as individuals and as a broader community with strong interconnections. As a result, the climate of business seems to be demanding once again talk and action with respect to moral matters.

However, countervailing forces such as short-term expectations and global competition have also been at work to make the ability to actually practice good values and behavior in the marketplace more difficult. These forces seem to make the climate of business more hostile to ethical change.

Investor fixation on quarterly financial results coupled with technology and its ensuing culture of speed can work to push corporate decision makers into short-term thinking. As some of the recent scandals reveal, the pressure can be overwhelming, even for executives long known for their character and devotion to faith. Rather than long-term value, corporate leaders find they have to appease investors by focusing on quarterly returns, which provide tempting incentives to cut a wide variety of ethical corners along the way in order to "make the numbers." CEOs who dare to go against the grain and take a longer term approach may find their positions in jeopardy.

Global competition has also rapidly increased, seemingly reducing the margin to maneuver and pursue ethical considerations. Domestic companies must not only compete with each other to achieve quarterly benchmarks, but with firms based in other parts of the globe, many of which may be provided with competitive advantages as a result of operating under different cultural and legal expectations on issues such as employee pay, safety, and environmental stewardship. Firms attempting to uphold higher standards than their competitors potentially face higher costs, lower profits, and the threat of "punishment" by the short-term orientation of financial markets.

These forces lead to reasonable questions about whether ethics will simply be cast aside as another management fad or buzzword if and when better economic times come along and whether the current level of attention being paid to ethics by business leaders is simply lip service to trick the public into believing their organizations genuinely care.

The fate of one company and its leader, who has often and rightfully been upheld as an exemplary model of good corporate ethical leadership, reflects these challenges and tensions. The company is Malden Mills, makers of Polartec, a popular fleece material used in outerwear. Two weeks before Christmas in 1995, the people of the town of Methuen, Massachusetts, watched a devastating fire destroy three out of four of the company's factories, the core of one of the last remaining large-scale textile mills in the region and the town's key employment and economic lifeline. The fire injured more than two dozen people, left fourteen hundred workers unemployed, and confirmed fears that the town would be destroyed economically — the plight suffered by many New England towns as other mills shut down in search of more cost-efficient labor sources overseas.

In a stunning surprise, the company's majority owner, Aaron Feuerstein (then seventy years old), who could have simply retired on the insurance money, immediately announced plans to rebuild with the goal of having his workers back in the mill within a few months. Furthermore, Feuerstein gave every employee a small Christmas bonus and a coupon for food at a local supermarket. Amid cheers from his employees, he then announced that for at least the next thirty days, he would pay every worker's salary in full, and that he had paid for their health insurance for the next ninety days. Citing his faith (Jewish) and his belief that difficult circumstances provide the real test of moral convictions, Feuerstein stated that collecting the insurance money and retiring was never a thought that crossed his mind. "My commitment is to Massachusetts, and New England. It's where I live, where I play, where I worship. Malden Mills will rebuild right here," he said at the time.[6]

After the announcement, Feuerstein followed through on his promises, receiving national attention for his actions. In the immediate years after rebuilding, the company experienced increased employee loyalty and production in the form of lower turnover and error rates. The Malden Mills story became one that was often shared as an example of extraordinary business citizenship and how it "pays" to prioritize people over profits.

A few years later, however, the story took an unfortunate and complex turn. Due in part to competitive forces and the cost of rebuilding and paying wages to idle workers, the company became mired in debt and filed for Chapter 11 bankruptcy in late 2001. The company eventually emerged from bankruptcy, however, Mr. Feuerstein's ownership of the company was significantly reduced, with banks and other creditors (who may not share Feuerstein's sense of social responsibility) assuming a controlling interest in the company. The company has also turned to more overseas production (in Shanghai, China) to remain competitive.

To be certain, the message here is not that nice guys finish last or that

[6] David Lamb, "Massachusetts Mill Town Gets Angel for Christmas," *Los Angeles Times*, December 19, 1995, A24.

it is impossible to exercise leadership that pursues goals other than profits. However, this story does put us on appropriate notice that ethics applied to competitive markets are more complex than simple, often-used platitudes, such as "Do the right thing" or "It all comes down to character" portray. Living out Christian convictions and improving the climate of business is a challenging and multidimensional task, and one that requires attentiveness to ethical norms and economic realities.[7]

This should come as no surprise to those familiar with the Christian faith as it does account for the fallen realities of human nature and the culture at large, providing a sense of realism in terms of what can be achieved. Yet Christian ethics are also about ideals, with a hopefulness based on faith that our work here on earth has ultimate significance (as partners or regents in the tasks of renewal and restoration), and that even the imperfect aspects of the world we live in will one day be redeemed.

Third Edition

While many readings, cases, and end-of-chapter editor's commentaries have been updated, much as in the first two editions, this book approaches business ethics in a manner that is grounded in Christian theology and takes realistic account of the complexity and changing nature of the practice of business. The reading selections include a wide variety of perspectives, some explicitly Christian and some that merely but clearly reflect Christian values. Other readings present viewpoints that are inimical to the Christian worldview but are included because they represent influential views worth engaging. Our goals are to make you think rigorously, to foster more dialogue with the world around you, and to instill values that are based soundly on the Christian faith.

[7] Another recent example involves Edun, a clothing company started by Paul (aka Bono) and Ali Hewsen. The company started as a "social venture" type project to bring jobs and economic development to poor areas in Africa. In 2010 the company announced it would be moving some of its operations to China.

PART ONE

FOUNDATIONS FOR CHRISTIAN ETHICS IN BUSINESS

ONE

Ethical Decision Making

Shelving hard decisions is the least ethical course.
Sir George Adrian Cadbury, CEO of Cadbury-Schweppes

Introduction

You work in sales for a major software manufacturer and are paid a base salary, commissions on all sales, and a quarterly bonus if you exceed the quota that management sets for you each quarter. Though your bosses view the quotas as demanding, it is expected that each salesperson will exceed his or her standard periodically and qualify for a bonus. If someone goes for some time without doing so, the person is considered to have done simply the minimum to keep his or her job. You are feeling some pressure to exceed your quota since everyone on your team has done so recently. They are experiencing the effects of the economy picking up after a harsh recession, and sales are starting to be encouraging again.

This particular quarter you have a good chance to surpass your expected sales figures and collect your first quarterly bonus in more than a year. You could really use the bonus to finish paying off some medical bills that your company's insurance plan did not fully cover. You are about to close a sizable sale of software to a large company, but it's beginning to look as if you won't wrap up the sale until after the close of the current quarter. You are discussing this unfortunate timing with one of your team members, and he suggests that you simply back-date the sales order to a date in the current quarter. Your colleague says that it's something that most salespersons have done at some point and that the chances of it being detected by upper management are quite low. As you consider this option, you realize that you are falsifying sales records and reaping a bonus you are not technically entitled to, but you have been assured by the customer that the sale will close in the first few days of the new quarter. Needless to say, the bonus will be very helpful to your family budget.

You are facing a moral issue that raises important questions about ethical decision making. The conclusion you reach about backdating the sales order is, of course, a key element of your moral deliberations. But equally important is the question of *how you reach your decision*. What are the elements that go into making a moral choice? What questions do you need to ask in order to resolve your dilemma? Rather than simply "trusting your gut," which is the uncritical process used by many businesspeople, we would encourage you to develop more thoughtful ways of thinking about moral issues.

The articles in this chapter will introduce you to important aspects of moral decision making and to ways of determining right and wrong in general. In the introductory article, business ethics professor David Gill helps us understand how complex ethical decision making can be in the workplace, and he rightly rejects simplistic and overly black-and-white views of ethical dilemmas. His article "Upgrading the Decision-Making Model for Business" will help you recognize when you are facing an ethical issue and give you a model for working through the dilemma. He is careful not to reduce ethics to decisions and dilemmas, and he rightly points out how important character and virtue are to your moral life in the workplace. He urges you to think beyond "damage control"—a reactive way of handling dilemmas.[1] Instead, he argues for a more proactive approach that connects ethics with the mission and core values of the organization. We will think more about this connection in chapter 11.

Bernard Adeney, in his article "The Bible and Culture in Ethics," insightfully teaches how to understand the use of the Bible in ethical decision making, particularly in cross-cultural contexts. He helps readers understand the cultural setting of the Bible and gives some sound advice for interpreting the Bible in its cultural context (Adeney rightly claims that some biblical mandates simply don't make much sense apart from the original setting for the command) and applying it properly to a very different culture today. As we'll see in chapter 5, economic life in biblical times (largely subsistence agriculture or a trade) was very different from the modern, information-age economy in today's developed world. He gives numerous concrete examples to help you understand and apply the Bible to economic life today. He emphasizes that the Bible is not a textbook on ethics, but that its moral wisdom is intertwined with the narrative story of God's redemption of the world. However, it does have moral rules (the Ten Commandments) and general principles that we can deduce from the narrative and wisdom material.

Professor Donald Schmeltekopf, in his article "The Moral Context of Business," provides some foundational material in which he argues that ethical issues are a necessary component of doing business well—this is because the proper functioning of business presumes a moral context. It presumes a

[1] For more discussion on this point of damage control in ethical decision making, see David Gill, "Business Ethics 2.0: Beyond Damage Control," *Cardus Comment* (May 14, 2010), http://www.cardus.ca/comment/article/1992/ (accessed January 17, 2011).

set of virtues that are both necessary and nurtured by a person's participation in business. He rightly criticizes the lack of preparation for ethical decision making in business schools and questions whether the secular academy has the intellectual resources to ground the virtues and values necessary for business to flourish.[2] He looks to the Christian worldview and the philosophical (Aristotelian) tradition of virtue to provide the framework for understanding business ethics but also for understanding the purpose and mission for business in general. He anticipates the articles by Dallas Willard ("The Business of Business") and Robert Sirico ("The Entrepreneurial Vocation") in the next chapters by affirming the intrinsic goodness of business as a part of the stewardship with which God has entrusted human beings.

An Introduction to Ethical Reasoning

In the workplace, people make moral decisions in a variety of ways. Some simply follow the law, insisting that "if it's legal, it's moral." Others simply follow their company's policies and assume that as long as they adhere to them, they are doing everything they need to do morally. Others follow their intuition, or "trust their gut." Or they may utilize a more structured method of moral reasoning, whether they are aware of that structure or not. That is, they employ one or more different formal modes of moral reasoning at different times as they wrestle with their moral obligation in any specific instance. Some people may actually move between different types of moral reasoning and not settle on any one in particular.

Take, for example, the following scenario:

Imagine that you are the CEO of a company that is launching into a new market, expanding your service to parts of Asia that your company has not previously served. You and your staff have prepared a proposal for a project that could amount to a $50 million contract over the next five years for your firm. The contract is to provide your services to a government agency in Southeast Asia. You are now flying to meet with government officials to bid on the deal. When you arrive to meet with the officials, you are told that you must submit a "pledge" to certain officials, in cash, in order to remain competitive in the bidding. When you ask if other bidders are also required to submit such pledges, you are told that that is not your concern. You must submit the money if you are to have any chance of securing the contract. You quickly realize that you have been asked to bribe the officials under the table in order to be considered for the contract. Your company has done this in the past, before you became CEO. Your principles tell you that this is wrong, but there are many other considerations, such as the jobs that will be created, as well as those that will be saved by getting this contract; the cultural

[2] For a more pointed discussion of this important point, see Charles Colson, "Why Harvard Can't Teach Ethics," speech given at Harvard Business School, April 4, 1991, available at BreakPoint, "The Problem of Ethics: Speech at Harvard Business School," http://www.breakpoint.org/features-columns/articles/entry/12/9649 (accessed January 17, 2011).

context in which bribery is a routine practice; and the fact that your interests would be clearly served by securing the contract. You agree to pay the bribe and submit your bid accordingly. On the flight home, you are troubled that you may not have done the right thing. After all, not only is your career in jeopardy if you fail to win the contract, but hundreds of jobs are also at stake for your company. Upon returning home, you are still bothered as you await word about the contract, so you bring the situation up for discussion at the next local chamber of commerce meeting. Many of your closest friends and associates are among the participants. They, however, seem only to add to your confusion, because each one approaches moral problems with a radically different methodology. The participants (with their respective approaches in parentheses) respond to you in the following ways:

Participant 1:
President of a Community Business (Ethical Egoist)

Why is this a moral discussion at all? I would have no problem doing anything that you have just stated. You see, for me it all boils down to the fact that I have a business to run, and the only thing that matters is if I can make a profit provided I stay within the bounds of the law. In fact, the only business ethic worth its weight is "Do unto others before they do unto you." There is no doubt that my competitors would also do this. After all, if my own job is dependent on this contract, what's my family going to do? Starve, so that I can feel good about myself? Forget it! My mortgage is not paid with someone else's moral principles. Aside from all of this, isn't capitalism based on self-interest anyway? You guys are so naïve. I mean, it's a rough and tumble world; if I don't look out for my needs, who will? A book that you all should read is *Looking Out for Number One*. It says it all!

Participant 2:
Head of the Local Chamber of Commerce (Utilitarian)

Wow, what a scenario! I admit, the prospect of bribing officials would bother me a bit. But if I were you, I think I could justify my actions based on the good that it will do for my employees and for the local community. Just think, without this contract, hundreds of jobs are at stake. That could devastate our local economy. But if we were to secure the deal, we could create jobs, expand our tax base, and go forward with those badly needed community improvement projects. I know that the competing company would be hurt, but their business just doesn't depend on government contracts to the degree that yours does. You see, I believe that it is not necessarily principles that determine right and wrong, but the consequences produced by the actions in question. If a particular course of action or decision produces the best set of consequences, then it seems to me that it should be allowed. To put it another way, the action that produces the greatest balance of benefits over harms is the one that is the most moral. So in this case, what is important to determine is whether offering the bribes would produce the greatest good for the greatest number of people. As I just pointed out, this could produce a lot of good for the people in your company. Now, there may be situations in which a similar action may produce, on balance, more negative than positive consequences. In those cases, it should not be allowed. We should be careful of setting hard and fast rules that don't take the consequences into account.

Participant 3:
President of the Area Christian Business Women's Chapter (Deontologist, or Principle-Based Ethics)

Hey, wait a minute! Doesn't this simply come down to bribery, which is designed to create an unlevel playing field for competition? This is clearly wrong. My moral authority, the Bible and common Western morality, is clearly opposed to this. Thus, it doesn't matter to me how many people would lose their jobs or what our community would gain from the contract. It equally doesn't matter if I might lose my job! Bribery is wrong, period! If torn between loyalty to my employer and loyalty to God, there's no question as to whom I will honor first. Likewise, you should instead trust that God will provide if you honor his principles first.

Participant 4:
Local Television Talk Show Host (Emotivist)

I hate to throw a monkey wrench into this whole discussion, but in my view, all of the participants so far are trying to do the impossible. Each person so far has attempted to make some kind of determination of what is right or wrong in this case. I don't think that's possible. They are really using the language of right and wrong to mask their own personal preferences. What I mean is that anytime a person says that something is right or wrong, all they are saying and can say about it is that they either like or dislike the action or position under consideration. We should be honest and admit that we're only talking about our preferences and using moral language to give greater persuasive power to our argument. In this specific case, you should ask yourself how you feel about it. Feelings are more important than any reasoning you could do. In my own view, my feelings would not be bothered by any of this, so I think I'm okay.

Participant 5:
Anthropology Professor (Relativist)

I clearly reject what my friend from the Christian Business Women's Fellowship says, because the Bible is not my moral authority! Now, I'm not prepared to say that there is no such thing as genuine right and wrong, but I do think that there is no universal, absolute standard of right and wrong. What is moral depends on the situation, and on what the cultural consensus of right and wrong is at that time. In this case, if the culture has reached a consensus that it should be allowed, then I see no reason why it should not be allowed. Conversely, if the culture is opposed to the practice, I see no good reason why any particular standard should be forced on them. I know that in most parts of the non-Western world, bribery is just a part of the game. Even though it may seem terrible to us, who are we to judge what is right for them? We should simply respect their norms. So, the operative question that we should be asking is whether this is an acceptable part of the business culture as opposed to the morality of other parts of life. You know, what is the right thing to do while in Rome?[3]

[3] Relativism will be addressed in chapter 6.

Participant 6:
Minister (Virtue Theory)

I'd like to put a slightly different slant on this issue. You see, I believe that there's more to morality than simply arguing about correct decisions when a person is faced with a moral dilemma. There is more to the moral life than simply doing the right thing and making the correct decision. Being the right type of person is more important. Thus, we cannot neglect the place of an individual's character or virtue when considering ethical questions. Simply debating issues is powerless if we continue to ignore the character traits that give people the ability to actually do the right thing. After all, most of the recent headlines of business ethics scandals involved participants that were educated at the nation's elite universities. So it couldn't have been just a matter of knowing right from wrong. You see, it was plainly a matter of character. As such, I believe that there are more important questions that need to be asked in this situation. For example, what does a person's attitude toward fair competition tell us about his or her character? What does support for paying the bribe or opposition to it say about our society? Does it say that as a society we no longer value fair competition on the merits of the product or the service? Besides, as I mentioned earlier, what good is only debating about ethics when our schools and communities no longer agree about or seek to equip our children with the character necessary to carry out what they know to be right? These are very important questions that cannot be ignored in any discussion of ethics in business.

•   •   •

Whew! A bit confusing, isn't it? No wonder we have so many disagreements about morality in society. Each person in this discussion has argued, using a distinctive style of moral reasoning, from a specific ethical system. The participants represent each of the predominant modes of moral reasoning that are used in the debates over today's current moral issues. Examples of the various styles of moral reasoning discussed in this chapter appear frequently in the media during discussions of moral issues. You will likely find most of these systems employed regularly if you are careful to watch for them. In what follows, we will analyze each of the ethical systems used by the participants in this panel, spelling out the positive elements of each system as well as offering a critique of each system.[4]

Ethical Egoism

Ethical egoism is the theory that the morality of an act is determined by one's self-interest. Those actions that advance self-interest are moral, and those that do not are not moral. To say that one is an ethical egoist is not to say that they are egotistical. This is a common confusion. Participant 1 in the discussion above is a clear example of an ethical egoist, as he makes his moral decision based strictly on his self-interest.[5] Other examples of egoism in business include individuals making moral decisions based solely on their ability to keep their jobs (their economic self-interest) or companies making decisions based on profit measures alone (corporate self-interest).

Although egoism has its appeal in the contemporary culture, there are problems with it as an all-encompassing ethical system. First, egoism does not provide any way to umpire conflicting interests without appeal to some other system. What happens when my self-interest conflicts with yours? All that the egoist can do to resolve that conflict is to reassert his basic premise of self-interest. It is naive to think that interests never conflict. Yet this assumption seems to be necessary if ethical egoism is to be a workable system.

A second problem with ethical egoism as a sufficient system of ethics is that the Bible calls believers and unbelievers both to a balance of self-interest and altruism. We are called to care about the needs of others because they are comparable to our own and because a significant part of being a disciple of Christ is following his altruistic example. Believers are called to be servants, and that invariably involves periodically putting others' needs

[4] For further reading on these moral systems, see Louis P. Pojman, *Ethics: Discovering Right and Wrong*, 5th ed. (Belmont, Calif.: Wadsworth, 2005); William Frankena, *Ethics*, 2nd ed. (Englewood Cliffs, N.J.: Prentice Hall, 1988); Scott B. Rae, *Moral Choices: An Introduction to Ethics*, 3rd ed. (Grand Rapids: Zondervan, 2009); Louis P. Pojman and Peter Tramel, *Moral Philosophy: A Reader*, 4th ed. (Indianapolis: Hackett, 2009).

[5] See the writings of Ayn Rand for examples of ethical egoism. See, e.g., Ayn Rand, *The Virtue of Selfishness* (New York: Signet, 1964), idem, "A Defense of Ethical Egoism," in Louis P. Pojman, *Moral Philosophy: A Reader*, 2nd ed. (Indianapolis: Hackett, 1998): 72–78.

ahead of our own. It does not, however, obligate believers to neglect their legitimate self-interest. *The Bible does not condemn the pursuit of self-interest.* Philippians 2:3 – 4 makes this very clear when it says, "In humility consider others better than yourselves. Each of you should look not only to your own interests but also to the interests of others" (NIV 1984 ed.). Exclusive pursuit of self-interest is what the Bible condemns, not self-interest balanced by the concern for the interests of others. The Bible does not call its followers to the kind of extreme altruism that ethical egoists claim it does. One should remember that at times, even Jesus walked away from the crowds in order to get time alone with his heavenly Father. Thus, there is a place for legitimate self-interest, to which the Bible periodically appeals, only balanced by a compassionate concern for the interests of others.

Utilitarianism

Utilitarianism is what is known as a teleological system (taken from the Greek word *telos*, meaning "end"), in which the end produced is what determines the morality of an act. In fact, sometimes utilitarianism and teleological ethics are used interchangeably. The most common form of utilitarianism today is that the act that produces the greatest good for the greatest number is the moral thing to do. That is, the course of action that produces the greatest balance of good consequences over harmful ones is the one to take. Thus, this type of moral reasoning is also called consequentialism because of its overriding emphasis on the consequences of an act.[6] Utilitarian modes of moral reasoning are widely applied in many of the current moral issues under debate. As is evident from Participant 2 in the discussion, a good deal of the discussion about morals in business is conducted on utilitarian grounds, in which cost-benefit analysis is common for a variety of strategic decisions. Utilitarianism is, for the most part, a *moral* application of cost-benefit analysis. If on balance the action provides more beneficial consequences for more people, then advocates consider it to be the most moral course of action. One example of this type of reasoning is involved when companies consider closing plants or laying off workers to maintain their competitive position in the marketplace. Often the firm will justify these measures by acknowledging that they are producing harm for some, but on balance they are safeguarding the jobs of the rest of the employees by keeping the company in business, thus producing a greater balance of benefit over harm.

Though utilitarianism has its appeal, especially in a secular society, it also has its shortcomings. The most common charge against utilitarianism is that it cannot protect the rights of minorities and sometimes can justify obvious injustices because the greater good is served. For example, slavery in

[6] Classical utilitarians include Jeremy Bentham and John Stuart Mill. For an anthology of Bentham and Mill's writings in moral philosophy, see Alan Ryan, ed., *Utilitarianism and Other Essays* (New York: Penguin, 1987).

the South during the Civil War era was clearly justifiable from a utilitarian point of view. It provided cheap labor that made the South very prosperous and clearly benefited more people than it harmed. But no one today would justify slavery on any grounds, let alone utilitarian ones, and the good consequences that it produced appear not only irrelevant, but callous toward the suffering that so many slaves endured. The reason that slavery was immoral has little to do with the balance of consequences. Rather, it has to do with a universal principle that directs us to safeguard the basic rights and dignity of each individual, ultimately because they are made in the image of God.

As with egoism, even though utilitarianism has wide popular appeal and is the basis for much public policy, other problems remain for this system. First, it requires that the decision maker be a good prophet, capable of predicting and measuring harms and benefits, which are difficult to predict and measure. Second, the notions of benefit and harm are not value neutral. For example, why is someone being laid off or killed considered a harm? It is clearly because of a prior commitment to a moral principle of human dignity and the sanctity of life, which says it's wrong to kill someone, regardless of the benefit. To explain why something should count as a benefit or a harm, one must appeal to principles. There is as much diversity and pluralism about what constitutes a benefit and a harm as there is about the definition of what is good. However, with those problems with utilitarianism, it is important to take the consequences of actions and decisions seriously, since there may be times when appeal to principles does not resolve a dilemma.

Deontological Systems

In contrast to teleological forms of moral reasoning, deontological moral systems are based on principles. In our view, this is the mode of moral reasoning that most people default to when making difficult decisions. *Deontological* is derived from the Greek term *dei*, meaning "it is necessary." From this comes the notion of moral obligations that are inherently necessary, not because of the ends or consequences they produce. Deontological obligations are one's moral duties because they are inherently the right thing to do. The deontologist would say, for example, that theft is wrong, period, irrespective of who benefits from it. The consequences of actions are not that relevant for determining right and wrong, since moral obligations come from principles, not ends. Participant 3 takes this approach in the discussion above.[7] There are a variety of types of deontological systems, both from religious perspectives and more secular views of the world. In fact, most religious traditions that are centered around a book, such as Judaism, Christianity, and Islam, are strongly deontological in their ethical outlook, since the principles come

[7] For further reading on the various types of deontological systems, see William Frankena, *Ethics*, 2nd ed. (Englewood Cliffs, N.J.: Prentice Hall, 1988).

from either the words or the ideas (or both) of the sacred book. This is usually called the "divine command theory" of ethics, in which the divine commands recorded in the inspired literature form the primary source of moral guidance for the particular religion's followers.[8] The Bible is clearly foundational for Christian ethics, and we will discuss how to use the Bible in ethics later in this chapter.

A second form of deontological morality is found in the use of natural law. In general, natural law refers to broad, general, objective, and widely shared moral values that are consistent with Scripture but revealed outside of Scripture. Values such as justice, fairness, respect for an individual's dignity, the obligation not to harm another, truth telling, and the respect for life in prohibitions against killing are some examples of virtually universally shared values that had an origin that predated Scripture.[9] Oxford University theologian John Macquarrie has put it this way: "In fact the very term 'natural law' is misleading if it is taken to mean some kind of code. The natural law is not another code or system of laws in addition to all the actual systems, but is simply our rather inaccurate way of referring to those most general moral principles against which particular rules or codes have to be measured."[10] To call them natural *laws* can be misleading, since they are the general principles on which our specific laws are based.

Perhaps the central passage in the Bible that affirms natural law is Romans 2:1 – 16. After Paul appeals to creation to point out the sin of the nonreligious and, interestingly, to oppose homosexuality in Romans 1:18 – 32, in 2:1 – 16, he proves that the moralistic person is also condemned before God because of his sin. The heart of this passage, as it applies to natural law is in verses 14 – 15, where Paul states: "Indeed, when Gentiles, who do not have the law, do by nature things required by the law, they are a law for themselves, even though they do not have the law. They show that *the requirements of the law are written on their hearts*, their consciences also bearing witness, and their thoughts now accusing them and at other times even defending them" (emphasis added).

God appears to hold those without the law accountable for their sin in the same way he holds the Jews accountable (Romans 2:17 – 29). It is difficult to see how this could be just unless those without the law had some way in which they could know what was right and wrong. In other words, for God to legitimately hold the world accountable for sin, they must have access to God's standard of morality, even if they are without special revelation. This would be natural law, or general revelation applied to morality. God has revealed these values outside of Scripture and made them accessible to those without access to Scripture.[11] Natural law makes it possible to build a bridge between the Bible and the culture that does not accept the Bible.

[8] For a helpful discussion of divine command views of morality, see Richard Mouw, *The God Who Commands* (Notre Dame: University of Notre Dame Press, 1991).

[9] For a catalog of these values traced historically, see the appendix in C. S. Lewis, *The Abolition of Man* (New York: Macmillan, 1947).

[10] John Macquarrie, "Rethinking Natural Law," in Charles E. Curran and Richard A. McCormick, eds., *Readings in Moral Theology, no. 7: Natural Law and Theology* (New York: Paulist, 1991), 239. Other reading on natural law includes J. Budziszewski, *Written on the Heart* (Downers Grove, Ill.: IVP Academic, 1997); and idem, *What We Can't Not Know* (New York: Spence, 2003).

[11] For further exegetical study on the biblical basis for natural law, see Alan F. Johnson, "Is There Biblical Warrant for Natural Law Theories?" *Journal of the Evangelical Theological Society* 27 (June 1982): 185 – 99.

To illustrate how natural law can apply to business ethics, consider employee rights. One of the most widely held universal moral principles is the dignity of the individual person and the corresponding duty to respect it. Human dignity is ultimately grounded in the image of God, but one does not need to be a religious believer to hold to genuine human dignity. This principle undergirds much of the Bill of Rights in the U.S. Constitution and declarations of human rights made around the world in this century. It is also the fundamental moral principle that obligates employers to provide safe and humane working conditions for employees. Workplaces that carry risk of injury to workers are problematic because they signify a lack of respect for the dignity of the individual worker. Firms employing workers in third world countries have the responsibility to provide wages and working conditions that are consistent with respect for human dignity. Further, when living arrangements are provided as part of the compensation, those quarters need to be consistent with human dignity. That is not to say that employers overseas must provide conditions similar to those in the United States, but that the conditions must not violate basic norms of human dignity. This principle comes from natural law and is central to the discussion of employee rights. The need of firms to make a reasonable profit must also be considered alongside respect for worker dignity. Of course, if workers willingly choose to work in substandard conditions, they are responsible for that choice. But in countries where workers have few employment choices, their vulnerability increases the moral obligation of employers to provide humane working conditions.

Respect for human dignity is also at the heart of society's concern over sexual harassment and workplace discrimination. Because both men and women possess fundamental dignity from being made in God's image, they are not to be the objects of sexual harassment. They are not to be treated as objectified sexual objects to be used for pleasure, but are to be respected as persons, significant because they bear God's image. Though there is disagreement on the definition of sexual harassment, whether the emphasis on it has gone too far, and how to protect the rights of the accused, virtually everyone agrees that sexual harassment is immoral because it violates a person's essential dignity. Similarly, discrimination on the basis of race, gender, or disability violates the respect for each person's dignity that demands that they be treated fairly.

Emotivism

Emotivism is an approach to morality that has made a significant resurgence in recent decades. Listening to callers and guests on popular radio

[12] For further commentary on this, see Thomas Sowell, "The Mushing of America," *Forbes*, July 18, 1994, 69. For more on emotivism, see Stephen Satris, *Ethical Emotivism* (New York: Springer, 1986); Mark Andrew Schroeder, *Non-Cognitivism in Ethics* (New York: Routledge, 2010).

and television talk shows, one could easily conclude that this is one of the dominant methods used to address ethical questions today.[12] Participant 4 in our discussion above represents this approach. According to emotivism, personal feelings are the most important determinant of right and wrong. Since feelings differ from individual to individual, however, morality quickly breaks down into a matter of personal preference. The emotivist holds that the judgments expressed by moral language simply communicate a person's emotions about a subject, and thus nothing anyone says in moral language can be true or false. Ethical statements are considered by the emotivist as attitudes masquerading as facts.

One of the primary criticisms of emotivism is that it cannot account for the place of reason in ethics. Emotivism sets up a false dichotomy that is as follows:

> a. Either there are moral facts, like there are facts about the sciences, or
> b. values are nothing more than expressions of our subjective feelings.

But there is another critical possibility, that moral truths are truths of reason, or a moral judgment is true if it is backed up by better reasons than the alternatives. We would also say as Christians that moral truths are truths of revelation, and that there is a strong connection between the facts of creation and the facts of morality. Good reasons usually resolve moral disagreements, but for the emotivist, giving good reasons and manipulation amount to much the same thing. There is no good reason to assume that moral language is not also factual language, and moral judgments are cognitive statements, not just expressions of emotion or preference. That ethical statements are not empirically verifiable should not be surprising, since right and wrong are not empirically observable qualities. But neither are they simply emotive expressions.

Virtue Theory

In view of the financial scandals in the early 2000s and the financial system meltdown in 2007–9, the consideration of character in ethics has made a resurgence. Works such as *The Book of Virtues* by William J. Bennett are evidence that the approach is making a comeback in popular circles as well. As is evident from the comments offered by Participant 6 in the preceding discussion, the virtue approach differs somewhat from the other methods.[13] All of the normative theories examined to this point are what are called action-oriented ethical systems. Every participant in the chamber of commerce discussion with the exception of the last participant uses one of these action-oriented methods. Most ethical theories in modern times have focused on doing the right action or making the right decision when con-

[13] To read further on virtue ethics, see Peter Kreeft, *Back to Virtue: Traditional Moral Wisdom for Modern Moral Confusion* (San Francisco: Ignatius, 1992); Jonathan R. Wilson, *Gospel Virtues: Practicing Faith, Hope and Love in Uncertain Times* (Downers Grove, Ill.: InterVarsity, 1998).

fronted by a moral dilemma. The virtue theorist holds that there is more to morality than simply doing the right thing. The foundational moral claims made by the virtue theorist are those about the person doing the action, not the act that he or she performs. *Virtue theory is an ethics of character, not duty.* These emphases are certainly consistent with the biblical emphasis on emulating the character of Christ, virtues that cannot be understood apart from the narrative of the life of Jesus and the broader story of his redemption of humankind. The tradition of virtue theory is a long one, going back to Plato and Aristotle, and includes the Gospels, Stoics and Epicureans, and Thomas Aquinas.

The virtue approach is essential to business ethics for several reasons. First, Participant 6 in the preceding discussion is correct in his statement that many of the most egregious business ethics scandals have involved participants who graduated from some of the country's elite schools and who almost certainly knew right from wrong. Thus, ethics has much to do with character. For example, Bernie Madoff knew that his Ponzi scheme that defrauded investors of billions of dollars was wrong—and he was a wealthy man when he engaged in that scheme. Similarly, Enron's accountants who "cooked their books" knew what they were doing was wrong but did it anyway.[14] Thus, it is not just a matter of moral reason, but of the will working in conjunction with knowledge of matters of right and wrong. It has been said that "reason without virtue is powerless, while virtue without reason is blind."[15] So there is a need for both reason and virtue in a comprehensive approach to ethics.

Second, as a system that requires virtues such as trust, honesty, and cooperation for its very functioning, the foundations of capitalism may be doomed without the character necessary to exercise self-restraint on the part of the participants. Indeed, the founders of our nation believed that the democratic experiment would work only if the citizens were virtuous. Contrary to popular belief, total liberty was never their intent. Rather, their vision was one of "ordered" or "restrained" liberty, that is, freedom tempered by morals and character. The alarming direction of many contemporary trends and their impact on society reveals the truthfulness of what they envisioned. Since business in a free-enterprise system is a cornerstone of democracy, we should all be worried about the future of the free-market economy if virtue isn't once again taken seriously in the public dialogue about morality.

Most of the ethical systems discussed above are still widely in use in the contemporary culture. As you read and hear about the different pressing moral issues being debated in public, be sure to watch for which of these styles of moral reasoning are used. The Bible gives examples of different types of moral reasoning from time to time, but nowhere does it suggest that

[14] To read more about the moral and legal failures in the Enron debacle, see Bethany McLean and Peter Elkind, *The Smartest Guys in the Room: The Amazing Rise and Scandalous Fall of Enron* (New York: Portfolio, 2003). On Bernard Madoff and his record-setting Ponzi scheme, see Erin Arvedlund, *Too Good to Be True: The Rise and Fall of Bernie Madoff* (New York: Portfolio, 2010).

[15] Adapted from William Frankena, *Ethics*, 2nd ed. (Englewood Cliffs, N.J.: Prentice Hall, 1973), 65.

any of the systems mentioned in this chapter are all-sufficient. As Bernard Adeney points out in his reading below, the Bible provides an overarching story, or narrative, of God's redemption of the world, and the general moral principles that can be applied to business emerge from that general story. For example, the Ten Commandments and the Mosaic law cannot be fully understood apart from narrative of the exodus and God's faithfulness to his people Israel. Similarly, the virtues that are to characterize men and women are rooted in God's character, which cannot be separated from the narrative story about his love and faithfulness to human beings. The biblical emphasis on principles that point back to the biblical story give it a deontological flavor. Furthermore, as mentioned above, Scripture also places a strong emphasis on moral character, the virtues that emerge from the character of God as revealed in the story of his relationship to his people. Thus, the Bible seems to support an approach to ethics that is a blend of virtues and principles; that is, principles that are ultimately grounded in the virtues of God's character and exemplified by Christ in their application, ultimately set in the context of the story of God's redeeming work.

READINGS

Upgrading the Ethical Decision-Making Model for Business

David W. Gill

Business and Professional Ethics Journal 23, no. 4 (Winter 2004): 135–51.

One of my favorite statements about decision-making was in Woody Allen's "My Speech to the Graduates" (1980): "More than at any other time in history, mankind faces a crossroads. One path leads to despair and utter hopelessness. The other, to total extinction. Let us pray we have the wisdom to choose correctly."[1] Often enough our options in business ethical decision-making seem to range from the unpleasant to the tragic. But, as in the case of Woody Allen's speech, we may not be seeing all the possibilities.

My paper proposes several ways of strengthening and enriching decision-making in business ethics. A major source for my own revisionist thinking about business ethics has been my work in Christian ethics over the years. Some of what I have learned in the business ethics guild has found its way across the bridge into my Christian ethics teaching and writing. But the other direction is fruitful as well, and some of the themes and emphases of Christian ethics can help strengthen our business ethics. Appropriating these ethical themes and insights from Scripture does not, however, require acts of faith and religious commitment; common sense and business experience point to the same conclusions.

There can be no doubt about the importance of decision-making. It is a basic human distinctive. We possess a capacity for self-transcendence, for reflection and choice. We do not just submit to our instinct or conditioning. Not to exercise that decision-making faculty, or not to be allowed to do so, is quite literally a dehumanizing experience. Philosophers, theologians, and others have paid a lot of attention to decision-making over the centuries. And, of course, decision-making is a critical part of business. The fate of companies and careers often turns on the quality of our decisions.

Ethical decision-making is concerned with matters of right and wrong, good and bad. The context is often one of dilemmas or quandaries in which it is not clear how one should decide (or what the right thing to do is in the circumstances). Certainly one obvious argument for renewed attention to our subject is the long and depressing list of bad decisions made by business leaders in the scandals of the past decade. Kenneth Lay, Andrew Fastow, Dennis Kozlowski, Martha Stewart, and so many others made wrong decisions with terrible consequences not just for themselves but for many others, most of them innocent.

It is worth asking, of course, whether Ken Lay and the other corporate malefactors failed because they lacked a good decision-making method. Perhaps that was part of the problem, but I'm not at all sure that the standard decision-making schemes would have saved them (or us). The critical decisions they mishandled were at a deeper level (What are my values? Am I above the law? What is my mission? What will be my legacy? Do I really want to serve my self-interest alone? Etc.). The standard account of decision-making may fail by being too narrow, that is, focused on immediate dilemmas and quandaries and neglecting more basic and fundamental matters. In any case, it is rare to open the daily newspaper and not find multiple reports of unethical and illegal business behavior—despite the growth of business ethics education and training in recent decades. So it is a very practical concern that drives our quest for improvement in our approach to ethical decision-making.

A second reason for another look at ethical decision-making in business is to provide something better than the pop business writers are offering. A fair number of business leaders out in the trenches must be reading things like *There's No Such Thing as "Business Ethics"—There's Only ONE RULE for Making Decisions* by best-selling "leadership" writer John Maxwell, whose various books occupy precious shelf space in the business sections of bookstores everywhere.[2] While Maxwell's various collections of thoughts on leadership may be helping some of his readers, I have to say that his approach to business ethics and decision-making is terribly misleading.

Maxwell writes: "An ethical dilemma can be defined as an undesirable or unpleasant choice relating to a moral principle or practice.... Do we do the easy thing or the right thing?" (p. 5). A dilemma is a problematic, difficult situation, but to describe it in terms of "undesirable" and "unpleasant" puts far too much emphasis on psychological factors (desire, pleasure) and fails to highlight the issue of *harm* that is at the core of ethics. Second, for Maxwell to pose the dilemma as "easy" versus "right" is also naive and misleading. Ethical dilemmas are such because of the difficulty in figuring out what is the right thing to do; what is right is not self-evident. For example, do we lay off these loyal workers and offshore their jobs? Maybe that will be good for our customers and shareholders, and good for the offshore economy. But it will likely be bad for our loyal workers, and may be bad for our long-term reputation and brand. It is ridiculous to say this is about "easy" versus "right."

Maxwell goes on to say "There are really only two important points when it comes to ethics. The first is a standard to follow. The second is the will to follow it" (p. 23). But what is the relevant standard in this situation? And how can we bring about the "will" to do the right thing once we figure it out? These are not simple questions, though Maxwell leaps past them as though they are. Maxwell overlooks the challenge of figuring out how we should apply our ethical values and guidelines to this or that situation and dilemma. What is our method? Who needs to be part of the decision process? Who are the stakeholders, and how do we respect their various interests and claims, especially when they conflict?

Maxwell argues that the one and only ethical guideline needed is the Golden Rule: "Do unto others as you would have them do unto you." No doubt this is a powerful, often helpful principle aiding our decision-making. But while Jesus, in his Sermon on the Mount, taught this "rule" to a band of disciples, not to an isolated, rugged individualist, Maxwell tears it out of its context and makes *self*-interest the criterion of right action. What I want done to me may (unless I am a masochist) prevent me from doing some injustice; but it would not, for example, prevent a tough guy–type from misapplying his tough guy tactics to all others. That is why Jesus and other wise teachers emphasize community discernment and action. Maxwell is also wrong to say that the Golden Rule is the one and only rule we need. It has wide *generality*, but not exclusivity or sufficiency, as Maxwell claims. It is not the only ethical principle. Unlike Maxwell, Jesus didn't limit his ethical teaching to the Golden Rule. Maxwell's decision-making model fails by being simplistic and naive. We need to find and promote a better way.

The textbook that I most often use in MBA ethics courses is Linda Trevino and Katherine Nelson's *Managing Business Ethics: Straight Talk about How to Do It Right*.[3] It is helpful to see their eight-step approach alongside what we have just seen from John Maxwell. Maxwell calls us to a little bit of their step 6 and a whole lot of their step 8 but dismisses explicitly or implicitly the rest of the process. Here are their eight steps in making sound ethical decisions in business:

1. Gather the facts. This is a critical point of departure for Trevino and Nelson and for anyone serious about ethics.
2. Define the ethical issues or values. What is it that is ethically at stake or in conflict?
3. Identify affected parties, stakeholders. This is partly a factual matter, but Trevino and Nelson also challenge the decision-maker to empathy, to see the dilemma from other stakeholders' perspectives.
4. Identify consequences. This step acknowledges the potential insights of utilitarianism and other consequentialist approaches.
5. Identify obligations. This step acknowledges the potential insight of Kantian and other non-consequentialist ethical approaches.
6. Consider your character and integrity. This step acknowledges the potential insight of virtue and character ethics.
7. Think creatively about potential actions. Imagination and creativity get lost in many accounts of ethics, but their role can be critical.
8. Check your gut. Your intuition, feelings, or conscience may help you resolve the dilemma.

Trevino and Nelson have outlined a fairly comprehensive, wise, and practical approach. They also urge managers to try to prepare themselves in advance, by learning the company's rules, asking lots of questions, and developing relationships that can help when facing tough challenges. The eight steps they outline are echoed by many other business ethics writers, though their presentation seems both more holistic and comprehensive and more practical and down-to-earth than most other accounts.

Toward More Practical and Comprehensive Ethical Decision-Making

The task of this essay is to reflect on the ethical decision-making process in business from a Christian perspective. What insights and perspectives might a Christian standpoint contribute? My own way of teaching decision-making to business students (and to people in the workplace, at any level of responsibility) has been to focus attention on four phases of the encounter with an (actual or possible) ethical problem.[4]

First, *recognize* whether you are facing a possibly serious ethical problem (or not). Six test questions provide what I believe is a reliable and comprehensive method for detecting serious issues (and leaving aside matters that are not specifically ethical in nature). Second, if a serious ethical issue has been recognized, we must then *strategize* about what to do. Third, if we cannot simply hand off the issue to the ethics department or to our supervisor, we must carefully *analyze* the issue and figure out our best options in terms of responses. Fourth, we must do our best to *resolve* the issue. How might Christian ethics bridge over to the business ethics arena and provide some insight on this process?

Mission, Purpose and Ethics

Before directly unpacking the four-stage recognize/ strategize/analyze/resolve method, three important preliminaries provide an essential texture for the whole enterprise. The first of these is mission, or "core purpose." Ethical decision-making, like all aspects of business, is (or ought to be) carried out in light of, and in service of, the overarching mission and purpose of the company. The ultimate, overarching mission both motivates and guides decision-making.

Jewish and Christian ethical reflection notes that the Decalogue, for example, begins with the clarification of "who is going to be god" here: "You shall have no other gods before me." The great rabbinical and theological commentators on the Decalogue have pointed out that the next nine commands are statements of the implications of having that god (Yahweh) on the throne. "Our gods determine our goods," we could say. Our purpose drives our ethics. The Bible is full of such teleological thinking: clarify your ultimate mission and purpose, then count the cost, prepare, plan, and execute. The negative lesson should also not be missed: put something like money on the throne, and don't be surprised by the negative ethical consequences that flow from such a mission.

Aristotle's teleological ethics and Jim Collins and Jerry Porras's "preserve the core" mantra in their *Built to Last* make the same basic point.[5] In an important and now classic essay on this topic, Douglas Sherman wrote, "The values that govern the conduct of business must be conditioned by the "why" of the business institution. They must flow from the purpose of business, carry out that purpose, and be constrained by it."[6] If businesses want to promote wise ethical decision-making and healthy corporate cultures, they should first get clear about why they are in business, what their purpose is.

The Character of the Moral Agent

Second preliminary point: moral agents are more than mere rational decision-making machines. You may be able to transfer logical reasoning skills to another person, but that does not guarantee wise ethical discernment or performance. Plato and Aristotle and most pre-Modern thinkers saw moral agency as more than decision-making skill. It is about character — the composite of who we are. Character is our ensemble of habits, traits, capacities, and inclinations. To use a sports metaphor: you cannot perform a given "play" unless you have the conditioning, the physical capac-

ity to carry it out. In ethics, you may know something intellectually but be unable to carry it out without the requisite strength of character.

The Christian-biblical perspective on this topic is clear. Jesus' program is not just "you need a new set of rules and a sharpened up decision-making method" — but rather, "you need to be born again." St. Paul writes about "putting off the old self" and "putting on the new" — not just about "correctly applying this moral rule." It is about *who* you are, what kind of person you are. It is not just that you memorize a moral rule forbidding embezzlement but that you develop a generous, honest character free of greed. It is not just recalling the rule against sexual or ethnic harassment but that you have a character that habitually respects and values all people as made in the image of God. It is not just that you can objectively categorize something as wrong or right, but that you "hate what is evil and cleave to what is good" (Romans 12:9). It is about multi-dimensional persons (with histories, feelings, personalities, etc.), not just reasoning machines. Christianity and the Bible are not the only sources for this stress on moral character, but anytime Christians are interested in improving the ethical health of organizations, this emphasis on recruiting and training for ethical character ought to be a central aspect of what they bring to the discussion.

Many business ethics teachers and writers make a category error when they list "virtue ethics" as an option in a decision-making theory parallel to the theories of Kant or Mill (Trevino and Nelson are partly guilty of this). They suggest that you first raise a Kantian question: what are our duties or others' rights in this case? Then a Millian question: how can we bring about the best consequences (for the greatest number)? Then, in the same way, a virtue ethics question: how does this affect or reflect on my character? This way of locating virtue/character ethics is not very helpful.

Our character is not just the source of a third theoretical question but is the backdrop and context behind all our reasoning and all our decision-making. Virtue ethics is about who you are whether faced with a dilemma or not. It is about your ongoing, habitual traits and capacities; it is not simply a decision-making theory or strategy like deontology or teleology provide; to treat it as such is to lose something very important.

The implication is that businesses should hire, train, and promote people of good character — not just people of high technical skill and reasoning skill — if they want to have good ethical decision-making and performance.

A Community of Ethical Discernment and Action

Third, the ethical life is a community affair, not an individual one. Ethics is a team sport not a solo one. "Let us (plural) make humankind (plural) in our image," the Creator says about the co-humanity he makes (Genesis 1). In fact, the only negative statement in the creation narratives of Genesis 1 – 2 is, "It is not good for one to dwell alone." All the great ethical instruction of Scripture was given to communities, not individuals. The Decalogue was given to a congregation, not an individual; the Sermon on the Mount was taught to the band of disciples, not an individual. Jesus sent his disciples out two-by-two, not one-by-one. He promised to be present "wherever two or three are gathered in my name," and charged them that "if two or three agree," what is bound on earth is bound in heaven. St. Paul taught that each person is one member of "the body of Christ," and that all such members are necessary. The wisdom literature urges that in the multitude of counselors there is wisdom.[7]

Anthropologists and sociologists have shown that morality is a social construction. The ancient philosophers saw ethics as embedded in politics, in the sense that the individual good is interdependent with well-ordered, just communities. The individualism of the Modern era, accentuated in America's cultural myths of the "Rugged Individual," runs radically counter not just to Christian thought but to the thinking and practice of most people in the history of the world.

Because their Scripture repeatedly teaches the critical importance of community, Christians must not fall into the individualist error of someone like John Maxwell. Ethical decision-making is not just an individual exercise in abstract logic. Determining the relevant rules, predicting the likely consequences, and arriving at the wisest decision — these challenges are always more effectively addressed if we are working in community. Community helps us *figure out* what is right and then helps us *carry out* what is right. The implication for business is to recruit team players and build and reward team effort, including the effort to make good decisions.

Recognizing Genuine Ethical Dilemmas

With these preliminary but essential features in place (mission, character, and community), the first phase of ethical decision-making will be to determine whether a particular question, issue, or action is of serious ethical importance. It may be that our concern is really a matter of taste and manners rather than ethics and morality. It may be a question of technical competence or managerial preference rather than ethics. There are many business dilemmas that are not really moral or ethical in nature. In these cases, of course, wise and good decision-making is still critical, but our concern is focused on detecting problems of ethical importance.

One simple test question is inadequate for this process. Just as there is no single, omniscient ethical czar or judge, there is not one single test question. Our best chance of not letting matters of ethical significance get past us is to use several tests. My proposal relies on six questions (or six criteria).

Legal and Ethical Codes. First, is there a potentially serious question of illegality? Second, does it violate company (or professional) ethics? These two initial tests rely on the values and judgments enshrined in ethics codes and standards articulated by governments and by organizational and professional groups. These are straightforward compliance tests. If something is happening that seems to violate laws and regulations — or the code of ethics of our company or our profession, a red flag should pop up and we may need to take the problem to the next phase and strategize what to do about it.

Generally speaking, our laws and regulations are the social compact we agree to about how we should behave in our society; anyone who lives within the jurisdiction of the law is expected to comply with it — or try to change it through constitutional means. So too, our acceptance of employment at a company usually means explicitly agreeing to observe its code of ethics. Membership in a profession also entails agreement with its code of ethics.

How do these compliance tests look in a Christian perspective? While the biblical teaching is that a Christian's primary "citizenship" and loyalty is in the "kingdom of God," Jesus, Paul, and others in the Bible counsel submission (in general) to the rule of the state and its laws. Such governing authorities are not merely to be tolerated but can be seen as the possible instruments of God to support the good and inhibit the bad (Romans 13:1–7). The exception to this general policy is when Caesar's requirements clearly contradict those stated by God, in which cases "We must obey God rather than human authority" (Acts 5:29).

Thus the laws of the state and the ethical guidelines of companies and professions are our first two guidelines, but they are not sufficient. There is a higher authority; a law may not be in accordance with the ethical right. No one nation or political entity or company or profession can claim perfection. Questioning moral authority is part of the Christian vocation. Sometimes laws are morally wrong, as when slavery or other morally repugnant activities have been legal. Sometimes they are morally silent, as when a government does not forbid dangerous toxic chemical discharges that endanger human or environmental health. Just because something is legal (or illegal), or the law is silent, does not make it right. We need some additional tests.

Individual Conscience.

The third test question is "Does it violate people's consciences and personal values?" Of course, people's consciences and personal values vary to some extent. A conservative Irish Catholic, a Muslim, a feminist, and a high school kid in the suburbs may be ethically sensitive to very different issues. But every person has some kind of interior moral "compass" that should be respected (though not necessarily agreed or complied with) by others. In Christian tradition, the source of this moral compass or conscience is the "tree of the knowledge of good and evil" eaten by our first ancestors. Though this was "Plan B" ethical knowledge, the Bible is clear that this knowledge also came from God and that it truly was appropriated by Adam and Eve (Genesis 2:16–17;

3:22). This "law written on the heart" or "common grace" or "natural morality" may not have been particularly effective throughout human history, but neither has been the revealed law and ethics of Scripture, according to St. Paul (Romans 1–2).

The point is to maintain an open moral dialogue in an organization and encourage persons (whole persons) to speak up whenever something seems to them seriously wrong. Some may be sensitive to issues about which others are dull. People should be invited to speak personally, from their own core values and conscience. Of course, it may be that the organization will, in the end, have to thank the person expressing the concern and then explain that their moral conviction cannot become the policy of the whole (diverse) organization. But it is all to the good to create an open and respectful environment in which people can share their deep convictions about right and wrong.

Golden Rule.

The fourth test question moves from inner conviction to outward behavior: "Would you like it done to you and yours?" (Matthew 7:12). This is the Golden Rule of Jesus' Sermon on the Mount, though it has close parallels in the Analects of Confucius and in other religious and philosophical teaching. Even Kant's "Categorical Imperative" is close to saying "Do unto others only what you could will everyone do to everyone." Of course, what you personally, individually would tolerate is a part of this test question. But the rule was given to a group of disciples, and it is best for us also to ask about our colleagues and loved ones. Would my colleagues and family tolerate this? Would I want them to? Would I myself, and my colleagues and children, take this new drug we are marketing? Drink the water we are polluting? Drive this car we are manufacturing? You can see that this fourth test goes further than question three's challenge to my conscience and thinking. Now it is about living, about action.

Publicity.

The fifth test question is "Would it happen if it was publicized?" If this were on the front page of our newspaper or the lead story on the evening news, would it be happening? This test assumes that the larger society has some kind of moral compass and that our shame and fear before the judgment of our society will help us avoid unethical choices. Jesus once said that "men love darkness rather than light because their deeds are evil" (John 3:19). Adam and Eve "hid from God" after disobeying him. Hiding and secrecy often accompany unethical acts; transparency and the light of day are great helps to keep things honest and ethical. This test is a little like the first (legal compliance) one. It anticipates that some kind of reliable moral guidance might reside in our society. Here, more than just the guidance enshrined in law, we are looking to public opinion to help guide us. Of course, we know that publics can be deceived and prone to evil. Just think of the well-educated German people who supported Hitler. So this publicity test is not adequate or fail safe by itself, but it is one more important screen for ethics.

Harm. The sixth and final test is "Could someone be seriously and irresponsibly harmed?" Many ethics codes repeat this "harm" guideline in one form or another. The ancient Hippocratic Oath of Physicians gives "Do no harm" as one of the first obligations of medical practitioners. In my judgment, harm is the bottom line question in ethics. Will we be harmed or will we flourish? The Ten Commandments, for example, were explained and justified as being guidelines "for our good," that their observers' lives would "go well," and they would "live long in the land" (Deuteronomy 5–6). Even the biblical teaching against the sins of the spirit (lust, greed, envy, etc.) emphasizes that these attitudes are wrong because they are the root of behaviors that harm others (as well as corrupting and harming those who harbor such attitudes).

Of course, "harm" must be debated and defined. Almost anything can potentially cause harm. The essential qualifiers here are "serious" and "irresponsible." These qualifiers are not always self-evident, so a discussion must take place, hopefully including all who may be affected by the decisions ("the stakeholders"). People should not be exposed to harms they do not choose or should not have to choose.

All of these six ethics tests are helpful in detecting serious ethical issues. None of them is all-sufficient all the time. Exceptional circumstances can occur. Interpretation is needed. Our character is tested. Some moral community is essential. But if we use these six

tests and start getting either some intense red lights or a number of blinking yellows, we had better take the next step and strategize about what to do. Certainly each of these six tests has been proposed by nonreligious thinkers so they are not "acts of faith" in any exclusive way. But as we have seen, Christian Scripture and tradition reinforce and emphasize these various themes in interesting ways.

Taking a Broader View of Ethical Decision-Making

Before leaving the "recognition" phase, however, we should note also that, while dilemma resolution is extremely important, a range of other decisions is also ethically critical. First, our day-to-day, mundane practices and decisions shape the long-term ethical health and performance of the organization. It is not just the big crises but the ordinary decision-making opportunities that are important. Second, our decisions regarding the mission and vision, the core values, and the ethical standards of our organization are more fundamental and significant than our decisions about what to do in a given dilemma. Third, our decisions about what kind of personal character we hire and what kind of corporate culture we build have everything to do with our ethical health and performance.

We need to avoid a narrow "decisionist" approach and take a broader, deeper, richer standpoint toward organizational ethics. If we think of ethics and ethical decision-making *only* or *primarily* in the crisis/dilemma context, it becomes little more than "damage control"—a reactive, mostly negative, enterprise. We must move beyond this reactive "dilemma" ethics to a proactive "practice" ethics, from a negative, "boundary" ethics to a positive "mandate" ethics. To put the process in a nutshell, we must first clearly identify the core mission and purpose of the organization. Then we carefully map out the important "practices" of the organization (e.g., research, marketing, financial reporting, meeting, communicating, etc., i.e., the activities that carry out and achieve the mission). Next we identify the principles that should guide each particular practice area so that (a) no boundaries are crossed which will harm people and (b) positive mandates and ideals are held up to indicate "how we do the things we do" in each aspect of organizational activity. Obviously, this process has decision-making at every turn; but it is proactive, positive, mission-driven decision-making.

Strategizing about Ethical Dilemmas: What Do We Do Next?

If we find that our six test questions are leading us to consider an issue or dilemma as a genuine and (at least potentially) serious ethical challenge, the next phase is to strategize: what should I do about this problem I see? With whom should I share this information? What should my next steps be? What are the things I must be especially careful about as I move forward on this? This is no time to be reckless. After all, if ethics is about protecting from harm, we do not want to react in a way that harms careers and companies and communities — including our own career and the well-being of those who depend on us.

Managers and organizational leaders can do a great favor to their company and its employees if they think about this strategy and create some guidelines and channels for response. Some companies specify that ethical questions and problems should (if possible) be brought immediately to the attention of one's supervisor, or to the compliance and law office, or the human resources, or to an anonymous ethics hotline. Some guarantee protection of anonymity. And some do nothing.

Christians may recall that Jesus suggested going to the offender first of all! If that doesn't satisfy, Jesus said, take another person with you. If that doesn't resolve the problem, then make it public ("to the church") (Matthew 18:15 – 17). Of course, in this instance Jesus was referring to interpersonal grievances more than breeches of organization standards, but there is certainly a general biblical theme that one ought to speak *to* someone rather than *about* them behind their back, and that this is intended to lead to resolutions of problems before they become bigger and more destructive. There is also biblical teaching about the need for witnesses, especially in cases of accusations of leaders whose positions make them especially vulnerable to false accusations. The strategic implications may be that one should consult with at least one or two others before making anything public.

Analyzing Ethical Issues

In some organizations, the recognition and strategy phases may be all that is required. You recognize a problem and refer it to the ethics committee or ombudsperson or your boss, and they take it from there. In other cases, though, you may need to proceed to the third stage and carefully analyze the problem. Four basic aspects of the problem need clarification and study before a resolution can be chosen.

First, clarify your own role and responsibility. Why are you pursuing this? What, if any, is your authority? You may be involved because it is a problem under your supervision. No controversy there. But what if, for example, you are pressing an issue of possible sexual or ethnic harassment outside your department or official responsibility? You may well be told to "butt out" and back off, that it is none of your business. On the other hand, you may feel as a human being, as a colleague, as a father, or whatever, that you can't let it go until you are assured that everyone is protected from harm. The point is to know from where you speak, for it may be challenged.

Second, the analysis requires that we clarify the relevant facts of the case. What happened exactly? When? Where? Who was involved? Who were the players, what did they do, and who was affected? Document these facts. Get witnesses. Make sure you get this part straight. Some apparent ethical dilemmas actually disappear at this fact-gathering stage. What appeared to be wrong, or what appeared to be a forced choice between two terrible options, turns out to be untrue.

Third, clarify the decisive values and principles at stake and in conflict. These values and principles may come from the organization itself, from your profession, from your conscience, or somewhere else. What is at stake? Is it a question of honesty? Fairness? Safety? What are the central value issues? It is in terms of these values that you raise the issue … and it is in terms of these values that you will later justify your response (e.g., now it is fair, now it is safe, now we are being honest, etc.).

Fourth, and finally, clarify the action options that are available — and their possible and probable consequences. No one can fully guarantee or know the consequences of our actions, but that does not excuse us from being as careful as possible to think about what might happen if we do this or that.

In all four phases of the analysis, we must be very careful—a lot may ride on our analysis. We must also be creative and imaginative, think win-win rather than "zero sum." And we must be collaborative: there is strength and wisdom in numbers.

Looking at this analytical scheme from a Christian point of view, the four "clarification" exercises all can find precedent in the Bible and Christian tradition—as in common sense and business experience. Perhaps the most distinctive Christian contribution lies in the final comments concerning (a) the seriousness and care directed at this analysis, (b) a call for creativity and imagination—rooted, as it could be, in the Christian virtue of hope, and (c) the call for collaboration, working together rather than as ethical "lone rangers."

Resolving Ethical Dilemmas

The fourth phase is the goal of the whole process: finding the best possible resolution of the ethical dilemma. Following our careful analysis and best possible thinking, we must choose the best, most responsible option we have come up with. How will we know our proposed resolution is the best we can do and is acceptable? We return to the earlier six test questions and to the core values and principles we clarified as being at stake in the dilemma. Our proposed resolution should be legal, in compliance with our ethics codes, respectful of our consciences, something we could live with ourselves and with our friends, something we could defend in public, and something that does not seriously or irresponsibly risk harm to others. The values that were in jeopardy (e.g., safety, honesty, fairness) are now observed.

Next? Drawing partly on the Jesus tradition, we could seek voluntary reform by the offenders—and blow the whistle only as a last resort. Unfortunately, too much ethical case discussion does not go further than the assignment of blame. A fuller resolution would require follow-through on those injured (employees, customers, whoever was harmed by the breech of ethics). We should also follow through on the offenders—perhaps by helping them reform, perhaps by warning others they may harm.

Finally, a full resolution would mean carrying through with organizational, structural, and procedural reforms to minimize the chances of recurrence of this kind of ethical dilemma. Maybe the compensation system is actually rewarding unethical behavior. Maybe better management would lessen the temptation to get into trouble.

Conclusion

While the Bible does not use the terms "ethics" and "morality," it is a book full of ethical interest and guidance, and this has resulted in a rich tradition of moral theology and ethical guidance for the people. The biblical themes concerning the "tree of the knowledge of good and evil" and the "law written on the heart"—and many other texts—make plain to Christians that they do not have a corner on moral wisdom. In fact, the first virtue of Christian moral character should be "poverty of spirit," i.e., humility—though the opposite is all too frequently the case.

Humble, open, teachable, respectful of the ethical convictions of others, Christians also have a particular ethical identity, centered on the values and ethics of Jesus, from which to speak. There is something valuable and insightful in the ethics of Jesus and Christian faith and tradition, even for the challenges in today's business milieu.

In summary, drawing on the business ethics literature and on the commonsense experiences of business leaders in the workplace, and now drawing on the insights and emphases of biblical and Christian ethics, our decision-making approach includes the following:

- Emphasizing corporate mission as motivator and guide for ethical decision-making
- Valuing good character, not just reasoning skills, as essential to good decision-making
- Stressing teamwork and community rather than individualism in decision-making
- Respecting laws and codes of ethics but not viewing simple compliance as necessarily equivalent to ethical rightness
- Respecting the consciences and values of everyone in our diverse marketplace
- Utilizing the Golden Rule test in a community rather than individualist way
- Promoting transparency and social responsibility as part of the ethical process
- Viewing the threat or presence of serious harm as the bottom line issue in ethics

- Creating advance strategies (processes, training) for handling questions and crises
- Approaching offenders first, whenever possible; blowing the whistle only as a last resort
- Being careful in analyzing ethical issues — getting facts, values, and options clear
- Valuing imagination and creativity alongside logic and rationality in decision-making

- Empathizing with all stakeholders, especially to ensure that those with less power have a voice in decisions that affect them
- Not viewing a verdict assigning blame as the resolution of an ethical problem but following through on those injured as well as those guilty of the offense
- Following through with organizational reforms to minimize recurrence of the problem

Notes

1 Woody Allen, *Side Effects* (New York: Ballantine, 1975), p. 76.
2 Warner Books, 2003.
3 Wiley, 3rd edition, 2004. Their "Eight Steps to Sound Ethical Decision-Making in Business" are provided on pp. 94–100.
4 Of course, if the pressure is on and one doesn't have the time to work through these four stages in any detailed way, the "one thing" to remember is to try to protect people from harm. Sometimes we have to keep it that simple.
5 James C. Collins and Jerry I. Porras, *Built to Last: Successful*

Habits of Visionary Companies (New York: HarperCollins, 1994), chapter 4, "Preserve the Core/Stimulate Progress," pp. 80–90.
6 "The Ethical Roots of the Business System," *Harvard Business Review* (Nov.–Dec. 1983), p. 186.
7 Genesis 1:26–27; 2:18; Exodus 20:1ff.; Matthew 5:1ff.; Luke 10:1; Matthew 18:19–20; 1 Corinthians 12:12ff.; Proverbs 11:14.

Questions for Discussion and Reflection

1. How does Gill suggest you recognize an ethical dilemma? What do you think of his six tests for an ethical dilemma?
2. Do you agree that simple compliance with the law is "not equivalent to ethical rightness," or do you believe that "if it's legal, it's moral"? Explain your answer.
3. Do you agree with John Maxwell that the only ethical guideline you need for business ethics is the Golden Rule? How does Gill react to Maxwell's view of business ethics?

The Bible and Culture in Ethics

Bernard Adeney

From *Strange Virtues: Ethics in a Multicultural World* (Downers Grove, Ill.: InterVarsity, 1995): 79–105.

Christians believe that the Bible is the primary, authoritative guide to faith and life. Cultural conventions do not have an authority that overrules Scripture. When Christians differ, whatever their culture, they rightly search the Scriptures to find wisdom.

William Dyrness has argued that "it is scripture, and not its 'message,' that is finally transcultural."[1] The message of the Bible, or the way it is interpreted, is always perceived and stated in human language that reflects the priorities of particular people in a particular culture. The entire canon of the Bible, on the other hand, is constitutive of what it means to be a Christian in every time and place. David Kelsey writes that to call a text "scripture" is to say:

> 1) that its use in certain ways in the common life of the Christian community is essential to establishing and preserving the community's identity.... 2) It is authority for the common life of the Christian community.... 3) It is to ascribe some kind of "wholeness" to it.... 4) The expression, "Scripture is authoritative for theology" has self-involving force.[2]

The term *scripture* implies commitment. In every time and place, believers define themselves in relation to Scripture. Whatever their differences in doctrine or practice, all accept a common written source as the vehicle of the revelation of God in Christ.

Yet the Bible is not self-interpreting. While all accept the text,[3] what they think it means differs widely.

The Cultural Context of the Bible

Not only the culture of the reader but also the many different cultures that lie within and behind the text compound the task of understanding. We can understand what we read only in relation to our cultural experience. But everything that is written in the Bible is located within the cultural experience of its author or editor.

There is an overlap between the cultures of the Bible and the cultures of its readers in every age. If there weren't, the task of reading such a foreign text would be impossible. But there are also pervasive differences. If we do not understand these differences, the ethical teaching of the Bible remains incomprehensible.

Christian commitment to the Bible reflects the conviction that God is revealed through this text. As Robert McAfee Brown has commented:

> Christians make the initially bizarre gamble that "the strange new world within the Bible" is a more accurate view of the world than our own and that we have to modify our views as a result. This means engaging in dialogue with the Bible — bringing our questions to it, hearing its questions to us, examining our answers in

its light, and taking its answers very seriously, particularly when they conflict with our own, which will be most of the time.[4]

The problem comes when the Bible's questions and its answers seem totally foreign and incomprehensible to us. Whatever their doctrine of Scripture, most Christians simply ignore the parts that seem irrelevant. But more difficult to ignore are differences in interpretation between different believers or even in the same person at different times.

Devout Christians sometimes marvel that each time they come to a familiar passage they learn something new. The Holy Spirit opens their eyes to new insight. Whenever a person reads a text again, she comes to it from a slightly different context. This week she has different problems and concerns from those she faced a year ago. As the context of her interpretation changes, she sees new things in the text. Just as two photographs of the same scene can look dramatically different because of how they are framed, what focus is used, the light setting chosen and the type of film and camera used, so a text looks different to us as we visualize it from different vantage points. With dramatically different cultures, the range of vantage points widens.

This does not mean that the text changes. The number and types of legitimate interpretations are controlled by what is really in the text.[5] What is in the text itself is ruled by the finite number of meanings possible in its original context. Ethical instructions, laws, examples, and narratives cannot be abstracted from the context without affecting their meaning. Whether the Bible says, "Do not kill," "Greet one another with a holy kiss," or "Jesus wept," the meaning of the text cannot be understood without the context.

Without this understanding, much of the Bible would be even more puzzling than it is. For example, in Exodus 23:19 the Israelites are commanded, "You shall not boil a kid in its mother's milk." Knowing that "a kid" means a baby goat does not get us much closer to understanding why there should be such a prohibition. While animal-rights activists might be delighted with this verse, it is unlikely that prevention of cruelty to animals was the motive for the law. Archaeological discoveries concerning Canaanite fertility practices provide a much more plausible explanation. Boiling a kid in its mother's milk was evidently part of a common fertility rite. Thus the law should be understood as forbidding syncretism with Canaanite religions. Those who have no connection with fertility rites may find the literal meaning of the law irrelevant. On the other hand, insofar as we can find analogies in our own culture, we may still learn from this rule.

In many parts of the world, rites to appease spirits and assure fertility are common. In such a context this law is very relevant. It teaches us how God viewed fertility magic in the context of ancient Canaan. Even in contexts where such rites are rare, the meaning within this law may have relevance today. For example, a cosmopolite might extrapolate that in some situations, use of a dangerous fertility drug (trust in the magic of science to manipulate what rightly belongs to God) is an unwarranted means of increasing fertility. Perhaps Asians who hunt the rhinoceros (and are threatening its extinction) because of the purported powers of its horn in Chinese medicine should also take note.

Some biblical commands cannot be understood apart from their original context. Others are clear enough but should not be followed in most places today because the cultural conditions that gave them meaning are no longer pertinent. Whether the command is Peter's instruction to "greet one another with a kiss of love" (1 Pet 5:14), Paul's observation that "any woman who prays or prophesies with her head unveiled disgraces her head—it is one and the same thing as having her head shaved" (1 Cor 11:5), or the Deuteronomic law that rebellious children should be stoned (Deut 21:18–21), the commandments of Scripture must be understood for what they meant to people in a specific time and place before we can begin to understand what they might mean in *our* time and place.

In the Old Testament, God does or commands many things that appear abhorrent today. It is hard to imagine anything good that can be learned from a law that allows parents to have their children executed. We might speculate that since the law provided for a legal procedure that involved the whole community, it was unlikely to be used except in very extreme cases. Thus, in addition to protecting the community from a youth who was entering a life of crime, the law protected children from arbitrary execution by parents who in that culture had unlimited power over their offspring. At the very least, the law required the agreement and participation of the entire community in the death sentence.

The meaning of the law can be understood only in relation to the actual conditions of its context. Possibly the law was intended to prevent even crueler practices. If so, like the divorce law ("because you were so hardhearted," Mt 19:8), it did not legislate something good but only prevented something worse.

Even so, I am not happy with this law and do not pretend to fully understand it. I don't think that under any circumstances disobedient children should be killed. Apart from the hazard of allowing my modern consciousness to stand in judgment on Scripture, I am culturally too distant from the events reported to fully understand them. But it is clear that the meaning of goodness is sometimes understood differently by the authors of the original text from the way we understand it today.

For example, in Numbers 15 Moses is instructed by God to have a man stoned to death for gathering wood on the Sabbath. Functionally the man was doing exactly the same thing as Jesus and his disciples did when they plucked grain to eat on the sabbath (Mt 12:1–8). But Moses, in accordance with the law, had the wood-gatherer stoned.

Korah, one of Israel's leaders, was outraged by Moses' seeming abuse of power. Korah said, in effect, "Moses, you have gone too far. Why should you have such power to act unilaterally? Are you the only one who knows the mind of God?" (Num 16:3).

Korah was not alone in his concern. He brought with him 250 well-known community leaders who had been appointed members of the council, a group meant to serve as judges of the people. Korah argued that all of God's people are holy. "All the congregation are holy, everyone of them, and the LORD is among them. So why then do you exalt yourselves above the assembly of the LORD?" (Num 16:3). As far as I know, this is the first biblical approximation of an argument for the priesthood of all believers.

When we read with modern eyes, Korah was admirable. He didn't grumble off in a corner but responsibly brought his concern to an appointed council. His concerns were ethical and related to human rights; his instincts were democratic; his methods were responsible; and his theological arguments were sophisticated by modern standards. Ah, therein lies the rub. Korah's actions cannot be judged by modern standards. Their meaning can be accessed only within the context of the birth of the nation of Israel in the early bronze age.

The meaning of Korah's action, in his cultural context, was rebellion against Moses and against God, threatening the very existence of the nation of Israel as a unified people of God. In this context, not only was Moses' leadership challenged, but God's leadership, God's law, and the discipline required for the formation of a nation were at stake. Apparently the Ten Commandments were also at stake, as gathering wood was a violation of the sabbath.

According to the account in Numbers, God considered Korah's sin so grave that Moses had to plead before God for the survival of the whole nation. As it was, God created an earthquake that scared the Israelites half to death. "The ground under [Korah and his family and followers] was split apart. The earth opened its mouth and swallowed them up.... And fire came out from the LORD and consumed the two hundred fifty men offering the incense" (Num 16:31–32, 35).

The point here is not whether Moses was intrinsically right or wrong to cast a death sentence on someone for gathering wood on the sabbath, but that Korah was horribly wrong to challenge Moses' leadership at this pivotal moment in the formation of Israel. Korah's action cannot be judged in itself, apart from his cultural context. This is the story of a power struggle. The action of God leaves no question that Korah's action was wrong in that time and in that place.

It does not follow from this that stoning people who gather wood on the sabbath is a good idea today. The conditions that existed during the time of the exodus will never be repeated. Does this mean that the passage has nothing to teach us? Of course not.

We might learn that keeping the sabbath is very important in the eyes of God—an important lesson for those enslaved by the twin gods of workaholism and materialism. We might learn that democracy is not an absolute good—an important lesson for those who think liberal political culture is the apex of civilization. We might learn that community solidarity and respect for leadership can be more important

than individual human rights or even the deaths of 251 people—an important lesson for those who have elevated individualistic autonomy to the central place in ethics.

The story is rich with ethical content. But the content cannot be abstracted into timeless truths that are alienated from real times and places. The story as a whole is far more fertile for ethical learning than any principles abstracted from it. The principles may prove false if they are applied at the wrong time, in the wrong place, by the wrong person. Fortunately, the lessons I drew from the story of Korah are not absolute. From other stories we might learn opposite kinds of lessons.

From the story of the disciples plucking grain, we might learn that human need can be more important than legalistic forms. From the story of Nathan the prophet's rebuke of David, we might learn that leadership should not have unlimited power and that it is important to stand up against leaders when they violate the rights of individuals (2 Sam 11–12). From the story of Jesus and the woman taken in adultery, we might learn that mercy in the judgment of sinners is wise for leaders who are also sinners (Jn 8:2–11). Even from other stories in the life of Moses, we might learn lessons balancing the story of Korah.

For example, when the people worship the golden calf, Moses pleads for their lives: "Alas, this people has sinned a great sin; they have made for themselves gods of gold. But now, if you will only forgive their sin— but if not, blot me out of the book you have written" (Ex 32:31–32). Presumably worshiping a golden calf was more serious than gathering firewood on the Sabbath, but in a different context, in a different life situation for God's people, a different ethical judgment is brought into play.

Does this mean that biblical ethics are relativistic, that there are no absolutes and we must make our decisions according to subjective criteria? By no means! Ethics in the Bible are contextual. They are incarnate words. But they derive from the character and will of God, which do not change.

Eugene Nida, followed by Charles Kraft, suggests that the Bible teaches a "relative cultural relativism."[6] The point is not that all truth is relative, but that all truth is enfleshed in specific language that relates it to specific cultural concerns. We can have an adequate but never an absolute understanding of moral principles: adequate because we can clearly see goodness and evil at work in biblical and modern times, never absolute because goodness and evil are grounded in specific realities of which we know only a tiny part. Nida goes so far as to say:

> The only absolute in Christianity is the triune God. Anything which involves [a human being], who is finite and limited, must of necessity be limited, and hence relative. Biblical cultural relativism is an obligatory feature of our incarnational religion, for without it we would either absolutize human institutions or relativize God.[7]

The poles of absolutism and relativism in ethics will be explored further [elsewhere]. For now we must turn to the question of how ethics are learned from the Bible.

Learning to See the World through the Stories of the Bible

The primary way we learn goodness from the Bible is by making the story of the Bible the interpretive framework through which we view all of life. This approach does not deny that we learn propositions or doctrines from the Scriptures. But unlike traditional conservative theology, we do not view these doctrines as propositions that we learn and then apply to various contexts. Rather, they are a lens through which we see reality. They help us to see the truth. The lens is not the truth, but it helps us to describe what is true.

George A. Lindbeck writes:

> A comprehensive scheme or story used to structure all dimensions of existence is not primarily a set of propositions to be believed, but is rather the medium in which one moves, a set of skills that one employs in living one's life. Its vocabulary of symbols and its syntax may be used for many purposes, only one of which is the formulation of statements about reality.[8]

Like a culture or language, it is a communal phenomenon that shapes the subjectivities of individuals rather than being primarily a manifestation of those subjectivities.[9]

Christians are inescapably influenced to see and experience the world through the lens of their culture. The reality we experience is socially constructed. It is difficult for even a strong-minded individual to maintain a belief that is contradicted by everyone else. There is a well-known story of an anthropologist who went to study a tribe and ended up becoming an animist. The story of reality the tribe told became the interpretive framework through which the anthropologist perceived all of reality.

A friend of mine experienced a radical loss of faith while studying for his Ph.D. One day he looked out the window in Cambridge and was overwhelmed with the feeling that the buses below, and all the material things he saw, were all that mattered, all that existed. The story of the universe he imbibed day after day from the university and from popular culture was in stark contradiction to his faith. The result was radical doubt.

Our lived morality is a result of the way we perceive reality. People usually act in relation to their interpretation of the way the world really is, far more than from a set of beliefs or principles. Iris Murdoch has observed that "we are not isolated free choosers, monarchs of all we survey, but benighted creatures sunk in a reality whose nature we are constantly and overwhelmingly tempted to deform by fantasy."[10] In this situation, morality is, as Simone Weil suggested, a matter of attention. We act in accordance with what we think matters, what we see as true. Our actions toward our family or colleagues, or employees or bosses, are more a natural outflowing of the story we are living than a rational choice of good or evil.

Our perception of reality derives from a tradition. In modern liberal culture, reality is perceived as an object accessible to universal, scientific, liberal rationality. In contrast, Alasdair MacIntyre argues that rationality itself is determined by particular traditions and by the social institutions and relationships that embody them. He writes, "What each person is confronted with is at once a set of rival intellectual positions, a set of rival traditions embodied more or less imperfectly in contemporary forms of social relationship and a set of rival communities of discourse, each with its own specific modes of speech."[11]

Modern liberals reject this position and continue to impose their own brand of rationality on everyone.

The great temple to universal, scientific rationality is the modern university. Adherence to any particular tradition, especially if it is explicitly religious, is ruled out of the classroom. In contrast, "postmodern" thinkers have radically "deconstructed" or destroyed the pretensions of universal, scientific rationality, along with its liberal institutions. They acknowledge diversity along with the assumption that there is no truth and every tradition is equally untenable.

MacIntyre critiques both the pretensions of liberalism and the cynicism of some forms of postmodernism.[12] He argues that we can be coherent about reality only if we perceive it out of a coherent way of seeing the world. Much of the incoherence of the modern world derives from the fact that people live out of half-believed liberalism, an incoherent mixture of traditions or no tradition at all. The fact that we need a tradition, along with its community of practices, does not imply that only one tradition is true or that all are false (or equally true). All traditions are limited by the perspective of their histories, their institutions, and their standpoint in time and place.

In order to escape the deformed fantasies of our age, Christians believe we must see the world from the perspective of God's work in history.[13] The stories of the Bible provide the language and categories through which we see the world truly. Lindbeck says:

> It is important to note the direction of interpretation. Typology does not make scriptural contents into metaphors for extra scriptural realities but the other way around. It does not suggest, as is often said in our day, that believers find their stories in the Bible, but rather that they make the story of the Bible their story. The cross is not to be viewed as a figurative representation of suffering nor the messianic kingdom as a symbol for hope in the future; rather, suffering should be cruciform, and hopes for the future messianic.... It is the text, so to speak, which absorbs the world, rather than the world the text.[14]

Christians learn to be good from the Bible by telling themselves and each other the story of their lives as a part of the story of the Bible. More important than the stories believers tell are the stories they live. Goodness comes by the work of the Holy Spirit when a person lives as part of the people of God. That happens when she has learned the story of Israel, of Jesus, and of the church so well that her life becomes a continuation of the story. Then a Christian becomes "a letter of Christ ... written not with ink but with the Spirit of the living God, not on tablets of stone but on tablets of human hearts" (2 Cor. 3:3).

The great problem for ethics is, of course, *How* do we learn the story of the Bible? There seem to be many stories in the Bible. The stories that are there do not all seem consistent with each other. The cultural contexts of the stories are often strange to us. And the way the same stories are related by different parts of the Christian community are sometimes unrecognizable to each other. These are very large questions which are beyond the scope of this book. As a start, however, let's consider several of the many ways in which we are formed by the biblical narratives.

Ethics in the Context of a Narrative

Stanley Hauerwas once commented that we can learn more ethics from reading novels than from reading ethics books. The Bible is not an ethics book. It does not contain many systematic treatises on ethics. Where ethics are explicitly addressed, it is usually in the context of a story. The Old Testament law is recounted in the context of the saga of the exodus; the Sermon on the Mount is an integral part of the story of Jesus. To borrow an expression that David Kelsey uses to describe Karl Barth's view of Scripture, the Bible is like a "vast, loosely structured, non-fictional novel."[15]

We learn ethics from a story by allowing its way of seeing the world to become our own symbolic structure of meanings. For example, when we read the story of the prodigal son, we may identify with the father, the prodigal, the elder brother, or even the riotous friends. As we identify with one or more characters, their behavior and relationships become symbols of our own behavior and relationships. The meaning and moral evaluation of our own behavior are clarified by the meaning assigned to the actions of the characters in the story. The prodigal son's riotous living may symbolize our own rebellion and teach us that forgiveness is really possible.

Within the biblical narrative, we see a moral outlook on life that is expressed in many literary forms. In stories, poetry, history, prophecy, apocalypse, law, sermons, proverbs, letters, songs, biography, prayers, and other kinds of literature, good and evil are revealed and symbolized within a particular cultural context.

When Christians read the rich profusion of biblical material, four common questions emerge: (1) How do we deal with all the intense and messy emotions expressed by biblical authors? (2) How relevant are biblical commandments for life today? (3) Are biblical principles the heart of Christian ethics? (4) Does the Bible tell us why we should live in one way rather than in another?[16] Many other questions could be added to these four, such as the place of moral examples (positive and negative), visions, aesthetic expression, tragedy, and so on. All are best understood in the context of a story. Nevertheless, in order to limit my task I will examine these four questions.

1. *Expressions of emotion.* The Bible is full of emotions. From the fear of Adam and Eve to the exultation of David, from the erotic love of Solomon to the anguish of Jeremiah, from the depression of Job to the calm courage of Esther, from the tears of Jesus to the joy of his disciples, every book of the Bible bears the mark of breathing human beings whose moral lives are expressed with emotion.

At the emotional level there can be no precise formulation of what are appropriate responses to specific situations. Usually such responses are recorded without comment. Emotional responses cannot be easily labeled good or bad. They are more amenable to the terms *honest* or *dishonest, appropriate* or *inappropriate.* For a priori reasons, only Jesus' emotive responses may be labeled good. The psalmist who expressed happiness at the thought of Babylonian babies having their brains smashed in is clearly not a guide for our emotional response to our enemies (Ps 137:9).

Nevertheless, the scope and range of emotions expressed by biblical writers gives valuable insight into the way God's people saw the world around them. In their emotions we see their honest response to what they saw as God's work in the world. Because they did not always see clearly, their emotions were not always appropriate. In many cases we are not able to judge whether the responses were appropriate. Their situa-

tion is too far from us. Their experience is too foreign. Even so, in most cases the emotions expressed enable us to identify with the biblical writer. While we may not uncritically imitate biblically expressed emotions, those emotions often provide a window into the heart of the situations the writers faced.

Sometimes within a story we see the destructive effects of negative emotions. Sometimes we see how God addresses human beings in the midst of their emotions. And sometimes human emotions are vehicles for the revelation of the heart of God. In Jeremiah, the prophet's own feeling of anguish at the coming destruction of Jerusalem is not distinguished from the Word of Yahweh. Gerhard von Rad comments that Jeremiah's unwanted vision contains a "darkness so terrible ... that it constitutes a menace to very much more than the life of a single man; God's whole way with Israel hereby threatens to end in some kind of metaphysical abyss."[17]

Unlike Jeremiah, we are not meant to curse ourselves and our parents and wish we had never been born. But if we ever do, if we ever experience despair that is even remotely like Jeremiah's, then his story and the way that God dealt with him in it may become vitally important to our moral life. Although Jeremiah's specific responses to his situation are not presented as a model for us to follow, within the context of the story of his life with God his emotions reveal the depths of evil and despair that exist in the world. We cannot judge him. Perhaps his response was far more appropriate than that of anyone else in the city of Jerusalem at the time. Certainly he saw more than anyone else. His emotions teach us to see.

2. *Moral rules and law.* It is tragic how many Christians try to reduce the Bible's moral teaching to the level of rules, commandments, and laws. When ethics and law are equated, the primary questions for biblical interpretation become, Am I bound by this law or may I safely ignore it? Is this commandment absolute, or is it relative to its original context? Is this instruction a commandment for all times and places, or is it a specific rule for a particular culture? Is this law relevant or irrelevant? Is this a moral or a ceremonial law?

The problem is not that these questions are invalid. But they do not go deep enough. Jesus said:

Do not think that I have come to abolish the law or the prophets; I have come not to abolish but to fulfill. For truly I tell you, until heaven and earth pass away, not one letter, not one stroke of a letter, will pass from the law until all is accomplished. Therefore whoever breaks one of the least of these commandments, and teaches others to do the same, will be called least in the kingdom of heaven; but whoever does them and teaches them will be called great in the kingdom of heaven. For I tell you, unless your righteousness exceeds that of the scribes and Pharisees, you will never enter the kingdom of heaven. (Mt 5:17–20)

There is no part of the law that is irrelevant. The common distinction between ceremonial and moral law has no substantiation in the Old or New Testament. So-called ceremonial laws are interspersed with clearly moral commandments. The ancient Israelites knew no distinction between the two. The religious and moral life of Israel were a single tapestry. Furthermore, as we have seen, some of the "moral" laws, including those calling for capital punishment, are the most difficult for modern people to understand.

The attempt by some "theonomists" to argue that all the laws of the Bible must be literally followed is in stark contradiction to a narrative reading of Scripture. When we abstract the laws from their context, their very source of meaning is lost. At the other extreme, some dispensationalists would discard some of the most profound teachings of Scripture by assigning them to a dispensation or period that does not concern Christians. For example, some say that the "Sermon on the Mount" is addressed only to Jews who will remain on the earth after the rapture.[18] The narrative structure of the law is honored, but at a cost of deleting some of its greatest insights. Theological liberals sometimes do the same but with different criteria.

Perhaps the most common and damaging "criticism with a penknife"[19] is the practice of rejecting the "difficult" Old Testament law in favor of New Testament grace. Not only does this contradict the practice and teaching of Jesus, but it deprives the believer of a great portion of the Old Testament. New Testament commandments are not necessarily more authoritative than Old Testament laws. Neither can be understood or blindly followed apart from their context. Their meaning is their source of authority and derives from God's will for God's people in a particular time and place.

Christopher Wright has classified the Old Testament law into five categories, each of which functioned within a specific sphere of ancient Jewish life. These categories include criminal law, civil law, family law, cultic law, and charitable law.[20] Each of these areas of law was relative to the specific social structures of Israel. The law helped create and maintain these social structures. Today our social structures are different. Insofar as our societies are not agrarian, monarchical, slave-based, patriarchal, tribal, theocratic, polygamous, Middle Eastern, and so on, we will have to develop our own laws to govern ourselves.

Laws are functional within their spheres of authority. They reflect an orientation toward love of God and neighbor within a specific social setting. Insofar as our setting is similar, these laws provide wisdom and instruction to us today.

Jesus said, "'You shall love the Lord your God with all your heart, and with all your soul, and with all your mind.' This is the greatest and first commandment. And a second is like it: 'You shall love your neighbor as yourself.' On these two commandments hang all the law and the prophets" (Mt 22:37–40). Every kind of biblical literature must be understood both in relation to its context and in relation to the great love commandments. These commandments are the motive that lies behind every other commandment. We can learn from every law in the Bible when we understand how each law makes the love commandment specific in a particular context.

Biblical moral rules are usually simple and outline the boundaries of acceptable conduct rather than the specifics. For example, the prohibitions of the Decalogue (Ten Commandments) mark the edges of God's will and must be understood within the context of God's liberation of the people from Egypt and their revelatory purpose for Israel. The command not to steal, for example, does not elucidate the details of Christian economic relations. It does provide a basic boundary for acceptable economic behavior which has significance in every society. But the meaning of stealing may differ from culture to culture with varying definitions of property rights.

The prohibition of theft, like the other nine commandments, is not a timeless ethical principle that we must translate into different cultural idioms. Still less is it a criminal law code. The Decalogue includes no detailed legislation or penalties. Rather it is a commandment that derives its meaning from the countless rules and regulations that are given in the criminal, civil, family, cultic, and charitable law. Taken together, these laws provide a picture of the kind of community God wanted Israel to be in the early bronze age.

In order to understand the kind of community God wants us to be today, we must understand the picture drawn by the biblical narrative of the people of God. The laws enflesh that paradigmatic picture. We are not freed from the laws in the sense that we need not follow them. Rather, we are bound to follow the *meaning* of the law as it is contained in the account of God's will for Israel. As we can see from Jesus' commentary on the prohibition of adultery, that task may be far more rigorous than merely obeying the law. Jesus suggested that the meaning of adultery encompasses all male lust which objectifies women in the secret of the heart (Mt 5:27–28).

All of the classic "four uses of the law" may be understood as elucidating the symbolic structure of meaning revealed in the biblical story. (1) The theological or revelatory use of the law shows us the nature of the world and the meaning of our relationships and actions. (2) The moral use of the law convicts us of sin and drives us to Christ. (3) The political/social use of the law utilizes the paradigm of society revealed by the law to help create modern legal norms that will function in our society with similar purposes to the biblical law. (4) The didactic, teaching use of the law seeks concrete, applicable rules that are as relevant today as when they were first given by God, because the contextual meaning of the law still holds.

Luther and Calvin had a classic debate over the four uses of the law. Both accepted the first three, but Luther argued that because of grace we are freed from the fourth. My position combines the two Reformers' positions. Like Calvin, I do not think we are freed from the law. Like Luther, I do not believe we are bound by its particulars without consideration of con-

text. Insofar as we can discover it, we are bound to the *meaning* to which the law points. The meaning of the law can be understood only in relation to the story of which it is a part.

3. *Moral principles and themes.* A common approach to ethics is to seek the basic moral principles that lie behind all the rules, laws, and instructions of the Bible. The rule may then be disregarded in favor of the principle. The strength of this approach is that it seeks the meaning of the law. The principles of the great commandment to love God and your neighbor are the foundation of all Christian ethics. We are to interpret all the moral instruction of the Bible through the lens of these great principles.

Jesus is very harsh in his condemnation of those who meticulously follow every biblical rule but have forgotten the meaning and purpose of the law: "Woe to you, scribes and Pharisees, hypocrites! For you tithe mint, dill and cumin, and have neglected the weightier matters of the law: justice and mercy and faith. It is these you ought to have practiced without neglecting the others. You blind guides! You strain out a gnat but swallow a camel!" (Mt 23:23–24).

Justice, mercy, and faith are foundational to a moral life. Through them we can understand the meaning of the law. But there is danger in seeing them as the basic meaning behind the law. Even the greatest principles are abstractions that live primarily in the world of thought and words. What does it mean to love God and do justice? The law tells you how in a specific situation. Even better, a story tells you how. If the great principles that may be deduced from the parable of the good Samaritan or the parable of the prodigal son are listed, some might think we have clearer teaching. But the principles listed are not more than the story. They are very much less. The idea that God loves sinners may leave a person cold. But the image of the father rushing to embrace his rebellious son grips the heart. It tells us how God loves us by giving us an image that relates to our experience and imagination.

Principles are indispensable to biblical ethics, but they should not be elevated to become the central source, still less the *only* source, of ethics. Principles are a tool for understanding the meaning of God's will, divorced from any specific situation or context. They lack the specificity of contact with cultural reality. Christians who make principles central often attempt to prioritize them to overcome situations of value conflict. For example, if the principle of protecting life is higher than the principle of telling the truth, then Rahab's lie can be justified.[21] Others absolutize certain principles in such a way that a sociocultural interpretation of the principle is treated like a moral rule that gives the same answer in every possible situation.[22]

With the exception of the great commandment, principles should not be rigidified into a strict hierarchy. It is not clear from the biblical record that a life is always of more value than the truth, or that, to quote Norman Geisler, "a complete person is more valuable than an incomplete person."[23] Nor should a particular cultural interpretation of a principle be taken as a rule for all time. Honoring parents (a principle) does not necessarily mean patriarchy (a sociocultural structure).

Just as principles help us see the meaning of biblical laws, so laws reveal the meaning of principles in a particular context. The real meaning of a principle can be understood only as it touches reality. But where it touches different realities, its incarnated meaning changes. The principle does not change at the level of abstract words. Justice and love remain the ideals. But whether they mean a person should be forgiven or stoned depends on the context.

Often moral rules point beyond themselves to principles. Take this moral rule: "If you take your neighbor's cloak in pawn, you shall return it to him by sunset, because it is his only covering. It is the cloak in which he wraps his body; in what else can he sleep? If he appeals to me, I will listen, for I am full of compassion" (Ex 22:26 NEB; this is categorized by Wright among the "charitable laws"). Taken as a moral rule, this may not give us much direct help for specific economic relations in the modern world. Coats are not usually taken in pawn today, and even if they were, they are not usually the only thing in which a person can sleep.[24] The law points beyond itself to the principle of compassion for the poor. The principle teaches us that God cares about the poor and how we treat them.

The meaning of the principle of care for the poor is derived from this and many other rules about how one

should treat a poor person in a particular situation. Principles are tools to help us reincarnate moral practice from one context to another. By abstracting some of the meaning from a law in simple form, they help us see how God's will in the biblical context might be relevant to us, even though our context is different. But the real meaning of the principle is revealed only in good practices in actual life.

The prophets continually appeal to ethical principles that go beyond the limited scope of moral rules. Often these appeals come in the form of warnings against evil practices. For example, "Woe ... to those who issue oppressive decrees, to deprive the poor of their rights and withhold justice from the oppressed of my people.... What will you do on the day of reckoning, when disaster comes from afar?" (Is 10:1–4 NIV). Legal oppression is denounced with an appeal to the principle of justice for the poor. The meaning of the principle derives from specific practices of oppression.

Moral rules and commandments should not be stripped of their power by abstraction into principles or dispositions, as if the rule could then be discarded as merely local. The rules put flesh on principles. It is more helpful to think of principles as abstractions from rules rather than rules as applications of principles. A theological, narrative understanding of the commandments protects them from ahistorical legalism and makes possible their application in altered form to new historical situations. Principles help transfer the meaning of good and evil from one context to another.

Principles lack the sharp definition of laws but provide an intermediate step through which contextual laws can be "reincarnated" in another cultural context. A good biblical example of this process is provided by Jesus in the Sermon on the Mount. "Eye for eye, tooth for tooth" (Ex 21:24) was an Old Testament law meant to protect a neighbor from excessive retaliation in the context of tribal warfare. Jesus does not simply discard the law but reformulates its deep, original meaning in terms of love for one's enemy. The original law protected the people against feuds and extremes of vengeance. Its meaning was rooted in respect for the rights of the enemy. Jesus does not eliminate that meaning but shows its logical implication.

4. *Why should we be good?* The fourth level of

moral discourse has been called the "postethical" or "meta-ethical" level. Here the question is asked, Why be moral? What is the foundation and meaning of goodness?

There is an extensive philosophical debate over whether theology and morality are interdependent.[25] The Bible does not offer logical or philosophical arguments for the meaning or basis of morality. Nor does it offer such arguments for the existence of God. Without entering into the debate over whether all morality is logically dependent on theology,[26] we can say it is clear that faith in the God of the Bible requires or entails moral behavior. In both testaments those who identify themselves as God's people are called to be like God in character and moral practice. God's people are to be holy because God is holy (Lev 11:45). They are to be merciful because God is merciful (Num 14:18–19; compare Hos 6:6). Jesus said, "Be perfect, therefore, as your heavenly Father is perfect" (Mt 5:48; compare 5:43–47).

But the basis of biblical morality is not an abstract demand that we imitate God; it is an appeal to respond to the inherent nature of who God is and what God has done. God is first of all presented in the Bible as our creator. Because God is both loving and creator, we are to be good because God made us to be good. Goodness is good for us because we were made in the image of God and can become who we are meant to be only by being like God. God created us as cultural creatures; therefore our goodness must be expressed in and through our cultures.

The Bible also pictures God as our parent. The Bible simply assumes that certain responses to one's creator and parent are appropriate and good. The definitions of creator, father, and mother are assumed to carry self-evident moral requirements. In the West, with its tremendous emphasis on individual autonomy and personal freedom, some may find this assumption more difficult to follow than those in other parts of the world. The majority of cultures in the world see obedience to parents as basic to membership within the community. Those who have been abandoned or abused by their father or mother may find the analogy of obedience to God as Father and Mother less than self-evident.[27] Nevertheless, whether or not the assumption of God's rights as parent are accepted, in

the Bible they are assumed as universal for all God's created offspring.

The biblical story of God's love for his children is the paradigmatic story from which we are to understand our rights and responsibilities in human families. God is pictured as both a father and mother to us, but we are not to see God primarily as like our earthly mother or father, who may or may not be good.[28] Rather, we should be parents who love our children the way God loves us. The image is transcultural and rooted in biology, even though its realization on earth will vary according to different cultural patterns of family structure. Matriarchal, patriarchal, egalitarian, nuclear, extended, and other family structures are all capable of reflecting God's love through the parents to the children.

Third, we are to be good because God is the lawgiver and judge of all the earth. God reserves the right as our creator and parent to judge the whole earth. As judge, God demands obedience. Richard Mouw has written a carefully nuanced book that argues that all Christian morality is founded on the idea of "moral surrender to the divine will."[29] As Mouw points out, surrender to God's authority need not be founded on fear of judgment; nevertheless, God's judgment is an inevitable aspect of God's authority. This image is prominent in Islam, which means submission.

The biblical picture of God as judge assumes that morality makes sense because there is goodness and justice at the heart of the universe. Justice and righteousness in the present make sense because, in the biblical story, God will someday establish them on earth. The coming kingdom of God is both motive and goal of Judeo-Christian ethics. The God of justice and the God of mercy are one and the same. God will judge the earth because God loves the earth.

Fourth, we are to be good because we are partners with God in a covenant. There is a paradox in the Bible on this point. On the one hand this covenant is a gift. It is unearned and eternal. On the other hand it is a mutual agreement that entails promises. The requirements of the covenant are religious fidelity (God is pictured as a husband and Israel as his bride) and social justice. In the New Testament, God's people have been accepted and forgiven through the new covenant sealed with the blood of Christ. Membership in this covenant is confirmed by obedience to Christ (Jas 2:17; see also Mt 25:31–46; Heb 6:4–8).

This points us to what I take as the central ethical image in the biblical story. We are to live well as the fitting response to God as our lover and redeemer.[30] Morality in the Bible is fundamentally seen as a response to God's grace in choosing, liberating, blessing, forgiving, and judging us. The focal point of revelation is the mystery of the incarnation. God's Son, Jesus, took upon himself the agony of history and died to set God's people free. If we are really free, then we must live in the true freedom of obedience (Gal 5:1).

Biblical goodness is linked to gratitude, reverence, loyalty, faith, and hope. These virtues transcend all cultures. Above all, goodness is revealed in love. The law of love opposes and denies the validity of every cultural custom that restricts the flow of God's love in the community. God's love in Christ breaks down all ethnic, social, economic, and sexual barriers that lead to the oppression of one group by another (Gal 3:28). The Bible tells us a story in historical, cultural terms of God's character and action in history. This story tells us why we should be good.

The Cultural Context of the Reader

It is not possible for us to understand the story of the Bible "objectively." As I have already indicated, all of knowledge is "subjective" in the sense that whatever we know, we know from a particular perspective. The goal of biblical understanding is not the formulation of some transcultural set of ethical principles but obedience to God in a particular time and place. People in different sociocultural situations may understand different things from the same story, in part because the will of God (but not the character of God) is different in different contexts.

The following story may raise disturbing new questions about a situation that had previously seemed clear and simple.

"Jane" taught English in a university in China. One day she saw "Kwei-feng" looking at someone else's paper on the final examination. Kwei-feng had often been in Jane's apartment, teaching her how to cook and engaging in deep conversations. They had

become good friends. Jane had threatened failure to anyone caught cheating, but if she failed Kwei-feng, she knew Kwei-feng's job prospects might well be destroyed for life. If Kwei-feng failed this class, she would be dismissed from the university with very slim possibilities for another chance at higher education or a decent job. Failure in the university could result in lifelong economic dependence on her parents. Her whole future might hang on this one exam. Besides, Kwei-feng was one of the most capable of Jane's students.

Jane could not recall any direct biblical passages on cheating, but she knew that dishonesty is wrong. The rules were clear, and academic standards were at stake. But was Kwei-feng really cheating, checking her answer with a friend, or just allowing her eyes to wander? If she was cheating, did it really warrant dismissal from the university? Did cheating mean the same thing here as in America? If it did, was it valued differently? Jane knew that her Chinese colleagues were very lax on cheating. But did the fact that they were lax mean she should be too?

What was the real meaning of Kwei-feng's wandering eyes? What was Jane's responsibility in the situation as a young American visiting teacher? Jane had gone to China with a very black-and-white view of right and wrong: rules should never be broken. But in this situation she was all at sea. When she confronted Kwei-feng in the hall and saw the anguished horror in her eyes, Jane's heart felt leaden and her rules hollow. Kwei-feng was her most promising student. How could she know what was good in this situation?

The question whether Kwei-feng was right to allow her eyes to wander is only a small part of the ethical dilemma in this story. In her own context, Jane would not have hesitated to fail a student caught cheating. She felt strongly about the biblical principle of honesty. Failure for cheating was simple justice. But did justice demand the same action in China?

Jane had to make a portentous decision quickly in a situation that she did not fully understand. If she had had more experience as a teacher in China, if she had understood the nature of the Chinese educational system better, if she had perceived a wider range of possible responses, if she had been able to consult a trusted Chinese Christian teacher, she would have been in a better position to know the will of God in this situation.

Jane approached the dilemma not only as a teacher in China but also as a North American with a well-established set of norms on things like cheating, plagiarism, intellectual property rights, academic competition, educational opportunity, and vocational freedom. None of these norms can be directly derived from the Bible, because in the biblical narrative there is no comparable sociocultural educational structure as now exists in the West. Nor, for that matter, is there a biblical educational structure comparable to that of China. Jane had to decide what to do based on a synthesis of educational values from her culture of origin, an understanding of the values of her new social situation and a critical assessment of both, based on the biblical story.

Since Jane's cultural situation in China was so far from the structures of education in the Bible, there were no concrete biblical laws or rules to tell her what to do.[31] General principles like honesty and justice seemed to be in tension with other principles like gentleness and mercy. Jane's emotions seemed to be in conflict with her rational, rule-oriented side. Perhaps of greatest importance was what kind of person Jane had become as a result of living her life in accordance with the Scriptures. If Jane was a person of integrity and compassion, a person of prayer and sensitivity, a person of self-control and wisdom, then she had a much greater chance of acting rightly in the situation. There is no law against the fruits of the Spirit (Gal 5:22–23). The guidance of the Holy Spirit might make up for her lack of cultural knowledge. On the other hand, even a godly person can make horrible mistakes. She would do well to learn the ropes of the Chinese educational system.[32]

The Bible is not an ancient puzzle to be solved but a narrative of God's action in history. As Brevard Childs has explained, "The central task is not the objective understanding of the Bible's ethical passages but the understanding of God's will."[33] It is impossible to know God's will apart from doing it in a particular human context. Knowledge is partial and dangerous when divorced from obedience and experience.[34] We cannot blithely say that we know what the Bible means before we have actually tried to do it.[35] In many instances we cannot know how to do God's will before we understand the sociocultural context in which we are placed.

The Sociocultural Context of the Bible: Model or Paradigm?

One of the knottiest problems for biblical social ethics is how to interpret the social structures assumed in the Bible. Are the structures of Israel an essential part of God's revelation? What is their ethical significance for us? The social, economic, political, and cultural structures assumed in the Bible are very foreign to most of us in the modern world. Most of us no longer live in a world of absolute monarchies, slavery, tribal and clan warfare, patriarchy (in its ancient Middle Eastern form), and animal sacrifice.

The entire Old Testament assumes that God's people are a political entity who are ideally ruled by God. Today most Christians assume that a theocracy is both impossible and undesirable. Apart from a few Islamic states, most countries of the world now assume a religious pluralism that is foreign to the world of the Bible.

Instead of the agrarian world assumed in much of the Old Testament, the world today is undergoing rapid urbanization. Instead of a world of assumed male superiority, many parts of the world have vigorous movements for women's equality. Instead of absolute monarchy, democracy is a pervasive ideal. Instead of an all-encompassing religious, economic, political, and social legal system, we have a patchwork of laws that govern different aspects of life in relation to social realities that are very different from those assumed in the Bible. Instead of face-to-face economic relations in which usury was forbidden, most of the world is structured around credit.

It is tempting to respond to these pervasive differences by simply rejecting at least the Old Testament as irrelevant to our time. The extent to which this is done by Christians of all theological convictions is one of the great tragedies of the church. Equally unacceptable are the attempts to require that all the Old Testament be literally followed or to limit the Old Testament to a source of "spiritual" typologies of Christ.

Christopher J. H. Wright offers a persuasive argument that the social shape of Israel is an essential part of its biblical theological significance.[36] The social laws of Israel cannot be easily separated from their theological motivation. Jewish law is continually justified with reference to the character of God. The revelation of God in the Bible is inseparable from an understanding of the kind of society Israel was meant to be. The story of God's work in the world cannot be divorced from the way God is revealed in the peculiar social structures of Israel.

In his massive study of the sociological world of the Old Testament prior to 1050 B.C., Norman Gottwald concludes that Israel was

> an egalitarian, extended family, segmentary, tribal society with an agricultural pastoral economic base ... characterized by profound resistance and opposition to the forms of political domination and social stratification that had become normative in the chief cultural and political centers of the ancient Near East.[37]

With the ancient law God offered Israel an opportunity to be different from the surrounding nations. Within the context of a social structure based on slavery, Israel was to free all slaves and give them a nest egg every seven years (Deut 15). Within the context of a political system of monarchy, Israel was to know that monarchy would become a vehicle of oppression (1 Sam 8) and that even its greatest king was not above the law of God (2 Sam 12). Within the context of an agricultural economy, Israel was to ensure that everyone had a fair share of land and that both land and animals would be respected (Lev 25). Within the context of patriarchy and polygamy, Israel was to protect the rights of women (Deut 21:10–14; 22:13–29).

It would be nice if all these points were unambiguous—even better, if the institutions that we find abhorrent were simply outlawed. The seeds of the destruction of monarchy, slavery, racism, sexism and polygamy are all found in the Old and New Testaments. But these seeds were beyond the perception of most of the biblical writers. In the Law and Prophets and the letters of Paul, structures of oppression are questioned, denounced, and ameliorated, but there are few calls for their abolition. In fact, these structures

were usually embedded in the thought patterns of the biblical writers.

The commandments of the Old and New Testament do not assume an ideal social structure for all time. Rather, they assume the social structure of *their own* time and outline ways in which Israel, or the church, was to be different. Israel provides a paradigm of God's will in relation to actual social conditions. Israel is not a model of how the church, still less any secular state, should be structured. The Old Testament tells a story of God's work in the ancient Near East that is relevant not only to the church but also to modern politics.

Theologians like Elisabeth Schüssler Fiorenza have argued that we need a "hermeneutic of suspicion" that ferrets out the influence of sexism on the biblical writers.[38] Fiorenza's hermeneutic of suspicion comes dangerously close to making her own subjective view of feminism into the critical standard by which everything else is judged. Nevertheless, a carefully used hermeneutic of suspicion can reveal how the social structures of the cultures of the Bible shaped its message in ways that are not relevant to our culture. Fiorenza suggests that in order to do this we must

> not understand the New Testament as an archetype but as a prototype. Both archetype and prototype denote original models. However, an archetype is an ideal form that establishes an unchanging timeless pattern, whereas a prototype is not a binding timeless pattern or principle. A prototype, therefore, is critically open to the possibility of its own transformation.[39]

The cultures of the Bible are no more authoritative than our own. Most of the Bible's moral exhortations were practically directed to people who were not living by idealized structures but according to the pagan practices around them. I suspect that things are not too different today. Biblical patterns of the extended family, home education, agriculture, usury, defense, and medicine are rarely seen as authoritative today. One of the great tasks of biblical interpretation is to distinguish between the will of God and the particular cultural homes in which it was biblically incarnated.

Bridging the Gap between Text and Today

The basic argument of this chapter has been that the biblical story, understood in context, teaches us to become good as we learn to see our lives as part of the same story. By guiding our interpretation, the story leads us to experience reality in a way that is consistent with God's work in the world. The story of God's work with Israel and revelation in Christ is our story too.

But it is not our only story. There is also the story of our lives that is inseparable from our cultural context. Our culture provides us with a symbolic meaning system from which we can never fully escape. We read the story of the Bible through cultural eyes. Our own cultural experience is not higher in authority than the Scriptures, but it is our starting place. It is also our goal. The Bible's teaching must be lived in our own cultural experience before we fully understand it.

This requires a process that is often called contextualization. We do not translate the Bible directly into a new cultural setting. Nor do we even "transculturate" it, as if the message of the gospel were an abstraction that could simply be expressed in different cultural forms.[40] It is the Bible, not an abstract interpretation of its message, that is authoritative. The message of the Bible can be understood only as it is perceived from a specific cultural standpoint. God's Word is always incarnated, and different parts of the church may incarnate it differently.[41] In other words, the content of the gospel cannot be separated from its cultural form.

The Reverend Nelly Hutahaean is a Batak pastor from North Sumatra, Indonesia. The following story relates how she tried to obey the God of the Bible in her own cultural context.[42]

> One day Ari, a close friend of Nelly, came to her to ask for help. Ari's father had been killed and her mother imprisoned for many years because of involvement with the communists. Ari was rescued as a baby and raised by a foster family. She was now eighteen years old and only two months away from graduation from high school. Ari was a conscientious student, well respected by her teachers and friends. Recently she had been chosen to represent the school in a traditional Batak dance performance. As Nelly met Ari, she saw that her eyes were swollen and her body covered with black and blue marks from the most recent beating she had received from her foster father.
>
> Every day Ari was required to come straight home from school and work in the house: washing clothes, cleaning, ironing, cooking, washing dishes, etc. She had been forbidden to take part in any extracurricular activities. Ari's foster father had very strict rules for her, and any deviation brought severe punishment. When the foster father found out she had accepted the honor of representing the school in the traditional dance, he locked all her school uniforms and books in the closet and forbade her to return to school.
>
> Ari could not stand the pain and degradation of her position in that house any longer. She received regular beatings and now was being denied the chance to finish high school. She asked Nelly to help her escape and run away to Jakarta. There she hoped to see her mother in prison and start a new life. Nelly's dilemma was over whether or not she should help Ari escape.

My first response to this story was outrage against the foster father and the conviction that Nelly should help Ari escape from such abuse. From my (Western) perspective, an eighteen-year-old had every right to flee from such a situation. Ari's foster family treated her like a slave. They would not allow her to finish high school. Her foster father abused her. And she wanted to meet her long-lost mother.

But Nelly was not so sure. She wanted to make sure that her response would be faithful to Scripture and wise in relation to the cultural situation. She pointed out that if Ari ran away and broke her relationship with her foster family, it would have a grave impact on the rest of her life. It would also bring severe repercussions on the whole foster family and even the whole community. Fleeing from the family would break one of the most basic taboos of the Batak people. It would be considered the greatest possible sin. Ari would be excommunicated not only from the family but from the entire community. Not only would she not finish high school, but she would be an outcast for life. As part of a Batak family, she was guaranteed material security for the future by the clan. If she ran away, she would become as one who is dead.

By breaking the most basic *adat* (tradition) of the society, Ari would also bring irreparable shame on the family and father who had raised her. Within the patriarchal, close-knit family structure of the clan, the father would be seen as having failed in his duty, and the whole family would suffer. He would be shunned. His business might well be boycotted and go bankrupt. The whole community would be divided and suffer the loss of his participation. The *adat* was so strong that no woman had ever dared flee before.

Nelly wanted to understand what she should do, both within this context and in the context of the Bible. On the one hand, the biblical story highly values the family. The fifth commandment requires that father and mother be honored and suggests that such honor brings with it a long and fruitful life (Deut 5:16). For almost eighteen years this family had raised Ari and paid for her schooling.

On the other hand, Ari seems to come under the category of an oppressed orphan. The Bible is full of commands like "Seek justice, rescue the oppressed, defend the orphan, plead for the widow" (Is 1:17). The God of the Bible is the defender of the weak.

Within the context of Batak culture, how could Nelly honor both themes in the Bible? Nelly believed that honor was due to the foster family that had raised Ari. On the other hand she knew Ari needed help and could not be abandoned to face her suffering alone.

After a process of reflection, biblical study, counsel with trusted members of the community, study of possible alternatives and repercussions, and planning,[43] Nelly arranged for Ari to be hidden with another local family. An elder of the community was selected to approach the foster father, reassure him of Ari's safety, tell him Ari's perspective, and ask him to forgive her and give his permission for her to finish school. Meanwhile, Nelly prayed that God would forgive her for her boldness and help Ari to be able to meet her mother. She also prayed for eventual reconciliation between Ari and her foster father.

In retrospect, Nelly reflected that within a paternalistic, collective, and family-oriented society such as hers, conflict such as this can seldom be solved by an individual. The leaders of the community are the only ones able to bring about a tolerable solution.

I learned much from this story. I saw that my Western, individualistic, human rights approach to a solution was inadequate. I also saw an example of a wise woman who took her culture and her faith very seriously. Nelly did not accept the patriarchal assumption that a father has unlimited power over his daughter. But she did not reject the communal resources of her culture for problem-solving. Nelly did not approach the Bible as a narrow rule book requiring a daughter always to obey. Nor did she simply resort to the popular "poor-and-oppressed" passages without consideration of the importance of family and communal structures. In her values and actions Nelly combined respect for authority, loyalty to the oppressed, and cultural sensitivity.

Because we live in a fallen world, we cannot be assured that stories such as this will all turn out right. In Ari's case the results were mixed. Ari is still not reconciled with her foster father, but she was able to finish high school and go on to university without being alienated from the community. Her mother is now free, and Ari is married and has children of her own. Nelly's story provides an example of someone who interpreted a moral crisis in her own culture through the lens of the biblical narrative. Nelly combined the story of the Bible with the story of her culture in such a way that her praxis was the product of wisdom.

Those of us who live in a foreign culture have a double task. We must continue to integrate the biblical story with the perspectives of our culture of origin. Beyond that, we must begin to understand our new home deeply enough so that its story may be seen and transformed through the Word of God.

Notes

[1] William A. Dyrness, *Learning about Theology from the Third World* (Grand Rapids, Mich.: Zondervan, 1990), p. 28. Of course the Bible itself is culturally located, but its original text functions cross-culturally for all Christians.

[2] David Kelsey, *The Uses of Scripture in Recent Theology* (Philadel-phia: Fortress, 1975), p. 89. Kelsey argues for an essentially functional definition of Scripture. That is, the Bible, or at least parts of the Bible, are Scripture because they function as authoritative for the Christian community. One may accept Kelsey's functional definition without denying (as Kelsey does) that "authori-

tative" is a judgment about Scripture in and of itself. I would hold that the entire canon of the Bible functions as authoritative for the Christian community because Christians believe God has made it the authoritative vehicle of revelation.

3 For the purpose of this chapter, I ignore the problems raised by textual criticism. There are extensive debates about just what is the original text of Scripture. These debates are important but lie beyond the scope of this chapter and the competence of its argument. There are also very significant differences in doctrines of the authority of Scripture, but whatever their differences, most Christians account for their beliefs and behavior in relation to Scripture.

4 Robert McAfee Brown, *Unexpected News: Reading the Bible with Third World Eyes* (Philadelphia: Westminster Press, 1984), p. 13. "The strange new world within the Bible" is a term borrowed from Karl Barth.

5 Unfortunately, sometimes translations of the text enshrine the interpretation of the (usually white male) translator. The text may then be narrowed in its meaning or even made to say what is not there, based on the cultural bias of the translator.

6 Kraft writes, "The Scriptures are like the ocean and supra cultural truth like the icebergs that float in it. Many icebergs show at least a bit of themselves above the surface, some lie entirely beneath the surface. Much of God's [self] revelation ... in the Scriptures is at least partially visible to nearly anyone who is willing to see it.... But much lies beneath the surface, visible only to those who search to discover what supra cultural truth lies beneath the specific cultural applications in Scripture" (Charles H. Kraft, *Christianity in Culture* [Maryknoll, N.Y.: Orbis, 1979], p. 131). Kraft's discussion of hermeneutical issues in chapter 7, "Supra Cultural Meanings via Cultural Forms," is very helpful. Still, I am not sure there are any "supracultural meanings" that exist denuded of cultural flesh. Every word of Scripture is itself a cultural form. If so, "supracultural meanings" may be more like molecules than like icebergs! Marvin Mayers, followed by Paul Hiebert, tries to improve on Eugene Nida's "relative cultural relativism" and proposes a model of ethical reflection based on "biblical absolutism and cultural relativism." While Mayers's approach has many helpful insights, it lacks the hermeneutical rigor displayed by Kraft. See chapter 16, "Cross-Cultural Ethics," in Marvin K. Mayers, *Christianity Confronts Culture*, 2nd ed. (Grand Rapids, Mich.: Zondervan, 1987), pp. 241–60). Also see Paul G. Hiebert, *Cultural Anthropology* (Grand Rapids, Mich.: Baker Book House, 1983), pp. 251–62.

7 Eugene A. Nida, *Customs, Culture and Christianity* (New York: Harper & Brothers, 1954), p. 282; see also pp. 48–53. Actually even this statement is questionable, since our understanding of the Triune God is far from absolute. But Nida's intention is to locate all that is infinite and absolute with God.

8 George A. Lindbeck, *The Nature of Doctrine* (Philadelphia: Westminster Press, 1984), p. 35.

9 Ibid., p. 33.

10 Iris Murdoch, "Against Dryness: A Polemical Sketch," in *Revisions*, ed. Stanley Hauerwas and Alasdair MacIntyre (Notre Dame, Ind.: University of Notre Dame Press, 1983), p. 49.

11 Alasdair MacIntyre, *Whose Justice? Which Rationality?* (Notre Dame, Ind.: University of Notre Dame Press, 1988), p. 393.

12 For the sake of brevity, I am simplifying MacIntyre considerably.

13 "The Christian tradition" is in fact many different traditions, each of which describes the world differently. When I speak of "Christians" as if they were all from one tradition, I am simplifying in order to make a point. By the word *Christians*, I assume a broad, central stream of the Christian tradition, including both Protestants and Catholics, which treats the Bible as Scripture.

14 Lindbeck, *Nature of Doctrine*, p. 118.

15 Kelsey, *Uses of Scripture*, p. 48. To approach the Bible like this is not to ignore the insights of biblical critical scholars. They may help us understand the story contained in the Bible. But the focus is not on some revelatory event that lies behind the text (as in Gerhard von Rad) nor on the experience of the community that transmitted it (as in Rudolf Bultmann), nor even on revelatory experience of the modern reader (as in Karl Barth), but on the story in the text of the canon as it now stands (see the work of Brevard Childs, such as *Introduction to the Old Testament as Scripture* [Philadelphia: Fortress, 1979]).

16 These four "levels of moral discourse" were first distinguished by Henry David Aiken but have been adapted many times since. Henry David Aiken, *Reason and Conduct* (New York: Alfred Knopt, 1962), pp. 65–87. Compare Allen Verhey, "The Use of Scripture in Ethics," *Religious Studies Review* 4 (January 1978); James Gustafson, *Theology and Christian Ethics* (Philadelphia: United Church Press, 1974), pp. 130–33. As a typology of ways of relating ethics to Scripture, the four levels are far too simplistic. We learn goodness from the Bible in many more ways than this. However, the four levels still capture four questions that trouble many Christians.

17 Gerhard von Rad, *Old Testament Theology* (San Francisco: Harper & Row, 1965), 2:204.

18 I have no written reference for this view but have often heard it expressed by believers within Plymouth Brethren circles. The dispensationalist approach pioneered by J. N. Darby has the advantage of trying to fit the law into a narrative structure of God's work in the world. On the other hand, some of Darby's followers have propagated an extreme literalism that does violence to the original meaning of the text in its context and results in a narrow legalism. Every instruction of the Bible that is not assigned to another dispensation must be followed to the letter.

19 The practice of cutting out any parts of Scripture that a person does not like. The prototypical example of this practice was the heretic Marcion (second century A.D.), who deleted the Old Testament and significant parts of the New which did not meet his approval.

20 Christoper J. H. Wright, *Living as the People of God* (Leicester, U.K.: InterVarsity Press, 1983), pp. 151–52; also published as *An Eye for an Eye* (Downers Grove, Ill.: InterVarsity Press, 1984). Wright's classification of the law was first proposed by A. Phillips, *Ancient Israel's Criminal Law: A New Approach to the Decalogue* (London: Blackwell, 1970).

21 Joshua 2:1–7. See John Jefferson Davis, *Evangelical Ethics* (Phillipsburg, N.J.: Presbyterian and Reformed, 1985), pp. 15–16. Norman L. Geisler is also an exponent of what he calls "ethical hierarchicalism"; see *Ethics: Alternatives and Issues* (Grand Rapids, Mich: Zondervan, 1971).

22 Bill Gothard's popular teaching on the principle of family hierarchy falls in this category. Gothard absolutizes the sociocultural system of patriarchy in the name of biblical principles.

23 Geisler, *Ethics*, p. 117. Geisler makes the absurd statement concerning those with physical limitations that "a person who is physically complete has a better manifestation of humanity than one who is not." By this measure Hitler showed more humanity than Helen Keller!

24 This observation does not apply to street people. But street people's coats are not usually worth enough to take in pawn. If they were, this rule might well be authoritative in its literal sense.

25 See, for example, Ian T. Ramsey, ed., *Christian Ethics and Moral Philosophy* (London: SCM Press, 1966), and Gene Outka and

John P. Reeder Jr., eds., *Religion and Morality* (Garden City, N.Y.: Anchor/Doubleday, 1973).

[26] This is a fundamental question of epistemology. It appears to me that the argument hinges on an evaluation of David Hume's familiar dictum "No Ought from an Is: no ethical conclusions from non-ethical premises." It is certainly possible to argue that the conception of a biblical God in itself requires some ethical conclusions. See Dewi Z. Phillips, "God and Ought," in *Christian Ethics and Moral Philosophy*, ed. Ian T. Ramsey (London: SCM Press, 1966), pp. 140–44. On the other hand, some argue that religious belief is itself dependent upon a priori moral judgments. See Kai Nielsen's article in the same volume, "Some Remarks on the Independence of Morality from Religion." Both of these positions may be argued without contradiction. A person can certainly make moral decisions about the goodness or existence of God without having belief or formal theology. But that does not imply that the person's moral ability or awareness did not come from God. If we begin with the assumptions of the biblical narrative, it is clear that God is the source of all morality. William Frankena is probably right in his assertion that a rational justification of ethics is possible without logically requiring a religious premise. See Frankena, "Is Morality Logically Dependent on Religion?" in *Religion and Morality*, ed. Gene Outka and John P. Reeder Jr. (Garden City, N.Y.: Anchor/Doubleday, 1973), p. 259. I would argue, however, that from Christian premises the ultimate meaning of both morality and reason is founded in the character of God. See C. S. Lewis, *Miracles* (New York: Macmillan, 1947).

[27] Those with painful family relationships should be reassured that God is not a parent like their parents, but rather their *mother* and *father* ought to be like their heavenly Father and Mother.

[28] Images of God as father are pervasive in both testaments. Images of God as mother are rarer because of the patriarchal structures of Israel. Nevertheless, there are a few mother images of God. See, for example, Isaiah 66:12–13. The terms *father* and *mother* are human symbols or signs of what God is like. Since God is a spirit and has no sexual organs, neither image should be taken as literal (see Jn 4:24).

[29] Richard J. Mouw, *The God Who Commands* (Notre Dame, Ind.: University of Notre Dame Press, 1990), p. 2. Mouw is careful not to base such surrender primarily on God's power to judge the earth, but God's absolute authority over the earth clearly entails judgment as one aspect of God's authority. Mouw's book helpfully restores obedience to a central place in ethics. Unlike Mouw, I do not think it is the central moral image of the biblical narrative.

[30] This is a pervasive theme in the writings of H. Richard Niebuhr.

[31] Perhaps the closest analogy is found in the book of Daniel, where Daniel is a student and teacher in a foreign context in which he must meet the demands of the Babylonian educational structure or face death. We are told that Daniel "responded with prudence and discretion" (Dan. 2:14). But this is still a far cry from Jane's situation.

[32] In this case Jane gave Kwei-feng a stern warning and allowed her to finish the examination in a different seat. But even a year later she was unsure if she had done the right thing. One reason cheating is common in many communal cultures is that individuals often have very little sense of the private ownership of ideas. An African student once commented, "Cheating is when one person withholds that which another person has need of."

[33] Brevard Childs, *Biblical Theology in Crisis* (Philadelphia: Westminster Press, 1970), p. 126.

[34] See, for example, the results of Pharaoh's knowledge of God's will prior to his obedience to God's will. The result of knowledge without obedience was "so the heart of Pharaoh was hardened" (see Ex. 9:27–35).

[35] The influence of Latin American theology can be discerned in these thoughts. For example, José Miguez Bonino says, "Correct knowledge is contingent on right doing," and "faith is always a concrete obedience" (*Doing Theology in a Revolutionary Situation* [Philadelphia: Fortress, 1975], pp. 89–90). The emphasis of liberation theology is on the movement from action (praxis) to thought (biblical ethics). This emphasis is good as a corrective but must not obscure the fact that the movement is dialectical and goes both ways.

[36] Wright, *Living as the People of God*.

[37] Norman K. Gottwald, *The Tribes of Yahweh: A Sociology of the Religion of Liberated Israel 1250–1050 BCE* (London: SCM Press, 1979), p. 10.

[38] Elisabeth Schüssler Fiorenza, *In Memory of Her: A Feminist Reconstruction of Christian Origins* (New York: Crossroad, 1983).

[39] Ibid., p. 33. This short discussion only scratches the surface of the hermeneutical issues raised. Fiorenza's book includes a very helpful overview of different feminist approaches. See also Phyllis Trible, *God and the Rhetoric of Sexuality* (Philadelphia: Fortress, 1978), and Letty Russell, *Human Liberation in a Feminist Perspective* (Philadelphia: Westminster Press, 1974).

[40] Charles H. Kraft, *Christianity in Culture* (Maryknoll, N.Y.: Orbis, 1979). See pp. 280–89.

[41] I understand this as one of the major points argued persuasively in Dyrness, *Learning about Theology from the Third World*.

[42] Nelly is a graduate student at Satya Wacana Christian University. She wrote out this story in Indonesian as one of the requirements for an ethics course I taught in the spring of 1992. With her permission I have paraphrased her story in English, shortening it and emphasizing portions that suit the needs of this chapter.

[43] These are elements in the well-known "hermeneutical circle."

Questions for Discussion and Reflection

1. What do you think are the main points Adeney is trying to make about the use of the Bible in ethics?

2. How do you think the Old Testament is relevant to ethics today? What does Adeney suggest about this?

3. What do you think Adeney means when he says, "It is not possible for us to understand the Bible 'objectively'?" Do you agree with Adeney on this?

4. How does Adeney use biblical principles in ethics? Do you agree that principles need to be understood from within the culture in which they were drawn?

5. Do you agree that "the prohibition of theft, like the other nine commandments, is not a timeless ethical principle that we must translate into different cultural idioms"? Why or why not?

The Moral Context of Business

Donald Schmeltekopf

(Waco: Baylor Business School, 2003).

I have entitled this lecture "The Moral Context of Business," and in it I argue that the ethical dimensions of business activity, from the large corporation to the small enterprise, can be fully understood and appreciated only if we have a clear, persuasive account of the meaning and purpose of business in the first place. And such an account requires us to move into theological and metaphysical territory, engaging subjects such as God, creation, the common good, vocation, and sin. The exploration of such matters will help us, I believe, illuminate the moral requirements and virtues that we generally believe should guide our lives, whether at home or work or play, and thus to situate and define the moral context in which business activity takes place. The deep problem that we face in business, both as practitioners and as those preparing to become practitioners, is the fragmented and divided life—the habit, namely, of separating our most important beliefs and convictions that we celebrate on Sundays from the practical realities of work on Mondays. This problem is not peculiar to business—it is the predicament of all modern secular people who daily breathe the ideological air of individualism and relativism—but it is an especially significant problem for business because of the dominant role that business plays in contemporary culture. In short, my thesis is that the activity of business, at its most basic levels, cannot be separated from its moral and religious context, and that it must meet the tests of moral and religious truth every bit as much as the tests of empirical facts and data that normally occupy our business thinking.

It is important to remember and to acknowledge at the outset the ways that business has contributed to our individual and collective life in America and around the world. American businesses employ approximately 55 percent of all United States citizens in the workforce, with government, education, the professions, and various cultural and religious institutions providing the remaining jobs for American workers.

Indeed, business activity constitutes the backbone of an economy that makes possible the high standard of living we enjoy in this country. Business has been responsible for the enhanced technology that has largely replaced the drudgery of most manual labor, a consequence in part of the inventiveness of business and its willingness to take and bear the burden of financial risk. Furthermore, perhaps no institution in our common life is more efficient in its operations and more rational in its organization than business. No institution is more responsive to the demands of its constituents than business. We must note as well that businesses pay a large share of the taxes that help to support our common defense, ensure safety in our homes and cities, and provide the necessary social services from which we all benefit. And there can be little doubt that most business firms conduct their affairs as good citizens of our various communities.

On the other hand, as we are all aware, business—especially in the form of some major corporations—has been guilty of some outrageous unethical and illegal conduct over the past twenty-five years or so. One thinks of the Ford Pinto case in the late 1970s that exemplified indifference to human safety issues within the American automobile industry; of management fraud in the savings and loan industry in the 1980s; of the insider trading scandals of large financial companies in the early 1990s; of the Ford and Firestone scandals in automobile safety; of cases of management fraud in companies such as Enron, Tyco, and WorldCom; of the avalanche of recent corporate accounting scandals in firms such as Adelphia Communications, Dynegy, Global Crossing, Reliant Energy, and Xerox, and the role played in those scandals by firms, such as Arthur Andersen, that were charged with ensuring the integrity of the accounting process; and of a spate of low-level scams by several major corporations, including a rigged marketing test by the head of Coca-Cola Company's fountain division. Other corporate actions, such as the extraordinary compensation packages of some CEOs, or disregarding environmental issues, while perhaps not illegal in themselves, nevertheless add to the public perception that a significant number of corporations in America today are driven solely by self-interest. These incidents have led many to conclude that a culture of greed infects much of corporate America today.

When asked recently if business maintained a reasonable balance between profits and the common good, 85 percent of the American public answered "No!" A September 2002 poll conducted by Peter Hart Research Associates found that Americans viewed large corporations in a more negative than positive light for the first time since such opinions have been surveyed. The report concluded that "Corporate scandals have left Americans angry at CEOs and skeptical about corporate America."[1] In addition, a survey conducted by the Gallup organization in 1988 revealed that of the ten major institutions in American life, business ranked last in public confidence and trust.[2] This cynicism regarding the institution of business is not only bad for business, but it is also harmful to our wider culture because it encourages the view that *no* human institutions can be trusted. From that attitude there is not much of a leap to the broader cynical claim articulated in our culture today, "Everyone should look out for himself, and let the devil take the hindmost." Can our nation's schools of business do anything to address this state of affairs, at least as it relates to the conduct and culture of business? On the positive side, schools of business across the country have worked hard in recent decades to enhance the quality of their programs, especially those who care about the professional and intellectual standards of their fields.

A century ago business programs in our nation's colleges and universities consisted of little more than a dash of economics, a sprinkling of accounting, and bits of business principles and management. Today, by contrast, all the disciplines and sub-disciplines in business programs are highly specialized and grounded in principles of scientific quantification, particularly taking into account empirical data regarding economic behavior. Students in our business schools, whether undergraduate or graduate, are expected to acquire the skills and knowledge associated with these special-ized disciplines. When these students graduate, they are not only "business smart," they are also prepared to manage day-to-day business operations—the processes of business activity. However, what is often still lacking in the curriculum of our business schools is a serious engagement with the moral and spiritual values that should inform the purpose and meaning of business. In a recent study of MBA student attitudes, only 22 percent of the respondents said that their schools were preparing them adequately for the ethical issues that arise in management.[3] Such ethical and spiritual issues must be taken seriously within the business curriculum, not because of the special pleading by a few outspoken critics in our universities and in the media, but because these issues are fundamentally important to us as human beings and because our desire to pursue them is deeply embedded in and motivated by our natural desire to understand the human condition, human flourishing, and the common good. For this reason, many academics advocate a strong liberal arts education for all students. The prevailing assumption in many business schools, however—and, in fact, in some universities as well—is that such moral and metaphysical questions are not susceptible to rational and empirical investigation, and hence are by definition private matters best left to "bull" sessions and sermons. This false assumption leads to the reductionist view that the ultimate ends of business activity are finally and of necessity individualistic in nature, that business itself is a mere instrumentality for each person to get whatever he or she can while the getting is good.

To repeat my question, can our schools of business address the value-related concerns of business in order to provide a genuine grounding in what I am calling "the moral context of business"? Fortunately, many recent developments indicate that schools of business are beginning to address these issues. American colleges and universities have offered business ethics courses for at least thirty years, and the number of such courses continues to grow annually. In fact, some accrediting bodies, such as the one for accounting, now require ethics courses for all majors in the respective fields. Many universities have established endowed chairs in the area. This growth in the field of business ethics has also led to the creation of three academic journals and the founding of a national professional association, the Society for Business Ethics.

One of the most thoughtful and influential attempts to address these value-related issues is taking place at the Harvard Business School. Several years ago, with the strong encouragement of the university administration and after extensive study by and preparation of the faculty, the Harvard Business School substantially revised the MBA curriculum to strike an appropriate balance between values, knowledge, and skills. The faculty and administration of the Harvard Business School recognized that any university holding a public trust has the obligation to teach more than knowledge and information; it must also provide opportunities for students to engage questions of value, because all of life, including business life, continually requires human beings to respond to such questions. The faculty at Harvard understood that value neutrality is not an option. Indeed, there is no such thing as value neutrality. We teach values even when we are silent about them. Therefore, the Harvard Business School developed and implemented a revised MBA program, at the heart of which was the required interdisciplinary study of "Leadership, Ethics, and Corporate Responsibility," now called "Corporate Governance, Leadership, and Values." This study comes through a significant module of the curriculum during the first semester of a student's enrollment, but it also spans the entire MBA curriculum. Harvard's vision here is a noble one. As Thomas R. Piper, one of the founders of the program, wrote: "[The goal] is to better fulfill our fundamental responsibility: that is, to educate professional women and men who possess not only certain basic skills and knowledge, and a broad managerial perspective, but also a heightened sense of the moral and social responsibility their education and future positions of power require."[4]

Implicit in Harvard's undertaking are unstated theological/metaphysical beliefs about human beings and the world. In attempting to provide a general justification for the vision inspiring the new MBA curriculum, Professor Piper employs phrases such as "failing faith" and "the joining of career and purpose," and he writes about overcoming cynicism with "a sense of purpose, worth, responsibility and accountability, and hope."[5]

This is the language of moral and religious truth being applied within the context of business. But Harvard's effort is undermined because, as a secular institution, it must avoid all overtly theological and metaphysical commitments. Thus, what I would like to do in the remainder of this lecture is discuss explicitly what I take to be the main lines of a Judeo-Christian understanding of the meaning and purpose of business, supplemented by some complementary themes from the ancient Greek tradition. Through a discussion of these fundamental beliefs and ideas, I hope to clarify what I have in mind by the moral context of business and its implications for business ethics.

First, let us begin with some theological background by recounting what many theologians refer to as simply the "Biblical story," the grand narrative of God's relationship to all the world. According to scripture, God created "the heavens and the earth." From this it follows, as the Psalmist said, that "the earth is the Lord's and the fullness thereof, the world and those who dwell therein." Regarding human beings we are told that God "created humankind in his own image, in the image of God he created them; male and female he created them" (Genesis 1:27). Furthermore, God gave these human beings a special responsibility to "have dominion over the fish of the sea, and over the birds of the air, and over the cattle, and over all the earth" (1:28). This dominion is not to be understood as ownership, but as stewardship, for the earth is the Lord's, not ours. According to scripture, the work given to man is good; indeed, God Himself worked, creating the heavens, the earth, and all therein, and on the seventh day of creation, God rested. Later in the story, we are instructed to worship God and God alone, to obey His commandments, and to live in covenant with Him and with one another.

However, we humans turned away from God, worshipping the creation rather than the creator. This sin not only separated us from God, but also caused us to be unfaithful stewards of the earth and its resources. Our idolatry—our disobedience to God's commandments to worship Him alone and to love our neighbors as ourselves—has left us humans in a moral and spiritual morass and thus at odds with the very nature of things. God's plan of redemption comes through the people of Israel and through His own son, Jesus of Nazareth, the one person who is both fully human and fully divine. His life, death, and resurrection made reconciliation with God possible and thus, through the Holy Spirit and in fellowship with other believers, we are given purpose and hope in this world and for the next.

There is much more to the Biblical story than this, of course. I have given only a sketch, and many more details might be filled in.[6] But if we believe this story, we can see within it an implicit theological/metaphysical foundation for a rich understanding of the meaning and purpose of business. What are these underlying and grounding convictions? First, since God is the creator, the earth is the Lord's, and He has commissioned us to take care of His world and of "those who dwell therein." Second, since we are called to be stewards of all that God has entrusted to us, we must use the just institutions established within society to facilitate that stewardship. Third, all worldly goods are a gift of God, and thus we must be good stewards of our economic resources while at the same time avoiding the desire to be rich, for, as the Apostle Paul wrote, "the love of money is the root of all evils." Fourth, because sin works actively in all of us, the stewardship we are called by God to render can be systematically corrupted by self-interest and the love of material things. We should not be deluded either by the pretensions of our own self-righteousness or by the illusion that the world of business is essentially value neutral. Fifth, because the freedom from such corruption is found in Christ, the Christian believer needs ongoing fellowship and worship in the life of the church.[7]

In the Christian tradition, we use the word "economy" to refer to God's plan for the ordering and management of our material well-being within a world which, on the one hand, God has created, but which, on the other hand, is broken and undone by human sinfulness. Taken in its simplest sense, the economy is that set of complex structures and activities that has as its purpose the governing of our business and working life in its totality, under the authority of God. Seen in this way, the economy is an institution alongside other institutions, such as the family, the church, government and law, hospital and other

health-related organizations, and cultural entities, such as the university, that God has established for the survival and flourishing of the human race. None of these institutions exists merely for itself. All exist for the good of humankind and the glory of God, are related to one another in significant ways, and reflect overall the "Divine Economy" of God's governance of the whole world in light of the human condition. As a specific institution, the economy, as understood in the Judeo-Christian tradition, has as its guiding and foundational starting point the grounding convictions I have already noted: that God is the creator of heaven and earth; that this world is His, not ours; that what we possess, including our wealth, is a gift from God; that we are charged by God to be good stewards of all that has been given and entrusted to us; that our labor and talents are to be offered in service to others, not merely in service to ourselves; that our work is the primary means by which we exhibit our stewardship of the earth and our service to others; that our tendency to self-love often causes us to fail in our responsibility to be good stewards; that we commit idolatry by worshipping the creation—material things, for example—or parts of it—money, for example—rather than the creator; and that the church, if it is to be relevant to our lives, must be a genuine community that not only calls us to the worship of the one true God, but also convicts us of our idolatry and self-love. Taken together, these foundational beliefs constitute the moral and spiritual framework for our lives in the economy, what I am calling the moral context of business.

Some may object at this point that (1) all these so-called "convictions" cannot be rationally believed, at least for us modern human beings; that (2) since apparently only a small number of people actually hold and live by these views, it would be foolish to take them seriously; and that (3) if one were to adopt such convictions, he or she would be palpably disadvantaged in the workplace—to put the matter bluntly, that he or she would appear naive and a bit foolish, a perpetual pauper as a Christian in business. My reply to the first objection is that these grounding convictions arise not out of mere suprarational mystery, but out of the living history of Israel and Jesus of Nazareth, as portrayed in the Biblical drama and as validated by two centuries of theological tradition and the moral teachings of the church. Yes, to believe in God and in the truth of the Biblical story is ultimately a matter of revelation and faith, but such belief is not without both rational and empirical evidence, as the testimony of the Christian ages attests. With regard to the second objection, no matter how few or how many people in the workplace actually live by these convictions, the Judeo-Christian understanding of business and the workplace nevertheless contains the truth with respect to all the fundamental and normative issues underlying the economy, irrespective of the historical time, place, or circumstance. And, finally, because I believe genuine and fully relevant truth is in this understanding, I do not think one would necessarily be disadvantaged in the workplace, although certainly at times one will need to make real sacrifices and may sometimes be considered naive. But this fact characterizes the life of Christian integrity in all spheres of human endeavor, not just within the economy.

I suspect that many people, perhaps the typical businessperson, might raise a fourth objection: that it is simply foolish for anybody in business to be concerned at all about theological notions and moral issues. Business is just business, they say. It has its own principles, methods, and practices, quite apart from theology and metaphysics. Business is sort of a game, with its own rules and system of scoring. One's primary goal in the game of business is to win against competitors, which means, at the least, to maximize profits for oneself or for the corporation and its shareholders. This line of thinking argues that as long as this is done within the law and with a sense of enlightened self-interest, one has really done about all that can be asked.

This is a recipe for the divided life, for separating what for most of us is the dominant part of our lives—work—from our most deeply held views about ourselves, others, and the world—about a flourishing life.[8] And the divided life is necessarily an impoverished and diminished life. It undercuts the moral and spiritual meaning of our daily labors, divorcing authentic meaning from our work and relegating it instead to the mere game of business with its rewards: money, possessions, and power. It also removes the grounds for distinguishing between the value of one kind of business over against another. In such a context, selling lottery tickets or pornographic magazines is as justifiable as repairing shoes or manufacturing computers. Moreover, the divided life is in one important respect a wasted life. It is a form of living that assumes that real meaning occurs only in those areas outside of work, in the Little League, in the social club, in the family, in the church, and in the neighborhood. While these aspects of life are vitally important, the one arena of life which occupies more of our waking hours than any other and substantially shapes our self-identity turns out to be largely empty of meaning and purpose.

This picture of the divided life draws us to an additional and central theme of the moral context of business, namely, the concept of vocation or calling. The word "vocation" comes from the Latin *vocatio*, a bidding, invitation, or calling. In the Judeo-Christian tradition, the creator-God of the universe also summons or calls each person not only to a redeemed life, but also to a life of service in a specific work—as a businessperson, as a doctor, as a homemaker, as a pastor, as an educator, as a student, and the like. Whether we realize it or not, God calls us all, not just priests or pastors, monks or missionaries, but all of us, to specific tasks according to the gifts and talents we have been granted by God. The theologian Max Stackhouse helpfully describes the idea of vocation in this fashion:

> Vocation is the answer to the question "Why am I?" Everyone has a vocation from God that he or she may choose to follow or ignore. From the calling of Abraham and Sarah, through the calling of the prophets and the apostles, to the profound sense of religious vocation in the Catholic monastic tradition and the sense of the priesthood of all believers of the Reformation, the idea that each of us is put into the world by God for a purpose and called to serve the whole of life in the economy of God is a profound and penetrating insight. It entails the belief that all of us are created in the image of God and that each of us has a role to play in fulfilling God's purpose.[9]

The calling of God is not only to individuals, but it is also, by implication, to institutions and organizations, a truth that Stackhouse emphasizes. He writes, "Schools and colleges, courts of law and hospitals, art museums and research institutes, manufacturing corporations and labor unions, churches and legislatures—all have distinctive vocations. They are called to fulfill certain functions of and for humanity, and they must do so with excellence and clarity of purpose."[10] Importantly, then, God's bidding applies to public and private institutions as well as to individuals. As I hope to show in a moment, this view has significant implications for business.

It is important to understand, then, that the idea of vocation or calling is what links God's purposes, as portrayed in the Biblical drama, to our actual concrete life in the economy. It enables us to integrate faith and work, thus overcoming the divided life. It also expresses the means by which we humans exercise our stewardship of the earth, our own labor, and our responsibility to care for others. Indeed, our vocation is a form of prayer—our way of honoring God in our daily lives. Although the secularists would have us believe that faith is strictly a private matter, hence of no relevance to any public conception of how we see ourselves or our businesses as participants in the economy or in any other aspect of our common life, it is clear that this denial of the moral and spiritual meaning of work is surely a road to nowhere.

A complementary alternative to the Judeo-Christian vision of the economy and an understanding of the moral context of business is that of the Greek tradition as expressed by Aristotle. Aristotle held that "every art and every inquiry, and similarly every action and pursuit, is thought to aim at some good; and for this reason the good has rightly been declared to be that at which all things aim."[11] Aristotle identifies the ultimate good for humans as happiness, defined as a life lived in accordance with intellectual and moral virtue. Aristotle adopted this view because he believed that such a life manifested the highest excellence of human beings. He argued that there can be no greater purpose for human beings than to live a life that fully realizes our natural potentialities as rational and social beings. Such a life, when lived in accordance with perfect virtue, is the meaning of happiness. It is its own

end and justification. Wealth, by contrast, cannot define happiness for us, although Aristotle acknowledges that "the general run of men" identify happiness with pleasure and wealth. But these are the "vulgar type," he declares. Wealth cannot be its own end; we do not desire it for its own sake. It must be seen only as a means, a means that is designed to support the pursuit of the virtuous life, both for individual persons and for the political society. Whatever specific economic activity one engages in should be performed virtuously and should produce goods possessing the quality of excellence. Thus, both performance and product are characterized by excellence. A product is excellent when it conforms perfectly to its function. For example, a cobbler is virtuous when he makes shoes that perform the function of shoes to the highest degree possible. A builder of houses, a carpenter, performs his work well when he constructs buildings that perform the function of physical safety and comfort for families in the best possible way. This is his excellence, his virtue as a builder. The ends or purposes in view are not those associated with the economic gain of the cobbler or builder, but are for the good and virtuous life of everyone. The living out of the moral virtues by the cobbler or builder is the prerequisite of happiness, the good which we all seek.

In the Aristotelian tradition, the moral context of business is seen in relation to human nature and our capacities and inclinations as rational and social beings. Our function in life is to maximize our potentialities as rational and social beings, to live a life of excellence as determined by intellectual and moral virtues. The purpose and meaning of business is to enhance such a flourishing life, whether the business activity be making shoes, building houses, constructing ships, or farming the land. Artisans, farmers, tradesmen, and shipmasters may not pursue the highest activity of the human soul, the life of the mind, but they nevertheless share in the virtuous life to the degree that they do their work excellently, and thereby actualize their potentialities as human beings.

Taken together, then, the Christian understanding of the moral context of business, supplemented by the Greek tradition, offers a radical alternative to our individualist idea of society and thus of business. For, in the Judeo-Christian and Greek traditions, human beings are seen as social beings, either created as such by God, as the Biblical story reveals, or else as being communal creatures by nature, as the Greeks held. Our relationships with others are not, therefore, primarily contractual, as many modern secular thinkers believe. That is, our obligations to others are not limited to the formal agreements that we may choose to make with them, as though prenuptial arrangements characterize all of life. Rather, we are bonded to one another by nature and by covenant, both giving and receiving in countless ways within human communities of responsibility to one another. Whether as individuals or as businesses, we exist in a state of mutual accountability. This is the meaning of the Biblical idea of covenant, an idea not to be perceived as a burden, but as a gift of God "that bonds the human will to God's justice and to ... [our] neighbor[s]."[12]

What, therefore, does this understanding of the moral context of business tell us about the purpose of business, its ethical self-understanding, and its desired corporate culture? Put differently, what should be the character of the moral life of business, both for the organization and the employees? It should be clear by now that the purpose of business, from a moral and religious standpoint, cannot be reduced to money or profits, whether for oneself or for shareholders. God is our final and lasting good, and this glad fact applies to all human activity, including business, whether this is acknowledged or not. Business is an institution belonging to God's governance of the world, a provision by which we human beings are commissioned to be good stewards of creation and to care for one another, all for our mutual well-being. The calling of business is to participate in this stewardship and to perform its tasks excellently. Yes, profits are necessary to continue to perform this work, at least in our modern economy, but they are not nor should they ever be the priority; they are merely a necessary condition for achieving the tasks at hand. The moral priority of business is and ever will be what we commonly refer to today as the production of goods and services, but not just any goods and services.

From the Judeo-Christian point of view, the goods and services we produce must reflect the proper stewardship of and care for the earth, our labor, our wealth, and our neighbors, as portrayed in the Biblical story. Every specific business, therefore, whether large corporation or small enterprise, should have a clear sense of mission which makes plain to its employees and to the public alike how the activity of that business serves the common good. Such a statement of mission need not employ religious language—indeed, it usually will not, but there should be no doubt that the corporation or enterprise draws its purpose out of the resources of a deeply communal understanding of the ends of business.

Any business with such a sense of moral and religious purpose will seek to accomplish its business tasks in an ethical manner. It will embrace a high code of conduct for itself and its employees, not for public relations purposes but because such a code reflects the integrity of the organization and its expectations of all workers, management and non-management alike. Moreover, any business undergirded by moral and religious purpose will create and sustain a corporate culture distinguished by openness, honesty, respect for all stakeholders, including employees with differentiated vocational goals, and a strong commitment to social responsibility and the covenant that bonds the human family. The corporate culture will also encourage high expectations of members of the organization, not as a means to weed out the less talented, but as an imperative for all to perform work excellently and for the common good. While some employees may have the capacity to work more efficiently and effectively than others, no one should be permitted to perform in a slipshod or indifferent manner—or in disregard for the well-being of others. Such lackadaisical work would not only violate the mission of the business, but it would also constitute unfaithfulness to the divine calling each of us has to be good stewards of all we have, including our gifts and talents. I want to mention as a final theme the place of virtue in business. A virtuous individual is a person of good and right character, one who possesses the understanding and conviction to do what is right in the proper way, with the proper spirit, and with the proper end in view—and one who does it faithfully, not just when it is convenient.

Within the virtue tradition, courage, temperance, prudence, and justice are the highest moral virtues, and faith, hope, and love are the highest spiritual virtues.

For one in business and the workplace, different activities demand different virtues, but whatever virtue is required can be inferred from one of the highest moral virtues. For example, the honesty required of the accountant is a kind of justice; the enterprise required of the farmer or manufacturer is an expression of courage; the discernment of the manager is a form of prudence; the refusal to prey upon the lust of the consumers is a manifestation of temperance.[13] How are these virtues developed? They are developed within the bonds of specific communities that are committed to the common good. If, for example, accountants are to be virtuous—honest—they will best develop that state of character within a community of accountants, the professionals who themselves exhibit the moral practice of honesty in their work.

The virtue tradition of ethics undoubtedly applies to individuals, but is it plausible to speak meaningfully about businesses themselves being virtuous? That is, while it makes sense to say of a given company that it conducts its affairs in an ethical manner, can we also say of a corporation or business enterprise that it is virtuous? I believe we can. When we speak of the ethical conduct of a person or business, we are referring primarily to a certain kind of behavior, behavior that conforms to the imperatives of the moral law. It is what we ought to do or ought not to do; or, more precisely, it is what we do or don't do as responsible agents. This suggests that ethical conduct qua conduct represents the external side of the moral life. The virtues, on the other hand, refer primarily to the internal dimension of the moral life, the character of an agent that produces right and good action or its opposite. As Jesus said, "Out of the heart come evil intentions, murder, adultery, fornication, theft, false witness, slander" (Mathew. 15:19).

Do businesses have something equivalent to a heart? We often speak of the "soul" of an organization or institution, and what we signify by that expression is the nature and quality of its character, what it is on the inside. The morally relevant inside of a business is defined primarily by its corporate culture and its operational policies. If it is a virtuous company or business, its culture will reveal it—through a sense of shared mission driven by the desire for excellence and the pursuit of the common good; through a commitment to all stakeholders and to its implicit covenant with the human family; and by the existence and felt presence of a moral tone that runs throughout the organization. Its policies will reflect and reinforce this quality of corporate culture through the regulatory guidelines that order the formal life of the business firm.

A truly ethical business, then, is virtuous on the inside and practices what is virtuous and right on the outside. The internal and the external are intimately related, as Jesus explained. But the presence of virtue and the practice of right conduct do not and cannot occur in a theological or metaphysical vacuum, either for the business practitioner or for the student of business ethics. Similarly, for business ethics programs to achieve their purpose, they cannot exist in a vacuum. Students may learn to refine their analytical skills or may become more adept at recognizing moral dilemmas—through a sort of "moral reasoning" approach using case studies of moral dilemmas—but without an understanding of the moral context of business they will not have any persuasive grounds for viewing business as part of our stewardship of the earth and our care for our neighbors, or for understanding the nature and justification of the moral life in business.

Notes

1 "Poll shows widespread distrust of corporation" (September 2002, Search Archive index, Calendar Directory), p. 1.
2 Thomas R. Piper, Mary C. Gentile, and Sharon Daloz Parks, *Can Ethics Be Taught?* (Boston: Harvard Business School, 1993), p. 2.
3 *New York Times* (May 20, 2003), p. C3.
4 Piper et al., ibid., p. 11.
5 Ibid., pp. 3–5.
6 Christians, because they embrace the Biblical story in its entirety, will be drawn to the theological/metaphysical foundation that I outline next. Many people in other religious traditions—Jews and Muslims, for example—may believe portions of the Biblical narrative as I have described it, while many others—Hindus, Buddhists, and non-believers, for example—may believe very little or none of it. Nevertheless, non-Christians may have other grounds for endorsing the same or a similar theological/metaphysical foundation for business activity. I will not explore those other grounds in this paper, but I recognize the importance of searching for various bridges connecting the religious traditions.
7 George N. Monsma, Jr., "Biblical Principles Important for Economic Theory and Practice," in *On Moral Business,* ed. Max L. Stackhouse, Dennis P. McCann, and Shirley J. Roels, with Pres-

ton N. Williams (Grand Rapids: Eerdmans Publishing Co., 1995), pp. 38–45.

8 See Helen J. Alford and Michael J. Naughton, *Managing as If Faith Mattered* (Notre Dame: University of Notre Dame Press, 2001), pp. 7ff.

9 Max L. Stackhouse, *Public Theology and Political Economy* (Grand Rapids: Eerdmans Publishing Co., 1987), p. 24.

10 Ibid., p. 25.

11 Aristotle, *Nicomachean Ethics*, in *The Basic Works of Aristotle*, edited by Richard McKeon (New York: Random House, 1966), p. 935.

12 Stackhouse, ibid., p. 26.

13 Alford and Naughton, ibid., pp. 88–94.

Questions for Discussion and Reflection

1. Do you agree with Schmeltekopf that business schools are not preparing students well for the ethical challenges they will face in the workplace? Why or why not?

2. What does Schmeltekopf think is the meaning and purpose of business, according to Judeo-Christian tradition? According to Aristotle?

3. What does Schmeltekopf mean by the idea of the virtuous business?

CASE STUDIES

Case 1.1: Keeping Secrets

Rumors have been swirling among employees after officials of a major airplane manufacturing company announced that a significant number of employees will be receiving layoff notices in the coming weeks. An economic recession has greatly reduced the number of commercial airplane orders, forcing the company to downsize.

While it is known that a specific number of employees will be laid off, the names of those who will be given notice are held in strict confidence. After the initial announcement, many employees have felt vulnerable and have been searching for employment at other firms. Given the status of the economy, jobs have been hard to find.

Only a few top executives, select members of the human resources department, and "group managers" know the names of those who have been targeted for layoff until the day the actual RIF (reduction in force) notices are issued (three weeks from now). As a group manager whose department will be affected, you are one of the few people in the firm privy to the names on the list. Once the layoffs are announced, employees have roughly four to six weeks to finish their tasks and look for other employment.

The company has a policy of strict confidentiality when it comes to layoffs. When word has gotten out early in the past, some employees left early to take other positions, leaving the company in the lurch. A few employees even resorted to sabotage of company equipment and computers during their last weeks on the job to "get even."

Normally your contractual obligation to uphold confidentiality is not a problem. However, you currently find yourself in a difficult situation. Seeing the name of one of your employees, John, on the list has made you somewhat depressed and wishing you could let him know his status ahead of time.

John is a computer systems analyst who has worked for the company for seven years. His area and level of expertise on his current project are critical to the company. If he were to leave early and not finish his tasks, your department would be hard pressed to finish the project according to schedule. This would result in substantial delays that could jeopardize future contracts with this particular client, a major airline, whose executives are already upset about delays in earlier stages of the project.

You and John have become close friends. In part, this is due to the fact that he is in a similar stage of life as you, in his mid-thirties and married with three children. Your daughters also play together on a soccer team, and your families have frequent social outings.

John and his wife, Margie, are about to welcome their fourth child into the world. At a soccer game one evening, John mentions that he has received an offer for employment by another company. "All things being equal, I would rather stay where I'm at. The pay and the commute are better," he says. "Knowing when the layoff announcement is coming, I tried to get more time to decide, but they need to fill the position. I need to let them know in a week. Do you think I should accept the position?" he asks with a wink.

Understanding the level of confidentiality required by your position (and employment contract), you remain silent. John replies, "I know you can't say anything directly about the layoffs, but am I safe to assume that your 'non-response' is good news? Given our relationship over the years, you would probably at least warn me in a roundabout way if the news were the opposite, right? Besides, by giving me some indication, you would be doing much more good than harm. No one gets hurt if you let me know. Think of what I stand to lose if you don't tell me."

Questions for Discussion

1. What will you do in response to John's inquiry about layoffs? Why?
2. Do you have to choose between confidentiality and loyalty to a friend? Explain your answer.

Case 1.2: Pay or Walk Away?

My name is Dan, and those who know me often tease me about being a "serial entrepreneur." I am in my late thirties, and I have already had a hand in starting four different businesses. Three were successfully grown and sold to larger companies, helping me (and several business partners) achieve a level of financial freedom I never imagined possible.

Throughout my career I have tried earnestly to make my faith a source of motivation and moral guidance. For example, when I have had the authority to do so, I have taken risks by hiring employees from the "margins of society." Often they have turned out to be highly responsible workers. I have taken great satisfaction in seeing their lives turn around, in part because of gainful, steady employment in a business I helped start. I have also strived to pay good wages, create challenging work, and enter businesses that make products or offer services with more direct social benefits (health care, recycling, etc.).

Although most of the organizations I have helped start have been successful, I, like most entrepreneurs, have learned some hard lessons through failure. One of the businesses I helped launch closed two years ago. After an abrupt down cycle, it became clear that the concept was not going to work and that we would simply be wasting more money and time to try to turn it around. So we (along with our major investors) decided to shut it down. The whole experience has left me humbled and wondering how far I need to go to make things right for those who have suffered as a result.

My partners and I together put several million dollars into the business and raised an additional $3 million from other investors (mostly from two venture capital firms and a handful of individuals). When we decided to close our doors, we had several significant bills outstanding. For instance, we owed money to suppliers, to a construction firm that had recently remodeled some of our facilities, and to several building owners (since we would be ending our leases early).

Almost a year after the closure, we went through bankruptcy proceedings. Because we had set up the business as a limited liability entity, the court distributed the remaining assets of the business to those whom we owed money. In the end, they each received about twenty-five cents on the dollar. This amount was nowhere near what would have "made them whole," but it was far better than what another one of my other businesses received when it was on the other side of a bankruptcy proceeding—ten cents on the dollar.

Since the court proceedings, one of the individual investors and the owner of the contracting firm have personally contacted me to let me know how much they have been harmed as a result of the failed business. The contractor has had to lay off several employees and has told me directly that without a fresh infusion of capital (money he would have, had we paid in full) to replace worn equipment and vehicles, his own business might fail soon. Both have told me how they are unsatisfied (although not nearly in such nice terms) that I have enough personal resources to repay them, but that the law allows me to just walk away.

I have consulted with my partners, and both tell me that we have done nothing wrong and that I should just ignore the "sore losers." One partner said that both the investor and the contractor have been around long enough to understand the risks involved and that any other assets I may have are not relevant to the failure of the business in question. Another partner believes that bankruptcy laws and limited liability help society overall by encouraging risk taking and innovation and thereby economic growth. If owners were always liable to the extent of other assets, far fewer people would accept the risks involved in starting businesses.

I don't know if my partners are right. Should I just walk away in good conscience and sleep well at night knowing full well I have the means to repay? In so doing, am I just making excuses and "hiding behind" the law?

The whole thing would not be a dilemma for me, except for the fact that as I stated at the beginning, I have tried to integrate my faith into my work. In consulting the Bible, one can find many passages instructing people to tell the truth (Ex. 20:16), repay what they owe (Ps. 37:21; Rom. 13:8), make restitution (Ex. 22) when they harm someone else (even accidentally), and maintain a good reputation (Acts 6:3).

I have enough understanding to know, however, that the Bible was written over a long time in contexts far different from our own, so not everything should be literally applied today. For example, the Bible condemns usury (charging interest on loaned money), but the context was very different. Money then was usually loaned to kin who had fallen on hard times. Charging them interest would have been to further oppress them. Applying Old Testament usury laws literally today would lead us to condemn capitalism outright. Yet, today's lending, especially for a business, goes to a productive asset, so a fair interest charge (and thereby responsible capitalism) seems justified.

I'm not trying to take the easy way out (though of course a part of me would rather not pay any more), but I wonder if passages written during times when simple agrarian economies existed still apply today to our modern, complex economy. Today, for better or worse, economic transactions are a lot less personal, and there are many more laws to govern conduct.

We did disclose all the risks and were diligent in how we ran the business, so I'm less inclined to repay the investor. But I feel differently about the contractor (who worked for us based on our past successes) and some of the other parties who recovered less than what they were owed.

Questions for Discussion

1. How would you advise me? Should I dip into my other assets to repay those who were hurt? Or, should I just take what happened in stride as a part of business and sleep soundly at night?
2. How do I correctly apply the Bible's instruction to this situation?

Case 1.3: Firing Undocumented Immigrants

You are president of a small company that manufactures products for remodeling kitchens — primarily manufacturing and installing kitchen cabinets and countertops. You have recently bought out a competitor, and as part of the due diligence prior to completing the sale, you learned that some of the long-time employees are in the country illegally. In fact, some of them have been with the company since it was founded. You didn't hire them; rather, you inherited them when you bought the company. As you have gotten to know them since the sale was closed, you have learned that they are also some of your best employees. They work very hard and put in long hours without complaining, and they will do virtually any type of job you ask them to do. You also have learned that all of them have families, including children who were born in this country, automatically making them citizens. You realize that if they were sent back to their country of origin, it would likely, though not necessarily, separate the family from one another. Since they are in the country illegally, they do not have social security numbers, and as a result, you have learned that you pay them in cash and do not withhold taxes or social security. This strikes you as unfair to the employees who are in the country legally and have those taxes regularly taken out of their paychecks. You also know that every time you pay them this way, you are violating the law, and every day you keep them employed, you are doing something illegal. If you were to require documentation from them concerning their immigration status, they would not be able to provide it. And if in some cases it were provided, it would be fairly clear that the documentation was fraudulent.

Questions for Discussion

1. What should you do with the employees who are in the country illegally? Is it right to let them go and risk their families' becoming impoverished? Or would you keep them employed and look the other way with their immigration status?
2. What do you think about the disparity created by the way you have to pay the illegal employees — not withholding taxes? Is that unfair? Or

is it acceptable that they don't pay social security since they would not
be able to collect it when they retire?

3. Do you believe that you have an obligation not only to let them go,
but also to report them to the immigration authorities? Why or why
not?

COMMENTARY

Ethical decision making is a complicated enterprise. David Gill is certainly correct when he criticizes popular leadership author John Maxwell for what Gill
considers a simplistic view of business ethics. Not only are there more principles
and virtues to consider besides the Golden Rule, but the application of those
elements is not always clear. You will find yourself in the midst of genuine
ethical dilemmas, in which there are legitimate gray areas, and when the right
thing to do may be somewhat ambiguous. To be sure, some decisions are more
black-and-white. Those are what we would call "temptations," in which there
is a conflict between your self-interest and a moral value or virtue. If all moral
decisions were temptations, Maxwell would be right to suggest that ethical
decision making is simple and straightforward. But moral dilemmas occur
regularly—in fact, given that we live in a flawed world, it's surprising that they
don't occur more often. Gill helps his readers to recognize when they are facing
a moral dilemma. We would suggest that *a moral dilemma occurs when you face
a conflict of values or virtues*. That is, when there is a collision between two or
more *value-driven interests*. If there are no values or virtues that undergird both
the competing interests in a given scenario, then you have some other kind of
dilemma—perhaps a strategic dilemma or a communication dilemma. Gill's
broader view of ethical decision making that includes matters of character is
consistent with a Christian virtue emphasis. He also rightly emphasizes the
formation of the corporate culture in which these decisions will be made. We
will address that subject further in chapter 11.

Implementing moral decisions is just as important as making the right
choice, since the goal is ultimately to facilitate change in the organization. It
is often tempting for a person facing a moral question to assume that once
the decision is made, by virtue of holding what is believed to be the moral
high ground, the implementation simply takes care of itself. Harvard Business School professor Joseph Badaracco, in a provocative book entitled *Leading Quietly*, suggests that implementing moral choices requires time, effort,
skill, wisdom, building organizational capital, and the willingness to settle

for limited objectives. Just because it's a moral matter doesn't mean that one can ignore the organizational culture and just "do the right thing." In other words, he argues for *an incremental approach* to putting moral decisions into practice, as opposed to an "all or nothing" tactic, which is often the view taken when people feel they have morality on their side. He suggests that leaders don't necessarily see ethical dilemmas as a "stark, yes-or-no choice or an inescapable test of basic principles. Quiet leaders recognize the ethical stakes in the situations they face, but they move beyond thinking about their situations in purely ethical terms and see them in another light: as challenges to their imagination, their managerial skills, and their ability to navigate difficult, sometimes treacherous waters."[16] He argues for an approach that resists using ethics as a "trump card" and insists that "the vast majority of important human problems (ethical ones included) are not solved by a swift, decisive stroke from someone at the top. What usually matters are careful, thoughtful, small, practical efforts by people working far from the limelight."[17] This is the kind of leadership, according to Badaracco, that brings long-term organizational change.

Donald Schmeltekopf lays more foundational groundwork for ethical decision making in his piece on the moral context of business. He rightly points out the danger for the businessperson of the "fragmented and divided life," which reduces all decision making in the workplace to strategic decisions. For if a person compartmentalizes his or her life and separates out the moral component to private life, then moral decision making in the workplace simply becomes a matter of adherence to the law and any applicable regulatory standards. Schmeltekopf anticipates a strong challenge to Christian ethics in the workplace that we will take up in more detail in chapter 2, particularly with the article by Albert Carr. Pay special attention to his view that the businessperson must compartmentalize his or her life in order to compete successfully. In our view, decision making has a moral component only when businesspeople reject Carr's thesis and intentionally bring values and virtues into the workplace. According to Schmeltekopf, the divided life "removes the grounds for distinguishing between the value of one kind of business over against another. In such a context, selling lottery tickets or pornographic magazines is as justifiable as repairing shoes or manufacturing computers." That is, to compartmentalize one's life and hold to a dual morality—morality for private life and business for business life—is to impoverish our view of business as a sacred calling and vocation.

Schmeltekopf is rightly critical of much of ethics education at the leading business schools, and he is not surprised at the statistics that show business students feeling unprepared to face ethical challenges when they finish their MBAs. He observes that the underpinnings of morality are either ignored or

[16] Joseph L. Badaracco Jr., *Leading Quietly: An Unorthodox Guide to Doing the Right Thing* (Cambridge: Harvard Business School Press, 2002): 160.

[17] Ibid., 9.

discounted, leading to moral decision making that is private and individualistic. Even Harvard's efforts to better prepare its students in leadership, values, and governance are undermined, according to Schmeltekopf, because they "must avoid all overtly theological and metaphysical commitments." We would suggest that they can't do that in reality, that they actually default to particular worldview commitments by necessity. But Schmeltekopf's observation about what schools can intentionally bring to the curriculum in the way of values is surely correct, and thus it reduces moral decision making to following models and procedures for decision making. He argues that ethical decision making has substance and content only when business is situated in a moral context, informed by Judeo-Christian morality (and supplemented, in his view, by Aristotelean notions of virtue).

Use of the Bible in Ethics

For the Christian, moral decision making in business begins with your biblically based view of the world. Specifically, Christian business ethics begins with God revealing his character and corresponding moral principles in the Bible. However, it is one thing to recognize that the Bible is the authoritative source for Christian ethics. It is quite another to use it correctly. To insist on the centrality of the Bible does not justify simplistic proof-texting, often done out of context, to address complex business ethics problems. Although the Bible does address some business practices, those practices occurred in the ancient world, in an economic system very different than a globalized market economy. All that is to say that applying the Bible in business ethics can be complicated. Even though we may agree on the Bible's authority for ethics, we may disagree on what the Bible teaches on a specific issue. We may further disagree on if and how that biblical teaching applies to the issue at hand. That is not to justify skepticism about the contribution of the Bible to business ethics, only to appreciate the complexity of using the Bible properly in addressing business ethics issues.

The Bible was written in an ancient context, in which life was predominantly agricultural. Most people lived in small villages, centered around their extended families. Government was usually by a monarch, and individuals had little if any input into the laws that regulated their lives. There were no stock markets, no sophisticated financial tools, no equivalent of the banking system, and nothing remotely resembling a mass communications network like the Internet. Though international trade did exist, most economic activity was directed at subsistence. The Bible records many instances of economic abuse, exploitation of the vulnerable, and the resulting cries for economic justice. The economic world of the Bible was very different than that of today.[18] It is unreasonable to expect that the Bible would directly

[18] For more background on economic life in biblical times, see Douglas E. Oakman, "Economics of Palestine," in *Dictionary of New Testament Backgrounds* (Downers Grove, Ill.: InterVarsity, 2000); Christopher J. H. Wright, *God's People in God's Land: Family, Land and Property in the Old Testament* (Grand Rapids: Eerdmans, 1990). This will be discussed further in chapter 5.

address complex issues such as insider trading, mergers and acquisitions, and consumer safety, since these are relatively new issues, far removed from the sociological world of biblical times. However, it does have a good deal to say about general principles of economic justice, fairness, and integrity in one's business dealings. As long as there have been human communities, there has been economic activity, and the Bible boldly addresses economic injustices of its time. Though the specific issues certainly have changed, there is nothing new about biblical ethics addressing economic life and business practices.

When interpreting the Bible and applying it to contemporary business, one should recognize that the Bible was written in different types of literature, each of which has its own distinctives.[19] Much of the Bible was written in story, or narrative, format, making its point by telling a story. Other types include poetry, such as the Psalms and much of the Prophets, using vivid figurative language that was designed to evoke an emotional as well as rational reaction from the reader. Wisdom Literature, especially the Proverbs, was intended as short, pithy sayings whose primary goal was to be memorable, not technically precise. The Proverbs are intended as "rules of thumb" that have periodic exceptions. The law of Moses, contained in the books of Exodus–Deuteronomy, records God's legislation to set up the nation of Israel, and is written as a body of laws in a unique time in biblical history, when Israel was what was called a theocracy, that is, when the law of God was automatically the law of the land. The Pastoral Letters, or epistles, of the New Testament use a combination of warm personal comments and compelling rational arguments to make their point.

In addition to reading the Bible in the light of its literary type, it is critical to read the specifics of the Bible through the lenses of the "big story" of the Bible—the narrative of God's love for and faithfulness to humanity and his work to redeem human beings and ultimately all of creation. That is the "big picture" of the Bible, and it is important to keep in mind that the moral principles and virtues were never intended to be understood as isolated moral codes. Rather, they are intertwined in the story of God's work to redeem and restore his world. Adeney is right to remind us never to lose sight of the grand narrative of the Bible and how the moral values and virtues emerge from that overall story.

To understand the intent of the biblical authors, you must realize that the Bible was written within a specific cultural context. Adeney is certainly correct when he insists that the Bible was enmeshed in a cultural context, so much so that some commandments make no sense at all unless you understand the original context. Adeney's example of the Hebrew commandment that "you shall not boil a kid [baby goat] in its mother's milk" is a clear case in point. That command is impossible to grasp without knowing its background in Canaanite religious practices, which Israel was prohibited from practicing. It

[19] For more discussion on hermeneutics—the study of biblical interpretation, particularly reading each of the different literary types of the Bible, see Gordon D. Fee and Douglas Stuart, *How to Read the Bible for All Its Worth,* 3rd ed. (Grand Rapids: Zondervan, 2003); and Walt Russell, *Playing with Fire: How the Bible Ignites Change in Your Soul* (Colorado Springs: NavPress, 2000).

is also difficult to appreciate a command like this apart from the overall purpose of God for Israel — to create a morally distinctive community that would bear corporate witness to God. Likewise, the command to wash one another's feet makes little sense in today's culture, since today roads are paved, we don't wear sandals as frequently, and we don't get places very often by walking long distances. Again, it would be shortsighted to take this command outside the overall story of Jesus and his mission "not . . . to be served, but to serve" (Mark 10:45). This overall narrative of the life of Jesus that culminated in his death for humankind is the ultimate form of servanthood, the context in which the command to wash one another's feet is set. Numerous commands in the Bible fit in this category. In fact, some of the commands that apply most clearly to business practices, such as the Year of Jubilee (which required that all land be returned to its original owners every fifty years — think of what that would do to today's real estate markets!), need to be understood within the context of a predominantly agricultural society in which raw land was the principal and often only tangible asset a person would have. Similarly, this command too is set against the backdrop of the overall story of God's ultimate ownership of the land and his work to take care of his people.

Adeney is also correct to insist that we apply the Bible in a specific context, and we read the Bible through the lenses of our own culture. In fact, most people are not aware of their cultural framework until they come into contact with a different culture. Though it sounds like relativism, it is not, and Adeney is right that no one is purely objective when it comes to reading and applying the Bible. That doesn't mean that we shouldn't try our best to overcome our cultural biases, and in many cases, we can. Reading the Bible in a community of people, preferably from other cultures, helps to minimize that. However, Adeney probably goes too far when he insists that the prohibition against theft and the other nine of the Ten Commandments are not timeless principles. It would be more accurate to say that what constitutes theft may vary from culture to culture depending on how property rights are viewed; but however theft is defined, that is prohibited by the command "thou shalt not steal."

Adeney correctly draws an important distinction between general principles and specific practices. In the Bible, most general principles are applied to specific situations. In other words, most biblical principles have "shoe leather" on them — that is, they are embedded in real life in that culture. *Usually the specific practice expresses a broader moral principle.* For example, believers in the New Testament are commanded to greet one another with a holy kiss, wash one another's feet, and work with their hands. A holy kiss applied the principle of hospitality, foot washing applied the principle of willingness to perform lowly service, and manual labor applied the principle of working hard to support oneself and one's family. Adeney says that "principles are tools to help us reincarnate moral practice from one context to another." Principles are the intermediate step between specific practices in the ancient setting and specific practices in today's setting.

To apply the Bible correctly, you should distinguish between general principles and specific practices. Many times the specific practice mandated by a biblical passage is conditioned by the culture and is not normative for today. Or the specific practice no longer exists today. But the general principle that underlies that specific practice is usually a moral norm for today and can be applied in a different specific situation, or situations, today. For example, to apply the principle of hospitality, we greet with handshakes instead of kisses. As a general rule, if the practice still communicates the underlying principle, it is likely that the practice is to be taken as a norm for today. So, for example, in many cultures, a greeting kiss does not communicate hospitality, so the principle can be expressed in a culturally appropriate way. Or working hard to support one's family can be expressed through many different ways, not simply through manual labor. Most of the commands of the Bible are culturally conditioned in this way. When that is the case, the goal of application is to seek the underlying principle and attempt to apply it to today's setting. Principles are not the end point, but the goal is the application of principles to real life. Of course, people of goodwill may disagree on what the general principles are and how they apply to the situation at hand.

The Old Testament law has factors besides cultural ones that also must be considered. Theological differences between the Old and New Testaments must be taken into account. For example, the ceremonial laws (laws dealing with the sacrifices and religious festivals) of the Old Testament no longer apply specifically to the Christian because of the death of Christ (Heb. 8–10). In addition, the New Testament is clear that the food laws of the Old Testament no longer apply specifically (Acts 8–12) and that no one is under the Old Testament civil law (Rom. 7:1–4). Thus numerous laws that were mandated for Israel are not directly applicable to Christians today. That is, they are indirectly applicable through the use of broader principles as intermediate steps. The challenge is to reapply them in a way that is relevant to today's culture and faithful to the intent of the law in the Old Testament. For example, we are not to offer the sacrifice of thanksgiving literally, but instead are to express thanksgiving to God in a variety of ways, including public testimony, generous giving, and private prayer. The principle underlying the sacrifice is to be applied in ways that are relevant today and that express the underlying principle accurately. Some of the most challenging laws to reapply include those that governed economic life, such as the Jubilee. We would suggest that most agricultural laws are designed to prevent fraud and to give people renewed opportunities to support themselves.

TWO

Christian Ethics in Business: Tensions and Challenges

A sudden submission to Christian ethics by businessmen would bring about the greatest economic upheaval in history!

Albert Z. Carr, "Is Business Bluffing Ethical?"

Introduction

During the past decade or so, interest in integrating spiritual values (especially Christian ones) into the workplace has exploded. Many books have been written and conferences organized; several academic research centers have been established at prestigious universities (such as Yale and Princeton); and a stand-alone academic journal (the *Journal of Management, Spirituality & Religion*) exploring this topic in depth has been launched. Cover stories on the topic have also been run by major industry magazines, such as *Business Week* and *Fortune*. The aim of "bringing" one's faith and values to work is a noble one and rightfully deserves this level of attention.

However, actual attempts to integrate faith and business can be challenging. Living the values derived from faith involves navigating terrain that is way more complicated than what simple platitudes infer. When the "darker" aspects of business, and the reality of economic competition are factored into the equation, a number of tensions come to light. In fact, some research supports the suspicion that many businesspeople do in fact live with two conflicting sets of rules—one for business and one for their lives outside of work.[1] More recently, the thunderous impact of numerous instances of egregious corporate misconduct has made questions about the essential compatibility of Christian values and business even more acute. Some have even gone so far as to argue that ethics and success in business have an *inverse* relationship[2]; that is, business demands shrewdness and the bending, if not

[1] O. C. Ferrell, "A Framework for Understanding Organizational Ethics," in *Business Ethics: New Challenges for Business Schools and Corporate Leaders*, R. A. Peterson and O. C. Ferrell, eds. (Armonk, N.Y.: M. E. Sharpe, 2004), 3–17.

[2] See James Michelman, "Some Ethical Consequences of Economic Competition," *Journal of Business Ethics* 2 (1983): 79–87.

outright breaking, of moral standards. Participants must leave their "private" moral convictions at the door or success will prove elusive. Conversely, success is achieved in direct proportion to the amount of moral compromise one is willing to make. Undoubtedly, "good" behavior still exists. When it occurs, however, the motivation behind it is economic self-interest, and not ethics, per se.

Organizations are trapped by similar deterministic laws. A "nice" company that engages in "restrained" competition or sacrifices profits for the benefit of higher wages for employees or charitable contributions to the local community beyond motivational or public relations value will soon find itself in decline if competitors don't operate with similar rules and intentions.[3] A choice then has to be made: compromise to succeed or get out of the game.

In stark contrast to these negative portrayals, some argue that ethics and business values are more aligned or can be made to be more so with some foresight.[4] Good ethics *is* good business, especially if a longer-term perspective is considered. Ethical lapses are shortsighted. Honesty and fairness, for instance, serve to attract loyal customers and motivated employees. Sound ethics then are a key element of strategy, with only short-term financial sacrifices required.

Given the complex moral nature of the marketplace, the central focus of this chapter will be on some of the tensions and challenges that are present when trying to live and act according to Christian ethics in business. Are Christian ethics a recipe for success, a naive prescription for failure, some of both, or something else altogether? In no small part, the answer to the foregoing question is predicated on our understanding of the relationship between Christian ethics and the demands of business. Are they in alignment, contradictory, or somewhere in between?

The first reading, "Is Business Bluffing Ethical?" is a classic from *Harvard Business Review*. Based on dark (perhaps realistic?) assumptions about business, Albert Z. Carr takes the posture that two sets of morals, one for business and one for private life, are an inescapable reality. Using the game of poker as an analogy to business, Carr argues that practices such as "bluffing" in business should be judged by their own set of standards and not by "the ethical principles preached in churches." He concludes that those who try to apply their private morals at the workplace will likely fail to be successful as businesspeople.

In the second article, titled "Why Be Honest If Honesty Doesn't Pay?" authors Amar Bhide and Howard H. Stevenson use qualitative research to try to find out more about the link between ethics and financial success in business. In particular, they set out to find evidence to support the popular notion that good ethics and good business are synonymous. Bhide and Ste-

[3] For a more thorough discussion of the power of competitive forces, see David Korten, *When Corporations Rule the World* (West Hartford, Conn.: Kumarian, 1995). See also John Dobson, "The Feminine Firm: A Comment," *Business Ethics Quarterly* 6, no. 2 (April 1996): 227–31.

[4] See, e.g., Norman Vincent Peale and Kenneth Blanchard, *The Power of Ethical Management* (New York: William Morrow, 1988). For a more scholarly argument (a Platonic one), see Manuel Velasquez, "Why Ethics Matters: A Defense of Ethics in Business Organizations," *Business Ethics Quarterly* 6, no. 2 (1996): 201–13. Read more at http://www.faqs.org/abstracts/Philosophy-and-religion/Why-ethics-matters-a-defense-of-ethics-in-business-organizations.html.

venson come to some surprising conclusions about the alignment (or lack thereof) of ethical behavior and financial success in business.

The third essay, "The Business of Business," by noted philosopher and theologian Dallas Willard, brings some insightful historical perspectives into the conversation. As Willard notes, modern business has largely lost its way in terms of a sense of social purpose and contribution. His key points offer a direct riposte to some of Carr's assumptions about what business is about and how true success within it should be measured.

READINGS

Is Business Bluffing Ethical?

Albert Z. Carr

Harvard Business Review (January–February 1968). Copyright © 1967.

The ethics of business are not those of society, but rather those of the poker game.

Foreword

"When the law as written gives a man a wide-open chance to make a killing, he'd be a fool not to take advantage of it. If he doesn't, somebody else will," remarked a friend of the author. Mr. Carr likens such behavior to the bluffing of the poker player who seizes every opportunity to win, as long as it does not involve outright cheating. "No one thinks any the worse of you on that account," says the author. "And no one would think any the worse of the game of business because its standards of right and wrong differ from the prevailing traditions of morality in our society."

Mr. Carr became interested in this subject when he was a member of a New York firm of consultants to large corporations in many fields. The confidences of many stress-ridden executives made him aware of the extent to which tensions can arise from conflicts between an individual's ethical sense and the realities of business. He was struck also by the similarity of the special ethical attitude shown by many successful and stress-free businessmen in their work to that of good poker players.

Mr. Carr was assistant to the chairman of the War Production Board during World War II and later served on the White House staff and as a special consultant to President Truman. He is now writing full-time. Among his books is *John D. Rockefeller's Secret Weapon*, a study of corporate development. This article is adapted from a chapter in his newest book, *Business as a Game*, to be published by New American Library in March 1968.

•   •   •

A respected businessman with whom I discussed the theme of this article remarked with some heat, "You mean to say you're going to encourage men to bluff? Why, bluffing is nothing more than a form of lying! You're advising them to lie!"

I agreed that the basis of private morality is respect for truth and that the closer a businessman comes to the truth, the more he deserves respect. At the same time, I suggested that most bluffing in business might be regarded simply a game strategy—much like bluffing in poker, which does not reflect on the morality of the bluffer.

I quoted Henry Taylor, the British statesman who pointed out that "falsehood ceases to be falsehood when it is understood on all sides that the truth is not expected to be spoken"—an exact description of bluffing in poker, diplomacy, and business. I cited the analogy of the criminal court, where the criminal is not expected to tell the truth when he pleads "not guilty." Everyone from the judge down takes it for granted that the job of the defendant's attorney is to get his client off, not to reveal the truth; and this is considered ethical practice. I mentioned Representative Omar Burleson, the Democrat from Texas, who was quoted as saying, in regard to the ethics of Congress, "Ethics is a barrel of worms"[1]—a pungent summing up of the problem of deciding who is ethical in politics.

I reminded my friend that millions of businessmen feel constrained every day to say *yes* to their bosses when they secretly believe *no* and that this is generally accepted as permissible strategy when the alternative might be the loss of a job. The essential point, I said, is that the ethics of business are game ethics, different from the ethics of religion.

He remained unconvinced. Referring to the company of which he is president, he declared: "Maybe that's good enough for some businessmen, but I can tell you that we pride ourselves on our ethics. In 30 years not one customer has ever questioned my word or asked to check our figures. We're loyal to our customers and fair to our suppliers. I regard my handshake on a deal as a contract. I've never entered into price-fixing schemes with my competitors. I've never allowed my salesmen to spread injurious rumors about other companies. Our union contract is the best in our industry. And, if I do say so myself, our ethical standards are of the highest!"

He really was saying, without realizing it, that he was living up to the ethical standards of the business game—which are a far cry from those of private life. Like a gentlemanly poker player, he did not play in cahoots with others at the table, try to smear their reputations, or hold back chips he owed them.

But this same fine man, at that very time, was allowing one of his products to be advertised in a way that made it sound a great deal better than it actually was. Another item in his product line was notorious among dealers for its "built-in obsolescence." He was holding back from the market a much-improved product because he did not want it to interfere with sales of the inferior item it would have replaced. He had joined with certain of his competitors in hiring a lobbyist to push a state legislature, by methods that he preferred not to know too much about, into amending a bill then being enacted.

In his view these things had nothing to do with ethics; they were merely normal business practice. He himself undoubtedly avoided outright falsehoods—never lied in so many words. But the entire organization that he ruled was deeply involved in numerous strategies of deception.

Pressure to Deceive

Most executives from time to time are almost compelled, in the interests of their companies or themselves, to practice some form of deception when negotiating with customers, dealers, labor unions, government officials, or even other departments of their companies. By conscious misstatements, concealment of pertinent facts, or exaggeration—in short, by bluffing—they seek to persuade others to agree with them. I think it is fair to say that if the individual executive refuses to bluff from time to time—if he feels obligated to tell the truth, the whole truth, and nothing but the truth—he is ignoring opportunities permitted under the rules and is at a heavy disadvantage in his business dealings.

But here and there a businessman is unable to reconcile himself to the bluff in which he plays a part. His conscience, perhaps spurred by religious idealism, troubles him. He feels guilty; he may develop an ulcer or a nervous tic. Before any executive can make profitable use of the strategy of the bluff, he needs to make sure that in bluffing he will not lose self-respect or become emotionally disturbed. If he is to reconcile personal integrity and high standards of honesty with the practical requirements of business, he must feel that his bluffs are ethically justified. The justification rests on the fact that business, as practiced by individuals as well as by corporations, has the impersonal character of a game—a game that demands both special strategy and an understanding of its special ethics.

The game is played at all levels of corporate life, from the highest to the lowest. At the very instant that a man decides to enter business, he may be forced into a game situation, as is shown by the recent experience of a Cornell honor graduate who applied for a job with a large company:

This applicant was given a psychological test which included the statement, "Of the following magazines, check any that you have read either regularly or from time to time, and double-check those which interest you most. *Reader's Digest, Time, Fortune, Saturday Evening Post, The New Republic, Life, Look, Ramparts, Newsweek, Business Week, U.S. News & World Report, The Nation, Playboy, Esquire, Harper's, Sports Illustrated.*

His tastes in reading were broad, and at one time or another he had read almost all of these magazines. He was a subscriber to *The New Republic*, an enthusiast for *Ramparts*, and an avid student of the pictures in *Playboy*. He was not sure whether his interest in *Playboy* would be held against him, but he had a shrewd suspicion that if he confessed to an interest in *Ramparts* and *The New Republic*, he would be thought a liberal, a radical, or at least an intellectual, and his chances of getting the job, which he needed, would greatly diminish. He therefore checked some of the more conservative magazines. Apparently it was a sound decision, for he got the job.

He had made a game player's decision, consistent with business ethics.

A similar case is that of a magazine space salesman who, owing to a merger, suddenly found himself out of a job:

This man was 58, and, in spite of a good record, his chance of getting a job elsewhere in business where youth is favored in hiring practice was not good. He was a vigorous, healthy man, and only a considerable amount of gray to his hair suggested his age. Before beginning this job search he touched up his hair with a black dye to confine the gray to his temples. He knew that the truth about his age might well come out in time, but he calculated that he could deal with that situation when it arose. He and his wife decided that he could easily pass for 45, and he so stated his age on his résumé.

This was a lie; yet within the accepted rules of the business game, no moral culpability attaches to it.

The Poker Analogy

We can learn a good deal about the nature of business by comparing it with poker. While both have a large element of chance, in the long run the winner is the man who plays with steady skill. In both games ultimate victory requires intimate knowledge of the rules, insight into the psychology of the other players, a bold front, a considerable amount of self-discipline, and the ability to respond swiftly and effectively to opportunities provided by chance.

No one expects poker to be played on the ethical principles preached in churches. In poker it is right and proper to bluff a friend out of the rewards of being dealt a good hand. A player feels no more than a slight twinge of sympathy, if that, when — with nothing better than a single ace in his hand — he strips a heavy loser, who holds a pair, of the rest of his chips. It was up to the other fellow to protect himself. In the words of an excellent poker player, former President Harry Truman, "If you can't stand the heat, stay out of the kitchen." If one shows mercy to a loser in poker, it is a personal gesture, divorced from the rules of the game.

Poker has its special ethics, and here I am not referring to rules against cheating. The man who keeps an ace up his sleeve or who marks the cards is more than unethical; he is a crook, and can be punished as such — kicked out of the game or, in the Old West, shot.

In contrast to the cheat, the unethical poker player is one who, while abiding by the letter of the rules, finds ways to put the other players at an unfair disadvantage. Perhaps he unnerves them with loud talk. Or he tries to get them drunk. Or he plays in cahoots with someone else at the table. Ethical poker players frown on such tactics.

Poker's own brand of ethics is different from the ethical ideals of civilized human relationships. The game calls for distrust of the other fellow. It ignores the claim of friendship. Cunning deception and concealment of one's strength and intentions, not kindness and open-heartedness, are vital in poker. No one thinks any the worse of poker on that account. And no one should think any the worse of the game of business because its standards of right and wrong differ from the prevailing traditions of morality in our society.

Discard the Golden Rule

This view of business is especially worrisome to people without much business experience. A minister of my acquaintance once protested that business cannot possibly function in our society unless it is based on the Judeo-Christian system of ethics. He told me:

> I know some businessmen have supplied call girls to customers, but there are always a few rotten apples in every barrel. That doesn't mean the rest of the fruit isn't sound. Surely the vast majority of businessmen are ethical. I myself am acquainted with many who adhere to strict codes of ethics based fundamentally on religious teachings. They contribute to good causes. They participate in community activities. They cooperate with other companies to improve working conditions in their industries. Certainly they are not indifferent to ethics.

That most businessmen are not indifferent to ethics in their private lives, everyone will agree. My point is that in their office lives they cease to be private citizens; they become game players who must be guided by a somewhat different set of ethical standards.

The point was forcefully made to me by a Midwestern executive who has given a good deal of thought to the question:

"So long as a businessman complies with the laws of the land and avoids telling malicious lies, he's ethical. If the law as written gives a man a wide-open chance to make a killing, he'd be a fool not to take advantage of it. If he doesn't, somebody else will. There's no obligation on him to stop and consider who is going to get hurt. If the law says he can do it, that's all the justification he needs. There's nothing unethical about that. It's just plain business sense."

This executive (call him Robbins) took the stand that even industrial espionage, which is frowned on by some businessmen, ought not to be considered unethical. He recalled a recent meeting of the National Industrial Conference Board where an authority on marketing made a speech in which he deplored the employment of spies by business organizations. More and more companies, he pointed out, find it cheaper to penetrate the secrets of competitors with concealed cameras and microphones or by bribing employees than to set up costly research and design departments of their own. A whole branch of the electronics industry has grown up with this trend, he continued, providing equipment to make industrial espionage easier.

Disturbing? The marketing expert found it so. But when it came to a remedy, he could only appeal to "respect for the golden rule." Robbins thought this a confession of defeat, believing that the golden rule, for all its value as an ideal for society, is simply not feasible as a guide for business. A good part of the time the businessman is trying to do unto others as he hopes others will *not* do unto him.[2] Robbins continued:

"Espionage of one kind or another has become so common in business that it's like taking a drink during Prohibition—it's not considered sinful. And we don't even have Prohibition where espionage is concerned; the law is very tolerant in this area. There's no more shame for a business that uses secret agents than there is for a nation. Bear in mind that there already is at least one large corporation—you can buy its stock over the counter—that makes millions by providing counterespionage service to industrial firms. Espionage in business is not an ethical problem; it's an established technique of business competition."

"We Don't Make the Laws"

Wherever we turn in business, we can perceive the sharp distinction between its ethical standards and those of the churches. Newspapers abound with sensational stories growing out of these distinctions:

- We read one day that Senator Philip A. Hart of Michigan has attacked food processors for deceptive packaging of numerous products.[3]
- The next day there is a Congressional to-do over Ralph Nader's book, *Unsafe at Any Speed*, which demonstrates that automobile companies for years have neglected the safety of car-owning families.[4]
- Then another Senator, Lee Metcalf of Montana, and journalist Vic Reinemer show in their book, *Overcharge*, the methods by which utility companies elude regulating government bodies to extract unduly large payments from users of electricity.[5]

These are merely dramatic instances of a prevailing condition; there is hardly a major industry at which a similar attack could not be aimed. Critics of business regard such behavior as unethical, but the companies concerned know that they are merely playing the business game.

Among the most respected of our business institutions are the insurance companies. A group of insurance executives meeting recently in New England was startled when their guest speaker, social critic Daniel Patrick Moynihan, roundly berated them for "unethical" practices. They had been guilty, Moynihan alleged, of using outdated actuarial tables to obtain unfairly high premiums. They habitually delayed the hearings of lawsuits against them in order to tire out the plaintiffs and win cheap settlements. In their employment policies they used ingenious devices to discriminate against certain minority groups.[6]

It was difficult for the audience to deny the validity of these charges. But these men were business game players. Their reaction to Moynihan's attack was much the same as that of the automobile manufacturers to Nader, of the utilities to Senator Metcalf, and of the food processors to Senator Hart. If the laws governing their businesses change, or if public opinion becomes clamorous, they will make the necessary adjustments. But morally they have in their view done nothing wrong. As long as they comply with the letter of the law, they are within their rights to operate their businesses as they see fit.

The small business is in the same position as the great corporation in this respect. For example:

- In 1967 a key manufacturer was accused of providing master keys for automobiles to mail-order customers, although it was obvious that some of the purchasers might be automobile thieves. His defense was plain and straightforward. If there was nothing in the law to prevent him from selling his keys to anyone who ordered them, it was not up to him to inquire as to his customers' motives. Why was it any worse, he insisted, for him to sell car keys by mail, than for mail-order houses to sell guns that might be used for murder? Until the law was changed, the key manufacturer could regard himself as being just as ethical as any other businessman by the rules of the business game.[7]

Violations of the ethical ideals of society are common in business, but they are not necessarily violations of business principles. Each year the Federal Trade Commission orders hundreds of companies, many of them of the first magnitude, to "cease and desist" from practices which, judged by ordinary standards, are of questionable morality but which are stoutly defended by the companies concerned.

In one case, a firm manufacturing a well-known mouthwash was accused of using a cheap form of alcohol possibly deleterious to health. The company's chief executive, after testifying in Washington, made this comment privately:

"We broke no law. We're in a highly competitive industry. If we're going to stay in business, we have to look for profit wherever the law permits. We don't make the laws. We obey them. Then why do we have to put up with this 'holier than thou' talk about ethics? It's sheer hypocrisy. We're not in business to promote ethics. Look at the cigarette companies, for God's sake! If the ethics aren't embodied in the laws by the men who made them, you can't expect businessmen to fill the lack. Why, a sudden submission to Christian ethics by businessmen would bring about the greatest economic upheaval in history!"

It may be noted that the government failed to prove its case against him.

Cast Illusions Aside

Talk about ethics by businessmen is often a thin decorative coating over the hard realities of the game:

Once I listened to a speech by a young executive who pointed to a new industry code as proof that his company and its competitors were deeply aware of their responsibilities to society. It was a code of ethics, he said. The industry was going to police itself, to dissuade constituent companies from wrongdoing. His eyes shone with conviction and enthusiasm.

The same day there was a meeting in a hotel room where the industry's top executives met with the "czar" who was to administer the new code, a man of high repute. No one who was present could doubt their common attitude. In their eyes the code was designed primarily to forestall a move by the federal government to impose stern restrictions on the industry.

They felt that the code would hamper them a good deal less than new federal laws would. It was, in other words, conceived as a protection for the industry, not for the public.

The young executive accepted the surface explanation of the code; these leaders, all experienced game players, did not deceive themselves for a moment about its purpose.

The illusion that business can afford to be guided by ethics as conceived in private life is often fostered by speeches and articles containing such phrases as, "It pays to be ethical," or, "Sound ethics is good business." Actually this is not an ethical position at all; it is a self-serving calculation in disguise. The speaker is really saying that in the long run a company can make more money if it does not antagonize competitors, suppliers, employees, and customers by squeezing them too hard. He is saying that over-sharp policies reduce ultimate gains. That is true, but it has nothing to do with ethics. The underlying attitude is much like that in the familiar story of the shopkeeper who finds an extra $20 bill in the cash register, debates with himself the ethical problem — should he tell his partner? — and finally decides to share the money because the gesture will give him an edge over the s.o.b. the next time they quarrel.

I think it is fair to sum up the prevailing attitude of businessmen on ethics as follows:

We live in what is probably the most competitive of the world's civilized societies. Our customs encourage a high degree of aggression as the individual's striving for success. Business is our main area of competition, and it has been ritualized into a game of strategy. The basic rules of the game have been set by the government, which attempts to detect and punish business frauds. But as long as a company does not transgress the rules of the game set by law, it has the legal right to shape its strategy without reference to anything but its profits. If it sets a long-term view of its profits, it will preserve amicable relations, so far as possible, with those with whom it deals. A wise businessman will not seek advantage to the point where he generates dangerous hostility among employees, competitors, customers, government, or the public at large. But decisions in this area are, in the final test, decisions of strategy, not of ethics.

The Individual and the Game

An individual within a company often finds it difficult to adjust to the requirements of the business game. He tries to preserve his private ethical standards in situations that call for time strategy. When he is obliged to carry out company policies that challenge his conception of himself as an ethical man, he suffers.

It disturbs him when he is ordered, for instance, to deny a raise to a man who deserves it, or fire an employee of long standing, to prepare advertising that he believes to be misleading, or conceal facts that he feels customers are entitled to know, to cheapen the quality of materials used in the manufacture of an established product, to sell as new a product that he knows to be rebuilt, to exaggerate the curative powers of a medicinal preparation, or to coerce dealers. There are some fortunate executives who, by the nature of their work and circumstances, never have to face problems of this kind. But in one form or another, the ethical dilemma is felt sooner or later by most businessmen. Possibly the dilemma is most painful not when the company forces the action on the executive but when he originates it himself — that is, when he has taken or is contemplating a step which is of his own interest but which runs counter to his early moral conditioning. To illustrate:

- The manager of an export department, eager to show rising sales, is pressed by a big customer to provide invoices which, while containing no overt falsehood that would violate a U.S. law, are so worded that the customer may be able to evade certain taxes in his homeland.
- A company president finds that an aging executive, within a few years of retirement and his pension, is not as productive as formerly. Should he be kept on?
- The produce manager of a supermarket debates with himself whether to get rid of a lot of half-rotten tomatoes by including one, with its good side exposed, in every tomato six-pack.
- An accountant discovers that he has taken an improper deduction on his company's tax return and fears the consequences if he calls the matter to the president's attention, though he himself has done nothing illegal. Perhaps if he says

nothing, no one will notice the error.

- A chief executive officer is asked by his directors to comment on a rumor that he owns stock in another company with which he has placed large orders. He could deny it, for the stock is in the name of his son-in-law and he has earlier formally instructed his son-in-law to sell the holding.

Temptations of this kind constantly arise in business. If an executive allows himself to be torn between a decision based on business considerations and one based on his private ethical code, he exposes himself to a grave psychological strain.

This is not to say that sound business strategy necessarily runs counter to ethical ideals. They may frequently coincide; and when they do, everyone is gratified. But the major tests of every move in business, as in all games of strategy, are legality and profit. A man who intends to be a winner in the business game must have a game player's attitude.

The business strategist's decisions must be as impersonal as those of a surgeon performing an operation—concentrating on objective and technique, and subordinating personal feelings. If the chief executive admits that his son-in-law owns the stock, it is because he stands to lose more if the fact comes out later than if he states it boldly and at once. If the supermarket manager orders the rotten tomatoes to be discarded, he does so to avoid an increase in consumer complaints and a loss of goodwill. The company president decides not to fire the elderly executive in the belief that the negative reaction of other employees would in the long run cost the company more than it would lose in keeping him and paying his pension.

All sensible businessmen prefer to be truthful, but they seldom feel inclined to tell the *whole* truth. In the business game truth-telling usually has to be kept within narrow limits if trouble is to be avoided. The point was neatly made a long time ago (in 1888) by one of John D. Rockefeller's associates, Paul Babcock, to Standard Oil Company executives who were about to testify before a government investigating committee: "Parry every question with answers which, while perfectly truthful, are evasive of *bottom* facts."[8] This was, is, and probably always will be regarded as wise and permissible business strategy.

For Office Use Only

An executive's family life can easily be dislocated if he fails to make a sharp distinction between the ethical systems of the home and the office—or if his wife does not grasp that distinction. Many a businessman who has remarked to his wife, "I had to let Jones go today" or "I had to admit to the boss that Jim has been goofing off lately," has been met with an indignant protest. "How could you do a thing like that? You know Jones is over 50 and will have a lot of trouble getting another job." Or, "You did that to Jim? With his wife ill and all the worry she's been having with the kids?"

If the executive insists that he had no choice because the profits of the company and his own security were involved, he may see a certain cool and ominous reappraisal in his wife's eyes. Many wives are not prepared to accept the fact that business operates with a special code of ethics. An illuminating illustration of this comes from a Southern sales executive who related a conversation he had had with his wife at a time when a hotly contested political campaign was being waged in their state:

"I made the mistake of telling her that I had had lunch with Colby, who gives me about half my business. Colby mentioned that his company had a stake in the election. Then he said, 'By the way, I'm treasurer of the citizens' committee for Lang. I'm collecting contributions. Can I count on you for a hundred dollars?'

"Well, there I was. I was opposed to Lang, but I knew Colby. If he withdrew his business, I could be in a bad spot. So I just smiled and wrote out a check then and there. He thanks me, and we started to talk about this next order. Maybe he thought I shared his political views. If so, I wasn't going to lose any sleep over it.

"I should have had sense enough not to tell Mary about it. She hit the ceiling. She said she was disappointed in me. She said I hadn't acted like a man, that I should have stood up to Colby.

"I said, 'Look, it was an either-or situation. I had to do it or risk losing the business.'

"She came back at me with, 'I don't believe it. You could have been honest with him. You could have said that you didn't feel you ought to contribute to a campaign for a man you weren't going to vote for. I'm sure he would have understood.'

"I said, 'Mary, you're a wonderful woman, but you're way off the track. Do you know what would have happened if I had said that? Colby would have smiled and said, "Oh, I didn't realize. Forget it." But in his eyes from that moment I would be an oddball, maybe a bit of a radical. He would have listened to me talk about his order and would have promised to give it consideration. After that I wouldn't hear from him for a week. Then I would telephone and learn from his secretary that he wasn't yet ready to place the order. And in about a month I would hear through the grapevine that he was giving his business to another company. A month after that I'd be out of a job.'

"She was silent for a while. Then she said, 'Tom, something is wrong with business when a man is forced to choose between his family's security and his moral obligation to himself. It's easy for me to say you should have stood up to him—but if you had, you might have felt you were betraying me and the kids. I'm sorry that you did it, Tom, but I can't blame you. Something is wrong with business!'"

This wife saw the problem in terms of man's obligation as conceived in private life; her husband saw it as a matter of game strategy. As a player in a weak position, he felt that he could not afford to indulge an ethical sentiment that might have cost him his seat at the table.

Playing to Win

Some men might challenge the Colbys of business—might accept serious setbacks to their business careers rather than risk a feeling of moral cowardice. They merit our respect—but as private individuals, not businessmen. When the skillful player of the business game is compelled to submit to unfair pressure, he does not investigate himself for moral weakness. Instead, he strives to put himself into a strong position where he can defend himself against such pressures in the future without loss.

If a man plans to take a seat in the business game, he owes it to himself to master the principles by which the game is played, including a special ethical outlook. He can then hardly fail to recognize that an occasional bluff may well be justified in terms of the game's ethics and warranted in terms of economic necessity. Once he clears his mind on this point, he is in a good position to match his strategy against that of the other players. He can then determine objectively whether a bluff in a given situation has a good chance of succeeding and can decide when and how to bluff, without a feeling of ethical transgression.

To be a winner, a man must play to win. This does not mean that he must be ruthless, cruel, harsh, or treacherous. On the contrary, the better his reputation for integrity, honesty, and decency, the better his chances of victory will be in the long run. But from time to time every businessman, like every poker player, is offered a choice between certain loss or bluffing within the legal rules of the game. If he is not resigned to losing, if he wants to rise in his company and industry, then in such a crisis he will bluff—and bluff hard.

Every now and then one meets a successful businessman who has conveniently forgotten the small or large deceptions that he practiced on his way to fortune. "God gave me my money," old John D. Rockefeller once piously told a Sunday school class. It would be a rare tycoon in our time who would risk the horse laugh with which such a remark would be greeted.

In the last third of the twentieth century even children are aware that if a man has become prosperous in business, he has sometimes departed from the strict truth in order to overcome obstacles or has practiced the more subtle deceptions of the half-truth or the misleading omission. Whatever the form of the bluff, it is an integral part of the game, and the executive who does not master its techniques is not likely to accumulate much money or power.

Notes

1 *The New York Times*, March 9, 1967.
2 See Bruce D. Henderson, "Brinkmanship in Business," *HBR*, March–April 1967, p. 49.
3 *The New York Times*, November 21, 1966.
4 New York, Grossman Publishers, Inc., 1965.
5 New York, David McKay Company, Inc., 1967.
6 *The New York Times*, January 17, 1967.
7 Cited by Ralph Nader in "Business Crime," *The New Republic*, July 1, 1967, p. 7.
8 Babcock in a memorandum to Rockefeller (Rockefeller Archives).

Questions for Discussion and Reflection

1. Do you agree with the executive's statement that "a sudden submission to Christian ethics by businessmen would bring about the greatest economic upheaval in history"? What do you think he means by that statement?
2. How do you evaluate Carr's analogy of business to a poker game, with its own distinct set of rules?

Why Be Honest If Honesty Doesn't Pay?

Amar Bhide and Howard H. Stevenson

Harvard Business Review (September–October 1990): 121–29. Copyright © 1990.

Business men and women keep their word because they want to, not because honesty pays.

We bet on the rational case for trust. Economists, ethicists, and business sages had persuaded us that honesty is the best policy, but their evidence seemed weak. Through extensive interviews we hoped to find data that would support their theories and thus, perhaps, encourage higher standards of business behavior.

To our surprise, our pet theories failed to stand up. Treachery, we found, can pay. There is no compelling economic reason to tell the truth or keep one's word—punishment for the treacherous in the real world is neither swift nor sure.

Honesty is, in fact, primarily a moral choice. Businesspeople do tell themselves that, in the long run, they will do well by doing good. But there is little factual or logical basis for this conviction. Without values, without a basic preference for right over wrong, trust based on such self-delusion would crumble in the face of temptation.

Most of us choose virtue because we want to believe in ourselves and have others respect and believe in us. When push comes to shove, hardheaded business-folk usually ignore (or fudge) their dollars-and-cents calculations in order to keep their word.

And for this, we should be happy. We can be proud of a system in which people are honest because they want to be, not because they have to be. Materially, too, trust based on morality provides great advantages. It allows us to join in great and exciting enterprises that we could never undertake if we relied on economic incentives alone.

Economists and game theorists tell us that trust is enforced in the marketplace through retaliation and reputation. If you violate a trust, your victim is apt to seek revenge and others are likely to stop doing business with you, at least under favorable terms. A man or woman with a reputation for fair dealing will prosper. Therefore, profit maximizers are honest.

This sounds plausible enough until you look for concrete examples. Cases that apparently demonstrate the awful consequences of abusing trust turn out to be few and weak, while evidence that treachery can pay seems compelling.

The moralists' standard tale recounts how E. F. Hutton was brought down by its check-kiting fraud.[1] Hutton, once the second largest broker in the nation, never recovered from the blow to its reputation and finances and was forced to sell out to Shearson.

Exxon's Valdez disaster is another celebrated example. Exxon and seven other oil companies persuaded the town of Valdez to accept a tanker terminal by claiming that a major spill was "highly unlikely." Their 1,800-page contingency plan ensured that any spill would be controlled within hours. In fact, when Exxon's supertanker spewed forth over 240,000 barrels of oil, the equipment promised in the cleanup plan was not available. The cost? According to recent (and still rising) estimates, Exxon's costs could exceed $2 billion, and the industry faces severe restrictions on its operations in Alaska.

But what do these fables prove? Check-kiting was only one manifestation of the widespread mismanagement that plagued Hutton and ultimately caused its demise. Incompetently run companies going under is not news. Exxon's under-preparedness was expensive, but many decisions turn out badly. Considering the low probability of a spill, was skimping on the promised cleanup equipment really a bad business decision at the time it was taken?

More damaging to the moralists' position is the wealth of evidence against trust. Compared with the few ambiguous tales of treachery punished, we can find numerous stories in which deceit was unquestionably rewarded.

Philippe Kahn, in an interview with *Inc.* magazine, described with apparent relish how his company, Borland International, got its start by deceiving an ad salesman for *BYTE* magazine.

Inc.: The story goes that Borland was launched by a single ad, without which he wouldn't be sitting here talking about the company. How much of that is apocryphal?

Kahn: It's true: one full-page ad in the November 1983 issue of *BYTE* magazine got the company running. If it had failed, I would have had nowhere else to go.

Inc.: If you were so broke, how did you pay for the ad?

Kahn: Let's put it that we convinced the salesman to give us terms. We wanted to appear only in *BYTE*—not any of the other microcomputer magazines—because *BYTE* is for programmers, and that's who we wanted to reach. But we couldn't afford it. We figured the only way was somehow to convince them to extend us credit terms.

Inc.: And they did?

Kahn: Well, they didn't *offer*. What we did was, before the ad salesman came in—we existed in two small rooms, but I had hired extra people so we would look like a busy, venture-packed company—we prepared a chart with what we pretended was our media plan for the computer magazines. On the chart we had *BYTE* crossed out. When the salesman arrived, we made sure the phones were ringing and the extras were scurrying around. Here was this chart he thought he wasn't supposed to see, so I pushed it out of the way. He said, "Hold on, can we get you in *BYTE*?"

I said, "We don't really want to be in your book; it's not the right audience for us." "You've got to try," he pleaded. I said, "Frankly, our media plan is done, and we can't afford it." So he offered good terms, if only we'd let him run it just once. We expected we'd sell maybe $20,000 worth of software and at least pay for the ad. We sold $150,000 worth. Looking back now, it's a funny story; then it was a big risk.[2]

Further evidence comes from professional sports. In our study, one respondent cited the case of Rick Pitino, who had recently announced his decision to leave as coach of the New York Knicks basketball team with over three years left on his contract. Pitino left, the respondent wrote, "to coach the University of Kentucky (a school of higher learning, that like many others, is a party in breaking contracts)." Pitino was quoted in the *New York Times* the week before as saying that he never broke a contract. But he's 32 years old and has had five jobs. What he neglected to say is that he's never completed a contract. The schools always let him run out, as they don't want an unhappy coach.

"The same thing is done by professional athletes every year. They sign a long-term contract, and after one good year, they threaten to quit unless the contract's renegotiated. The stupidity of it all is that they get their way."

Compared with the ambiguity of the Hutton and Exxon cases, the clear causality in the Kahn and Pitino cases is striking. Deceiving the *BYTE* salesman was crucial to Kahn's success. Without subterfuge, Borland International would almost certainly have folded. And there is a hard dollar number (with lots of zeros in it) that professional athletes and coaches gain when they shed a contract.

What of the long term? Does treachery eventually get punished? Nothing in the record suggests it does. Many of today's blue chip companies were put together at the turn of the century under circumstances approaching securities fraud. The robber barons who promoted them enjoyed great material rewards at the time—and their fortunes survived several generations. The Industrial Revolution did not make entirely obsolete Machiavelli's observation, "Men seldom rise from low condition to high rank without employing either force or fraud."[3]

Power can be an effective substitute for trust. In theory, Kahn and Coach Pitino should suffer the consequences of their deceits and incomplete contracts: scorned by its victims and a just society, Borland shouldn't be able to blow a whistle. But they continue to prosper. Why do reputation and retaliation fail as mechanisms for enforcing trust?

Power can be an effective substitute for trust.

Power—the ability to do others great harm or great good—can induce widespread amnesia, it appears. Borland International's large ad budget commands due respect. Its early deceit is remembered, if at all, as an amusing prank. Pitino's record for winning basketball games wipes out his record for abandoning teams in midstream.

Prestigious New York department stores, several of our respondents told us, cavalierly break promises to suppliers:

"You send the department store an invoice for $55,000 and they send you $38,000. If you question it, they say, 'Here is an $11,000 penalty for being two days late; here is the transportation tax and a dockage fee.... You didn't follow our shipping instructions, Clause 42, Section 3C. You used the wrong carrier.' And half the time they call the order in and send the 600-page confirming document later, and they say you didn't follow our order."

"Department stores are horrible! Financial types have taken control, the merchants are out. The guy who keeps beating you down goes to his boss at the end of the year and says, 'Look at the kind of rebates I got on freight reduction—$482,000. I delayed payments an average of 22 days from my predecessor at this kind of amount, and this is what I saved.'"

Nevertheless, suppliers still court their tormentors' orders.

"Don't tell me that department stores will go out of business because they treat their suppliers like that! I don't believe that at all. They have too much power—they screw one guy, and guys are waiting in line to take a shot at them again."

Heroic resistance to an oppressive power is the province of the students at Tiananmen Square, not the business-folk in the capitalist societies the students risk their lives to emulate. Businesspeople do not stand on principle when it comes to dealing with abusers of power and trust. You have to adjust, we were told. If we dealt only with customers who share our ethical values, we would be out of business.

A real estate developer we interviewed was blunt:

People are really whores. They will do business with someone they know they can't trust if it suits their convenience. They may tell their lawyers: "Be careful, he's dishonest; he's not reliable and he will try to get out of the contract if something happens." But those two do business with each other.... I've done transactions with people knowing that they were horrible and knowing that I'd never talk to them. But the deal was so good, I just accepted it, did the best I could, and had the lawyers make triply sure that everything was covered.

Sometimes the powerful leave others no choice. The auto parts supplier has to play ball with the Big Three, no matter how badly he or she has been treated in the past or expects to be treated in the future. Suppliers of fashion goods believe they absolutely have to take a chance on abusive department stores. Power here totally replaces trust.

Usually, though, power isn't quite that absolute, and some degree of trust is a necessary ingredient in business relationships. Pitino has demonstrated remarkable abilities in turning around basketball programs, but he isn't the only coach available for hire. Borland International's business is nice to have, but it can't make or break a computer magazine. Nevertheless, even those with limited power can live down a poor record of trustworthiness. Cognitive inertia— the tendency to search for data that confirm one's beliefs and to avoid facts that might refute them—is one reason why.

To illustrate, consider the angry letters the mail fraud unit of the U.S. Post Office gets every year from the victims of the fake charities it exposes. Apparently donors are annoyed that they can't keep sending contributions to a cause they believed in. They want to avoid information that says they have trusted a fraud.

When the expected reward is substantial and avoidance becomes really strong, reference checking goes out the window. In the eyes of people blinded by greed, the most tarnished reputations shine brightly.

Many a commodity broker's yacht has been financed by cleaning out one customer after another. Each new doctor or dentist who is promised the moon is unaware of and uninterested in his or her predecessor's fate. Such investors want to believe in the fabulous returns the broker has promised. They don't want references or other reality checks that would disturb the dreams they have built on sand. Thus can the retail commodity brokerage business flourish, even though knowledgeable sources maintain that it wipes out the capital of 70% of its customers every year.

The search for data that confirm wishful thinking is not restricted to naive medical practitioners dabbling in pork bellies. The *Wall Street Journal* recently detailed how a 32-year-old conglomerateur perpetrated a gigantic fraud on sophisticated financial institutions such as Citibank, the Bank of New England, and a host of Wall Street firms. A Salomon Brothers team that conducted due diligence on the wunderkind pronounced him highly moral and ethical. A few months later—

Even with a fully disclosed public record of bad faith, hard-nosed businesspeople will still try to find reasons to trust. Like the proverbial "other woman," they'll reason, "It's not his fault." And so it comes to pass that Oscar Wyatt's Coastal Corporation can walk away from its gas-supply contracts;[4] then, with the consequent lawsuits not yet settled, issue billions of dollars of junk bonds. Lured by high yields, junk bond investors choose to believe that their relationship will be different: Wyatt *had* to break his contracts when energy prices rose; and a junk bond is so much more, well, *binding* than a mere supply contract.

Similarly, we can imagine, every new Pitino employer believes the last has done Pitino wrong. Their relationship will last forever.

Ambiguity and complexity can also take the edge off reputational enforcement. When we trust others to keep their word, we simultaneously rely on their integrity, native ability, and favorable external circumstances. So when a trust appears to be breached, there can be so much ambiguity that even the aggrieved parties cannot apprehend what happened. Was the breach due to bad faith, incompetence, or circumstances that made it impossible to perform as promised? No one knows. Yet without such knowledge, we cannot determine in what respect someone has proved untrustworthy: basic integrity, susceptibility to temptation, or realism in making promises.

The following example, in which we hear the buyer of a company who was taken in by the seller's representations, is instructive:

"The seller said: 'We have a technology that is going to be here for a long time. We own the market.' We liked this guy so much, it was funny. He's in the local area, he knew my father. He's a great guy to talk to, with all sorts of stories.

"He managed to fool us, our banks, and a mezzanine lender, and he ended up doing quite well on the deal. Then the company went on the skids. The funny thing is, afterwards he bought the business back from us, put a substantial amount of his own capital in, and still has not turned it around. I'm just not sure what was going on.

"I guess he believed his own story and believed it so much that he bought the business back. He was independently wealthy from another sale anyway, and I think he wanted to prove that he was a great businessman and that we just screwed the business up. If he was a charlatan, why would he have cared?"

Where even victims have difficulty assessing whether and to what extent someone has broken a trust, it is not surprising that it can be practically impossible for a third party to judge.

That difficulty is compounded by the ambiguity of communication. Aggrieved parties may underplay or hide past unpleasantness out of embarrassment or fear of lawsuits. Or they may exaggerate others' villainies and their own blamelessness. So unless the victims themselves can be trusted to be utterly honest and objective, judgments based on their experiences become unreliable and the accuracy of the alleged transgressor's reputation unknowable.

Businesspeople learn not to get hung up about other people's pasts.

A final factor protecting the treacherous from their reputations is that it usually pays to take people at face value. Businesspeople learn over time that "innocent until proven guilty" is a good working rule and that it is really not worth getting hung up about other people's pasts.

Assuming that others are trustworthy, at least in their initial intentions, *is* a sensible policy. The average borrower does not plan million-dollar scams, most coaches do try to complete their contracts, and most buyers don't "forget" about their suppliers' bills or make up reasons for imposing penalties.

Even our cynical real estate developer told us:

"By and large, most people are intrinsically honest. It's just the tails, the ends of the bell-shaped curve, that are dishonest in any industry, in any area. So it's just a question of tolerating them."

Another respondent concurred:

"I tend to take people at face value until proven otherwise, and more often than not, that works. It doesn't work with a blackguard and a scoundrel, but how many total blackguards and scoundrels are there?"

Mistrust can be a self-fulfilling prophecy. People aren't exclusively saints or sinners; few adhere to an absolute moral code. Most respond to circumstances, and their integrity and trustworthiness can depend as much on how they are treated as on their basic char-

acter. Initiating a relationship assuming that the other party is going to try to get you may induce him or her to do exactly that.

Overlooking past lapses can make good business sense too. People and companies do change. It is more than likely that once Borland International got off the ground, Kahn never pulled a fast one on an ad salesman again. Today's model citizen may be yesterday's sharp trader or robber baron.

Trust breakers are not only unhindered by bad reputations, they are also usually spared retaliation by parties they injure. Many of the same factors apply. Power, for example: attacking a more powerful transgressor is considered foolhardy.

"It depends on the scale of the pecking order," we were told. "If you are a seller and your customer breaks promises, by and large you don't retaliate. And if you are an employee and your employer breaks promises, you usually don't retaliate either."

Where power doesn't protect against retaliation, convenience and cognitive inertia often do. Getting even can be expensive; even thinking about broken trusts can be debilitating. "Forget and move on" seems to be the motto of the business world.

Businesspeople consider retaliation a wasteful distraction because they have a lot of projects in hand and constantly expect to find new opportunities to pursue. The loss suffered through any individual breach of trust is therefore relatively small, and revenge is regarded as a distraction from other, more promising activities.

Retaliation is a luxury you can't afford, respondents told us.

"You can't get obsessed with getting even. It will take away from everything else. You will take it out on the kids at home, and you will take it out on your wife. You will do lousy business."

"It's a realization that comes with age: retaliation is a double loss. First you lose your money; now you're losing time."

"Bite me once, it is your fault; bite me twice, my fault.... But bite me twice, and I won't have anything to do with you, and I'm not going to bite back because I have better things to do with my life. I'm not going to litigate just for the pleasure of getting even with you."

Only those who have their best years behind them and see their life's work threatened actively seek to retaliate. In general, our interviews suggested, businesspeople would rather switch than fight. An employee caught cheating on expenses is quietly let go. Customers who are always cutting corners on payments are, if practicable, dropped. No fuss, no muss.

Our interviewees also seemed remarkably willing to forget injuries and to repair broken relationships. A supplier is dropped, an employee or sales rep is let go. Then months or years later the parties try again, invoking some real or imaginary change of circumstances or heart. "The employee was under great personal strain." "The company's salesman exceeded his brief." "The company is under new management." Convenience and cognitive inertia seem to foster many second chances.

"Retaliation is a double loss. First you lose your money; then you lose your time."

What about the supposed benefits of retaliation? Game theorists argue that retaliation sends a signal that you are not to be toyed with. This signal, we believe, has some value when harm is suffered outside a trusting relationship: in cases of patent infringement or software piracy, for example. But when a close trusting relationship exists, as it does, say, with an employee, the inevitable ambiguity about who was at fault often distorts the signal retaliation sends. Without convincing proof of one-sided fault, the retaliator may get a reputation for vindictiveness and scare even honorable men and women away from establishing close relationships.

Even the cathartic satisfaction of getting even seems limited. Avenging lost honor is passé, at least in business dealings. Unlike Shakespeare's Venetian merchant, the modern businessperson isn't interested in exacting revenge for its own sake and, in fact, considers thirsting for retribution unprofessional and irresponsible.

"There is such a complete identification in my mind between my company's best interests and what I want to do that I am not going to permit anything official out of spite. If I can't rationalize [retaliation] and run it through my computer brain, it will be relegated to my diary and won't be a company action."

We would be guilty of gross exaggeration if we claimed that honesty has no value or that treachery is never punished. Trustworthy behavior does provide protection against the loss of power and against invisible sniping. But these protections are intangible, and their dollars-and-cents value does not make a compelling case for trustworthiness.

A good track record can protect against the loss of power. What if you stop being a winning coach or your software doesn't sell anymore? Long-suppressed memories of past abuses may then come to the fore, past victims may gang up to get you.

A deal maker cited the fate of an investment bank that was once the only source of financing for certain kinds of transactions.

"They always had a reputation for being people who would outline the terms of the deal and then change them when it got down to the closing. The industry knew that this is what you had to expect; our people had no choice. Now that the bank has run into legal problems and there are other sources of funds, people are flocking elsewhere. At the first opportunity to desert, people did—and with a certain amount of glee. They are getting no goodwill benefit from their client base, because when they were holding all the cards they screwed everybody."

Another entrepreneur ascribed his longevity to his reputation for trustworthiness:

"The most important reason for our success is the quality of my [product] line. But we wouldn't have survived without my integrity, because our lines weren't always very successful. There are parabola curves in all businesses, and people still supported me, even though we had a low, because they believed in me."

Trustworthiness may also provide immediate protection against invisible sniping. When the abuse of power banishes trust, the victims often try to get their own back in ways that are not visible to the abuser: "I'm not in business just to make a profit. If a client tries to jerk me around, I mark up my fees." "The way to get even with a large company is to sell more to them."

On occasion, sniping can threaten the power it rebels against. The high-handedness of department stores, for example, has created a new class of competitors, the deep discounter of designer apparel.

"Ordinarily, manufacturers don't like to sell their goods at throwaway prices to people like us," says one such discounter. "But our business has thrived because the department stores have been systematically screwing their suppliers, especially after all those leveraged buyouts. At the same time, the manufacturers have learned that we treat them right. We scrupulously keep our promises. We pay when we say we'll pay. If they ask us not to advertise a certain item in a certain area, we don't. If they make an honest mistake in a shipment, we won't penalize them.

"The department stores have tried to start subsidiaries to compete with us, but they don't understand the discount business. Anyone can set up an outlet. What really matters is the trust of the suppliers."

How can you quantify the financial repercussions when suppliers you have abused ship hot items to your competitors first?

Neither of these benefits can be factored easily into a rational business analysis of whether to lie or keep a promise. Sniping is invisible; the sniper will only take shots that you cannot measure or see. How could you possibly quantify the financial repercussions when suppliers you have abused refuse your telephone orders or ship hot items to your competitors first?

Assessing the value of protection against the loss of power is even more incalculable. It is almost as difficult to anticipate the nature of divine retribution as it is to assess the possibility that at some unknown time in the future your fortunes *may* turn, whereupon others *may* seek to cause you some unspecified harm. With all these unknowns and unknowables, surely the murky future costs don't stand a chance against the certain and immediate financial benefits from breaking an inconvenient promise. The net present values, at any reasonable discount rate, must work against honoring obligations.

Given all this, we might expect breaches of trust to be rampant. In fact, although most businesspeople are not so principled as to boycott powerful trust breakers, they do try to keep their own word most of the time. Even allowing for convenient forgetfulness, we cannot help being swayed by comments like this:

"I've been in this business for 40 years. I've sold two companies; I've gone public myself and have done all kinds of dealings, so I'm not a babe in the woods, OK? But I can't think of one situation where people took advantage of me. I think that when I was young and naive about many things, I may have been underpaid for what my work was, but that was a learning experience."

One reason treachery doesn't swamp us is that people rationalize constancy by exaggerating its economic value.

"Costs have been going up, and it will cost me a million dollars to complete this job. But if I don't, my name will be mud and no one will do business with me again."

"If I sell this chemical at an extortionate price when there is a shortage, I will make a killing. But if I charge my customers the list price, they will do the right thing by me when there is a glut."

Just as those who trust find reasons for the risks they want to run, those who are called on to keep a difficult promise cast around for justification even when the hard numbers point the other way. Trustworthiness has attained the status of "strategic focus" and "sustainable competitive advantage" in business folklore—a plausible (if undocumented) touchstone of long-term economic value.

But why has it taken root? Why do businessmen and -women want to believe that trustworthiness pays, disregarding considerable evidence to the contrary? The answer lies firmly in the realm of social and moral behavior, not in finance.

The businesspeople we interviewed set great store on the regard of their family, friends, and the community at large. They valued their reputations, not for some nebulous financial gain but because they took pride in their good names. Even more important, since outsiders cannot easily judge trustworthiness, businesspeople seem guided by their inner voices, by their consciences. When we cited examples to our interviewees in which treachery had apparently paid, we heard responses like:

"It doesn't matter how much money they made. Right is right and wrong is wrong."

"Is that important? They may be rich in dollars and very poor in their own sense of values and what life is about. I cannot judge anybody by the dollars; I judge them by their deeds and how they react."

"I can only really speak for myself, and to me, my word is the most important thing in my life and my credibility as an individual is paramount. All the other success we have had is secondary."

The importance of moral and social motives in business cannot be overemphasized. A selective memory, a careful screening of the facts may help sustain the fiction of profitable virtue, but the fundamental basis of trust is moral. We keep promises because we believe it is right to do so, not because it is good business. Cynics may dismiss the sentiments we heard as posturing, and it is true that performance often falls short of aspiration. But we can find no other way than conscience to explain why trust is the basis for so many relationships.

At first, these findings distressed us. A world in which treachery pays because the average business-person won't fight abusive power and tolerates dishonesty? Surely that wasn't right or efficient, and the system needed to be fixed! On further reflection, however, we concluded that this system was fine, both from a moral and a material point of view.

The moral advantages are simple. Concepts of trust and, more broadly, of virtue would be empty if bad faith and wickedness were not financially rewarding. If wealth naturally followed straight dealing, we would only need to speak about conflicts between the long term and the short, stupidity and wisdom, high discount rates and low. We would worry only about others' good sense, not about their integrity. It is the very absence of predictable financial reward that makes honesty a moral quality we hold dear.

Trust based on morality rather than self-interest also provides a great economic benefit. Consider the alternative, where trust is maintained by fear.

A world in which the untrustworthy face uncertain retribution is a small world where everyone knows (and keeps a close eye on!) everyone else. A village,

really, deeply suspicious not only of commodities brokers but also of all strangers, immigrants, and innovators.

No shades or ambiguities exist here. The inhabitants trust each other only in transactions in which responsibilities are fully specified — "deliver the diamonds to Point A, bring back cash" — and breaches of trust are clear. They do not take chances on schemes that might fail through the tangled strands of bad faith, incompetence, over-optimism, or plain bad luck.

A dark pessimism pervades this world. Opportunities look scarce and setbacks final. "You can't afford to be taken in even once" is the operating principle. "So when in doubt, don't."

In this world, there are no second chances either. A convicted felon like Thomas Watson, Sr. would never be permitted to create an IBM. A Federal Express would never again be extended credit after an early default on its loan agreements. The rules are clear: an eye for an eye and a tooth for a tooth. Kill or be killed.

Fortunately, our world is full of trusting optimists—a Steve Jobs with no track record to speak of can start an Apple.

Little, closed, tit-for-tat worlds do exist. Trust is self-reinforcing because punishment for broken promises is swift—in price-fixing rings, loan-sharking operations, legislative log rolling, and the mutually assured destruction of nuclear deterrence. Exceed your quota and suffer a price war. Don't pay on time and your arm gets broken. Block my pork barrel project and I'll kill yours. Attack our cities and we'll obliterate yours.

At best such a world is stable and predictable. Contracts are honored and a man's word really does become his bond. In outcome, if not intent, moral standards are high, since no one enters into relationships of convenience with the untrustworthy. On the other hand, such a world resists all change, new ideas, and innovations. It is utterly inimical to entrepreneurship.

Fortunately, the larger world in which we live is less rigid. It is populated with trusting optimists who readily do business with strangers and innovators. A 26-year-old Steve Jobs with no track record to speak of or a 52-year-old Ray Kroc with nearly ten failures behind him can get support to start an Apple or a McDonald's. People are allowed to move from Maine to Montana or from plastics to baked goods without a lot of whys and wherefores.

Projects that require the integrity and ability of a large team and are subject to many market and technological risks can nonetheless attract enthusiastic support. Optimists focus more on the pot of gold at the end of the rainbow than on their ability to find and punish the guilty in case a failure occurs.

Our tolerance for broken promises encourages risk taking. Absent the fear of debtors' prison and the stigma of bankruptcy, entrepreneurs readily borrow the funds they need to grow.

Tolerance also allows resources to move out of enterprises that have outlived their functions. When the buggy whip manufacturer is forced out of business, we understand that some promises will have to be broken—promises that perhaps ought not to have been made. But adjustments to the automobile age are more easily accomplished if we don't demand full retribution for every breach of implicit and explicit contract.

Even unreconstructed scoundrels are tolerated in our world as long as they have something else to offer. The genius inventors, the visionary organizers, and the intrepid pioneers are not cast away merely because they cannot be trusted on all dimensions. We "adjust"—and allow great talent to offset moral frailty—because we know deep down that knaves and blackguards have contributed much to our progress. And this, perhaps unprincipled, tolerance facilitates a dynamic entrepreneurial economy.

Since ancient times, philosophers have contrasted a barbaric "state of nature" with a perfect, well-ordered society that has somehow tamed humankind's propensity toward force and fraud. Fortunately, we have created something that is neither Beirut nor Bucharest. We don't require honesty, but we honor and celebrate it. Like a kaleidoscope, we have order and change. We make beautiful, well-fitting relationships that we break and reform at every turn.

We should remember, however, that this third way works only as long as most of us live by an honorable moral compass. Since our trust isn't grounded in self-interest, it is fragile. And, indeed, we all know of organizations, industries, and even whole societies in which trust has given way either to a destructive free-for-all or to inflexible rules and bureaucracy. Only our individual wills, our determination to do what is right, whether or not it is profitable, save us from choosing between chaos and stagnation.

Notes

1 The HBR Collection *Ethics in Practice* has six citations (Boston: Harvard Business School Press, 1989).

2 "Management by Necessity," *Inc.*, March 1989, p. 33. Reprinted with permission. Copyright © 1989 by Goldhirsh Group, Inc., 38 Commercial Wharf, Boston, Mass. 02310.

3 *The Discourses*, Chapter XIII, Book 2, Modern Library Edition, 1950.

4 "In the early 1970s," reports *Forbes* (Toni Mack, "Profitable If Not Popular," May 30, 1988, p. 34), "Wyatt found himself squeezed between rising natural gas prices and low-priced contracts to supply gas to cities like San Antonio and Austin. His solution? Renege. He simply refused to honor the contract."

Questions for Discussion and Reflection

1. Do you agree with Bhide and Stevenson that honesty doesn't pay? Why or why not?
2. What do you think is the connection between good ethics and good business ("good business" being defined as profitability)?

The Business of Business

Dallas Willard

Provocations, October 11, 2006, http://www.ttf.org/index/journal/detail/business-of-business

Business is a profession, and professions have a moral role in society.

What is business (manufacturing, commerce) for? Today the spontaneous response to this question is: The business of business is to make money for those who are engaged in it. In fact, this answer is now regarded as so obvious that you might be thought stupid or uninformed if you even ask the question. But that is only one of the effects of the pervasive miseducation that goes on in contemporary society, which fosters an understanding of success essentially in terms of fame, position, and material goods.

This response, however, only reflects a quite recent view of the professions—of which we will here assume business to be one—and even today it is definitely *not* the view of success in professional life shared by the public in general. No business or other profession advertising its "services" announces to the public that it is there for the purpose of enriching itself or those involved in it. All will say with one accord that their purpose is service. I have never met any professionals who would tell their clients that they were there just for their own self-interest. Still, many professionals today are dominated by self-interest, and that is the source of the constant stream of moral failures that occupies our courts and what we now call the "news." Many, too, who would never say it publicly really do think of their success in terms of self-advancement, and will say so "after hours." But the "professional" yet holds a moral role in society, not just one of technical expertise in the marketplace of untrammeled competition.

The older tradition of the profession as having, at bottom, *a moral role in society* was more obvious and defensible before the days of mass society and urban anonymity. Today an individual doctor, lawyer, or other such figure more or less disappears as a person living together with other persons. In other days, they received special training, position, and respect as an appropriate response to the special and potentially self-sacrificing good that they made available to the ordinary people around them—to the public or "common" good, as it used to be called. Considered with respect to the merchant and manufacturer, there has always been less clarity about this role than with the traditional professions of clergy, medicine, and law, but their elevated position and power in the community was nonetheless understood to bring with it unique and unavoidable moral responsibilities.

Writing of this in 1860, John Ruskin remarks: "The fact is that people never have had clearly explained to them the true functions of a merchant with respect to other people."[1] He then puts what we today would call "business" in the context of the "five great intellectual professions" necessary to the life of "every civilized nation." With respect to that nation:

> The Soldier's profession is to *defend* it.
> The Pastor's, to *teach* it.
> The Physician's, to *keep it in health*.
> The Lawyer's, to *enforce justice* in it.
> The Merchant's, to *provide* for it.

He appends to this list: "And the duty of all these men is, on due occasion, to *die* for it." The soldier to die "rather than leave his post in battle," the physician "rather than leave his post in plague," the pastor "rather than teach falsehood," the lawyer "rather than countenance injustice," and the merchant ... rather than ... *what*? It is here, Ruskin acknowledges, that people are apt to be unable to finish the thought. What is it that the "merchant" would die rather than do?

The answer to this question is supplied by the merchant's or manufacturer's function and the good that it supplies to the people in his community. His task is to *provide for* the community. His function is not to pluck from the community the means of his own self-aggrandizement. "It is no more his function," Ruskin continues, to get profit for himself out of that provision than it is a clergyman's function to get his stipend. The stipend is a due and necessary adjunct, but not the object of his life, if he be a true clergyman, any more than his fee (or *honorarium*) is the object of life to a true physician. Neither is his fee the object of life to a true merchant. All three, if true men, have a work to be done irrespective of fee.... That is to say, he [the merchant] has to understand to their very root the qualities of the thing he deals in, and the means of obtaining or producing it; and he has to apply all his sagacity and energy to the producing or obtaining it in perfect state, and distributing it at the cheapest possible price where it is most needed.

Ruskin proceeds to emphasize the responsibility of the "merchant" for the well-being of those in his employ. The merchant has a direct governance over those who work for him. So "it becomes his duty, not only to be always considering how to produce what he sells in the purest and cheapest forms, but how to make the various employments involved in the production or transference of it most beneficial to the men employed." Hence the function of business requires "the highest intelligence, as well as patience, kindness, and tact, ... all his energy ... and to give up, if need be, his life in such way as it may be demanded of him." As the captain of a ship is duty-bound to be the last to leave the ship in disaster, "so the manufacturer, in any commercial crisis or distress, is bound to take the suffering of it with his men, and even to take more of it for himself than he allows his men to feel; as a father would in a famine, shipwreck, or battle, sacrifice himself for his son."

That Ruskin may not be left to stand alone in the field, we also cite the words of Louis Brandeis, one of the greatest of past American leaders of thought and government. In his Commencement Day address to Brown University of October 1912, titled "Business — A Profession,"[2] Brandeis remarks that

the recognized professions ... definitely reject the size of financial return as the measure of success. They select as their test, excellence of performance in the broadest sense — and include, among other things, advance in particular occupation and service to the community. These are the basis of all worthy reputations in the recognized professions. In them a large income is the ordinary incident of success; but he who exaggerates the value of the incident is apt to fail of real success.

He continues, "In the field of modern business, so rich in opportunity for the exercise of man's finest and most varied mental faculties and moral qualities, mere money-making cannot be regarded as the legitimate end."

Brandeis gives most of his lecture to illustrating "real success" in business, "comparable with the scientist's, the inventor's, the statesman's," from the careers of contemporary businessmen around the turn of the last century. He, like Ruskin, emphasizes the *nobility* of the "merchant's" function. If we take such careers as models, he says, "then the term 'big business' will lose its sinister meaning, and will take on a new significance. Big business will then mean business big not in bulk or power, but great in service and grand in manner."

Well, needless to say, this change of meaning has not yet happened. Texts by Ruskin and by Brandeis, along with similar ones,[3] are not popular references in our schools of business today. These schools, for all their good, are instead far too much given to "the excuses which selfishness makes for itself in the mouths of cultivated men,"[4] to quote another person from the times of Ruskin and Brandeis.

Certainly in business one must make a profit, and one's business must survive if it is to serve. But not at the expense of the public good and the well-being of individuals who depend on you — not, for example, if you must sell tainted food or shoddy furniture or electronic devices to stay afloat or thrive. And certainly not as *the* aim or goal of those involved in business.

It is not enough to say that "the market" will drive you out if you don't do what is right. That slogan, with its grain of truth, is brain surgery with a meat cleaver, at best; and in fact it rarely turns out to be true. It serves at all only because, at this particular time in our history, *moral calling* and *moral character* have no weight and are thus unable to serve as established points of reference for individual practice and public policy. They are not treated as aspects of *reality* which must be appealed to in judgment and with which any decent person must come to terms. There is no legitimating support, therefore, for the idealism of young people who go into the professions, nor for the justifiable demands of the public to be served.

It is *a convincing framework of calling and character* that must be restored if professional life is to be directed in a manner which—surely everyone deep-down knows—is suited to its function as provider

and protector of the public good and thus of individuals throughout our neighborhoods and beyond. The greatest challenge facing an officially post-Christian world is to provide that framework. To this point it is not doing very well with the task.[5]

Surely the best course—find a better who may—is to take up one's profession as an appointment from God, through intelligent discipleship to Jesus Christ. This provides a time-tested and experiential foundation and framework for professional life that yields the nobility seen by Ruskin and Brandeis—and much more.

Notes

[1] All quotations are from "Lecture I" of Ruskin's book, *Unto This Last*. Many editions. This lecture is titled "The Roots of Honor."

[2] First published in *Business—A Profession* (Boston: Small, Maynard & Company, Publishers, 1914); also available via Google Book Search.

[3] The "Progressive Movement" of the latter nineteenth century and the first part of the twentieth century was, in large part, an effort to implement in the political and social life of America the kind of idealism, somewhat toned down to be sure, expressed by Ruskin, T. H. Green, and Brandeis. What happened to that movement—how it went sour through the course of events, and was gutted of its genius by currents of thoughts without viable moral content—would be a highly instructive study for any person devoted to understanding our current social and personal situation in America. A good place to start might be *Who Were the Progressives?*, Glenda Gilmore, editor (Boston: St. Martin's Press, 2002), and Michael McGerr, *A Fierce Discontent: The Rise and Fall of the Progressive Movement in America, 1870–1920* (New York: Oxford University Press, 2003).

[4] The words of T. H. Green in §208 of his *Prolegomena to Ethics* [Google Book Search].

[5] But see, by contrast, Os Guinness's indispensable book, *The Call* (Nashville: Word Publishing, 1998). See, as well, the many treatments of the spiritual life by Phillips Brooks (1835–93). [*Editor's note:* One book, *Phillips Brooks' Addresses*, which includes a sermon called "The Duty of the Christian Business Man," is available via Project Gutenberg or on Google Book Search, which has several other full-text editions of Brooks's works, including this reader, which collects passages from many sources.]

Questions for Discussion and Reflection

1. According to Willard, what is the business of business? Do you agree with his view of the purpose of business?
2. How does Willard's view of business differ from Carr's? Which view of business do you tend to favor more? Explain why.
3. What is Willard's view of profit? Do you agree with this view? Why or why not?

CASE STUDIES

Case 2.1: Borland's Brave Beginning

Philippe Kahn, the colorful former CEO of Borland International, built a powerful software company from the ground up with a series of brilliant business moves, including the 1991 acquisition of Ashton-Tate, one of the software industry's biggest companies, for $440 million. At one point

[5] Julie Pitta, "The Barbarian Steps Down," *Los Angeles Times*, January 12, 1995, D1.

the company was extremely successful, culminating in building a palatial headquarters complex costing nearly $100 million. At one point, Kahn even entertained thoughts of challenging Microsoft as the world's top software manufacturer.[5] While the company has recently fallen on hard times, its beginning is one that some would consider morally questionable while others would denote as being "smart moves within the game."

In an interview with *Inc.* magazine in 1989 (see p. 95), Kahn told the story of Borland's humble beginnings. Operating out of two small rooms and strapped for cash, he couldn't afford to place an ad in *BYTE* magazine, the best forum to reach his target market. To convince the ad salesman to extend credit terms, Kahn hired "extra people" to scurry around and made sure the phones were ringing in order to look busy. He prepared a media plan on a chart in which *BYTE* was crossed out but made sure the salesman "accidentally" saw the chart. When the salesman asked if they wanted to advertise in *BYTE*, Kahn replied that it was not the right audience and that they couldn't afford it. The salesman pleaded and eventually gave good terms of credit. The ad ran once and sold $150,000 worth of software, launching a successful venture.[6]

[6] "Managing by Necessity," *Inc.*, March 1989, 33.

Questions for Discussion

1. What do you think about Kahn's actions? Do his actions amount to shrewd business ("within the rules of the game"), deception, or both?
2. How would Kahn's actions be seen in light of Carr's description/ assumptions about business versus Willard's?
3. Some might argue that since everyone "won" in the end, Kahn's decision was ethical. Do you agree? Why or why not?

Case 2.2: Giving Advice Where It Doesn't Belong[*]

* This case was authored by Michael Peterson, an undergraduate student at Seattle Pacific University, as a class project for Business Ethics (BUS 4899), Spring 2010.

Historically, the high cost of using a stockbroker has prevented many people from investing in the stock market. Due in part to technological advancements such as the Internet, the discount brokerage industry (with lower fees and commissions on trades) has made stock market investment accessible to more people. The lower costs, however, come with a catch: discount brokers cannot provide personalized advice to their clients. Discount brokers are meant to serve investors who want to do their own research or who cannot afford the high prices charged by full-service brokers.

For the past year (my senior year of college) I have been working part-time as an intern at a branch of a national discount brokerage. I hope to get into the industry full-time upon graduation, as I truly believe the service we provide is beneficial to our customers. One of my primary responsibilities is to open up accounts for clients and educate them about my company's services. We have a wide range of customers, in terms of age and economic status, who use our services.

Recently a customer in his early eighties came into our branch to open an individual trading account. This fact in and of itself is not unusual, but as I realized his intentions, I became deeply concerned. He stated that his plans were to transfer his life savings into this new account and invest it in the stock market. Many people have large portions of their savings invested in the market, but his age combined with the level of economic volatility was unsettling to me. Furthermore, this client was intent on investing all of his money in one particular penny stock that was trading on the pink sheets. When a stock is listed on the pink sheets, the company is going through the process of filing for bankruptcy, which makes the investment extremely risky. In short, this customer was adamant about leveraging his entire future on the performance of this one risky security.

Besides myself, there was one other person working in the office that afternoon, a licensed broker. While I am assisting customers, the broker's responsibility is to oversee my work and to provide assistance when needed. In addition to supervising me, the broker is also responsible for answering calls and helping other customers. Even though it was clear he overheard the conversation and understood my hesitations and concerns, the broker did not intervene other than to remind me to show the client how to use our website and to make sure all of the paperwork was properly completed.

How should I proceed? How should I integrate my faith into my work in this situation? I care deeply about trying to live my Christian values at work, but in this case, doing so might put me at odds with what's legal. Should I violate the law and potentially jeopardize my future career (I really like working here, and we are in a deep recession that is making jobs scarce) by advising this customer not to invest in penny stocks? Should I try to contact his daughter (which would probably violate his confidentiality), whom he listed as a contact on his forms, and try to get her to talk some sense into him? Or should I stay within the scope of my job and open up the account, take his money, and send him on his way, knowing he is severely endangering his financial well-being? What is the ethical thing to do? How can I act as "my brother's keeper" while also honoring the proper authorities (in this case, the law and my employer)? My supervisor has acknowledged my concerns but is not willing to stick his neck out to resolve the issue and has now moved on to assisting another client. How I choose to proceed is now up to me, and I fully expect that any consequences are my responsibility.

Questions for Discussion and Reflection

1. What should this intern do, given what seems to be a conflict between the legal requirements of his position and the ethical obligation to the elderly client?
2. Should he abide by the rules of his workplace, or should he conduct himself according to broader duties and obligations?

COMMENTARY

Many businesspeople feel an uneasy tension between the moral values that seem to permeate commercial dealings and the standards that govern their lives outside of work. Nagging suspicions that financial success may actually "require" the abandonment of moral convictions is one of the most troubling aspects of a business career. Act honestly or compassionately, you may fear, and find yourself (or your organization) at a great disadvantage vis à vis your competitors. In fact, some research finds that people often live with two sets of values, one for "private life" and one for work.[7] Albert Carr's description of business as a game and the Borland case are somewhat humorous yet poignant illustrations of these tensions.

Given these troubling issues, how should we approach our work in business? Should we live by two sets of ethics as Carr claims? Carr relies on rather dark assumptions about the moral nature of business. Especially provocative are his statements about the inverse Golden Rule and that "a sudden submission to Christian ethics by businessmen [*sic*] would bring about the greatest economic upheaval in history." By this, he meant the economy would actually fall apart, since it is structurally dependent on mistrust and deception for its survival.

Though common, are these types of depictions correct? Is business so broken that deception and mistrust are the norm? Was Kahn "forced" to choose a less than transparent path in order to successfully launch his venture? Does one *have to* compromise or compartmentalize one's convictions in order to succeed?

Business is comprised of many different people, organizations, and industries, each with varying patterns of acceptable behavioral standards. Therefore, overgeneralizing is always a danger when business is spoken of as a singular entity. However, there are good reasons to believe that a more optimistic account may be more accurate, at least for some parts of business. Could an economy based on mistrust actually work for as long and as efficiently as it has?

[7] John P. Fraedrich, "Philosophy Type Interaction in the Ethical Decision-Making Process of Retailers" (Ph.D. diss., Texas A&M University, College Station, Tex., 1988).

As noted in Bhide and Stevenson's article, honesty and trust are probably more the norms of business practice than the rare exceptions. This is especially noteworthy given their findings that while the idea that "honesty is the best policy for economic gain," makes intuitive sense, it is an unsubstantiated claim from a rational, economic standpoint. They point to cases in which breaking one's word is actually handsomely rewarded or, at the very least, seldom punished. Even so, they conclude that the trust necessary for business relationships is alive and well, because for many businesspeople, honesty is a matter of conscience and morality rather than strategy.

The Borland case may well capture our attention, because it is an extreme example of how far someone was willing to go to launch a venture. Normal business activities (that occur billions of times on a daily basis) in which trust is a necessary foundation (like buying and selling) and in which fair dealing is taken for granted (like offering good value to customers, paying bills on time, and engaging in community service projects) don't make for good entertainment, whether in the form of magazine stories, television programs, or movie plots.

As attested to by recent large-scale breaches (accounting fraud, subprime mortgages) of trust, trust is necessary to keep an economy running. A cursory look around the globe further reveals that countries without solid moral foundations tend to have very slow, inefficient economies—as everything has to be verified and verified again.[8]

While common assumptions of the moral nature of business may be too pessimistic (though of course some businesspeople, organizations, and/or whole industries may be deeply flawed), our point isn't to offer an overly optimistic defense of the marketplace. The relationship between ethics and business success is complex. There is no perfect correlation between ethics (whether good or bad) and "successful" business. In fact, it might be most accurate to say that business (like the rest of "the world" in Christian theology) is good and evil (broken yet retaining some of God's image/presence). Some people have built careers through time-tested reputations for fair dealing while others have done so through ruthlessness and cunning. Some have "made it" through a mix of both. Truth telling may build reputational capital and encourage return business in some cases while leading to lost sales in others. Through the course of a career, however, there is no doubt that real choices (and tradeoffs/sacrifices) between living the right kind of story and gaining financially will have to be made. As Bhide and Stevenson note, however, this is something for which we should be thankful. The fact that honesty often goes unrewarded makes us have to choose to do the right thing (and be the right kind of people) for the right reasons.

Setting aside the question of economic alignment, another, perhaps more

8 See Transparency International Corruption Perception Index. www.Transparency.org..

important, point to consider is how "success" in business is measured in the first place. Carr solely defines it in terms of economic self-interest. In our culture today, this is a given. In fact, most people would be hard pressed even to begin to describe an alternative definition. In "The Business of Business," Dallas Willard challenges us to think of it in very different terms. He asks, "What is business for?" What indeed? Success is ultimately tied to purpose. If viewed as a "profession," the purpose of self-interest falls far short of the mark. Think of how odd it would be if physicians, pastors, teachers, leaders of nonprofit organizations, and artists described the primary purpose of their work as acquiring wealth. Why do we accept anything less noble from business? A much better approach is to view business as having a moral role in serving society (or "the common good") through providing (goods and services) for and through taking care of the well-being of employees.[9] In this view, business is far more than a "game."

Defined in this way, one can be quite successful in business while failing to "accumulate much money or power," as Carr states it. A businessperson can be successful by creating a sustainable enterprise that makes life-enhancing goods and services for the community and creates challenging, rewarding work for employees. Of course, there may well be further obligations and/or ways to serve society too (such as volunteer work, philanthropy, environmental protection, etc.).

[9] Also see Charles Handy, "What's a Business For?" *Harvard Business Review* (December 2002). See also Jeff Van Duzer, *Why Business Matters to God: (And What Still Needs to Be Fixed)* (Downers Grove, Ill.: InterVarsity Press Academic, 2010).

Bluffing and Games

The story of Borland's launch is entertaining, especially for the entrepreneurial audience (readers of *Inc.* magazine) for which it was originally told. However, former CEO Philippe Kahn's decisions serve to illustrate some of the inadequacies of Carr's view of business, namely, the fact that unlike in poker, many people who are impacted are not "at the table" by choice.

Although the outcome in this case was "good" for everyone, judging the morality of a decision or action based on consequences alone is inadequate (as noted in chapter 1). If the ending had been different and Borland failed on making good on the credit, there would be nothing endearing about the tale at all. *BYTE* would have lost money, the salesman would have suffered some negative consequences, and Kahn may have sullied his reputation too. While the actual losses would have been small as measured by money, the principle (not principal) is what is at stake. Kahn deceived the salesperson into getting *BYTE* to bear risks without their knowledge or consent.

Probing deeper, one has to wonder if success at deception, even on a small scale, is truly beneficial, especially in the long term. Will an even more desperate situation lead to more lies but on a grander scale? Can employees be counted on to uphold sound ethics when a story about the questionable actions of the company's founder circulates as a part of the company lore? How did this impact Kahn's career? Although he went on to start other companies, he was later forced out by Borland's board (for different reasons).

A similar story may serve to reinforce these points. Barry Minkow was once touted as a wonder boy for launching a commercial building restoration business called ZZZZ Best in the 1980s. By age twenty Minkow had become a millionaire through the seemingly overnight success of his business. Media appearances on magazine covers and major television shows soon followed. Just as quickly as the company (and Minkow's fame) soared, however, its demise came.

After applying for a multimillion-dollar loan, Minkow cleverly deceived the bank by falsely inflating future financial projections. He brought auditors performing due diligence on the loan application to a large building during off-hours to show them an example of a large ZZZZ Best account. In reality, the building was not a company account at all. Minkow paid off a security guard to gain access and had several colleagues wear company uniforms and pretend they were working on the building in order to trick the auditors. ZZZZ Best secured the loan but couldn't pay it back. In the end, Minkow (along with several other ZZZZ Best executives) served several years in prison for his role in defrauding investors and lenders out of more than $100 million.[10] While former Borland CEO Philippe Kahn's actions may not amount to illegal fraud and the stakes were significantly lower in his case, the ethical principles are parallel.

Carr's arguments, though provocative, fall apart with some scrutiny. As Willard points out, business is far from a mere "game." There are good reasons to see business as a profession with a moral role of service to the common good as its central purpose. Moreover, to treat business like a game of poker with its own special set of rules is to abrogate the calling for responsible action in the world. Carr is emphatic that we never should allow Christian ethics (or any other value system that is external to business) to influence our work in business in which we cease to be "private citizens." This goes directly against Christ's mandate to be salt and light in the world.

[10] Minkow's story has taken some interesting turns. After prison he became a pastor and then started an organization, the Fraud Discovery Institute, that helps the government detect fraud. Tragically, Minkow returned to prison in late 2011 for conspiracy to commit securities fraud.

THREE

Christian Engagement in Business

Introduction

Historically, the Christian church has had an uneasy relationship with business. For example, Augustine flatly declared, "Business is in itself an evil," and Tertullian observed that trade is "scarcely adapted for a servant of God." Luther also decried the "trading companies" (akin to modern corporations) of his day.[1] Today it has been well documented that many businesspeople feel as though their work is not viewed as befitting "kingdom work" by their church leaders, though it is valued for the economic wealth it creates to fund what is presumed to be the "real work" of God—that which takes place in churches and missionary endeavors.

More recently, troubling revelations about corporate misconduct (accounting fraud, subprime mortgage lending, environmental disasters) coupled with debates about the potentially pernicious effects of "globalization" have once again heightened centuries-old questions about engagement in business. Can commerce be a legitimate means of participating in divine work in the world when it appears to be conducted within a system riddled with values that are in tension with the Christian tradition?

The focus of this chapter will be on the development of a theologically informed perspective on Christian engagement with business. In particular, the important issue of how Christians in business should thoughtfully, and faithfully, approach their work will be addressed. Should commercial activity be abandoned for the sake of moral and spiritual purity, seen primarily as a means to support the "real" or "proper" work of the church, or embraced as a legitimate spiritual vocation or calling in which to serve as a "faithful presence" or to help transform society into kingdom ideals?

Proper engagement with business will be investigated through the broader discussion of how Christians should interact with contemporary culture (of which business is a part). As cataloged long ago in H. Rich-

[1] See Martin Luther, "Treatise on Trade and Usury," in Theodore Tappert, ed., *Selected Writings of Martin Luther* (Philadelphia: Fortress Press, 1967), 85ff.

ard Niebuhr's influential (though flawed) book, *Christ and Culture*, various theological traditions hold widely diverging views about the relationship between Christianity and culture. Some traditions (and theologians who have influenced them) emphasize the gap between Christian values and those of the surrounding culture, and lean toward separatist tendencies in their interactions. Others see harmony between the values of Christ and those of culture and tend to emphasize common moral ground between them. Yet others fall somewhere in between, giving different emphasis on the fallen, "graced," and "to be redeemed" aspects of culture, and participate within it accordingly.

The first essay in this chapter, "Christ and Business: A Typology for Christian Business Ethics" by Louke van Wensveen Siker, sets the stage for examining appropriate Christian engagement with business by creating a set of organizing categories. Based on Niebuhr's *Christ and Culture*, Van Wensveen Siker develops a typology that categorizes a range of beliefs about the relationship between the competing moral authorities of "Christ" and "Business." She describes five "ideal types" in which patterns of thought regarding this relationship are detected. The remaining essays in this chapter bear distinctive marks of the various strands of thought described by Van Wensveen Siker.[2] The second essay presents an optimistic account of business and the sanctity of participation within it. Robert Sirico's "The Entrepreneurial Vocation" attempts to correct some unflattering assumptions about the world of commerce. In so doing, he undermines the tacit assumption that business is not an arena in which the "proper work" of the church can take place. Sirico argues that business has *intrinsic* value because entrepreneurial activity (broadly understood) is reflective of God's creative nature.

In the third essay, "Tough Business: In Deep, Swift Waters," executive Steve Brinn says that we should accept difficult ethical tensions as a fact of life in the fallen, imperfect world of business. He asserts, however, that Christians should not leave an arena simply because they face moral danger. The model lived by Christ, Brinn observes, is one of cultural engagement rather than abandonment.

The cases probe the issue of cultural engagement through examining situations in which participation in business may advance ethically questionable outcomes yet in which abandonment may actually be worse. These examples of what author Steve Brinn refers to as "deep, swift waters."

As you read the case studies, assess which "type" or "types" (as presented in the essay "Christ and Business") your thinking most closely identifies with. Consider how your thinking is being challenged, changed, or confirmed by what you read.

[2] To be certain, the remaining essays do not perfectly fit the categories developed in the typology. Any typology has limits. It is quite likely that many authors (and readers) hold parts of two or more of the "types." However, typologies are extremely helpful tools to categorize and describe basic thought patterns.

READINGS

Christ and Business:
A Typology for Christian Business Ethics

Louke van Wensveen Siker

Journal of Business Ethics 8 (1989): 883–88. Copyright © 1989 Kluwer Academic Publishers.

Introduction

As the field of business ethics is becoming more defined, the sub-discipline of Christian business ethics is taking on a multifaceted shape. In this paper I shall take stock of the variety of ways in which Christian business ethicists currently conceive of ethical change in business. In order to do so, one needs an appropriate set of organizing categories. Simply adopting the traditional categories used by applied philosophers to organize the field—utilitarian, Kantian, etc.—will not do, for Christian ethicists rarely structure their work along these lines. Rather, I shall show that traditional theological categories can go a long way in helping one appreciate the scope and variety of Christian business ethics as a relatively new area of inquiry. The categories I have chosen are inspired by the typology set forth in H. Richard Niebuhr's classic study, *Christ and Culture*.[1]

The Typology

Before I proceed, let me briefly call to mind the main features of Niebuhr's typology. The book *Christ and Culture* explores how Christians over the centuries have dealt with what Niebuhr calls "the enduring problem of the relation between the authorities of Christ and culture."[2] Niebuhr discerns a pattern of recurring answers to this problem, which he proceeds to organize in the form of five types. First he presents the most extreme answers. Here one finds the views of radical Christians, who stress the presence of evil in culture to such a degree that they can see Christ only in opposition to it ("Christ against Culture"). At the opposite end of the spectrum one finds the position of cultural Christians, who see no

basic contradiction between the demands of culture and the demands of Christ ("The Christ of Culture"). Between these extremes, Niebuhr locates three other typical positions. So-called synthesist Christians tend to establish a hierarchy in which the authority of culture is affirmed, yet also superseded by the authority of Christ ("Christ above Culture"). Dualist Christians struggle with the ambivalence created by seeing culture as both fallen and preserved by God ("Christ and Culture in Paradox"). Finally, conversionist Christians tend to affirm culture insofar as it is the arena of Christ's transforming work ("Christ the Transformer of Culture").

Niebuhr's typology is well suited to serve as a heuristic device for understanding the rich variety inherent in the work of Christian business ethicists. Its focus, the relation between the authorities of Christ and culture, must naturally also be a main theme in an area of inquiry characterized as both Christian and concerned with business. In fact, for the purposes of this study, Niebuhr's five types can simply be narrowed down into the following subset: Christ against Business, the Christ of Business, Christ above Business, Christ and Business in Paradox, and Christ the Transformer of Business. In each case, "Business" refers to the prevailing capitalist business culture. These categories will provide a uniquely theological way of identifying various approaches in Christian business ethics. While the categories used by applied philosophers reflect different foundations of moral authority, an adaptation of Niebuhr's typology will show various ways in which *one* ultimate moral authority, Christ, is thought to relate to an area of life that also claims human loyalty, business. In other words, these categories will highlight a range of beliefs about the ramifications of Christ's work and being for the possibility and dynamics of ethical change in business.

As we shall see, each of Niebuhr's five types is indeed clearly represented among Christians reflecting on ethics in business. This is not to say, however, that any one approach exactly fits a particular type. As Niebuhr observes, "When one returns from the hypothetical scheme to the rich complexity of individual events, it is evident at once that no person or group ever conforms completely to a type."[3] Yet to the extent that the typology can provide a rough background against which various approaches may be grouped (and exceptions noted!), it will serve a useful purpose. Given this qualification, I will now proceed to show what a Niebuhrian typology of Christian business ethics might look like.

Type I: Christ against Business

At some point in time, every Christian business ethicist is likely to encounter the skepticism or even opposition of those among the faithful who assume that the business world can never be salvaged from its corruption. The arguments sound familiar, all variations on the theme, "Business ethics, isn't that an oxymoron?" Niebuhr himself points to an early proponent of this attitude, the church father Tertullian, who argued that trade "is scarcely 'adapted for a servant of God,' for apart from covetousness, which is a species of idolatry, there is no real motive for acquiring."[4]

The skepticism of the radical Christian about ethical change in business seems to be a permanent motif among the various ways of relating Christ and business, akin to the attitude Niebuhr has described with his "Christ against Culture" type. Theologically speaking, such skepticism is rooted in the assumption that the current business culture must be marked off as a realm of evil and idolatry, a realm that must be destroyed rather than changed. As a Christian, one must dissociate oneself as much as possible from the corruption of the business world, while focusing on the new order established by Christ. A modern example of such radical skepticism about ethical change in business can be found in the writings of Franz Hinkelammert, a Marxist theologian who has been working in Costa Rica. Hinkelammert describes a capitalist busi-

ness world marked by idolatry, where commodities and corporations are treated as independent agents, requiring the total subjection of all businesspeople. He concludes that Christians confessing faith in God clearly have no choice but to repudiate this realm of idolatry.[5]

Overall, it is fair to say that the "Christ against Business" type forms the anti-type of any method in Christian business ethics. It denies the validity of the discipline because it denies the legitimacy of anything resembling the prevailing form of business enterprise.

Type II: The Christ of Business

In a scene from *The Power of Ethical Management* by Kenneth Blanchard and Norman Vincent Peale, a minister says to a bewildered businessman, "When you have patience, you realize that if you do what is right—even if it costs you in the short run—it will pay off in the long run."[6] The minister also explains that having patience means trusting in the timing of a higher power, which could be called God. If you do that, things will always work out. This scene epitomizes the assumption that God's aims and the aims of business are essentially in harmony. While the business world may still contain a fair share of corruption, the argument goes, in essence it bears the stamp of goodness. Overcoming the corruption is not only possible, but also relatively easy. After all, most businesspeople have good intentions and basically know right from wrong. They only need some guidance in making concrete moral decisions. Business ethicists, in the role of consultants, can provide such guidance and thus facilitate ethical change. This familiar approach to business ethics can be classified as the "Christ of Business" type.

Niebuhr's observations regarding cultural Christians help to highlight further the features of the "Christ of Business" type. Niebuhr notes, for example, that "the cultural Christians tend to address themselves to the leading groups in a society."[7] Similarly, the "Christ of Business" approach involves targeting mainly top-level managers as the agents of ethical change. Niebuhr notes also that cultural Christians use the language of these sophisticated circles. Similarly, Christian business ethicists often swap theological categories for a mixture of generally accepted ethical terms and the straight business talk of the corporations they consult. A most notable example of this kind of adaptation is the catch phrase "good ethics means good business." Finally, Niebuhr notes that, in their zeal to recommend Christ to the cultured, cultural Christians "want to make discipleship easy."[8] Similarly, the "Christ of Business" approach makes ethics look simple and attractive, a matter of positive thinking, a message that sells at a two-day management retreat. All in all, Niebuhr's "Christ of Culture" type helps us to understand how the specific features of this widely practiced approach to business ethics flow from the basic assumption that Christ and business are essentially aligned.

Type III: Christ above Business

Niebuhr's third type, "Christ above Culture," helps us gain perspective on a somewhat less optimistic, yet even more widespread Christian approach to business ethics. The so-called synthetic type is based on the largely Thomistic assumption that ethical change resembles step-for-step elevation to a higher level of existence, a process guided by the rational discernment and application of natural law and, ultimately, divine law. In Christian business ethics, this assumption finds expression in the method of applying general norms to specific situations by means of careful deductive reasoning. The general norms, such as human dignity, justice, and co-creation, are thought to have universal moral authority. They provide the unequivocal basis for the field of business ethics. The main task of the discipline is to guide the transformation of business according to these ultimate foundations, usually by means of rationally developed medial norms, such as subsidiarity and proportionality. A perfect example of this approach can be found in an essay by Theodore V. Purcell, S.J., entitled "Management Development: A Practical Ethical Method and a Case."[9]

In sum, unlike the radical Christians, synthesist business ethicists do not assume that the modern business world needs to be destroyed. After all, it is still part of the created order. Nor, on the other hand, do they follow the cultural Christians in believing that

business already carries the full potential of goodness within its own laws. Rather, they assume that business life needs to be elevated by means of authoritative, external guidelines. This may not be an easy task. For example, as Thomas McMahon has asked, how does one apply the justice-based concept of a family living wage in a business world guided by the notion of compensation based on comparable worth?[10] Yet despite such difficulties, adherents of the synthesist view of transformation believe that with thorough and imaginative reasoning, it is possible to find authoritative direction.

Type IV: Christ and Business in Paradox

"Christ and culture stand in a relation of paradox," observes Robert S. Bachelder, a congregational pastor. As a result,

> executives should expect that their general and personal callings will exist in tension. But this tension need not create defeatism and cynicism. It can give rise to alertness and moral imagination. What executives must do is accept the moral ambiguities of their companies and yet fully participate in them, trusting all the while in God to open the way to new moral possibilities.[11]

Niebuhr's "Christ and Culture in Paradox" type could not have been more adequately expressed in relation to a business context. And, as we shall see, Bachelder is not the only one to perceive ethical change in business as a matter of tension and paradox. Once again, we are dealing with a distinctive motif in Christian business ethics.

In describing the paradox type, Niebuhr observes that dualist Christians are highly sensitive to the fallenness of culture. Yet at the same time they feel called to participate in culture. After all, God continues to sustain the world in its sin, so to escape it would mean to counter God's plan. Living with this tension between judgment and participation, dualist Christians tend to have only limited expectations of social transformation. The sins of this world can be kept in check through laws and countervailing force, yet the Kingdom of God is not of this world. Meanwhile, God's grace does work transformation in individuals. Yet even forgiven sinners are left to juggle the imperfect options of social life, being always forced again to "sin boldly" with no positive rules to guide their actions.

In a business context, one finds this type expressed in various ways. One manifestation, at a social level, is the activist attempt to channel the power of big business by means of external pressure, such as strikes, boycotts, shareholder resolutions, publicity, and legislation. I am thinking, for example, of the work of the Interfaith Council on Corporate Responsibility under the direction of Tim Smith. At a personal level, one recognizes the type when business ethicists, like Robert Bachelder, stress the necessity to live with compromise and ambiguity, and the need to use one's best personal judgment in the absence of clear-cut rules. My favorite example along these lines comes actually not from a business ethicist, but from Dietrich Bonhoeffer, who observes in his *Ethics* that in extreme situations, one may sometimes have to opt for "the destruction of human livelihoods in the interest of the necessities of business."[12]

All in all, dualist business ethicists are likely to speak the realistic language of power struggles and necessary compromises. Yet with all the stress on freedom of judgment and the absence of fixed rules, this realism can just as easily express itself in liberal as in conservative recommendations (witness the examples mentioned above!). Thus dualist business ethicists are not likely to excel in predictability. But then, of course, their strength lies in providing a witness to the courage and freedom found in a living faith.

Type V: Christ the Transformer of Business

Niebuhr's fifth type, the conversionist approach to the problem of Christ and culture, is marked by nuances rather than tensions. It expresses awareness of the perversion of culture, combined with affirmation of culture as the arena of God's transforming work. Conversionists see transformation as a process which begins with a conversion of the human spirit, and ends in action and social change. Given these inner-worldly

possibilities of change, they believe, it is appropriate for Christians to focus more on positive practice than on negative action toward sin.

Conversionist business ethicists will combine awareness of serious evil in the business world with hope for actual historical transformation of business life. In their attempts to seek out this transformation, they will try to work *with* business, rather than always *against* it. Also, they will take a holistic approach, paying attention to the spiritual as well as the material, the individual as well as the communal. Notions such as character, embodiment, and story may well appear in their work.

A good example of a conversionist approach can be found in Max Stackhouse's book *Public Theology and Political Economy*.[13] In chapter 7, entitled "Spirituality and the Corporation," Stackhouse argues:

> the ideal of social democracy borne by the ecumenical church ... must, without extensive political [*sic*], economic, or technological power, develop a new spirituality, based on a public theology, to transform the materialist and reductionist preoccupation of all present economic forms and ideologies. This is possible because already within the modern corporation are residual ecclesiological elements wherein spiritual matters are intrinsically related to social ones, and therefore are potentially related to new patterns of material and organizational embodiment.[14]

This brief passage captures the main features of the conversionist type in almost a textbook manner, showing both concern for economic distortions and hope for a spirit-based, yet fully historical transformation.

Evaluation

... Now let me turn to the payoff for Christian business ethics. Most obviously, Niebuhr's typology could assist Christian business ethicists in their efforts at maintaining methodological self-awareness in a new area of inquiry. Taken one step further, Niebuhr's typology could also provide fresh opportunities for approaching the work of colleagues in the field. After all, the nuances of the various types prevent the kind of black-and-white vision that does not do justice to the work of another. For example, one is less liable to lump together dualists with the radical approach, or conversionists with the cultural approach, to mention some common errors. On that basis, the typology may even become the occasion for an open discussion on the relative adequacy of each approach....

This leads to my final observation. Niebuhr's typology may ultimately challenge Christian business ethicists to investigate how their methods may be complementary. Niebuhr himself carefully avoided designating any one of his types as the most authoritative answer to the enduring problem of the relation between Christ and culture.[15] He advocated what we

might nowadays call a reflective equilibrium approach, arguing that each type contributes something indispensable and yet insufficient in itself. Thus the radical Christian reminds one of the force of Christ's authority, the cultural Christian shows how the gospel can be brought to leading groups in society, the synthesist reminds one that salvation affirms creation, the dualist adds a healthy dose of suspicion and realism, and the conversionist calls one to positive, confessional action. In a similar vein, the various theological approaches to seeking ethical change in business may well complement each other in unexpected ways. In that case, we should be listening carefully to Norman Vincent Peale as well as to Tim Smith!

Notes

[1] H. Richard Niebuhr, *Christ and Culture* (Harper & Row, New York, 1951).

[2] *Christ and Culture*, 11. Niebuhr's statement of the problem can be criticized for implying that Christ and human life may potentially be conceived of apart from culture. Yet, as Charles Scriven argues in his recent study, *The Transformation of Culture* (Herald Press, Scotsdale, PA, 1988), Niebuhr generally seems to refer to the authority of the *prevailing* culture. Given this understanding, statements concerning Christ's opposition to culture, or Christian withdrawal from culture, make more sense.

[3] Ibid., 43–44.

[4] Ibid., 54. Citation from Tertullian, *On Idolatry*, xi.

[5] Franz Hinkelammert, "The Economic Roots of Idolatry: Entrepreneurial Metaphysics," in *The Idols of Death and the God of Life: A Theology*, ed., Pablo Richard et al. (Orbis Books, Maryknoll, NY, 1983), 165–93.

[6] Kenneth Blanchard and Norman Vincent Peale, *The Power of Ethical Management* (William Morrow, New York, 1988), 60.

[7] *Christ and Culture*, 104.

[8] Ibid., 126.

[9] Theodore V. Purcell, S.J., "Management Development: A Practical Ethical Method and a Case," in *Doing Ethics in Business*, ed. Donald G. Jones (Oelgeschlager, Gunn & Hain, Cambridge, MA, 1982), 187–202.

[10] Thomas F. McMahon, "The Contributions of Religious Traditions to Business Ethics," *Journal of Business Ethics* 4 (1985): 344.

[11] Robert S. Bachelder, "Ministry to Managers," *The Christian Ministry* 15 (September 1984): 14.

[12] Dietrich Bonhoeffer, *Ethics* (Macmillan, New York, 1955), 239.

[13] Max L. Stackhouse, *Public Theology and Political Economy: Christian Stewardship in Modern Society* (Eerdmans, Grand Rapids, 1987).

[14] Ibid., 131. In this passage Stackhouse uses dialectical language to throw a different light on an earlier developed argument. Overall, his argument does not depend on a dialectical reading of history.

[15] Yet, personally Niebuhr seems to prefer the conversionist type. See, for example, Paul Ramsey, *Nine Modern Moralists* (Prentice-Hall, Englewood Cliffs, N.J., 1962), 149–79.

Questions for Discussion and Reflection

1. What are the primary ways that Van Wensveen Siker views the relationship between Christianity and business?
2. Which of these do you think of as the dominant paradigm of the Christian businessperson today?
3. Which of these do you think is most consistent with the Bible, and why?

The Entrepreneurial Vocation*

Robert Sirico

Journal of Markets and Morality 3, no. 1 (Spring 2000): 1–21.

Introduction

There was a time, in the not too distant past, when prejudice was an acceptable social posture. However, stereotypes, which typically function as shortcuts to knowledge, are today considered offensive. This is so, regardless of whether they elucidate a group characteristic. People ought not be judged merely by the associations they keep, without regard for their person or individual qualities. Such a tendency is properly objectionable to anyone with moral sensibilities. Despite the laudable attitude of popular culture against prejudice of any form, there remains one group upon which an unofficial open season has been declared: the entrepreneur! One sees vivid evidence of this prejudice at nearly every turn, particularly in terms of popular forms of communication. Consider, for example, classic literary works (say, of Dickens[1] or Sinclair Lewis[2]), television programs (such as *Dallas* or *Dynasty*), films (*China Syndrome, Wall Street*, and some versions of *A Christmas Carol*), cartoon strips (such as *Doonesbury* and *Dilbert*), and even sermons in which entrepreneurs are depicted as greedy, immoral, and cutthroat.[3]

On the rare occasion when opinion-makers, especially moral leaders, refrain from denouncing the "rapacious appetite" and the "obscene and conspicuous consumption" of these capitalists, about the best one can expect is that businesspeople be tolerated as a necessary evil. Most news editors, novelists, film producers, and clergy assume that commerce requires a broad and complicated network of controls to serve genuine human needs. Even friends of capitalism frequently display the same attitude! Religious leaders and critics of the market often suffer from confusion in their economic and moral thinking. This can be seen, for example, in their refusal to grant any moral sanction to the entrepreneur. Thus, instead of praising the entrepreneur as a person of ideas, an economic innovator, or a provider of capital, the average priest or minister thinks of people in business as carrying extra guilt. Why? For owning, controlling, or manipulating a disproportionate percentage of "society's" wealth.

While entrepreneurs should not be unfairly criticized for making money, they also must not be treated as victims of unjust discrimination who deserve a special blessing. However, it is also true that their chosen profession deserves to be legitimized by their faith. The public must begin to acknowledge the value of the entrepreneurial profession, the wise stewardship of talents, and the tangible contributions that entrepreneurs make to society. The consequences of a divorce between the world of business and the world of faith would be disastrous in both arenas. For the world of business it would mean not acknowledging any values higher than expediency, profit, and utility, which would result in what has been described as bloody or savage capitalism.[4] It would lead to a truncated view of consumers as well as producers, whose sole value would be measured by utility. It does not require much imagination to gauge the effect such attitudes would exert on a wide range of social and civic norms. Similarly, the preconceived notions of religious leaders must be challenged to avoid the charge of "being so heavenly minded they are no earthly good." Forgetting that enterprise requires insight or intuition, and not merely a transcendent reference point directing it to the overall good of society, religious critics disregard the implicit spiritual dimension of enterprise.

Some moralists[5] seem to view business ethics as either an oxymoron or an effort to subordinate what is intrinsically an ethically compromised mechanism to moral norms. To this way of thinking, ethics and business stand in fundamental tension with one another. However, I see matters differently. Working with a wide array of successful business leaders, extensive

---

*This paper was originally delivered as the closing address at CEO retreat weekends and "Toward a Free and Virtuous Society" conferences sponsored by the Acton Institute for the Study of Religion and Liberty.

reading in the fields of economics and business ethics, and a fair amount of meditation and prayer on these matters, have led me to the conclusion that searching for excellence is the beginning of a search for God. Put succinctly, the human thirst for the transcendent is what drives people to seek excellence, whether they acknowledge it or not. Nonetheless, this does not preclude our initial impulse and intuition from being a (divine) tug in the right direction. This is also the case with the human capacity for knowledge. Various philosophers and theologians contend that the human quest for knowledge reveals that human beings are ontologically oriented toward the truth.[6] The human mind was originally designed to have an immediate awareness of the truth. The principal argument of this article is that the pursuit of excellence, like the mind's original constitution, discloses humanity's ontological orientation toward the highest and most supreme good, namely, the perfect apprehension of God in heaven (cf. 1 Cor. 13:12).

Stewardship of Talents: The Intellectual Divide between Religious Leaders and Entrepreneurs

The time has come for religious institutions and leaders to treat entrepreneurship as a worthy vocation, indeed, as a sacred calling. All laypeople have a special role to play in the economy of salvation, sharing in the task of furthering the faith by using their talents in complementary ways. Every person created in the image of God has been given certain natural abilities that God desires to be cultivated and treated as good gifts. If the gift happens to be an inclination for business, stock trading, or investment banking, the religious community should not condemn the person merely on account of his or her profession. In response to my writings in a variety of business journals, people of a particular profile contact me. The following story illustrates a typical encounter.

On one occasion a gentleman called to let me know that he had just finished reading an article of mine in *Forbes*. It was, as he explained, both a shocking and emotional experience. Shocking, because in all of his Catholic school education and regular

church attendance, he had never before heard a priest speak insightfully of the responsibilities, tensions, and risks inherent in running a business. Was there, he wondered, no spiritual component at all in what occupied so much of his life? In reading the article he felt affirmed—for the first time—by a religious leader at the point in his life where he spent most of his time and effort: in the world of work.

This man represents many others, whose stories are too numerous to recount here. Very often they are relatively successful individuals with deep moral and religious convictions. However, each experiences a moral tension, not because what they do is somehow wrong, but because religious leadership has usually failed to grasp the dynamics of their vocations and thus provide relevant moral guidance and affirmation.

These people represent a variety of Christian traditions, and they each expressed a sense of being disenfranchised and alienated from their churches. I recall one man in particular, who described himself as a conservative Christian, saying that he no longer attended church services because he refused to sit in the pew with his family and, in effect, be chastised for his business acumen. How many critical sermons can a small business owner or investment banker hear before he or she loses heart and decides to sleep in on the Sabbath? Michael Novak relates another experience demonstrating the almost impenetrable resistance some clergy exhibit to conceding the moral potential of market liberalism. His experience occurred at a conference on economics in which several Latin American priests were participating. The conference went on for several days, during which a persuasive case was made for how the free economy is capable of lifting the poor from poverty through the productive means of the market. The priests remained silent until the final day of the conference, and Novak offers an interesting account of what happened next:

> At the last session of what had been a happy seminar, one of the priests arose to say that his colleagues had assembled the night before and asked him to make a statement on their behalf.
>
> "We have," he said, "greatly enjoyed this week. We have learned a great deal. We see very well that capitalism is the most effective means of producing wealth, and even that it distributes wealth

more broadly and more evenly than the economic systems we see in Latin America. But we still think that capitalism is an immoral system."[7]

Why does this state of affairs exist? Why is it so common that businesspeople hear nothing better from a religious leader than something to the effect, "Well, the way to redeem yourself is to give us your money"? Why is it that many of those who form the moral conscience of our world simply do not grasp either the moral foundation or basic principles of the market?

An obvious reason for this ignorance is the astonishing lack of any economics training in virtually all seminaries. It is rare to find a single course explaining fundamental economic principles, the complicated world of stock trading, or microeconomic dynamics. Seminarians are accustomed to hearing in most social ethics courses the empty slogans of liberation theology proponents who believe that developed nations exploit less-developed nations, thus keeping them in a perpetual state of poverty.[8] Generally, these arguments are put forth by theologians with little grasp of economics.

The Practical Divide between Religious Leaders and Entrepreneurs

In addition to an intellectual or academic gap, there is a kind of practical divide between religious leaders and entrepreneurs in their understanding of market operations. This is because the two groups tend to operate from different worldviews and employ different models in their daily operations. Notice how these differences are typically manifested. On Sunday morning a collection basket is passed in most churches. On Monday the bills are paid, acts of charity attended to, and levies paid to denominational headquarters. However, when the collection regularly comes up short, making it difficult to pay the bills, most ministers will preach a sermon on the responsibility of stewardship.

In the minds of many clergy, economic decisions resemble dividing up a pie into equal slices. In this view wealth is seen as a static entity, which means that for someone with a small sliver to increase his or her share of the pie, someone else must necessarily receive a slightly smaller piece. The "moral solution" that springs

from this economic model is the redistribution of wealth, what might be called a Robin Hood morality.

Nevertheless, entrepreneurs operate from a very different understanding of money and wealth. They speak of making money, not collecting it; of producing wealth, not redistributing it. Entrepreneurs must consider the needs, wants, and desires of consumers, because the only way to meet their own needs peacefully—without relying on charity—is to offer something of value in exchange.

These people, then, view the world of money as dynamic. In referring to the free market as dynamic, it is easy to get the impression that we are describing a place or an object. However, the market is actually a process, or a series of choices made by independently acting persons who themselves place monetary values on goods and services. This process of assigning subjectively determined values is responsible for producing the "wealth of nations," a phrase that is typically associated with the title of Adam Smith's classic eighteenth-century work,[9] but was actually first employed in the book of Isaiah (60:5).[10] The creative view of economics taken by business people is also illustrated in Scripture.

Unfortunately, the preceding argument may be misconstrued as urging that religion adopt a bottom-line, profit-and-loss mentality with regard to its mission, but this would be a grave distortion. I agree that there is a significant place for the sharing of wealth and resources within Christian practice. With their transcendent vision, communities of faith recognize that some matters cannot be placed within the limited calculus of economic exchange or evaluated solely in terms of "dollars and cents." It is equally true, however, that to maintain credibility in the world of business and finance, clergy must first understand the inner workings of the market economy, for only then will such moral guidance be helpful.

But there is another, if somewhat misleading, factor that contributes to the hostility toward capitalism one frequently encounters in religious circles. Many religious leaders spend a great portion of their lives personally confronting the wretchedness of poverty. Poverty saddens and angers us, and we want to put an end to it. This sentiment is entirely proper, not to mention morally incumbent upon Christians. However, a problem develops when this sentiment is combined with the economic ignorance described above. When this happens, the just cry against poverty is converted into an illegitimate rage against wealth as such, as though the latter created the former. While this reaction is understandable, it is nevertheless ill-informed, and can lead to overreactions. Persons who react in this way fail to acknowledge that the amelioration of poverty will be achieved only by producing wealth and protecting a free economy.

The Propriety of Moral Outrage

There is understandable moral resistance to the image of successful business enterprise if one presumes that the engine of such activity is animated by greed, acquisitiveness, selfishness, or pride. The issue is not that some entrepreneurs are greedy or proud, but whether these character flaws are the norm for successful practitioners of enterprise. The intent here is not to gloss over the fact that there are serious temptations associated with wealth and success, but to come to a more balanced assessment of the moral character of entrepreneurs.

For some reason, moral critics often focus on the personal gains of entrepreneurs—as if wealth itself is somehow unjust—but lose sight of the many personal risks shouldered by these individuals. Long before entrepreneurs see a return on their idea or investment, they must surrender their time and property to an unknown fate. They pay out wages even before they know whether their forecast has been accurate. They have no assurance of profit. When investments do return a profit, much of it is usually reinvested (though some of it goes to charities and religious institutions). Sometimes entrepreneurs make errors of judgment and miscalculations, and the business suffers financial loss. The nature of the vocation is such that entrepreneurs themselves must accept the responsibility for their losses without shifting the burden onto the public. For the person with a true vocation to be an economic agent of change, he or she must remain vigilant, for economic conditions are ever changing.

Religious professionals should wonder, when economic risk proves to have been a mistake, whether it is not better to encourage than to condemn. Or, should economic losses suffered by capitalists be viewed as their just deserts? Why not make such occasions opportunities to extend sympathy or pastoral care instead? Whether they win or lose, by putting themselves and their property on the line, entrepreneurs make the future a little more secure for the rest of us.

What is unique about the institution of entrepreneurship is that it requires no third-party intervention either to establish or maintain it. It requires no government program or government manuals. It does not require low-interest loans, special tax treatment, or public subsidies. It does not even require specialized education or a prestigious degree. Entrepreneurship is an institution that develops organically from human intelligence situated in the context of the natural order of liberty. Those with the talent, calling, and the aptitude for economic creativity are compelled to enter the entrepreneurial vocation for the purpose of producing goods and services and providing jobs.

Truly, the gifts that entrepreneurs offer society at large are beyond anything either themselves or others can fully comprehend. Entrepreneurs are the source of more social and spiritual good than is generally recognized, but this is not to underestimate a pastor's proper function of providing spiritual direction (with strong admonition for moral failure) and counseling for misplaced priorities or neglect of one's family or spiritual development through overwork. Clergy must remind all people of the seriousness of sin and call them to virtue, which means they must likewise challenge entrepreneurs when they go astray. To be authentic, this spiritual direction must be grounded in an understanding of what Judaism and Christianity have traditionally understood as sin, not in some "politically" or "theologically correct" economic ideology masquerading as moral theology.

This is a difficult transition for many religious leaders to make, especially given the fact that their traditional moral framework for understanding economic productivity was developed in a pre-capitalist world. It is an arduous undertaking to translate and apply pre-modern Christian social teaching to the dynamic environment of a modern, post-agrarian, post-industrial, and now, post-Communist world. It is especially difficult because, while human nature does not change, the socio-economic context in which human nature exists is radically different from those cultures and societies where the principles of moral theology were first developed.[11]

Entrepreneurs and Economists: Family Squabble or Sibling Rivalry?

Economic theory itself has long had difficulty coming to terms with the nature of entrepreneurship, probably because it does not fit well into the equations and graphs of econometrics that picture the economy as a large machine. Entrepreneurship is too human to be understood by science alone. That is where religion can be helpful in reconciling such people to the life of faith. Religious leaders must seek to understand entrepreneurs and encourage them to use their gifts within the context of faith. Of course, with wealth comes responsibility, and Pope John Paul II insists that even the decision to invest has an inescapable moral dimension.[12] Yet entrepreneurs, by taking risks, serving the public, and expanding the economic pie for everyone, can be counted among the greatest men and women of faith in the Church.

Anti-Capitalist Capitalists

Even more puzzling than the anti-capitalist bias among the clergy is the bias found among capitalists themselves! In misguided attempts to achieve a high level of "social responsibility" for their companies, some business leaders have succumbed to false views of the marketplace. While creating wealth for society through their successful businesses, they simultaneously support causes antithetical to economic growth, free enterprise, and human liberty. Why does the rhetoric of "corporate social responsibility" seem to have such an anti-capitalistic bias? In the mid-1990s it became increasingly apparent that otherwise successful chief executive officers were using their corporations to fund politically interventionist causes under the rubric of corporate social responsibility. This could be seen particularly in the cases of Patagonia, Inc., Ben & Jerry's ice cream, and The Body Shop cosmetics chain.

Yvon Chouinard is the founder of Patagonia, Inc., successful producers of functional outdoor sports clothing. Chouinard told the *Los Angeles Times* that he can "sit down one-on-one with the president of any company, anytime, anywhere, and convince [him or her] that growth is evil." His words, in fact, match his actions. In 1991 the company sent a letter to its dealers, announcing that it was "curtailing domestic growth" for economic and moral reasons. "We've taken a public stand in favor of more rational consumption in order to benefit the environment," the statement read. But, as *Los Angeles Times* reporter Kenneth Bodenstein relates, the situation in 1991 was quite different from Chouinard's public statements. It was not that Patagonia "curtailed domestic growth" to maintain a high standard of social responsibility. "The company actually fired 30% of its staff, not because [it] was in deep financial trouble but because Yvon Chouinard's personal wealth was threatened." Interestingly, in Bodenstein's appraisal, Patagonia's situation resulted from ill-informed economic decisions such as Chouinard having "surrounded himself with managers with too little experience."[13]

Patagonia is, indeed, an unusual company. Chouinard donates 1 percent of Patagonia's total sales to environmental groups, including one known as Earth First!, an organization that gained notoriety for its sabotage of logging machinery and infringement of private property rights. Patagonia also supports abortion purveyor Planned Parenthood on the grounds that an increase in population presents a threat to the future well-being of the planet. Chouinard desires his company to be a shining moral example to the corporate world. "If we can take the radical end of it and show it's working for us, the more conservative companies will take that first step. And one day they'll become good businesses, too," he quips.

Ice cream entrepreneurs Ben Cohen and Jerry Greenfield, of Ben & Jerry's fame, though enormously successful as entrepreneurs, promote burdensome environmental controls and advocate giving welfare recipients broader rights to the public purse. Cohen and Greenfield have been leaders in the movement to restrict the production of bovine growth hormone, a drug that, when injected into cows, can increase milk output by up to 15 percent. They oppose the drug on economic grounds, because they believe it poses a threat to small-scale dairy farmers. However, the hormone, which was approved by the Food and Drug Administration on August 4, 1997, would also push down the price of milk, something that would be particularly helpful to poor families, if not ice cream producers.

The Body Shop, the cosmetics chain with a naturalist bent, has been a vociferous supporter of animal rights and other left-wing causes. The company's founder and managing director, Anita Roddick, is a self-appointed preacher to the corporate world, chiding business people who are not "doing their share." "I am not talking about people who are just scraping up a living ... I am talking about people who have huge, huge profits," she told the *Arizona Republic*. "You know, these CEOs with compensation packages bigger than the GNPs of some African countries."[14]

There are countless companies run by former 1960s-style radicals who try to reconcile their business success with the values of their youth. Everyone, including businesspeople, has a right to advocate a chosen cause, as all customers have the right not to fund their causes by boycotting their products. But the pattern of these entrepreneurs displays an internal incoherence and suggests an attempt to do penance for capitalist "sins," which are not really sins at all.

These penitent capitalists castigate businesses that do not give enough back to society. A misplaced sense of guilt has clouded their understanding of how their own businesses do good for society—independent of social activism. Patagonia produces top-quality sporting goods. Ben & Jerry's serves up a superior ice cream. The Body Shop sells inexpensive all-natural cosmetics. Each of these companies brings satisfaction to millions, providing good products for consumers, as well as jobs and investment opportunities. Their market success does not—and should not—need to be justified by support of anti-market causes.

The cynic might suggest such postures are little more than marketing gimmicks. Socially aware chief executive officers such as Chouinard, Cohen and Greenfield, and Roddick have packaged 1960s idealism and are selling it for profit. When you buy a pint of Ben & Jerry's Rain Forest Crunch ice cream, you can feel good about helping save what used to be called "the jungle." The left-wing political slogans that adorn the Body Shop franchises are part of the image of cosmetics for the young and "socially aware." Benetton's ads featuring colorful condoms sell the cause of promiscuity along with the conservative cardigans. Such companies as Patagonia, Inc., Ben & Jerry's, The Body Shop, and so forth, sell a mingled sense of moral superiority. The businesspeople, using politically correct advertising slogans, can believe that despite their material success, they are giving something back to the world. Yet their "social responsibility" campaigns often become an irresponsible recipe for economic ruin.

These companies, and others like them, certainly profit from their association with left-wing causes. Meanwhile, they advocate strict environmental controls, restrictions on Food and Drug Administration-approved growth hormones, and permissive attitudes toward sexual conduct that cause taxpayers to suffer in order to protect the environment and fund new regulations and welfare programs, which inhibit would-be future entrepreneurs. We may commend business when it supports charities that lift people out of poverty, or purchases land to be preserved, or explores cures for diseases; legitimate causes do not impede the market or push for more ill-conceived government action to solve social problems. However, capitalism does not need more guilt-ridden leftists, publicly flogging themselves and others for making money. Rather, capitalism needs more businesspeople who understand that their greatest contribution lies in making profits, expanding jobs, boosting investment, increasing prosperity—doing so in a way that promotes a wholesome, stable, and virtuous culture. The proper moral response to capitalist success is both praise for the Creator who provided the material world as a gift for all and support of the economic system that allows prosperity to flourish. Rather than doing needless penance, entrepreneurs such as Chouinard, Cohen, Greenfield, and Roddick should study basic economics (not to mention sound moral theology).

• • •

The Biblical Case for Entrepreneurship

Those who consider the entrepreneurial vocation a necessary evil, who view investment capital and profits with open hostility, should realize that Scripture lends ample support to entrepreneurial activity. The Bible teaches us eternal truths but also provides surprising practical lessons for worldly affairs. In Matthew 25:14–30, we find Jesus' Parable of the Talents. As with all parables, its meaning is multilayered. Its eternal meaning relates to how we use God's gift of grace. With regard to the material world, it is a story about capital, investment, entrepreneurship, and the proper use of economic resources. It is a direct rebuttal to those who insist that business success and Christian living are contradictory. What follows is the text of the Parable of the Talents (NRSV) with commentary that applies principles taken from the parable to the entrepreneurial vocation.

For it is as if a man, going on a journey, summoned his slaves and entrusted his property to them; to one he gave five talents, to another two, to another one, to each according to his ability. Then he went away. The one who had received the five talents went off at once and traded with them, and made five more talents. In the same way, the one who had the two talents made two more talents. But the one who had received the one talent went off and dug a hole in the ground and hid his master's money. After a long time the master of those slaves came and settled accounts with them. Then the one who had received the five talents came forward, bringing five more talents, saying, "Master, you handed over to me five talents; see, I have made five more talents." His master said to him, "Well done, good and trustworthy slave; you have been trustworthy in a few things, I will put you in charge of many things; enter into the joy of your master." And the one with two talents also came forward, saying, "Master, you handed over to me two talents; see, I have made two more talents." His master said to him, "Well done, good and trustworthy slave; you have been trustworthy in a few things, I will put you in charge of many things; enter into the joy of your master." Then the one who had received the one talent also came forward, saying, "Master, I knew that you were a harsh man, reaping where you did not sow, and gathering where you did not scatter seed; so I was afraid, and I went and hid your talent in the ground. Here you have what is yours." But his master replied, "You wicked and lazy slave! You knew, did you, that I reap where I did not sow, and gather where I did not scatter? Then you ought to have invested my money with the bankers, and on my return I would have received what was my own with interest. So take the tal-

ent from him, and give it to the one with the ten talents. For to all those who have, more will be given, and they will have an abundance; but from those who have nothing, even what they have will be taken away. As for this worthless slave, throw him into the outer darkness, where there will be weeping and gnashing of teeth."

This is a story that many religious leaders do not often apply to real life. When people think of Jesus' parables, the Parable of the Talents is not usually the first to come to mind. Perhaps this is because most religious leaders hold to an ethic where profit is suspect and entrepreneurship is frowned upon. Yet the preceding story relays an immediately apparent ethical meaning, not to mention even deeper lessons for understanding economic accountability and proper stewardship.

The word *talent* in this parable has two meanings. First, it is a monetary unit, perhaps even the largest denomination of Jesus' time. The editors of the *New Bible Commentary* agree that a talent was the name for a very large sum of money, which in modern terms would have been equivalent to several thousand dollars.[15] So we know that the amount given to each servant was considerable. Second, more broadly interpreted, talent refers to all of the various gifts God has given us to cultivate and multiply. This definition embraces all gifts, including our natural abilities and resources as well as our health, education, possessions, money, and opportunities.

I do not pretend to build an entire ethic for capitalism from this parable. To do so would be to commit an egregious exegetical and historical error, similar to those committed by the liberation and the dominion theologians. Yet one of the simplest lessons from this parable has to do with how we use our God-given capacities and resources. This, I contend, must be part of an ethic that guides economic activity and decision making in the marketplace. On one level, in the same way the master expected productive activity from his servants, God wants us to use our talents toward constructive ends. We see here that in setting off on his journey, the master allows his servants to decide upon the best manner of investment. In this regard, they have full liberty. In fact, the master does not even command them to invest profitably; instead, he merely assumes their goodwill and interest in his property. Given this implicit trust, it is easier to understand the master's eventual disgust with the unprofitable servant. It is not so much his lack of productivity that offends the master, as it is the underlying attitude he exhibits toward the master and his property. One can imagine the servant's reasoning: "I'll just get by; I'll put this talent out of sight so that I don't have to deal with it, monitor it, or be accountable for it." Leopold Fonck observes, "It is not the misuse only of the gifts received which renders the recipient guilty in the sight of God, but the non-use also...."[16] The master invited each of the diligent servants to rejoice in his own joy, once they had shown themselves to be productive. They were handsomely rewarded; indeed, the master gave the lazy servant's single talent to the one who had been given ten.

The Parable of the Talents, however, presupposes a local understanding of the proper stewardship of money. According to rabbinical law, burying was regarded as the best security against theft. If a person entrusted with money buried it as soon as he took possession of it, he would be free from liability should anything happen to it. For money merely tied up in a cloth, the opposite was true. In this case, the person was responsible to cover any loss incurred due to the irresponsible nature of the deposit.[17] Yet in the Parable of the Talents, the master encouraged reasonable risk-taking. He considered burying the talent—and thus breaking even—to be foolish, because he believed capital should earn a reasonable rate of return. In this understanding, time is money (another way of speaking about interest).

A second critical lesson from the parable is this: It is not immoral to profit from our resources, wit, and labor. Though writing for an entirely different audience and context, Austrian economist Israel Kirzner employs the concept of entrepreneurial alertness to show the significance of cultivating one's natural ability, time, and resources. Building on the work of Ludwig von Mises, Kirzner acknowledges that by seeking new opportunities and engaging in goal-directed activity, entrepreneurs strive "to pursue goals efficiently, once ends and means are clearly identified, but also with the drive and alertness needed to identify which ends to strive for and which means are available."[18] Without overstating the similarity between Kirzner's concept and the Parable of the Talents, there seems to be a natural connection between the discovery of entrepreneurial opportunities

and the master's (the Lord's) admonition to be watchful of his return and caretakers of his property in Matthew 25. Thus, with respect to profit, the only alternative is loss, which, in the case of the third servant, constitutes poor stewardship.[19] However, the voluntary surrender of wealth, such as in almsgiving or in its more radical form of renouncing the right to ownership of property (as in the traditional vow of poverty taken by members of certain religious orders),[20] should not be confused with economic loss. In the former case a legitimate good is foregone in exchange for another to which one has been uniquely called. In the latter case, to fail deliberately in an economic endeavor, or to do so as a result of sloth, is to show disrespect for God's gift and for one's responsibility as a steward.

Nevertheless, we must distinguish properly between the moral obligation to be economically creative and productive, on the one hand, and to employ one's talents and resources prudently and magnanimously, on the other. It is clear from our discussion of the Parable of the Talents and the cultural mandate in Genesis 1 that in subduing the earth, people need to be attentive to the possibilities for change, development, and investment. Furthermore, because humans created in the image of God have been endowed with reason and free will, human actions necessarily involve a creative dimension. Thus, in the case of the third servant who placed his single talent into the ground, it was the non-use of his ability to remain alert to future possibilities—which precluded any productive return on the master's money—that led to his being severely chastised. There is, perhaps, no clearer illustration of employing one's talents and resources prudently for the good of all than the monks of the medieval Cistercian monasteries. Insofar as monasteries were ruled by a religious constitution that divided each monk's day into segments devoted to prayer, contemplation, worship, and work, the amount of time available to spend on productive activities was tightly regulated. This constraint, along with the typical monastic emphasis on self-sufficiency, according to Ekelund et al., motivated monasteries to develop more efficient farm-production techniques, which provided a natural incentive to embrace technological development. In addition to the early and frequent use of mills, Cistercian monks also experimented with plants, soils, and breeding stocks, thus enabling them to use their God-given creativity wisely and productively in order to accumulate money for the monastery and to aid the poor.[21]

Economics shows that the rate of return (profit) on capital over the long run is likely to equal the interest rate. The rate of interest, in turn, is the payment given for putting off present consumption for future consumption (sometimes called the rate of time preference). For the master in Jesus' parable, it was not enough merely to recover the original value of the talent; rather, he expected the servant to increase its value through participation in the economy. Even a minimal level of participation, such as keeping money in an interest-bearing account, would have yielded a small rate of return on the master's capital. Burying capital in the ground sacrifices even that minimal amount of return, which was what incensed the master about his servant's indolence.

In the book of Genesis, we read that God gave the earth with all its resources to Adam and Eve. Adam was to mix his labor with the raw material of creation to produce useable goods for his family.[22] Similarly, the master in the Parable of the Talents expected his servants to use the resources at their disposal to increase the value of his holdings. Rather than passively preserve what they had been given, the two faithful servants invested the money. But the master was justly angered at the timidity of the servant who had received one talent. Through this parable, God commands us to use our talents productively. The principal emphasis of the parable, I believe, is on the need for work and creativity and the rejection of idleness.

Conclusion

Throughout history, people have endeavored to construct institutions that ensure security and minimize risk—much as the failed servant tried to do with the master's money. Such efforts range from the Greco-Roman welfare states, to the Luddite communes of the 1960s, to full-scale Soviet totalitarianism. From time to time, these efforts have been embraced as "Christian" solutions to future insecurities. Yet uncertainty is not just a hazard to be avoided; it can be an opportunity to glorify God through wise use of his gifts. In the Parable of the Talents, courage in the face of an unknown future was generously rewarded in the case of the first servant, who had been entrusted with the most. He used the five talents to acquire five more. It would have been safer for him to deposit the money in a bank and receive a nominal interest rate. For taking reasonable risks and displaying entrepreneurial acumen, he was allowed to retain his original allotment and his new earnings. Furthermore, he was even invited to rejoice with the master. The lazy servant could have avoided his dismal fate by demonstrating more entrepreneurial initiative. If he had made an effort to increase his master's holdings, but failed in the process, he may not have been judged so harshly.

The Parable of the Talents implies a moral obligation to confront uncertainty in an enterprising way. There is no more apt example of such an individual than the entrepreneur. Entrepreneurs look to the future with courage and a sense of opportunity. In creating new enterprises they open up new options for people to choose from in earning a wage and developing their skills. But none of what has been argued should be taken to imply that the entrepreneur, because of the importance that he or she holds for society, should be exempted from spiritual accountability. Immoral behavior can be found among entrepreneurs no less often than among any other group of sinful human beings. However, it is important that the biblical categories of sin not be applied to this group more severely than to any other, specifically the accusation that businesspeople are motivated solely by greed.

Notes

[1] Charles Dickens, *Hard Times for These Times* (London: Oxford University Press, 1955 [1854]); *Dealings with the Firm of Dombey and Son, Wholesale, Retail, and for Exportation* (London: Oxford University Press, 1964 [1847–48]).

[2] Sinclair Lewis, *Babbitt* (New York: Harcourt, Brace and Company, 1922).

[3] For a fuller description of how businessmen have been depicted in literature, see Michael J. McTague, *The Businessman in Literature: Dante to Melville* (New York: Philosophical Library, 1979).

[4] Ibid., 63–71.

[5] The quintessential historical representative of this position would be Bernard Mandeville, who thought that economic prosperity resulted from the actions of self-seeking and amoral individuals. He argued that to achieve economic success, people

must be liberated from the restraints of conventional morality. This relegated the prescriptions of business ethics to the status of useful fictions created to maintain order and ensure predictable results. *The Fable of the Bees*, vol. 1, ed. F. B. Kaye (London: Oxford University Press, 1924 [1705]), 46. For a criticism of Mandeville and his contemporary followers, see Norman P. Barry, *Anglo-American Capitalism and the Ethics of Business* (Wellington, New Zealand: New Zealand Business Roundtable, 1999), 8–16; also cf. *The Morality of Business Enterprise* (Aberdeen: Aberdeen University Press, 1991), 3–6.

6 John Paul II, *Crossing the Threshold of Hope*, ed. Vittorio Messori (New York: Alfred A. Knopf, 1994), 32–36; *Encyclical Letter Fides et Ratio* (September 14, 1998), nos. 4–5, 27.

7 Michael Novak, *This Hemisphere of Liberty: A Philosophy of the Americas* (Washington, D.C.: The AEI Press, 1990), 38.

8 According to Gregory Baum, then professor of theology and religious studies at St. Michael's College, University of Toronto, "… the economic dependence of the Latin American countries on the system of corporate capitalism, with its center in the North Atlantic community and more especially in the U.S.A., has not only led to the impoverishment of the mass of the population in the city and country but also affected the cultural and educational institutions and through them the consciousness of the people in general." *The Social Imperative: Essays on the Critical Issues That Confront the Christian Churches* (New York: Paulist Press, 1979), 10. Or, as Northwestern University professor Rosemary Ruether writes: " … it is only in Latin America that the real theology of liberation can be written, whereas Europeans and North Americans, who remain encompassed by their own status as beneficiaries of oppressive power, can only comment upon this theology from outside." *Liberation Theology: Human Hope Confronts Christian History and American Power* (New York: Paulist Press, 1972), 181. Comment she does. For a cogent critique of these approaches, see Michael Novak, *Will It Liberate? Questions about Liberation Theology* (New York: Paulist Press, 1986).

9 Adam Smith, *An Inquiry into the Nature and Causes of the Wealth of Nations*, ed. R. H. Campbell and A. S. Skinner (Oxford: Oxford University Press, 1976 [1776]).

10 The text of the verse reads (NRSV):

> Then you shall see and be radiant;
> Your heart shall thrill and rejoice,
> because the abundance of the sea
> shall be brought to you,
> the wealth of the nations shall
> come to you.

11 In the two years preceding his reception into the Roman Catholic Church (1843–45), John Henry Cardinal Newman wrote his now famous work, *An Essay on the Development of Christian Doctrine* (London: J. Toovey, 1845). Unfortunately, then as now, it is all too common that well-meaning and faithful Catholics associate a growing Christian self-understanding and maturity in the area of doctrine and morals with a relativist worldview. It is true that some theologians are in jeopardy of slipping into relativism; however, to argue, as some do, that any doctrinal emendation will necessarily lead to relativism is false. In the case of Cardinal Newman, he was called upon to respond to the Protestant argument that justified separation from Rome because the teaching of the early church had become corrupted through a series of doctrinal additions. The main task of the Essay, then,

was to examine the principal differences between a doctrinal corruption and a doctrinal development. He insisted that a true and fertile idea is endowed with a certain vital and assimilative energy of its own, which without experiencing substantive change, attains a more complete expression as it encounters new aspects of truth or collides with new errors over time. Thus, Cardinal Newman employs an organic metaphor to describe how doctrinal ideas develop over the course of time through the Church's new experiences, discoveries, and revelations. To bolster his argument, he provides a series of tests for distinguishing a true development from a corruption, the chief of which are the preservation of type and the continuity of principles. It is important to grasp, therefore, that the essence of the doctrine — both in its earlier and later forms — was contained in the original revelation given to the Church by Christ and the Apostles, and guaranteed by its Magisterium.

12 John Paul II, *Encyclical Letter Centesimus Annus* (May 1, 1991), nos. 29, 32.

13 Kenneth Bodenstein, "Pure Profit; For Small Companies That Stress Social Values as Much as the Bottom Line, Growing Up Hasn't Been an Easy Task," *Los Angeles Times Magazine* (February 5, 1995): 4.

14 Jodie Snyder, "Social Awareness: Corporate America Cultivates Conscience," *Arizona Republic* (May 12, 1994): 6.

15 G. J. Wenham, J. A. Motyer, D. A. Carson, and R. T. France, eds., *New Bible Commentary*, 21st Century Edition (Downers Grove, Ill.: InterVarsity Press, 1997), 938.

16 Leopold Fonck, *The Parables of the Gospel: An Exegetical and Practical Explanation*, 3rd ed., ed. George O'Neill, trans. E. Leahy (New York: F. Pustet, 1914 [1902]), 542.

17 According to the teaching of Rabbi Gemara, "Samuel said: Money can only be guarded [by placing it] in the earth. Said Raba: Yet Samuel admits that on Sabbath eve at twilight the Rabbis did not put one to that trouble. Yet if he tarried after the conclusion of the Sabbath long enough to bury it [the money] but omitted to do so, he is responsible [if it is stolen]." *The Babylonian Talmud (Seder Nezikin), Baba Metzia*, vol. 1, trans. H. Freedman (New York: The Rebecca Bennet Publications Inc., 1959), 250–51. Also, cf., the very next section (pages 254–59) for a detailed discussion of liability surrounding the deposit of money with a bailiff, private individual, or a third party.

18 Israel M. Kirzner, *Competition and Entrepreneurship* (Chicago: University of Chicago Press, 1973), 33.

19 Kirzner points out that entrepreneurial responses to changes in information should not be understood as a process of calculation. Rather, the entrepreneurial dimension concerns that element of a decision involving "a shrewd and wise assessment of the realities (both present and future) within the context of which the decision must be made." *Discovery and the Capitalist Process* (Chicago: University of Chicago Press, 1985), 17. Samuel Gregg comments incisively on Kirzner's statement: " 'Assessment' is the key word here. It highlights the reality that each person's knowledge is limited and that each individual's acts consequently take place in, and contribute to, a context of uncertainty. For if there was no uncertainty, decision-making would merely call for the precise calculation of facts and options, in which case humans would be nothing more than robots. The reality is, however, that no matter how accurate one's calculations, a decision will be poor if its entrepreneurial-speculative component involves poor judgment." "The Rediscovery of Entrepreneurship: Developments in the Catholic Tradition," in *Christianity and Entrepreneurship: Protestant and*

Catholic Thoughts (Australia: The Center for Independent Studies, 1999), 65.

[20] Monasteries were originally conceived to be a refuge from worldly concerns and a place where spiritual matters dominated daily life. Medieval monasteries were regulated by a constitution or set of internal rules, which among other things, required that a vow of chastity, poverty, and obedience be taken by the monks. One of the most widespread constitutions was the Rule of St. Benedict that applied to both the Benedictine and Cistercian Orders. This rule set forth specific guidelines that controlled the organization and operation of monasteries and regulated the daily activities of the monks. For a recent translation with an excellent introduction and explanatory notes, see *The Rule of St. Benedict*, trans. Anthony C. Meisel and M. L. del Mastro (Garden City, N.Y.: Image Books, 1975).

[21] Robert B. Ekelund, Jr., Robert F. Hébert, Robert D. Tollison, Gary M. Anderson, and Audrey B. Davidson, *Sacred Trust: The Medieval Church as an Economic Firm* (New York: Oxford University Press, 1996), 53–54.

[22] The Second Vatican Council's Decree on the Apostolate of Lay People (November 18, 1965) expands this argument in the following lengthy quotation:

"That men, working in harmony, should renew the temporal order and make it increasingly more perfect: such is God's design for the world.

"All that goes to make up the temporal order: personal and family values, culture, economic interests, the trades and professions, institutions of the political community, international relations, and so on, as well as their gradual development—all these are not merely helps to man's last end; they possess a value of their own, placed in them by God, whether considered individually or as parts of the integral temporal structure: 'And God saw all that he had made and found it very good' (Gen. 1:31). This natural goodness of theirs receives an added dignity from their relation with the human person, for whose use they have been created. And then, too, God has willed to gather together all that was natural, all that was supernatural, into a single whole in Christ, 'so that in everything he would have the primacy' (Col. 1:18). Far from depriving the temporal order of its autonomy, of its specific ends, of its own laws and resources, or its importance for human well-being, this design, on the contrary, increases its energy and excellence, raising it at the same time to the level of man's integral vocation here below" (no. 7).

Questions for Discussion and Reflection

1. Sirico refers to entrepreneurship as a sacred calling. What are the reasons he gives for this view? Do you agree with his view of entrepreneurship?
2. Do you agree with Sirico that entrepreneurs are regarded by religious leaders with hostility and skepticism? Why or why not?
3. What is the biblical case for entrepreneurship, according to Sirico? Do you agree with his understanding of the Bible in this case?

Tough Business: In Deep, Swift Waters

Steve Brinn

Vocatio 2, no. 2 (July 1999): 3–6. Copyright © 1999.

"Tough business" is the stuff that causes us to say, "There must be a fifth solution to this, because the first four stink." Or it causes us to say, "God, I don't really know the right answer—I see a range of options and not one of them gives me any comfort that I know the right thing to do." Put yet another way, tough business is the kind of business engagement that, in spite of our very best effort, causes some other Christian bystander to say, "And she considers herself a Christian!"

Tough business is a tough road to travel. Still, Christ calls many of his followers to this journey. More pilgrims on this path should talk honestly about our experiences, including fears and failures. To that end, I would like to address three "tough business" questions.

Why Not Tough Business?

The first question is "Why shouldn't Christians be up to their ears in tough stuff—and aren't most of our reasons for shying away from it shallow or false?"

From the time I entered business more than 22 years ago, Christ to me has been a model of engagement. Dangerous engagement in life, where there was high exposure with questionable people and complicated issues, entailing prospects for great conflict and trouble. Christ's invitation to be like him led me, in the business context, from safe harbors to open water. Do we, as Christians, belong out there, where we are bound, often, to get wet?

I row a scull. Usually novice rowers, on a river, will cleave to the shore. The water is shallower there, and the currents are less strong. By custom, rowers on one side of the river row upstream and on the other side downstream, so collisions are far less likely. Should you pitch out of your boat, by chance, the swim to shore is easier. All in all, it is a place to begin, with much less exposure than out in the middle.

As rowers progress, they are challenged to move to deeper water. They do this because the shortest, fastest run is down the middle of a river; there the current is swifter. Rowers are moving in both directions, so the chance for collision is greater (especially as scullers face backward!) and, if you go for a swim, it is much further away to the safety of the shore.

If Jesus were a rower, he would move to deeper water as his skills progressed. If Jesus were a businessman, he would get his feet down and learn the basics. Then he would push out and take his faith to the place where the action is. But is this what Christians do? Too often, I think, people come into the church, experience its safe harbor—and then just stay there, rather than moving out in faith. This is true in every direction. And it seems to be very true in the case of Christians in the marketplace.

Why is this? I suppose the reasons are as diverse as people in the church. But it seems clear that for many people of faith stepping into business at all is stepping into Babylon, and "less is better." In this spirit, Christians may steer away from large stakes, fast-paced transactional situations, controversy, or exposure by their selection of employment—or by their response to team members, if these circumstances arise.

> If Jesus were a businessman, he would get his feet down and learn the basics. Then he would push out and take his faith to the place where the action is.

Here is an example of these predicaments from my own experience. Some years ago, just after I joined the company where I am now a senior executive, it came to my attention that one of our associates was proposing a deal involving our property on a river and riverboat gambling. I was stunned and unsure what to do. Though I do not believe gambling to be a categorical sin, participating in a gaming enterprise even indirectly was about the last thing under heaven I would choose to do.

Tough business situation: Do I (1) resign, (2) threaten to resign if the proposal is adopted, or (3) keep my place at the table and express my own strong reservation, using my business sense as well as my moral convictions, and see how things actually develop?

I chose option (3). Another executive who is a Christian immediately resigned from his position as CFO and from the board in order to "hear no evil," and, presumably, avoid participating directly in one.

As things played out over months, I was teased as a prude, told of my hypocrisy, and accused of worrying about my reputation. But I held my ground, asked tough-minded questions about the durability of the business, the business implications, and the involvement in gaming and how it fit with the core principles of our company. In the end, the deal faded—and the proponent left the company.

The moral of the story isn't that, if you stay at the wheel and don't abandon ship bad things won't happen. (I've stayed at the wheel other times and the thing I disliked still came to pass.) But it does illustrate how I was able to retain a vote, while my colleague surrendered his chair and, in my view, made it even more difficult for our shared objections to be spoken with greatest force.

I think Christ wanted my voice in that discussion. What's more, I think he wants our voices in many "tough business" exchanges which may never have ideal outcomes, but only relatively better rather than worse results in the best case. But Christians shy away from these situations, consciously and subconsciously, every day. They abdicate the role and think they are avoiding the chance of failure and sin. In the past few years, I've come to see that this crucible, this high-wire act of being in but not of the world, just can't be avoided. We all face it, in different roles. And counting degrees is only within the ken of God himself.

This last point is crucial. For 20 years I have struggled to reconcile my heart for heaven with the reality of the work world and its chances and outcomes. I could never put them together! I never experienced resolution of the tension, and therefore thought I was in the wrong place, which led me to consider career changes, new tactics, different decision-making strategies, and leaving the marketplace altogether! Then it finally struck me: We are children of God living our lives in a world hostile to our Father, and we are never in our lifetime going to experience a resolution of the conflict between the Kingdom of God and the powers of this earth. In other words, this is not heaven—but we are not in the wrong place.

Jesus incarnated this truth. Wherever he went, the will of heaven and the will of the world confronted each other, kicking up all kinds of disturbances and storms. Our lives will, in a fractional way, resemble His walk. Tough business is a place where heaven and earth meet and tussle just like any other point we occupy. Some of us are called to be there, working in the tensions that will only be resolved in glory.

Avoiding tough business out of concern for our reputation is ungodly if we are called to the role by God. Abdicating the role is also a false solution if we do so to escape the tension basic to our existence, between the will of God and the powers controlling this world. (There is no place really to escape it!) Finally, though there is little support for, or understanding of tough business in the church, the church's failure in this area is not an excuse for shunning God's call. Christians should be right in the middle of tough business, as followers of the one true God. Who better to make tough choices without any good outcomes?

Where God Is

The second question worth pondering is: "Will God meet us there?" Obviously, from what already has been said, the answer is "Yes!" God calls many Christians into these situations. Followers of Jesus aren't supposed to go spoiling for trouble, but if we put our oars into deeper water, we are going to get drawn into situations involving pain, disappointment, and compromise. Other believers may end up saying, "And he calls himself a Christian!"

To judge from church practices, there is little grace available to followers of Jesus who understand their calling to be tough business. Much in church is said about the difficulties of marriage and family, health, aging and poverty, and as to those things words and symbols all say grace abounds. But what about reducing, but not stopping, adverse impacts of logging, or providing two weeks rather than one week of severance pay to 100 people laid off in a corporate restructuring? Are these kinds of issues ever the stuff of group prayer? Do sermons ever fully recognize the compromises all of us who are in the marketplace face? When they do, do they provide assurances that our work has meaning—and when we fail, that we may receive grace? Sadly, across the church, these supports for marketplace Christians are lacking.

Oddly, we may feel more confidence in God's mercy toward the penitent assassin than the slick but reportedly reborn casino manager. Yet the God who can wash cardinal sins white as snow is more than capable of forgiving the businesswoman implicated in a corporate injury to a third party resulting from a breached contract! And despite the compunctions about business in the North American church today, church-goers who do engage in business can receive both God's guidance and forgiveness as they wrestle with limited options, misinformation and misunderstanding, the painful reality of scarce resources and the zero-sum games endlessly played out in a competitive economy. God will meet Christians in the crucible of tough business as often as they follow Him there in faith.

> ## God will meet Christians in the crucible of tough business as often as they follow Him there in faith.

C. Everett Koop, the former Surgeon General of the United States, once commented that his most painful injuries, while attempting with all his heart to perform his best as a person of faith, arose from the vicious insults of Christian critics. Those of us who follow Jesus, who always push into deep water, should thank God when we see a person of faith tackling tough jobs in the marketplace or in government. And we should hope for their courage, wisdom, and perseverance, rather than thinking the worst and attacking like jackals. We have a long way to go. God is already there, waiting for us.

> ## We should thank God when we see a person of faith tackling tough jobs in the marketplace. And we should hope for their courage, wisdom, and perseverance, rather than thinking the worst and attacking like jackals.

Tips and Tools

It is dangerous to prescribe any nostrum for the troubles confronted in tough business. But we all learn lessons that may be helpful to other pilgrims. So here are a few my own life freely offers the reader:

- We should figuratively stand on our heads every morning, to remember all the mystery in the world before we enter the 20th-century business realm, which is so much predicated on science and efficiency. In fact, the daily sacrament of this kind of irreverence on the way into the office gets us oriented toward heaven's part in all that will face us the rest of the day, no matter how mundane or hopelessly separated from heaven itself.

- Read fairy tales. This is a complement to standing on one's head. Fairy tales defy limits. Up can suddenly meet down. Animals can talk. And, if we restore our belief in heaven's ability to exceed all rules, we start to lift our sights away from the way it is done, to truly be "in, but not of" the world in which we are working. Deals, then, can be at least partly shaped by mercy. Hopes for improving a hopelessly tarnished prospect may not be abandoned, but rather rekindled. Nothing is ever completely over when we look at things through the eyes of faith. Fairy tales help restore the child, even in businesspeople.

- Don't flee from the scenes of your failure. Christian businesspeople hate failures as much as anyone, and perhaps more, because we feel called to results not achievable in this lifetime. It is tempting to sweep our failures out of sight and rush on to the next challenge. Yet, by admitting our shortcomings and experiencing forgiveness for them, we find our relationship with God in tough business grows. And He will give us new visions, which often grow out of the ashes of our failures.

- Give yourself time. It takes time to find out what really is your calling, and then to learn the ropes. This may take decades. I am 46 and just beginning to get a clearer sense of the gifts I've been given and where to put them to work.

- Beware of life-style enclaves. Just like every other "group" in our society, business folks tend to hang out too much with each other. Find friends who aren't called to tough business and let your world overlap with theirs. Both of you will be better off.

- Join a revolutionary movement at some point. Sooner or later business causes anyone to become established, just as professional ministry does. Do something that shocks your friends and tests your own fences.

- Never give up on things that matter. God doesn't. Why should we?

- Finally, carry a token. It will go with you into the marketplace and call you back to the memory of God when you would least expect it.

I imagine that many of you soon will be in the knot-hole of tough business again, alone and wondering why you can't build a bridge that really works between heaven and earth. That's not your job. That job belongs to Jesus. But my prayer is that He will meet you in the bind, give you courage and wisdom there, and heal your wounds and worries as you stay in the world, where you are meant to be, as salt and light.

Questions for Discussion and Reflection

1. What does Brinn mean by the phrase "tough business"?
2. What would you have done if your company were considering the property deal that involved riverboat gambling and you had some decision-making authority on the project?

CASE STUDIES

Case 3.1: The Assignment

Upon graduation from college, Sarah takes a position at a small firm (twenty employees) that specializes in web design and management services for business clients. Sarah loves both the work that she does as a web designer and her place of employment. The owners of the company have treated her well, and her coworkers are very collegial and are fun to be around.

After nine months on the job, Sarah is given the opportunity to take the lead role on a project for a new client that everyone around the firm has referred to as "the big kahuna." It's an honor to be asked to take this role, since it is very clear that if this client is impressed with the work done on the initial project, much more work may be directed to the firm.

Sarah is well aware of the positive light in which senior executives of the firm view her and of the career opportunities presented by being asked to lead the design team on this particular project. However, the nature of the client company's business and some of its past marketing campaigns are troubling to her.

The company is a leading apparel manufacturer and retailer that has sought to create an edgy and somewhat rebellious image. One marketing campaign, which used posters in dormitories and full-page ads in college newspapers featured "drinking games" and "party drink" mixes, prompting some activists to accuse the company of encouraging under-aged drinking. While the company was initially concerned about the negative publicity, clothing sales actually increased.

At an initial project conceptual design meeting, Sarah meets marketing executives from the client company who express their desire for a website that "attracts a lot of traffic by capitalizing on the brand identity and image we have worked so hard to successfully create."

After the meeting, Sarah meets with a senior executive of her firm named Lynn. Lynn is a seasoned veteran of the advertising industry and has served as an informal mentor to Sarah. Sarah shares with Lynn that this assignment is especially giving her trouble because her cousin was killed in a car accident in which underage drinking was involved a few years ago.

Lynn replies, "I understand your reservations, Sarah; but consider the positive impact you can make on the campaign. Someone will end up directing the design work. It may as well be someone with a conscience. For years I worked on ad campaigns for a tobacco company and was able to help curb some possible 'spill-over' that would have impacted kids. I suggest you accept the assignment."

Questions for Discussion

1. In light of concepts developed in this chapter, should Sarah accept the assignment? Why or why not?
2. Do you agree with Sarah's boss that if she walks away from this assignment, she will be succeeded by someone with a less sensitive conscience than hers?

Case 3.2: Bad Boy Executive

Derek Ferguson is a Harvard Business School–educated entertainment industry executive who serves as the CFO of Bad Boy Worldwide Entertainment, headquartered in New York City. Bad Boy, founded and led by entertainer Sean ("Diddy") Combs, produces musical acts such as the late Notorious B.I.G., Gorilla Zoe, and Jordan McCoy. The company also markets the Sean John clothing line and operates two restaurants. According to Yahoo Finance, Bad Boy "sells attitude and image."[3]

Given the controversial nature of Combs, some of the musical acts the company produces, and the rap/hip-hop musical genre (known for explicit, misogynistic, and sometimes violent lyrics), some may be surprised to learn that Ferguson is a committed Christian who is involved in a number of urban development ministries. He even leads a well-attended weekly Bible study for employees of Bad Boy. While he is bothered by some of the messages of hip-hop, he says, "I don't think we're called to run away from controversial environments. We're called to run to them and try to create change." He continues, "You can be in the corporate world and still incorporate goodness and righteousness in your work.... At the end of the day, what really matters is using your skills in a way that has a lasting benefit."[4]

[3] Yahoo! Finance: Bad Boy Entertainment, Inc. Company Profile, http://biz.yahoo.com/ic/53/53318.html (accessed January 20, 2011).

[4] Julia Hanna, "Derek Ferguson: Bad Boy's Good Man," *Harvard Business School Bulletin* 80, no. 1 (March 2004). Also see "Derek Ferguson, CFO, Bad Boy Worldwide Entertainment," *Bain & Co. Global Alumni Newsletter*, http://www.bain.com/alumni/newsletter/May2010/alumni_features.htm#Ferguson.

Questions for Discussion

1. Is Ferguson's industry and company an appropriate venue to engage business? Some might argue that in attempting to create change, he is compromising his beliefs and likely has to contribute to producing products that are damaging. Others might argue that every industry, company and/or job in a broken world has something wrong with it, so what Ferguson is doing is not all that unusual in terms of its moral content. And, what better place for a light to shine than in one that is "dark" (the biblical examples of Nehemiah, Joseph, and Daniel come to mind).
2. What do you think of the way that Ferguson attempts to balance his Christian beliefs and the lyrics of some of the music that the label produces? Do you agree with his view of his business? Or is this a kind of business that you would have difficulty staying involved in for the long term? Explain your view.

COMMENTARY

The weight of historical Christian thought seems to lean against wholehearted participation in business. Comments such as those by Augustine and Tertullian cited in this chapter's introduction portray commerce as "worldly" and unsanctified. Since many of these types of negative sentiments were written from within the context of premodern economies, which were primarily zero-sum in nature, they are understandable.

Even today, however, Christian involvement in business is still viewed with skepticism. At best, business is commonly viewed as a means of supporting the "real" work of the church. This is reflected in the fact that many Christian businesspeople justify their involvement in business by citing opportunities for evangelism or by what they do outside the scope of their regular work responsibilities (or "on the side"), whether it is volunteering, giving money, or going out of their way to assist a troubled colleague or employee. In contrast, there is much difficulty in explaining how business activity by itself can be proper "kingdom" work. Current headlines and negative portrayals of business only contribute to nagging suspicions that business is spiritually suspect.

The commercial marketplace is commonly seen as a murky realm that is fraught with values and activities that run counter to traditional Christian ethics. Practices that appear essential for success, such as hiding negative aspects of products, ruthlessly undermining the competition, and eliminating jobs held by people who need employment are quite difficult to reconcile with values such as honesty, civility, and compassion. Such negative depictions of the marketplace are troublesome for those attempting to live their lives under the guidance of Christian ethics.

Given these troubling issues, how should we engage business? Should we seek to separate ourselves from it, embrace it wholeheartedly, live with two separate sets of values, work to transform it, or some combination of the foregoing? The question of Christian engagement in business can be seen as part of a broader and longstanding theological conversation about how Christians should interact with contemporary culture (of which business is a part).

As described by Van Wensveen Siker (based on the classic book *Christ and Culture* by H. Richard Niebuhr), different theological subtraditions hold diverging views about the relationship between Christianity and culture. For Niebuhr, "culture" "comprises language, habits, ideas, beliefs, customs, social organization, inherited artifacts, technical processes, and values."[5]

[5] H. Richard Niebuhr, *Christ and Culture* (New York, Harper & Row, 1951), 32.

Some traditions emphasize the gap between Christian values and those of the surrounding culture, and lean toward separatist tendencies in their interactions. Others see harmony between the values of Christ and those of culture and tend to emphasize common moral ground between them. Yet others fall somewhere in between, giving different emphasis on the fallen, "graced," and "to be redeemed" aspects of culture, and participate within it accordingly.

One pivotal issue that may influence our stance toward culture (and business) is our assumptions about the gap between the claims of Christ and the claims of the culture/business. If the gap is large and business is broken beyond repair, then the stances of separation, of dualism within paradox, make sense. If, however, the chasm is narrow, synthesis or elevation seems more appropriate. Alternatively, even if the gap is wide, a posture of transformation may offer another method of engagement.

So then, how broken is business? As we said in chapter 2, much care should be taken in making generalizations, because variances exist within departments, organizations, and entire industries. If negative anecdotal depictions and recent headlines about corporate conduct told the whole story, the case for an engagement stance toward business as a legitimate calling would be difficult to make. However, even if business were as dark and "fallen" as portrayed, this alone may not be reason enough to abandon it as a place of Christian engagement. In "Tough Business: In Deep, Swift Waters," Steve Brinn (reflecting a Niebuhr type 4 and 5) insightfully points out that Christians should be at the forefront of business *because* (and not despite the fact that) moral tensions exist.

Pessimistic accounts of business, though common, may not present a comprehensive or truthful picture. As Robert Sirico (reflecting a Niebuhr type 3 stance) eloquently states in "The Entrepreneurial Vocation," "Christ is no stranger to the world he has created." To some degree, the world of business already bears the imprint of the goodness of its creator. For example, sound ethics in business are probably more the rule than the exception. Underneath the headlining scandals (which make for high entertainment value), an efficient economy rests on a largely invisible but solid moral foundation. Since it is largely taken for granted, we are most aware of this footing when it is undermined. Indeed, recent stock market declines perpetuated by corporate accounting scandals remind us of the existing but fragile trust needed to buoy an efficient economy.

Furthermore, good ethics, in some cases, make sound long-term financial sense. Although not a guarantee nor a proper motive for ethical behavior, a reputation for honesty can be a strategic asset. While far from aligned (the tendency of "type 2" in *Christ and Business*), there is some degree of overlap between Christian values and most common business practices.

If, in fact, these more optimistic accounts are true and Christian values are woven to some extent into the fabric of business, eager participation in business is far less problematic. However, a proper theology of business (and cultural) engagement must move well beyond the mere avoidance of evil/sin and into a deeper realization of how economic activity may be a "calling" that directly participates in God's work in the world.

The primary or general calling of all Christians is to live a godly life. In addition, Christians may have specific callings into occupations, many of which are "worldly" in nature. In contrast to the view widely held during the medieval age in which only clergy and monks were called, the Protestant Reformers (and many subsequent scholars) have pointed out that since all of creation is the theater for God's glory, all biblically consistent work can serve as a legitimate vocation.

On what basis can business be considered a specific calling? First, business activity can help fulfill the creation mandate given in Genesis 1:26–28. The mandate contains community ordering and cocreativity with God as key components. Many theologians, including R. Paul Stevens, have pointed out that the creation mandate has been tragically separated from the Great Commission, leading to the erroneous conclusion that evangelism is all that matters.[6] Second, business is one means by which God provides for his people. As noted in chapter 2, business provides goods and services, creates employment opportunities, and with market capitalism's unique ability to create new wealth, may (if properly done) be the best means of mitigating poverty in the world.

Third, one's work in business may reflect two other related and important, but generally underemphasized, theological concepts. Theologian Miroslav Volf makes a strong case that one's calling is an outworking of

[6] R. Paul Stevens, "The Marketplace: Mission Field or Mission?" *Crux* 37, no. 3 (September 2001): 11.

spiritual giftedness (pneumatological) and a means of active participation in God's transforming work of the world in preparation for the new creation (eschatological).[7] While each of the "types" presented in the essay "Christ and Business" contribute important insights, type 5 ("Christ the *Transformer* of Business") is most helpful in terms of giving us a better understanding of Christian engagement with business as a calling. While acknowledging the fallen nature of business and its institutions, God's work in transforming and redeeming the world he created is also recognized. Christians then bear a significant responsibility to participate in business (and other parts of culture) in order to contribute to this transformative agenda.[8]

A Multifaceted Calling

Especially since it is a highly influential part of our culture, business should be viewed as a legitimate place of calling for Christians. As Steve Brinn ("Tough Business") conveys, if Christians (assuming they are acting ethically) were simply to pull out of what are perceived to be fallen parts of culture, the invariable course would be further decline (a distinct possibility in several of the case studies in this chapter). A blanket strategy of withdrawal or separation also neglects the fact that there are no "pure" venues in which one can participate. The whole world bears the staining effect of the fall. Moreover, there is no realistic way to completely withdraw from "business" for the sake of moral or spiritual purity. Just about everyone interacts with business as a consumer or investor. Looking at the case studies in this chapter, an alternative to hip-hop music is "Christian" music. An alternative to business is church work. Of course, there are many alternatives in between, but every genre of art, every industry, every subculture bears marks of brokenness of its own. Working in "Christian" music or film and/or in a church has its place if one is called there, but the choice to separate from the "world" raises legitimate theological questions of its own.

To be certain, not every part of business is in need of transformation. With respect to practices and areas of commerce that already reflect Christian values, the task is to uphold and promote them. Neither is it correct to say that Christians can or should be involved in every aspect of business. Clearly, some values and practices and some entire industries would be more appropriately engaged and changed through external "prophetic" means, such as withdrawal and/or modeling a different way of thinking and acting.

Business activity should not be seen as second class in terms of its spiritual value if participation is done with proper aims and motives in mind. In fact, it should be seen as a legitimate and important calling and as a proper

[7] Miroslav Volf, *Work in the Spirit: Toward a Theology of Work* (New York: Oxford University Press, 1991).

[8] For a more complete discussion of this idea, see James Skillen, "Conclusion," in Bob Goudzwaard, *Globalization and the Kingdom of God* (Grand Rapids: Baker, 2001). For more recent work on cultural engagement, see James Davidson Hunter, *To Change the World: The Irony, Tragedy, and Possibility of Christianity in the Late Modern World* (New York: Oxford University Press, 2010). Also, see Andy Crouch, *Culture Making: Recovering Our Creative Calling* (Downers Grove, Ill.: InterVarsity, 2008).

venue to exercise one's giftedness and, above all, to advance God's kingdom on earth.[9]

To be certain, a type 5 is not a stance without risks. Getting involved in changing the structures of the world may mean getting one's hands too dirty, and it leaves one vulnerable to using too many of the surrounding culture's methods and getting captured by its agendas. And like several of the subjects of the case studies in this chapter, you may find yourself doubted by your friends and peers (though this may not indicate you are in the wrong place).

[9] For further discussion of this important point, see Kenman L. Wong and Scott B. Rae, *Business for the Common Good* (Downers Grove, Ill.: IVP Academic, 2011), chapter 1, "Your Work Is an Altar."

PART 2

ETHICS, CORPORATIONS, AND THE GLOBAL ECONOMY

FOUR

Corporate Social Responsibility

Introduction

Public expectations of corporations are shifting rapidly. Shortly after being named *Fortune* magazine's "Most Admired Company" (in 2004), Walmart became the target of intense criticism and boycott activism. Often cited as examples of the company's pernicious practices were the relentless pursuit of reduced costs (by squeezing price concessions from suppliers, paying employees low wages, and allegedly failing to provide many with health care benefits), and methods of competing that allegedly harmed local retailers. The fact that several heirs of founder Sam Walton were regularly found near the top of the list of "wealthiest Americans" added even more fuel to the fire.

Contributing to Walmart's transition from being the most respected to perhaps the most reviled corporation was, according to management scholar R. Edward Freeman, that Walmart got caught living under the "old story" of business, under which shareholder wealth was all that mattered.[1] Company executives could claim the achievement of financial objectives but were at a loss as to explain how they advanced the well-being of many other "stakeholders" (i.e., employees, suppliers, and local communities). To be sure, Walmart has its ardent defenders, among them those who argue a business *should* focus on maximizing profit and those who point out that the company saves consumers money and drives down overall inflation.

In contrast, another retailer, Costco, has been offered as an example of a corporation that is living well according to an "emerging story" of business. Under this newer narrative, a corporation should be financially successful but must be so while advancing the interests of other stakeholders too. Costco, it is said, creates wealth for shareholders and excellent value for customers but does so while paying good wages to employees and treating suppliers fairly. Not everyone buys into this new story, of course. Although

[1] R. Edward Freeman, "The Wal-Mart Effect and Business, Ethics, and Society," *Academy of Management Perspectives* 20, no. 3 (2006): 38–40.

Costco was a darling of Main Street, its practices have been criticized by Wall Street analysts for being too generous with employees and customers at the expense of shareholders.

Whether fair or not (Walmart has since made large efforts to change both its reputation and its practices, and Costco may not be all that it is made out to be), the foregoing comparison illustrates shifting expectations of corporate social responsibility, or CSR. CSR concerns itself with questions such as, What purposes and whose interests should shareholder owned corporations serve? Should they primarily seek to maximize profit for shareholders (allegedly Walmart's practice), or should they intentionally and more directly serve other constituents (purportedly Costco's practice), especially when these pursuits may reduce financial gain for shareholders?

Although these questions have been around for a long time, corporate social responsibility has become an increasingly prevalent, perhaps almost omnipresent, part of business during the past two decades. Once the domain of only a small number of progressive companies, such as Ben & Jerry's and Starbucks, many corporations (including the likes of Shell, Starbucks, Timberland, and Ford Motor Company) claim to integrate CSR concerns into their core operations, going to the extent of posting CSR reports that purportedly account for social and environmental performance. Efforts are also under way to ensure measurability and accountability to guarantee these reports are more than mere public relations devices.[2] Whether genuinely motivated by an ethos of service, by the need to win over public opinion, or some of both, the evolving rhetoric and practices of many corporations seem to indicate that the philosophical debate is over and that stakeholder oriented capitalism (the emerging story) has been declared the victor. In fact, Harvard professor and the United Nations Secretary General's Special Representative for Business and Human Rights, John Ruggie, claims the "theological question" of whether corporations should engage in CSR has been settled (in favor of stakeholder capitalism).[3] While rhetorical debates about whether corporations have "social responsibilities" may well be extinct, the belief that profit maximization is the single overriding objective of corporations still dominates business school curricula.[4] And more importantly, questions over what these responsibilities are and how they should play out in business practices and decisions are still quite contentious.[5] For example, should a company with a profitable and legal but arguably harmful product or manufacturing technique cease production or modify its process if it comes at a higher cost? Likewise, should a corporation pay a living wage or provide medical benefits beyond their motivational or public relations value when competitors do not do so and it is clear customers will not pay higher prices to make up the difference? Or would these companies achieve more

[2] See, e.g., The Global Reporting Initiative, http://www.globalreporting.org.

[3] "The Next Question: Does CSR Work?" *The Economist*, January 17, 2008.

[4] Aspen Institute Initiative for Social Innovation through Business, "Where Will They Lead? MBA Student Attitudes toward Business & Society," 2002.

[5] See, e.g., "Just Good Business," *The Economist*, January 17, 2008; see also Aneel Karnani, "The Case against Corporate Social Responsibility," *Wall Street Journal*, August 23, 2010; and Michael Jensen, "Value Maximization, Stakeholder Theory, and the Corporate Objective Function," *Business Ethics Quarterly* 12 (2002): 235–56.

social good by maximizing gains for the owners, who could then direct these funds as they see fit: whether spending it (and thereby contributing to economic growth), saving it for noble goals such as retirements and educations, and/or giving it to charitable causes?

Moving more into the territory of philanthropy, should a pharmaceutical company dramatically reduce the price (and thereby cut into its profits) of medications so that health care (in both wealthy and developing countries) can be more accessible?

Questions about the purpose and duties of corporations, and thereby the content of their "social responsibilities," are important to explore. The answers create the context and guiding narrative for business practices and inform what is considered ethical versus unethical behavior. If, for example, the central mandate of business is wealth creation, decisions will be evaluated in light of this objective. In contrast, if the central purpose is something else, then the same decisions will be seen much differently.

The first reading in this chapter, "Rethinking the Social Responsibility of Business," is a spirited—and sometimes inflammatory—debate about the central purpose of corporations. Nobel laureate Milton Friedman, the author of the classic essay "The Social Responsibility of Business Is to Increase Its Profits," argues that the primary duty of managers of a publicly held company is to increase wealth for its shareholders. When managers act in "socially responsible" ways that effectively reduce profits, they violate their fiduciary duties to the owners of the enterprise. Friedman's perspective has become known as the "shareholder wealth" or "finance" model of corporate social responsibility. T.J. Rodgers, the CEO of Cypress Semiconductors, supports Friedman's views and offers a searing critique of the legitimacy of stakeholder theory.

John Mackey (founder and CEO of Whole Foods) presents one model of an alternative philosophy known as the "stakeholder" approach (more accurately approach*es*), which has gained much popularity in recent years among both academicians and corporate executives.[6] Proponents of this model argue that the lone consideration of shareholder interests is morally insufficient. Instead, corporations must broaden their obligations to a wider group of "stakeholders." Unlike many stakeholder theorists, however, Mackey is arguing from a libertarian viewpoint, which makes the consideration of stakeholder interests (other than for instrumental profit purposes) voluntary rather than obligatory. Other management thinkers use different philosophies (i.e., pragmatism, communitarianism) as a driving "normative core" and would thus develop their versions of stakeholder theory in a different way.

Deborah Doane's article, "The Myth of CSR" is a critique of these efforts from a very different perspective. She doesn't question the moral legitimacy

[6] R. Edward Freeman notes that it may be more accurate to speak of stakeholder "theories," since organizations can choose from a number of viable "normative cores" to guide the process of balancing the claims of various stakeholder groups. See R. E. Freeman, "Stakeholder Theory of the Modern Corporation," in T. Donaldson, P. Werhane, and M. Cording, *Ethical Issues in Business: A Philosophical Approach*, 7th ed. (Englewood Cliffs, N.J.: Prentice Hall, 2002).

of CSR as an issue of violating the property rights of shareholders, but she expresses deep concerns about whether corporations can effectively deliver the type of change CSR's proponents hope it can. Markets and current ownership structures may simply be too powerful to allow for large-scale change, and, she argues, CSR may well be little more than a public relations tool lulling the public into a false sense of security.

The third article in this chapter, "A Long-Term Business Perspective in a Short-Term World," is a conversation with Jim Sinegal, the CEO of Costco. Interviewers Albert Erisman and David Gill pose thoughtful questions about how ethics and corporate responsibility play out in the retailing business. Sinegal describes the centrality of corporate values in building a sustainable enterprise that benefits a wide group of stakeholders, including shareholders.

While much of this debate has been carried out along secular philosophy and economics lines, it is interesting that John Ruggie poses it (though somewhat dismissively) as a "theological question." In this chapter's commentary section, we will explore a direction in which Christian ethics could address this issue.

READINGS

Rethinking the Social Responsibility of Business
Milton Friedman, John Mackey, and T.J. Rodgers
Reason (October 2005): 3–10.

Thirty-five years ago, Milton Friedman wrote a famous article for *The New York Times Magazine* whose title aptly summed up its main point: "The Social Responsibility of Business Is to Increase Its Profits." The future Nobel laureate in economics had no patience for capitalists who claimed that "business is not concerned 'merely' with profit but also with promoting desirable 'social' ends; that business has a 'social conscience' and takes seriously its responsibilities for providing employment, eliminating discrimination, avoiding pollution and whatever else may be the catchwords of the contemporary crop of reformers."

Friedman, now a senior research fellow at the Hoover Institution and the Paul Snowden Russell Dis-

tinguished Service Professor Emeritus of Economics at the University of Chicago, wrote that such people are "preaching pure and unadulterated socialism. Businessmen who talk this way are unwitting puppets of the intellectual forces that have been undermining the basis of a free society these past decades."

John Mackey, the founder and CEO of Whole Foods, is one businessman who disagrees with Friedman. A self-described ardent libertarian whose conversation is peppered with references to Ludwig von Mises and Abraham Maslow, Austrian economics and astrology, Mackey believes Friedman's view is too narrow a description of his and many other businesses' activities. As important, he argues that Friedman's take woefully undersells the humanitarian dimension of capitalism.

In the debate that follows, Mackey lays out his personal vision of the social responsibility of business. Friedman responds, as does T.J. Rodgers, the founder and CEO of Cypress Semiconductor and the chief spokesman of what might be called the tough love school of laissez faire. Dubbed "one of America's toughest bosses" by *Fortune*, Rodgers argues that corporations add far more to society by maximizing "long-term shareholder value" than they do by donating time and money to charity.

Putting Customers Ahead of Investors
John Mackey

In 1970 Milton Friedman wrote that "there is one and only one social responsibility of business—to use its resources and engage in activities designed to increase its profits so long as it stays within the rules of the game, which is to say, engages in open and free competition without deception or fraud." That's the orthodox view among free market economists: that the only social responsibility a law-abiding business has is to maximize profits for the shareholders.

I strongly disagree. I'm a businessman and a free market libertarian, but I believe that the enlightened corporation should try to create value for *all* of its constituencies. From an investor's perspective, the purpose of the business is to maximize profits. But that's not the purpose for other stakeholders—for customers, employees, suppliers, and the community. Each of those groups will define the purpose of the business in terms of its own needs and desires, and each perspective is valid and legitimate.

My argument should not be mistaken for a hostility to profit. I believe I know something about creating shareholder value. When I co-founded Whole Foods Market 27 years ago, we began with $45,000 in capital; we only had $250,000 in sales our first year. During the last 12 months we had sales of more than $4.6 billion, net profits of more than $160 million, and a market capitalization over $8 billion.

But we have not achieved our tremendous increase in shareholder value by making shareholder value the primary purpose of our business. In my marriage, my wife's happiness is an end in itself, not merely a means to my own happiness; love leads me to put my wife's happiness first, but in doing so I also make myself happier. Similarly, the most successful businesses put the customer first, ahead of the investors. In the profit-centered business, customer happiness is merely a means to an end: maximizing profits.

In the customer-centered business, customer happiness is an end in itself, and will be pursued with greater interest, passion, and empathy than the profit-centered business is capable of. Not that we're only concerned with customers. At Whole Foods, we measure our success by how much value we can create for all six of our most important stakeholders: customers, team members (employees), investors, vendors, communities, and the environment.

There is, of course, no magical formula to calculate how much value each stakeholder should receive from the company. It is a dynamic process that evolves with the competitive marketplace. No stakeholder remains satisfied for long. It is the function of company leadership to develop solutions that continually work for the common good.

Many thinking people will readily accept my arguments that caring about customers and employees is good business. But they might draw the line at believing a company has any responsibility to its community and environment. To donate time and capital to philanthropy, they will argue, is to steal from the investors. After all, the corporation's assets legally belong to the investors, don't they? Management has a fiduciary responsibility to maximize shareholder value; therefore, any activities that don't maximize shareholder value are violations of this duty. If you feel altruism towards other people, you should exercise that altruism with your own money, not with the assets of a corporation that doesn't belong to you.

This position sounds reasonable. A company's assets do belong to the investors, and its management does have a duty to manage those assets responsibly.

In my view, the argument is not *wrong* so much as it is too narrow.

First, there can be little doubt that a certain amount of corporate philanthropy is simply good business and works for the long-term benefit of the investors. For example: In addition to the many thousands of small donations each Whole Foods store makes each year, we also hold five 5% Days throughout the year. On those days, we donate 5 percent of a store's total sales to a nonprofit organization. While our stores select worthwhile organizations to support, they also tend to focus on groups that have large membership lists, which are contacted and encouraged to shop our store that day to support the organization. This usually brings hundreds of new or lapsed customers into our stores, many of whom then become regular shoppers. So a 5% Day not only allows us to support worthwhile causes, but is an excellent marketing strategy that has benefited Whole Foods investors immensely.

That said, I believe such programs would be completely justifiable even if they produced no profits and no P.R. This is because I believe the entrepreneurs, not the current investors in a company's stock, have the right and responsibility to define the purpose of the company. It is the entrepreneurs who create a company, who bring all the factors of production together and coordinate it into viable business. It is the entrepreneurs who set the company strategy and who negotiate the terms of trade with all of the voluntarily cooperating stakeholders—including the investors. At Whole Foods we "hired" our original investors. They didn't hire us.

We first announced that we would donate 5 percent of the company's net profits to philanthropy when we drafted our mission statement, back in 1985. Our policy has therefore been in place for over 20 years, and it predates our IPO by seven years. All seven of the private investors at the time we created the policy voted for it when they served on our board of directors. When we took in venture capital money back in 1989, none of the venture firms objected to the policy. In addition, in almost 14 years as a publicly traded company, almost no investors have ever raised objections to the policy. How can Whole Foods' philanthropy be "theft" from the current investors if the original owners of the company unanimously approved the policy and all subsequent investors made their investments after the policy was in effect and well publicized?

The shareholders of a public company own their stock voluntarily. If they don't agree with the philosophy of the business, they can always sell their investment, just as the customers and employees can exit their relationships with the company if they don't like the terms of trade. If that is unacceptable to them, they always have the legal right to submit a resolution at our annual shareholders meeting to change the company's philanthropic philosophy. A number of our company policies have been changed over the years through successful shareholder resolutions.

Another objection to the Whole Foods philosophy is where to draw the line. If donating 5 percent of profits is good, wouldn't 10 percent be even better? Why not donate 100 percent of our profits to the betterment of society? But the fact that Whole Foods has responsibilities to our community doesn't mean that we don't have any responsibilities to our investors. It's a question of finding the appropriate balance and trying to create value for all of our stakeholders. Is 5 percent the "right amount" to donate to the community? I don't think there is a right answer to this question, except that I believe 0 percent is too little. It is an arbitrary percentage that the co-founders of the company decided was a reasonable amount and which was approved by the owners of the company at the time we made the decision. Corporate philanthropy is a good thing, but it requires the legitimacy of investor approval. In my experience, most investors understand that it can be beneficial to both the corporation and to the larger society.

That doesn't answer the question of *why* we give money to the community stakeholder. For that, you should turn to one of the fathers of free-market economics, Adam Smith. *The Wealth of Nations* was a tremendous achievement, but economists would be well served to read Smith's other great book, *The Theory of Moral Sentiments*. There he explains that human nature isn't just about self-interest. It also includes sympathy, empathy, friendship, love, and the desire for social approval. As motives for human behavior, these are at least as important as self-interest. For many people, they are more important.

When we are small children we are egocentric, concerned only about our own needs and desires. As we mature, most people grow beyond this egocentrism and begin to care about others—their families, friends, communities, and countries. Our capacity to love can expand even further: to loving people from different races, religions, and countries—potentially to unlimited love for all people and even for other sentient creatures. This is our potential as human beings, to take joy in the flourishing of people everywhere. Whole Foods gives money to our communities because we care about them and feel a responsibility to help them flourish as well as possible.

The business model that Whole Foods has embraced could represent a new form of capitalism, one that more consciously works for the common good instead of depending solely on the "invisible hand" to generate positive results for society. The "brand" of capitalism is in terrible shape throughout the world, and corporations are widely seen as selfish, greedy, and uncaring. This is both unfortunate and unnecessary, and could be changed if businesses and economists widely adopted the business model that I have outlined here.

To extend our love and care beyond our narrow self-interest is antithetical to neither our human nature nor our financial success. Rather, it leads to the further fulfillment of both. Why do we not encourage this in our theories of business and economics? Why do we restrict our theories to such a pessimistic and crabby view of human nature? What are we afraid of?

Making Philanthropy Out of Obscenity
Milton Friedman

By pursuing his own interest [an individual] frequently promotes that of the society more effectually than when he really intends to promote it. I have never known much good done by those who affected to trade for the public good.

—Adam Smith, *The Wealth of Nations*

The differences between John Mackey and me regarding the social responsibility of business are for the most part rhetorical. Strip off the camouflage, and it turns out we are in essential agreement. Moreover, his company, Whole Foods Market, behaves in accordance with the principles I spelled out in my 1970 *New York Times Magazine* article. With respect to his company, it could hardly be otherwise. It has done well in a highly competitive industry. Had it devoted any significant fraction of its resources to exercising a social responsibility unrelated to the bottom line, it would be out of business by now or would have been taken over.

Here is how Mackey himself describes his firm's activities:

1. "The most successful businesses put the customer first, instead of the investors" (which clearly means that this is the way to put the investors first).

2. "There can be little doubt that a certain amount of corporate philanthropy is simply good business and works for the long-term benefit of the investors."

Compare this to what I wrote in 1970:

Of course, in practice the doctrine of social responsibility is frequently a cloak for actions that are justified on other grounds rather than a reason for those actions.

To illustrate, it may well be in the long run interest of a corporation that is a major employer in a small community to devote resources to providing amenities to that community or to improving its government....

In each of these ... cases, there is a strong temptation to rationalize these actions as an exercise of "social responsibility." In the present climate of opinion, with its widespread aversion to "capitalism," "profits," the "soulless corporation" and so on, this is one way for a corporation to generate goodwill as a by-product of expenditures that are entirely justified in its own self-interest.

It would be inconsistent of me to call on corporate executives to refrain from this hypocritical window-dressing because it harms the foundations of a free society. That would be to call on them to exercise a "social responsibility"! If our institutions and the attitudes of the public make it in their self-interest to cloak their actions in this way, I cannot summon much indignation to denounce them.

I believe Mackey's flat statement that "corporate philanthropy is a good thing" is flatly wrong. Consider the decision by the founders of Whole Foods to donate 5 percent of net profits to philanthropy. They were clearly within their rights in doing so. They were spending their own money, using 5 percent of one part of their wealth to establish, thanks to corporate tax provisions, the equivalent of a 501c(3) charitable foundation, though with no mission statement, no separate by-laws, and no provision for deciding on the beneficiaries. But what reason is there to suppose that the stream of profit distributed in this way would do more good for society than investing that stream of profit in the enterprise itself or paying it out as dividends and letting the stockholders dispose of it? The practice makes sense only because of our obscene tax laws, whereby a stockholder can make a larger gift for a given after-tax cost if the corporation makes the gift on his behalf than if he makes the gift directly. That is a good reason for eliminating the corporate tax or for eliminating the deductibility of corporate charity, but it is not a justification for corporate charity.

Whole Foods Market's contribution to society — and as a customer I can testify that it is an important one — is to enhance the pleasure of shopping for food. Whole Foods has no special competence in deciding how charity should be distributed. Any funds devoted to the latter would surely have contributed more to society if they had been devoted to improving still further the former.

Finally, I shall try to explain why my statement that "the social responsibility of business [is] to increase its profits" and Mackey's statement that "the enlightened corporation should try to create value for all of its constituencies" are equivalent.

Note first that I refer to *social* responsibility, not financial, or accounting, or legal. It is social precisely to allow for the constituencies to which Mackey refers. Maximizing profits is an end from the private point of view; it is a means from the social point of view. A system based on private property and free markets is a sophisticated means of enabling people to cooperate in their economic activities without compulsion; it enables separated knowledge to assure that each resource is used for its most valued use, and is combined with other resources in the most efficient way.

Of course, this is abstract and idealized. The world is not ideal. There are all sorts of deviations from the perfect market — many, if not most, I suspect, due to government interventions. But with all its defects, the current largely free-market, private-property world seems to me vastly preferable to a world in which a large fraction of resources is used and distributed by 501c(3)s and their corporate counterparts.

Put Profits First

T.J. Rodgers

John Mackey's article attacking corporate profit maximization could not have been written by "a free market libertarian," as claimed. Indeed, if the examples he cites had not identified him as the author, one could easily assume the piece was written by Ralph Nader. A more accurate title for his article is "How Business and Profit Making Fit into My Overarching Philosophy of Altruism."

Mackey spouts nonsense about how his company hired his original investors, not vice versa. If Whole Foods ever falls on persistent hard times — perhaps when the Luddites are no longer able to hold back the genetic food revolution using junk science and fear — he will quickly find out who has hired whom, as his investors fire him.

Mackey does make one point that is consistent with, but not supportive of, free market capitalism. He knows that shareholders own his stock voluntarily. If they don't like the policies of his company, they can always vote to change those policies with a shareholder resolution or simply sell the stock and buy that of another company more aligned with their objectives. Thus, he informs his shareholders of his objectives and lets them make a choice on which stock to buy. So far, so good.

It is also simply good business for a company to cater to its customers, train and retain its employees, build long-term positive relationships with its suppliers, and become a good citizen in its community, including performing some philanthropic activity. When Milton Friedman says a company should stay "within the rules of the game" and operate "without deception or fraud," he means it should deal with all its various constituencies properly in order to maximize long-term shareholder value. He does not mean that a company should put every last nickel on the bottom line every quarter, regardless of the long-term consequences.

My company, Cypress Semiconductor, has won the trophy for the Second Harvest Food Bank competition for the most food donated per employee in Silicon Valley for the last 13 consecutive years (1 million pounds of food in 2004). The contest creates competition among our divisions, leading to employee involvement, company food drives, internal social events with admissions "paid for" by food donations, and so forth. It is a big employee morale builder, a way to attract new employees, good P.R. for the company, and a significant benefit to the community—all of which makes Cypress a better place to work and invest in. Indeed, Mackey's own proud example of Whole Foods' community involvement programs also made a profit.

But Mackey's subordination of his profession as a businessman to altruistic ideals shows up as he attempts to negate the empirically demonstrated social benefit of "self-interest" by defining it narrowly as "increasing short-term profits." Why is it that when Whole Foods gives money to a worthy cause, it serves a high moral objective, while a company that provides a good return to small investors—who simply put their money into their own retirement funds or a children's college fund—is somehow selfish? It's the philosophy that is objectionable here, not the specific actions. If Mackey wants to run a hybrid business/charity whose mission is fully disclosed to his shareholders—and

if those shareholder-owners want to support that mission—so be it. But I balk at the proposition that a company's "stakeholders" (a term often used by collectivists to justify unreasonable demands) should be allowed to control the property of the shareholders. It seems Mackey's philosophy is more accurately described by Karl Marx: "From each according to his ability" (the shareholders surrender money and assets); "to each according to his needs" (the charities, social interest groups, and environmentalists get what they want). That's not free market capitalism.

Then there is the arrogant proposition that if other corporations would simply emulate the higher corporate life form defined by Whole Foods, the world would be better off. After all, Mackey says corporations are viewed as "selfish, greedy, and uncaring." I, for one, consider free market capitalism to be a high calling, even without the infusion of altruism practiced by Whole Foods.

If one goes beyond the sensationalistic journalism surrounding the Enron-like debacles, one discovers that only about 10 to 20 public corporations have been justifiably accused of serious wrongdoing. That's about 0.1 percent of America's 17,500 public companies. What's the failure rate of the publications that demean business? (Consider the *New York Times* scandal involving manufactured stories.) What's the percentage of U.S. presidents who have been forced or almost forced from office? (It's 10 times higher than the failure rate of corporations.) What percentage of our congressmen have spent time in jail? The fact is that despite some well-publicized failures, most corporations are run with the highest ethical standards—and the public knows it. Public opinion polls demonstrate that fact by routinely ranking businessmen above journalists and politicians in esteem.

I am proud of what the semiconductor industry does—relentlessly cutting the cost of a transistor from $3 in 1960 to *three-millionths* of a dollar today. Mackey would be keeping his business records with hordes of accountants on paper ledgers if our industry didn't exist. He would have to charge his poorest customers more for their food, pay his valued employees less, and cut his philanthropy programs if the semiconductor industry had not focused so relentlessly on increasing its profits, cutting his costs in the process. Of course, if the U.S. semiconductor industry had been less cost-competitive due to its own philanthropy, the food industry simply would have bought cheaper computers made from Japanese and Korean silicon chips (which happened anyway). Layoffs in the nonunion semiconductor industry were actually good news to Whole Foods' unionized grocery store clerks. Where was Mackey's sense of altruism when unemployed semiconductor workers needed it? Of course, that rhetorical question is foolish, since he did exactly the right thing by ruthlessly reducing his record-keeping costs so as to maximize his profits.

I am proud to be a free market capitalist. And I resent the fact that Mackey's philosophy demeans me as an egocentric child because I have refused on moral grounds to embrace the philosophies of collectivism and altruism that have caused so much human misery, however tempting the sales pitch for them sounds.

Profit Is the Means, Not End
John Mackey

Let me begin my response to Milton Friedman by noting that he is one of my personal heroes. His contributions to economic thought and the fight for freedom are without parallel, and it is an honor to have him critique my article.

Friedman says "the differences between John Mackey and me regarding the social responsibility of business are for the most part rhetorical." But are we essentially in agreement? I don't think so. We are thinking about business in entirely different ways.

Friedman is thinking only in terms of maximizing profits for the investors. If putting customers first helps maximize profits for the investors, then it is acceptable. If some corporate philanthropy creates goodwill and helps a company "cloak" its self-interested goals of maximizing profits, then it is acceptable (although Friedman also believes it is "hypocritical"). In contrast to Friedman, I do not believe maximizing profits for the investors is the only acceptable justification for all corporate actions. The investors are not the only people who matter. Corporations can exist for purposes other than simply maximizing profits.

As for who decides what the purpose of any particular business is, I made an important argument that Friedman doesn't address: "I believe the entrepreneurs, not the current investors in a company's stock, have the right and responsibility to define the purpose of the company." Whole Foods Market was not created solely to maximize profits for its investors, but to create value for all of its stakeholders. I believe there are thousands of other businesses similar to Whole Foods (Medtronic, REI, and Starbucks, for example)

that were created by entrepreneurs with goals beyond maximizing profits, and that these goals are neither "hypocritical" nor "cloaking devices" but are intrinsic to the purpose of the business.

I will concede that many other businesses, such as T.J. Rodgers' Cypress Semiconductor, have been created by entrepreneurs whose sole purpose for the business is to maximize profits for their investors. Does Cypress therefore have any social responsibility besides maximizing profits if it follows the laws of society? No, it doesn't. Rodgers apparently created it solely to maximize profits, and therefore all of Friedman's arguments about business social responsibility become completely valid. Business social responsibility should not be coerced; it is a voluntary decision that the entrepreneurial leadership of every company must make on its own. Friedman is right to argue that profit making is intrinsically valuable for society, but I believe he is mistaken that all businesses have only this purpose.

While Friedman believes that taking care of customers, employees, and business philanthropy are means to the end of increasing investor profits, I take the exact opposite view: Making high profits is the means to the end of fulfilling Whole Foods' core business mission. We want to improve the health and well-being of everyone on the planet through higher-quality foods and better nutrition, and we can't fulfill this mission unless we are highly profitable. High profits are necessary to fuel our growth across the United States and the world. Just as people cannot live without eating, so a business cannot live without profits. But most people don't live to eat, and neither must a business live just to make profits.

Toward the end of his critique, Friedman says his statement that "the social responsibility of business [is] to increase its profits" and my statement that "the enlightened corporation should try to create value for all of its constituencies" are "equivalent." He argues that maximizing profits is a private end achieved through social means because it supports a society based on private property and free markets. If our two statements are equivalent, if we really mean the same thing, then I know which statement has the superior "marketing power." Mine does.

Both capitalism and corporations are misunderstood, mistrusted, and disliked around the world because of statements like Friedman's on social responsibility. His comment is used by the enemies of capitalism to argue that capitalism is greedy, selfish, and uncaring. It is right up there with William Vanderbilt's "the public be damned" and former G.M. Chairman Charlie Wilson's declaration that "what's good for the country is good for General Motors, and vice versa." If we are truly interested in spreading capitalism throughout the world (I certainly am), we need to do a better job marketing it. I believe if economists and business people consistently communicated and acted on my message that "the enlightened corporation should try to create value for all of its constituencies," we would see most of the resistance to capitalism disappear.

Friedman also understands that Whole Foods makes an important contribution to society besides simply maximizing profits for our investors, which is to "enhance the pleasure of shopping for food." This is why we put "satisfying and delighting our customers" as a core value whenever we talk about the purpose of our business. Why don't Friedman and other economists consistently teach this idea? Why don't they talk more about all the valuable contributions that business makes in creating value for its customers, for its employees, and for its communities? Why talk only about maximizing profits for the investors? Doing so harms the brand of capitalism.

As for Whole Foods' philanthropy, who does have "special competence" in this area? Does the government? Do individuals? Libertarians generally would

agree that most bureaucratic government solutions to social problems cause more harm than good and that government help is seldom the answer. Neither do individuals have any special competence in charity. By Friedman's logic, individuals shouldn't donate any money to help others but should instead keep all their money invested in businesses, where it will create more social value.

The truth is that there is no way to calculate whether money invested in business or money invested in helping to solve social problems will create more value. Businesses exist within real communities and have real effects, both good and bad, on those communities. Like individuals living in communities, businesses make valuable social contributions by providing goods and services and employment. But just as individuals can feel a responsibility to provide some philanthropic support for the communities in which they live, so too can a business. The responsibility of business toward the community is not infinite, but neither is it zero. Each enlightened business must find the proper balance between all of its constituencies: customers, employees, investors, suppliers, and communities.

While I respect Milton Friedman's thoughtful response, I do not feel the same way about T.J. Rodgers' critique. It is obvious to me that Rodgers didn't carefully read my article, think deeply about my arguments, or attempt to craft an intelligent response. Instead he launches various ad hominem attacks on me, my company, and our customers. According to Rodgers, my business philosophy is similar to those of Ralph Nader and Karl Marx; Whole Foods Market and our customers are a bunch of Luddites engaging in junk science and fear mongering; and our unionized grocery clerks don't care about layoffs of workers in Rodgers' own semiconductor industry.

For the record: I don't agree with the philosophies of Ralph Nader or Karl Marx; Whole Foods Market doesn't engage in junk science or fear mongering, and neither do 99 percent of our customers or vendors; and of Whole Foods' 36,000 employees, exactly zero of them belong to unions, and we are in fact sorry about layoffs in his industry.

When Rodgers isn't engaging in ad hominem attacks, he seems to be arguing against a leftist, socialist, and collectivist perspective that may exist in his own mind but does not appear in my article. Contrary to Rodgers' claim, Whole Foods is running not a "hybrid business/charity" but an enormously profitable business that has created tremendous shareholder value.

Of all the food retailers in the *Fortune 500* (including Wal-Mart), we have the highest profits as a percentage of sales, as well as the highest return on invested capital, sales per square foot, same-store sales, and growth rate. We are currently doubling in size every three and a half years. The bottom line is that Whole Foods stakeholder business philosophy works and has produced tremendous value for all of our stakeholders, including our investors.

In contrast, Cypress Semiconductor has struggled to be profitable for many years now, and their balance sheet shows negative retained earnings of over $408 million. This means that in its entire 23-year history, Cypress has lost far more money for its investors than it has made. Instead of calling my business philosophy Marxist, perhaps it is time for Rodgers to rethink his own.

Rodgers says with passion, "I am proud of what the semiconductor industry does — relentlessly cutting the cost of a transistor from $3 in 1960 to *three-millionths* of a dollar today." Rodgers is entitled to be proud. What a wonderful accomplishment this is, and the semiconductor industry has indeed made all our lives better. Then why not consistently communicate this message as the purpose of his business, instead of talking all the time about maximizing profits and shareholder value? Like medicine, law, and education, business has noble purposes: to provide goods and services that improve its customers' lives, to provide jobs and meaningful work for employees, to create wealth and prosperity for its investors, and to be a responsible and caring citizen.

Businesses such as Whole Foods have multiple stakeholders and therefore have multiple responsibilities. But the fact that we have responsibilities to stakeholders besides investors does not give those other stakeholders any "property rights" in the company, contrary to Rodgers' fears. The investors still own the business, are entitled to the residual profits, and can fire the management if they wish. A doctor has an ethical responsibility to try to heal her patients, but that responsibility doesn't mean her patients are entitled to receive a share of the profits from her practice.

Rodgers probably will never agree with my business philosophy, but it doesn't really matter. The ideas I'm articulating result in a more robust business model than the profit-maximization model that it competes against, because they encourage and tap into more powerful motivations than self-interest alone. These ideas will triumph over time, not by persuading intellectuals and economists through argument but by winning the competitive test of the marketplace. Someday businesses like Whole Foods, which adhere to a stakeholder model of deeper business purpose, will dominate the economic landscape. Wait and see.

Questions for Discussion and Reflection

1. Of the three views presented, Friedman, Mackey, and Rodgers, which one do you think is the most compelling? Explain your answer.
2. What do you think of Friedman's view that "the social responsibility of business is to increase its profits"?
3. How does Mackey defend his stakeholder view of corporate responsibility?

The Myth of CSR

Deborah Doane

Stanford Social Innovation Review (Fall 2005): 3-9.

The Corporate Social Responsibility (CSR) Movement has grown in recent years from a fringe activity by a few earnest companies, like The Body Shop and Ben & Jerry's, to a highly visible priority for traditional corporate leaders from Nike to McDonald's. Reports of good corporate behavior are now commonplace in the media, from GlaxoSmithKline's donation of anti-retroviral medications to Africa, to Hewlett-Packard's corporate volunteering programs, to Starbucks' high-volume purchases of Fair Trade coffee. In fact, CSR has gained such prominence that the *Economist* devoted a special issue to denouncing it earlier this year.

Although some see CSR as simply philanthropy by a different name, it can be defined broadly as the efforts corporations make above and beyond regulation to balance the needs of stakeholders with the need to make a profit. Though traces of modern-day CSR can be found in the social auditing movement of the 1970s, it has only recently acquired enough momentum to merit an *Economist* riposte. While U.S. and European drivers for CSR have differed slightly, key events, such as the sinking of Shell's Brent Spar oil rig in the North Sea in 1996, and accusations of Nike and others' use of "sweatshop labor," triggered the first major response by big business to the uprisings against the corporate institution.

Naomi Klein's famous tome, *No Logo*,[1] gave voice to a generation that felt that big business had taken over the world, to the detriment of people and the environment, even as that generation was successfully mobilizing attacks on corporate power following the Seattle anti-globalization riots in 1999. Rather than shrink away from the battle, corporations emerged brandishing CSR as the friendly face of capitalism, helped, in part, by the very movement that highlighted the problem of corporate power in the first place. NGOs, seeing little political will by governments to regulate corporate behavior, as free-market economics has become the dominant political mantra, realized that perhaps more momentum could be achieved by partnering with the enemy. By using market mechanisms via consumer power, they saw an opportunity to bring about more immediate change.

So, organizations that address social standards in supply chains, such as the Fair Label Association in the United States or the United Kingdom's Ethical Trading Initiative, have flourished. The United Nations partnered with business to launch its own Global Compact, which offered nine principles relating to human rights and the environment, and was hailed as the ethical road map for the future. And while socially responsible investment had been popular in some circles for years, eventually the mainstream investment community cottoned onto CSR: In 1999, Dow Jones created the Dow Jones Sustainability Indexes, closely followed by the FTSE4Good.

All of these initiatives have been premised on the notion that companies can "do well" and "do good" at the same time—both saving the world and making a decent profit, too.

The unprecedented growth of CSR may lead some to feel a sense of optimism about the power of market mechanisms to deliver social and environmental change. But markets often fail, especially when it comes to delivering public goods; therefore, we have to be concerned that SR activities are subject to the same limitations of markets that prompted the movement in the first place.

Making Markets Work?

At face value, the market has indeed been a powerful force in bringing forward some measurable changes in corporate behavior. Most large companies now issue a voluntary social and environmental report alongside their regular annual financial report; meanwhile the amount of money being poured into socially responsible investing (SRI) funds has been growing at an exponential rate, year over year. Some socially linked brands, such as Fair Trade, are growing very quickly. Ethical consumerism in the United Kingdom was worth almost £25 billion in 2004, according to a report from the Co-operative Bank.[2]

The *Economist* article argued that the only socially responsible thing a company should do is to make money—and that adopting CSR programs was misguided, at best. But there are some strong business incentives that have either pushed or pulled companies onto the CSR bandwagon. For example, companies confronted with boycott threats, as Nike was in the 1990s, or with the threat of high-profile lawsuits, as McDonald's is over obesity concerns, may see CSR as a strategy for presenting a friendlier face to the public.

Once launched, CSR initiatives may provoke changes in basic practices inside some companies. Nike is now considered by many to be the global leader when it comes to improving labor standards in developing-country factories. The company now leads the way in transparency, too. When faced with a lawsuit over accusations of sweatshop labor, Nike chose to face its critics head-on and this year published on its Web site a full list of its factories with their audited social reports. And Nike is not alone. A plethora of other brands have developed their own unique strategies to confront the activists, with varying degrees of success. But no one could reasonably argue that these types of changes add up to a wholesale change in capitalism as we know it, nor that they are likely to do so anytime soon.

Market Failure

One problem here is that CSR as a concept simplifies some rather complex arguments and fails to acknowledge that ultimately, trade-offs must be made between the financial health of the company and ethical outcomes. And when they are made, profit undoubtedly wins over principles.

CSR strategies may work under certain conditions, but they are highly vulnerable to market failures, including such things as imperfect information, externalities, and free riders. Most importantly, there is often a wide chasm between what's good for a company and what's good for society as a whole. The reasons for this can be captured under what I'll argue are the four key myths of CSR.

Myth #1: The market can deliver both short-term financial returns and long-term social benefits.

One assumption behind CSR is that business outcomes and social objectives can become more or less aligned. The rarely expressed reasoning behind this assumption goes back to the basic assumptions of free-market capitalism: People are rational actors who are motivated to maximize their self-interest.

Since wealth, stable societies, and healthy environments are all in individuals' self-interest, individuals will ultimately invest, consume, and build companies in both profitable and socially responsible ways. In other words, the market will ultimately balance itself.

Yet, there is little if any empirical evidence that the market behaves in this way. In fact, it would be difficult to prove that incentives like protecting natural assets, ensuring an educated labor force for the future, or making voluntary contributions to local community groups actually help companies improve their bottom line. While there are pockets of success stories where business drivers can be aligned with social objectives, such as Cisco's Networking Academies, which are dedicated to developing a labor pool for the future, they only provide a patchwork approach to improving the public good.

In any case, such investments are particularly unlikely to pay off in the two-to-four-year time horizon that public companies, through demands of the stock market, often seem to require.

As we all know, whenever a company issues a "profits warning," the markets downgrade its share price. Consequently, investments in things like the environment or social causes become a luxury and are often placed on the sacrificial chopping block when the going gets rough.

Meanwhile, we have seen an abject failure of companies to invest in things that may have a longer-term benefit, like health and safety systems. BP was fined a record $1.42 million for health and safety offenses in Alaska in 2004, for example, even as Lord John Browne, chief executive of BP, was establishing himself as a leading advocate for CSR, and the company was winning various awards for its programs.

At the same time, class-action lawsuits may be brought against Wal-Mart over accusations of poor labor practices, yet the world's largest and most successful company is rewarded by investors for driving down its costs and therefore its prices.

The market, quite frankly, adores Wal-Mart. Meanwhile, a competitor outlet, Costco, which offers health insurance and other benefits to its employees, is being pressured by its shareholders to cut those benefits to be more competitive with Wal-Mart.[3]

CSR can hardly be expected to deliver when the short-term demands of the stock market provide disincentives for doing so.

When shareholder interests dominate the corporate machine, outcomes may become even less aligned to the public good. As Marjorie Kelly writes in her book, *The Divine Right of Capital*: "It is inaccurate to speak of stockholders as investors, for more truthfully they are extractors."[4]

Myth #2: The ethical consumer will drive change.

Though there is a small market that is proactively rewarding ethical business, for most consumers ethics are a relative thing. In fact, most surveys show that consumers are more concerned about things like price, taste, or sell-by date than ethics.[5] Wal-Mart's success certainly is a case in point.

In the United Kingdom, ethical consumerism data show that although most consumers are concerned about environmental or social issues, with 83 percent of consumers intending to act ethically on a regular basis, only 18 percent of people act ethically occasionally, while fewer than 5 percent of consumers show consistent ethical and green purchasing behaviors.[6]

In the United States, since 1990, Roper ASW has tracked consumer environmental attitudes and propensity to buy environmentally oriented products, and it categorizes consumers into five "shades of green": True-Blue Greens, Greenback Greens, Sprouts, Grousers, and Basic Browns. True-Blue Greens are the "greenest" consumers, those "most likely to walk their environmental talk," and represent about 9 percent of the population. The least environmentally involved are the "Basic Browns," who believe "individual actions (such as buying green products or recycling) can't make a difference" and represent about 33 percent of the population.[7]

Joel Makower, co-author of *The Green Consumer Guide*, has traced data on ethical consumerism since the early 1990s, and says that, in spite of the overhyped claims, there has been little variation in the behavior of ethical consumers over the years, as evidenced by the Roper ASW data. "The truth is, the gap between green consciousness and green consumerism is huge," he states.[8]

Take, for example, the growth of gas-guzzling sport-utility vehicles. Even with the steep rise in fuel prices, consumers are still having a love affair with them, as sales rose by almost 8 percent in 2004. These data show that threats of climate change, which may affect future generations more than our own, are hardly an incentive for consumers to alter their behavior.[9]

Myth #3: There will be a competitive "race to the top" over ethics amongst businesses.

A further myth of CSR is that competitive pressure amongst companies will actually lead to more companies competing over ethics, as highlighted by an increasing number of awards schemes for good companies, like the Business Ethics Awards, or *Fortune*'s annual "Best Companies to Work For" competitions.

Companies are naturally keen to be aligned with CSR schemes because they offer good PR. But in some cases businesses may be able to capitalize on well-intentioned efforts, say by signing the U.N. Global Compact, without necessarily having to actually change their behavior.

The U.S.–based Corporate Watch has found several cases of "green washing" by companies, and has noted how various corporations use the United Nations to their public relations advantage, such as posing their CEOs for photographs with Secretary General Kofi Annan.[10]

Meanwhile, companies fight to get a coveted place on the SRI indices such as the Dow Jones Sustainability Indexes. But all such schemes to reward good corporate behavior leave us carrying a new risk that by promoting the "race to the top" idea, we tend to reward the "best of the baddies." British American Tobacco, for example, won a UNEP/Sustainability reporting award for its annual social report in 2004.[11] Nonetheless, a skeptic might question why a tobacco company, given the massive damage its products inflict, should be rewarded for its otherwise socially responsible behavior.

While companies are vying to be seen as socially responsible to the outside world, they also become more effective at hiding socially irresponsible behavior, such as lobbying activities or tax avoidance measures. Corporate income taxes in the United States fell from 4.1 percent of GDP in 1960 to just 1.5 percent of GDP in 2001.[12] In effect, this limits governments' ability to provide public services like education. Of course, in the end, this is just the type of PR opportunity a business can capitalize on.

Adopting or contributing to schools is now a common CSR initiative by leading companies, such as Cisco Systems or European supermarket chain Tesco.

Myth #4: In the global economy, countries will compete to have the best ethical practices.

CSR has risen in popularity with the increase in reliance on developing economies. It is generally assumed that market liberalization of these economies will lead to better protection of human and environmental rights, through greater integration of oppressive regimes in the global economy, and with the watchful eye of multinational corporations that are actively implementing CSR programs and policies.

Nonetheless, companies often fail to uphold voluntary standards of behavior in developing countries, arguing instead that they operate within the law of the countries in which they are working. In fact, competitive pressure for foreign investment among developing countries has actually led to governments limiting their insistence on stringent compliance with human rights or environmental standards, in order to attract investment. In Sri Lanka, for example, as competitive pressure from neighboring China has increased in textile manufacturing, garment manufacturers have been found to lobby their government to increase working hours. In the end, most companies have limited power over the wider forces in developing countries that keep overall wage rates low. Nevertheless, for many people a job in a multinational factory may still be more desirable than being a doctor or a teacher, because the wages are higher and a worker's rights seem to be better protected.

What Are the Alternatives to CSR?

CSR advocates spend a considerable amount of effort developing new standards, partnership initiatives, and awards programs in an attempt to align social responsibility with a business case, yet may be failing to alter the overall landscape. Often the unintended consequences of good behavior lead to other secondary negative impacts, too. McDonald's sale of apples, meant to tackle obesity challenges, has actually led to a loss of biodiversity in apple production, as the corporation insists on uniformity and longevity in the type of apple they may buy—hardly a positive outcome for sustainability.[13]

At some point, we should be asking ourselves whether or not we've in fact been spending our efforts promoting a strategy that is more likely to lead to business as usual, rather than tackling the fundamental problems. Other strategies—from direct regulation of corporate behavior, to a more radical overhaul of the corporate institution, may be more likely to deliver the outcomes we seek.

Traditional regulatory models would impose mandatory rules on a company to ensure that it behaves in a socially responsible manner. The advantage of regulation is that it brings with it predictability, and, in many cases, innovation.

Though fought stridently by business, social improvements may be more readily achieved through direct regulation than via the market alone, as some examples show in Table 1.

Other regulatory-imposed strategies have done more to alter consumer behavior than CSR efforts. Social labeling, for example, has been an extremely effective tool for changing consumer behavior in Europe. All appliances must be labeled with an energy efficiency rating, and the appliances rated as the most energy efficient now capture over 50 percent of the market. And the standards for the ratings are also continuously improving, through a combination of both research and legislation.[14]

Perhaps more profoundly, campaigners and legal scholars in Europe and the United States have started to look at the legal structure of the corporation. Currently, in Western legal systems, companies have a primary duty of care to their shareholders, and, although social actions on the part of companies are not necessarily prohibited, profit-maximizing behavior is the norm. So, companies effectively choose financial benefit over social ones.[15] While a handful of social enterprises, like Fair Trade companies, have forged a different path, they are far from dominating the market. Yet lessons from their successes are being adopted to put forward a new institutional model for larger shareholder-owned companies.

Red Tape Realities

Regulation	Prediction	Reality
National Minimum Wage	Would result in over one million job losses within two years	Unemployment fell by 200,000
EEC Introduction of Catalytic Converters	The cost of technology would be £400–£600 per vehicle, with a fuel consumption penalty of top	Real costs of around £30–£50 per convertor; technological innovation led to smaller cars
US Clean Air Act	Would cost the US $51 to $91 billion per year and result in anywhere from 20,000 to 4 million job losses	Yearly cost £22 billion to business, but employment in areas affected up by 22 percent the benefits arising are between £120 and £193 billion
Montreal Protocol	Opposed by industry on economic cost grounds, but no projected figures	No impact; substitute technologies may have saved costs according to follow up studies

D. Doane, "From Red Tape to Road Signs: Redefining Regulation and Its Purpose" (London: CORE Coalition, 2004).

In the United Kingdom, a coalition of 130 NGOs under the aegis of the Corporate Responsibility Coalition (CORE), has presented legislation through the Parliament that argues in favor of an approach to U.K. company law that would see company directors having multiple duties of care—both to their shareholders and to other stakeholders, including communities, employees, and the environment. Under their proposals, companies would be required to consider, act, mitigate, and report on any negative impacts on other stakeholders.[16]

Across the pond, Corporation 20/20, an initiative of Business Ethics and the Tellus Institute, has proposed a new set of principles that enshrines social responsibility from the founding of a company, rather than as a nice-to-have disposable add-on. The principles have been the work of a diverse group including legal scholars, activists, business, labor, and journalism, and while still at the discussion phase, such principles could ultimately be enacted into law, stimulating the types of companies that might be better able to respond to things like poverty or climate change or biodiversity. Values such as equity and democracy, mainstays of the social enterprise sector, take precedence over pure profit making, and while the company would continue to be a profit-making entity in the private realm, it would not be able to do so at a cost to society.

Of course, we are a long way from having any of these ideas adopted on a large scale, certainly not when the CSR movement is winning the public relations game with both governments and the public, lulling us into a false sense of security. There is room for markets to bring about some change through CSR, but the

Corporation 20/20 Draft Principles

1. The purpose of the corporation is to harness private interests in service of the public interest.
2. Corporations shall accrue fair profits for shareholders, but not at the expense of the legitimate interests of other stakeholders.
3. Corporations shall operate sustainably, helping to meet the needs of the present generation without compromising the ability of future generations to meet theirs.
4. Corporations shall distribute their wealth equitably among those who contribute to its creation.
5. Corporations shall be governed in a manner that is participatory, transparent, and accountable.

(See www.corporate-responsibility.org.)

market alone is unlikely to bring with it the progressive outcomes its proponents would hope for. While the *Economist* argument was half correct—that CSR can be little more than a public relations device—it fails to rec-

ognize that it is the institution of the corporation itself that may be at the heart of the problem. CSR, in the end, is a placebo, leaving us with immense and mounting challenges in globalization for the foreseeable future.

Notes

1 N. Klein, *No Logo: Taking Aim at the Branding Bullies* (United Kingdom: HarperCollins, 2001).

2 Co-operative Bank, 2004 Ethical Purchasing Index, http://www.co-operative-bank.co.uk/servlet/Satellite?cid=107761004 4424&pagename=CoopBank%2FPage%2FtplPageStandard& c=Page.

3 A. Zimmerman, "Costco's Dilemma: Be Kind to Its Workers, or Wall Street," *Wall Street Journal*, March 26, 2004.

4 M. Kelly, *The Divine Right of Capital: Dethroning the Corporate Aristocracy* (San Francisco: Berrett-Koehler, 2003).

5 U.K. Institute of Grocery Distributors, 2003.

6 "Who Are the Ethical Consumers?" Co-operative Bank, 2000.

7 Green Gauge Report 2002, Roper ASW, as related by Edwin Stafford.

8 http://makower.typepad.com/joel_makower/2005/06/ideal_ bite_keep.html.

9 http://money.cnn.com/2004/05/17/pf/autos/suvs_gas/.

10 "Greenwash + 10: The U.N.'s Global Compact, Corporate Accountability, and the Johannesburg Earth Summit," *Corporate Watch*, January 2002.

11 "The Global Reporters 2004 Survey of Corporate Sustainability Reporting," SustainAbility, UNEP, and Standard & Poor's.

12 J. Miller, "Double Taxation Double Speak: Why Repealing Tax Dividends Is Unfair," *Dollars & Sense*, March/April 2003.

13 G. Younge, "McDonald's Grabs a Piece of the Apple Pie: 'Healthy' Menu Changes Threaten the Health of Biodiversity in Apples," *The Guardian*, April 7, 2005.

14 Ethical Purchasing Index, 2004.

15 E. Elhauge, "Sacrificing Corporate Profits in the Public Interest," *New York University Law Review* 80, 2005.

16 http://www.corporate-responsibility.org.

Questions for Discussion and Reflection

1. Do you believe that business can provide short-term financial returns and long-term social benefits at the same time? Why or why not?
2. What do you think of the Corporation 20/20 draft principles for social responsibility?
3. Do you believe that Doane is too skeptical about the ability of ethical consumers to drive change in companies, or is she right that that is a myth? Explain your answer.

A Long-Term Business Perspective in a Short-Term World

A Conversation with Jim Sinegal

Albert Erisman and David Gill

Ethix 9 (March–April 2003): 6–9, 16. Copyright © 2003.

James D. Sinegal is president, CEO, and a director of Costco Wholesale Corporation, America's top warehouse retailer, based in Issaquah, Washington. Costco operates more than 400 stores, employs more than 100,000 people, tallied $38 billion in sales to more than 23 million members, and made $700 million

in profits in fiscal 2002. Sinegal was founding CEO of Costco in 1983 (with cofounder Jeffrey Brotman, who serves as chairman) and has remained at the helm through its transitions and growth, including its merger with the Price Company in 1993. From 1954 to 1977 Mr. Sinegal worked his way up the ladder at San Diego–based discount retail chain Fed-Mart from bagger to executive vice president. Early on at Fed-Mart, he abandoned studies at San Diego State after getting a job promotion. *Business Week* magazine featured Sinegal along with five others in their September 23, 2002, cover story on "The Good CEO."

•   •   •

Low Prices and High Wages: Why?

*Ethix: Costco is distinctive among its competitors with its policies of never marking anything up more than 14 per cent (with an average mark-up of only 10%). You have been known to lower prices on items when the wholesale price went down—even if market competition and customer awareness didn't require it, even if you had purchased the item at an earlier, higher price. Costco also is determined that its employee wages and benefits lead the industry. **Business Week** reported that a Costco cashier with four years experience can earn more than $40,000 with full benefits. Where do these policies come from? How did you decide to run your business this way?*

Jim Sinegal: Part of it is just sound business thinking. It shouldn't surprise anyone that if you find good people, give them good jobs, and pay them good wages, good things will happen.

Part of the reason may also have to do with the kind of business we have. When we opened our first warehouse in downtown Seattle with forklifts running through stacks of tires and electronics, food and mayonnaise and cranberry juice, people would naturally ask the question, how can they sell things for such low prices? What are these guys doing?

We decided that we would take away any objections or questions a customer might have, such as perhaps we could be treating our employees unfairly in order to sell things at low prices. We also decided to establish a stronger and better "guarantee of satisfaction" on every product we sold, that would exceed the warrantee offered by any other company.

We have the same attitude toward our suppliers and everyone else who has contact with our business. We operate this way because we believe philosophically that this is what we should be doing—but we also do it because of the nature of

our business. People would always ask, "What's the catch?" We wanted to make it clear that there were no catches.

Ethix: Don't investors pressure you to increase quarterly profits and raise shareholder value by cutting wages and raising prices as the market dictates or allows? How do you and your Board resist that?

Sinegal: We get it every day. That's not an unreasonable question for someone in the business of making money. Their job is to buy low and sell high. But that's not our job. Our job is to build the company, hopefully one that's going to be here fifty years from now. You don't do that by changing every time the wind blows in a different direction.

The things that we do are basic and intrinsic to our business and our company. Our reputation for pricing is an example. We have sweated over this for years. Why would we sacrifice that just to make a quarterly target? It wouldn't make sense—sacrificing everything, risking our whole reputation. We believe our strategy will maximize shareholder value over the long term.

We have a reputation for pricing. Why would we sacrifice that just to make a quarterly target?

Ethix: Customers have price and quality incentives to come to Costco. Employees have wage and satisfaction incentives to work at Costco. What is the incentive for investors? Must they always share your long-term view?

Sinegal: The record shows clearly that we are successful over the long term. I don't know what the exact number is, but look at our return over the past five or ten or fifteen years. Our mission is to do four essential things: obey the law ... take care of our customers ... take care of our people ... and respect our suppliers. If we do these four things, and do them consistently, we will succeed as a business enterprise that is profitable and rewarding to our shareholders.

It is possible for some to ignore these things and reward their shareholders in the short term—but not for the long term. We feel an obligation to build businesses so that communities can count on us being there, suppliers can count on us being there, employees can count on the security of jobs, and customers who shop with us know that they can count on us. When they buy a washing machine or a television, we're still going to be around a couple of years from now.

Ethix: *This all seems pretty obvious, but many are not doing business this way. Why?*

Sinegal: In the past year public attention has been focused on the "crooks in business" and how to stop them. The result has been a bunch of new legislation and rules. You know as well as I do that the crooks are going to go on "crooking"—they're going to figure it out. But I believe that, by and large, most businesses are running on a basis similar to ours.

The Good CEO

Ethix: **Business Week** *called you one of the good CEOs. What in your view makes a good CEO? As you look for a successor some day at Costco, what characteristics matter most?*

Sinegal: I'm flattered of course that *Business Week* included me in that group. Characteristics? Good leaders make the determination how to run the company and then communicate it to everyone in the company so that they all understand it. Honesty and doing the right thing cannot be the responsibility of management alone. Every level of the company should understand what the rules are, and every employee in the company should be mortified if the company and its people don't do what they are supposed to do. The attitude has got to be pervasive throughout the organiza-

tion: "We don't do that kind of stuff around here! Period!"

Ethix: *So first you're looking for character and ethics?*

Sinegal: You're looking for a lot of things. You look for intelligence, industriousness, integrity, for someone faster than a speeding bullet—all of those things you want in a manager. If you start off with integrity, financial integrity as well as intellectual integrity, you're starting on a pretty good base.

Values and Integrity through the Ranks

Ethix: *How do you make sure that integrity and company values are part of the culture all the way down to the forklift driver and the mail delivery person?*

Sinegal: As an organization, make sure that you are consistent. You put in place simple guidelines on how you run your business and then follow them.

One guideline we follow at Costco is that no employee who has been with us for more than two years can be fired without the approval of a senior officer in the company. We think an employee who has been with us two years is entitled to that. No manager can come in on a bad day and decide some employee is history. There has got be a review process. Is it perfect? Of course not. We're fallible. But it is one of the things that we do to show respect to our employees.

Another example is our open-door policy. People have a way to voice their grievances and get them addressed. All 100,000 employees cannot run to me (although sometimes it feels like they do), but I do take on some. It would be a very rare day that I don't get a couple of calls from employees. But think about this: if warehouse managers know that their own regional bosses have open door policies and will talk to any employees about their issues, then they are going to be a little faster to talk to the troubled employees themselves. They don't want the problems to come back to them through their bosses. They are smart enough to figure out that it is their responsibility to take care of things at their level.

Ethix: You can't know 100,000 employees personally and you can't visit all your stores as frequently. What do you do differently now to maintain consistency in your culture and values?

Sinegal: It's clearly much more difficult than in the early days. That rule about the two-year employee termination review used to apply just to my partner Jeff Brotman and me. When the company got too big, we had to say the review will be by one of our senior officers. I used to pride myself on visiting every one of our warehouses between October and December. Now that is impossible. Some locations take two days of travel just to get there. I still try to get to every warehouse at least once a year. Why? That's what I do for a living. I love the business and I enjoy doing it. It is important that those in management get out there and understand where the business is. Otherwise your business is going to fall apart on you.

Technology at Costco

Ethix: Does information technology help you to stay in communication?

Sinegal: Technology has made us much more productive. With computers, fax machines, and cell phones, we have more productive time during the course of the whole day and can react to situations more immediately.

Ethix: When I think of technology and retail, I think of what Amazon has done at the front end of their business—and what WalMart has done at the back end of their business. How does Costco's use of technology compare with what Amazon and WalMart have done?

Sinegal: We have a relatively sophisticated computer system and lots of technology. We have wireless recording of purchases and can go into any of our warehouses anywhere and check on how any given item is selling during the day. Sometimes we have so much information it's more than we can deal with. Our web site and our e-commerce business are also profitable on a fully allocated basis, and that is somewhat of a milestone.

Technology helps us become more efficient

and productive, but our business still has a lot of art as opposed to strictly science. The reason the dot-com companies didn't succeed is that they were very good at the science end but they didn't understand anything about the art of buying and selling merchandise. They thought that was the easy part, but it turned out to be the most difficult. Time will tell whether Amazon.com is going to turn a profit. My guess is that they will succeed. They are pretty sophisticated guys, and there is a reason why they survived when the others were falling by the wayside. But buying and selling merchandise is the business. These other things augment your running the business, but they aren't the driving force. If you don't have the right merchandise in the right place at the right time, you can forget about everything else. All the satellites in the world aren't going to help you.

The reason the dot-com companies didn't succeed is that they were very good at the science end but they didn't understand anything about the art of buying and selling merchandise.

Retail in the Future

Ethix: How do you see the retail world thirty years from now? Any dramatic changes?

Sinegal: I think there will continue to be the huge hypermarket types of businesses. People have been going to the marketplace for thousands of years for its social significance as much as for replenishing household needs.

Ethix: It won't all be done on-line?

Sinegal: I don't think so. People are still going to want to go out and have that social exchange. I think there probably will be more hypermarkets. I think that WalMart-style, 200,000 square foot superstores that carry everything will become the norm as time goes on. We could see shopping malls turn into superstores where there are independent stations within one superstore with one check-out. The expertise within those walls will reside in the little stores and boutiques inside the superstore.

Ethix: Part of it is that people want to associate with people. But another part must be that people want to see and touch the merchandise. I'm not sure that even if you could make something holographically present in my living room it would be a satisfying substitute for going to a store and seeing and touching the thing itself.

Sinegal: A good example of that is that ninety percent of our book sales are unplanned. A customer walks by the book table, sees a book, picks it up, looks at the jacket, says, "Hey this looks kind of interesting," and buys it.

Ethix: Is anything being lost, in your view, by the replacement of local merchants by huge national franchises in cookie cutter malls everywhere you go? There are certainly some efficiencies of scale with the Home Depots, SportMarts, Office Maxes, and Costcos in every community, but can the smaller neighborhood store survive? Should we mourn its loss?

Sinegal: It comes down to the quality of the individual merchant. Those who run their businesses in an efficient manner are going to survive. But we need to ask also, what's the difference between a 200,000 square foot WalMart superstore and a 200,000 square foot shopping center with shops carrying the same merchandise?

Ethix: It may be that most traditional downtown shopping districts, especially in rural America, were smaller than the typical WalMart or Costco.

Sinegal: Some of these power centers have a drugstore, a supermarket, a sporting good store, a coffee shop, a clothier, and a couple of restaurants. All together they add up to a lot of square footage.

Costco and Small Businesses

Ethix: How big is your emphasis on supplying small businesses? Maybe Costco is actually supplying (and preserving) small businesses rather than replacing them entirely.

Sinegal: The business customer is the key member that we service. We also supply a lot of nonprofits like churches, schools, and sports teams. Sixty percent of our business is with business customers.

Ethix: Where Home Depot comes in, local hardware stores disappear. But where Costco comes in, it sounds like you might replace some stores, but you're also helping others to survive by being their supplier.

Sinegal: Our business was founded so that small businesses could come in and buy essentially everything they needed for their business under one roof. Cafe owners could purchase all of their food and drink, cigarettes and candy, cleaning supplies, pots and pans, toilet paper and towels, pads and pencils, and so on. They also might buy a television set for home or work.

Ethix: Would you sell them a pick-up truck to drive all their stuff back to the office or home also?

Sinegal: Actually, I think on a referral basis we sell about 100,000 cars a year. That's pretty substantial.

*Ethix: In the December 2002 issue of your magazine, **The Costco Connection**, I noticed an article about ethics in business. Is this to help small businesses improve their operating structure? Is that part of your work with small businesses?*

Sinegal: Absolutely. Small businesses are our key customers, and you will find articles in most issues that revolve around the businesses: advice on how to run a business, how to get staff, how to hire consultants, and so on.

Globalization Challenges

Ethix: Costco has gone global both in terms of its supply chain and its sales outlets. What challenges have you seen in moving from an American company to a global company?

Sinegal: Every country is different. The one constant is value. Value is appreciated no matter where you go, though how you make it work can vary by country.

After we started our business in Seattle, we had an opportunity to go up to Canada. We thought "Canada is only 140 miles away, how different could it be?" Well, we found out! They have a different system of weights and measurements, a different currency system, different laws, and a different language. Everything had to be printed in two languages. We found out very quickly that there was a lot to doing business in a different country even if it was only 140 miles away.

That experience helped prepare us to do business in countries that are much more difficult than Canada. Today we do business in 61 Costcos in Canada and we have 15 in the UK. We have 21 in Mexico, three in Japan, five in South Korea, and three in Taiwan. So, we've got an international presence in various places and we will continue to grow internationally, especially in Japan, the UK, and Mexico.

The keys to doing international business are to understand local rules and laws, recognize what customers want to buy, and take care of our employees. Whether in the UK or Canada or in Mexico, we're going to measure ourselves against every other retailer and make sure that we're paying higher wages than anyone else. We would like to be able to turn our inventory faster than our people, because excessive turnover of people is very costly.

Expanding into New Product Areas

Ethix: You manufacture some of the things that you sell, such as bakery goods. How do you decide what to make? For example, have you thought about becoming a book publisher? Is the process simply that somebody in your organization gets the idea, proposes it, and then you decide whether it's cost-effective or not?

Sinegal: That's pretty generally the way it starts.

Ethix: Do you have a strategy to go out and aggressively build up your own manufacturing industry?

Sinegal: We get calls all the time from people who want us to do ancillary businesses and all sorts of deals or proposals coming to us about getting involved in salons or healthcare in our warehouses. It's not our business, and we think that probably it winds up just taking up valuable parking spaces.

We do have a strategy of trying to bring new products and new services to our customers on an ongoing basis. The question in our minds is whether we can do it well and provide value for the customer. If we think we can, we're prepared to try it.

Ethical Screening of Products

Ethix: Are there products where you could make money, but you would not pursue for ethical reasons? For example, how would you decide whether to sell pornography? Do you have stated policies on these things?

Sinegal: Yes, we do. We determined that we're not going to carry any pornographic materials. We also don't carry violent video games. We don't carry guns or ammunition. These decisions came from those of us who run the company.

Ethix: But you do have cigarettes.

Sinegal: We do have cigarettes. Obviously it's a dilemma today. But it was a big portion of how we started our business taking care of wholesale customers. A lot of them sell tobacco in their stores, cafes, machines, and lunch trucks.

If you don't have the right merchandise in the right place at the right time, you can forget about everything else. All the satellites in the world aren't going to help you.

Ethix: Do you have policies for your buyers to investigate how products are manufactured, i.e., that there is no child labor or slave labor? How would you enforce this?

Sinegal: There are lots of laws in the US and other countries. We also have a code of conduct for our suppliers that demands that they have to meet the laws of their own country, pay the right wages, and not use child, slave, or prison labor, etc.

Ethix: *What about bribery?*

Sinegal: Bribery is clearly the worst. As an American company we can't get involved in bribery because of the Foreign Corrupt Practices Act. We have a conduct policy for our suppliers. We visit our supplier factories on a regular basis to make certain they are complying with our standards and values.

What Went Wrong in Corporate America?

Ethix: *As you look back on the corporate scandals of the last couple years, what would you say has gone wrong in American business? What is the problem and the solution from where you sit?*

Sinegal: I think the gates were too wide open, with too many opportunities. Clearly that's something that has to be taken care of. But no matter what types of rules and regulations, no matter how many committees are set up, bad guys are still going to figure out some way to do wrong. The good news is that there aren't that many bad guys. Most business leaders are trying to run their businesses in an ethical fashion. I think the biggest single thing that causes difficulty in the business world is the short-term view. We become obsessed with it. But it forces bad decisions.

Ethix: *But you can't regulate against it.*

Sinegal: It's a process. It's the way our system works. The system is a very good one. I'm not knocking it. The pressure from analysts and Wall Street is good because it forces us to think carefully about our business. Reflection and thinking from another point of view is not bad at all.

Finding Time to Reflect

Ethix: *How do you find time for reflection, given the pace of life, the quantity of information, and competitive pressures?*

Sinegal: You have to schedule it. You have to plan the opportunity to think about your business and plan what you're going to do. Otherwise you're just a hamster running on a treadmill; you're never going to get anywhere. You've got to schedule it. Strategic planning is an important part of running any business and the more so for businesses that operate in multiple states and countries.

Ethix: *In the future, will Costco be in the Middle East, Africa, South America—or other places that might be a little more difficult than Mexico, Japan, or the UK?*

Sinegal: There are lots of places for us to go that don't have really severe problems, but I could see a time where we might enter areas of greater challenge.

Ethix: *Do you have a grand vision for what you'd like to do with this company before you hand it off to somebody else?*

Sinegal: We're not kamikaze pilots. We want to do things in a sensible fashion. If we can speed up our growth, without outdistancing our management team, and provide a quality product, then we will do so. Aside from the quality issues and wanting to grow the business in a sensible fashion, we don't have any grand scheme that says, for example, that we have to be in Latin America by the year 2015 or have 1000 Costco's in ten years.

Questions for Discussion and Reflection

1. How well do you think Jim Sinegal has done in integrating good business practices with being a good corporate citizen?
2. What do you think of Costco's decision not to carry potentially profitable products such as pornography, guns, and violent video games? Are they being consistent in their decision to sell cigarettes? Why or why not?

CASE STUDIES

Case 4.1: Violent Video Games

"Shoot a snitch in the kneecaps, or snuff out a rival with a single head shot and watch them bleed."

From the jacket of the video game Kingpin

As computer games become more realistic in graphical appearance, controversy is growing as the games also become more violent in thematic content. A proposed California law (the constitutionality of which was rejected by the United States Supreme Court in 2011) would ban the sales of violent games to minors.

One popular game series, Grand Theft Auto, has participants scoring points by killing people, stealing cars, and dealing drugs. Players receive new life by having implied sexual contact with prostitutes. An ad for the teen-rated game Wargasm reads, "Kill your friends guilt-free."

Of course not all video games contain questionable content. Many, including several top sellers, have educational or other nonviolent themes. However, many violence-themed games that push the envelope on tastefulness and morality sell well and provide solid profits for their manufacturers.

Thousands of studies link violent behavior among children to watching violence on television. While research to examine the effect of computer-simulated violence on real-world violence is in earlier stages (some studies show a positive link with more aggression while others show no correlation), some observers say that computer activity is much more compelling than other forms of media because the players participate and become engaged in the game through the role of one of the characters. Pomona College professor Brian Stonehill claims that this is a big change from other types of spectator violence, because "this takes you out of the role of spectator and into the role of murderer."[7] Some electronic gaming industry executives respond that their products should not be taken so seriously. Steve Race, a former president of Sony Computer Entertainment once told a reporter, "I just sell games, lady. To make me responsible for the mores or values of America, I don't think I'm ready for that."[8] Other industry spokespersons state that the more violent M-rated (Mature) games are intended for nineteen- to twenty-two-year-old males who clearly know the difference between fantasy and reality.

The industry also adopted a self-imposed rating system (www.esrb.com) to help parents make informed choices to keep the games in the hands of age-appropriate audiences. Defenders of the industry state that given the

[7] Amy Harmon, "Fun, Games, Gore," *Los Angeles Times*, May 12, 1995, A28.

[8] Ibid.

rating system, parents are at fault if the games wind up in the wrong hands, since they are the ones who purchase the games for their children.

Critics of these types of games in turn point out that enforcement of the rating system is spotty at best. Some retailers don't enforce the code at all, while others do so in an inconsistent manner. Moreover, the industry isn't really sincere about working with parents as seen by the way the games are marketed. Ads for violent teen-rated games have been placed in *Sports Illustrated for Kids*. And games rated for all ages are often sold right next to those earning an M rating.[9]

[9] Susan Nielsen, "A Beginner's Guide to Becoming a Video Game Prude," *Seattle Times*, February 21, 1999.

Questions for Discussion

1. Despite the demand for these games and the high profit margins they create, are these companies being socially irresponsible?
2. Do the companies that make the games have responsibilities to other stakeholders, or should they seek to maximize profit for shareholders alone?
3. Is it mostly up to parents and retailers to keep the games out of the hands of younger audiences, or do the manufacturers also have responsibilities in this area?

Case 4.2: Charity or Theft?

You are the president of a medium-sized, publicly traded furniture manufacturing company that has production facilities all over the world but is headquartered in New York City. Following the devastating Haitian earthquake (2010), you immediately contact the Red Cross and offer a donation of $500,000 of company funds to aid in the relief work. You did what numerous other companies and individuals did on that day. The urgency you felt to make this contribution came from the fact that many of the company's customers and their families were affected by the catastrophe.

You understand that this is an emergency, and though it would probably be better to wait until the monthly board meeting to get approval, this is not a normal time. The Red Cross needs the funding today, not a month from now when the board next convenes. Somehow word gets out to the media that your company has made such a generous contribution, and you are asked to appear on CNN and other media outlets and are congratulated for your company's generosity and responsiveness to the tragedy.

The next day you are summoned by the chairperson of the board and told that he is furious with you for making the contribution without board approval, especially in light of declining profits due to the recession (the $500,000 amounts to 3 percent of after-tax profit for the fiscal year). You are offended and angered by the chairperson's complaint and remind him that you have a discretionary fund of $2 million that is at your disposal for company emergencies. You argue that if ever there was an emergency that needed a response, this was it.

The chairperson replies that it is neither fair nor a proper discharge of your fiduciary responsibilities to use the shareholders' money for anything other than efforts to directly increase the profitability of the company. "Doing anything else is theft from their coffers," he says. The chairperson tells you that if the shareholders want to contribute to the Red Cross, they should do so with their own money, and that the same thing holds true for the company's management — that if they want to donate to charity, they should do it with their own money, not the shareholders' money. He also reminds you that in order to trim costs this past year, "we've had to lay off 15 percent of our workforce — giving that kind of sum to charity is an insult to the workers we have had to let go of and to their families."

You somewhat understand where the chairperson is coming from, but one of the company's key cornerstones has always been community involvement. You are also having a hard time believing that the shareholders wouldn't agree with your decision to donate the money.

Questions for Discussion

1. Who do you think is right here — the chair of the board or the president? Defend your answer.
2. Reflect back to the debate earlier in this chapter between Milton Friedman, John Mackey, and T.J. Rodgers. Who do you think Friedman would support? Mackey? Explain your answer.

Case 4.3: Google in China

Google is a company that really needs no introduction. The company name is nearly an eponym for Internet searches, its products delight users and quickly grab market share from rivals, and it regularly appears on "best places to work" type lists. The company was started in 1996 by two Stanford University graduate students, Larry Page and Sergey Brin. The founders sought to make it a different kind of company from the very beginning, including a well-known operating philosophy of "Don't be evil."

Operating in China, however, has been nothing short of challenging. To enter what will probably be its largest market for expansion in the future, Google executives had to consider how it would operate, given strict government rules. Unlike many countries, the Chinese government does not welcome the free flow of information that comes with the Internet. Relying on

10 For a detailed description of China's laws and technical filtering capabilities, see Kirsten E. Martin, "Google, Inc. in China," Business Institute for Corporate Ethics, 2006, http://www.darden.virginia.edu/corporate-ethics/pdf/Case_BRI-1005_Google_in_China_condensed.pdf.

its "Great Firewall," China's government regularly blocks access to websites that promote democracy and/or report on human rights abuses within the country, and those that offer objectionable material such as pornography. The government tracks sites visited by its citizens, relies on self-filtering by Internet providers, and employs thousands of "Internet police" to enforce laws.[10] A company like Google that seeks to operate within China would need to be licensed and would thereby be required to engage in filtering of search results and possibly to turn over information about political dissidents when requested to do so.

In its first foray in 2005, Google decided to put up a Chinese language version of its website that was housed outside of the country so that China's laws would not need to be followed (filtering would be left to China's government). Within a short period after its startup, however, the site began to experience severe technical problems (including a two-week shutdown that some suspect the Chinese government was behind). Over time, Google could not gain significant traction on Baidu, China's largest such search engine.

After much deliberation and careful planning and the hiring of several key leaders, company executives decided it would launch a search site housed on servers based in China, Google.cn, in 2006. This new venture would require compliance with China's Internet policies, but company executives believed it would make their engine faster and more reliable and would thus give them a better chance of gaining a foothold in the country. Even though Google decided to keep some functions such as Gmail out of China to protect the privacy of users, the decision still created controversy. Critics attacked the company for selling out on its core values of "do no evil" and said it would be cooperating with China and, thereby, be complicit in denying human rights to Chinese citizens for the sake of increasing profit.

Google.cn was a challenging effort from the beginning. There were constant misunderstandings with government officials and some serious cases of hacking (at least one traced back to China), in which some of the company's back end code was stolen and the Gmail accounts of US government officials and Chinese political activists were targeted. In 2010 Google officials announced it would likely stop its filtering activities in China and thus would be in effect closing its China-based site.

This latest decision also created controversy. While those concerned about human rights were no doubt pleased, some shareholders were upset that the company abandoned the effort, fearing future efforts to have a presence in China would be made much more difficult. Looking at the vast market for growth in the country, one writer argued, "Google is effectively abandoning its customers and partners in China and harming its American shareholders in the process. To me, that's poor business ethics. To me, that's doing evil ... business evil. Once they made the commitment, I think they were bound to stay the course."[11]

Questions for Discussion

1. Were Google's decisions (both to enter China's search market and then to withdraw from it) "responsible"? Should the company have created Google.cn in the first place?
2. How should Google executives weigh the company's core operating philosophy with financial duties to shareholders?

Sources:

"Google in China: Timeline," *The Telegraph*, June 7, 2011. http://www.telegraph.co.uk/technology/google/8551639/Google-in-China-timeline.html.

Steven Levy, "Google and Its Ordeal in China," *Fortune*, May 2, 2011, pp. 95-100.

Kirsten E. Martin, "Google, Inc. in China," Business Institute for Corporate Ethics, 2006, http://www.darden.virginia.edu/corporate-ethics/pdf/Case_BRI-1005_Google_in_China_condensed.pdf.

J. P. Raphel, "Google in China: How It Came to This," *PC World*, January 10, 2010. http://www.pcworld.com/article/187426/the_googlechina_challenge_how_it_came_to_this.html.

Clive Thompson, "Google's China Problem (and China's Google Problem)," *New York Times*, April 23, 2006. http://www.nytimes.com/2006/04/23/magazine/23google.html.

COMMENTARY

One of the central questions of debate about Corporate Social Responsibility regards the central purposes and obligations of publicly held corporations. While the Michigan State Supreme Court famously argued in *Dodge v. Ford* (1919) that "a business organization is organized and carried on primarily for the profit of stockholders," it is clear that social expectations are shifting. In addition to avoiding wrongdoing, repairing harm directly caused, and steering clear of capitalizing on injustice, corporations are also being called on to use their financial resources, expertise, and distribution networks to solve social problems proactively, even ones they do not cause.[12]

When corporate managers are confronted with decisions (ones with ethical dimensions or ones concerning whether to undertake social initiatives) that may jeopardize earnings for shareholders for the sake of another stakeholder, should they take the course of action that maximizes profit, one that favors the other objective, or attempt to strike some sort of harmonious balance (if one can be found)? In large part, the answer depends on how the legitimate purposes and duties of corporations are conceived of. The day-to-day moral latitude managers have in decision making is greatly influenced by this conception since it plays an important role in shaping factors such as corporate

---

[11] Steve Tobak, "Google in China: Should Corporate Ethics Trump Profits?" BNET. March 25, 2010, http://www.bnet.com/blog/ceo/google-in-china-should-corporate-ethics-trump-profits/4215.

[12] See Joshua Margolis and James P. Walsh, "Misery Loves Companies: Rethinking Social Initiatives by Business," *Administrative Science Quarterly* 48 (2003): 268–305; see also Michael Porter and Mark Kramer, "Creating Shared Value," *Harvard Business Review*, January–February 2011, 1–17.

mission, identity, and objectives; consumer purchasing and employment decisions; and the legal and regulatory context in which business operates.

One approach (taken by Milton Friedman and T.J. Rodgers) is to conceive of a firm's only proper objective ("social responsibility") as profit maximization (within legal boundaries and "ethical custom"). This view is known as *shareholder capitalism*, the custodian of wealth or the finance model of the firm. To be certain, supporters of this perspective are not advancing a case for short-term greed (i.e., "putting every nickel possible on the quarterly bottom line," as Rodgers puts it). Nor are they arguing that stakeholders should be overlooked. Financially successful managers must work with stakeholders. Of course the primary ("singular") objective is to maximize profit with stakeholder interests receiving only "instrumental" (means to an end) consideration.[13]

While giving to charity, volunteering, and engaging in many other activities that resemble CSR can be good for business, supporters of the finance model (like Friedman and Rodgers) challenge the legitimacy of CSR efforts that reduce shareholder value. Exceeding standards set by law and "ethical custom" and directly spending corporate profits on social causes represent a form of misappropriation of resources or "taxation without representation."[14]

Another approach that has emerged over the past twenty-five years is stakeholder theory, or more accurately, theories. At the heart of these theories is the belief that corporations can and should advance the interests of multiple groups (customers, employees, shareholders, suppliers, and local communities) that have a "stake" (typically characterized by a reciprocal relationship) in the firm at once. While John Mackey shows what stakeholder theory might look like if driven by a libertarian set of beliefs, stakeholder theory and practice is often shaped by a more communitarian philosophy. Communitarians tend to deemphasize individualistic conceptions of property rights and focus more intentional and direct efforts on benefiting various stakeholder groups (beyond what is required by law) as better paths to achieve social good. As members of larger communities and as "moral communities" themselves, corporations are bound by the practice of good citizenship, which minimally means refraining from harm, and at times may mean deploying their resources for the benefit of others.

Though itself not a distinct theory of CSR, another growing agenda (we will call it the convergence approach, for the sake of discussion) is represented by attempts to escape the shareholder-stakeholder paradox by finding an overlapping path. For example, Michael Porter and Mark Kramer encourage moving beyond ways of seeing the relationship as a zero-sum game and into thinking of it as a "source of opportunity, innovation and competitive advantage."[15] Along these lines, a growing body of research attempts to make a "business case" for CSR and thereby relax the tensions between shareholder

[13] See Michael Jensen, "Value Maximization, Stakeholder Theory and the Corporate Objective Function," *Business Ethics Quarterly* 12 (2001): 235–56.

[14] Milton Friedman, "The Social Responsibility of Business Is to Increase Its Profits," *New York Times Magazine*, September 13, 1970, 122–26.

[15] Michael Porter and Mark Kramer, "Strategy and Society: The Link between Competitive Advantage and Corporate Social Responsibility," *Harvard Business Review*, November–December 2006.

and stakeholder interests. Well over a hundred studies over the past thirty years have tried to establish a link between corporate social performance and corporate financial performance.[16] And a number of recent studies have also looked at the net impact of CSR activities on the bottom line.[17]

Christian Ethics and CSR

While this debate has largely proceeded based on secular grounds, John Ruggie rightly calls it a "theological question."[18] What light, then, might Christian theology/ethics shed on the central CSR question of corporate purpose and duties? To be certain, developing a theologically informed model of the firm is a challenging task. The Scriptures were written in a time when the primary basis of economics consisted of farmers, artisans, and makers of small crafts. Modern shareholder-owned corporations did not exist then, nor have they been in operation throughout much of the history of the church. So, sorting out contextual issues and ethical guidance for individuals versus collective entities, and principles and commands meant for the ancient Hebraic community and/or the Christian community versus secular communities/organizations make the task even more challenging. However, there are biblical resources (i.e., moral instruction given in the form of laws, commandments, and principles to individuals and communities on topics such as justice, stewardship, and duties to others) that enable critical and constructive engagement with these questions.

The Finance Model

In examining the finance model of the firm, a few points of clarification are in order. It's a mistake to believe that the model is a fancy way to advance an argument for short-term greed. The model should be properly seen as an extension of a philosophical viewpoint about what makes a *good society*. This view (perhaps best captured as "market libertarian") emphasizes the primacy of private property rights and unfettered markets regulated by "the invisible hand." Allowing "business to be business" by doing what it uniquely does best — create wealth — and passing that wealth along to shareholders and allowing them to decide what to do with it is the best means to maximize social good.

This model has also been blamed for many recent scandals by allegedly encouraging a fixation on short-term share price, which thereby led to fraudulent activities. While a misapplication of the finance model may be partially to blame, the real culprit appears to be managerial capitalism (managing the firm for the interests of insiders). Had executives of the Enrons of the world actually looked out for the interests of shareholders, the outcomes might have been much different.

[16] See Margolis and Walsh, "Misery Loves Companies."

[17] See, e.g., Remi Trudel and June Cotte, "Does It Pay to Be Good?" *Sloan Management Review*, Winter 2009, 61–68.

[18] John Ruggie, Harvard Professor and UN Special Representative on Human Rights, Transnational Corporation and Other Business Enterprises. See "The Next Question: Does CSR Work?" *The Economist*, January 17, 2008.

With these points of clarification in mind, the model itself needs to be examined. By itself, the goal of increasing shareholder wealth is not problematic. Much social good comes from corporations earning a profit—that is, job creation, increasing a tax base that pays for public services and creating wealth for shareholders. To further illustrate, consider the negative impact brought about by the destruction of shareholder wealth during "the Great Recession." Many other secondary benefits also accrue from increasing profit. Investors save for retirement, college educations, and charitable giving. Philanthropic foundations also own shares of corporations, and the endowments of many nonprofit organizations (namely universities) depend on companies increasing shareholder wealth.

The emphasis on property rights also has some resonance with the biblical tradition. Earthly ownership is certainly implied by the commandment against theft. While "property" today is quite different than in biblical times (often taking the form of paper representation rather than tangible physical assets), the concept is still applicable. At face value, shareholders are among the legally recognized owners who provide (at risk) capital for the success of the corporation. Their economic interests should be honored as a matter of contractual fairness. Unless stated otherwise, increasing the value of shareholder ownership should be a high (though not the only) priority item on the list of managerial objectives.

Profit is an important aim for corporations for other reasons too. At the risk of stating the obvious, even organizations working for the primary benefit of other (nonshareholder) stakeholder groups need to achieve a sustainable level of returns. As the old saying goes, "No margin, no mission." In the absence of strong financial results, a corporation will see its costs of borrowing increase and may jeopardize its abilities to attract investment capital, recruit and retain top-notch employees, and invest in capital improvements and research and development efforts.

The finance model has some serious limitations, however. Jeff Van Duzer argues that a biblical case cannot be made for profit as an end goal of business.[19] The limitations of wealth maximization come into clearer focus in cases in which the quest to increase profit harms another stakeholder group, conflicts with other forms (noneconomic) of human well-being, or takes advantage of injustice. While Scripture does recognize and legitimizes the idea of "private" property, it is a limited "right."[20] Along with the privileges of ownership come special duties or "social responsibilities" for the larger community.

In the Old Testament, land owners were instructed to avoid harm by not exploiting workers and to advance the common good by making provisions for impoverished members of their surrounding community. Scripture also makes it clear that God retains "transcendental title" to "private"

[19] See Jeff Van Duzer, *Why Business Matters to God: (And What Still Needs to Be Fixed)* (Downers Grove, Ill.: IVP Academic, 2010).

[20] To be clear, the emphasis on "rights" in contemporary dialogue is more a product of the Enlightenment rather than the biblical tradition.

property. "The land must not be sold permanently, *because the land is mine*" (Lev. 25:23, emphasis added). Humans are merely stewards, greatly curtailing our freedom to simply view our use of property as an exclusively individualistic and/or private matter. From the biblical tradition, ownership is a spiritual and moral matter. Property is to be used in service to God, primarily for the benefit of others. While biblical teaching (especially laws and commands) cannot be directly applied to modern economics, paradigmatic moral guidance can still be strongly implied. In today's context, one implication seems to be that shareholders cannot legitimately exercise a "right" of ownership and expect corporate managers to earn profits while harming others.

In addition to overelevating ownership/property rights, the finance model has other weaknesses. Friedman, for example, makes broad assumptions about the economic "rationality" of shareholders, assuming they are only interested in maximizing profit. This runs counter to a Christian understanding of human nature as fallen/selfish but still bearing a reflection God's image and thus capable of other motivations.

While some shareholders may favor increased profit at any cost, most support a more tempered approach if the question is directly put in front of them. Consistent with a Christian understanding of human nature, moral concerns often accompany self-interested pursuits. Among them are sentiments toward the well-being of others. Any theory that reduces human motivations and behaviors to narrow self-interested economic ones is inconsistent with Christian values.[21] In fact, some research into voting patterns confirms that shareholders value contributions to social causes over financial gain. They will often cast votes for courses of action that produce social benefits at the expense of profit.[22] The growth of socially responsible mutual funds, investor funded social enterprises, and "conscious" consumer movements present more evidence that humans are not entirely motivated by economic concerns.

Another point that is often overlooked is that even if shareholders are solely motivated by maximized wealth, do they have the right to be? Corporate legal charters and mission statements typically do not list wealth maximization as a singular objective. Most say something to the effect of "quality products/services, community citizenship, in exchange for a reasonable or healthy profit." Therefore, investors may have no right (legal or moral) to be upset about a firm run for objectives that depart from profit maximization, a point emphasized by John Mackey.[23]

Stakeholder Models

While the finance model falls short, does a stakeholder approach fit better within the contours of Christian ethics, especially as it may well be emerging as the dominant ("new story of business") model? A singular evaluation

[21] For a thoughtful critique of economic reductionism, see Robert H. Nelson, "Economic Religion versus Christian Values," *Markets & Morality* 1, no. 2 (October 1998).

[22] See Pietra Rivoli, "Ethical Aspects of Investor Behavior," *Journal of Business Ethics* 14 (1995): 265–77. For a further discussion of complex human motivations and behavior, see Robert Frank, "Can a Socially Responsible Firm Survive in a Competitive Environment?" in David Messick and Ann Tenbrunsel, *Codes of Conduct: Behavioral Research into Business Ethics* (New York: Russell Sage Foundation, 1996), 86–103.

[23] See Charles Handy, "What's a Business For?" *Harvard Business Review*, November–December 2002, 49–55. Handy notes that corporate owners are more akin to investors or even gamblers, given the fact they don't bear any of the traditional responsibilities associated with ownership. For a similar argument, see Marjorie Kelly, *The Divine Right of Capital* (San Francisco: Berrett-Koehler, 2009).

of stakeholder theory is bound to be limited given the fact that it can come in many individual forms depending on the "normative core" or central philosophy that drives it. (John Mackey offers a version that he describes as based in libertarianism, although Friedman and Rodgers disagree with how consistent his version is with this philosophy.) Stakeholder theory can also be driven, for example, by pragmatism or environmentalism or a host of other philosophies. Though well past its nascent stage, stakeholder theory has a way to go in terms of development and refinement. [24]

What the theory does do, in effect, is create the space necessary for more direct and intentional decisions that benefit a wider range of stakeholders. It allows managers to honor the interests of a broad range of groups without subordinating these decisions to a singular objective of maximizing shareholder wealth. Many Christian theological subtraditions construe social institutions such as government, schools, and families as entities ordained by God to promote his purposes in the world. Business can be categorized as another one of these entities. Therefore, profit should not be viewed as an end in itself, but as a means to promote other goods, such as human well-being and flourishing. Thus, depending on the central guiding philosophy employed as the "normative core," stakeholder theory in theory and in practice may be more consistent with Christian values.

While the stakeholder approach leaves more room for ethical/social considerations, it too suffers from some limitations. Foremost, objectives for managerial decision making may be less clear when compared to the seemingly formulaic nature of the wealth maximization view of the firm. More specifically, the criticism has been raised that the stakeholder approach creates too much room and thereby gives managers little guidance as to how they should balance the competing claims of stakeholder groups.

For example, the timber industry continues to be controversial in areas such as the Pacific Northwest. While timber harvesting provides vital economic lifelines for some small towns, some interest groups want to end logging because of the adverse impact on the environment. Managers are then left without clear direction in terms of achieving a proper balance. The result is likely to be some type of consensus among the competing interests. While not problematic in its own right, the reached consensus may or may not reflect company values and/or may not be ethically defensible in terms of broader conceptions of the common good.[25]

Others are concerned that stakeholder theory offers no boundaries with respect to the claims society can make on the owners of a corporation. Particularly difficult are cases in which a corporation has not caused a certain social harm nor benefited from that harm, but may have the expertise and resources to address it. For example, what obligations do corporations have

[24] See Bradley Agle et al., "Dialogue Toward Better Stakeholder Theory," *Business Ethics Quarterly* 18:2 (2008), 153–90.

[25] For a thoughtful discussion of these and other shortcomings of the stakeholder approach, see Helen Alford and Michael Naughton, *Managing as If Faith Mattered* (Notre Dame, Ind.: University of Notre Dame Press, 2001).

to address human suffering in the form of AIDS, hunger, or lack of health care? While stakeholder theory creates the space to legitimate a response, it offers very limited guidance as to whether the corporation is actually obligated to respond and how many resources should be devoted to the objective.

A stakeholder model provides more "space" for managers to address social concerns and is thereby necessary but not sufficient. Managers still need other sources of moral guidance to make good decisions. To be certain, there may be times when perfect answers may not be available, and the appropriate balance between profit and other social goods could fit into a range of morally defensible options.

Despite its weaknesses, the stakeholder approach pushes the concept of corporate responsibility in the right direction. A philosophy of the firm that deemphasizes profit as a singular objective and broadens the scope of moral duties to a wider range of constituents seems more consistent with biblical tradition, especially the part of the divine agenda that is concerned with human flourishing on earth.[26] While shareholders should undoubtedly receive significant consideration, other stakeholder interests also merit attention, primarily when harm may accrue to them. Legal standards for corporations are currently evolving to allow for these broader concerns.[27]

Convergence Approaches

As noted in this chapter's introduction, an emerging way to approach CSR is to try to relax the tensions between shareholder and stakeholder interests by finding points of convergence. This may come in the form of using data to establish a link between corporate financial and social performance, studying consumer behavior to determine if consumers are willing to pay a premium for "socially responsible" products and/or by finding win-win "sweet spot" activities (i.e., using energy efficient vehicles for delivery) that benefit stakeholders and shareholders simultaneously.

Most of the (more than one hundred and growing) studies actually find a positive association between social and financial performance.[28] So shareholders may well be made better off in the end and misgivings of misappropriation of corporate resources allayed. These types of studies are helpful especially since it is difficult to imagine how large-scale movements toward socially responsible behavior could occur in the absence of an established link. It may well be the case that lasting and sustainable CSR efforts will be those that are financially rewarding or at least do not require too much sacrifice. However, researchers have identified problems with every study, so care must be taken in establishing their conclusiveness.

[26] For a further description of the links between business and human flourishing, see Kenman Wong and Scott Rae, *Business for the Common Good* (Downers Grove, Ill.: IVP Academic, 2011). See also Van Duzer, *Why Business Matters to God*.

[27] See Richard Marens and Andrew Wicks, "Getting Real: Stakeholder Theory, Managerial Practice and the General Irrelevance of Fiduciary Duties Owed to Shareholders," *Business Ethics Quarterly* 9, no. 2 (April 1999): 273–93.

[28] Joshua Margolis and James P. Walsh, *People and Profits?: The Search for a Link between a Company's Social and Financial Performance* (Mahwah, N.J.: Erlbaum, 2001).

Several notable concerns with the convergence approach exist. First, it may unintentionally imply that these interests can always be harmonized (leading to "a good ethics is good business construct"). Managers are then left without guidance on how to act in cases in which interests are truly competing and may give in to the short-term demands of the market.

The link studies also have the unintentional effect of confirming the philosophical assumptions of the finance model of the firm as they insinuate that in order to be legitimate, socially responsible behavior must increase wealth for shareholders.[29] Finally, the question of motives arises. Doesn't true CSR require some level of sacrifice? Is "socially responsible" behavior that converges with profitability real CSR, or is it simply strategy posing as social concern?

[29] Margolis and Walsh, "Misery Loves Companies," 278.

Social Responsibility in the "Real World" of Competitive Markets

A major criticism of stakeholder-oriented CSR is that it is naive and not representative of the real world. As argued by the likes of Doane, ("The Myth of CSR"), most, if not all, firms exist to maximize profit. Even if executives have other intentions, competition, the short-term nature of markets, and shareholder ownership forces them to value profit above all. Executives who do not act to maximize profit or at least give it a very high priority will soon find the organizations they are entrusted with run out of business by competitors who do not expend similar levels of resources on "socially responsible" endeavors. Rhetoric to the contrary is mostly window dressing or branding to seek a competitive advantage given current public tastes for dealing with socially responsible firms.

Motives are rarely pure and cannot be openly read; nevertheless, some CSR efforts seem to be genuine and sacrificial. While good public relations may have ensued or profit increased in the long run with respect to some of these decisions, it would be difficult to make a "rational" case for some decisions based on cost-benefit analysis before the fact.

Doane is right, however, to question the genuineness of many CSR efforts. Undoubtedly some (perhaps most) are just public relations strategies and/or "green-washing" strategies. Current corporate structures and the short-term orientation of markets do in fact make it difficult for firms to act outside of the win-win space. If there are truly competing interests, the dice are loaded in favor of profits over social good.

Of course, Doane's suspicions must be held up against the evidence of the link between social and financial performance. Moreover, socially responsible behavior may result in financial gains in unanticipated and indirect ways.

For example, corporations may attain advantages in recruiting and retaining talented employees who wish to work for an organization that shares their values. Or consumers or business partners may be attracted to the firm for similar reasons.[30] While considering stakeholder interests for the sake of profit may not be "socially responsible" behavior in the true sense of the word, this is some evidence to discount the idea that the "real world" of economics is comprised of a set of iron-clad laws that prevent ethical considerations.

Another assumption within some of the CSR literature is the power of consumers to drive change, which Doane properly questions. The gap between intention and actual consistent purchase decisions may well be large at this point. However, the fact that consumer demand has led Walmart to become a large distributor of organic food may paint a slightly more optimistic picture.[31] To address some of these concerns, taking steps toward actual measurability and accountability of CSR is a must if CSR (and CSR reporting) is to be more than public relations spin.

Costco may well be an outstanding example of a firm that is trying to honor the interests of a broad range of stakeholders while managing shareholder expectations and the tensions produced by operating in competitive markets. CEO Jim Sinegal clearly describes the importance of emphasizing company values in building an organization that is sustainable and profitable for the long term.

Norman Bowie, professor emeritus of strategic management and philosophy at the University of Minnesota, has observed a dynamic of irony in the pursuit of profit. Much like the way individuals find the intentional pursuit of happiness elusive, firms that just focus on profit may never acquire it. Rather, those that focus on treating stakeholders well, and for its own sake, may well achieve profit much as individuals who focus on other matters find happiness as a by-product. Borrowing from an old philosophical idea known as the "Hedonic paradox," Bowie has referred to this dynamic as the "profit paradox."[32]

Bowie's observations find some support in the conclusions drawn in the well-known book *Built to Last*, in which authors Jim Collins and Jerry Porras find that companies managed around a deep sense of mission and core values are often more profitable than those operated with the direct goal of profit maximization.[33]

From a Christian perspective, corporate social responsibility entails much more than economic profit. Any model that mandates the maximization of profit (with only law and a nod to "ethical custom" as boundaries) is much too narrow. The central philosophical assumptions supporting this model are questionable in light of Christian values, and managers would be trapped into making some very poor decisions within its confines.

[30] See Remi Trudel and June Cotte, "Does It Pay to Be Good?" *Sloan Management Review* (Winter 2009): 61–68.

[31] Melanie Warner, "Walmart Eyes Organic Food," *New York Times*, May 12, 2006, http://www.nytimes.com/2006/05/12/business/12organic.html.

[32] Norman E. Bowie, "New Directions in Corporate Social Responsibility," *Business Horizons* 34 (July–August 1991): 55–65.

[33] Jim Collins and Jerry Porras, *Built to Last: Successful Habits of Visionary Companies* (New York: HarperCollins, 2004).

Corporations (like all other social institutions) exist to enable human flourishing in all of its dimensions. While profit is necessary and a highly important part of the sustainability of an organization, the direction of the causal arrow should be reversed. Instead of treating stakeholders well for instrumental reasons, profit should be seen as a means to support the achievement of objectives such as the production and distribution of life-enhancing quality products and services, the creation of challenging and rewarding work, and the improvement of local communities. Profit may also be seen as a way to serve shareholders who risk capital but should not be seen as *the* goal of business.

FIVE

Globalization and Christian Ethics

Introduction

Imagine yourself attending one of the economic summits of the G8 or G20 nations (the industrialized nations of the world) in the past few years. As you make your way into the summit, you see numerous protesters with their signs and slogans articulating their objections to key aspects of globalization. You see criticism, for example, of child labor, exploitation of workers, environmental damage, destruction of local communities, and the rich becoming richer at the expense of the world's poor. Though you may not see their presence on the streets, you are surely aware that globalization has its proponents too. They suggest that participation in the global economy is the best hope for the poor to escape poverty and that trade encourages peaceful relations between nations. They may also point out that the competition has increased efficiencies and has contributed to lower prices for many goods that are produced more efficiently and inexpensively around the world.[1]

Globalization refers to the process of tighter economic, political, and social integration/cooperation. This involves a freer flow of ideas, products, services, investment, and labor, and has been made possible by many technological advances, such as the Internet. For example, due to the prevalence of electronic communications, companies can employ people around the world, and it matters less where they live. Electronic and data technology have also enabled the virtually instantaneous flow of investment capital around the world. Barriers to trade have been lowered, and the world economy is more integrated than ever before. The global supply chain for manufacturing has become commonplace. It is not uncommon for manufactured goods to be assembled in steps, with each successive stage taking place in another part of the world. Entrepreneurial activity now has a global focus, and products, services, and capital can all be distributed globally and efficiently, thus lowering prices and making more goods and services available to more people.

[1] For an introduction to the subject of globalization, see Manfred Steger, *Globalization: A Very Short Introduction* (Oxford: Oxford University Press, 2003; 2nd ed., 2009); George Ritzer, *Globalization: A Basic Text* (Malden, Mass.: John Wiley and Sons, 2009). For works on globalization with a distinctly Christian framework, see Peter Heslam, ed., *Globalization and the Good* (Grand Rapids: Eerdmans, 2004); Steven Rundle, ed., *Economic Justice in a Flat World: Christian Perspectives on Globalization* (Colorado Springs: Paternoster, 2009).

2 See, e.g., Colin Read, *Global Financial Meltdown: How We Can Avoid the Next Economic Crisis* (New York: Palgrave Macmillan, 2009), esp. 144–48, "When America Sneezes, the World Catches a Cold."

3 Some of the proponents of globalization include Jagdish N. Bhagwati, *In Defense of Globalization* (New York: Oxford University Press, 2007); Johan Norberg, *In Defense of Global Capitalism* (Washington, D.C.: Cato Institute, 2003); Martin Wolf, *Why Globalization Works,* 2nd ed. (New Haven, Conn.: Yale University Press, 2005).

4 For further reading on some of the overall criticisms of globalization, see Amy Chua, *World on Fire: How Exporting Free Market Democracy Breeds Ethnic Hatred and Global Instability* (New York: Anchor, 2003). For a more guarded criticism of globalization, see Joseph E. Stiglitz, *Globalization and Its Discontents* (New York: W. W. Norton, 2003).

5 For this strand of the globalization literature, see John H. Dunning, ed. *Making Globalization Good* (New York: Oxford University Press, 2004).

6 Walter L. Owensby, *Economics for Prophets: A Primer on Concepts, Realities, and Values in Our Economic System* (Grand Rapids: Eerdmans, 1988). See also Samuel Gregg, *Economic Thinking for the Theologically Minded* (Lanham, Md.: University Press of America, 2001); Victor V. Claar and Robin J. Klay, *Economics in Christian Perspective: Theory, Policy and Life Choices* (Downers Grove, Ill.: InterVarsity, 2007).

This has allowed the benefits of economic growth to spread to regions with heretofore relatively stagnant economies. Critics of globalization have argued that the process has left the poor further behind and simply increased the profits of already large, profitable, and powerful corporations. Further caution about globalization has also come in the aftermath of the global financial meltdown, as concerns about the vulnerability of such a highly interdependent economy have grown substantially.[2]

This chapter and the next one take up the complicated subject of globalization. In this chapter, we will focus on the broader issues of Christian ethics and economics. In the chapter that follows, we will address the more specific ethical issues that arise as a result of doing business in a global context, such as child labor and bribery. The readings in this chapter reflect the broader economic discussion on globalization. Lord Brian Griffiths brings both a European and a Christian perspective on the subject in his article "Globalization, Poverty, and International Development." Griffiths is a former adviser to British Prime Minister Margaret Thatcher and Goldman Sachs and a former director of the Bank of England. Griffiths reflects the more positive assessment of globalization that is characteristic of its proponents.[3] Griffiths draws heavily on the influential Catholic encyclical *Centesimus Annus* of Pope John Paul II. In a second reading, "Globalization and the Poor: Reflections of a Christian Economist," University of San Francisco economist Bruce Wydick articulates some concerns about globalization. Like Griffiths, he approaches the subject from his Christian worldview, but he expresses concerns about unfair trading practices and the impact of globalization on the poorest of the poor.[4] A third selection in this chapter comes from economist Steven Rundle, who essentially accepts that globalization is here to stay and articulates a new vision of corporate responsibility in a global economy. His article "Corporate Social Responsibility in a Globalizing World: What's a Christian Executive to Do?" represents a strand of the literature on globalization that acknowledges the reality of globalization, with a focus on making it as constructive and positive for the world as possible.[5] Rundle's article also provides a link to the previous two chapters in that he provides specific prescriptions for how one can carry out social responsibility amid a competitive global economy.

Economics 101

Before you get into the readings in this chapter, it might be helpful to introduce you to some of the primary concepts that define an economic system. One writer has creatively called his introduction to economics, "economics for *prophets*," in his book by that title.[6] Keep in mind that every economic system in the world today is a mixed system. Since the collapse of socialism in the late 1980s, there is no longer much debate between capitalism and socialism as economic systems, since there are only a handful of avowedly socialist economies remaining around the world (North Korea, Cuba). Rather, the current debate is about whether the global expansion of free market mechanisms is, on balance, harmful or beneficial, particularly to the poor and the developing world. More specifically, the current debate concerns whether economic and social problems (some created by globalization) can be solved by reliance on the market, or whether more government intervention in the market is the solution.[7] These questions are far more complicated given the rapid globalization of the economy in the past two decades, in what author Thomas Friedman calls the "flattening" of the world's economy.[8]

In any economy, the system must address certain basic questions. The most basic questions concern how the goods of society will be distributed and on what basis. That is, as long as theft is illegal, trading of goods and services in the marketplace remains the most efficient way of distributing those goods and services. Other important questions concern ownership of property, deciding which goods and services get produced and what price is charged for them, what wages will be, how to ensure the quality and safety of products, how wealth will be distributed, what level of unemployment is acceptable, and how competition is viewed. In pure market systems, property, particularly the means of production and businesses, is all privately owned. In pure command systems, which characterize socialism, most businesses are owned by the state. In most systems, there are degrees of private ownership, and the differences in the systems have to do with how much is owned or controlled by the state and how much is owned privately. An economy in which government owns a sizable portion of economic assets or controls certain markets is more command oriented. For example, countries that have nationalized health care are command oriented in that segment since government is the employer of doctors and supplier of health care. In some European countries, governments own large portions, and in some cases all, of the airline and energy industries. Some economies tend to be somewhat of a hybrid, as is the case with China, which combines an emphasis on market mechanisms and state ownership of many industries. We would call it a "state-owned market economy." In the United States, business tends to be far more privately owned, and government tends not to be a shareholder in American companies, though in the aftermath of the 2007–9 financial meltdown, the government became a shareholder in General Motors, Chrysler, and some financial firms.

In market-oriented systems, the forces of supply and demand determine what goods and services will be produced, how much they cost, and what workers will be paid. That is, the market determines these elements. In pure

[7] See Rebecca M. Blank and William McGurn, *Is the Market Moral?: A Dialogue on Religion, Economics and Justice* (Washington, D.C.: Brookings Institution, 2004).

[8] Thomas L. Friedman, *The World Is Flat* (New York: Farrar, Straus, and Giroux, 2005). See also idem, *Hot, Flat and Crowded* (New York: Picador, 2009).

command systems, the state, or whatever authority is responsible for economic central planning, decides what will be produced as well as the price level and the wage scale for workers. Again, most economic systems are a mixture of market and command styles when it comes to prices and wages. For example, wages are not entirely determined by market forces in most developed countries due to minimum wage laws set by government. Though formal price controls are rare, tariffs (taxes on imports) are routinely imposed to protect domestic markets from outside competition, which in effect helps determine what products are made and their price.

In pure market systems, competition insures product safety and quality, since consumers will not continue to buy from manufacturers who produce shoddy or unsafe products, ultimately driving them out of business if they do not meet the standards of the marketplace. In command systems, the state with its regulatory agencies is responsible for ensuring safety. In the United States, which has a predominantly market system, this aspect of ensuring safety is highly command oriented. This is even more the case in Europe and Japan. There is relatively little confidence that the market will guarantee consumer safety. Even in market systems where society trusts competition to effect product safety, there is an information time lag during which consumers are unprotected. That is, it takes time for a company's reputation for building unsafe products to become widespread in the marketplace, during which time consumers are unknowingly buying risky products. Other industries, such as energy production and banking, are heavily regulated. In fact, one could argue that the money supply and interest rates are largely controlled by the central bank (the Federal Reserve in the United States) and not set by market forces.

In pure market systems, wealth is distributed according to merit as measured by money, that is, income and net worth. As a result, wealth tends to be more concentrated in fewer hands in this system. In pure command-oriented systems, wealth is distributed more equally, often based on need or on a person's social contribution, such as the way Olympic athletes were rewarded in former Communist countries. But most systems are mixed. In the Western developed world, wealth is redistributed through a progressive tax system, and need plays a significant role in determining who gets certain resources. Politics as well as need influences the distribution of wealth, as the decades of "corporate welfare" and farm subsidies indicate. Some have argued that the more wealth is distributed on grounds other than merit, the fewer incentives there are for people to take risks in starting or expanding businesses, because the tax system takes a higher share of their income the more successful they are.

In market systems, competition is viewed as one of the chief positive elements, encouraging quality and innovation, thus giving consumers better access and cheaper goods and services. Even though competition can at times be cutthroat and go beyond the bounds of civility and even beyond the law, proponents of the market system would argue that the benefits of having an economy based on competition far outweighs the costs. This is what is commonly meant by economist Joseph Schumpeter's "creative destruction."[9] This refers to competition and innovation rendering some products and services, not to mention entire industries, obsolete. For example, the invention of the automobile destroyed the entire horse and buggy industry. The jobs that were lost were considered an acceptable cost of the innovation of the car, which is widely regarded as a net gain.

Market critics counterargue that competition has many destructive elements, which include, for example, jobs being exported overseas with their clear human costs and social dislocations. Again, most systems are mixed and governments frequently restrict competition or minimize its harmful effects. Trade is frequently restricted in order to protect domestic industry. Governments subsidize what they consider key businesses, and in some cases, government subsidies actually give incentives for people not to produce, as in the case of farm supports for agriculture around the world. Governments also intervene periodically to "bail out" companies that have been hurt by normal market forces. For example, many of the largest banks and insurance companies (not to mention U.S. automakers) around the world were bailed out by their governments in the aftermath of the financial meltdown, having been deemed "too big to fail."[10]

[9] This term was coined in Joseph Schumpeter, *Capitalism, Socialism and Democracy* (New York: Harper & Row, 1942), 82–85.

[10] For further reading on these bailouts, see Andrew Ross Sorkin, *Too Big to Fail: The Inside Story of How Wall Street and Washington Fought to Save the Financial System—and Themselves* (New York: Viking, 2009).

READINGS

Globalization and World Poverty
Brian Griffiths
Globalization, Poverty, and International Development (Grand Rapids: Acton Institute, 2007).

When the subject of globalization and world poverty arises, globalization invariably becomes a contentious issue. Its supporters tend to be those who benefit, and its detractors those who have either been bypassed by it, such as numerous sub-Saharan African countries, or those who lose out, such as service workers and farm lobbies in America and the European Union. Many who take part in the debate have an ideological axe to grind, while others are clearly defending vested interests. If, however, the debate is to be rational, it is surely necessary to establish common ground regarding the facts.

This is complicated by the fact that attempts at a definition of globalization tend to be fuzzy although the basic idea is fairly straightforward. *Globalization is the increasing integration or connectedness of nations through increased trade, investment, and the migration of labor.* While the economic dimension is critical to understanding globalization, the process is not limited to the economic realm. In the social sciences, globalization is commonly regarded as multidimensional, crossing cultural, political, military, social, and ecological spheres. At the same time, globalization has led to the emergence of a global consciousness, which is linked to the growth of movements concerned with eradicating poverty and disease, preserving the environment, and maintaining peace.

We should also remember that globalization is not a new phenomenon. The growth of trade in the sixteenth and seventeenth centuries following the voyages of Columbus and Vasco da Gama and the growth in the world economy following the Napoleonic wars associated with the growth of railroads, steam power, and the telegraph were all instances of globalization. Perhaps the belle époque of globalization was the quarter century before World War I. The fact that the two decades following 1918 saw the reemergence and growth of protectionism, economic isolationism, and populism ought to remind us that there is nothing inevitable about globalization.

The Pace of Globalization

The pace of economic integration in the past fifteen years has been simply staggering. Global merchandise exports in recent years have been over 20 percent of world gross domestic product compared with 8 percent in 1913 and less than 15 percent as recently as 1990. Production processes have become increasingly fragmented. Instead of producing goods in a single location, firms have broken the process down into discrete steps and produced or purchased them from the most cost-effective locations. Take, for example, the production of the Barbie doll.

The doll is designed in Mattel's headquarters in El Segundo, California. Oil is refined into ethylene in Taiwan and formed into plastic pellets that produce the doll's body. Nylon hair is manufactured in Japan, while the cotton for her clothing comes from China. The molds for the doll are made in the US as are the paint pigments used to decorate it and the cardboard used for packaging. Assembly takes place in Indonesia and Malaysia. Finally, the dolls are quality tested in California and marketed from there and elsewhere around the globe.[1]

Increased trade has taken place in services as well as goods. There has been dramatic growth in the outsourcing (especially to India) of what were formerly thought of as nontradable services. Companies established in Bangalore have become call centers for retail financial services and railway timetable enquiries, back offices for international accounting and law firms, sources of computer assistance and software development and places at which hospital X-rays, tax returns, and stock market behavior can be analyzed. Over the same period, international financial flows have expanded even more rapidly than trade as have the developments of new, sophisticated financial instruments. The decisions by China, India, and former Communist bloc nations to enter the global economy have amounted to what one commentator has described as a doubling of the world labor force over the past twenty-five years, with the former Soviet bloc adding 260 million people, India 440 million people, and China 760 million people.

Economic Liberalization, Capital Flows, and New Technology

The driving force behind globalization has been a combination of three factors: economic liberalization, increased capital flows, and new technology. In the past twenty-five years, governments have taken deliberate steps to strengthen their economies through deregulation, privatization, and liberalization. These have reduced government ownership and controls and extended the scope of markets. Privatization only started in 1980, yet today most countries in the world have privatized companies and large sectors of their economies. At the same time, entrepreneurs and companies have increasingly invested in emerging markets in their search for higher returns. Two enormous new pools of capital have grown up, each between one and two trillion dollars in size; namely, hedge funds and private equity. Hedge funds are able to make investments using strategies and investments that were not open to traditional institutional investors, such as pension funds and mutual funds. Private equity, namely, investment in private unquoted companies, is playing an important role in the transformation of economies as companies change ownership and are made more efficient through being restructured. In the past, foreign investment tended to finance countries' infrastructure projects and government deficits. Today, however, the growth of hedge funds and private equity has allowed foreign capital to be invested in a broad range of sectors and in a variety of instruments, including equity, debt, and derivatives.

These developments would not have been possible without the new technology associated with the development of microelectronics and the convergence of computers, telecommunications, and information technology. New technology is based on new ideas. In his *The World Is Flat* (2005), Thomas Friedman illustrates how the power of new ideas has produced the Internet, software developments, and search engines and led to advances in digital, mobile, personal, and virtual communication technologies.[2] These in turn have created a much more level playing field between countries and resulted in outsourcing, new supply chains, and new methods of inventory control, which in turn have lowered costs dramatically worldwide.

New technology, in turn, has speeded up the pace of change. To provide some concrete examples:

- The number of people traveling from one country to another doubled between 1980 and 1996, from 260 million to almost 600 million, roughly equivalent to one-tenth of the world's population each year.
- The time spent on international telephone calls rose from 23 billion to 70 billion minutes between 1990 and 1996.
- The cost of a three-minute telephone call from London to New York fell from $50 in 1960 to $3 in 1990 to 35 cents in 1999.[3]

The Global Antipoverty Movement

The scale and impact of globalization has simultaneously highlighted the persistent poverty of many countries, especially in sub-Saharan Africa. Global poverty has been of concern to the international community ever since the reconstruction following World War II, which, among other things, established the International Bank for Reconstruction and Development (World Bank), the International Monetary Fund (IMF), and the General Agreement on Tariffs and Trade (GATT)—the precursor of the World Trade Organization (WTO). Foreign aid was launched by President Truman's Marshal Plan in 1948.

Until the 1990s, foreign aid grew steadily, as did the influence and balance sheet of the World Bank. Foreign aid, however, began to attract increasingly adverse criticism. Not only did it fail to diminish poverty in developing countries, but it facilitated the politicization of economic life and the growth of corruption. The average growth in per capita GDP for the forty-seven sub-Saharan African countries for which data is available for the period 1980–2004 was one-third of 1 percent. Twenty-three of these nations averaged zero or negative growth. Reacting against these problems, foreign aid as a percentage of the GDP of donor countries fell throughout the 1990s.

The advent of the third Christian millennium provided many people with the desire to address these and related issues. In the years running up to 2000, the Jubilee Campaign pressed the G8 countries to restructure and in some cases cancel the debt of a number of poor countries. At the UN Millennium Summit of 2000, 147 heads of state and 189 countries signed a Millennium Declaration making a joint commitment to reduce world poverty by 2015. The Declaration set out a series of goals committed to reducing hunger and poverty, providing universal primary education, tackling disease, and supplying clean water. Funds were set up to fight HIV/AIDS, tuberculosis, and malaria and provide elemental schooling. The United States also set up the Millennium Challenge Account. All of the G8 countries also expressed support for the Doha Development Round of trade liberalization, which was specifically targeted at reducing trade barriers to help developing countries.

Progress in meeting the Millennium Development Goals has been patchy. In some countries, especially in sub-Saharan Africa, the goals will not be met for many years to come. In response to this, Britain's then-Chancellor of the Exchequer Gordon Brown proposed the International Finance Facility, while former British prime minister Tony Blair joined Gordon Brown in creating the Commission for Africa in 2004. In 2005, Britain's presidency of the G8 made Africa one of the two key items on its agenda. This issue was also the reason for the campaign "Make Poverty History," led by Bono and Bob Geldof, and the reason why the series of Live Aid concerts in 2005 focused on Africa more than any other continent. In 2006, over $200 million was pledged by global business leaders in support of President Clinton's initiative for economic development and the fight against HIV-AIDS in Africa.

The movement to act now against global poverty expresses the aspirations of people from all continents, political persuasions, ethnic backgrounds, social classes and across the generations. President Bush spoke on behalf of all rich countries in an interview just before the Gleneagles Summit in July 2005 when he said, "To whom much is given, much is required."

Criticisms of Globalization

Globalization has proved extremely controversial and been subject to enormous criticism. These range from violent protests on the streets of Genoa, Gothenberg, and Washington at meetings of the IMF and World Bank to more reasoned arguments from people such as David Held of the London School of Economics and Joseph Stiglitz, Nobel laureate and former chief economist at the World Bank. Stiglitz has been an outspoken critic of globalization. While he is not opposed to globalization per se, he is critical of the manner in which it has occurred.

> For much of the world, globalization as it has been managed seems like a pact with the devil. A few people in the country become wealthier; GDP statistics, for what they are worth, look better, but ways of life and basic values are threatened. For some parts of the world the gains are even more tenuous, the costs more palpable. Closer integration into the world economy has brought greater volatility and insecurity, and more inequality. It has even threatened fundamental values.[4]

These criticisms are not dissimilar to those expressed by the World Commission on the Social Dimension of Globalization:

> Globalization is generating unbalanced outcomes both between and within countries. Wealth is being created but too many countries and people are not sharing in its benefits. They have little or no voice in shaping the process ... these global imbalances are morally unacceptable and politically unsustainable.[5]

Twelve years after the publication of *Centesimus Annus*, Pope John Paul II returned to the subject of globalization. While recognizing "that globalization in itself is not the problem" he contended that it "exacerbates the conditions of the needy, that [it] does not sufficiently contribute to resolving situations of hunger, poverty and social inequality, that [it] fails to safeguard the natural environment." These difficulties arise, he suggested, because it lacks effective mechanisms of governance for giving proper direction.[6] The more common criticisms made of globalization are the following:

- The rules of the game governing globalization are biased towards the rich countries and against poor countries.
- It has undermined democracy in developing countries because it has compromised their sovereignty in key areas.
- It is facilitating an apparent environmental crisis.
- It is not a win-win situation as the process creates losers in developed as well as developing countries.
- It has forced governments of developing countries to implement polices such as privatization, liberalization and the removal of capital controls which have been inappropriate and damaging.
- It has failed to force rich countries to remove protectionist policies against the exports of developing countries.
- It threatens the international order established after World War II with the founding of the United Nations, as evidenced by the invasion of Iraq in 2003.

Whatever the merits or otherwise of these criticisms, globalization has unquestionably had an impact on culture.

Changing technology has led to changing work practices and changing lifestyles that are often markedly different to local traditions. English has emerged as the dominant language of globalization, but its increasing use poses a challenge for minority languages. Globalization has enabled unprecedented contact between people of different countries, ethnic groups, and cultures. Satellite and cable television have meant that world news in real time can be accessed anywhere in the world.

Pope John Paul II expressed the Church's particular concern over the impact of globalization on culture in the following terms:

> The market as an exchange mechanism has become the medium of a new culture. Many observers have noted the intrusive, even invasive, character of the logic of the market, which reduced more and more the area available to the human community for volunteering and public action at every level. The market imposes its way of thinking and acting and stamps its scale of values upon behavior. Those who are subject to it often see globalization as a destructive flood threatening the social norm which had protected them and the cultural points of reference which had given them direction in life.[7]

He went on to argue that globalization has resulted in changes in technology with relationships moving so rapidly that cultures are unable to respond. "Social, legal and cultural safeguards—the result of people's efforts to defend the common good—are vitally necessary if individuals and intermediary groups are to maintain their centrality." But because globalization introduces new styles of working and living, it risks destroying these safeguards.

Has Globalization Been Successful in Economic Terms?

Centesimus Annus recognized that globalization created "unusual opportunities for greater prosperity." The encyclical notes that whereas it was once thought that poor countries would develop by isolating themselves from the world market, "this view has been proved wrong" (CA 58). It adds that "recent experience has shown that countries which did this have suffered stagnation and recession, while the countries

which experienced development were those which succeeded in taking part in the general interrelated economic activities at the international level" (CA 35). This judgment was subsequently tempered by a statement in May 2003 that, although globalization in itself is not the problem, nevertheless it was "disturbing to witness a globalization that exacerbates the conditions of the needy, that does not sufficiently contribute to resolving situations of hunger, poverty and social inequality, that fails to safeguard the natural environment."[8]

Although the evidence of globalization and economic growth is far from being unambiguously clear, some fairly strong statements can be nevertheless made with confidence. The present period of globalization began in the 1970s, symbolized by China's decision in 1978 to introduce economic reforms, especially in agriculture, and to open its economy gradually to trade and investment. Since then other countries have followed suit and two trends have been apparent. One is that those countries that have chosen to open up their economies to trade and investment have by and large benefited through higher rates of economic growth. The other is that the major factor reducing poverty has been the country's rate of economic growth: the faster the growth rate of a country, the more rapid the decline in poverty.

The evidence for the link between trade liberalization and increased growth comes from three sources. One is the experience of individual countries. Under Chairman Mao, the Chinese economy was a model of socialist economics: it involved public ownership of firms, the mass collectivization of agriculture and land, centralized state planning, price and wage controls, barriers to trade and foreign investment, and a rather inward-looking foreign policy that cut China off from the rest of the world. Since Deng Xiaoping decided to reverse this policy, not least by introducing major reforms in agriculture and liberalizing foreign trade and investment, the Chinese economy has taken off in a spectacular way. Since 1978, China has averaged a growth in real per capita GDP of 9.6 percent per annum. Exports have grown even faster. Foreign investment into China today is around $50 billion per year, roughly equal to the total of all foreign aid given by the wealthier nations of the world to the poorer.

While the results have not been as dramatic, India's experience is not dissimilar. India's economic policy pre-1991 was heavily influenced by Fabian socialism. It was based on wholesale controls of almost every aspect of economic life. Licenses were needed for exports, imports, and production. In the 1960s, growth was modest at 1.4 percent per year and far worse in the 1970s with an annual reduction of –0.3 percent. In 1991, the government decided to change and introduce far-reaching reforms that involved abolishing most licenses, reducing tariffs, and allowing successful companies to expand. In the 1990s, India's growth in real GDP rose to an average of around 4 percent, and since the millennium the figure has risen to over 6 percent. India and China are the most recent and dramatic examples of the benefits which countries have experienced from opening up to trade. Other current examples include Mexico, Vietnam, and Uganda. These were preceded by Hong Kong, Singapore, South Korea, and Taiwan in the 1950s and 1960s. It was the latter countries' experience that played a major role in leading Deng Xiaoping to introduce far-reaching reforms.

A second source of evidence concerning the link between openness to trade and increased growth is cross-country statistical analysis. Countries with noticeably increased exports and imports have also experienced an acceleration in their growth rates. In their analysis of 137 countries, World Bank economists David Dollar and Aart Kraay find that increased trade is associated with more rapid growth and that the poor share proportionately in the rise in incomes.[9]

A final piece of information comes from studies of individual firms. One characteristic of many developing countries is that firms within a particular industry have markedly different levels of productivity. Some firms are very efficient while others are not, the reason being that competition between firms tends to be limited. When trade liberalization is introduced, it becomes much easier for new firms to enter the industry and drive out high-cost, inefficient producers. Trade liberalization, when accompanied by privatization and deregulation, will typically create greater competition and act as a spur to innovation. The net result will be more rapid economic growth.

The second overall trend from empirical research is the way that the increased growth which proceeds from globalization has had a major impact in reducing poverty. David Dollar estimates that in 1977–1978 there were roughly one billion people in India and China living on less than one dollar per day. By 1997–1998 this figure had fallen to roughly 650 million. What is even more remarkable is that over the same period the population of these two countries grew by 700 million. To put the same point differently, the percentage of the population of India and China living on less than one dollar per day fell from 62 percent in 1977–1978 to 29 percent in 1997–1998. Even someone as critical of globalization as Stiglitz has this to say about the poverty reduction in China that has resulted from globalization:

> China's poverty reduction has been truly remarkable. At the one-dollar-a-day standard, the number in poverty has fallen from 634 million to 212 million — more people have been brought out of absolute poverty than the total number living in Europe or America.[10]

Dollar and Kraay also studied the impact of globalization on the poorest fifth of society in eighty countries and found that it directly improves the lot of the poor. As average income rises, they noted, incomes of ordinary poor people rise proportionately. In other words, growth directly benefits the poor. They also found that the more a country opened itself to trade and investment, the better the poor tend to fare.

> This is not some process of "trickle down" which suggests a sequencing in which the rich get richer first and eventually the benefits trickle down to the poor. The evidence, to the contrary, is that private property rights, stability and openness directly and contemporaneously create a good environment for poor households and increase their productivity and income.[11]

Globalization: A Christian Analysis

The growth and acceleration of globalization and the emergence of an antipoverty consensus are clearly two major new developments since the publication of *Centesimus Annus*. I would now like to suggest five distinct Christian perspectives on these developments.

1. Globalization has moral legitimacy, and this is the foundation of its success.

Centesimus Annus rightly observes that one reason for Communism's defeat was the inefficiency of its socialist economic system. The encyclical recognized that "on the level of individual nations and of international relations the free market is the most efficient instrument for utilizing resources and effectively responding to needs" (CA 34). It elaborated upon this by stating that "the mechanisms of the market offer secure advantages: they help to utilize resources better; they promote the exchange of products; above all they give central place to the person's desires and preferences, which, in a contract, meet the desires and preferences of another person" (CA 40). It then posed the question whether establishing a market economy[12] should be the goal not only of former Soviet bloc countries but also of third world countries. The answer was clear but complex.

> If by "capitalism" is meant an economic system which recognizes the fundamental and positive role of business, the market, private property and the resulting responsibility of the means of production, as well as free human creativity in the economic sector, then the answer is certainly in the affirmative.... But if by "capitalism" is meant a system in which freedom in the economic sector is not circumscribed within a strong judicial framework which places it at the service of human freedom in its totality, and which sees it as a particular aspect of that freedom, the core of which is ethical and religious, then the reply is certainly negative. (CA 42)

This statement is based on a theological-anthropological insight, not simply an economic observation. The reason the market economy is successful in producing wealth is that it respects the dignity and freedom of the human person, the importance of property rights, the creativity and enterprise of people, and the duty and dignity of work. All of these biblical principles for economic life are central to Catholic social teaching. The reason for the success of market economies in Europe in the second half of the twentieth century is that they embodied these principles, and the reason for the failure of communist economies over the same period is that they rejected them.

Globalization is the natural extension of the market economy to economic relations between countries. The reasons for the success of globalization in China since 1978 and in India since the early 1990s, and the failure of socialism in these countries before those dates, are precisely those which *Centesimus Annus* identified in recognizing the success of market economies and the reasons for socialism's self-immolation in twentieth-century Europe. Third world countries, and not just India and China, which have successfully reduced poverty by embracing globalization, have done so by enlarging their economies' private sector, strengthening private property rights, opening themselves to trade and investment, and providing incentives for enterprising people to reap the rewards of their own work and risk-taking.

Of course, markets by themselves are not enough. They need to be embodied within a moral culture that respects the dignity of each person, embodies norms of social justice, and has at its core a prevailing ethos that Leo XIII termed "friendship," Pius XI "social charity," Paul VI "a civilization of love," and John Paul II "solidarity." But even with those principles in mind, we ought to note that the implication of *Centesimus Annus'* analysis of capitalism and communism is surely to welcome globalization and to recognize that its moral legitimacy is directly comparable to that of market economies because it is built on the same foundations. Globalization has shortcomings, but the starting point must be the recognition of its moral legitimacy.

2. Liberal market philosophy is an inadequate basis for globalization because it fails to provide a moral and cultural foundation that respects fully the dignity of the human person.[13]

Centesimus Annus insists that the whole of economic life is part of a moral order that is based on Christian revelation and right reason. By contrast, what might be called a "liberal market philosophy" is basically a secularist worldview that is at odds at many points with a Christian perspective. If the market is embodied in an ethical and cultural system that is thoroughly materialistic and in which economic liberty has become autonomous, completely unrelated, and unattached to the objective moral order knowable through faith and reason, then the consequence will be economic injustice and human alienation. To the extent that globalization is embedded in a thoroughly materialistic and libertarian vision of man that has little regard for distributive justice and a circumscribed view of the human person, globalization will be found wanting.

The scenario I have in mind is one in which the market is considered autonomous of any external standard and exists in a society considered to be made up solely of utility-maximizing individuals, who, as buyers or sellers, make their choices free from any of the demands of morality. Perhaps the clearest recent exposition and defense of this position is the work of the Austrian philosopher and economist Friedrich Hayek. Although Milton Friedman popularized this position, it was Hayek who has been its most penetrating philosopher. Despite the origins of economic life being cloaked in the mists of time, Hayek views the growth of capitalism — by which he means not just economic life but also the moral systems and institutions that underpin it — as a spontaneous order, something that evolved without there being any overall plan or design to it. This spontaneous order in the economic sphere is comparable to the growth of language, money, and law in the social sphere, or the growth of crystals, organic compounds, and the evolution of biological species in the physical world.

The crucial point is that Hayek does not believe that this spontaneous order has any ultimate purpose. It has no end to which it is working. It simply expresses the wishes of myriad individuals in the pursuit of their particular objectives. As a consequence, the outcomes of a spontaneous order, namely, what is produced and what is consumed and the consequent distribution of income and wealth find their justification in terms of utility or appeals to "progress." Hayek himself wrote that his own faith in freedom did "not rest on the foreseeable results in particular circumstances but on the belief that it will, on balance, release more forces for the good than for the bad."[14] His justification for minimizing coercion is therefore somewhat utilitarian. Leaving aside the obvious difficulties with the utilitarian basis for Hayek's defense of liberty as essential for progress, it should be stated that Hayek has surprisingly little to say about the content of progress. He even concedes that progress "in the sense of the cumu-

lative growth of knowledge and power over nature is a term that says little about whether the new state will give us more satisfaction than the old." Such a question, Hayek comments, is "probably unanswerable."[15]

For Hayek, however, this does not matter. More important is "successful striving for what at each moment seems attainable," or "movement for movement's sake."[16]

This leaves unanswered some very important questions. Toward what are people moving? What are they becoming in the process of doing so? Moreover, within this framework, globalization becomes understood purely as a natural, spontaneous process, independent of any reference to the morality knowable through reason and, Christians add, divine revelation. It is thus best left to itself.

Hayek is right to point out the complexity of economic development. His observations concerning the often unintended but disastrous consequences that flow from the attempts of well-meaning politicians to improve humanity's lot also repay careful reading. Hayek's basic thesis, however, regarding the autonomy of the market is difficult to reconcile with Christian teaching. Beyond vague appeals to utility and progress and sometimes custom, Hayek is very clear that he rejects any external moral standard by which economic activity should be judged. For Hayek, the demands of the moral life are not "immutable and eternal," determined "outside" the system. Rather, they result from a process of adaptation to changing circumstances and an almost Darwinian process of cultural selection.

If globalization and the culture promoted by globalization are rooted solely within this vision of man, his nature, and his destiny, globalization is likely to take the following forms. First, it will have no external standards of what is right and wrong, just and unjust, moral and immoral, by which its results can be judged. Second, there will be no guarantee that, in the absence of outside intervention, globalization will be a benign process — it will be viewed as simply "evolving" in an almost amoral manner. Third, it provides no assurance that, in a free society shorn of the moral and cultural truth imparted by faith and reason, we can count on globalization producing an evolution of moral beliefs which will generate the values necessary for the success of the market order.

Hayek has relatively little to say about the nature of the human person other than that we are the product of biological and cultural evolution. With the exception of his last work, *The Fatal Conceit*, Hayek's writings also reflect relatively little interest in a range of religious and secular traditions that contain powerful insights into what makes human life distinct from that of other species and which confer upon man a dignity that makes him innately greater than all other earthly creatures. If, however, a person has no capacity for transcendence, or if work in a globalized world is undertaken in what Max Weber called the "iron cage of modern capitalism," or if globalization ultimately results in the development of a hegemonic culture of consumerism, then however successful globalization may be in economic terms, life will be stripped of any noneconomic, nonmaterial meaning and will bring man face to face with the reality of his alienation from what makes man truly human—his moral, spiritual, and cultural dimensions. As John Paul II noted in *Centesimus Annus*:

> Economic freedom is only one element of human freedom. When it becomes autonomous, when man is seen more as a producer or consumer of goods than as a subject who produces and consumes in order to live, then economic freedom loses its necessary relationship to the human person and ends up by alienating and oppressing him. (CA 30)

3. Growing globalization implies a need for improved global governance.

Centesimus Annus acknowledges that globalization creates unusual opportunities for greater prosperity. It adds, however, that "there is a growing feeling that this increasing internationalization of the economy ought to be accompanied by effective international agencies which will oversee and direct the economy to the common good" (CA 58), something which an individual state is not in a position to do. If the type of governance envisaged by John Paul II is to be achieved, three changes are necessary:

1. Increased coordination among powerful countries.
2. Adequate representation from poor countries in the governance of international agencies.

3. International agencies should give sufficient consideration to the needs of the desperately poor in their decision making, even though such countries have little weight in the international markets.

Pope John Paul II returned to this theme a decade later. He observed that in the globalized world in which we live, "the market economy seems to have conquered virtually the entire world" and noted that "it enshrines a kind of triumph of the market and its logic." He later added:

> Globalization in itself is not the problem. Rather difficulties arise from the lack of effective mechanisms for giving it proper direction. Globalization needs to be inserted into the larger context of a political and economic program that seeks the authentic progress of all mankind.[17]

Calls for improved governance have come from many other sources: national governments, international commissions, central bankers, academics, think tanks, journalists, and NGOs. Some of the most radical have come from social democrats such as David Held,[18] who has proposed grandiose schemes for a new "global social contract" and a new "global covenant" between developed and less-developed countries. These would involve democratic reforms of existing global institutions, the creation of new international institutions to deal with the environment, immigration, and security, and the reform of the United Nations itself.

Closely linked to this is the idea of justice. For the Christian, justice is about more than making sure the rules of the game are fair. It is also about the results. It is about what happens to those who are not qualified to play the game. It is also about those who play but get injured. Justice is about the common good of all, not just the rewards of the successful. If globalization is to be just, it is not enough that the poor be heard; the poor must be empowered. Each person created in the image of God is created as a responsible human being. "Love your neighbor as yourself" assumes a legitimate self-love as the basis of responsibility. From the individual, responsibility extends first to the family, then the community, the nation and, ultimately, the world.

4. The scandal of world poverty—the scar on our conscience—should be urgently tackled.

World poverty remains a scar on our conscience. The responsibility of Christians to the poor and the marginalized—the "preferential option for the poor"—did not originate with "liberation theology" and its associated Marxist apparatus. Rather, it is a recurring theme throughout *Centesimus Annus*, two thousand years of Christian tradition and practices, and faithfully reflects the teaching of Jesus himself. At the beginning of his public ministry, Jesus returned to Nazareth where he had been raised and made a public declaration on the Sabbath based on the Old Testament prophecy of Isaiah:

> The Spirit of the Lord is on me,
> because he has anointed me
> to preach good news to the poor.
> He has sent me to proclaim freedom
> for prisoners and recovery of sight
> for the blind; to release the oppressed
> to proclaim the year of the Lord's favor.
> (Luke 4:18, 19)

Spurred by the millennium, most countries of the world have responded by committing themselves to the Millennium Development Goals. In view of the fact that these goals look as if they will be missed by wide margins, especially in sub-Saharan Africa, what can be done?

Economic Development Begins at Home

Centesimus Annus makes it clear that economic development begins at home. Pope John Paul stated:

> Economic activity, especially the activity of a market economy, cannot be conducted in an institutional, juridical or political vacuum. On the contrary, it presupposes guarantees of individual freedom and private property, as well as a stable currency and efficient public services. Hence the principal task of the state is to guarantee this security, so that those who work and produce can enjoy the fruits of their labors and feel encouraged to work efficiently and hon-

estly. The absence of stability, together with the corruption of public officials and the spread of improper sources of growing rich and of easy profits deriving from illegal or purely speculative activities, constitutes one of the chief obstacles to development and to the economic order. (CA 48)

This suggests a number of priorities for the developing countries themselves. One is the need for cutting the cost of doing business. Each year, the World Bank publishes an index of the cost of doing business for most countries of the world and then ranks them from 1 (least cost) to 155 (highest cost). The index measures government regulation and the protection of property rights and is based on ten key characteristics: start-up costs, obtaining licenses, hiring and firing people, registering property, access to credit, protecting investors, paying taxes, trading across borders, enforcing contracts, and closing businesses. In 2005, the number one country on the list was New Zealand, followed by Singapore, the United States, Canada, Norway, Australia, Hong Kong, Denmark, the United Kingdom, and Japan.

The first African country to be listed was Botswana (40) followed by Zambia (67), Kenya (68), Uganda (82), and Nigeria (94). Of the bottom twenty, no less that fourteen were African, and all but one were from sub-Saharan Africa. Nigeria is almost the worst for registering property, Tanzania is very bad for obtaining licenses, hiring and firing, and registering property, while Burkina Faso and the Democratic Republic of Congo are bad at almost everything. Using this information, economists at the World Bank have estimated that countries with better business environments grow faster. They estimate that if a country moved from its position in the worst 25 percent of all countries surveyed to the top 25 percent, this would imply a 2.3 percent increase in its annual growth rate. The conclusion of this work, therefore, is that if countries wish to grow faster and remove poverty, they should seriously reduce the cost of doing business. The Church has conducted successful campaigns to cancel debt, remove trade barriers, and increase foreign aid. An urgent need at present is for the Church to take a lead in campaigning for developing countries to reduce the cost of doing business.

A second priority is the need to tackle corruption. Corruption has a corrosive effect on markets and undermines economic growth. Certain countries are recognizing this and are taking action. The president of the World Bank, Paul Wolfowitz, should be applauded for his courage in making rooting out corruption a priority for the World Bank in 2006.[19]

According to the World Bank, as much as one trillion dollars in U.S. currency changes hands each year in bribes and the bank has uncovered two thousand cases of alleged fraud, corruption, and other misconduct related to its projects since 1991 and has sanctioned more than 330 companies and people. Wolfowitz suggested that World Bank money should not be given to countries that are not serious in tackling this issue. As a result, the World Bank has suspended loans to projects in Kenya, India, Bangladesh, Cameroon, and other countries.

The response of the UK government and the European Union, which publicly criticized Wolfowitz's proposals, was extraordinary. Despite knowing the damage done by corruption, they nevertheless insist on lending taxpayers' money to corrupt governments. Such policies beggar belief, and it should be the Church which speaks out loudly and clearly against them. Thus far, the Church's voice has been largely silent on this matter.

A third priority is building a lean but effective public administration in developing countries that will produce timely statistics; deal efficiently with the issue of licenses and the registering of property; develop explicit standards for company law, governance, and the protection of investors; and ensure an effective legal system for the enforcement of contracts and banking supervision. This should be complemented by the development of independent judiciaries, a free press, and vibrant civil societies.

Trade and Aid

G8 countries have a responsibility to help developing nations undertake the necessary reforms. There are two areas where action especially needs to be taken: trade liberalization and foreign aid. The potential benefits from trade liberalization far outweigh those from foreign aid for two reasons. First, the magnitude of the gains from trade is much greater than that from doubling aid. Global free trade would mean continuing benefits of up to $350 billion per year compared to only $50 billion per year from doubling aid. Second, trade liberalization creates permanent jobs, attracts foreign investment, and, consequently, new technology and innovation.

Another matter requiring attention is the issue of foreign aid. There have been a number of proposals to increase foreign aid dramatically. The UN Millennium Project commissioned by UN Secretary General Kofi Annan in 2002 advocated "a big push of basic investments between now and 2015 in public administration, human capital, and key infrastructure."[20] To meet the Millennium Development Goals, Jeffrey Sachs in *The End of Poverty* proposed a transfer of $100–180 billion each year from 2005 to 2015.[21]

World Bank studies dealing with foreign aid have found, however, that while foreign assistance strengthens growth in countries with good economic policies such as free markets, fiscal discipline, and the rule of law, countries with poor economic policies have not experienced sustained growth regardless of the amount of foreign aid.[22] Other research demonstrates that aid can only help growth temporarily and in certain circumstances. Moreover, if countries fail to strengthen the rule of law, fight corruption, and remove heavy state intervention, then foreign aid will not help. Some studies have even questioned whether there is evidence that aid can improve growth at all.[23]

For the Christian, the problem is how to reconcile the "preferential option for the poor" and hence the need to reach out to the poor, with the research evidence of the ineffectiveness of aid in promoting economic growth. There should be general agreement that God has given the earth for the benefit of the whole of the human race, or what the Catholic Church calls "the universal destination of material goods." Even if we argue that the wealth of G7 countries has been legitimately created by the resourcefulness of its people, given the scale of human suffering, there is still a moral case for some transfer of resources from the rich to the poor countries. But Official Development Assistance — namely funds given by one government to another government — is only one route for effecting such a transfer. If aid is given, it should be given in creative, radical, and more demanding ways. This entails grants, not loans, the continuing importance of conditionality, the use of the private sector and Christian NGOs in the delivery of services, and bilateral rather than multilateral donations that creates greater accountability. Aid should be granted in a more transparent fashion, such as all aid programs should come under independent external scrutiny, which should be open to the public to examine.

One initiative in foreign aid, which embodies some of these features — and which was championed by Gordon Brown as Chancellor of the Exchequer — is the International Finance Facility for Immunization (IFFIm). IFFIm is a new multilateral development institution whose primary purpose is to provide funding for the immunization programs of the Global Alliance for Vaccines and Immunization (GAVI), which covers seventy-two of the poorest countries of the world. Funds are raised on the capital markets against the commitments of the governments of the United Kingdom, Italy, Norway, Spain, Sweden, and France to provide contributions over the next twenty years. GAVI, which was set up in 2000, is a public-private partnership between the WHO, World Bank, UNICEF, the Bill and Melinda Gates Foundation, and others. The objective of IFFIm is to raise $4 billion in U.S. currency between 2006 and 2015, which could lead to the vaccination of more that 500 million people over the next ten years with the objective of preventing the deaths of five million children and five million adults.

5. The Church has the potential to tackle world poverty and to change the culture of globalization in ways that governments and international institutions do not.

It is very easy in considering the challenges of globalization and international development to enter a secular debate, on secular terms, in which the Christian faith has seemingly limited relevance and is reduced to the margins. Jesus, however, was under no illusion of the claims He was making when He declared, "I am the Way, the Truth and the Life." While Christ's kingdom is "not of this world," Scripture makes clear that Christ's kingdom is nevertheless relevant to every aspect of our life in this world. The Church is a witness to that kingdom and because of

that has great potential to influence our world for the better.

Let me provide two concrete examples of what this might mean: the Church in Africa and the leadership of business. All of the initiatives proposed by G8 countries to help sub-Saharan Africa — dealing with debt, aid, trade, and so forth — are "top-down" initiatives. The decisions made at the Gleneagles meeting in 2005 were all "top-down" proposals. The report of the Commission on Africa made eighty recommendations. Of these, seventy-eight recommendations were addressed exclusively to African governments, the governments of donor countries, or a combination of these. The question that needs to be asked concerning such top-down initiatives is how they translate into tangible results affecting the lives of ordinary people in the villages and small towns of rural Africa. Sadly, the perception is that they do not.

It is here that the Church scores highly. If we take sub-Saharan Africa as an example, the Christian Church numbered around sixty million people in 1960. Today that figure is between 350 – 400 million. The Church in Africa is in closer touch with the poor — those living on less than one dollar per day — than any other institution. Moreover, the Church has a stable administrative infrastructure through its provinces, dioceses, and parishes, which is unrivalled and is in marked contrast to the often-failed structures of local government. The Church has a highly respected leadership (unlike the political class in Africa) who are trained, experienced, and live permanently in the communities they serve. This is a vivid contrast to aid workers and officials of international institutions. Through the provision of schools, hospitals, clinics, dispensaries, and more recently, micro-finance initiatives, the Church has a proven track record in helping the poor.

This should not surprise us. In *Deus Caritas Est*, Pope Benedict XVI stated:

> For the Church, charity is not a kind of welfare activity which could equally well be left to others, but is part of her nature, an indispensable expression of her very being. (DCE 25)

The Church in Africa is a sleeping giant with enormous potential. The challenge faced by Christians in wealthy countries is how we can serve the Church in Africa so that in turn it can most effectively serve its people.

Another area of enormous potential influence is business leadership. We have argued that the sine qua non for economic development is the creation of a vibrant private sector in developing countries. Successful private sector companies provide jobs, training, exports, and community involvement. Christians ought to be committed to shaping companies in ways that allow people to develop and pursue excellence. Throughout G7 countries, there are thousands of Christians in positions of business leadership, not least in those companies that are at the heart of globalization. There will be others, maybe of other faiths or even no faith, who will have equally high ideals for corporate life. Once again, I believe that the Church is in a unique position to mobilize its members to take responsibility and leadership. To cite Benedict XVI again:

> In today's complex situation, not least because of the growth of a globalized economy, the Church's social doctrine has become a set of fundamental guidelines offering approaches that are valid even beyond the confines of the Church. (DCE 27)

Conclusion

To conclude these reflections, I would like to summarize my thoughts:

1. Globalization and the scandal of world poverty are two of the most important "new things" on the global agenda since the publication of *Centesimus Annus*.
2. Globalization has been an economic success. It has reduced poverty and raised per capita income in countries such as China, India, Mexico, Vietnam, Brazil, Russia, and Uganda.
3. Globalization has moral legitimacy because its foundations rest on principles such as respect for the dignity of the individual; the creativity and enterprise of persons; the responsibility to work; and the need for equity and justice, private property rights, and wealth creation.
4. A narrow liberal philosophy that is ultimately reducible to the slogan "free to choose" is an inadequate basis for globalization because it has no external points of reference. It has no absolute moral standards; it has no concept of truth; and it promotes a deficient anthropology of man.
5. Globalization is in danger of stalling because of powerful vested interests. The Church has made it clear that it has never opposed globalization as such. Its criticisms are: (a) that it has not been managed properly, and (b) that it could become the vehicle for a "libertarian" consumerist culture.
6. If globalization is not to stall, it urgently needs legitimacy in terms of a moral framework that explains and promotes not just wealth creation as a moral imperative but also the ways in which poor countries can benefit and the environment can be protected.
7. The architecture and governance of international institutions have simply not kept pace with globalization. The G8 group of countries needs to be enlarged. The IMF needs to return to its original and rather narrow mandate. The World Bank needs to focus its attention on technical assistance, with loans being replaced by grants.

    International institutions need to be more transparent, more accountable, and need to require greater representation in their governance by developing countries.
8. Global poverty is an international scandal and its removal should be a priority for the Christian Church. Fighting poverty must start with developing countries themselves by establishing an independent judiciary, a free press, and a vibrant market economy open to trade and foreign investment. Corruption is a major problem facing poor countries and a major constraint on growth and prosperity. The Christian Church could and should do far more to fight corruption than it has done to date.
9. The G8 countries must show the political will to make globalization acceptable to all countries. Trade liberalization is the priority, though there is some role for aid. The Doha Round should be revived and completed to help developing countries

increase their exports and access to international markets. The current manner in which foreign aid is given needs to change radically. It should be given conditionally, as grants not loans, and primarily through the private sector. Government to government aid should be radically reduced.

10. The Church has an enormous opportunity to shape the culture of globalization through the proclamation of the Christian gospel and through the creation of faith-based institutions that can fight poverty, disease, hunger, ignorance, and war.

Notes

1 Another example was given in the 1998 Annual Report of the World Trade Organization that describes the production of a typical "American" car. "Thirty percent of the car's value goes to Korea for assembly, 17.5 percent to Japan for components and advanced technology, 7.5 percent to Germany for design, 4 percent to Taiwan and Singapore for minor parts, 2.5 percent to the UK for advertising and market services and 1.5 percent to Ireland and Barbados for data processing." This means that 63 percent of a typical American car is made outside of the United States in eight different countries.

2 Thomas L. Friedman, *The World Is Flat: A Brief History of the Twenty-First Century* (New York: Farrar, Straus and Giroux, 2005).

3 1990 prices.

4 Joseph E. Stiglitz, *Making Globalization Work* (London: Allen Lane, 2006), 292.

5 World Commission on the Social Dimension of Globalization, "A Fair Globalization: Creating Opportunities for All" (2004). http://www.ilo.org/public/english/wcsdg/docs/report.pdf.

6 John Paul II, Address to the Members of the Pontifical Academy of Social Sciences (2 May 2003). http://www.vatican.va/holy_father/john_paul_ii/speeches/2003/may/documents/hf_jp-ii_spe_20030502_pont-acad-sciences_en.html.

7 John Paul II, Address to the Members of the Pontifical Academy of Social Sciences (27 April 2001). http://www.vatican.va/holy_father/john_paul_ii/speeches/2001/documents/hf_jp-ii_spe_20010427_pc-social-sciences_en.html.

8 John Paul II, Address to the Members of the Pontifical Academy of Social Sciences (2 May 2003).

9 David Dollar and Aart Kraay, "Growth Is Good for the Poor," World Bank Policy Research Working Paper 2587 (Washington, D.C., 2001).

10 Stiglitz, *Making Globalization Work*, 294.

11 Dollar and Kraay "Growth Is Good for the Poor," 26.

12 I strongly support *Centesimus Annus'* recommendation that phrases such as "market economy," "business economy," or "free economy" should be used instead of the word *capitalism*. The latter carries excessively negative overtones in many countries and is, after all, a Marxist term.

13 This section draws heavily on a part of my essay, "The Challenge of Global Capitalism—A Christian Perspective," in *Making Globalization Good*, ed. J. H. Dunning (London: Oxford University Press, 2003).

14 Friedrich Hayek, *The Constitution of Liberty* (London: Routledge & Kegan Paul, 1960), 31.

15 Ibid., 41.

16 Ibid.

17 John Paul II, Address to the Members of the Pontifical Academy of Social Sciences (2 May 2003).

18 See David Held, *Global Covenant: The Social Democratic Alternative to the Washington Consensus* (Cambridge: Polity Press, 2004).

19 See "Wolfowitz's Corruption Agenda," *Washington Post*, 20 February 2006.

20 *United Nations Millennium Project Overview Report* (New York: United Nations, 2005), 19.

21 Jeffrey Sachs, *The End of Poverty* (New York: Penguin Press, 2005).

22 See, for example, Craig Burnside and David Dollar, "Aid, Policies & Growth" (World Bank Policy Research Department, June 1997).

23 See, for example, William Easterly, "Can Foreign Aid Buy Growth?" *Journal of Economic Perspectives* 17, no. 3 (2003): 23–48.

Questions for Discussion and Reflection

1. Do you agree with Griffiths that globalization has been an economic success? Why or why not?

2. Griffiths observes that globalization has made the poor better off, and it has also increased the disparity in wealth between the rich and the poor. Do you see this disparity as a problem, or is it acceptable as long as the poor are better off than before?

3. Griffiths asserts that "globalization has moral legitimacy." On what basis does he make that statement? Do you agree with his view?

4. Griffiths suggests that democratic institutions such as a free press, protection of private property, and an independent judiciary supporting the rule of law are essential for globalization to benefit a country. Do you agree with Griffiths? What do you think of the example of China, which has achieved remarkable economic growth while retaining its authoritarian political structure?

Globalization and the Poor: Reflections of a Christian Economist

Bruce Wydick

Prism 32 (2007): 8–12, 15.

Globalization has brought about a level of economic contact between nations that is unparalleled in our world's history. In the last 20 years, international trade has increased nearly fourfold, and foreign direct investment has increased nearly tenfold. This has created relationships between rich and poor countries that have become both complex and controversial. How should a Christian think about the difficult issues surrounding economic globalization?

I would like to consider economic globalization from the standpoint of three major principles that run throughout the Scriptures, the objective being to help us as Christians to think more clearly and critically about globalization and to consider our roles in the midst of it.

The first biblical principle is that God clearly cares about the poor and about the response of the rich to the poor among them. We see this clearly throughout the Bible, from Deuteronomy 15:4, Psalm 82:3, and Amos 2:7 to Acts 10:4 and innumerable references in the Gospels and Epistles, such as Matthew 19:21 and James 2:3. Psalm 82 summarizes these texts well with its exhortation to "defend the cause of the weak and the fatherless, and maintain the rights of the poor and the oppressed." The implication is unequivocal: Christians cannot support social and economic structures that systematically degrade the poor and cause them to remain mired in poverty.

The second biblical principle is that interdependence between people is a community ideal. Throughout the Bible, God consistently upholds people who offer their specialized skills for the benefit of the community, whether it be in construction (Exod. 35:10), metalworking (1 Kings 7:14), woodcutting (Eccles. 10:10), poetry (Ps. 45:1), or music (Ps.150:3), not to mention spiritual gifts (Rom. 12:6 and 1 Cor.12:4).

This is also clear from the way that God expects his church to function, not as a collection of autono-mous clones but as distinct individuals, each endowed with different gifts to offer the larger community. As the apostle Paul writes, "Each person has his own gift from God; one has this gift, the other has that" (1 Cor. 7:7). These gifts are offered and exchanged with the presumption that everyone in the community benefits from the exchange. It is clear that, wherever possible, God values interdependence over independence.

The third biblical principle is that God is not a patriot. God loves and cares for people from all nations: "There is neither Jew nor Greek ... for all are one in Christ Jesus" (Gal. 3:28); "make disciples of all nations" (Matt. 28:19); "from every nation standing before the Lamb" (Rev. 7:9). Again, the implication from this principle is clear: Christians cannot favor social and economic structures that provide dispro-portionate benefit to those within their own nation. Everybody in the world is equally valuable and impor-tant to God. This is a tough one for many who would like to base economic and foreign policy on "American interests." (I like the bumper-sticker response to the ubiquitous "God Bless America" stickers: "God Bless Everyone—No Exceptions.")

Other important principles are also manifest in Scripture; however, I would contend that none of these other principles trumps those I have men-tioned as a lens through which we can critically analyze issues of economic globalization. And from these three principles I first would like to propose that trade and exchange are inherently good things that—in the vast majority of cases—should win the support of Christians who share God's concern for all of the world's people. Here we see a clear intersection between faith and reason, for it has long been under-stood that exchange is a fundamental building block to the well-being of any community. Interestingly, the first great economist, Adam Smith, believed that exchange would only be mutually beneficial if two parties each held a mutual absolute advantage over the other at producing a certain good. This would imply that specialization and exchange could only benefit a highly endowed party if it exchanged with a second highly endowed party and if the second was more skilled at producing something than the first. Following this line of reasoning, we can easily see how the poor could get left out: What if a person or country with low skills doesn't have an absolute advantage over anybody else at producing any one thing?

Fortunately, the 19th-century economist David Ricardo demonstrated that Adam Smith was wrong. What he showed (and what has remained convincing to this day) was that it is comparative advantage rather than absolute advantage that yields the mutually beneficial gains from exchange. This is very good news for the poor, because what it means is that no matter how low a person or country's relative level of skills may be, that person or country still has something valuable to offer the rest of the community. This is also good news for trade, based on biblical principle #1. It says that endowments in skills (while they do help determine the level of a party's income after exchange) are irrelevant to one's attractiveness as an exchange partner. In other words, the poor have an equally important role in trade and exchange, and the poor can benefit by exchanging with the rich and vice versa (as well as the rich with the rich and the poor with the poor).

Consequently, it is hard to find a trained economist anywhere who fundamentally disagrees with biblical principle #2. Some on the left, including the Christian left, have argued that trade between rich countries and poor countries is inherently exploitative. The truth is that the basis for international trade is no different from the basis for specialization and exchange between individuals. At a fundamental level, you can think of your purchase of a good or service as involving the trade of your money for someone else's time and the other person trading his time for your money.

The basis for exchange, then, is in harnessing relative differences in people's productivity between various economic activities. For example, suppose you are both a very good computer programmer and a very good lawn mower. You can earn $20 per hour building web pages. Alternatively, you could mow your lawn, which would take you one hour. Suppose the cost of my time is only $5 per hour (which I earn for, say, babysitting), but it would take me two hours, or twice as long, to mow your lawn as it would for you. However, it would take me forever to design a web page because my technical skills are low and I don't know how.

Based on this example, you are more productive than I in both activities, yet it will benefit both of us for you to hire me for somewhere between $10 and $20 to mow your lawn, between the opportunity cost of my time to mow your lawn and the opportunity cost of your time. In fact, given that a bunch of people like you and me exist out there, the market rate for lawn-mowing will lie somewhere in this range, and for any price in between we are both going to benefit — you will pay less than the opportunity cost of your time, and I will get more than the opportunity cost for my time. These simple kinds of transactions constitute one of the foundational building blocks of an interdependent society (which is a good thing by the standards of biblical principle #2).

The application of the analogy to trade between rich and poor countries is plain, since international trade is just a more complicated extension of this example. International trade leverages differences in relative productivities between countries to create an outcome after exchange that is better for both than in the absence of exchange. The level of each country's income after trade, however, is going to be a function of the productivity of that country's workers. This is determined by education, the amount of capital and technology people work with, and the relative scarcity of labor in a country relative to its capital and technology.

Terms like "fairness" and "exploitation" are problematic when talking about trade, and should be used with more care than they usually are. In our example, we could say that our exchange is not fair unless I end up making the same wage as your $20 after the transaction. On the other hand, we also could say that paying me a wage equal to yours is not fair because of your relatively higher education. We could also say that our exchange is not fair unless the lawn-mowing wage splits the surplus between our reservation points at $15. We could say that our exchange is not fair unless you pay me a wage upon which I could live comfortably, by your definition of comfortably or mine, or that you are exploiting me unless any one of these conditions are met, or that I am exploiting you if the standard is exceeded.

The real issue, which is obscured in most discussions about trade and globalization, is related to a cognitive bias. We are often unaware of the extent of poverty in the developing world until we come into contact with it, which has happened more frequently through economic globalization. We think that trade has caused poverty when it has really just exposed us to it. On a missions trip to Guatemala a few years ago, we took a break from what we were doing to take a five-mile hike up a very steep volcano. Getting close to the top, we encountered a Mayan peasant family carrying wood back down to the village to cook their food and heat their home. They carried the wood lashed to their backs. The father was carrying perhaps 100 pounds, the mother maybe 75 pounds, and the children 30–50 pounds each, an agonizing journey down to the village several miles below that would make any chiropractor cringe. The desperate poverty of rural peasants is largely hidden; the 50-cents-an-hour wage in textile manufacturing plants (i.e., "sweatshops") to make the shoes we import may be less so.

However, the latter reflects the former: Most people in developing countries are extremely poor. International trade does not make them worse off. It typically makes them better off—but starting from a tragically low base. By no means am I suggesting that the typical export-driven textile firm in a developing country represents a pleasant work environment. But I have been in many foreign manufacturing plants, and I have never seen labor performed that was as punishing and degrading as what I have seen in the rural areas of developing countries. Sadly, this is probably why such jobs are so often highly sought after.

But if international trade offers so many improvements, then why do so many people seem to oppose it? The answer is that while trade increases social welfare overall in a trading country, within countries there are both winners and losers from trade.

The winners in the typical pattern of today's economic globalization include (1) consumers in both rich and poor countries; and (2) workers who possess skills that are associated with a country's actual or potential exports, which would include, say, aircraft workers in the United States, automobile workers in Mexico, and garment workers in Asia.

The losers in the typical pattern of today's economic globalization essentially consist of one group: workers who possess skills that are associated with a country's actual or potential imports. Examples of these would be garment workers in the United States, corn farmers in Mexico, and vegetable growers in France. In these examples, productivity relative to wages is too low compared to other places in the world, resulting in a diminution of these industries under trade and an often painful dislocation of these workers to other industries.

The pain of the relatively small group of losers from trade is more sharply felt than the gain of the larger number of winners. As a result, the voice of the losers is disproportionately factored into the formulation of trade policy. Part of the issue is, again, a cognitive bias with respect to the benefits and costs of international trade. When a plant closes due to pressures from international competition, it makes newspaper headlines. However, when a handful of jobs are added to thousands of previously existing firms, or when a new firm starts up and creates a few jobs due to expanded international opportunities, no one notices much—even if, on the whole, the benefits to people outweigh the costs.

Here is how trade affects the poor across the world today: Trade typically hurts poor workers by putting downward pressure on wages in rich countries like the United States and helps poor workers by putting upward pressure on wages in developing countries. This would seem to then create an ethically ambiguous effect of trade based on biblical principle #1, but this is where biblical principle #3 comes into play. As Christians, we cannot oppose economic globalization because we favor the well-being of our workers over workers in other countries.

As such, "Buy America" campaigns are inconsistent with a biblical view of justice. On the contrary, because workers in other countries are poorer than even the poorest of our displaced workers, we should welcome new opportunities that arise for workers in the developing countries while supporting a strong social-safety net and generous retraining and educational programs for our own displaced workers at home. We should also advocate for the humane treatment of workers everywhere, through political pressure and being wise about the products we buy. Low wages in developing countries do not have to equal human degradation.

Where else can Christians play an active role in ensuring that economic globalization develops in a way that is consistent with God's concern for the poor in all countries? One obvious action that Christians can take is to support the interests of the developing countries in the Doha Round of the world trade talks. The Doha Round was initiated in late 2001 to incorporate the poorest countries of the world into a free and fair global trade system and to address issues that were neglected by the previous Uruguay Round, concluded in spring 1994.

As the Doha Round began, the World Bank had estimated that better poor-country access to rich-country markets would increase world income by $520 billion and would lift 144 million people out of poverty by 2015. But both the United States and the European Union have consistently formulated policies based on the special interests of their own producers over their own consumers and the welfare of poor farmers in developing countries. Such policies violate all three biblical principles that I mentioned: God's concern for the poor, favoring interdependence over independence, and the fact that God is not a patriot.

Support of economic justice in trade negotiations implies taking a strong stand against trade policies that favor domestic interests, especially of the rich, over the welfare of the poor in developing countries. One clear example of this is the system of subsidies, tariffs, and non-tariff barriers in rich-country agriculture. In many instances, agriculture represents a comparative advantage for poor countries. When rich governments shower their (often corporate) farmers with subsidies and import-killing tariffs at the taxpayer's expense, it is devastating to peasant farmers in developing countries, who otherwise would enjoy a comparative advantage in the export of such crops.

Agricultural trade protection in the United States and the European Union amounts to a staggering $300 billion per year, approximately six times the amount these nations spend on foreign aid. In fact, some African leaders have even stated that they would be happy to have their foreign aid budget cut to zero if only the rich countries would remove these oppressive trade barriers in agricultural products.

The U.S. share of this $300 billion is mighty. In no small part this is a result of the Bush administration-sponsored Farm Bill 2002, which represented an 80-percent increase in agricultural spending to subsidize and protect U.S. agricultural products such as barley, corn, cotton, rice, and wheat. Because votes from senators in the low-population farm states have a disproportionate impact on trade policy and these senators are heavily lobbied by corporate farming interests, agricultural subsidies have come to represent an egregious form of U.S. corporate welfare that exacts a destructive toll on farmers in the developing countries.

One of the more appalling examples is the $4 billion in agricultural subsidies that 25,000 U.S. cotton farmers receive to grow $3 billion worth of cotton. According to the International Cotton Advisory Committee, an international consulting organization, these U.S. cotton subsidies have caused a 26-percent decline in world cotton prices. These massive cotton subsidies help keep 15 million cotton farmers mired in poverty from some of the poorest countries in West Africa, including Benin, Chad, Mali, and Burkina Faso. Notice that if farming costs for cotton farmers in these countries are, say, one-half of revenues, this means that U.S. cotton subsidies cut household income by more than half for these rural families! Such policies clearly contradict biblical principles #1 and #2 but are ironically supported by the "Bible Belt" states of the Midwest.

Concerned Christians should support the efforts of the WTO to force the removal of the subsidies for the benefit of impoverished farmers in developing countries, particularly in West Africa, and should vote senators and representatives out of office who favor U.S. agricultural protection.

Another crucial role that Christians can play is to consistently support policies and programs that provide economic opportunities for the poor in developing countries. The remedy for poverty is not to discourage international trade but instead to raise wages and living standards in developing countries by helping them to invest in education, improve health, foster appropriate technology transfer, empower the entrepreneurial poor with microfinance, and create stable and just governance structures that promote indigenous economic activity, along with a host of other potentially helpful approaches. Any effort to empower the poor and make them more economically productive, even in domestic industries, will put upward pressure on wages and working conditions in export industries.

Christians concerned about the poor need to think smart about globalization. We need to learn to partner with the poor in developing countries by allowing them access to our markets and promoting policies that allow them to thrive in an environment with increasing levels of productivity and economic opportunity.

Action Steps for Christians in an Age of Globalization

1. Let globalization work directly for the poor by directly purchasing the products of artisans in developing countries through online websites such as PEOPLink.org. Encourage indigenous artisanship and artistic creativity in developing countries at all levels.

2. Christians must support efforts to protect the environment during the process of economic development and globalization. Develop a long-term relationship with an organization that is doing ongoing work to protect the environment in developing countries, such as EarthCare, Floresta (a wonderful Christian NGO promoting reforestation), Evangelical Environmental Network, or Oxford's Christian environmental group, Sage.

3. Support efforts to empower entrepreneurs in developing countries via microfinance. Directly provide a microloan to an entrepreneur in a developing country via Kiva.org.

4. Sponsor a child through a Christian NGO such as Compassion International, World Vision, or Proyecto Fe, and visit your child in his or her home country. This is one of the most basic ways to make a difference. Children receiving a quality education in developing countries are more likely to acquire the skills that enable them to reap the positive gains from a globalizing world.

5. Write your senators and representatives, urging them to oppose U.S. domestic agricultural subsidies. Write letters to the editor of your local newspaper articulating your support for the Doha Round of the WTO trade talks as they seek to eliminate agricultural tariffs, quotas, and subsidies in Europe, Japan, and the United States that discriminate against poor farmers in developing countries.

6. Reflect on the teachings of Scripture about God's love for all peoples of the world. Eschew a patriotism that favors domestic interests over the interests of the poor in other countries.

7. Pray for a globalization that yields equal access to markets for the poor, protects the global environment, and promotes the common good rather than the interests of the few.

Questions for Discussion and Reflection

1. What are the three main principles that Wydick uses to evaluate globalization?
2. What do you think of the notion that "God is not a patriot"?
3. How does Wydick view international trade affecting the poor today?
4. Do you agree with Wydick that "Buy American" campaigns are inconsistent with a biblical view of justice?

Corporate Social Responsibility in a Globalizing World: What's a Christian Executive to Do?

Steven Rundle

Business and Professional Ethics Journal 23, no. 4 (2004): 171–83.

Introduction

Several years ago John Houck and Oliver Williams (1996) produced a book entitled *Is the Good Corporation Dead?* It was prompted by the question of whether globalization is changing—or worse—eliminating, our modern sense of corporate social responsibility (CSR). As is often the case with edited compilations, there was a range of opinions expressed, both about what defines CSR and what should be done to save it. But if there was a common theme, it was that while the "good" corporation is not dead, it is certainly facing new challenges because of globalization. To this I would add that new *opportunities* for CSR are emerging as well. Globalization is expanding the reach of even the smallest businesses, and with that comes the capacity to do great harm or great good. The CSR debate more often emphasizes the former; this essay will focus on the latter.

Anyone familiar with the CSR debate knows that the only real difference between the concerns being raised today—corporate obligations toward employees and other stakeholders, the ethics of outsourcing, downsizing, and so on—and those raised in past decades, is the global nature of today's marketplace. Where once the debate focused on the ethicality of, for example, outsourcing certain stages of the production process to low-wage states like South Carolina or Mississippi, now the sharpest criticism is reserved for those who use overseas sources.

There is one more difference that is of particular interest to Christians: Many of the countries that are now wide open to foreign trade and investment have been the most challenging for Christian missionary efforts. Christians in these countries often represent small, persecuted minorities, and the countries themselves are often plagued by problems stemming from social and economic underdevelopment. Because of globalization, a new route is opening by which the church can pursue its transformational calling.

Specifically, Christian businesspeople are doing what was once the exclusive purview of missionaries; that is, they are having a material, social, *and even a spiritual* impact in some of the poorest and most isolated places in the world. This essay will elaborate on how this is happening, and specifically on how corporate executives can pursue this mission while remaining faithful to their moral and legal responsibility to shareholders.

Before making that case, let me begin by saying that there is no inherent contradiction—with one qualification—between the norms of the Christian faith and the so-called "classical" view of CSR. This view maintains that corporate executives are responsible, first and foremost, to their shareholders. Not only is corporate law in this country unambiguous on this point, but such a position is entirely consistent with biblical teachings on stewardship and the proper roles of owners and managers; or, if you will, principles and agents.[1] The caveat, as Rae and Wong (1996) correctly observe, is that sometimes the classical view is construed as justification for adhering only to the minimum legal requirements, even when such a position conflicts with biblical standards of justice and integrity. There are clearly times when doing "the right thing" conflicts with "the most profitable thing," and the stricter moral laws should be brought to bear in cases where local or national laws are ambiguous or nonexistent.

For people of faith, this "higher standard" argument goes even further, because moral standards are themselves often hard to define. Take the CSR debate for example. If corporations simply "do no harm," have they fulfilled their responsibilities as members of society? Or does social responsibility require something sacrificial (like philanthropy, or above average employee benefits, or a "no layoff" policy) that has a measurably negative impact on the corporate bottom line? As it turns out, the definition of CSR, like pornography, is in the eye of the beholder. Reasonable people can and do disagree, sometimes sharply. This is why I prefer the term "significance" over "responsibility." The absence of significance is *insignificance*, and it is hard to imagine any Christian being satisfied with that. To be significant is to have a lasting, positive impact on people. Yet some businesses, while legally and socially responsible according to the minimalist definition, add little in the area of significance. In fact, they may even have a *negative* impact on people. Significance therefore represents a higher standard because it connotes some level of proactive involvement in the needs of others.

This higher standard argument is also consistent with biblical teachings about our purpose in this world. Specifically, the Bible says that we were created for good works, that we should use our resources, opportunities, and even our positions of authority in ways that benefit others.[2] Good works will not get us *into* heaven, but once our relationship with God is made right, good works become central to our life's purpose. How does a Christian, particularly one working for a company that is indifferent to the teachings of the Bible, reconcile this responsibility to do good works with his or her legal and moral responsibilities to shareholders?

It starts by recognizing that self interest is also consistent with biblical teachings. For example, in the New Testament we are told to look after *not only* our own interests, *but also* the interests of others.[3] Indeed, the Bible frequently either appeals to our self-interest or encourages us to take care of ourselves, both individually and collectively. In business, this means making sure the company we work for remains profitable. Obviously this should not be taken to mean profitability at any cost, but still, doing business well and doing it profitably is not inherently inconsistent with living a life of service unto others, as we will see.

I am convinced that at some level most Christian executives understand this and try to faithfully carry out their dual mission of serving shareholders and doing good unto others, especially the less fortunate. The challenge is in finding appropriate ways

to integrate both responsibilities into a single business strategy. Given the increasing pressure on firms to "go global," this means understanding how global business strategies such as offshore outsourcing and foreign direct investment can be used not only for the firm's benefit, but also for the material and spiritual benefit of the world's less fortunate. Accordingly, this essay begins with a brief look at why businesses, even relatively small ones, are "going global," followed by a discussion about how, even without any overt Christian motivation or influence, a global business strategy can contribute to the economic and social development of a nation. We then look at specific ways a company can benefit others while pursuing a global business strategy.

Globalization and the Disintegration of the Production Process

The progressive integration of the global economy has led, ironically, to a progressive *disintegration* of the production process (Feenstra, 1998). Large, vertically-integrated firms, which were the hallmark of the so-called "Fordist" approach to manufacturing, have given way to global networks of smaller, more entrepreneurial firms. Behind this trend have been several factors. One, as Hoogvelt (1997) explains nicely, is the inherent rigidity of Fordism itself; the cost advantages were critically dependent on being able to produce long runs of identical products, and growth depended on the "continuous and uninterrupted expansion of market demand" (p. 93). Over time the system proved vulnerable to fluctuations in the business cycle and the fleeting nature of consumer tastes, which led to a vicious cycle of overproduction, underutilization of fixed capacity, layoffs, losses, and ultimately, factory closures. The deathblow to Fordism was dealt when the Japanese began producing customized products that also benefited from the cost savings of mass production.

A second and perhaps more obvious reason behind the disintegration of production is economic liberalization, particularly in the developing world. The shortcomings of the many post-colonial era experiments in protectionist, inward-oriented development strategies are well known.

These strategies, which restricted the inflow of foreign investment and foreign-made goods, not only failed to deliver economic prosperity, but ultimately led to a *reduction* in the overall quality of life for the average citizen. Today, all but the most autocratic governments have rejected those strategies and are now aggressively seeking to attract foreign investment as a means of catching up with the rest of the world. Indeed, according to the United Nations Conference on Trade and Development (UNCTAD, 2004), there were nearly 1,900 regulatory changes made worldwide between 1991 and 2003 in the area of foreign investment. Of these, an overwhelming ninety-four percent of these changes were aimed at making national economies more attractive to foreign companies.

The increasing sophistication of today's consumer is a third reason why the production process is becoming more globalized and disintegrated. The freedom that businesses now have to compete almost anywhere, combined with the ability to efficiently customize, means that consumers have more choices and more information than ever before. They are using their increased bargaining power to demand higher quality, greater variety, better service, and lower prices. In order to remain competitive, firms have little choice but to pay close attention to the specialized needs of their customers. The change is particularly striking overseas. In the past, multinational corporations (MNCs) treated developing countries with what Prahalad and Lieberthal (1998) describe as an "imperialist mindset," that is, as places where they could squeeze new profits out of outdated products.

This mindset is now giving way to a realization that market share can no longer be built by remaining indifferent to the specialized needs of foreign customers. Instead, the firms must become a trusted part of the local communities in which they hope to do business, which in turn requires having a significant investment in the form of service, marketing, and research and development capabilities in each market.

The cumulative result of these trends has been a marked increase in competition, both at home and abroad. The pressure to innovate and improve service is unrelenting. Geographical distance is no longer the defense against competition that it once was. The small manufacturing operation in Indiana is not only competing against other Midwestern firms, but also against manufacturers from the other side of the globe. This part of the globalization challenge is well known. What is often overlooked in the furor over globalization, however, is that not only are foreign firms competing in our home turf, but our own firms are competing—often successfully—in foreign markets. Economic liberalization cuts both ways, and firms of all sizes are discovering that their very survival often requires thinking more globally in terms of their competition, and their suppliers. In short, "going global" is no longer as risky as it once was; *avoiding* globalization more often carries the greater risk today.

For developing countries, multinational corporations represent instant credibility and access to the global economy. Yet, in the realm of the popular media (not to mention much of the ethics and theological literature), MNCs are more often portrayed as inherently exploitive and harmful to society, indifferent to workers' rights, environmental concerns, and anything else that stands in the way of profit maximization. Clearly there have been some egregious examples over the years to support this view, examples brought to light thanks to the unrelenting watchfulness of activists and the media. However, such a broad brush portrayal is not only patently unfair, but is unjust if it discourages firms from investing in challenging and dangerous parts of the world. Theologian Michael Novak (1981) made a similar point when he said, "The absence of investment from abroad may be *more morally damaging* to traditional societies than is the activity of MNCs" (p. 20, emphasis added).

Good corporations, like well-behaved children, rarely receive the same attention that bad ones do. Corporate misconduct is far more sensational and, frankly, more interesting. The imbalance in press coverage is therefore hardly surprising, but neither is it an accurate portrayal of the positive influence corporations can have in a society. Thus, before describing the specific role of Christians, it is necessary to first show how MNCs in general can contribute to a nation's economic and social goals.

Doing Good by Going Global

Foreign investment by MNCs contributes to a country's social and economic well-being in many ways. One of the most obvious and immediate benefits is the inflow of capital, a scarce resource in many developing countries that is essential for economic growth. Properly motivated and structured, the new or expanded businesses not only contribute to the development goals of the host government, but the inflow of capital also helps shore up the country's balance of payments, making the country a better credit risk for international lending agencies like the International Monetary Fund and World Bank.

MNCs also facilitate economic growth and social transformation by linking up with local suppliers for their inputs. It is common, in fact, for MNCs to work closely with those suppliers — even to the point of sharing technology with them — to improve productivity and bring their products up to international standards (OECD, 2002; Moran, 2002). These so-called "backward linkages" trigger a gradual process throughout the economy that raises the overall level of competence and efficiency in local firms, helping them compete more effectively both at home and abroad. It is not uncommon for the more enterprising employees to start companies of their own — a process that ultimately leads to even more jobs and greater efficiencies (Lynn, 2003).

Another benefit can be seen in the local labor markets. Researchers are finding that, with the notable exception of low-skill and low-margin industries such as toys, clothing, and sporting goods, linkages between MNC and local suppliers usually lead to *improvements* in the working conditions, pay, and training of local workers (Moran, 2002; OECD, 2002; Santoro, 2000). The explanations given for these trends, interestingly, have more to do with corporate self-interest than with altruism. For example, Spar (1998) maintains that avoiding the unrelenting and unforgiving "glare of public scrutiny" is an important factor in explaining why subsidiaries of Western MNCs tend to hold closely to Western standards.

When local producers in Vietnam, Pakistan, or Honduras exploit their workforce, few in the West hear of it, especially if the products are not exported to Western markets. But when those same producers become suppliers to Reebok, Levi Strauss, or Walt Disney, their actions make headlines in the United States. Changing their behavior becomes, increasingly, a bottom-line concern of Reebok, Levi Strauss, and Disney (p. 12).

Other researchers make an invisible hand argument, pointing to the link between self-interest and the need to attract and retain a well-trained workforce in an increasingly competitive and technology-driven environment (Lynn, 2003; OECD, 2002; Moran, 2002). In other words, these and other studies show that working conditions in most industries are improving, and are likely to continue improving, even without any public scrutiny.

Perhaps the most subtle, and controversial, impact Western MNCs are having is in the area of culture. For example, in his ten-year study of MNCs in China, Santoro (2000) found that MNCs are imparting ideas and values that are quite radical in that country. More specifically, the democratic ideals that are often taken for granted in the West are firmly embedded in our corporate culture, and often transferred unwittingly. He and others claim that this transfer of ideas and values ultimately leads to even broader social reforms, including reductions in corruption and higher levels of corporate and government transparency (see also Friedman, 2000; Moran, 2002; OECD, 2002). Critics might see this as a form of cultural imperialism. Yet, without such reforms, developing countries are at a distinct disadvantage when trying to attract foreign investment. Thus we can see why, as Thomas Friedman (2000) points out in his book *The Lexus and the Olive Tree*, "there is now a growing awareness among leaders of developing countries that what they need in order to succeed ... is not just an emerging market but ... an emerging *society*" (p. 162). This recognition of the need for social as well as economic change has important implications for corporate executives in general and Christians in particular.

There is no denying that sweatshops and other examples of exploitive business practices exist. The "glare of public scrutiny" is therefore necessary and good. Yet, as we work toward improving the lives of the less fortunate, we must keep in mind that most MNCs genuinely want to be good citizens, and work hard at being law-abiding and respected members of the community. If for no other reason, it is in their self interest to do so. What follows is a look at how some Christians have taken this one step further. That is, they not only behave as responsible corporate citizens for its own sake, but have found ways to have a humanitarian and spiritual impact through their sourcing, investment, and philanthropy decisions.

Global Sourcing

One way an executive can please shareholders while also looking after the interests of others is through the supply chain. It is no secret that the search for ways to cut costs and improve service often leads to developing countries. Yet, while it is common to weigh such factors as working conditions, wages, and the like when doing business with foreign suppliers, many Christians in this position have never considered the impact their sourcing decisions can have toward assisting local churches. Indeed, it often comes as a shock to people in the West that there are Christians in developing countries who own or manage world-class, multinational businesses. Consider, for example, Semiconductor Manufacturing International Corporation (SMIC), a Shanghai-based semiconductor foundry that employs over 8,000 people. In addition to developing its own proprietary integrated circuitry (IC) products, SMIC provides IC foundry services for some of the leading names in consumer electronics. Company founder and chairman Richard R. Chang is unequivocal about his dual purpose for starting the company: to become China's largest semiconductor producer and to share the love of Christ. He pursues the latter in a variety of ways, such as by providing subsidized housing and education for his employees, and by establishing, with government permission, a church—now 300 worshipers strong—for the local and foreign Christians.

Transcription Services, Inc. provides another example of how partnerships with overseas suppliers can benefit Christians in the developing world.[4] This small but fast-growing American company—with annual revenues of about three million dollars—was struggling in 2000 to increase its capacity and the turnaround speed for its medical reports. Sending some of its work to India therefore was a survival strategy having more to do with serving customers better than with cutting costs. When considering different Indian partners, quality control was the company's main concern, although the deciding factor ultimately hinged on the benefit this relationship would have for Indian Christians. Today nearly a quarter of the company's work is performed in India by a company managed by a Christian woman who makes no distinction between her business career and her "ministry." In addition to treating her nearly 100 employees as a pastor would his or her "flock," the company directs a sizeable share of its net profits to local Christian ministries.

When it comes to promoting social and economic development, Christians in the West tend to think of nongovernmental organizations (NGOs) or microenterprises rather than large, multi-million or multi-billion dollar companies. This could be why corporate executives rarely give any thought to the matter: What can a microenterprise realistically offer a company like Dell or Motorola or General Motors? But the truth of the matter is that because of globalization there are Christian-owned, world-class companies springing up almost everywhere—in Asia, Latin America, parts of Africa, and many parts of the former Soviet Union—all sharing an interest in helping promote a stable and prosperous society and in supporting Christian ministry. This is not to suggest that Christian executives should make compromises for the sake of doing business with other Christians, although under some circumstances compromises may be appropriate.

Rather, sometimes with little effort and no compromise at all in terms of price and quality, Christian executives can get "ministry leverage" out of their routine sourcing decisions.

Foreign Direct Investment

Another way a Christian executive can fulfill their obligation to shareholders while also looking after the interests of others is through foreign direct investment (FDI), that is, the building or buying of corporate assets in other countries. UNCTAD estimates that there are now over 900,000 foreign firms that have ownership linkages to some 61,000 parent companies worldwide, a figure that has *more than tripled* in less than ten years. Not included in these figures are the large but unknown number of firms that are linked to each other through non-equity arrangements such as franchise agreements, management contracts, partnerships, and so forth (UNCTAD, 2004).

Few Christians have given much thought to how FDI can specifically benefit Christians in the developing world. One notable exception is Dwight Nordstrom, founder of Pacific Resources International (PRI), a company that helps Western MNCs establish world-class manufacturing operations in China. His track record includes dozens of factories that now collectively employ over two thousand people and generate more than $200 million per year. Clearly, the job and wealth creation is a significant contribution in its own right. But PRI also takes steps to ensure that Christians are treated fairly on the job and in the hiring process. Again, this is not to suggest that one should compromise his or her responsibility to shareholders. But foreign investment decisions often have a way of coming down to choices between two equally attractive locations, two equally qualified plant managers, and so on. The attentive executive can turn those choices into opportunities for helping local Christians.

Corporate Good Deeds

A third way Christian executives can promote the company's interests while also looking after the interests of others is through corporate good deeds. Many companies are eager to find ways to make high-profile philanthropic investments in the local community, and some are even *required* to do so by the local government as a condition for their approval (a practice known as "offsetting"). Voluntary or not, there is no denying the self-interest motive involved in many of these "charitable" acts. Nevertheless, these opportunities represent another way Christians can use their influence within the company to pursue activities that are beneficial both to the community as a whole, as well as to the local Christian population.

Here one is limited only by one's imagination. Some companies, such as S&K International, a Korean-owned company in northern China, offer free self-improvement classes to their employees, such as computer training, foreign language training, and the like. Others, such as India-based Olive Technologies, support local charities such as community centers, orphanages, schools, and so on. One Malaysia-based company allows its employees to co-manage a fund used to support local charities. For many employees of this Christian-owned company, this is the first time they have ever taken a serious look at the needs in their own community. This unusual arrangement also creates opportunities for the Christians to explain their own motivation for reaching out to the less fortunate.

While the examples above involve Christian-owned companies, there is no reason why, with a little creativity, similar low-cost social benefit programs cannot be pursued within any company seeking to maintain good community relations.

Starting a Company That Has a Broader Social Purpose

Finally, there is the most challenging but potentially most rewarding way to combine one's passions for business and social concerns—starting a company that aims to meet a specific social or spiritual need. Many case studies and books are starting to appear on this topic under the general heading of "Social Entrepreneurship," so I will limit myself to just two examples.[5] The first is Pura Vida Coffee, a company that is profiled in greater detail in Rundle and Steffen (2003). This young, fast-growing American company was *founded for the express purpose* of supporting Christian ministries that are meeting the physical, emotional, and spiritual needs of children in Costa Rica and other coffee-growing countries. Its social purpose is evident in many ways: in its promotion of fair trade coffee, its donation of 100 percent of its net profit to needy kids, and its alliances with other like-minded, charitable organizations such as World Relief, Sojourners, and Habitat for Humanity.

The second example is China-based Meixia Arts, a producer of inlaid stained glass that was started by an American who wanted to make a difference in one of the poorest parts of the world. One of the many ways he does that is by hiring from the local population of handicapped, homeless, or beggars (a population that is often one-and-the-same). The owner's efforts at restoring dignity to people's lives through work has earned him recognition by the mayor as the city's most admired corporate citizen several years in a row. What is most significant about this story, however, is that some of the people who have been helped are *themselves* starting to reach out to the downtrodden in their communities by providing food, shelter, and meaningful work. The company founder sees this "second generation activity" as a vital step toward sustainable social change.

Conclusion

There is no question that globalization is forcing companies of all sizes to take a more global view of their competition, their markets, their suppliers, and their strategies. The underlying forces that are driving this are also making it possible for firms to do considerable harm or considerable good virtually any-

where in the world. It follows that any discussion of a corporation's social responsibility must also become more global in its scope. I have argued that the moral and legal responsibility of corporate executives to be faithful stewards has not changed. What is different today is that good stewardship often requires a well-conceived global business strategy. While this clearly creates problems for those who once benefited from political and geographical barriers, it also presents many opportunities for praiseworthy corporate conduct. Many of those opportunities can be found in surprising places—in the sourcing, investment, and philanthropy decisions that are intended to improve the firm's bottom line. Corporate executives, and particularly Christians, should be mindful of those opportunities to leverage a profitable business strategy into opportunities to contribute to the social and spiritual welfare of some of the neediest countries.

Notes

[1] The Sarbanes-Oxley Act of 2002 has only reinforced this responsibility.

[2] See, for example, Proverbs 3:27, Galatians 6:10, Ephesians 2:10 and 5:16, Colossians 4:5, and Titus 2:14.

[3] Philippians 2:4.

[4] Because of occasional violence directed against Christians in India, the company founders have asked to remain anonymous.

[5] See, for example, Brinckerhoff (2000), Bomstein (2003), Dees, Emerson and Economy (2001), and Rundle and Steffen (2003).

References

Brinckerhoff, P. C. 2000. *Social entrepreneurship: The art of mission-based venture development.* New York, NY: John Wiley & Sons.

Bomstein, D. 2003. *How to change the world: Social entrepreneurs and the power of new ideas.* New York, NY: Oxford University Press.

Dees, J. G., J. Emerson, and P. Economy. 2001. *Enterprising nonprofits: A tool kit for social entrepreneurs.* New York, NY: John Wiley & Sons.

Feenstra, R. C. 1998. "Integration of trade and disintegration of production in the global economy," *Journal of Economic Perspectives* (Fall), pp. 31–50.

Friedman, T. 2000. *The Lexus and the olive tree: Understanding globalization.* New York, NY: Anchor Books.

Hoogvelt, A. 1997. *Globalization and the post-colonial world: The new political economy of development.* Baltimore, MD: Johns Hopkins University Press.

Houck, J. W., and O. F. Williams (eds.). 1996. *Is the good corporation dead? Social responsibility in a global economy.* Lanham, MD: Rowman and Littlefield Publishers.

Lynn, S. R. 2002. *Economic development: Theory and practice for a divided world.* Upper Saddle River, NJ: Prentice Hall.

Moran, T. 2002. *Beyond sweatshops: Foreign direct investment and globalization in developing countries.* Washington, DC: Brookings Institution Press.

Novak, M. 1981. *Toward a theology of the corporation.* Washington, DC: American Enterprise Institute for Public Policy Research.

OECD. 2002. *Foreign direct investment for development: Maximising benefits, minimising costs.*

Prahalad, C. K., and K. Lieberthal. 1998. "The end of corporate imperialism." *Harvard Business Review* (July/August), pp. 69–79.

Rae, Scott, and K. Wong (eds.). 1996. *Beyond integrity: A Judeo-Christian approach to business ethics.* Grand Rapids, MI: Zondervan.

Rundle, Steve, and T. Steffen. 2003. *Great commission companies: The emerging role of business in missions.* Downers Grove, IL: InterVarsity Press.

Santoro, M. 2000. *Profits and principles: Global capitalism and human rights in China.* New York, NY: Cornell University Press.

Spar, D. L. 1998. "The spotlight and the bottom line: How multinationals export human rights." *Foreign Affairs* (March/April), pp. 7–12.

UNCTAD. 2004. *World investment report.* Washington, DC.

Questions for Discussion and Reflection

1. According to Rundle, what factors contribute to production becoming more globalized?
2. How does Rundle believe that companies can do good by going global? Give some examples that he cites. Do you know of other examples of companies that are doing good by going global?

CASE STUDIES

Case 5.1: Walmart and Globalization

A 2004 *Frontline* documentary on PBS chronicled the rise of Walmart to the global giant it has become (available at http://www.pbs.org/wgbh/pages/frontline/shows/walmart/). In the past few decades, Walmart has been transformed from Sam Walton's "5 & 10" stores to the model for companies operating in a global economy. Duke University business professor Gary Gereffi said, "Walmart is one of the key forces that propelled global outsourcing—offshoring of U.S. jobs—precisely because it controls so much of the purchasing power of the U.S. economy." The rise of Walmart has changed the balance of power in the world economy from manufacturers to global retailers. Walmart's defenders argue that their unprecedented efficiency and productivity that keeps costs as low as possible and enables them to keep prices lower, not only gives them a competitive advantage but is good for the poor who must make every dollar stretch as far as possible. They have experienced growth in sales from $1 billion in 1979 to roughly $250 billion in 2005, which the company argues cannot be considered in any other way but as good for the world economy.

But critics of Walmart and other stores like it insist that these benefits to the consumer come at a cost to workers, not only at Walmart but at many of their suppliers. Their wages are lower than the industry standard (in fact, the pay and benefits are so low that store managers have all the public assistance agencies on their Rolodexes so that they can easily refer to them), and according to critics, they pay virtually no pension or retirement benefits, have substandard health care benefits, and buy a high percentage of their merchandise from low-cost producers in China. Critics argue that the way in which they use their leverage to squeeze suppliers forces American manufacturers to export their jobs overseas in order to keep their costs down. In addition, they are charged with being primarily responsible for the trade deficit with China. Critics argue that on balance Walmart is not good for America.

Questions for Discussion

1. After viewing the *Frontline* program, do you think that Walmart is good for America? Why or why not? Considering some of the arguments in this chapter, is "good for America" the right question to ask? Why or why not?
2. Do you think that Walmart has any obligation to preserve American jobs? If so, on what basis?
3. If Walmart is good for consumers by keeping prices low, do you believe that the impact on workers is acceptable, given Walmart's benefits to poor consumers? Why or why not?

Case 5.2: Outsourcing Production

You are a member of your company's executive leadership team that is facing a decision about laying off employees and sending their jobs to other parts of the world where wages are much less than at home. Your company is in the software design and implementation business, and you are finding it increasingly efficient to send some of the design work to India, to software engineers who charge a fraction of what it costs to do the design in the United States. The company is making a healthy profit at present, and prospects for the future look bright. With the efficiency of the Internet and electronic communications, it is not necessary today to have many of your software developers working together in close proximity in an office. You have heard of many companies sending more unskilled work overseas, such as call center operations and manufacturing work. In the past you have had little sympathy for workers whose jobs are sent to other parts of the world because you have accepted that "it's just business" and "we have to stay competitive." In addition, you have regarded these lower skilled workers as the ones who are responsible for developing new skills to keep them employable.

The jobs that your executive team is considering sending overseas are different from those lower skilled jobs that have traditionally been sent overseas. These are well-educated software developers who have done everything a productive employee is supposed to do — get a good education and work hard at a job that requires specific skills. You know many of these individuals personally — they have families and mortgages, and they will be significantly impacted by being laid off. Some of them are a bit older, too, and may have more difficulty finding other jobs. But you also realize that your company has to cut costs regularly to stay competitive. You also see the benefit to the employees who will get these jobs in India — they are emerging from poverty and will greatly benefit by getting the work. But you have questions about your obligation to domestic workers and wonder if keeping jobs at home is a worthy goal that ought to be pursued.

Questions for Discussion

1. When asked for your vote in the executive committee of your company about laying off the software engineers and sending their jobs to India, how will you vote? Explain your rationale for your vote.
2. Do you think your company has any obligation to the domestic employees to keep their jobs at home? Why or why not?
3. Does it matter that your company is making strong profits at the present time? Does the fact that the company is currently profitable and its survival is not threatened give a greater obligation to domestic employees? Why or why not?

COMMENTARY

A moral evaluation of globalization is quite a complicated undertaking, involving economics, political philosophy, ethics, and for the Christian, theology. Some of the charges against globalization are not new at all, but are long-standing criticisms of capitalism as an economic system, made more acute and pressing by the global setting in which business takes place today. Some of these allegations have a specifically theological basis, such as Wydick's charge that some aspects of globalization violate a primary biblical principle—that God cares for the poor. Griffiths, by contrast, bases his claim of the moral legitimacy of globalization partly on his theology—that "it respects the dignity and freedom of the human person, the importance of property rights, the creativity and enterprise of people and the duty and dignity of work." This is an extension of his earlier work defending capitalism in general as a moral enterprise.[11]

[11] See Brian Griffiths, *The Creation of Wealth: A Christian's Case for Capitalism* (Downers Grove, Ill.: InterVarsity, 1985).

Economics in the Bible and the Ancient World

However, before we can apply the Bible and theological principles to business today, we need to recognize that the Bible's teaching on wealth and commerce was set in an ancient system that was very different from today's system. That doesn't mean that the Bible has nothing of relevance for today, only that we must use the Bible carefully in applying its general principles of economic life now. A direct application of many of the commands of the Bible relating to business would be impossible today, since the system to which those commands were addressed has dramatically changed. Take, for example, the command to keep the Year of Jubilee, in which all land returned to its original owners every fiftieth year. It is virtually impossible to conceive how this could be done today in an Information Age setting. Rather, we are seeking from Scripture more general principles, or norms that govern economic life, that can be applied to different economic arrangements. As we mentioned in chapter 1, these norms are more fundamentally grounded in the overall biblical narrative of God's care for his people, particularly the least advantaged.

A significant part of the "big picture" of the Bible when it comes to economic life has to do with a person's view of wealth and possessions. Though the Bible does have quite a bit to say about the economic life of the community, an individual's view of money is often seen as the starting point for understanding the Bible's teachings. At first glance, the Bible appears to condemn the accumulation of wealth. Classic teachings of Jesus, such as "it is easier for a camel to go through the eye of a needle than for someone who is rich to enter the kingdom of God" (Luke 18:25), and "Blessed are you who are poor" (Luke 6:20), suggest that possession of wealth is suspect and poverty is a virtue. Of course, these texts should be balanced by others that present wealth in a different perspective. These include the sayings of the Old Testament Wisdom Literature, which regard wealth as God's blessing and to be enjoyed (Eccl. 5:18–20) and a result of one's diligence (Prov. 10:4–5). Similarly, in the New Testament, Paul counsels Timothy to keep wealth in proper perspective (1 Tim. 6:6–19). He acknowledges that God gives liberally to his people for their enjoyment (v. 17). Yet this is balanced by admonitions not to trust in one's wealth because of the temptation to arrogance and due to the uncertainty of wealth (see also Eccl. 5:8–6:12) and to be content with one's economic station in life. The Bible does make a distinction between possession of wealth and the love of wealth. Only the latter is condemned (1 Tim. 6:10). The love of wealth and desire to become wealthy bring a variety of temptations and have the potential to shipwreck one's spiritual life (1 Tim. 6:9). Yet the members of the early church and the crowds who followed Jesus represented the socioeconomic spectrum from the very poor to the wealthy. It does not appear that the possession of wealth per se is problematic in Scripture, but hoarding one's wealth when surrounded by poverty is a sign of selfishness and greed.

Throughout the Bible, the wealthy are condemned for their callousness to the needs of the poor (Amos 4:1–4; James 2:1–7). The early days of the church were characterized by an extraordinary generosity toward the less fortunate, who constituted the majority of the membership in the early church (Acts 2:45). Though the pattern of the early church probably did not involve a socialistic style of holding property in common, it did involve heightened sensitivity to the needs of the economically vulnerable.[12] Though the Bible

[12] For further reading on the early church holding their goods in common, see Justo L. Gonzalez, *Faith and Wealth: A History of Early Christian Ideas on the Origin, Significance, and Use of Money* (San Francisco: Harper & Row, 1990).

does affirm the right to private property, it is not absolute. It is tempered by the responsibility to use one's wealth to meet the needs of the poor in the community. It is further tempered by the notion that we are trustees, or stewards, of God's property, which he entrusts to us both for our needs and enjoyment and use for God's purposes.

The pursuit of wealth in the ancient world was fraught with potential problems, which made it easy to view those who possessed wealth with moral and spiritual skepticism. Though we should be careful not to minimize the temptations facing the pursuit of wealth today, there are some important differences between the modern and ancient economic systems that may partially account for the strong cautions about wealth. For example, in the ancient world, as a general rule, people became wealthy differently than in today's market system. The ancient economic system was largely centered around subsistence agriculture with some commerce and trade. Real estate was the predominant productive asset. The ancient economy is best described as what is called a "zero sum game." That is, there was a relatively fixed pool of economic resources, so that when one person became wealthy, it was usually at the expense of someone else. To put it a different way, there was a fixed economic pie, and when someone received a larger piece, that meant that someone else received a smaller piece. This set up numerous opportunities to become wealthy at someone else's expense by theft, taxation, or extortion. One of the most common ways this was done in the ancient world was for those who had resources to loan money to the poor (frequently to pay for basic needs) at terms they could not repay, with what little land they owned as collateral. Then when they inevitably defaulted, the lender would appropriate their land, thereby increasing his wealth, and the debtor would become a tenant farmer or slave or be reduced to dependence on charity. This kind of taking advantage of the poor occurred regularly in the ancient world and is why the Bible so frequently condemns exploitation of the poor. In these cases, literally, the rich became richer at the expense of the poor, and when someone was wealthy, more often than not that person had acquired it through some immoral means. Thus, the wealthy were viewed with suspicion and there was great emphasis on the potential temptations of becoming wealthy because there were so few morally legitimate avenues to become wealthy in the ancient world.[13]

Though it is certainly true that the poor continue to be exploited, some in economic systems around the world that resemble those of the ancient world, in the developed market system, there is no longer the zero-sum type of economic arrangement in which there is a necessary connection between winners and losers. It is true that the market system is in various stages of development in different parts of the world, but in more mature market

[13] For further reading on economic life in biblical times, see Douglas E. Oakman, "Economics of Palestine," in Craig A. Evans and Stanley E. Porter, eds., *Dictionary of New Testament Backgrounds* (Downers Grove, Ill.: InterVarsity, 2000), 304–8. See also Scott B. Rae, "Views of Wealth in the Bible and the Ancient World," *Religion and Liberty* 12, no. 4 (November–December 2002), reprinted in 20, no. 3–4 (Summer–Fall 2010): 10–11.

systems, the economy is anything but a zero-sum game. In modern information economies, the size of the financial pie is constantly increasing with economic growth. Wealth is being created instead of simply being transferred. In fact, in the vast majority of cases, when a company makes a profit, wealth is created and the size of the pie grows larger. That is why people can become prosperous while at the same time the poor can also be better off. That is why the incomes of the less fortunate can increase and have done so at the same time as the wealth of the rich accumulates, though admittedly, at very different rates. But simply because someone like Bill Gates or Warren Buffet has extraordinary wealth, it does not follow that the poor are necessarily worse off. Nor does it necessarily follow that Gates's and Buffet's affluence was gained at the expense of someone else. This principle applies to nations as well as individuals. In a modern market economy, wealth is constantly being created, which is why it is possible for someone to become prosperous without necessarily succumbing to the temptations about which Scripture warns. It is far easier to be well off and virtuous in today's market economy than it was in the ancient world. Of course, the same admonitions about not giving in to the temptations that accompany the pursuit of wealth apply today, as do the commands to share generously with those in need. A person's attitude toward wealth as well as his or her generosity are fundamentally conditions of the heart that have not changed since the ancient world. Regardless of one's net worth, one is still expected to depend on God, not on money, for one's hope, to share God's heart for the poor and be generous toward those in need.

A Biblical Paradigm for Economic Life

The Bible both addresses specific economic practices and lays out broader moral norms for economic life that transcend time and culture. These norms are grounded in the biblical story of God's provision and generosity toward humanity and form the basic principles guiding economic arrangements in whatever culture or time period is relevant. Though the practices of a fundamentally agricultural society are very different from an industrial or information economy, the norms from Scripture are applicable to a new set of practices and can be used to evaluate the economic arrangements of any economic system at any time.

The biblical narrative that is the context for economic justice begins in Genesis 1–2. God's creation of the world out of nothing and his pronouncement that the world is "good" teach that the created world is inherently good. Genesis 3 indicates that the created realm is also subject to the entrance of sin into the world, is fallen, and as the New Testament describes, eagerly awaits its redemption (Rom. 8:19–23). Not only will human beings be released from the influence of sin, but so will the creation. From the beginning of the biblical story, human beings are a part of creation but are also stewards over it. The Bible is clear that God owns all the land and that human beings are simply trustees over it. That is why in the Old Testament, real estate could not be permanently bought or sold (Lev. 25:23–24). God is the owner, and human beings are his stewards, having been charged with dominion over creation. Part of the dominion mandate over creation is the opportunity and responsibility to put the creation to use for the common good, particularly for the benefit of human beings. God's common grace is available to all human beings to aid them in the work of establishing dominion over the creation, bringing it under control and unlocking its potential. This responsibility gives a high place for traits such as freedom, initiative, and creativity in utilizing creation responsibly for the benefit of humankind. As Griffiths points out, responsible wealth creation is a part of the dominion mandate and a tangible way in which one can honor God.[14]

[14] Griffiths, *Creation of Wealth*, 25–31.

Human beings were created both with freedom and with a fundamental need for community, the aspect of community rightly emphasized by Wydick. Being made in God's image, human beings are more than material beings and more than merely economic agents in a marketplace. Economic systems that deny freedom and initiative are just as problematic as those that elevate individual freedom at the expense of community. Wydick's principle #2 — that interdependence between people reflects a community ideal — also emerges from the Genesis account of the community being engaged in dominion, or wealth creation.

Work in the Bible was instituted prior to the introduction of sin into the world. Adam and Eve were commanded to work the garden in order to care for it and realize its benefits (Gen. 2:15). Thus, work is not a result of the fall into sin, but since it was commanded prior to the fall, it is inherently good and not a curse. After the fall, work became more arduous and taxing, but the fundamental goodness of it was not destroyed. Work is fundamental to human flourishing, which suggests that economic systems must provide access to productive labor for as many people as possible.[15] All work is flawed due to sin, which suggests that alienation can occur in any economic system. That is, the criticisms of work are more due to its fallen nature than to the contribution of any specific economic system.

[15] Stephen Mott and Ronald J. Sider, "Economic Justice: A Biblical Paradigm," in David P. Gushee, ed., *Toward a Just and Caring Society: Christian Responses to Poverty in America* (Grand Rapids: Baker, 1999), 15–45.

It is presumed throughout the Bible that human beings are responsible for engaging in the work necessary to provide for themselves and their families. Though the spirit of community is very strong in both the Old and New Testaments, people do not have a claim on the community's resources unless they are incapable of supporting themselves. For those capable of working, the Pauline admonition that "the one who is unwilling to work shall not eat" (2 Thess. 3:10) strongly suggests that if one is unwilling to work, that person has no claim on the resources of the community.

However, the Bible makes generous provision for the poor, for those who cannot support themselves and are economically vulnerable. God's heart for the poor is a significant part of the narrative of his love and care for his people. The Mosaic law set up institutions that provided an ample safety net for the poor, and the prophets roundly condemned those who took advantage of the economically vulnerable. The Prophets regularly connect one's spiritual maturity and growth to tangible commitments to caring for the poor. For instance, in Isaiah 58:6–7, the type of religious service acceptable to God is not a fast or other ceremony, but service to the poor. Likewise, Isaiah identifies the signs of the coming kingdom by the fact that the gospel is preached to the poor and the vulnerable are rescued (Isa. 61:1–2; Luke 4:18–19). Service to the poor reflects what it means to know God, according to Jeremiah (Jer. 22:16), and the Wisdom Literature connects one's heart for God with service to the poor. Proverbs 14:31 puts it strikingly: "Whoever oppresses the poor shows contempt for their Maker, but whoever is kind to the needy honors God." Similarly, Proverbs 19:17 insists that "whoever is kind to the poor lends to the LORD, and he will reward them for what they have done."

Numerous Mosaic laws supported the poor, including the Jubilee (Lev. 25:8–18); the law of redemption (Lev. 25:35–43); the right of gleaning, in which the poor could harvest from the fields of the community (Lev. 23:22); the provision of no-interest loans, which could be forgiven at the Jubilee (Ex. 22:25); the release of slaves every seven years and their being sent away with sufficient capital to be self-supporting (Deut. 15:12–14); and a portion of the tithe for the poor as well as for the priests and Levites (Deut. 14:28–29). The tithe, in the form of a "transfer payment" went to the dependent poor, those incapable of working, while the loans went to the working poor. Stephen Mott and Ronald Sider insightfully summarize the notion of economic justice taken from these laws concerning the land: "Justice demands that every person or family has access to the productive resources (land, money, knowledge) so they have the opportunity to earn a generous sufficiency of material necessities and be dignified participating members of their community."[16] Economic justice does not suggest, as some have supposed, an equality of outcome, but rather an equality of opportunity to earn a sufficient living in order to engage in full, dignified participation in the life of the community. That is, economic justice does not presume that everyone must achieve the same level of prosperity, only that they have equal opportunity to get there. In terms of distributive justice, it would appear that

16 Ibid., 34.

the Bible uses both need and merit as criteria for distributing the goods of society. Those who can work earn their share based on their merit, consisting of their initiative, creativity, and hard work. Those incapable of self-support are entitled to a share of the goods of society on the basis of their need.

We could summarize the primary moral principles governing economic life as follows:

1. Even though marred by sin, the created world is inherently good since it is God's good creation.
2. God is the ultimate owner of all productive resources.
3. Human beings are stewards of these resources charged with responsible and productive use of them.
4. Responsible wealth creation is part of the dominion mandate and is a way of honoring God.
5. Human beings are created with freedom and a need for community, making them more than autonomous economic agents.
6. Work is inherently good, though marred by sin.
7. Human beings who are capable of working are responsible for supporting themselves and their families.
8. The community is responsible for taking care of the poor—those who cannot support themselves.
9. Human beings are not to exploit the economically vulnerable, but to take care of them.
10. Economic justice is the provision of access to the productive resources necessary for self-support.
11. Distributive justice in the Bible is based on a combination of merit and need.
12. God is more concerned with how the global economy affects those at the bottom of the ladder than those at the top.

Moral and Theological Critique of Global Capitalism

Over the years, a variety of criticisms have been leveled against capitalism as an economic system, particularly since it is, with a handful of socialist exceptions, the only viable economic system in operation. Many of the most common criticisms of market capitalism have become more pointed due to globalization. As a result of a global economy, what happens in one country's economy can have immediate and catastrophic impact on the rest of the world. This interdependence of the global economy is one of the primary lessons of the 2007–9 financial crisis (and several other episodes over the past several decades). Even though the economic world has changed dramatically in the past few years, from manufacturing to more of a globalized, knowledge-based economy, the fundamental criticisms of the market system have remained consistent.

The most common critique of global capitalism concerns its foundational motive — greed.[17] It is often alleged that it is a system based on greed, or what Adam Smith called the invisible hand of self-interest. Defenders of the system argue that multinational enterprises (MNEs) are run by individuals seeking their self-interest, or maximizing their profit, and the assumption is that to succeed they must make a useful product or perform a useful service and in so doing contribute to the common good. Yet critics observe that greed and individual acquisitive self-interest have not contributed to the common good, but have undermined it. They have, for example, created enormous disparities in the distribution of income and concentrated wealth in the hands of a relative few at the expense of the majority of the poor of the world. Global capitalism, critics charge, involves large corporations uprooting communities, outsourcing jobs around the world, and spoiling the environment, all in the name of increasing their profits. Critics of capitalism insist that a system fueled by a trait that the Bible clearly identifies as a vice cannot possibly be consistent with Christian ethics. Expansion of corporate profit and power, the rise of the consumer society, and overconsumption all assume that greed fuels the economic system.

A second critique is that capitalism leads to an unjust concentration of wealth and global inequalities in resource use.[18] Critics of globalization claim that the global economy has made these inequalities worse. For example, the developing world has far more people yet far fewer of the world's resources. Critics cite the growing concentration of economic and political power in the hands of a few large multinational enterprises (MNEs) that control a disproportionate amount of wealth and power and exercise it unjustly to maintain their "empires," often at the expense of the poor.

This leads to a third major criticism of global capitalism, that the economy of the developed world is responsible for the poverty of the developing world.[19] Critics argue that the inequalities in the distribution of wealth are exacerbated by global capitalism, not alleviated by it. Griffiths points out that although the poor may be better off, the gap between rich and poor has increased dramatically. Wydick suggests that though there are clear winners in the global economy, there are numerous losers as well. He insightfully points out that the winners are those who have skills in the goods and services that a country is exporting, while the losers are the ones who have skills in the products and services that a country is importing, and that the gap between winners and losers is growing. Both Griffiths and Wydick argue

[17] This criticism came out most clearly in Michael Moore's 2009 film *Capitalism: A Love Story*. See also Jim Wallis, *God's Politics* (San Francisco: HarperCollins, 2005), 259–69.

[18] Wallis, *God's Politics*, 265. See also Wallis, *Rediscovering Values: On Wall Street, Main Street, and Your Street* (New York: Howard, 2010), 81–92.

[19] See, e.g., Richard Gillett, *The New Globalization* (Cleveland: Pilgrim, 2005), 11. See also Wallis, *God's Politics*, 270–95.

that protectionist trade arrangements that close off the developing world from the developed world's markets are a significant part of the problem in growing inequality. Wydick actually asserts that "Buy American" campaigns are inconsistent with a biblical view of justice and undermine the access of the poor to consumer markets.

A fourth criticism is that global capitalism fosters materialism and nurtures overconsumption.[20] Critics of globalization charge that the primary export of the developed world to the developing world is middle-class materialism. Goods are produced and consumed that would appear to have no socially redeeming value simply because in the market system, supply follows demand. If there is market for a certain good, someone will make it, regardless of its social value. The only value of a product that counts is its economic value, as measured by the market. Products like pornography, a billion-dollar business annually in the United States, and cigarettes, which kill thousands of people each year and cost billions in medical care, are examples of products that society would undoubtedly be better off without, yet are produced in mass quantities simply because the market demands it. Critics charge that this kind of consumerism leaves a person and a society spiritually impoverished.

The advocates of global capitalism have responded to each of these critiques, arguing that its critics have either misunderstood the system or misinterpreted the Bible.[21] First, they insist that greed and self-interest are not the same thing. When Adam Smith wrote of self-interest fueling capitalism, he had nothing like "greed is good" in mind. He advocated *enlightened* self-interest — that is, self-interest restrained by Judeo-Christian morality and a concern for the common good, in which everyone benefits.[22] As Steven Rundle pointed out, globalization has given companies many new ways in which to do good by going global, ranging from partnerships with overseas suppliers to foreign investment and starting companies with broader social purposes that assist the poor around the world. Global capitalism was never intended to operate apart from the virtue of its participants. Yet the critics of capitalism reply that the conditions under which Smith envisioned capitalism are so foreign today that perhaps capitalism is not capable of being a moral system, with self-interest properly restrained.[23] Whether or not that is true is open to debate, but the key point here is that greed does not equal self-interest and that there is nothing wrong with individuals pursuing their self-interest if regulated by virtue. In addition, greed is fundamentally a matter of the heart, not specific to any economic system. Greed can and does flourish under any economic system.

The second and third critiques, that the concentration of economic power inherent in capitalism is responsible for third world poverty, assume

[20] See, e.g., Nafeez Mosaddeq Ahmed, "Capitalism, Consumerism and Materialism: The Values Crisis," *OpEd News* (February 28, 2008), at opednews.com. See also Jim Wallis, *Rediscovering Values*, 53–79.

[21] For more developed responses to these criticisms of global capitalism, see Austin Hill and Scott B. Rae, *The Virtues of Capitalism* (Chicago: Northfield, 2010), 56–74; and Jay W. Richards, *Money, Greed, and God: Why Capitalism Is the Solution and Not the Problem* (New York: HarperCollins, 2009).

[22] For further reading on Adam Smith, see Patricia H. Werhane, *Adam Smith and His Legacy for Modern Capitalism* (New York: Oxford University Press, 1991).

[23] This is one of the primary criticisms of the popular critic Michael Moore in his film *Capitalism: A Love Story*.

[24] Richards, *Money, Greed and God*, 59 – 82.

that the world's supply of goods is a "zero-sum game."[24] That is, when someone gains, inevitably someone else loses, because the pie is the same size for everyone. So, according to the critics, if someone gets a bigger slice of the economic pie, someone else will inevitably get a smaller slice. Those who defend global capitalism have responded that the world is not necessarily structured this way. In fact, global capitalism is capable of making the pie bigger for everyone, particularly lifting the poor in the developing world out of poverty as they become integrated into the global economic system. An honest assessment of global capitalism should acknowledge that there are situations that can be categorized as win-lose. For example, trading of financial instruments, such as bonds and derivatives, seems to fit this pattern. In addition, some economic systems in the developing world resemble a zero-sum situation — those in which we would suggest that the market system has yet to be fully implemented. The merit of global capitalism is that it seems to be the only economic system that is capable of consistently creating wealth, and as Griffiths points out, it has clearly been an economic success in raising millions out of poverty.

However, both Griffiths and Wydick rightly denounce the protectionist trade measures taken by the developed world to protect its markets from competition. Trade in the global economy is a long way from being free. Griffiths argues that trade liberalization is essential for the developing world to participate fully in the global economy and is a much more effective way of helping the poor than financial aid. Wydick argues that agricultural trade protection of American and European farmers is "devastating to peasant farmers in developing countries, who would otherwise enjoy a comparative advantage in the export of such crops." Wydick argues that there is no justification for trade policies that favor domestic interests over the developing world, and urges Christians to support policies and programs that economically empower the poor and give them access to economic opportunity through free trade. Whether "Buy American" campaigns are at odds with a biblical view of justice, as Wydick claims, is open to debate, but he is correct to point out the hypocrisy of the developing world's support for market competition and protectionist trade policies at the same time.

Griffiths rightly points to decades of empirical data to show that participation in the global economy is the best means of lifting the poor out of their poverty. He cites the Pacific Rim miracles of economic development as evidence and the numbers of people from India and China who have emerged from poverty into the middle class. Nations such as Singapore, South Korea, Taiwan, and Japan have few natural resources on which to build an economy. Yet they all are prosperous because of a system that allowed initiative and creativity to flourish and protected them with a political system that respected property rights and the rule of law. The contrast between the prosperity of South Korea and the continuing poverty of North Korea is another particularly vivid case in point.[25] Both have roughly the same endowment of natural resources, yet the capitalist system has enabled people to prosper, and per capita income is substantially higher in the south.

On the fourth critique, the charge of overconsumption, advocates of global capitalism admit that the free market allows for production of many goods and services that do not have socially redeeming value. Christian defenders of the market system would surely agree that society would clearly be better off without some products. But they argue that the presence of such products and services is an acceptable price to pay for the greater good of economic freedom that is consistent with human beings created in God's image. However, overconsumption is not morally neutral, but is a genuine indictment on one's character. The Bible speaks clearly to the responsible use of one's wealth, but that is a matter of the heart and not the economic system per se. It is true that the global market system does provide more goods and services, and corporations need vast numbers of consumers to sustain growth, thus increasing temptations to overconsume. Yet materialism can occur in *any* economic system because of human sin and selfishness.

Overconsumption and the rise of the global middle class do have clear environmental implications that critics of globalization point out.[26] Bringing millions of people into the consumer culture of the global economy raises significant environmental issues, from climate change to the disposal of waste. It seems to us that even if a person is skeptical about the climate change alarm being sounded, the other environmental issues that emerge from the growing middle class joining the consumer society are equally pressing. Moving to a sustainable economy while at the same time lifting large numbers of the poor out of grinding poverty is one of the most significant challenges that advocates of globalization face. If it is true, as Griffiths claims, that global economic growth is the best hope for the poor, then insuring that such growth is environmentally sustainable is essential. We explore this notion of sustainability further in chapter 10.

Conclusion

Maintaining that the Bible is neutral is difficult when it comes to economics. The prophets voiced searing criticism of the nation of Israel and its surrounding neighbors for its economic injustices, neglect of the poor, and exploitation of the economically vulnerable. Yet God's mandate at Creation gave humankind the opportunity to create wealth and so further exercise dominion over the creation. The emphasis on individual initiative, creativity, and

[25] See also, Michael Novak, *The Spirit of Democratic Capitalism*, rev. ed. (New York: Madison, 1990), 16–18.

[26] See, e.g., the work of Bill McKibben, *Earth: Making a Life on a Tough New Planet* (New York: Times, 2010); *Deep Economy: The Wealth of Communities and the Durable Future* (New York: Times, 2007).

economic freedom are rooted in the command to have responsible dominion over creation and in the notion that human beings are made in God's image.

However, some concerns are raised by the collision of biblical values with global capitalism. One well-placed concern is about the overconsumption and materialism encouraged by an economic system that generates so much wealth. The Bible saves some of its clearest condemnation for those who have succumbed to the temptation of materialism. There is a further concern about the ability of global capitalism to fairly distribute the goods of society, particularly given the protectionist trade policies that are designed to protect local markets from competition. It should be troubling to see the growing disparities in the distribution of income, especially the accumulation of wealth that is way beyond what a person will ever need or is willing to give away. Finally, the potential abuses of global capitalism illustrate the need for society in general and religious leaders specifically, to encourage the development of virtue and character to provide the necessary internal restraints of self-interest and urge tempering self-interest in favor of the common good.

SIX

Global Business Practices

Introduction

Working in a globalized economy can raise complicated ethical dilemmas for business people. To start focusing on these issues, put yourself in the following situations and think about what you would do:

1. Your company manufactures glue that is used for shoe repair and shoe making. You export it all over the world. In the United States, the law requires an additive that is a very effective deterrent to prevent kids from sniffing the glue. Most of the countries to which you export the glue do not require this additive. Adding it to your glue will likely price you out of the market. Do you continue to sell the glue around the world without the additive?

2. You are doing business in parts of the world where bribery and corruption are common. You are often required to pay bribes to officials in order to get equipment into the country for manufacturing your products. It's technically illegal to make these payments (and to solicit them), but it is generally regarded as the cost of doing business. Do you pay them when they are demanded? In addition, sometimes you must pay bribes to obtain certain contracts for your business. Would you pay?

3. You are a buyer for a major clothing retailer, and much of the clothing you purchase for your stores is manufactured in other parts of the world in what are commonly called "sweatshops." The wages are low, conditions are far from what would pass OSHA standards in the United States, and children are routinely hired to work twelve-hour days. You have been to these plants, and the people seem glad to have the work, but you are troubled about the conditions and the fact that children are working instead of going to school. Your company does not own the factories, but you can have some limited influence over the conditions. Would you continue to do business with these sweatshops?

4. You walk into you neighborhood coffee shop for your morning jolt of caffeine, and you see signs that advertise the shop's support for "fair trade"

coffee, which involves paying higher than market prices for coffee to enable smaller, developing world coffee growers to support families, thus mitigating the harsh disruptions of the globalization that forces farmers to leave a livelihood that has been in their families for generations. You have friends who have put a bit of guilt on you in the past for not buying fair trade coffee. It is more expensive, and you're not sure if it's the same quality as the coffee you normally buy, but you feel an obligation to help these coffee growers if you can. Should you buy the fair trade coffee?

In chapter 5, we outlined some of the positive elements of the general globalization of business as well as some of the concerns it raises. In this chapter, we want to look more specifically at the ethical issues raised by global business practices. First, we will examine the controversial issues involved with "sweatshop" manufacturing. Sweatshops have been widely criticized for exploitation — namely, low wages, substandard working conditions, and child labor.[1] But there is a side to sweatshop labor that is sometimes overlooked and underpublicized — that it provides badly needed jobs that the employees are grateful to have and provides the first steps out of grinding poverty. University of San Diego philosopher Matt Zwolinski defends sweatshops in his "Sweatshops: Definitions, History, Morality." He argues that the employees choose to work in these places, and that even though they have limited choices for employment, it is still their choice to work there. He argues that governments' and activists' efforts to shut down sweatshops or severely regulate them end up harming the very people the activists most want to help.

A second very common ethical issue faced around the world has to do with bribery. *Bribery* is often an umbrella term that can describe gifts, tips, premiums, or even extortion payments. Bernard Adeney analyzes bribery from the perspective of both culture and the Bible in "Ethical Theory and Bribery." Adeney comes to this discussion out of long experience as a missionary in Indonesia and provides a helpful balance of culture traditions and the biblical insistence on the immorality of bribery.

A third set of issues revolves around some of the well-publicized attempts to use business to aid the poor in the developing world. In chapter 5, Steven Rundle addressed some of the ways in which companies can exercise their social responsibility around the world. In a set of contrasting articles, we address the fair trade movement, particularly as it relates to the production of coffee and support for smaller coffee growers. Paul Chandler, the CEO of Traidcraft, a Christian-based fair trade organization, argues in "Moving the Fair Trade Agenda Forward" that the movement is helping the poor in the developing world and has a set of objectives that are both good for the poor and honoring to God. He points out that the fair trade movement was origi-

[1] For more on the connection between sweatshops and exploitation, see Jeremy Snyder, "Exploitation and Sweatshop Labor: Perspectives and Issues," *Business Ethics Quarterly* 20, no. 2 (April 2010): 187–213. For an example of the common critique of sweatshops, see Denis G. Arnold and Norman E. Bowie, "Sweatshops and Respect for Persons," *Business Ethics Quarterly* 13, no. 2 (April 2003): 221–42.

nally faith based and was designed to lessen some of the severe consequences of the movement toward a more global economy—which forced small farmers to abandon their traditional way of making a living. By contrast, economist Victor Claar, in an excerpt from his book *Fair Trade? Its Prospects as a Poverty Solution*, maintains that fair trade practices actually hurt the poor by distorting market incentives and creating a set of "golden handcuffs" that prevent the poor from moving into more productive and profitable sectors of the economy. He too views the issue from a distinctly Christian perspective.

READINGS

Sweatshops — Definitions, History, and Morality
Matt Zwolinski

From James Ciment, ed., *Social Issues in America: An Encyclopedia* (Armonk, N.Y.: M. E. Sharpe, 2006).

Introduction

The term "sweatshop" is heavy with emotional, historical, and moral significance. It calls to mind images of women and children working long days in cramped, rat-infested quarters, abused by their supervisors and paid barely enough to survive and work another day. To others it will suggest the horrors of Mexican *maquiladoras*, where young female apparel workers are often subject to sexual harassment from the local supervisors and punished severely for any attempt to organize.

Perhaps most frighteningly of all, the term suggests that the *responsibility* for these situations falls squarely on the shoulders of the average consumer. By as simple an act as buying a dress for oneself or running shoes for one's children, the story goes, one is providing economic support to the system which leads to the sorts of oppression described above. The only difference between the consumer who buys sweatshop-made products and the supervisor who runs the sweatshop his or her self is physical proximity to the offense. Morally speaking, we are all guilty.

But guilty of what, exactly? The term "sweatshop" undoubtedly connotes something objectionable. But what precisely are the conditions which have to be met by a business before this term is appropriately applied? What makes a sweatshop a sweatshop?

Definitions

Unfortunately, the issues surrounding sweatshops and their economic context are so contentious that not even the definition of the term is free from controversy. As we will see in the next section, the term has a historical reference, which picks out a particular method of production in the apparel industry in the early part of the 1900s. But we do not want our definition to rule out the possibility that sweatshops might exist *today*, in *other* industrial contexts. To tie the term "sweatshop" to a particular industry in a particular historical era is to put too strict a limit on the broader social criticism that term was intended to invoke.

The term also has a legal meaning. The U.S. General Accounting Office defines a sweatshop as "an employer that violates more than one federal or state law governing minimum wage and overtime, child labor, industrial homework, occupational safety and health, workers compensation, or industry regulation."

The advantage of this definition is that it provides a clear, quantifiable standard with which to assess the status of sweatshops within the United States, and a basis for pursuing legal action against them.

In certain contexts, this definition may be entirely appropriate. Its disadvantage is much the same as that found in the historical definition discussed above—it seems too narrow to serve as a *general* definition. In the history of the United States, many sweatshops existed *prior* to the enactment of many of the worker-protection laws referenced in the GAO's definition. Does this mean they were not really sweatshops? Similarly, many of today's sweatshops exist outside of the United States, in countries where legal protection for labor is minimal at best. Often, these companies operate without breaking any of the laws of their home country at all. If we wish to condemn these operations as "sweatshops," the legal definition will be inadequate.

Ultimately, then, the precise meaning of the term "sweatshop" will vary depending on context. Historical and legal definitions have their place, but usually our description of a certain producer as a sweatshop will reflect a *moral* judgment. In other words, it will reflect our judgment that the producer is treating its employees inhumanely, or that it is violating their basic human rights or simple standards of decency. This definition, too, is not without its problems, for it raises a whole host of complicated moral questions such as what moral obligations employers have toward their employees, or what constitutes a fair wage for a day's work. Furthermore, by building moral wrongness into the definition, this approach rules out from the start the question of whether sweatshops might ever be morally permissible. Nevertheless, understanding "sweatshop" as a moral term seems to best fit the way in which the term has been used in the context of social criticism in which it arose.

Apparel and the Origins of the Sweatshop

In America, sweatshops can be traced back to the rise of industrialization in the nineteenth century, when millions of European immigrants flooded the nation's cities seeking a better life for themselves and their families. Many of these immigrants went to work in large factories, where they played their part in the division of labor under a fairly centralized, hierarchical system of management. The factory was not the only place where work was to be found in the city, however, and many workers, especially women and children who lacked the physical strength demanded by factory work, sought employment in apparel.

It is in the apparel industry that the form of production we now think of as "sweatshops" originally took form. Unlike the factory system, the production of apparel tended to be relatively decentralized. This is because unlike the sort of manufacturing which took place in the factories, the manufacture of apparel required little in the way of large, expensive pieces of equipment. The manufacture of apparel was, and remains, essentially a low-tech, and thus labor-intensive process. Essentially, the only start-up cost involved, apart from rent and utilities, was a simple sewing-machine. Manufacturers could thus contract out the sewing of pre-produced pieces of fabric to small companies which specialized in such tasks, or simply assign it directly to their workers themselves. In this latter arrangement, referred to as "homework," workers would either buy or lease the needed tools and equipment—sometimes even the materials themselves—and perform the work out of their own homes.

The inherent volatility of the market for fashionable apparel rendered this system of homework economically efficient for manufacturers. Weather, season and, most of all, changes in taste, can have a dramatic impact on the sorts of apparel demanded by consumers on any given day. A trendy outfit which can sell for hundreds of dollars one month can easily lose over 50% of its value over the next several months. Fashion retailers are thus faced with the risk of winding up with large stocks of goods for which there is no longer any consumer demand. Not unexpectedly, most retailers react to this risk by trying to shift its cost to elsewhere in the production cycle. By placing orders for only as many clothes as they can reasonably expect to sell in a short time, retailers push the risk down to manufacturers. Instead of retailers facing the prospect of being stuck with clothes they cannot sell, manufacturers are forced to adjust their production processes to the quickly-changing demands of retailers, and to run their businesses on the basis of the unpredictable revenue streams such orders produce. Manufacturers thus limit their production to so-called "short-runs," producing relatively few articles of clothing at a time. This system of production, where apparel is produced in small amounts and only when demand is relatively secure, is another reason that most apparel production has not been mechanized. The short-runs needed for the production of fashionable apparel simply do not justify the investment in expensive capital equipment.

Thus the risk is passed down from retailer to manufacturer, and likewise from manufacturer to contractor and subcontractor, until ultimately it is borne by the individual worker. In the homework system, workers themselves are responsible for many of the costs of doing business (rent, heat, etc.). Though these costs will be reflected to a certain extent in their wages, this system frees manufacturers from the burden of paying for the cost of a labor pool they do not need. In periods when demand is low, manufacturers simply do not place orders with homeworkers, who must therefore find some other way of paying for their sustenance. A similar motivation lies behind the system in which workers are paid by the number of pieces they produce, rather than by salary or even hourly wage. If manufacturers cannot be sure of steady orders from retailers, then why pay for workers they may not need?

Early Reform

Because the persons employed by sweatshops tended to be those with few other options for economic advancement—mostly women, children, and immigrants—employees were willing to put up with low wages, cramped and unsanitary working conditions, and unsteady employment, all without much protest. This is not to say that those outside the system were complacent. In 1900, New York State License Superintendent Daniel O'Leary was reported to be so shocked by "workers toiling in dark, humid, stuffy basements on Division St., children of eight years and women, many of them far from well, sweating their lives away in these hellholes," that he appealed to the trade union for help and advice. But the unions would not be much help for some time.

The first moves for reform came from the workers themselves. In 1909, 20,000 shirtwaist makers throughout the country went on strike in support of a walkout at the Triangle Shirtwaist Factory in New York. This event, sometimes called "The Uprising of the 20,000," became a national cause as community leaders joined picket lines and raised funds in support of the strike.

After the Uprising, labor leaders and manufacturers came together to forge the first prototype collective bargaining agreement—the "Protocol of Peace." This agreement, shaped largely by jurist and strike-mediator Louis D. Brandeis, required manufacturers to recognize the union and a union shop, and to set up a grievance procedure and a board to oversee health conditions in the workplace. The agreement was widely praised and viewed as a model for future reform, but the reform would not come quickly.

In 1911, a fire at that same Triangle factory resulted in the deaths of 146 garment workers. This fire, exacerbated by the unsafe conditions at the factory, was viewed as a setback to the hope inspired by the Protocol. Still, progress was being made. More and more workers were being unionized into the International Ladies' Garment Workers' Union (ILGWU), and its counterpart in textiles and menswear, the Amalgamated Clothing and Textile Workers Union (ACTWU). According to labor historian Alan Howard, total membership in these unions between 1931 and 1933 climbed from less than 40,000 to over 300,000. This dramatic rise in union membership, combined with worker-friendly New Deal legislation, helped eliminate sweatshops as a major factor in garment production in the United States. Sweatshops remained on the margins of industry until the mid-1970s.

The Re-emergence of Sweatshops

The return of sweatshops is usually seen as a by-product of globalization. The rise of the multinational corporation, manufacture for export in many developing countries, the elimination of barriers to trade, and increasing freedom of migration have all served to lessen the cost of labor for corporations. Perhaps the most important development is the way in which increasing access to foreign labor pools has enabled industries to move production offshore so as to take advantage of lower costs of doing business. This access to foreign labor also affects U.S. labor directly, insofar as it causes domestic manufacturers to look for ways to lower their costs in order to compete effectively. They do this either "above-board" by attempting to weaken the power of trade-unions through political action or hard negotiating, or "below-board" by moving production to illegal, unregulated and un-unionized sweatshops.

The result of this process of globalization is dramatic. According to New York University American Studies professor Andrew Ross, more than 60% of the garments now sold in the United States are imported, mostly from Asian countries. In 1997, apparel imports totaled $42 billion, up from $21.9 billion in 1990, $5.5 billion in 1980, and $1.1 billion in 1970. How exactly did this state of affairs come to be?

In the United States, apparel manufacture has long benefited from various protectionist measures. One such benefit has been a series of exemptions from various free-trade agreements, such as the General Agreement on Tariffs and Trade (GATT). Founded in 1947, GATT designed various rules against trade discrimination, import restrictions, and tariff protectionism. The motivating belief is that free trade, in general, makes all parties better off, and that restrictions on free trade should therefore be limited. From 1947 until the Uruguay Round in 1994, many of these restrictions were eased for textile and apparel. The 1974 Multi Fiber Agreement, for instance, regulated the international trade in apparel and textiles through an elaborate quota system, thus preventing domestic producers from being overrun by more cheaply produced imports.

The re-emergence of the sweatshop has generally paralleled the decline of these protectionist measures. In 1963, a special provision in the U.S. Tariff Schedule (Item 807) allowed manufacturers to export cut garments for foreign assembly, and to re-import them into the United States with duties paid only on the (relatively small) value added to the garment in the assembly process. In 1983, the Caribbean Basin Initiative (CBI) extended tariff-free access for most products to twenty-two (later increased to twenty-seven) countries. While this did not initially apply to apparel, in 1986 the 807A ("super 807") provisions extended the benefit to products assembled in the Caribbean but made and cut in the United States. Probably the most significant development for apparel manufacture in the Western hemisphere has been the North American Free Trade Agreement (NAFTA), which, implemented in January 1994, sought to eliminate all tariffs on industrial products traded between the United States, Mexico, and Canada by 2004. The MFA, too, is now being phased out, with the goal that by 2005 all trade in apparel will be quota-free.

Part of the motivation for these developments, as we saw above, was a belief that free trade would be beneficial for all nations involved. For many, this conclusion was the result of a straightforward application of a basic economic principle: what 18th – 19th century economist David Ricardo called the "principle of comparative advantage." This principle holds that a nation benefits most from trade when it focuses its productive energies on those tasks in which it is *relatively* more efficient, even if it does not have an absolute advantage in the area. For instance, if a country is better at making electronic devices than at making cars, it should focus its resources on making electronic devices, and use the revenue generated to pay for imports of cars. This is true, the principle holds, even if the country is the world's best car maker. (Bill Gates may be a better typist than his secretary, but it nevertheless makes sense for him to pay his secretary to do his typing *for* him, so that he can focus on running Microsoft.) Even relatively undeveloped countries, then, will have a comparative advantage in *some* field. Free trade allows nations to specialize and reap the benefits of the efficiencies this generates.

Free-market mechanisms were also believed to have the virtue of "flexibility." Large factories engaged in the mass-production of goods require massive capital investment, and often have difficulty responding to new developments in technology or consumer demand. The new system of production was to be based on a more decentralized model, where specific tasks would be contracted out to whomever could most efficiently produce them. In the long run, it was argued, this would lower costs, better enable manufacturers to satisfy the desires of consumers, and even liberate workers by freeing them from the repetitive burden of the Fordist assembly line.

The actual consequences, critics charge, have not been so rosy. Instead of simply freeing workers from the monotony of the factory, trade liberalization policies have increased job insecurity, shifted workers toward more part-time and temporary work, and made it more difficult for workers to unionize. And instead of bolstering the economies of developing nations, critics continue, the CBI has been a disaster on almost every front. It has shifted the productive focus of developing economies from local consumption to export, but this has not yielded the gains in trade promised by Ricardian economics. Instead, it has undermined political sovereignty and any hope of sustainable development, creating undiversified economies vulnerable to even a mild recession in the U.S. Meanwhile, U.S. firms are able to enjoy the benefits of a production process unhampered by the sorts of environmental, worker safety, and union regulations imposed by their own domestic government. Much of the production work that was once assigned as "homework" is thus now contracted out to foreign firms.

Anti-Sweatshop Activism

For most Americans, awareness of sweatshops as a social issue started when Kathie Lee Gifford cried on television. On April 29, 1996, National Labor Committee (NLC) director Charlie Kernaghan testified before a congressional committee about conditions at Global Fashion, a Honduran factory where sportswear bearing Kathie Lee's name was produced for sale at Wal-Mart. Most of the women employed in this plant, Kernaghan testified, were teenagers, and 10% were just thirteen to fifteen years old. These girls worked exceedingly long hours, usually from 7:30 in the morning until 9:00 at night. 75 hour work-weeks were not uncommon. Trips to the restroom were limited to two per day, and a prohibition on non-business related conversation was enforced by verbally and sometimes physically abusive supervisors. Pay for overtime work was often difficult to obtain. Regular wages were 31 cents per hour.

At first, Ms. Gifford seemed unrepentant. Two days after Kernaghan's testimony, Gifford wept on the air as she castigated him for his "vicious attack." Eventually, however, public outrage became too powerful for her to resist. While still maintaining that the subcontractors were acting without her or Wal-Mart's knowledge, Gifford pledged to devote herself to campaigning against sweatshops, and to allow independent monitors to visit all factories that make her clothes.

Ms. Gifford's embarrassment by the issue of sweatshops was probably the most visible result of anti-sweatshop activism in the late 1990s, but it was only one element of the beginnings of a newly-energized campaign. In September 1994, U.S. Secretary of Labor Robert Reich began taking legal action against sweatshops under the Hot Goods Provision of the Fair Labor Standards Act (FLSA). This clause allowed the Department of Labor to fine and seize the goods of those manufacturers and retailers who knowingly sell merchandise manufactured by companies violating the FLSA. However, with only 800 federal inspectors to cover the nation's over 20,000 cutting and sewing jobs, this sort of direct legal action was soon seen to be largely ineffective. In 1995, Reich switched to a strategy trying to solve the problem of sweatshops through the power of public opinion. The DOL began publishing a so-called "Fashion Trendsetter List," which purported to provide consumers with a directory of retailers and manufacturers who had made outstanding efforts in the fight against sweatshops. In May 1996, the Department of Labor began to issue reports of health and safety violations in the domestic apparel industry in a publication titled the "No Sweat Garment Enforcement Report." Inclusion on this list did not entail any legal action against the individuals responsible, but was rather intended as a method to publicly shame them into correcting their behavior.

A similar sort of campaign for public education on the issue of sweatshops would take place on the campuses of America's colleges, through the activism of an organization called United Students Against Sweatshops (USAS). Students in this organization focused their efforts on manufacturers of university licensed apparel, such as Nike, in an effort to ensure their adherence to codes of conduct prohibiting worker exploitation. Nike was especially singled out for focus because of its name recognition and dominance of the sports-apparel market, the fact that almost all of its production is outsourced, and because some of the most egregious reports of worker abuse had come from companies with which Nike had subcontracted. For instance, one Nike contractor in Jakarta, Indonesia, is charged with paying workers less than a living wage (employees are paid $2.00 per day when $4.00 per day is necessary to purchase adequate food, clothing, and shelter). More worrisome still are the results of an audit of the Tae Kwang Vina factory outside Ho Chi Minh City, Vietnam. This audit, conducted by Ernst & Young and commissioned by Nike itself (but released only when leaked to CorpWatch), found that workers in the factory were exposed to the toxic chemical toluene at levels 6 to 177 times that allowed by Vietnamese law.

USAS, founded in 1998, relied for its support on a coalition of student and labor activism. It drew support from labor mostly through the Union of Needletrades, Industrial and Textile Employees (UNITE), the union formed from the merger of ILGWU and ACTWU. Its most significant struggle since its inception has been the fight to establish an effective method for monitoring conditions in companies manufacturing university licensed apparel. The first response to student pressure on the issue was a code of conduct put forward in January 1999 by the Collegiate Licensing Company (CLC), a company which controls the use of university trademark logos and serves as a legal go-between for universities and clothing manufacturers. This code of conduct, which was adopted by many of the 150 colleges and universities then represented by the CLC, was criticized by USAS on the grounds that it (1) lacked a provision for full public disclosure of findings, (2) lacked a provision guaranteeing that workers be paid a living wage, and (3) lacked a provision to guarantee the protection of women's rights. In response to what they saw as an effort by universities to satisfy public opinion while avoiding the real issues, USAS members at Duke University and elsewhere staged sit-ins at the office of the university president. At Duke, this sit-in eventually won the promise of full disclosure.

A similar fight emerged over the attempts of the Clinton administration's Fair Labor Association (FLA), a group composed of apparel companies and NGOs which sought to address the sweatshop issue through the use of voluntary company monitoring.

More protests and sit-ins ensued, this time beginning with the University of North Carolina (Chapel Hill) and the University of Arizona, with students protesting that voluntary, industry-sponsored monitoring would be insufficient to stem abuses in sweatshops. Instead, USAS urged that universities enroll in the Worker Rights Consortium (WRC), an organization which deliberately shunned industry representation on its governing board in order to establish itself as a genuinely independent monitoring organization.

Despite suffering from occasional internal struggles, USAS has been remarkably successful in its efforts. By January 2003, 176 schools had enrolled in the FLA, and 112 had enrolled in the WRC. Many schools chose to enroll in both.

Moral Questions

For all the controversy that surrounds the issue of sweatshops, one thing is perfectly clear: conditions in sweatshops are usually horrible. There may be debate about *how* horrible conditions are: whether wages are enough to maintain an adequate diet, whether physical abuse takes place in a particular factory, whether manufacturers are living up to their contractual and legal agreements, and so on. But no matter how significant these details may be, they are dwarfed by the broader conclusion: by any first-world standard of decency, sweatshop conditions are atrocious.

But are first-world standards of decency the appropriate standard to apply to industries in third-world countries? Even if we agree that conditions in sweatshops are horrible, we still must answer two important questions in order to reach any settled moral conclusion. First, are companies who contract with sweatshop manufacturers doing anything *wrong*? And second, whether they are wrong or not, what should we *do* about the situation of sweatshops?

Let us begin by considering the first question. Certain individuals, especially economists, have defended sweatshops on the grounds that they currently constitute the best available alternative for people living in developing countries. The wages paid by Nike's firm in Jakarta, they point out, might seem low by U.S. standards, but they are actually fairly high by the standards of the local economy. People freely choose to work at these factories because they can make more money there than they can anywhere else.

If Nike were to close down the factory and begin producing exclusively in the United States, the situation of the workers it would have to lay off would not be improved—it would be worsened. They would either need to seek lower-paying employment elsewhere in the legitimate economy or try to make money by illicit means, often by prostitution or theft.

This argument draws its support from the claim that individuals *choose* to work at sweatshops. If those individuals had a better alternative, they would have taken it. Of course, this argument only holds where workers are not physically coerced into working at a particular plant. Cases of sweatshops hiring armed guards to ensure that their workforce does not leave exist, but they are rare. For the rest, the argument runs, the fact that employees chose to work at sweatshops shows that they view sweatshops as the best employment available. Taking that option away by forcing sweatshops to shut down would end up harming precisely the people the anti-sweatshop activists are trying to help.

Not only would shutting down factories harm the individuals who would lose their jobs as a result, the argument continues, it would also slow down the development of the economy as a whole, and thus prevent the development of better options for future generations. Sweatshops, economists are quick to point out, tend not to dominate an economy for very long. Often, they are the first step in a long path of economic development, injecting capital and management training into an economy where it can serve as the basis for the creation of new domestic industries. In Korea and Taiwan, for instance, Nike is no longer able to maintain manufacturing operations because, as one source reports, "workers in these quickly developing economies are no longer interested in working in low-paying shoe and textile factories." Sweatshops, according to this argument, are a *symptom* of poverty, not a *cause* of poverty. But moreover, they are a *hopeful* symptom: for they signal the beginning of an economic development which will eventually bring that poverty to an end.

These arguments are powerful and caution those opposed to sweatshops to think carefully about the results of the policy they advocate. But it is not clear that they are decisive. We began this section with two questions, and the sorts of arguments described above might give us reason to suppose that we have arrived at an answer to the first. If companies who contract with sweatshops thereby provide individuals in developing countries with better opportunities than they would otherwise have had, then maybe they are not acting wrongly, or at least, not as wrongly as some have supposed them to be.

But this still leaves us without an answer to the second question: what should we *do* about sweatshops? The arguments given above seem to leave this question largely unaddressed. After all, by and large, anti-sweatshop activists are not calling for U.S. companies to pull out of third-world countries altogether. They do not want sweatshops to be shut down; they want them to be *improved*. Students who agitate for code of conduct programs want U.S. companies to ensure that their subcontractors pay a living wage, that they provide safe and sanitary working conditions for employees, and that they respect workers' basic human rights. Sophisticated anti-sweatshop activists recognize that companies are making employees better off by their providing individuals with jobs. They simply demand that companies ensure that those jobs be provided in a way which meets some basic ethical guidelines.

Still, the issue of what guidelines companies, consumers, or international organizations should impose on sweatshops is a complicated matter. Many of the proposals to regulate sweatshops suffer from the same sort of problem as proposals to abolish them. In 1992, for instance, the U.S. Congress considered a bill known as the Child Labor Deterrence Act, which sought to prohibit the importation of any product made in whole or in part by individuals under the age of 15 who are employed in industry or mining. Proposals such as this seem not to recognize that in a developing economy, child labor can play a vital role. For families living in such conditions, almost all income is directed toward the basic necessities of life: food, medicine, shelter, clothing. When parents grow too old or sick to work, children often become the main breadwinners of the family. An effective ban on products made by child labor would mean that these children would lose their jobs. Because developing countries generally have little in the way of social welfare programs for families to fall back on, the effect of this loss can be devastating.

In dealing with sweatshops, then, good intentions are simply not enough. Well-intentioned proposals to provide workers with a living wage, or health or maternity benefits, can raise the amount of money companies are forced to spend on each worker, and in so doing create a pressure to lay off all but the most essential. But these considerations do not settle the matter in favor of sweatshops; they simply caution that close empirical research is necessary before drawing any conclusion.

Sweatshop critics Edna Bonacich and Richard Appelbaum are quick to respond to the above arguments, for instance, by pointing out that in the case of a typical $100 dress sold and made in the United States, only 6% of the purchase price goes to the individual who actually made the garment. 25% goes to profit and overhead for the manufacturer, 50% goes to the retailer, and the remaining is spent on raw materials. Using similar reasoning, the National Labor Committee pointed out to Disney Chairman Michael

Eisner in 1996 that the effect of raising the pay of workers at the Classic Apparel facility in Haiti from their then-current 35 cent per hour wage to 58 cents an hour would be a mere 3 cent raise in price for an $11.99 garment. And if certain economists are right, raising wages in many circumstances might actually *lower* costs, or at least have no negative effect. Workers who are not paid enough to provide for their nutritional needs might not be as productive as those who are able to afford a steady and reliable diet.

It is difficult, then, to come to any generally applicable conclusions about the wrongness of sweatshops or the desirability of any sort of regulatory or consumer-driven alternative. By way of general principle, we can only say that any reasonable policy will need to pay careful attention to the way in which alternative stances towards sweatshops actually affect the persons they are intended to help. Discovering what helps and what doesn't is less a matter of applying a pre-packaged ideology (free-market or anti-sweatshop) than it is of doing careful research into the unique local conditions of particular sweatshops and their political and economic contexts.

References: Print

Arnold, Denis. "Exploitation and the Sweatshop Quandary," *Business Ethics Quarterly* 13:2 (April 2003).

Arnold, Denis, and Norman Bowie, "Sweatshops and Respect for Persons," *Business Ethics Quarterly* 13:2 (April 2003).

Becker, Gary S. "Is There Any Way to Stop Child Labor Abuses?" *Business Week*, May 12, 1997.

Bliss, C. J., and N. H. Stern. "Productivity, Wages, and Nutrition, 2: Some Observations." *Journal of Development Economics* 5 (1978): 363–398.

Bonacich, Edna, and Richard P. Appelbaum. *Behind the Label: Inequality in the Los Angeles Apparel Industry.* Berkeley: University of California Press, 2000.

Boukhari, Sophie. "Child Labour: A Lesser Evil?" *The Unesco Courier*, May 1999.

Donaldson, Thomas. "Multinational Decision Making: Reconciling International Values," *The Ethics of International Business*, Oxford University Press, 1989.

Featherstone, Liza, and United Students Against Sweatshops. *Students Against Sweatshops.* New York: Verso, 2002.

Hayek, Friedrich. *Capitalism and the Historians.* Chicago: University of Chicago Press, 1954.

Khoury, Jean-Claude. "The Re-Emergence of Sweatshops." *Business Ethics* 7:1 (January 1998): 59–62.

Kristol, Nicholas D., and Sheryl WuDunn. "Two Cheers for Sweatshops," *The New York Times Magazine*, September 24, 2000.

Lopez, Luis F. "Child Labor: Myths, Theories and Facts," *Journal of International Affairs*, 55:1 (Fall 2001).

Maitland, Ian. "The Great Non-Debate over International Sweatshops," reprinted in Tom L. Beauchamp and Norman E. Bowie, *Ethical Theory and Business*, 6th ed. (Englewood Cliffs: Prentice Hall, 2001), p. 595. First published in *British Academy of Management Conference Proceedings* (September 1997), pp. 240–265.

Moran, Theodore H. *Beyond Sweatshops: Foreign Direct Investment and Globalization in Developing Countries.* Washington, D.C.: Brookings Institution Press, 2002.

Nardenelli, Clark. *Child Labor and the Industrial Revolution.* Bloomington: Indiana University Press, 1990.

Rosen, Ellen Israel. *Making Sweatshops: The Globalization of the U.S. Apparel Industry.* Berkeley: University of California Press, 2002.

Ross, Andrew. *No Sweat: Fashion, Free Trade, and the Rights of Garment Workers.* New York: Verso, 1997.

Santoro, Michael A. *Profits and Principles: Global Capitalism and Human Rights in China* (Ithaca: Cornell University Press, 2000).

Stein, Leon. *Out of the Sweatshop.* New York: Quadrangle/New York Times Book Co., 1977.

Varley, Pamela, ed. *The Sweatshop Quandary: Corporate Responsibility on the Global Frontier.* Washington, D.C.: Investor Responsibility and Research Center, 1998.

Williams, Mary E. *Child Labor and Sweatshops.* San Diego: Greenhaven Press, 1999.

References: Electronic

American History Sweatshop Exhibition: http://americanhistory.si.edu/sweatshops/.

Clean Clothes Campaign: http://www.cleanclothes.org/.

Collegiate Licensing Company: http://www.clc.com.

CorpWatch: http://www.corpwatch.org.

Fair Labor Association: http://www.fairlabor.org.

Maquila Solidarity Network: http:// www.maquilasolidarity.org/.

National Labor Committee: http://www.nlcnet.org.

"Nike Is Right"—article by William Stepp defending Nike's use of sweatshops: http://www.mises.org/fullstory.asp?control=628.

No Sweat: http://www.nosweat.org.uk/.

PBS Feature on Battling Sweatshops: http://www.pbs.org/newshour/bb/business/jan-june97/sweatshops_4-14.html.

Stop Sweatshops!: http://www.uniteunion.org/sweatshops/sweatshop.html.

Sweatshop Watch: http://www.sweatshopwatch.org.

Triangle Factory Fire (online exhibit): http://www.ilr.cornell.edu/trianglefire/.

United Students Against Sweatshops: http://www.usasnet.org.

U.S. Department of Commerce Information on the Caribbean Basin Initiative: http://www.mac.doc.gov/CBI/webmain/intro.htm.

U.S. Department of Labor Information on the Garment Industry: http://www.dol.gov/esa/garment/index.htm.

Worker Rights Consortium: http://www.workersrights.org.

Questions for Discussion and Reflection

1. What do you think of the countries mentioned in this article that allow and even encourage children to work?
2. How do you balance the family's need for income and the need for children to get an education? Do you think that children working so young undercuts their opportunity for an education?
3. What do you think of the claim that refusing to buy goods made in sweatshops is actually harmful to the poor in the developing world?

Ethical Theory and Bribery

Bernard Adeney

From *Strange Virtues: Ethics in a Multicultural World* (Downers Grove, Ill.: IVP, 1995), 142–62.

In interviews with Christians from all parts of the world working in "Third World" countries, the most commonly cited moral problem is corruption or bribery. This chapter explores how Western ethical theory of moral choice might contribute to a sharpened perception of the nature of moral reality in relation to this thorny issue. I will examine a case study in order to consider how classical ethical categories and more recent conceptions contribute to an understanding of what is at stake in a particular cross-cultural problem. This will provide both an in-depth ethical analysis of bribery and the outlines of an ethical method for evaluating other cross-cultural dilemmas.

As an individual case, the situation presented in the following story is relatively trivial. But behind it lies a much larger problem of how to "act well" in a bureaucratic, patronage-based, social structure in which relationships, and even survival, are structured through the giving and receiving of gifts.

The Case Study: Elusive Justice

Bill looked at the police officer with uncertainty and frustration. The officer had asked him for 200,000 rupees for the return of his driver's license. It was Bill's twelfth weekly visit to the headquarters since the license had been confiscated, and his resentment rose as he faced the possibility of yet another wasted week clouded with uncertainty and unpleasantness, unable to use his car. Must he sacrifice his principles in order to resolve the matter?

The problem began when Bill had returned from a missionary assignment out of town. He was coming into Bandung, West Java, along the main highway from Cirebon, the same road on which he had left the city two days before. The chaotic congestion was about normal in this heavily populated part of town. Animals, trishaws, and people were weaving their way in and out among the motorized traffic that crawled along the road toward the urban open market. For some time Bill had been caught behind a slow-moving, overcrowded bus, and there was little chance of getting past it, even when it stopped to allow passengers to alight.

Suddenly Bill was jolted to attention when something hit the side of the car. Before he knew what had happened, he caught sight of a policeman approaching the car and shaking his fist. By the time the officer had picked up his baton from the street, Bill was out of the car and prepared for the worst. Fellow missionaries had warned him never to tangle with the police. In fact, it was missionary policy not to call the police, even in the case of a house burglary. Experience had shown that it was cheaper to sustain the losses of robbery than to bear the frustration of red tape and loss of further property taken to headquarters to test for fingerprints.

Bill did not have to wait long to find out what he had done wrong. For several hundred yards approaching the market area, the highway became a one-way street. Buses and other public vehicles were permitted to use it in both directions, but private vehicles had to detour around back streets and rejoin the highway several blocks beyond the market. Bill pleaded that he had seen no sign and had simply followed the bus. The officer walked Bill back twenty yards and pointed out to him a small, mud-spattered sign obscured by a large parked truck. This did not seem to concern the officer at all. There was a law and a sign, and Bill was guilty.

Officer Somojo escorted Bill to the local police post in the market. Five other officers materialized from the stalls in the market, so Somojo began to explain how very embarrassing it was for him to have to prosecute a foreigner, and how he regretted that Bill had put him in this difficult position. After some time, Somojo suggested that the whole thing might be smoothed over quietly and without further awkwardness if Bill would pay a token fine of 2,000 rupees ($1.20) on the spot. Bill had been expecting just such a request. Without even asking if it was a formal, legitimate fine for which a receipt would be given, Bill quickly protested that although he might be technically guilty, Indonesian law had a system of justice and courts where such matters were to be settled. He would go through proper channels and requested to be allowed to do so. The officer scowled and told Bill that he would have to hold his driver's license until the case was settled. Bill could come to the police headquarters the following week to get it back. Since no receipt was issued for the license, Bill secretly feared that he would never see it again.

The following week, Bill went to the appointed office, only to be informed that the license had been sent to another department on the other side of the city. After a slow trip by trishaw, Bill finally found his way to the other office. The policeman in charge had a record of Bill's offense and said Bill could talk to the captain who would probably be prepared to settle the issue for 4,000 rupees. Bill suspected dishonesty and requested an official receipt for the money. The man just smiled. Bill told the policeman that he had come to Indonesia to build efficiency, justice, and a high standard of morality in the country. He would prefer to go through official channels. At that, he was told to return in a week's time. So week followed weary week, with hours wasted in travel and more hours spent waiting in offices. Each time the amount requested for settlement rose higher.

Bill worried about what he should do. He didn't want to be a troublemaker, but as a missionary he had to take a stand for honesty. His Christian witness depended on it. His whole upbringing as the son of an evangelical pastor had been one of strict integrity, and he had managed, so far, to maintain this standard in previous encounters with immigration officers and postal clerks. Yet, while he felt he had done the right thing, he still felt uneasy, for he knew full well that government officials were so poorly paid that they had to make at least double their official salaries on the side if they were to feed and clothe their families. The whole system was unjust, and he was caught in it. Bill talked to some other missionaries. They just laughed and said, "Let us know how you get on!"

Now it was the twelfth week, and he still did not have his license. Moreover, the amount being asked to settle the case had risen to 200,000 rupees (U.S. $120). Should he pay the official and end the case? Or should he appeal to a higher-level officer in hopes of a just settlement? Bill looked at the officer and said....

Responses to the Case Study

As I have presented this case study to Christians from various countries, most felt that "Bill" should have paid the bribe or fine in the first place. Others, including Indonesians, Filipinos and a few North Americans, thought "Bill" should stand firm.

Of the minority who said Bill should refuse to pay, the Americans appealed to a moral principle: "Bribery is always wrong." The Filipinos explained that the only way for Christians to escape the straightjacket of corruption is for them, as a community, to become known as people who never compromise in such matters, no matter how trivial the situation. Some Indonesians suggested that because of his role as a Westerner and a missionary, Bill should not pay. But of course Indonesian Christians would just pay; they would have no choice.

The majority from all nationalities felt that in this situation the money should have been paid in the first place. Various reasons were given in justification: (1) The situation involves a conflict of values—the values to be gained by paying are greater than the values lost by compromise. (2) Since the police are paid so poorly, the money should be thought of as a tip for services rendered rather than a bribe. (3) Bribery is an accepted mechanism for legal transactions in this context. Westerners have no right to impose their own legal norms on a context in which small-scale bribery has almost the status of customary law. (4) Corruption should be fought, but you must choose your enemy. If you refuse to compromise at such a trivial level, you will waste all your time struggling with the victims of the system and have no time to address the real

villains—the structures of the system and those who enforce them at a high level. (5) Unless Bill has friends in high places, he has no choice. He must pay and should be considered a victim of petty extortion, not a criminal.

Sources of Moral Decision-Making in Ethical Theory

How does Western ethical theory correspond to the reasons stated in these various opinions? The concern of this chapter is to clarify why some people think one way and others another way. What follows is a brief description of theoretical ways of moral thought. I will use two traditional, philosophical approaches to moral decision-making and see how far they take us in understanding why people differ on their opinions. More recent ethical theory attempts to move beyond the "decision" by focusing on the moral qualities of the person(s) within their particular tradition and social structure.

Deontological ethics: absolute right and wrong. The first traditional approach is often called "deontological" ethics, from the Greek *ontos*, which means "that which exists by itself." A deontological approach to ethics argues that goodness and evil are intrinsic to an act or an actor. Certain actions and attitudes are right or wrong in and of themselves, no matter what their effect on the world. Some Christians argue that we must do or not do certain things, regardless of culture, and leave the results in God's hands.

For example, a Christian pacifist may argue that it is always wrong to kill another human being. Even if by killing a person you save ten lives, it is still wrong. Some would say the same for lying. George MacDonald said, "I would not favor a fiction to keep a whole world out of hell. The hell that a lie would keep any man out of is doubtless the very best place for him to go to. It is truth ... that saves the world."

In this quote, lying is seen as deontologically wrong. A deontological approach draws the line at a certain point and suggests that if your behavior crosses this line it is wrong, no matter what your motives are or how salutary the outcome.

A simplified deontological approach to Christian ethics is sometimes labeled "moralism." There are clear moral rules derived from Scripture, reason, or society. These are moral absolutes that should never be violated under any circumstances: don't lie, don't bribe, don't kill, don't drink alcohol, turn the other cheek, and so on. A value of this approach is that it is clear, uncompromising and objective, and it precludes rationalization. Some students who argued that "bribery is always wrong" exhibit this approach.

The biggest problem with moralism is that a person's choice of moral rules is likely to be deeply related to culture. No one follows all the rules of the Bible, so determining what is absolute requires selection. Bribery may feel wrong to me because it is considered illegal and "sleazy" in my culture. To someone from another context, small-scale bribery may seem perfectly all right. One Third World pastor told me that he felt great relief and peace after paying a small bribe to a police officer who stopped him for a minor infraction. He felt that God had rescued him from a potentially very dangerous situation!

Moralism ignores the fact that sometimes moral rules conflict with each other or with broader moral principles. Moralism can lead to legalistic self-righteousness and concentration on trivial rules at the expense of larger, less definable issues. For legalists, all morality is flattened out. All rules are equally important. Those in the fourth group, who argued for ignoring the small-scale problem and fighting against corruption at a higher level, were trying to avoid this problem. Similarly, those who felt a Westerner could afford to resist but they could not were applying different rules to different people according to their power in the situation: it is better not to pay, but for some it is just too costly.

Moralism is a shallow example of a deontological approach that insufficiently recognizes the complexity of reality. The narrow rigidity of legalism is an inherent danger of deontology.

Teleological ethics: goodness determined by the outcome. The second philosophical stream is called "teleological" ethics, from the Greek *telos,* which means end, result, or goal. Teleological ethics argue that goodness lies not in an act or actor but in the act's real effect on the real world. People and actions are judged good or evil not by some inner quality but by the results of their action in human history. As Jesus said, "You will know them by their fruits" (Mt 7:20).

For example, some Christians would object to an absolutist interpretation of the commands not to kill or to lie. To kill or lie in order to save the lives of innocent people may be seen as good. Of course the results or "fruit" of an action cannot be measured only for the short term; the long term must also be considered. If the judgment of God is factored into a teleological approach, its distance from deontology is lessened. God's sovereign final judgment is the ultimate guarantee that good action produces good results and sin leads to death.

Situation ethics is a popular attempt to escape the dangers of moralism. Joseph Fletcher argued that since Christians are not "under the law," there are no moral rules, only the law of love. Every situation should be judged uniquely on the basis of love: what is the most loving thing to do in this situation? On the one hand, goodness is determined by motivation—does the action spring from love? On the other hand, it is based on realistic calculation of what action will most effectively show love to those involved. Situation ethics recognizes the primacy of love and the uniqueness of each individual circumstance. In regard to the case study above, those who considered the low pay of the police and the conventional acceptance of the system of "gift giving" exhibit a situational rather than a moralistic approach.

Situation ethics has many problems. There is the obvious danger of subjective rationalization. Almost anything can be justified by an appeal to love. As Stanley Hauerwas observed, "the ethics of love is often but a cover for what is fundamentally an assertion of ethical relativism. It is an attempt to respond to the breakdown of moral consensus by substituting the language of love for the language of good and right as the primary determinate for the moral.... Love becomes a justification for our own arbitrary desires and likes." The short- and long-term effects of an action rarely can be accurately predicted. The true situation ethicist chooses the good by calculating what course of action will have the most loving results. Morality by calculation assumes that it is possible to know the moral results of an action. But the moral results of action are often unknowable, even after the event. What can scarcely be known in retrospect can hardly be known beforehand. Situations do not stand alone but are part of a larger historical, sociocultural and economic context that is impossible to master.

An Indonesian professor responded to the story of Bill by writing out his own hypothetical story of the policeman, showing how hard his life was and the desperate material needs of his family. His conclusion was that Bill should have paid out of love and respect for the policeman. But his imagined circumstances are just the sorts of things that a person cannot know on the spot, when a decision has to be made.

Situation ethics promotes an individualistic approach that exchanges the absolutism of rules for an absolutism of the personal conscience. By doing so, it ignores the usefulness of moral rules as a shorthand for judgments of society or the Christian community on right and wrong. Situation ethics devalues all principles except love and oversimplifies the relational meaning of morality. Love may be our highest norm, but it is not the only one. In a case of bribery, other principles such as justice, honesty, gentleness, and obedience to the state cannot be ignored.

Finally, situation ethics is too time-consuming. To judge every situation afresh, without the benefit of rules, is impossible for human beings, for we must all categorize reality in order to avoid being overwhelmed by data. To be sure, emotivist situationalism is easy and quick. But if a situationalist is serious about calculating the most loving action, each decision could be long and torturous.

The dangers of a situational approach were recognized by respondents to the case study who argued for a principled rejection of all bribery. They saw a principled approach as the only way for a community to resist the enslavement of corruption. Some even argued that it was working, that officials no longer tried to receive payments from the Christian community because they knew it was futile.

On the other hand, the Indonesians who said that Bill should refuse to pay but that Indonesians would have to pay were not situationalists. Their conclusion was based not on the love commandment but on a power assessment of the situation: a Westerner might be able to get away without paying, but they could not. Furthermore, they thought it was appropriate for Bill to go through all the hassle of refusing to pay because of his role as a Western missionary who would

be expected to bring unexpected values into the situation. At the very least they did not want to judge Bill in his decision to take a costly stand.

Situation ethics is a shallow example of a teleological approach that overestimates the power of an individual to calculate and bring about loving results without the restraints of law and community.

Distinctions, Synthesis, and the Problem of Bribery

Deontological and teleological ethics are often treated as mutually exclusive. The polarization of means and ends, the antithesis between principles and results, is a characteristic weakness of Western dualistic thought. It leads to a war between the absolutists and the relativists. The absolutists are thought to be too narrow and rigid. The relativists are thought to be too wishy-washy.

Actually, the distinctions between deontology and teleology helpfully show two necessary and contrasting elements in moral choice. These are not contradictory but complementary. The way they fit together cannot be determined by abstract philosophical principle. The concrete situations in which moral choices are embodied reveal the ways in which principles and results interact.

Absolute moral principles. As a Christian I believe there are absolute moral principles and rules that reflect the character of God. These moral principles underlie all human behavior and are based in the fact that we live in a moral universe. Human beings were created in the image of God and have an intrinsic value. In the words of the Westminster Confession, we were created "to glorify God and to enjoy him forever." While these deontological absolutes are expressed and emphasized differently in different places and times, they are clearly affirmed by Christians in all cultures.

The central moral absolute that follows from these Christian affirmations is "The Lord our God, the Lord is one; you shall love the Lord your God with all your heart, and with all your soul, and with all your mind, and with all your strength. You shall love your neighbor as yourself. There is no commandment greater than these" (Mk 12:29–31).

Out of love for God and neighbor come the deontological proscriptions against idolatry and covetousness. From love of neighbor and the inherent dignity of the human person (rooted in creation and confirmed by redemption) come the absolutes of beneficence (the quality of charity or kindness) and the commands to seek justice and love mercy. Most would accept the further implication that one should never torture or degrade a human being made in the image of God.

Some Christians see bribery as one of these absolutes. Bribery is seen as a form of dishonesty, of cheating, which favors the rich. They reject any compromise and are willing at any cost to resist the pressure to smooth their way with money. An American businessman in the Middle East has told me some marvelous stories of his absolute refusal to compromise on the issue of bribery. Though he faced enormous obstacles to his business, he always kept his priorities straight. He knew he was there not primarily to make money but to serve God.

Bribery as a general concept may be fit into this absolute category if a moral condemnation is included in the definition of bribery. If a bribe is defined as a gift intended to corrupt an official and cause him to act unjustly, then it must always be wrong to bribe. Some have tried to rigidly define bribery as only gifts given to obtain illegal favors. Given that definition, gifts to obtain just or legal service can be called tips.

But this is an unfortunate solution to a complex dilemma, because it allows proscriptions against bribery to be considered absolute while it disregards the most common kind of bribery in the modern world. By this definition there is nothing amiss when individuals or corporations pay large sums of money for special treatment, provided the treatment is not illegal.

Certainly gifts, especially large gifts given to obtain basic services, easily become a means of oppression. As a result of such gifts, those who cannot or will not pay may be denied even minimal justice. Similarly, gifts given by large foreign companies to win contracts routinely squeeze out the local industries that cannot afford such gifts. As John Noonan has observed, size is an important clue to whether a payment is a tip or a bribe.

But what about small gifts? Is there anything wrong with small gifts given to induce a poverty-stricken civil servant to bypass mountains of (quite legal) red tape? Whether such gifts are considered a bribe or a legitimate tip may amount to a matter of definition. The word *bribery* has strong moral connotations. Characterizing a transaction as a gift, tip, or bribe makes a great deal of difference. Our tradition, our culture, and the assumptions embedded in our experience usually determine how we describe a given activity.

Some Christians reject an absolute prohibition on bribes because they believe that what a Westerner calls a bribe may be a necessary mechanism for sharing wealth in poor countries. A prominent scientist of unquestionable Christian integrity suggested to me that paying a bribe in the Soviet Union is permissible if it is really an accepted part of a person's salary. Where salaries are low, everyone knows that officials must require gifts in order to survive. The money is not meant to corrupt but to expedite a sluggish process. People need money to live, and you have to make small gifts in order to get things done.

A moral distinction may be made on the basis of whether a person has the freedom to give or not to give. If a small gift is freely given to obtain better service and there is no fear or threat involved, it is possible to consider it a tip. Presumably the service would be given in any case but would probably take a little longer. The tip speeds up the process and benefits both parties. Little or no harm is done to the poor who either do not need the service or can obtain it with a little more time.

On the other hand, if fear or force is involved, or if the expected delays are extreme, the freedom that characterizes a gift or a tip is removed. A gift or a tip is never compulsory.

While a gift is never compulsory, it may be strongly expected. When my neighbors bring me a bunch of bananas from their tree, they expect that sooner or later I will share with them the papayas that grow in our yard. Yet I would never suspect them of bribery! As Anthony Gittins has pointed out, gift giving is a rule-governed activity in which obligations are a constant. The obligations, however, are not usually to be seen as the requirement to pay the person back on a tit-for-tat basis. Rather, the obligation is to continue the relationship that is symbolized by the gift: "gift exchange is seen to be patterned behavior embodying clear moral values; it creates and maintains personal relationships, not simply between private individuals, but between groups and between 'moral persons 'or 'statuses.'"

This is a far cry from bribery, in which either the briber buys special service from the bribee through an illegal gift or the bribee forces an illegal payment by refusing to give fair treatment. A gift helps create or maintain a moral relationship, while a bribe undermines it.

Small gifts paid to poor officials are ambiguous because they occupy a gray area between a gift, a tip, and a bribe. Usually they are not compulsory, but neither are they free. They may help establish a relationship of trust and mutual help, but they are also underlined with the threat of poor service and time delays. Certainly they are a part of the establishment of status relationships, but they are also sometimes a pure economic exchange that takes place outside the law.

This ambiguity was echoed by many Christians I interviewed. For example, a Christian who worked in the Dominican Republic suggested that the clear definitions we assume in the West do not apply to some other countries. He suggested, "In the U.S. there is a clear line between a bribe and a non-bribe. But in many places it is a continuum. In the States a person may get a 30% commission while their counterpart in the third world receives only 5% but expects a bribe. Sometimes you don't know you are paying a bribe. You may receive a bill for 125% import duty where 25% of it is a bribe. The equivalent of not paying the customs officer a tip is not paying a waitress a tip. He deserves a tip as payment for his services because his salary is so low."

The complexity of the meaning and value of gift giving is reflected in the book of Proverbs, where there are three negative and three positive references to bribery (Prov. 15:27; 17:8; 17:23; 18:16; 21:14; 22:16). John Noonan Jr., in his massive historical study of bribery, faults the Old Testament for having a double standard. He suggests that while the extortion of bribes is roundly condemned, the giving of bribes (or gifts to officials) is not condemned in the Old Testament. Such equivocation in the Old Testament seems to reflect a recognition of the power differential between a poor person who gives a gift in order to stave off injustice and the rich who uses his power to exploit the poor. The powerful and the powerless are not judged by the same abstract absolute, but by the relationships and intentions of their situation. Thus, if you close your ear to the cry of the poor, you will cry out and not be heard. A gift in secret averts anger and a concealed bribe in the bosom, strong wrath. When justice is done, it is a joy to the righteous but dismay to evildoers (Prov. 21:13–15). The way a moral act is described is part of the texture of a narrative. If the narrative experienced is of a righteous poor person who escapes injustice by giving a culturally appropriate gift to his or her potential oppressor, the reality described is very different from the narrative of a policeman who threatens torture unless he is given a large gift. The definition of what is going on springs not from a philosophical category such as "deontology" or "teleology" but from a much larger tradition and narration of experience. The positive references to bribery in the Bible appear to reflect a utilitarian approach to ethics for those who have no other means of receiving justice. However, Proverbs unequivocally condemns those who accept bribes in order to do wrong: "The wicked accept a concealed bribe to pervert the ways of justice" (Prov. 17:23). It also warns that giving gifts does not always work "Giving to the rich will lead only to loss" (Prov. 22:16). A single perspective on bribery cannot be forced on the Bible, because different verses were written at different times for different contexts and different people.

Certainly the great majority of Old Testament references to bribery are negative. The God of the Bible is one who does not accept *sohad* (bribes), who judges impartially. We are called to be like God in love of righteousness. Nevertheless, there is enough ambiguity in the biblical record to allow for hesitancy in making the prohibition of bribes an absolute.

Right and wrong "on the face of it." A helpful intermediate category between the relativism of teleology and the absolutism of deontology has been developed by Roman Catholic moral theology. The concept of prima facie moral rules and principles is founded in the recognition that we live in a fallen, sinful world where what ought to be is sometimes impossible. Prima facie means "on the face of it" or "on first assessment." Prima facie rules ought to be absolutes in all cultures and all times. On the face of it, all things being equal, one must always obey these rules.

If you break a prima facie command or principle, you cannot escape doing evil. Nevertheless, there are tragic circumstances where, because of sin, values come into conflict and one commandment must be sacrificed if we are to uphold a higher value. Such an action, even though justified, should never be done without regret. In a real sense it still remains wrong. For there are tragic consequences from such a violation that undermine the fabric of society. Evil still clings to the act, even if it is morally justifiable.

William Frankena suggests that if certain actions are prima facie wrong, they are "intrinsically" wrong. In other words, they are always actually wrong when they are not justified on other moral grounds. They are not in themselves morally indifferent. They may conceivably be justified in certain situations, but they always need to be justified; and, even when they are justified, there is still one moral point against them.

Commonly cited prima facie rules include the prohibitions against killing, lying, work on the Sabbath, and divorce. If you kill to stop a maniac gone amok, lie to save an innocent person hiding in your house, overwork to meet an urgent deadline, or divorce to end a situation of physical and mental abuse, in each case your action may be necessary and morally justifiable. But your action is not good; it is a necessary evil. Tragic consequences will follow. A fellow human will be dead, truth and human trust will be undermined, the quality of your inner harmony and worship will be threatened, what God has joined together will be torn apart.

The "necessary" evil that is done in all these cases will affect the actor, the immediate people involved, and the broader society. Their effect is not only personal but also social. That is why these moral rules, on the face of it, should never be broken.

Some Christians deny this category and treat examples such as the above as absolutes never to be broken. But the prima facie category has the virtue of taking moral rules seriously without trivializing the power of evil to frustrate the best intentions of law. Prima facie principles may only be broken to avert some greater evil. Unlike in situation ethics, prima facie rules and principles are not nullified by moral calculation. They remain strong guides for behavior which must be reckoned with even when we tragically break them.

How can we determine when a prima facie moral law must be set aside in favor of a higher value? Some ethicists reject the implication that a Christian may face unavoidable evil. Instead of a prima facie category of morality, they suggest a fixed hierarchy of values in which to choose a higher value over a lower is not a lesser evil but a higher good. For example, to lie to save innocent life is in no sense wrong, but the highest possible good in the situation. Others admit the tragedy implied by the prima facie category but also suggest a fixed hierarchy of values to guard against creeping relativism.

Unfortunately, no fixed hierarchy of values can be demonstrated from Scripture, reason, or experience. Where is it written that death is worse than deceit? Is divorce worse than lying? Is neglecting the needs of your family worse than neglecting a friend in despair? Is stealing a car more honorable than allowing a criminal to escape? There is no abstract answer to such questions apart from detailed knowledge of the situations in which they are embedded. The fact that there is no fixed hierarchy of values does not imply that such values are relative, subjective, or changeable. All of the actions in this paragraph are intrinsically wrong. But their relative seriousness depends on many factors not revealed in the moral principle itself. Cowardice may sometimes be worse than killing.

One thing can be known for certain. The double love command does not admit exception. Augustine suggested that every other command of God must be filtered through the eyes of the command to love God and your neighbor. "On these two commandments hang all the law and the prophets" (Mt 22:40). The love commandment does not set aside the other commands but interprets their true meaning in a concrete situation. Unlike in situation ethics, love is not all that matters, but love is a part of all that matters. All moral situations receive their true weight in relation to the love of God and neighbor.

The category of prima facie rules is helpful for thinking about bribery. If bribery is defined as the giving of gifts in exchange for privileges or services that either are illegal or are meant to be administered impartially, then bribery is a prima facie evil. Each case of bribery undermines the cause of justice in society by making it difficult for the poor to be treated fairly. Bribery is officially illegal in almost every country in the world. On the other hand, it is possible to conceive of situations where greater harm may be done by refusing to pay a bribe. In the case of Bill, were fifteen hundred rupiahs ($1.50) and the principle of not paying an unofficial gift to an impoverished police officer worth the weeks or months of frustration and the possible permanent loss of private transportation? Should Bill be fighting other battles?

Whatever your answer, the effects are not simple. The escalating amount of money required symbolizes a growing alienation between Bill and the authorities. Is this a case of justice holding out against tyranny or a case of a foolish neo-colonialist foreigner insisting that his hosts conform to his rules? In either case Bill is unable to ensure that justice is done. If he pays, he violates his own conscience and may well reinforce the structural injustice of a society that treats those with money better than those without. If he doesn't pay, he may end up without a car because he quibbled over paying less than two dollars to a poor official.

Our individual actions cannot always overcome evil that is a structural part of a situation. Many Christians have told me stories of instances where they paid a small bribe to avoid what they understood as a far greater evil. Were they without sin in doing so? Perhaps not. The prima facie category does not absolve the lawbreaker from guilt. It only allows us to recognize our weakness in the face of a sinful world. Sometimes we are not wise enough or strong enough to act well in situations of ambiguity. Sometimes we cannot see any good course of action. Sometimes the law we break seems insignificant in the face of the enormity of our situation. If so, we dare not claim innocence. Nor may we rescind or denounce our action. It throws us on the mercy of God.

Relative moral situations. Many moral situations are not determined either by absolute principles or by prima facie commandments. One need not be a relativist to see that many decisions are relative to a particular situation. Those who argued that the "bribe" was really a tip with the status of customary law are suggesting that what is a bribe in a Western legal context is best considered a tip in an Indonesian context. In that case Bill simply misunderstood the meaning of his situation in a foreign context. His refusal to pay was not so much wrong as unwise.

While in the case of Bill this argument may be oversimplified, there are many moral choices we make that are unique to a particular person, time, or place. Such relative situations are not trivial. They may have large moral consequences. But they are not subject to abstract definition. They require deep understanding of a context and the subject's role in it. They require calculation of what actions will bring the most good and prevent the most evil in a particular context. They require the capacity of character and the commitment to care about what matters most. And they require the wisdom of God's Spirit so that we may choose the good.

Culture plays a major role in making morally relative decisions. How do we treat time? How do we decide how to live and at what socioeconomic level? How directly and forcefully do we communicate? How individualistic or communalistic are we in decision-making? How competitive are we? How do we spend our money? When do we give to those in need? How much time do we spend with our family? How do we honor our parents? How do we plan for emergencies? How authoritarian are we with our subordinates? Do we reach out to those in prison? How do we work for justice in society? How do we share the good news of our faith with people in need?

These, and many other questions like them, may be the most important moral questions of our lives. But there are no simple answers to them that are directly based on absolute or prima facie commandments.

An American evangelist once told a wealthy audience that a person could not be a Christian and drive a BMW luxury sedan. While such a statement could be considered neither an absolute nor a prima facie moral command, it provocatively dramatized what is at stake in our relative moral decisions. It is our relative moral decisions that demonstrate what we mean when we claim to love God and our neighbor.

In some cases the definition of a bribe and the meaning of a particular gift may be relative to the cultural intentions and expectations of those involved.

In the Middle East the value of a service or a thing is often defined through emotional bargaining. The normal fee for installing a telephone may not be fixed but variable. Appeals to relationship, need, the ability to pay, and other subjective factors are a vital part of defining the value of all goods and services. After all, why should we think something (like a telephone) has an objective value outside the relationships of those involved in the transaction?

A study by E. Glen, D. Witmeyer, and K. Stevenson of negotiation styles within the United Nations showed that Arabs argued with an intuitive-affective style, expressing their positions through appeals to strong emotion. Compromises were often "indicated by strong expressions of personal friendship and esteem towards the intermediary."

If relationships are the key to negotiations, it is not hard to see how the value of a service might be understood as contextual. For many people, relationships outweigh efficiency. If the feelings are right, for example, a seller may be willing to take a loss. While in economic terms it is a loss, in affective terms there is a gain—an established relationship of indebtedness. At the least the customer may come back, and she may encourage her friends to do so as well. On the other hand, if the feeling of relationship is wrong, the seller may pass up a profit. An economic profit may not outweigh the cultural alienation of dealing with someone perceived as rude and arrogant.

What Westerners see as bribery or deceit may be understood in some countries as ways of maintaining or achieving the right relationships. The market conditions of modern capitalism are not necessarily a more moral way of setting price than a bargaining relationship between two people.

Sometimes if a right relationship is established with someone, the necessity for a monetary exchange is eliminated. The right word or the meeting of eyes (or the humble averting of eyes!) may signal the kind of respect or "in-groupness" that establishes relationship.

In our case study, Bill might have been able to avoid the situation of conflict altogether. By showing the policeman genuine love, by expressing greater respect, by demonstrating true humility, by a wise use of trust, by an appropriate invitation or nonmonetary gift, by speaking with meek authority, Bill (or Jesus) might have reached the policeman in his place of greatest need. He might have been able to avoid the request for a bribe and initiate a friendship.

Many situations that appear to be either-or moral dilemmas may have hidden within them a third way. A godly Indonesian pastor shared his surprise with me that one time when he was stopped by the police for a traffic infraction, he was released with no payment or charge after he had apologized with genuine humility for his error. The right word spoken by the right person in the right way at the right time may bridge the chasm to another human being.

Most people do not have such deep power for good in their character. Most do not have the wisdom to overcome the deep divisions in society which lead to conflict. Sometimes human evil or structural injustice cannot be overcome by goodness. Sometimes the best of people end up on one cross or another. The best course of action for one person may be disastrous for another.

The relative moral decisions we make are ultimately grounded in the absolute core values that guide our lives. They grow out of our habitual praxis, our knowledge (or ignorance) of our context, our relationship to a community and the gift of God's wisdom and guidance.

Bribery and social structure. Why is bribery so much a part of some societies and not of others? Are some countries more dishonest than others? Does poverty make people corrupt? The prevalence of bribery in poor countries may contribute to the paternalism or even racism of some Westerners who see it as evidence of "Third World" backwardness or moral inferiority.

One Englishman suggested that in India it stemmed from a Hindu culture in which there are no moral absolutes. Religion undoubtedly influences ethics, but if Hinduism is the culprit, why is there so much graft in many Roman Catholic and Muslim societies? Certainly moral relativism is no part of Catholicism or Islam. Moreover, it seems unlikely that the "Protestant" West is more honest or less greedy than other parts of the world. A better explanation is that the social structures of some countries makes gift giving a far more extensive practice than in others. In Indonesia one seldom pays a visit without bringing a gift. In North Africa relationships are secured through mutual indebtedness. In Egypt nothing is done without a tip. In Latin America trust is ensured by a gift. In China connections are established through presents. Gift giving is not bribery; but when gifts become an obligatory mechanism for major social functions, the possibilities for corruption are obvious.

In many parts of the world, gift giving is radically shaped by a historical marriage between the structures of patronage and bureaucracy. Gift giving is an integral part of a patriarchal society. It is expected that the superior should care for the people under him by giving them gifts. Gifts are a means of buying loyalty and service. In the Marcos palace in Manila there were whole rooms full of merchandise for giving as gifts. Gifts mitigate an unjust and harsh social system. People are honored to have a patron, a protector. A person may be exploited, but he or she is also protected by the "father."

The word "patron" is originally from Rome. But the idea of responsibilities that accompany patriarchy must go back to the dawn of history. When a bureaucracy is added to a patronage system, both systems are modified but continue to operate. Modern bribery is related to this historical marriage. In Latin America a semifeudalistic hacienda system was grafted onto a bureaucracy derived from the French. In Indonesia the feudalistic javanese state was consciously married to the Dutch colonial bureaucracy. In the process, both were changed.

Bureaucracy is a different system from the hacienda system or the javanese rule of the divine king, but a gift is still the accepted mechanism to buy loyalty or silence or service. Gifts are expected not only from the social superior but also from anyone who needs the "loyalty" or service of the bureaucrat.

In the traditional society, services were rendered and protection was given according to a strict hierarchical order. Gifts were simply a means of strengthening established relationships and rewarding good work. In a modern bureaucracy, relationships have to be established without the benefit of a clear social order. If the country is very poor, with high unemployment and a large, underpaid bureaucracy, civil servants are effectively paid with power and prestige rather than money. They must use their power

to receive gifts if they are to support a family. The "patron" must demonstrate by gifts her worthiness of being served. This, of course, lends itself to corruption. But it is more than bribery in the Western sense. It also serves the social functions of sharing wealth and clarifying relationships. An Ethiopian church leader remarked, "In Africa we do not have such a defined world as you do in the States. We give weight to different issues. It's not that bribery is OK, but it's not so central. In America money changes hands by different rules. People still get a share of the wealth that passes through their hands, but it is done by more highly defined rules. On the other hand, it can be very irritating in Africa."

When Bill refused to pay the policeman a small sum, he also refused to recognize the status and power of the man. In America a police officer is ideally a servant of the people and an agent of the law. But in Indonesia he is an important, powerful man (albeit a very poor one) whose dignity must be upheld.

The linking of patronage and bureaucracy might be considered morally neutral if it were not for the poor. Not only the relatively rich are served by the bureaucracy but the poor as well. An Indonesian professor remarked to me that the Dutch ideal was that the bureaucrat was meant to serve the people. But here the bureaucrat does not serve the people, he serves the state. Or more accurately, he serves his superiors in the bureaucracy. This can become very oppressive to the poor who have nothing. It takes great sacrifice, or is simply impossible, for someone who earns fifty dollars a month to scrape together a bribe. Of course the poor are seldom expected to pay as much as the rich. To someone used to the rule of law, this too feels unjust. Actually it mitigates the injustice of the system.

The ability to break the bribery system depends on the power you have, what is at risk and what values are at stake. Those who can afford to go without the services of the bureaucrat, who can afford to wait, who have the power and education to appeal to higher levels, whose goodwill and service are needed by the country or who have connections to a powerful elite in the country can break the system. Such people also "earn" the service they receive, though they do it in an indirect manner.

Conclusion. Moral choice in every society is founded in the cultural character of a person and the way he or she sees the world. We are cultural creatures who make sense of our lives by means of a narrative that distinguishes between the good and the evil, the important and the insignificant. What we pay attention to shapes our ability to choose. This chapter suggests that neither relativism nor absolutism is an adequate approach to moral choice. The structures of society are fallen and pervaded by evil as well as infused with good. To cooperate with the good while exposing the evil is a task that requires character, sensitivity, and knowledge.

First of all, we need to know our core, absolute values. These may never be compromised, though they may be expressed in different ways. Certain types of bribery are absolutely wrong. Paying money to subvert justice or hide our own evil is clearly wrong. The size of a gift is significant. Very large gifts that are given or demanded in exchange for services that are intended to be free signal serious injustice. Needless to say, gifts to secure illegal services are also wrong.

Second, we need to avoid situations of value conflict. When confronted with tragic circumstances we cannot control, we need to know how to choose higher values over lesser values. While some kinds of bribery are absolutely wrong, some may be wrong but unavoidable. They are wrong on the face of it, but less significant than the values that would be lost if we refused to pay. Some people have more power to break the bribery system than others. Therefore it is important not to judge those who make different decisions about what is a "lesser evil." Nevertheless, the greatest danger of the prima facie category is that it may become an easy way out, a means of justifying actions we know are wrong. Most of what we call bribery is evil and cannot be done without consequences that hurt other people more than the bribery. If we bribe or kill or lie for what we consider a higher cause, repentance is advisable, for judgment lies ahead.

Third, we must constantly weigh our priorities and decisions on the basis of what fits our particular role in a particular context. Some things that look like bribes to Western eyes may be appropriate tips or gifts that serve a positive role in a given social structure. When there is ambiguity, the Westerner would do well

to get advice from someone native to the culture. Bill might have gotten better advice from an Indonesian than he did from other missionaries. But to do so he would have to have the humility to be a learner and not a teacher in the situation.

Conversely, some kinds of payment that look perfectly legitimate to Westerners look like bribery to others. An Asian woman complained that some of the worst corruption comes when large Christian mission organizations lure gifted national leaders away from urgently needed, indigenously controlled work. The offer of a relatively enormous salary tempts gifted people to abandon locally controlled organizations to serve a Christian multinational. Local leaders may become discouraged as their gifted young leaders are made subservient to foreign organizations. Thus the power of money can perpetuate another form of colonialism.

Sometimes patterns of foreign aid serve the same function as bribery. Aid brings dependence, fostered by a patronage system in which the foreigner has all the financial power. Paternalism may take the place of partnership.

Obviously these issues are not cut and dried. What may be right for one situation may be wrong for another. Gifts may be empowering or enslaving. The fact that some values are relative does not mean that all values are relative. The fact that there are some situations of structural evil where one cannot escape without fault does not suggest that whenever we feel tension we should give in.

Bribery is a serious evil in the modern world. The person who successfully navigates the shoals of corruption is likely to be someone who is living the right kind of story. At the point where we have to make a decision, we are unlikely to reflect on whether deontology, teleology, or prima facie thinking is more appropriate. The kind of person we are and the way we are oriented to God, to our neighbor, and to our own self-interest will most likely decide for us.

The God of Job and the God of Jesus does not accept bribes. Bribes are the opposite of true gifts. Bribes seek to dominate and control. Bribes subvert justice for the poor. Gifts are given freely and establish a reciprocal relationship. Gifts are a sign of love. Gifts are at the heart of the gospel. Those who love God bring gifts, not bribes, to their neighbor.

Questions for Discussion and Reflection

1. How does Adeney view bribery? How does he distinguish between gifts and bribes? Do you agree with that distinction, or are there some other categories that you would use to describe what is occurring in many of these countries?
2. If you were Bill, the missionary in the article, how would you have responded to the demand for a bribe?
3. Do you think there is any difference between bribes in business transactions and the bribe that Bill the missionary was forced to pay?

Moving the Fair Trade Agenda Forward

Paul Chandler

Ridley Hall Cambridge, 2005.[1]

These are undoubtedly exciting times for those of us in the Fair Trade movement. Fair Trade products have never been more popular with the general public, nor more readily available. Supermarkets and other commercial organisations are not only stocking products from fair trade organisations, but are increasingly developing their own fair trade product ranges. Politicians now regularly pay lip service to the importance of what we do, and in the wake of the Asian tsunami, the importance of addressing the issues of world poverty with a new urgency has been recognised.

But this success brings with it a range of challenges. Having become more significant commercially, Fair Trade is rightly becoming subject to greater scrutiny, and a range of vested interests are beginning to launch counter-attacks in an attempt to undermine the momentum of the Fair Trade sector. At the same time, the Make Poverty History campaign is heightening public awareness of wider trade justice issues, but is also experiencing challenges from economists, businesses and others—who feel threatened by the challenges being made to free market orthodoxy, or who consider the trade justice arguments to be ill-founded for one reason or another. Arguments on both sides are often over-simplified and overpolarised, making it difficult for more neutral observers to know where they should stand.

Against this background it is important that Christians contribute to the debate, understanding the arguments and reflecting on Christian perspectives on these issues. As a small contribution to this process, I propose to explore the understanding of fair trade and trade justice that has been developed by Traidcraft over the 25 years that it has been a leading practitioner of fair trade. I shall then consider some of the bigger challenges facing the fair trade movement over the coming five to ten years, and suggest several ways in which the movement needs to move on. Finally I shall consider what might be the role of churches and individual Christians in the fight for fair trade and trade justice.

Background

First I would like to say a few words about my own background and about Traidcraft. I joined Traidcraft as Chief Executive in mid 2001, having spent the previous nine years as General Secretary of SPCK, the Anglican mission agency, publisher and bookseller. Before that I worked for nine years in Barclays plc, initially as a graduate entrant, and then, after studying for an MBA, as manager in a City of London branch, as manager responsible for Group long-term strategic planning, and finally as Assistant Director responsible for branch network changes and sales to personal customers in the southwest London region. I have thus worked both within the multinational capitalist system (and enjoyed it!), and within two mission-driven businesses that have combined the need to make sufficient profits to survive and grow with strong Christian and "third world" connections. I am a practitioner rather than a theorist; a businessman rather than a theologian.

Traidcraft is a Christian response to poverty, dedicated to "fighting poverty through trade" since its foundation in 1979. It is best known as the UK's leading fair trade organisation, but in fact operates within a much broader sphere than simply "Fair Trade", being a leading advocate of wider trade justice and corporate responsibility issues. Traidcraft runs many pro-poor trade-related projects around the world.

Traidcraft is an unusual organisation in that it brings together a public limited company—Traidcraft plc—and a development charity—Traidcraft Exchange. The two share the same senior management team, have overlapping Boards and, most importantly, share the same mission of fighting poverty through trade, through support activities in the Southern hemisphere and through influencing governments, businesses and the general public. The combination of being a business and a charity has proved very fruitful, with each able to inform the thinking and development of the other, giving Traidcraft a unique voice and an ability to understand both business and development perspectives on the various arguments around poverty and trade.

Traidcraft plc is the trading arm of the family, and the best known part of Traidcraft. It sources fairly traded foods, gifts and paper products from about 100 producer groups in some 30 countries, seeking both to generate income for those producers and to help them develop the capacity to establish sustainable businesses that can thrive in local as well as export markets. In 2004/5 our turnover was £16 million, double the figure in 2000/1. In the last three years Traidcraft plc has begun to generate a healthy level of profits, in line with norms for UK industry, which is vital both to sustain future growth and to demonstrate the viability of fair trade as a commercial (rather than a charitable) model.

Traidcraft Exchange raises money from the general public and institutional donors to support trade development projects, especially in East and Southern Africa, India, Bangladesh and South East Asia. It has a training and consultancy arm which makes our expertise available to producers who do not supply Traidcraft plc, to NGOs and to businesses. A London-based Policy team is the leading think tank in the international fair trade movement, and is highly respected within the UK and Brussels for its wider advocacy of fairer approaches to trade rules and corporate ethical behaviour.

Underpinning both parts of Traidcraft is a substantial supporter community of shareholders, Fair Traders, donors and campaigners, who are drawn particularly (but not exclusively) from the UK Christian community. As a non-denominational Christian organisation all senior staff and Board members must be practising Christians, but Traidcraft seeks to work with and through people of all faith backgrounds and does not have an evangelistic agenda: rather it seeks to offer a practical expression of Christian love and concern for the poor and marginalised.

What Is Fair Trade?

Many debates on fair trade are bedevilled by different understandings of what the phrase means. There are at least three commonly used definitions, and care is needed to identify which one is being referred to if discussions are not to become confused and unproductive.

"Free and fair trade" is a phrase increasingly used by politicians and business leaders in support of the trade liberalisation agenda. Fairness in this context refers primarily to establishing a "level playing field" between countries (*Faith in Business Quarterly Journal,* Volume 9, No. 2, Summer 2005, 27) and companies, removing protectionist tariffs and subsidies.

"Fair trade not free trade" is a slogan much used by campaigners within the Trade Justice and Make Poverty History coalitions. In this context it means allowing weaker countries to have greater access to developed country markets, whilst at the same time allowing them to use differing degrees of protection to prevent themselves being dominated by multinational companies or flooded with cheap (and often subsidised) goods from developed countries. This is

"fair" because it seeks to redress the balance between weak and strong.

"Fair Trade" (or "FairTrade" for those products for which labelling criteria have been developed) refers to a specific form of pro-poor trade, paying above-market prices and premiums where needed to ensure a respectable standard of living for producers. This includes a commitment to investing resources in capacity building, to ensuring good working conditions and rights for workers in Fair Trade producer groups, and to seeking long-term relationships between suppliers and fair trade companies in the North. Fair Trade relates particularly to trade with smallholder farmers, cooperatives and rural crafts workers, although there are a number of plantations and private sector models emerging as well.

Where does Traidcraft stand on the various issues implicit within these definitions?

Our starting point is to recognise that trade is the most sustainable way of addressing global poverty, and is essential if other initiatives such as aid and debt relief are to be followed through to good effect. Some of the more extreme advocates of "fair trade" merge into elements of the anti-globalisation and anti-capitalist movements, but Traidcraft believes that business, whilst it has the potential to do harm, also has significant potential to do lasting good, and indeed will be the most essential part of any programme to combat world poverty effectively. On issues of trade liberalisation, we recognise that no western economy has developed without the use of protection during the early stages of its development, and although once sufficiently developed economies benefit hugely from more open markets, undue liberalisation at an early stage will tend to consign less developed countries to volatile and low margin commodity production and to other low added-value activities. Free markets are an illusory theoretical concept, given the huge imbalances of power that exist in today's world, and no developed country truly believes in free trade. All shelter their vulnerable groups and industries behind tariff and non-tariff barriers and subsidy programmes.

Turning to the most specific usage of the term, "Fair Trade" might in many ways be more accurately named "Biased Trade"! It represents pro-poor trade with a developmental intention. Whilst establishing a gold standard for showing how trade can benefit the poor and marginalised, and providing much direct assistance to those groups supplying fair trade products, Traidcraft believes that it should be seen primarily as an incubator—allowing additional resources to be channelled to the most needy groups until they have built the expertise and resources to survive in mainstream markets (which then allows fair trade companies to switch their attention to other poor producer groups). It is thus essential to ensure that fair trade producers develop sustainable businesses, with strong local markets as well as exports, and diversified product ranges and customer bases. Fair Trade should not be about creating cosy niche markets between a few fortunate producers and small dedicated ethical consumers!

As well as helping producers develop, Fair Trade is also to be seen as an effective tool for changing attitudes in the North. Fair Trade products on shelves and in churches raise popular awareness of world poverty issues. By providing a moral choice for consumers, it allows them both to put their money where their hearts are and to send powerful signals to companies and politicians about the importance of ethical business and trading behaviour. The recent and welcome expansion of Tesco, Sainsbury and Asda into Fair Trade products reflects not a moral conversion experience for their boards, but a recognition of growing consumer demand for ethically sourced goods. Fair Trade also demonstrates that all businesses can afford to take ethical concerns seriously—that being a "good business" can make good business sense, and that not to respond to growing consumer pressure will be to court financial disaster.

Christian Perspectives on Fair Trade and Trade Justice

All the above arguments make sense from a purely practical point of view, reflecting the experience of Traidcraft's 25 years of trading. But how do the arguments look from a more explicitly Christian and theological perspective?

Our starting point must be the Biblical call for justice, repeated throughout the Old and New Testaments. God has a heart for the poor and marginalised—the widow, the orphan and the alien—and as Christians we should be seeking to reach out to help. Warnings against rich oppressors and unscrupulous exploitation of the poor are clear, whether expressed in Micah, Amos or James. Economic justice is a biblical imperative, and the fight for fair trade and trade justice should thus be seen as a key expression of the Christian message of love and justice for all. I believe it is a necessary part of our Christian discipleship.

As Christians we must look beyond concepts of poverty that focus only on income and consumption. People are more than economic creatures. As Christ himself teaches us, man lives by more than bread alone. Thus alongside our concern for the provision of adequate food, water, shelter and basic levels of education and health care provision—all of which are clearly essential—we must always place a strong premium on addressing more intangible dimensions of poverty. Promoting dignity, self-esteem, participation in decisions, and having opportunities to develop one's God-given potential are all aspects of the Fair Trade model that are profoundly Christian. Models of economic development require a deeper understanding of what contributes to real human well-being.

Central to the Christian perspective is our recognition of the value of each individual in God's eyes. Each of us is made in the image of God, and he cares for every one of us. Too often in the arguments about economic development we are told that in the interests of market efficiency there is bound to be transitional restructuring pain, as people are forced out of one activity into more productive areas. This pain is allegedly worthwhile, because it will ultimately contribute to the creation of greater wealth that will reduce overall poverty. Yet in the context of extreme poverty, people often lack the resources, skills or opportunities to reallocate their efforts to new areas of production. Neutral sounding "structural adjustments" can mean utter penury and even starvation when you look at the implications for particular families and communities. From a Christian perspective we should surely not simply stand by and accept this as a necessary evil in the pursuit of greater long-term efficiency. Where human lives are concerned, the means may not justify the ends.

Traidcraft recognises that business and the operation of markets have great potential for good through wealth creation. Too often in Church and development circles there is an inbuilt suspicion of business, and an assumption that profit must always be at someone else's expense. We believe that enterprise is a God-given aspect of human creativity, and one of the ways in which we are able to be good stewards of the world's resources. Without human enterprise and the benefits of business, we do not believe that we will be able to create the wealth to reduce world poverty. However, like any other human activity, it has the potential to be turned to bad ends as well as good. This need not always be a question of conscious decisions to be exploitative or harm the poor, but may be the result of unforeseen and unintended consequences of actions on people further down the supply chain.

As Christians we therefore need to be conscious of our own complicity in economic systems that may have an adverse impact on others. We need to think about the people behind the products we buy, rather than simply buying the cheapest of most attractively branded products without further thought. How we spend our money is a key moral issue, and Christians need to inform themselves and think about how they allocate their expenditure. Whilst welcoming the positive dimensions of business, Christians need to be aware of the need to create and support structures that will help mitigate the more negative aspects of corporate activity. Supporting steps that promote corporate responsibility and encourage all companies to find out about the impact their supply chains are having on the poor is an important part of our witness.

Central to all of this, is the need for the Church to speak out prophetically against the tendency in modern societies to judge everything by its financial worth. Wealth creation, efficiency and cost-effectiveness have become the constant mantras of our leaders in political and business spheres. Yet so often this ignores wider human and Christian values: the values of community and of human well-being, for which growing wealth may not be an adequate proxy measure. Is our society in too great an abeyance to Mammon? When church leaders speak out on economic justice they are told not to interfere in areas they don't understand—we must obey the dictates of economists in the world of economics for only they know how to maximise wealth. But surely we should be bringing to the fore arguments that society should be focusing on wider values than money. That is a key prophetic message for our age.

Future Challenges for Fair Trade

So what does the future hold for those of us engaged in the world of Fair Trade, and what in particular should be the role and contribution of churches and Christians? In my opening remarks, I spoke of the great opportunities that are arising, as Fair Trade is becoming fully embedded in mainstream business, with growing levels of commercial involvement bringing a new scale of opportunities—albeit with greater competition for dedicated fair trade organisations and increased scrutiny of everything that we do.

Within this environment Traidcraft will need to continue to advocate best practice in Fair Trade. We will need to ensure that standards are not diluted or corners cut as multinationals place ever greater pressure on the limits of Fair Trade practices. We need to push for the raising of the bar: the bringing in of higher standards, the extension of fair trade to new areas of the supply chain. Our role as pioneer and innovator will come to the fore.

To ensure that we are still able to survive to carry out this role, Traidcraft will need to develop new commercial strategies—linking to markets with commercial allies, and developing expertise in providing ingredient supply and producer support services on behalf of others. There are real opportunities in all of these areas. For example, Traidcraft has recently decided to licence its successful Geobar brand to a commercial partner. This partner now owns the product and the risk associated with it, releasing a lot of capital for Traidcraft, whilst ensuring we have a strong income stream from the profits of the trade. But they also bring their much bigger sales force to bear, offering the scope for volume growth that will drive up business for our Fair Trade suppliers. Our partner's new product development team is also coming up with suggestions for new products that could use Fairtade ingredients and still hit important price points in supermarkets. This offers further scope to expand volumes for our producers—something that Traidcraft alone would struggle to achieve.

At the same time we need to differentiate our offer from that of commercial fair trade suppliers, making it clear that we go beyond the minimum standards that are guaranteed by the Fair Trade mark, investing far more in relationships, capacity building and other benefits for producers. For Traidcraft in particular we need Christian consumers to recognise that we are seeking to bring a distinctively Christian approach to bear on the market, calling on them to buy our products and to support us in other ways to ensure we can continue to speak out prophetically.

Traidcraft will also continue to work in the wider sphere of corporate social responsibility, building on its strong reputation as one of the leading plcs in the sphere of social accounting and ethical approaches to business. But any advocacy work we can carry out at this level needs to be underpinned by consumer pressure—for it is ultimately only the demands of consumers that will force business to take such matters seriously.

The Role of Churches and Christians

So what can Churches and Christians contribute to all this?

First, we must continue to proclaim a prophetic challenge to the rule of money in our lives, arguing that moral choices over the structures of world trade must be assessed on the basis of their impact on people rather than being purely arguments about the most effective means of wealth creation.

Second, by encouraging churchgoers to think seriously about these issues, and to take an active interest in trade justice and Fair Trade, the Church can play an important part in mobilising public opinion. The leadership of the Church was a key element in the success of the Jubilee 2000 campaign, and we believe the fight for trade justice is in some ways a natural extension of this leadership role.

Third, churches and Christians who are convinced of our cause can show in a practical way that they are serving the needs of the poor by opting to buy and use Fair Trade products and encouraging others to do so too. Whilst each purchase seems insignificant in itself, cumulatively they send powerful signals to the business world—all the more effective if underpinned by constant prayer.

Is the challenge too enormous to offer the hope of

success? Surely not. The campaigners for the abolition of slavery faced many similar arguments to those being wielded in today's debate over trade, yet through persistent efforts they managed to overturn that system.

Arguably, the fight against global economic injustice is the moral crusade that our generation needs to take up if we are to live out gospel values. With God's help we will make a difference.

Notes

1 http://www.ridley.cam.ac.uk/documents/fib/2005/agenda.html (accessed January 5, 2011).

Questions for Discussion and Reflection

1. What do you think of Traidcraft's mission and use of fair trade to assist the poor around the world? Would you want to be an investor in this company? Why or why not?
2. What do you think of Chandler's insistence that we participate with fair trade and spend our money in ways that assist the poor?
3. How do you assess Traidcraft's practice of paying above market prices for fair trade goods in order to ensure that the poor have a minimal living standard?

Fair Trade? Its Prospects as a Poverty Solution

Victor V. Claar

From *Fair and Free Trade* (Grand Rapids: Acton Institute, 2010), 49–59.

When Jesus was anointed at Bethany, he reminded us of what is written in Deuteronomy 15:11: "There will always be poor people in the land. Therefore I command you to be open-handed toward your brothers and toward the poor and needy in your land."[1] In Matthew 25:40, he tells us that when we serve the poor we also serve him. Through both word and example, Christ calls us to care for the poor and also to welcome them as we would welcome our Master.

Given the extent of poverty in the world today and its miserable depths in some nations, surely we are called to be agents for change on their behalf. Even though we can never personally know every person who may be most pressed by economic circumstances, we must nevertheless serve him. We cannot serve our Master directly, but we serve him when we come to the aid of others.

Our response must be thoughtful, careful, and prayerful. Surely we do not want to serve our Master in some slapdash, haphazard effort. This requires responding to urgent needs both with speed and with an understanding of what is needed most. Too often we simply throw things at a problem—because we do indeed have much to give—rather than find out first what is needed most and where we can serve most effectively.

When needs are persistent rather than temporary, we must stay focused on our hope for the long-term improvement of the prospects of the subjects of our care. Just as we must treat others as we would treat our Lord, sometimes it is helpful to ask ourselves what we would do if a specific individual we already know and care for were in similar circumstances. The modern fair trade movement has marvelous intentions.

This author has dear friends who are also dedicated brothers and sisters in the faith who believe they are saving the world by purchasing Equal Exchange's coffees and chocolate or by staffing the Equal Exchange coffee concession between church services. They carry out those duties with joy, love, good humor, and the belief that they are agents for change acting on behalf of the "least of these."

Yet, the fair trade movement, for all its good intentions, cannot deliver on what it promises. Simply put, coffee growers are poor because there is too much coffee. Fair trade simply does not address that fundamental reality. In fact, by guaranteeing a price to growers that is higher than the world price of coffee, fair trade makes the supply of coffee even larger than it would otherwise be. As we have already seen, whenever coffee prices increase, there will be another coffee grower, and another, and another.

There is no question that some people benefit from the fair trade movement. Beginning in your neighborhood and moving outward, your local coffee bar benefits, as does Equal Exchange or some other fair trade company that supplies your coffee shop. Transfair USA benefits by charging aspiring cooperatives an entrance fee, and Transfair USA benefits by charging companies such as Equal Exchange for use of their fair trade mark—the primary source of Transfair's income. Of the extra dollar or two that you pay for a bag of coffee, at least some tiny part remains by the time it travels all the way back through the entire supply chain to the needy growers you are seeking to serve.[2] At least we hope so. Kate Bird and David Hughes state that "... due to lack of data and the low volumes of coffee exported using fair trade marketing systems, a causal relationship between fair trade and enhanced producer welfare cannot be proved categorically."[3]

Further, because we know little if anything about the people we attempt to help through fair trade—the actual individuals who have names and faces—it is nearly impossible for each of us to know whether or not we are righting some past wrong or correcting some harm. We certainly know little if anything at all about what a given country's best long-term development strategy might be. Perhaps the best face that may be put on the realities of fair trade is one provided by Malgorzata Kurjanska and Mathias Risse:

... a difficulty arises when consumers cannot distinguish between situations in which they ought to buy Fair Trade and when they ought not to do so. What, then, ought one to do? ... From a first-person standpoint, we can resolve this situation by noting that Fair Trade does not occupy large market shares.... So even if supporting particular producers is not a good development strategy, the potential harm is minimal.... [O]ne does little harm while benefitting somebody immediately.... [P]ermissibility to purchase Fair Trade products hinges on the movement's improbability of hindering more feasible development strategies. This might be less force than defenders of the Fair Trade movement might hope for, but it is hard to see how to make their case stronger.[4]

The Promise of Free Trade

Despite its marvelous intentions, as well as the good-faith monetary contributions that consumers make when they choose higher-priced fair trade coffee over other coffee, Fair Trade will never lead to the long-term enrichment of the poor. Instead, it creates an additional incentive for the poor to continue to soldier on in a line of work that will never pay much better than it does right now. As long as coffee prices remain low, growing coffee—even if it is fair trade coffee—will not pay well. The reason that coffee prices remain low is because there is too much of it. The fair trade movement does no favors for the poor by encouraging even more poor people to grow even more coffee, but that is precisely the effect that a higher fair trade price is having, leading to the FLO's reluctance to take on any more cooperatives.

Low coffee prices, like low prices for any other commodity, normally are a signal to producers to make less of it and move on to something else instead. Yet, fair trade frustrates this signal, with unfortunate consequences. First, fair trade encourages even more coffee production. Second, fair trade makes nonfair trade growers poorer because nonfair trade prices fall as new growers in places such as Vietnam are attracted into the market by artificially high prices.[5] Entry by new growers increases the supply, and bigger supplies of anything drive prices downward.

Another unintended consequence of fair trade agreements is that they weaken the incentives of coffee growers to increase the market appeal of their beans through quality improvements, or to reduce their production costs through improved techniques. Unlike Colombia, a nation that improved demand for its coffee by focusing on its quality, fair trade growers have little incentive to do likewise.[6] This is especially distressing because all market research regarding fair trade agrees that coffee quality nearly always trumps fair trade for consumers as a reason to pay a higher price, even among the Fair Trade Lovers described earlier.[7] Generally speaking, coffee drinkers buy first on quality.[8]

Thus, fair trade agreements act like golden handcuffs that bind the wrists of fair trade cooperatives and their member growers. Fair trade discourages member growers from trying Fair Trade, something new that they would certainly otherwise try if they did not have the security of the fair trade price.[9] As John Wilkinson puts it, "North-South Fair Trade ... could never itself be a sufficient strategy for rural development," reminding us that fair trade coffee accounts for only 20 percent of all coffee sold by fair trade cooperatives. Further, while there are about five hundred groups worldwide in forty-nine countries, this implies that we are talking about an average of just ten groups per country.[10]

The moral shortcoming of the fair trade movement is that it keeps the poor shackled to activities that, while productive, will never lead to poverty reduction on a large scale—or even a modest one. Further, if our purchases of fair trade really do retard the long-term rate of poverty reduction, then buying fair trade might rightly be viewed as causing harm.[11]

As a case for comparison, Malgorzata Kurjanska and Mathias Risse point to Costa Rica. Costa Rica has shifted its production of goods away from traditional fair trade products such as bananas and coffee, and toward new exports and ecotourism. As a result, Costa Rica's exports of nontraditional goods rose from just 38.6 percent in 1982 to 87.0 percent by 2003. Fair Trade loving northern consumers, despite their good intentions, would have resisted such a shift in production. Yet, the shift is one that over time has led to conditions even better than those that fair trade alone could deliver.[12]

When the price of something is low, like coffee, market forces normally direct people to make less of it and move on to something else, but fair trade interferes with the signal that prices ordinarily provide; it can never serve as a sustainable long-term development strategy. Paul Collier, a former World Bank director of development research puts it this way in his bestselling *The Bottom Billion*:

> The price premium in fair trade products is a form of charitable transfer, and there is evidently no harm in that. But the problem with it, as compared with just giving people the aid in other ways, is that it encourages recipients to stay doing what they are doing—producing coffee. A key economic problem for the bottom billion is that producers have not diversified out of a narrow range of primary commodities. Raising their prices (albeit infinitesimally, since fair trade is such a small component of demand) makes it harder for people to move into other activities. They get charity as long as they stay producing the crops that have locked them into poverty.[13]

Tim Harford echoes Collier, observing that coffee farmers will never be rich until everyone else is first; that is, until coffee growing becomes rare enough that it can command a higher price. Because fair trade creates more coffee, and not less, coffee will never pay well. Thus, only long-term growth and development will help the poor grow rich.[14]

What, then, can lead to real and lasting economic gains for the poor? The good news is that we have considerable information about this question, and a rich feast of evidence confirming the answer that economics provides. When prices are free to act as a signal showing people what to make either more or less of, poor people begin to flourish. For example, even though there continues to be income inequality within nations, inequality across the entire globe has decreased over the last quarter century. More importantly, the rate of extreme poverty has declined. Columbia University's Xavier Salai-Martin estimates that between 1976 and 1998, the number of people living on one dollar or less per day fell by 235 million. Further, the number living on two dollars or less per day fell by 450 million.[15] That is improvement worthy of our rejoicing!

How does it happen? Why has it happened so quickly in China and India, while much of Africa has grown slightly poorer over the same period, even as we have given massive amounts of foreign aid to Africa? Simply put, in places where markets operate freely, prices act as a signal — to all of us — to stop doing things that pay little and begin doing things that pay more. In the case of the coffee market, the reason that coffee continues to be cheap is that we keep making too much because we choose to ignore the price signal.

Putting at least some faith in markets to be a powerful force for change in the lives of the poor does not amount to abdicating our concern for the poor; instead our opting to cavalierly put our hope in little more than fairies and magic dust does. Just as we trust gravity to keep us all affixed securely to the ground and just as principles of particle physics assure you that the chair you are sitting in right now will not let you slip through its seat to the floor, markets work invisibly in ways that we understand reasonably well. Although this author is no physicist, he trusts what a physicist tells him regarding what can and cannot work in our physical world, though the forces themselves cannot be easily observed; we see only the effects of such forces.

The laws of physics are part of God's providence; so are the laws of economics. In fact, many Christian economists have seen the providence of God in Adam Smith's famous invisible hand of the marketplace. Two quotes wonderfully and beautifully illustrate. Consider first the words of Robin Klay and John Lunn, two economics professors from Hope College in Holland, Michigan:

> Just as God-given productivity of the soil, combined with human labor and ingenuity, blesses societies with abundant crops, so also does the productivity of gifted human beings bless all humanity through markets. The somewhat mysterious way in which markets accomplish this without any one person directing it suggests to us the providential hand of God at work.[16]

More recently, in a book reflecting on John Calvin's thought regarding markets, David Hall and Matthew Burton write:

> God's providence is present in all events. We need to learn to see his "invisible hand" working in all things. He is truly sovereign over all of history. To doubt that is to reject God's lordship. Such repudiation is not merely based on an absence of information; it is also a rebellion of the heart against one's Creator. Happy is the person who learns to see God's hand in all of life.[17]

A key role for concerned Christians, then, is to permit and even encourage the power of markets to do the heavy lifting of the poor from poverty. One encouraging tool that is already making a difference in the lives of poor coffee and soybean growers is the Internet and mobile phone access. For years, coffee sellers everywhere and soybean growers in India have fallen victim to greedy middlemen by settling for a selling price that is below the going rate simply because growers did not have access to potential buyers other than their local coyote and also because they lacked accurate information regarding the going market value of their crops.

In a new piece of research, Aparajita Goyal presents significant evidence that the introduction of Internet kiosks in the Indian state of Madhya Pradesh has allowed soybean farmers to access alternative marketing channels that had never before been available to them, as well as learn about current movements of soy prices. The presence of the kiosks has resulted in significantly higher soy prices, even after controlling for other potential explanatory factors.[18] In this case, it appears that the presence of kiosks has accomplished far more for poor soy farmers than any fair trade program could, because the kiosks supplied valuable information that allowed the pricing system to work as intended. Sellers possessed reliable information about prices and traded accordingly. Philip Booth, writing for the *Catholic Times*, forecasts a similar role for mobile phones: "There are many other mechanisms [besides Fair Trade] around in the market for achieving similar objectives. Just to give one example, the mobile phone probably does more in Africa today to spread information about the best prices that primary producers can achieve than the fair trade movement. Its impact is tremendous."[19]

Speaking more generally, when poor countries grow rich, it rarely has anything at all to do with how many mouths they have to feed or the abundance of natural resources. Instead, across the globe, poor countries of all sizes, climates, and endowments begin to grow rich as two key factors increase. First, countries grow rich as their human capital improves. Human capital is the term economists use to describe the value that a country's people possess through their accumulated experience and education. For example, there is little doubt that India's recent growth explosion is due in large part to the education—including the knowledge of the English language—of its people. Second, countries grow rich as they invest in and accumulate physical capital: the machines, tools, infrastructure, and other equipment that make the product of each hour of physical labor more valuable.

That which both human capital and physical capital share is that they both transform the result of an hour of a person's hard work into something of even greater value. As the value of an hour of labor rises, employers gladly pay higher hourly rates, knowing that their bottom lines will be the better for it. If we want to be effective agents in aiding the poor, we should focus our efforts in directions leading to the enhanced value of an hour of labor. That is, we should help poor countries wisely grow their stocks of human and physical capital, all the while bearing in mind that markets and their prices send the best available signals regarding where our efforts can have the greatest impact. The newfound success of innovative microlending efforts such as Kiva can help show us ways to effectively invest in the accumulation of physical capital by the global poor. Compassion International is a marvelous organization that works to further the education—the human capital—of poor children worldwide, with a financial accountability record above reproach.

Further, markets work best when economic systems maintain the dignity of human beings. First, human beings grow and flourish—and accumulate human and physical capital—in systems that afford them considerable economic freedom. Economic freedom means that people are able to make personal choices, that their property is protected, and that they may voluntarily buy and sell in markets. Yet, economic freedom requires the protection of private property. When property rights are clearly defined and protected, people will work harder to create and

to save. When they are confident that the fruits of their labors cannot be taken away arbitrarily or by force, people everywhere have greater assurance that their labors will lead to better lives for themselves and their families. Today's rich collection of NGOs that work toward basic human rights play a critical role in this regard. Finally, we should be outraged at the protectionist agricultural policies of already-rich nations such as the United States.

When we allow the agricultural lobby to garner sweetheart deals from the U.S. House and Senate, the poor in other nations simply cannot compete with American growers of many crops because the trade rules are so utterly slanted against those in other nations. For example, it is illegal for sugar buyers in the United States to purchase their sugar from sources outside the United States, even though the world price of sugar lies below the federally mandated price of sugar in the United States. This is wonderful, though, for U.S. sugar beet growers in the United States; it means they have a captive supply of buyers at a price that is being kept artificially high by federal decree. If the United States were to abandon such self-centered policies, sugar growers everywhere would have access to our markets, and the price of sugar would fall for all of us. Moreover, confectioners and soft-drink makers in the United States would be able to produce their goods at lower costs, thereby adding to their job security. In one well-publicized case in 2002, Beatrice closed its Life-Savers factory in Holland, Michigan, and relocated to Canada, though the Michigan factory had been in operation for over thirty-five years and employed six hundred or so American workers. By moving to the northern side of the U.S.–Canada border, Life-Savers slashed its input costs dramatically because, in Canada, Life-Savers was free to buy cane sugar at the world price: sugar grown by those who need the income most.

Sugar is not the only market we currently protect to keep out lower-priced commodities in an effort to help poor farmers in the United States. We have erected similar barriers that turn a blind eye to the plight of the global poor in markets for cotton, peanuts, and several other products that we can grow at home. In fact, by now you can probably see another reason why coffee prices are low. Because coffee cannot be grown in Ohio, or in France, rich northerners have not erected protectionist barriers to keep out the coffee that foreigners make.

If we really care about the global poor, we should work to make trade freer for everyone in our global community: a level playing field for all. That means tearing down all of the barriers we use to keep the global poor from working in the very jobs in which they are perfectly positioned to make the greatest lasting gains.

Notes

[1] All scripture quotations taken from the New International Version.

[2] Jeremy Weber, "Fair Trade Coffee Enthusiasts Should Confront Reality," *Cato Journal* 27 (2007): 109.

[3] Kate Bird and David R. Hughes, "Ethical Consumerism: The Case of 'Fairly-Traded' Coffee," *Business Ethics: A European Review* 6 (1997): 166.

[4] Malgorzata Kurjanska and Mathias Risse, "Fairness in Trade II: Export Subsidies and the Fair Trade Movement," *Politics, Philosophy, & Economics* 7 (2008): 49.

[5] *Economist*, "Voting with Your Trolley" (December 7, 2006).

[6] Ibid.

[7] Margaret Levi and April Linton, "Fair Trade: A Cup at a Time?" *Politics & Society* 31 (2003): 420.

[8] Brink Lindsey, "Grounds for Complaint? Understanding the 'Coffee Crisis,'" Trade Briefing Paper No. 16 (Washington, D.C.: Cato Institute, 2003), 6.

[9] *Economist*, "Voting with Your Trolley."

[10] John Wilkinson, "Fair Trade: Dynamic and Dilemmas of a Market Oriented Global Social Movement," *Journal of Consumer Policy* 20 (2007): 233.

[11] Kurjanska and Risse, "Fairness in Trade II," 47.

[12] Ibid., 46.

[13] Collier, *The Bottom Billion: Why the Poorest Countries Are Failing and What Can Be Done about It* (Oxford, U.K.: Oxford University Press, 2007), 163.

[14] Tim Harford, *The Undercover Economist* (Oxford, U.K.: Oxford University Press, 2006), 229.

[15] Robin Bade and Michael Parkin, *Foundations of Microeconomics*, 4th ed. (Boston: Addison-Wesley, 2009), 55.

[16] Robin Klay and John Lunn, "The Relationship of God's Providence to Market Economies and Economic Theory," *Journal of Markets & Morality* 6 (2003): 559.

[17] David W. Hall and Matthew D. Burton, *Calvin and Commerce: The Transforming Power of Calvinism in Market Economies* (Phillipsburg: P&R, 2009), 158.

[18] Aparajita Goyal, "Information, Direct Access to Farmers, and Rural Market Performance in Central India," *American Economic Journal: Applied Economics* (forthcoming).

[19] Philip Booth, "Fair Trade Proponents Should Have More Humility," *Catholic Times* (January 28, 2008), http://www.iea.org.uk/record.jsp?type=pressArticle&ID=350.

Questions for Discussion and Reflection

1. What is Claar's critique of the fair trade movement? Do you agree with his assessment? Why or why not?
2. According to Claar, what do low coffee prices signify? What does he suggest coffee growers do in response to these low prices? Do you agree with his suggestion?
3. Claar claims that the laws of economics are part of God's providence? Do you agree with his claim? Why or why not?
4. How does Claar view protectionist policies like those applied to sugar?

CASE STUDIES

Case 6.1: Sweatshops

You are employed in the human resources department of a large international company that manufactures athletic clothing and shoes. Over the course of several years, the company has closed down a dozen or so manufacturing plants in the United States. Most of the company's manufacturing and assembly operations have been moved overseas to subcontractor owned factories located in developing countries. Wages are much lower and local regulations governing worker safety and factory conditions are significantly less restrictive in third world countries than in the United States.

Recently your company has become the target of groups who protest against globalization. Members of these groups have been quoted in major media stories and have set up websites accusing your company of "selling out" American labor by moving jobs overseas. They have also accused your organization of running sweatshops and exploiting poor workers by paying low wages, exposing workers to dangerous working conditions, and employing young children at some plants. You are asked by company executives to lead a team of human resources personnel to visit some of these factories and to write a report offering your thoughts about the company's actions.

After visiting five different factories, you find that the average wage is thirty dollars (U.S.) for a six-day week, which averages fifty-five hours. (In the United States, a worker doing comparable work earns about seventeen dollars per hour.) This wage scale is in compliance with minimum-wage scales set by local laws. Most workers are young women (ages sixteen to twenty-two) who live in poor conditions and cannot save much money or afford many items we would consider necessities in the United States. However, the employees you interview tell you that they are satisfied with the wages they earn and the hours they work. Judging by the long line of job seekers at each factory's gates each morning, you can also tell that there is heavy local demand for jobs in the factories.

You also find that working conditions are much different than in the United States. One factory had inadequate ventilation and no source of clean drinking water. When you were inside this particular factory, the temperature was 98 degrees and very humid. At another factory, you witnessed a number of workers handling chemicals without wearing masks or gloves, which does not necessarily violate local laws but goes against your company's code of conduct. About 25 percent of the 100 or so workers you interviewed at this factory had no knowledge of your company's code of conduct, which is supposed to be posted. In fact, several workers had not even heard of your company.

During your trip, you also speak with several youthful appearing employees who told you they were only thirteen years old. Local laws permit them to work at this age, and it is clear to you that their families need the income they produce. However, protesters are particularly vocal about firms employing children under the age of fourteen.

Questions for Discussion

1. Which of your company's practices can you defend in good conscience?
2. Which practices are in need of modification?
3. If no changes are made to working conditions, will you continue to do business with this particular factory?

Case 6.2: When in Rome, Do as the Romans?

Upon graduation you take a position with an organization setting up Internet/coffee houses in countries with developing economies. One of your first assignments is to spend a month in Southeast Asia to assist in opening stores near large university campuses.

During your first week, your supervisor (a citizen of the country you are in) asks you to look into acquiring electricity and phone service for the stores. After you stand in a long line, a local government official informs you that the wait for such services can take six to nine months, a delay that would make it impossible to open the stores by the start of the school year. When told of the waiting period, your supervisor informs you that the proper procedure is to go back and recognize the government official's position and authority by offering him a gift (approximately $1,000 U.S.) in order to receive faster service.

Upon hearing this suggestion, you raise the question of whether such a payment would constitute bribery since these types of payments are not legally acceptable in the United States and seem to contribute to corruption. Furthermore, they seem to give you an unfair advantage over a local citizen who cannot pay the amount in question.

Your supervisor replies in a joking manner that "you should take off your 'red, white, and blue' glasses, because this is the way things are done here." "Besides," he explains in a more serious tone, "there is a vast difference between a 'gift' or 'tip' to ensure promptness and a true bribe. A gift is perfectly legal here, especially considering the small amount in question. It simply speeds up the process."

"It's like paying more for first-class service in your country," he says.

"We are not corrupting anyone. It's a common, known practice. In fact, the gifts are considered part of the compensation of government employees, who are paid very poorly, so you could look at it as a form of charity," he concludes. His answer sounds reasonable, but you are still troubled.

Questions for Discussion

1. Based on the readings, which of the practices could you support from an ethical perspective? Why?

2. On what basis should we make decisions about matters of right and wrong when another culture's practices differ from our own?

3. Do you think that the payment in question constitutes bribery? Or would you refer to it as something else—a gift, tip, or premium?

Case 6.3: Starbucks and Fair Trade Coffee

After receiving much publicized pressure from activist organizations such as *Transfair USA*, Starbucks officials announced in April 2000 that the company would begin to sell Fair Trade coffee in all of its retail stores. Specifically, the company announced that it would sell coffee certified by the Fair Trade Federation by the pound and would feature it as its "coffee of the day" on the twentieth day of every month.

Starbucks is a company that prides itself on being "socially responsible." The company is heavily involved in community service and philanthropic activities and has its own charitable foundation, the Starbucks Foundation.

The concept behind fair trade originated as a faith-based initiative in Europe during the late 1980s. The goal is simply to ensure that suppliers and growers of products in poor countries receive fair prices for their goods.

Fair trade coffee beans are purchased directly from cooperatives owned by Latin American farmers. In effect, profit-taking by export middlemen, often labeled "coyotes," has been greatly reduced, and the growers are allowed to take home a much higher profit from the sales of beans. For example, under traditional trade arrangements, coffee sells for a variable price on the world market (as low as 50 to 60 cents per pound recently). Farmers in Central America receive as little as 25 to 40 cents per pound of coffee, which (after roasting and packaging) sells in stores in the United States for as much as $9 to $10 retail.

In contrast, coffee beans are sold at guaranteed and precontracted prices (recently $1.26 to $1.62 per pound) under fair trade purchase agreements. Growers receive up to 50 to 60 cents more per pound than they would receive under traditional arrangements, allowing many farming families to escape poverty.

Promoters of fair trade coffee claim that another important benefit of the product is that a high percentage of it is organically grown through sustainable and earth-friendly farming practices.

Starbucks's announcement was initially seen as a leadership stance. However, some critics still believe that the company continues to "exploit" coffee farmers in Latin America, since the total amount of fair trade coffee is a small percentage of total sales. These critics are pressuring Starbucks (and other coffee retailers) to use more fair trade coffee.

The reluctance on the part of coffee retailers such as Starbucks to carry more fair trade coffee may be partially explained by the readiness and willingness of consumers to pay more. Since fair trade coffee is more expensive to purchase, some (or most) of the cost is usually passed along to consumers in the form of higher prices. For example, a pound of "house blend" retails for approximately $10 in Starbucks stores. The price of a fair trade blend is approximately $11.45. While the company could use much more fair trade coffee, prices would have to be raised, and price-conscious consumers could simply purchase coffee from competing retailers. Alternatively, Starbucks could "absorb" some of the higher costs, leading to a reduction in profit.

Critics of fair trade coffee claim that the practice has some inconsistencies. For example, some cooperatives set a size limit (i.e., twelve acres) for the farms that qualify for the programs. Farmers who exceed that amount of land may not qualify for some fair trade programs even though they may treat workers fairly and otherwise qualify.

Also, some critics argue that the additional money going to farmers amounts to an artificial "wage support" that is not sustainable over time, and that rather than teaching farmers how to compete in the global marketplace, this creates an unhealthy dependence.

Finally, fair trade coffee often comes up short in taste tests, which likely means that most current purchasers buy the product for the social benefits rather than for quality or price. Critics claim that prenegotiated higher prices may effectively create disincentives to improve quality.

Questions for Discussion

1. Do you support Starbucks' fair trade coffee efforts? Why or why not?
2. How do you think Victor Claar would view the fair trade emphasis?
3. Would you buy fair trade coffee? Why or why not?

Resources

Transfair website: http://www.transfair.org
Bradley Meacham, "How Fair Is Fair Trade Coffee?" *Seattle Times*, September 11, 2002.

Case 6.4: Cultural Sensitivity at Hong Kong Disneyland*

As Disney, Inc. was set to open the gates to its Hong Kong theme park, the company was broadsided by protests and calls for boycotts by environmental groups. Sparking the controversy was the pre-park opening release of its food menu, which included shark fin soup as an option for wedding banquets held at the park. Spokespersons for organizations such as Greenpeace and

* We are indebted to Albert Chan for bringing this case to our attention and for providing useful background information.

[2] Patricia Leigh Brown, "Soup without Fins? Some Californians Simmer." *New York Times*. March 5, 20011. http://www.nytimes.com/2011/03/06/us/06fin.html?_r=3&hp

[3] Keith Bradsher, "Disneyland in China Offers a Soup But Lands in a Stew." *New York Times*, June 17, 2005. http://www.nytimes.com/2005/06/17/business/worldbusiness/17shark.html

[4] "Environmentalists Fume over Disney Decision to Serve Fins." *Taipei Times*. May 24, 2005. http://www.taipeitimes.com/News/world/archives/2005/05/24/2003256404

[5] "Disney Hong Kong insists on shark's fin-soup meals." *Taipei Times*. May 29, 2005. http://www.taipeitimes.com/News/biz/archives/2005/05/29/2003257104

[6] Bradsher, "Disneyland in China Offers a Soup But Lands in a Stew."

[7] Keith Bradsher, "Shark Fin Soup Is Off the Menu at Hong Kong Disneyland." *New York Times*, June 25, 2005. http://www.nytimes.com/2005/06/25/business/media/25disney.html

the World Wildlife Fund expressed deep concern about the environmental impact of harvesting fins for the soup. To meet worldwide demand, they say, many sharks (up to 73 million per year according to the *New York Times*[2]) are killed each year, putting some species at risk. "Finning," a practice in which the fins are cut off and the rest of the shark is thrown back into the ocean to die, is another common occurrence. The Sea Shepherd Conservation Society went as far as making T-shirts showing Disney characters such as Mickey Mouse and Donald Duck brandishing knives over bleeding sharks that had their fins removed.[3]

Hoping to avoid some of the cultural insensitivity that contributed to the failure of its European theme (in Paris) to hit attendance goals, Disney took great pains to fit its Hong Kong venture in with local cultural customs. Shark fin soup has been served at festive Chinese occasions, especially weddings, for hundreds of years. The soup is fabled for its medicinal powers and symbolizes power and wealth. Serving the dish also shows respect and honor to guests. "Hong Kong Disneyland takes environmental stewardship very seriously, and we are equally sensitive to local cultures. It is customary for Chinese restaurants and five-star hotels to serve shark's fin soup in Hong Kong, as the dish is considered an integral part of Chinese banquets," said Hong Kong Disneyland spokeswoman Irene Chan.[4] Some supporters of Disney say that it would be shameful for those holding special events to not offer shark fin soup to their guests. David Ng, the president of the Hong Kong Federation of Restaurants and Related Trades, said, "This is the traditional culture of the Chinese people, and you can't say it's right or wrong."[5] Another restaurateur blamed Westerners for stirring up the controversy. "It's a cultural difference—they don't eat it, so they see it differently," he said.[6]

At first, Disney stuck to its decision to serve the soup. Just a short while later, however, executives announced that they would not offer the soup, citing the fact that they could not source the fins in a sustainable manner.[7]

Discussion Questions:

1. In deciding to pull the soup from its banquet menu, did Disney executives make the right decision? Why or why not?
2. If you were a Disney executive or someone faced with a similar choice, how would you incorporate cultural differences into your decision?

COMMENTARY

With the expansion of business across global boundaries has come an increase in the level of awareness of conflicting ethical standards between cultures. While simply adapting to local culture and "doing as the Romans do" might make sense from a strictly practical standpoint, many are uncomfortable with engaging in practices that would constitute a departure from familiar moral standards, but which may be necessary in order to operate successfully in a different culture.

While cultural sensitivity is undoubtedly important, there are many instances in which simply following the popular mores of the land, including your own, is clearly wrong. Yet there are many other situations in which a conflict of ethics is only apparent. Upon closer examination, many instances that resemble moral conflicts may really be arguments over facts, procedures, and/or as Bernard Adeney points out, culturally laden interpretation of events, instead of underlying ethical principles. In these instances, one can adapt while not violating true moral standards.

Many who hold to the view that people should behave "like the Romans while in Rome" base their position on a moral philosophy known as ethical relativism. Ethical relativism became popular in the early 1900s as a result of the observations of cultural anthropologists who observed that different cultures have widely varying moral codes and concepts of right and wrong.[8] As they studied different cultures, they were struck by the lack of a uniform concept of right and wrong. For example, some cultures practice polygamy, while others practice monogamy. Some cultures consider it a moral obligation to give one of their children to an infertile couple. Some cultures, such as certain groups of Eskimos, practice euthanasia and infanticide in ways that seem ghastly and immoral to many in other cultures. Some parts of the world have very strict sexual taboos, while other areas have widespread sexual freedom. Among the Sawi people of New Guinea, treachery was considered the highest virtue, and when missionaries brought the gospel to them, they were horrified to learn that the hero of the gospel message was not Jesus, but Judas.[9] These are just a sample of the great variety in the way morality is conceived and practiced.

As a result of these observations, new conclusions were being drawn about the nature of morality. It was suggested that in view of such diversity, belief in universal values that applied irrespective of culture could not be maintained. Such ethical diversity called into question systems that held to absolute, unchanging principles that could be universally applied. The more "enlightened" way of viewing right and wrong was to see it as relative to the

[8] The main works in this area are as follows: William Graham Sumner, *Folkways* (New York: Ginn and Co., 1906); Ruth Benedict, *Patterns of Culture* (New York: New American Library, 1934); Melville Herskovits, *Cultural Relativism* (New York: Random House, 1972); John Ladd, ed., *Ethical Relativism* (Belmont, Calif.: Wadsworth, 1973).

[9] This is documented in Don Richardson, *Peace Child: An Unforgettable Story of Primitive Jungle Treachery in the 20th Century*, 4th ed. (Ventura, Calif.: Regal, 2005).

culture in which one found himself or herself. Morality was seen as relative to the cultural consensus, with ethical standards as merely cultural conventions. This way of viewing ethics has become more popular in recent times due to the emphasis on multiculturalism and the way in which the global economy is shrinking the world.

As Adeney points out, some of our cultural values are formed in reaction to or affirmation of the social conditions of the time. Unfortunately, these have been and are mistaken for absolute/objective standards, when in reality they are little more than the biases of a particular (often dominant) culture dressed up in moral language.

A good example of this dynamic at work is the practice of slavery before the Civil War. Though it was clearly immoral for human beings to own other human beings, and in many cases, treat them like animals, many in the South attempted to justify slavery as an institution, sometimes using biblical grounds. Slavery, which was created as a result of the agricultural conditions in the South, was treated as moral, and the right to own slaves was regarded as an absolute right. Of course, it was nothing of the sort, and a cultural creation was regarded as an absolute moral right, mistaking the absolute for the sociologically relative.

Frequently relativism is presented as though it and its polar opposite, called absolutism, were the only two valid alternatives. The absolutist holds to absolute moral principles rigidly and does not allow for any exceptions regardless of the circumstances. As Adeney points out, this position simplistically "flattens out" all morality and neglects the fact that a person's choice of moral rules is often highly related to culture. This is clearly not an attractive or realistic position to hold, and if relativism is presented as the only alternative to this kind of absolutism, it is not hard to see why people would prefer relativism.

However, it is better to see morality on a continuum, with absolutism at one extreme and relativism at the other. One can hold to objective moral principles and not be an absolutist; that is, one can be what is called a prima facie absolutist, or an absolutist "on the surface," allowing for periodic exceptions to general principles when they conflict with other important moral values.[10] For example, if someone comes into your house with a gun ready to shoot and asks where your husband or wife is, you are not obligated to tell him the truth.

In spite of its appeal and widespread use in the popular culture, relativism has some commonly held flaws.[11] First, consider that many of the observations of moral diversity were actually differences in moral *practices*. That is, someone could hold to universal moral absolutes but allow for cultural flexibility in their application. For example, in some parts of the world, taxes are

[10] This is developed further in William K. Frankena, *Ethics*, 2nd ed. (New York: Prentice Hall, 1988).

[11] For more on the critique of relativism, see Francis J. Beckwith and Gregory Koukl, *Relativism: Feet Firmly Planted in Mid-Air* (Grand Rapids: Baker, 1998).

computed based on exact figures, whereas in other areas, a person's taxes are more of a negotiation in which the tax return is considered a first position in the discussion. The overall principle is fairness in the distribution of the tax burden, but the procedure for getting there varies widely depending on the culture. One should recognize that diversity in practice does not necessarily equal diversity in *underlying values or principles.*

Second, there is a leap in logic—ethical relativism as a system does not follow from the empirical data of moral diversity among cultures. Simply because different cultures have different moral standards, it does not follow that there is no such thing as absolute values that transcend culture. For instance, although bribery is supposedly "commonly practiced," so what? Drawing normative conclusions ("ought" from descriptive observations ["is"]) is an error known as the naturalistic fallacy.

Third, relativism provides no way to arbitrate among competing cultural value claims. This is critical as business begins to expand across national boundaries and countries are attempting to create trade agreements. For example, in the absence of transcendent norms, the United States cannot rightfully accuse China of wrongdoing in its alleged failures to crackdown on the piracy of intellectual property such as computer software.

Fourth, the relativist cannot morally evaluate any clearly oppressive culture or, more specifically, any obvious tyrant when those practices reflect the cultural consensus. In the absence of absolutes, no one can rightfully claim the existence of *international* human rights. Cultures that relegate women to the status of second-class citizens cannot be evaluated by the relativist since morality is dependent on the cultural context. Similarly, the relativist cannot pass judgment on someone like Hitler, who oppressed a minority with the permission, if not approval, of the majority, since there is no moral absolute that transcends culture to which the relativist can appeal as a basis for that judgment.

While these objections to relativism can seem quite abstract, they are critical when considering particular situations that arise in international business settings. Clearly, some cases of "doing as the Romans do" can violate a universal norm for moral behavior. For example, without apparent consideration of the interests of their citizens, some governments will accept toxic chemicals from industrialized countries and unsafely dispose of them in exchange for large sums of money. For a company to "export death" in such a manner is irresponsible and immoral, knowing the risks involved and that the money is probably going to the private wealth of a few government officials.

Low-wage, low-skill factories (sweatshops) in developing nations provide some insight into the complex nature of behaving ethically in international business. Many factory workers have no other options than to accept low wages in exchange for their labor, which usually takes place under poor conditions. For some young women, the available alternatives are unemployment, farming, or prostitution. As Zwolinski points out in his article, in sweatshops, a job in a factory is seen as an "opportunity" within this broader context. He insists that efforts to close down these factories would "end up harming precisely the people that anti-sweatshop activists are trying to help." In addition, he argues that sweatshops do not cause poverty, but are rather an indication of economic growth and emergence from poverty — seen as hopeful signs for an economy. He suggests that "they are the first step in a long path of economic development."[12]

With the surplus of available labor in many of these countries, these employees cannot simply quit and take another position. In some cases, when some workers tried to unionize, they were fired immediately. Thus, to treat these workers poorly and to pay them the minimum amount possible fits a textbook definition of exploitation, in which a party with all of the power forces another to abide by their rules.

However, when it comes to wages, the issue is very complex, as it would be impractical to pay a rate much more than the market set price. The incentive to employ people in the developing world would be diminished and the economic disruption caused by paying much higher wages could be significant. In addition, there is a risk of some professionals, such as teachers, leaving their positions for higher-paying factory work.

Paying lower wages to workers based on geographical location is not necessarily immoral. In our own country, there are sometimes large wage variations for similar positions based on cost-of-living differences. The goal should be, however, to provide a level of pay that provides a minimal necessary standard of living, a "moral wage" so to speak. Although there are clear limits, the term *minimal* can be defined somewhat flexibly depending on the culture and the stage of economic development of a particular place.

The issue of safe working conditions and how employees are treated, however, offers far less flexibility. On these issues, ethics demands that human health and well-being serve as universal standards wherever they may live and work. Zwolinski recognizes that most anti-sweatshop activists do not desire that they be shut down, only that conditions be improved to accord with basic human dignity. It seems clear that the companies that operate these factories are responsible for insuring that the workplace is safe, sanitary, and free from physical and sexual harassment.

What remains controversial is child labor. Zwolinski argues that regulations on employment of children hurt the families they are trying to help, since the money children earn is essential to families surviving financially.

[12] For further development of the opportunity of sweatshop employment, see Matt Zwolinski, "Sweatshops, Choice and Exploitation," *Business Ethics Quarterly* 17, no. 4 (October 2007): 697–98.

What prohibitions on child labor are meant to protect for the children is not entirely clear. It may be an education, but in much of the developing world, education is either not widely available or exists only in private schools that are financially out of the reach of many families. If one is trying to protect something about the innocence of childhood, that is likely more of an affluent, Western ideal that is culturally driven, since throughout most of the history of civilization, children have worked from young ages. We recognize that children working is necessary for their family's economic survival in some parts of the world and see some efforts to curtail child labor as hurting these struggling families. On the other hand, we realize that children are more vulnerable to abuse and see child labor as problematic if it comes at the expense of an opportunity for education.

When it comes to bribery, trying to adopt local standards of behavior while staying within the bounds of Christian ethics and U.S. law is undoubtedly challenging. However, we earlier stated that one could consistently abide by Judeo-Christian morals and succeed in international business settings. Some companies are actually making it public that they will not pay or solicit bribes and are becoming well known for their stance. For example, the global engineering firm Fluor has what it calls "anti-corruption language" in all its contracts, making it clear that bribes will not be paid under any circumstances.[13]

Moreover, as the second shortcoming of relativism described above notes, many instances in which ethical conflicts appear may actually be disagreements over facts and interpretations rather than underlying moral principles. The common situation of small monetary payments to government officials serves as a good example. On the surface, these situations pit conflicting standards against each other. However, upon closer examination, these may be conflicts over definition and/or culture, rather than underlying ethical principles. When these types of conflicts occur, the immediate question that must be asked is whether a real conflict of underlying moral principles is taking place. As Adeney points out, these types of payments may represent gifts, tips, bribes, or something in between all of them. We would suggest that the term *bribery* is often used as the umbrella term but is inaccurate to describe all of these morally questionable payments. The payment that Adeney describes as going to the police officer is probably more correctly called extortion, since the police officer is using a position of power to extract a benefit (a financial one) from the driver. Though it is generally wrong to demand extortion payments, it is not obvious that it would be wrong to pay it, analogous to paying a ransom. One is being victimized and using money to extricate oneself from further victimization.

[13] Gail Dutton, "Do Strong Ethics Hurt U.S. Global Competitiveness?" *World Trade* 21, no. 3 (March 2008): 36–41. The article concludes that sometimes competitiveness is hurt but that an anticorruption consensus is emerging.

It is best to see payments that we commonly call bribery along a continuum, with gifts at one end and extortion at the other, and tips, premiums, and bribes somewhere in between these extremes. Gifts are payments that are made with no expectations or strings attached—they are unconditional. Tips are generally seen as rewards for good service, though the original acronym for tips—"to insure prompt service," suggests that the payment comes before, not after the service. Premiums are payments that insure expedited service—Adeney's example of the payment made to the service technician to guarantee utilities being turned on in a few days as opposed to a few months, is probably best termed a premium. Bribes are payments that give one a competitive advantage in a contractual setting. They are fundamentally exclusive of other competitors and give someone the "inside track" to obtaining a piece of business.[14] They are unethical because they undercut fair competition. Bribes are illegal under U.S. law, though enforcing that law in other parts of the world can be difficult.

Though many of the major ethical issues relate to companies and their global supply chains, some efforts are being made to involve consumers more directly. The fair trade movement is one of those examples. Fair trade began as a faith-based movement to try to mitigate the harsh and disruptive consequences of the global economy. As worldwide coffee prices plummeted after the collapse of the International Coffee Agreement in 1989, many farmers simply had to walk away from plots of land that in some cases had been worked by multiple generations of family. Paul Chandler argues that out of our concern for the poor in the developing world, the developed world should support local growers through fair trade organizations. Fair trade coffee is certainly the best known, but just one of the products (e.g., chocolate, clothing, flowers, soccer balls) for which consumers can pay slightly higher than market prices to support a living wage for producers in the developing world. Chandler insists that support for fair trade products, provided they don't become "cozy niches," helps the growers, who have few other skills and for whom changing occupations would be quite challenging if not impossible.

By contrast, Victor Claar argues that the reason that coffee prices are too low to support a living wage has to do with conditions of supply and demand—there is simply too much coffee on the market. Claar maintains that fair trade movements actually hurt the poor by distorting market incentives that are set by prices. He insists that current market prices should act as a signal for producers to move into other, more productive segments of the economy, as he suggests has been the case in Central American countries such as Costa Rica moving into eco-tourism. He argues for free trade and market incentives being allowed to set the signals to the producers without

[14] For more on business bribery, see "Bribery: Not Only Wrong, but Costly Too?" *Academy of Management Perspectives* 21, no. 3 (August 2007): 86–87.

distortion from nonmarket forces. He would also include protectionist measures as harmful distortions of market forces.

Though both Chandler and Claar agree on the moral *ends*—assisting the poor in the developing world, they disagree on the most effective *means* to accomplish those ends. We advocate the market being allowed to function freely as much as possible, though we are deeply concerned about the difficulty of farmers and other less skilled workers transitioning into other, more productive occupations. Many of these farmers and producers also lack the type of "safety nets" enjoyed in wealthier countries.

In the long run, we would hold that distorting market forces is generally unwise and counterproductive, but recognize the substantial short-term dislocation caused to farmers and their families should they have to change occupations. Moreover, fair trade is not a government set price floor but is in fact market based, since it is up to the preferences of consumers. Thus, an "incubation" type use of fair trade, as suggested by Chandler, might be a justifiable and useful application of the practice. We would note, however, that the Fair Trade brand has been subjected to much criticism (too many narrow requirements and high cost of certification) that it has evolved in the cozy arrangement that Chandler warns about. Some coffee retailers (including Starbucks) have instituted their own programs to pay "fair" prices for coffee without the Fair Trade brand certification. Thus, one might well be able to "trade fairly" without the Fair Trade brand.

When ethical dilemmas are created by the collision of cultures, it is important to have some criteria in place to help you make ethical decisions, to decide whether to follow the standards of the home country in which you are based or the host country in which you are operating. For example, business ethics professor Thomas Donaldson has suggested that there are ethical norms that transcend culture and must be followed regardless of the culture in which one is doing business. He calls these core human values that must always be followed—respect for human dignity, respect for basic human rights, and good corporate citizenship.[15] We agree that there are cross-cultural moral values that do not depend on cultural acceptance for their validity. We would add values such as "do no harm," fairness, nondiscrimination, and justice to Donaldson's. Though this is not an exhaustive list, we acknowledge that there are moral principles that transcend culture, that form the criteria for making decisions when cultures clash. We would suggest that when a cultural practice clearly violates one of these core moral principles, it cannot be followed and you must follow the core moral value. For example, unsafe working conditions in sweatshops violate the "do no harm" principle. Bribery violates the principle of fair competition and the obligation to follow the law (for U.S. companies). However, child labor, in our view, may not necessarily involve violation of core moral values.

[15] Thomas Donaldson, "Values in Tension: Ethics Away from Home," *Harvard Business Review* 74, no. 5 (September–October 1996): 48–62; and Thomas Donaldson and Thomas Dunfee, "When Ethics Travel: The Promise and Peril of Global Business Ethics," *California Management Review* 41, no. 4 (Summer 1999): 45–63.

Conclusion

"When in Rome, do business as the Romans do," is an inadequate guide to moral action while operating in different cultures. Cultural relativism as a theory has some significant shortcomings, and simply adapting to the norms of a host country can lead to serious ethical problems. However, narrow "absolutism" is not the correct answer either. There are other instances in which mere apparent and not real conflicts of underlying ethical principles can be resolved (though perhaps not easily) with a closer look at the facts, including our cultural assumptions. Thus, it is possible to be successful in international business while remaining consistent with your ethical standards, though you will have to be open minded and cautiously, but appropriately, flexible in the process.

PART 3

CONTEMPORARY ETHICAL ISSUES IN BUSINESS

SEVEN

Ethics and the Management of Talent

Introduction

Successfully mobilizing the people who make up an organization's "talent" or "human capital" to achieve an organization's mission and objectives is a critically important and challenging part of business. In fact, the word *management* is commonly defined as "(1) the process of planning, organizing, leading and controlling human and other organizational resources with the aim of (2) the effective achievement of organizational goals."[1]

While this definition sounds value neutral, there are in fact many latent values assumptions. Influential management theorist and author Peter Drucker once said, "Management is deeply involved with spiritual concerns—the nature of man, good and evil."[2] Moreover, conflicts often occur between what may help accomplish an organization's objectives and what is in the best interests of employees as people. For example, long working hours and/or constant connectivity through technological devices may serve (at least in the shorter term) the financial interests of an organization, but may not serve to better the lives of employees. Many other "people management" decisions, such as hiring and promotion, the distribution of financial rewards, employee input into decisions, work conditions, job design, and performance measurement pose similar questions and conflicts. Organizational policies and practices with respect to these matters reflect philosophical and theological assumptions and values about such matters as organizational purpose and priorities, human dignity, human nature, fairness, and justice.

Throughout much of the modern history of work, the tenor of the prevailing "social contract" between employers and employees was a "fair day's work for a fair day's pay." Employees, especially nonmanagerial ones, were primarily seen as labor, prompting such infamous exclamations as the one attributed to Henry Ford: "Why is it that I always get the whole person when all I really want is a pair of hands?"[3]

[1] Bruno Dyck and Mitchell Neubert, *Management: Current Practices and New Directions* (Boston: Houghton Mifflin Harcourt, 2010), 7.

[2] Peter Drucker, "Management as a Social Function and Liberal Art," in Peter Drucker, *Management*, revised and updated by Joseph A. Maciariello (Harper & Row, 1974; repr., New York: HarperCollins, 2008).

[3] Quip commonly attributed to Henry Ford; see C. William Pollard, "Mission as an Organizing Principle," *Leader to Leader* 16 (2000): 3 (reprinted in this chapter).

Much has changed today. Many employees, especially in developed economies, are increasingly engaged in creative, knowledge-based work, typically requiring very little physical use of their hands (other than to type their thoughts on keyboards), and much more engagement with the "whole person" that Ford decried. The nature of contemporary work is no longer something easily "left at the office." In addition to long hours spent in exchange for a salary, work has become a source of identity, purpose, and meaning. A reconceptualized "social contract" and new approaches to management and leadership are needed to reflect these realities and to exercise responsibility in properly stewarding the human capital of organizations.

Not surprisingly, a focus on people and how they should be treated is a central theme within Christian ethics. In addition to duties to neighbors, family members, and strangers, the Bible offers some direct guidance on how employees should be treated. For example, employers were to pay wages on the day they were earned, likely to ensure that interest was not being earned at the expense of the worker. In the New Testament, landowning employers are the subject of several parables. For example, Jesus condemned farmers who mistreated their servants in the field (Mark 12:1–12). He also used justice in a day's pay in the fields as an example of the "last shall be first" (Matt 20:1–16). In addition to specific principles, there is much more in the form of paradigmatic-level guidance in the Bible that is applicable for today's complex marketplace.

This chapter will focus on the implications of Christian ethics for managing people. The subjects discussed are often categorized under the auspices of "human resources management." However, managers across various functions and levels have input into these types of decisions. So our aim is to explore issues that are broadly applicable across an organization as opposed to the formal human resources or talent management offices alone.

Among the many issues that could be covered in this chapter (as noted in the brief listing of possible conflicts above), we have chosen to focus on a few key ones for their ability to bring to the surface some key assumptions and values that influence management theories and practices. Focusing on these issues will help us in developing an overall narrative or broader ethic of managing people—which can then be applied to other issues as they arise.

The first reading in this chapter, "Mission as an Organizing Principle," by noted author and former ServiceMaster CEO Bill Pollard, sets the tone by identifying the deep-seated, nonmaterial needs (i.e., purpose and meaning) of employees and the role and responsibilities of leaders to meet them. Notably, Pollard argues that developing people is an "end goal," while profitability is a mere "means goal" of the organization he led for many years.

The following article, "Building Healthy Organizations in Which People Can Flourish" by Richard Beaton and Linda Wagener (formerly faculty members at Fuller Seminary, now consultants), is a thoughtful exploration of how

Christian theology (and ethics) can inform the shaping of organizational policies to maximize human well-being. The authors explore the Scriptures to develop theological insights into how work can be designed and managed in a manner that represents a win-win for both the organization and its employees.

The third article, "Technology and the New Challenges of Management," by Albert Erisman (former director of research and development for computing and mathematics at Boeing, and now an executive in residence at Seattle Pacific University) offers insights into managing organizations and people amid the challenges brought about by emerging technologies. Erisman takes a look at challenges in organizational communications, assessing and controlling behavior, measuring the work product, and managing the new generation of "technology natives."

The fourth article is an interview (conducted by Al Erisman and Kenman Wong) with Cheryl Broetje, the cofounder of one of America's largest privately owned apple farms, First Fruits. The company sees one of its primary objectives as people development, with a special eye toward the vulnerable. The Broetjes manage their entire operation (with roughly 1,000 year-round employees) with a servant leadership approach and have made substantial and innovative investments into employee development and well-being.

The final article, "The Ethics of Executive Pay: A Christian Viewpoint," by Richard Higginson (the director of Faith in Business at Ridley Hall, Cambridge) and David Clough, addresses excessive executive pay, an issue that has received much attention during the past several years. While the distribution of pay seems value neutral (market based), the authors insightfully point out how it is also driven by values and how it directly intersects with biblical conceptions of fairness and justice.

READINGS

Mission as an Organizing Principle
C. William Pollard
Leader to Leader 16 (Spring 2000).

To say that today's leaders must learn to initiate rapid and continuous change is to state the obvious. Such change is a fact of life. The problem is, the people who make up organizations are not built for rapid and continuous change. In the absence of a meaningful mission and purpose that transcends the change and includes a caring and nurturing of people, rapid change can bring discontinuity, dislocation, and demoralization.

People need a hope beyond the change. They need

an anchor, a purpose that does not change and that provides meaning for their life and for their work.

What is the role of our organizations in responding to this need for meaning? What will be the social contract between an employer and employee as we move to the 21st century? Have we defined the mission of our organizations to include bringing purpose and meaning to those who are fulfilling the mission? How do we measure the effectiveness of our organizations? Can our organizations become moral communities to help shape the human character and behavior of our people? Can our mission be an organizing principle?

The first job of leaders is to ask, and try to answer, such questions. But our ultimate job is to be champions of the mission of the firm and, more important, to live that mission. We also must recognize that our values and character will be tested in the process.

I ask these fundamental questions not as a philosopher or educator but simply as a businessperson — someone who, with my colleagues, is seeking to lead a fast growing, dynamic service company. ServiceMaster has experienced rapid growth, doubling in size every 3½ years for over 25 years, with systemwide revenues now exceeding $6 billion. Yes, we have experienced massive change. Over 75 percent of our current business lines we did not do just ten years ago. And we face the same pressures as every public company. Revenue and profits must be reported quarterly. The shareholders to whom we are responsible vote every day on our leadership — they have the choice to buy, hold, or sell.

But a business leader's success cannot be limited to the calculation of profit or a return on equity. My success must be measured by the 240,000 people with whom I work — the people who deliver value to customers and shareholders every day.

Much of our business may be seen as routine and mundane. We clean toilets and floors, maintain boilers and air-handling units, serve food, kill bugs, care for lawns and landscapes, clean carpets, provide maid service, and repair home appliances. Our task as leaders is to train and motivate people to serve so they will do a more effective job, be more productive in their work and, yes, even be better people. But how does one go about motivating so many people — most of whom are scattered about the locations of our 10 million customers? Although we work hard at developing our training programs and management systems, no amount of training or management can effectively motivate others to serve. Unless we align the values of our people with the mission of the firm, and unless we continue to develop and care for people in the process, we will fail.

A Reason for Being

When you visit our headquarters in Downers Grove, Illinois, you walk into a large, two-story lobby; on your right is a curving marble wall, 90 feet long and 18 feet high. Carved in stone on that wall are four statements that constitute our mission: To Honor God In All We Do, To Help People Develop, To Pursue Excellence, and To Grow Profitably. It's a statement simple enough to be remembered, controversial enough to require continuous dialogue, and profound enough to be lasting.

The first two objectives are end goals. The second two are means goals. All of them provide a reference point for people seeking to do that which is right and avoiding that which is wrong. Our goals remind us that every person has been created with dignity, worth, and great potential. They remind us, too, that our core principles, like the wall itself, do not change.

In a pluralistic society, some may question whether our first objective is an appropriate goal for a public company. However, we do not use that goal as a basis of exclusion. It is, in fact, the basis for our promotion of diversity, as we recognize that different people are all part of God's mix, in whatever way (and whether or not) they choose to worship.

Our beliefs do not mean that everything in the business will be done right. We experience our share of mistakes. But because of a stated standard and our reason for that standard, we cannot hide our mistakes. They are brought into the open for correction and, in some cases, for forgiveness.

The New World of Work

Fifty years ago pundits were predicting that by the year 2000, everyone would be enjoying a 30-hour work week. The balance of our time would be spent in rest and leisure. But now it seems that most of us work harder. Others retire earlier or are in transition because their job is no longer needed. We use words like *downsizing* and *rightsizing* to mask the reality that people lose jobs for reasons other than performance. In fact, it has been suggested that we now live in a post-job world.

People want to contribute to a cause, not just earn a living.

In this new world of work we have found that people want to contribute to a cause, not just earn a living. When we create alignment between the mission of the firm and the cause of its people, we unleash a creative power that results in quality service to the customer and the growth and development of the people who do the serving. People find meaning in their work. The mission becomes an organizing principle of effectiveness.

While we work with many accomplished people seeking new ways to contribute, we also have many workers coming to us with little or no formal training, social skills, or understanding of standards of civility. As a result, the workplace is increasingly becoming—or must become—a place of training and education, a University of Work. The distinctions we once made between going to school during part of our life and then working for the other part are no longer meaningful. For all people, the lines between school and work are blurring.

As we recognize the importance of dealing with the whole person, we seek to link the performance of the task with the development of the person, and to assume responsibility for what happens to the person in the process. What are they becoming in their work? Are the task as defined, the tools as designed, and the training so provided contributing to or detracting from the work and the worker? Are there opportunities for personal and professional advancement? These questions force a self-energizing, self-correcting, ongoing process that is the basis for continuous improvement in how we serve customers.

Of course, any task can be seen as drudgery or self-expression. A given job, no matter how mundane, is not determinative. The difference is to be found within the person doing the task, in that part of our being that seeks a meaning for life and work. It is the desire to accomplish something significant. A person who sees a rewarding purpose and a genuine opportunity beyond the task can bring creativity, productivity, quality, and value to any job. The job of the leader, then, is to articulate a mission that brings deeper meaning to work, and to assure that the organization's mission is in alignment with people's own growth and development.

Bringing Meaning to Work

Why is Shirley Nelson, a housekeeper in a 250-bed community hospital, still excited about her work after 15 years? She certainly has seen some changes. She actually cleans more rooms today than she did five years ago. The chemicals, the mop, and the housekeeping cart have all been improved. Nevertheless, the bathrooms and the toilets are the same. The dirt has not changed nor have the unexpected spills of the patients or the arrogance of some of the physicians. So what motivates Shirley?

Shirley sees her job as extending to the welfare of the patient and as an integral part of a team that helps sick people get well. She has a cause that involves the health and welfare of others. When Shirley first started, no doubt she was merely looking for just a job. But she brought to her work an unlocked potential and a desire to accomplish something significant. As I talked with Shirley about her job, she said, "If we don't clean with a quality effort, we can't keep the doctors and nurses in business. We can't serve the patients. This place would be closed if we didn't have housekeeping." Shirley was confirming the reality of our mission. She was in command of her work, of herself, and of her own small piece of our business. And in a very real sense she was leading me, by talking about her work, her customers, and her role in our shared mission.

Leading the Whole Person

People are not just economic animals or production units. Everyone has a fingerprint of personality and potential and desire to contribute. When we define people solely in economic terms, our motivational and incentive schemes tend to become mechanical and manipulative. We try to define a system that will idiot-proof the process, which can in turn make people feel like idiots. *Fortune* magazine recently described the soulless company as suffering from an enemy within, citing Henry Ford's quote as descriptive: "Why is it that I always get the whole person when what I really want is just a pair of hands?"

The scope of training must include more than teaching a person to use the right tools or to complete an assigned task within a defined period. It also must include how people feel about their work, about themselves, and how they relate to others at work or at home.

Thus, if I am involved in the leadership process, then as part of my training, I should also experience what it is like to do the hands-on work and to feel the emotions of those I am going to manage. That is why every manager in ServiceMaster spends time actually doing the tasks he or she will ultimately manage others to do.

When we define people solely in economic terms, incentive schemes become mechanical and manipulative.

Over 20 years ago, when I started as senior vice president responsible for the legal and financial affairs of the company, I spent the first three months of my training doing cleaning and maintenance tasks in hospitals, factories, and homes. It was a learning and serving experience that helped me to identify with the needs and concerns of our service workers. It was a great lesson in servant leadership and the role of a leader in implementing the mission of a firm. It has been a constant reminder that I must always be prepared to serve and should never ask anyone to do something that I am not willing to do myself. As a leader in such an environment, I should always be ready to be surprised by the potential of people.

A colleague tells of an experience that has been a great reminder to me of this point. It is often the custom for firms to hand out service pins in recognition of years of service. As my friend was involved in such an event,

he was surprised by the response of one of the recipients. The young man opened the box, took out the sterling silver tie tack, said thanks, and with a wide grin proudly put the pin into his ear lobe, not on his lapel.

We should never be too quick to judge potential by appearance.

People are different, and we should never be too quick to judge potential by appearance or lifestyle. It is a leader's responsibility to set the tone, to learn to accept the differences of people, and to foster an environment where different people can contribute as part of the whole and achieve unity in diversity.

When Work Is Only a Job

Several years ago I was traveling in what was then the Soviet Union. I had been asked to give several talks on the service business and our company objectives. While I was in the city then called Leningrad, now St. Petersburg, I met Olga. She had the job of mopping the lobby floor in a large hotel, which at that time was occupied mostly by people from the West. I took an interest in her and her task. I engaged her in conversation through an interpreter and noted the tools she had to do her work. Olga had been given a T-frame for a mop, a filthy rag, and a bucket of dirty water. She really wasn't cleaning the floor; she was just moving dirt from place to place. The reality of Olga's task was to do the least amount of motions in the greatest amount of time until the day was over. Olga was not proud of what she was doing. She had no dignity in her work. She was a long way from owning the result.

I knew from our brief conversation that there was a great unlocked potential in Olga. I am sure you could have eaten off the floor in her two-room apartment—but work was something different. No one had taken the time to teach or equip Olga. She was lost in a system that did not care. Work was just a job that had to be done. She was the object of work, not the subject.

But think back to Shirley—what makes her experience of work so different from Olga's? Yes, one was born in Moscow and the other in Chicago, and their cultures, language, and nationalities were different. But, their basic tasks were the same. They both had to work for a living. They both had limited financial resources. One was proud of what she was doing. Her work had affected her view of herself and others. The other was not, and had a limited view of her potential and worth.

The difference, I suggest, has something to do with how they were treated, loved, and cared for in the work environment. In one case, the mission of the firm involved the development of the person, recognizing their dignity and worth. In the other case, the objective was to provide activity and call it work.

Everywhere one looks today, there is more freedom and more choice in our lives — but also more confu-

sion and uncertainty. A corporate mission cannot be viewed as a panacea, nor applied like a mathematical formula. It can, however, provide a foundation, a reference point for action. It offers a living set of principles that allows us to confront the difficulties and contradictions of work life. When our mission becomes an organizing principle, our organizations become communities of people caring for each other and for those they serve. As we continue to define and refine that mission and seek to lead in its fulfillment, let us not forget the people who are serving and making it happen — they are the soul of our organizations.

Questions for Discussion and Reflection

1. Do you agree with Pollard that a person's work needs to provide him or her with meaning? Or is that too much to ask of the workplace? Explain your answer.
2. How do you balance the need to be competitive and efficient with what Pollard suggests is a need to provide opportunities for workers for self-improvement?

Building Healthy Organizations in Which People Can Flourish

Richard Beaton and Linda M. Wagener

Theology, News and Notes 57, no. 1 (Spring 2010): 1–4.

Synopsis

In this essay, Wagener and Beaton propose that the idea of human flourishing ought to be expanded from individuals to the organizations that often claim most of their time and creativity. Bemoaning the lack of resources on the theology of organizational life, the authors suggest that creating organizations — such as businesses, churches, governments, and clubs — in which people can flourish is uniquely suited to the Judeo-Christian theological imagination.

• • •

A recent poll returned the surprising result that over 60 percent of people were seriously interested in changing their jobs and only 15 percent were fully committed to staying in their current position. This is due to the economy and the treatment of employees and degrading working conditions that the 60 percent observed (see sidebar below). The manner in which layoffs occurred in almost every sector and form of organization provided a visual language about corporate values. The way your colleague has been treated is more than likely how you will be treated as well. We all give much of our lives to organizations of various types, and we all hope for more when we are in them.

This is not surprising since organizations play a significant role in the lives of most of the human population. Organizations are places we invest ourselves for a large part of our lives. We work, develop relationships, use our skills, capacities, even sacrifice our families and future. For this we, in turn, receive something: a salary, an identity, meaning, purpose, and hopefully a place to do meaningful, creative work. Involvements at work, church, nonprofits, government, school boards, clubs, and so on, shape not only our experience of life and society, but also impact our personal growth and development.

While not a recent phenomenon, organizations have changed much in the modern era, becoming more focused on strategy, mission, and efficiency. But in reality they are made up of people. It is people who do the work within them, people who run them, people who shape them. The human capital present and the responsibility of leadership/management for this resource are sobering. It is surprising that as much as people write about leadership, there are virtually no books and few articles specifically writ-

Job poll results ...

The fourth annual survey of job satisfaction conducted by Salary.com in 2009 revealed that 65% of employed survey respondents said they are looking for different jobs (up more than 17%); 60% said they plan to intensify a job search despite the economy; 65% were "somewhat satisfied," but only 15% were extremely satisfied. Online public membership organization Conference Board reports in January of 2010 that job satisfaction in the U.S. is at its lowest level in two decades since the first year in which their survey was conducted.

ten about a theology of organizational life. We are consumed with the leader and his or her growth and capacity and seemingly less than interested in running healthy organizations. This disconnect is an odd one, especially since it is in organizational life that we see our values, beliefs, and practices expressed most vividly.

Organizations today function in a diverse, pluralistic world, and this complex context demands a more thoughtful consideration about what it means to live out one's faith within the world. As a result, how we understand work and the relationships between the church, believers, and society are also in flux. We are finally moving beyond the notion that calling is reserved for pastors, missionaries, or other such pursuits (as though a vocation and work were lesser things), to a more holistic notion that we can glorify God in the vocations of good work. This is an important shift, since it pushes us towards a more holistic understanding of life, work, faith, and practices. And it forces us to finally begin thinking about a theological view of organizational life and how to participate in, build, manage, and lead it. To do this, we need a more robust theology of humanity—what Max DePree calls our "concept of persons."

The Judeo-Christian theological imagination provides several ways into thinking about creating organizations in which people can flourish. The biblical documents do help us a great deal, but perhaps not in the way many of us think. If organizations are fundamentally about people working together to accomplish a mission, then the context we are interested in involves issues that surround being human. Any manager or leader that takes on responsibilities within an organizational context may be swayed by the work of strategy, organizing, problem solving/decision making, delegation, self-management, reporting, or budgeting, but the work has to be done by and through people. Thus, the leader/manager must be a keen student of the human person and be able to create a relationship-based model that promotes optimal human functioning. The Old and New Testaments have much to say on the human person, and it is here that they contribute most.

When we think of understanding the human person, Genesis 1:26–29 is an important passage.

It contains a rich theological landscape from which to draw. We learn in this text that humanity, men and women equally, have dignity and value, being created in God's image. Similarly, we learn that humanity is given a profound role of responsibility within the created order, to manage it—which one assumes includes human society and the institutions found therein. Thus, part of our mandate is to create healthy systems in which humans can flourish. Paul's understanding of the new creation is similar. His eschatology suggests that the church is to live out the values of the future in the present. If we are a new creation and old things have passed away and all things are new, there is a sense in which the future order has broken into the present. Surely this includes creating organizations that reflect those beliefs, values, and practices.

Genesis 3 chronicles humanity's separation from God, climaxing in the expulsion from the Garden. Paul draws on this passage for his argument in Romans 1–3, which argues that all humanity is fallen, broken, and separated from God. This situation has sometimes been interpreted too negatively, however, as though little or no goodness or beauty remains in the created order. Quite the contrary. The human person retains the dignity of being made in God's image and is capable of developing in amazing ways. The goodness that God proclaimed at the original creation can be caught in glimpses in a beautiful aria, work of art, nature, and in people fully alive and thriving. This fact alone ought to suggest a different way of being in the world, especially when one also considers the salvation, justice, mercy, and goodness of God. Irenaeus captures this in relationship to humanity in the oft-quoted thought that humanity fully alive honors God, because it is when people's capacity is fully developed and is functioning that their creator is honored. Organizations, leaders, and managers all have a role to play in this regard.

A biblical understanding of the human person teaches that people have tremendous capacity for good and evil. It also suggests that people need to be developed, that we need accountability, and that we need challenge and adversity in order to grow. This changes our expectations of people and the way in which we manage and construct organizations. But how do we bring this understanding of humanity into public discourse in a pluralistic, diverse society?

The cultural shift we are currently experiencing in the West further complicates the public square and issues of faith and religion, values and beliefs. In early modernism, there was a clear boundary between what was viewed as private and public. Religion, for example, belonged to the private sphere. And as a result, people could be somewhat confused as they walked out their doors to work: Are their values of the family and their faith going to work with them? Or do they become some other person at work? In this new era, people are seeking to live more holistically and integrate their private and public worlds. As a result, their private belief systems and values are increasingly entering organizational life—which makes sense, since they take their whole selves to work. And some organizations are following suit, as they push to maximize human capacity/performance and create healthy, productive workplaces. Management studies are following this trend. Recent issues of the *Harvard Business Review* are implicitly exploring this topic.[1]

Organizations have become an important locus of this intersection, especially as they seek to create learning communities that are innovative, creative, efficient, productive, and profitable, but also enhance human capacity and well-being that engenders this productivity and creativity. The message is that one can and must do both. Further, organizations do not exist in a vacuum, rather they are connected to society in very intricate ways both dependent and contributing. This social contract is something that has been resisted, but the work of systems theorists has changed how we think about these matters. As a result, new models of management and organizations need to be rather more sophisticated in their understanding of what it means to be human and what humans need to live productive, healthy, meaningful lives. This should be placed front and center in any discussion of management, organizations, and leadership.

It is at this point that theology and religion have much to contribute. But it is a challenge. It may be that the theological construct of human flourishing provides an important bridge between the two worlds and offers a helpful start in building an ecological model that is sustainable.

Religion in the Public Square

We live in a diverse, pluralistic society in which there are many faiths, belief systems, values, and cultures. Organizations generally reflect this diversity, creating a complex environment in which to work and lead. How we think about the public expression of our belief system becomes very important. If piety is the focus, or the inward journey of the soul, evangelism, and other such pursuits, it creates tension in organizations since these expressions are in competition with other belief systems and behaviors. This is in general why public corporations are scared of religion. We really need a different way of viewing reality than this traditional construct allows. Of necessity it becomes a more practical discussion that revolves around how the mission of the organization can be furthered and the human capital be developed. The esoteric theological discourse, while necessary and interesting, has not helped much. Nor have the many books and talks on a general philosophy of leadership, calling, or other such matters. People need to know how exactly to live, work, and practice their faith in public.

How one understands work and faith, and the content of faith, is vital. In popular Christian literature, faith and work are often at odds. And even among those attempting to bridge the two, there is still talk about the separation of Sunday from Monday to Friday, losing Saturday in the cracks. The implication is that work is part of the curse, and something we can hopefully lose in our spiritual existence in eternity with God. Included in this struggle is tension with the material world. We have resorted to having to label the various domains a calling, much like a pastor's call to the ministry. This re-sacrilizing of the public sphere seems at times an attempt to bring meaning into people's daily mundane existence, who were not fortunate to be called into the ministry. It might be easier to argue that all work is sacred and part of God's design in creation and that it does not need to be designated a calling, high or otherwise. Rather, it is part of our earthly sojourn that can be very meaningful when it taps into our capacities. The Flow research and the Good Work project provide the evidence that work can be meaningful when it is excellent, socially responsible, and engaging.[2] To

flourish as individuals, we need to tap into these resources and organizations if we seek to maximize human capital.

Many have now suggested that Western Christianity has become fundamentally gnostic or neoplatonist, in the sense that it focuses upon a dualism that emphasizes the spiritual at the expense of the physical, material world. If one listens to sermons and popular language, much of it emphasizes devotion, pietism, living apart from the world. Yet, we have bodies, we work in the physical world, we participate in culture and society for work, income, and other such things. Human flourishing as a construct seeks to bring these together in a more holistic fashion. The tension between the two is obvious, as more than one conservative evangelical author/preacher has opined that the new emphasis in human flourishing is nothing more than a renewal of the onslaught of "humanism" upon the gospel and church. This challenge reveals more than it realizes. It demonstrates their antipathy for and defensive struggle with broader culture, the spiritual vs. material separation, and a very negative view of humanity.

If we accept human flourishing as a way of constructing reality, then we need to articulate a theology of being human and the basics for a meaningful life. There is not room to argue the case in this short essay, but we think that people, once they are more integrated, will understand their work, play, and faith as a single piece that is an important part of their personal development and growth, their relationships, and contributions. They are living out their lives to the glory of God in the midst of the world. And as a result, they are becoming more self-aware, and growing and developing through education, experiences, and encounters with others.

In public discourse it is important to find areas of common ground and contribute to practices that support the construction of society. While we might disagree on the nature or origins of humanity, we can agree that we all seek to contribute to building a good society in which people can reach and express their full capacity. A reading of Genesis 1:26–27 and Paul's understanding of new creation both point in this direction. In order to do this, however, we need coherence between message and practice. The organizational culture and values that result in both corporate and individual behavior make powerful statements about core beliefs and values. How this works out in practical terms is developed in the section that follows.

Human Flourishing and Organizations

The work context is core to the capacity of people to flourish. Beyond the simple fact that we spend so many hours of each week at work, much of our identity as humans is tied up in the nature of the work we do. Three elements of work seem to be particularly related to flourishing: work that enables people to perform to high standards, requires their full capacity and resources, and is socially responsible is linked to the construction of a meaningful life. Managers who are concerned about both the productivity and the well-being of their teams will recognize the win-win nature of emphasizing these three dimensions. How then is it possible to develop people so that they improve in these areas of excellence, ethics, and engagement?

Having argued that a theology of what it means to be human has a place in the public square, we now turn our attention to issues of practical implementation. In what remains of this essay, we will explore five specific areas in which our humanness needs to be incorporated into how we shape and run organizations. These include being known, communication, scaffolding, autonomy and accountability, and the problem of entropy. Attending to these dimensions of the workplace will enhance the capacity of organizations to be more intentional about developing their human capital and ultimately to prosper.

Being Known: Intimacy

Too often all we see of the people who are part of an organization are the ways they fit the job they were hired to do. We hire or incorporate people into organizations based upon need and function. They may have an MD, but if they are hired to photocopy, that's all they are expected to do. When people in organizations are typecast like actors and limited in their opportunity to contribute to much-needed creativity

and innovation, the result is amazing underutilization of human capital. Theologically, the challenge in the Garden to steward creation includes organizational life. Leadership/management has a responsibility before God for not just the organization, but also the various people in their care. For people to flourish in an organization, we need to create structured ways through which to know and understand the potential of each member of the team. It's essential as well to provide structures, systems, and processes for them to be developed and promoted. Giving even a very gifted employee too much responsibility without support and training is risky at best.

Leadership and management need an additional set of sensibilities and skills to care for those in their organizations. The rapidly changing technological, global, and diverse marketplace requires a toolset of leadership skills that include direct, instrumental, and relational skills.[3] Younger workers of the Gen-X and Millennial generations expect and thrive in lateral rather than vertical structures. Drucker saw this when he argued that workers must be led and not managed. In order to maximize what they bring to an organization, leaders need to know their people much better than before. Failure to know their human capital, that is, the capacity, character, and competence of people, is as risky as failing to understand their financial capital. It places the organization's mission in jeopardy. Understanding the human side of the organization requires high emotional and social intelligence in addition to the specialized competencies related to the mission of the organization.[4]

Communication

In order to protect and develop the human capital of an organization there must be explicit processes, policies, and strategies for performance review, supervision, training, and delegation of new responsibilities. These policies must be accurately understood throughout the organization. The success of each of these processes depends on effective communication. Professional and personal boundaries are protected by clarity, transparency, and practices that are coherent with the verbal and written statements. Job descriptions, compensation, promotion policies, and expectations for performance ought to be communicated in a direct and clear manner. There should be no surprises when it comes time to fire, promote, or reward any member of an organization.

The nonverbal side of communication is equally important in shaping the people and culture. Whether conscious or unconscious, coherence between the practices and stated values of an organization speaks volumes. When verbal communication is at odds with real practices, policies, and values, organizations can be places in which mistrust and dishonesty come to rule. Passive aggressive communication practices such as gossip and triangulation are signs of toxicity. At times, these indirect forms of communication can stem from values that otherwise seem to be positive. For example, in an attempt to be nice or out of a fear of hurting feelings, people may fail to directly communicate about problem behavior.

To this point, we have been discussing primarily the contractual aspects of organizations. However, there is also a covenantal aspect to communication that stems from a theological understanding of human dignity. All persons being created in God's image are equal before God and are owed justice and respect. They ought to also be accorded the opportunity to speak with honesty and integrity without fear of retribution.

There is a link between good communication, the affirmation of a person's dignity, the development of people, creating a healthy organizational culture, and the values of the people of God. Christians are not the only ones who share these values, but they are central to the Christian belief system. Part of the broader goal for the people of God ought to be the construction of a good society. A just, peaceable society is good for everyone and consistent with the gospel.

Scaffolding: How to Develop People

Rarely do managers receive formal training in mentoring processes, which include supervision, performance review, and delegating responsibility to others. All of these routine managerial activities are opportunities to increase the human resources of organizations by developing the gifts and capacities of team members.

As background, it is perhaps helpful to think about the components that go into a good mentoring relationship in which a more experienced person takes on the role of helping another develop in a specific domain. Of primary importance are the advanced competencies of the mentor. They have the knowledge, skills, and attitudes that are not yet fully matured in the other. They must also have sufficient awareness of the proficiency level of the person whom they are encouraging. Finally, they must be able to form a bridge between their own level of performance and that of the junior team member. The concept of scaffolding is a useful metaphor for describing the temporary support that more experienced players provide as others gain the skills needed to take on additional role assignments. Note that scaffolding is meant to be a temporary support structure that is gradually dismantled as the skill is constructed. Through the provision of sufficient support during the construction phase, the less-experienced team member is more likely to experience success and less likely to make a serious mistake.

For those invested in developing themselves, being mentored is a unique relational experience that adds dimensionality to our human experience. There are attitudes and behaviors that can enhance the mentoring relationship. These include letting ourselves be known; openness to feedback; actively pursuing what we need; and expressing our gratitude to those who give us the gift of their mentoring attention.[5]

Autonomy and Accountability

There is a delicate balance in organizations between giving people space to exercise their autonomy and providing appropriate oversight and accountability. When the sweet spot is found, good work is the result; both in its excellence and in its ethics. Organizational cultures vary in their ability to tolerate mistakes. Highly creative and innovative cultures by necessity need to be able to follow rabbit trails that will often lead nowhere. On the other hand, assembly line production depends upon precision and exact replication of each step in the process. Accountability serves to protect both individuals and the organization from mistakes but also, stated more positively, allows them to continue to develop and improve.

Entropy

If we accept that people have limitations and a capacity for sin (broadly defined), then the natural pattern of human performance is not towards excellence but mediocrity. Challenge, adversity, and even suffering are essential for healthy growth, though we don't normally seek them out. Entropy is difficult to keep at bay.

To maintain a flourishing organization, leadership needs to be fully aware of the human factor. Rather than looking for entrepreneurial keys, lead-ership models, and other such things in Scripture, a reading that informs our theological imagination and allows us to participate in a constructive man-ner to the construction of healthy organizations, their systems, processes, and practices, and ultimately to a good society is what we need. Granted this is a more challenging model, but ultimately it is more satisfying. Stewardship involves more than money and ideas; it also involves the immense human capital that is part of every organization.

Notes

1 *Harvard Business Review*, http://hbr.org.
2 M. Csikszentmihalyi, *Flow: The Psychology of Optimal Experience* (New York: Harpers, 1990); H. Gardener, M. Csikszentmihalyi, and W. Damon, *Good Work: When Excellence and Ethics Meet* (New York: Basic Books, 2001).
3 J. Lipman-Blumen, *Connective Leadership: Managing in a Chang-ing World* (Oxford: Oxford University Press, 2000).
4 D. Goleman, *Emotional Intelligence: Why It Can Matter More Than IQ* (New York: Bantam, 2002).
5 J. Nakamura and M. Csikszentmihalyi, "The Construction of Meaning through Vital Engagement," in *Flourishing: Positive Psychology and the Life Well-Lived*, by C. M. Keyes and J. Haidt (Washington, DC: American Psychological Association, 2003), 83–104.

Questions for Discussion and Reflection

1. What is the underlying view of a person that is the basis for Beaton and Wagener's idea that organizations should serve human flourishing?
2. Do you agree that an organization is responsible for providing an environment where the employees can flourish, or is the organization only responsible for getting its job done efficiently? Explain your answer.
3. Beaton and Wagener insist that employees desire leadership, not simply management. How do you balance employees' need for autonomy in getting their jobs done well and accountability to insure that they are done in a cost effective way?

Technology and the New Challenges of Management
Albert Erisman
Previously unpublished material.

The 1960 movie *The Apartment* has a scene that characterizes old school management. The boss is seated behind a glass partition and his people (and it was always *his*) were in a sea of desks in a large bay in full view. Managing people was done in person, where every action could be seen. More than likely the manager could do the work of most of the employees. Time spent sitting at a desk was a significant measure of productivity.

Today, a manager may have a team of people

located around the world. Some are working from their homes, some in remote offices, and others are temporarily parked at places like Starbucks. Much of the work is comprised of the creative contributions of the individual or teams, and "desk time" is becoming increasingly irrelevant. Today, many of the tasks being done could not be completed by the manager and the details may not even be understood by him or her.

This new construct, made possible by the development of telecommunications and information technology, parses out work in new ways toward the accomplishment of often very complex ends. These shifts raise important questions about managing people in what might be considered a new age of technology. For example, how can we take advantage of what technology has to offer while also honoring and respecting the dignity of employees and allowing them to develop into all that God intends for them to be? Two challenging realities make these questions even more difficult to answer. First, technology will continue to develop and transform the workplace. Today's leader cannot simply settle into a new way of doing things, but must be constantly prepared to accept changes and to ask challenging questions again tomorrow. Second, many business leaders are not, and do not want to be, experts in technology. Hence managers are challenged to operate effectively amidst a sea of change that he or she might wish would simply go away.

After a 30+ year career managing a large research and technology organization for Boeing, working in academia for the last decade, and as a Christian who is deeply concerned with the intersections of ethics and business, I have spent a considerable amount of time pondering these types of questions and interviewing senior executives to get their perspectives.[1] I have been asked to share some of my thoughts and findings in this essay.

In what follows, I will focus on four particular managerial challenges:

1. Communications
2. Measuring and controlling behavior
3. Assessing the work product and putting it into use
4. Effectively managing the new generation of "technology natives"

I will use the Team Performance Model for communications to help address the first issue. In considering the next three challenges, I will propose a five-layer model that examines the different ways technology affects the business itself. From this model, I will then develop areas of guidance for managing people in this new environment.

In addressing these challenges, I will keep the double-edged nature of technology in view. Technology offers tremendous opportunity for enhanced communications, motivation, measurement, and employee development. But for every opportunity there is a possible shadow side that impinges on the task at hand.

Communications

Communications technology brings a whole new array of tools to the manager. From email to social networks to Twitter to instant messaging, managers have new and rapid ways of staying in touch and gaining responses. Indeed, without this technology, the job of managing a workforce distributed around the world would be undoable. All of this sounds good, but is there a downside?

The movie *Up in the Air* provides an interesting case study for business communications in an age of technology. Ryan Bingham (played by George Clooney) works for a larger company that does the work that many companies do not want to do themselves. In particular, the company goes to client locations to implement layoffs on their behalf. Ryan travels more than 300 days per year, building his frequent flyer mileage and living out of a suitcase.

Then one day the company hires a young, newly minted MBA who makes the pitch for efficiency. Rather than traveling to a company to do these layoffs, she suggests they set up the technology to allow them to do this work without travel, using video conferencing technology and saving millions of dollars in travel costs. Ryan is personally lost in this new world, but it turns out that the technologically efficient solution has some downside risks for the organizations involved as well. Given the fact the employees are about to lose not only their economic livelihoods, but also a key contributor to meaning, purpose, and community in their lives, is this truly the best way to convey the difficult news of a layoff? Has something been lost in this technological translation?

Although cheaper and faster, communicating electronically is not the same as doing so face-to-face. A helpful model to help us understand how the applications of these new tools fit into the bigger picture of communications is the Team Performance Model.

In the 1990s, the Institute for the Future developed a guiding model to help clarify effective communications through technology. I continue to find this model helpful in thinking through the types of questions that need to be asked about the use of new communication tools.[2] The architects of the Team Performance Model argue that there are three different kinds of conversations we have in the workplace, and that these conversations (and the technologies that enable them) fall into three groupings: "same time, same place"; "same time, different place"; and "different time, different place." Each of these groupings brings its own attributes contributing to overall communications.

Face-to-face communication is the most expensive (in terms of time and travel) but offers a richness unattainable in the other environments. When two people are together in relationship, nuances are easy to pick up. The conversation can wander from the immediate task, building other bridges of a deeper relationship. Trust is a key attribute that is developed here, the authors argue. When people meet face-to-face in a meeting, they may have a cup of coffee afterwards, further building the relationship. When they travel to a meeting, they share a meal. The structure of the meeting is the start of the conversation, not the end.

A second type of communication takes place in the "same time, different place" category. Here the two parties can interact over an idea, with the kind of give-and-take that is helpful in reaching resolution on a difficult issue. When images are included, as in a video teleconference or a Skype session, nuances and body language can add to the communications. The authors argue that this type of communications can be very effective in setting direction and gaining agreement on how to carry out a particular task. And if this session is carried out after the face-to-face relationship has been established, then it can be done faster and better because of the foundation of trust.

With the understanding and direction accomplished through the "same time" approaches, it is then easy to use email, blackboards, or other types of asynchronous messaging to carry on the work. These tools have the advantage that they are not intrusive, interrupting people in the other work they are doing. The weakness is exposed when people try to use a "different time, different place" tool like email to resolve a difficult issue, particularly if the relationship has not been adequately developed and does not have the level of trust that comes from face-to-face communication.

With respect to this issue, Pat Gelsinger, president and COO of EMC Corporation, and former executive vice president of Intel remarked:

> We work to have everything online [for our virtual teams], in databases, so that there truly can be shared workspaces. Then we focus on regular face-to-face interactions. Instant messaging to someone that you know well is a very powerful form of communication. A six-word instant message to a person that you don't have a relationship with is a very inadequate form of communication. IM and other more technologically oriented communication are only efficient when they are built on top of good teams and good relationships.
>
> I have a personal rule. If I go back and forth with somebody in email more than four or five times on the same topic, I stop. No more. We get on the phone, or we get together face to face. I have learned that if you don't resolve something quickly, by the time you get together one of you is mad at the other person. You think they are incompetent since they could not understand the most straightforward thing that you were describing. But it is because of the medium, and it is important to account for this.[3]

Communications does not always move in a single linear direction, starting with face-to-face and progressing to more indirect forms. Sometimes a person joins a team and first hears of the issues through "different time, different place" communication. In my experience, teams rooted in trust developed in a face-to-face environment are able to move faster and more effectively.

A wide variety of tools from technology are available for the leader to use in communicating with people. But it is not simply a choice of picking the ones most comfortable for the manager. Rather, it requires understanding of the nature of communication and the type of tool so that the right tool is used for the right task.

The Other Issues

Addressing the other three questions of managing with technology requires us to understand how technology affects the work itself. I propose a model to help us better understand the different ways technology affects a 21st-century business.

5. People Transformed by Technology
4. Transformation of Products and Processes through Technology
3. Management of the Technology Infrastructure
2. Development of Technology Products
1. Base Technology Development

In what follows, I briefly review the meaning of the different layers, and then will build on this to address the three management issues.

In *the first layer*, information technology has been tracking what is known as Moore's Law since the early 1960s. Named for Gordon Moore, the founder of Intel, it is a law of innovation, not a physical or legal law. Moore's Law says that the capability coming from IT will double in its cost/performance every 18 months. Technology companies need to know this because they continue to manage their product development (the basic capability of the microchip) against this law. What a general business manager needs to know is this: new capability will continue to come at the business, and it will not stop or go away. Preparation for continued change is required.

The second layer represents that collection of tools that comes from this rapidly developing technology. These tools might change the way a company does business, or might simply be a waste of time and money. The pressures to effectively evaluate these tools that generally nobody in the organization asked for, and make decisions about them, are relentless.

The third layer is often regarded as the province of the IT department: making all of these systems work in a reliable, secure, and cost effective way. But what is done here affects every person in the business. Examples of these decisions include safeguarding information, monitoring employee use of computing, identifying who has the need to access which information, and the personal use of company computing resources.

The fourth layer is where the business gets reshaped. The products and processes of the company are transformed through technology, supported by the infrastructure, and enlightened by the new ideas that are explored from layer 2. Because of the highly technical nature of some of the work at this (and the third) layer of the model, we must find ways of assessing quality of work and risk from that work in new and uncomfortable ways.

The fifth layer is the way technology impacts society. The people we hire and the customers of a business are often changed by technology. For example, it has been well documented that people have shorter attention spans, read less, and try to do two things at once. One consequence is that the employees may be culturally different from the manager because of the effect of technology. This is often (though not always) the case if there is an age gap between the manager and his or her employees (digital immigrants vs. digital natives).[4] Another point of tension is when an "old school" manager is overseeing knowledge work, where the value of the work comes from the ideas that are created rather than the number of widgets produced.

With this model in mind, let's turn our attention to the remaining three issues.

Assessing and Controlling Behavior

The old-school manager had a number of tools available to assess behavior. Having the boss looking out over the workers was a natural deterrent to playing games, goofing off, slipping out for coffee. Time cards measured the all-important attendance in the office. Standardized work made it possible to assess and compare workers — numbers of standard contracts produced each hour was not much different in the office than it was in the factory. Further, there was a clear line between "company work" and personal work, so businesses often had policies assuring the workers did not use company equipment (telephone, copy machines, later fax machines, later yet PCs and access to the Internet) at work for personal things.

Line of sight and time cards don't help the manager with people distributed over a geographical area doing fundamentally creative tasks. That is not to suggest that there are no traditional tasks left to manage. Certainly there are, but the relative percentage of creative work is growing as technology automates many of the more mundane jobs.

As a higher percentage of work becomes "knowledge based," measuring amounts accomplished becomes more difficult as well. Early in my career managing a research organization at Boeing, I read a book about this task. I have long since forgotten the title or author, but I remember one of the situations. The boss stopped by the office of a researcher and saw the person with his chair tilted back and his feet on the desk. "What are you doing?" the boss asked. "I'm thinking," the researcher responded. After a pause, the boss responded, "Well think on your own time—get back to work!" Indeed, the old measures fail.

Even the line between work time and personal time has been blurred by technology. Many businesses have expectations that their people are available to respond to customers and the boss through email or other technology-enabled communications, creating the 24/7 work environment. With respect to personal use of company equipment, a lot has also changed. Unlike the copy machine (one of the most abused pieces of equipment in the past), which uses real paper resources (not to mention toner), the PC will likely become obsolete before it is worn out.

What kinds of policies should be established (generally at the third layer of our model) regarding the personal use of technology owned by the company? In the early 1990s Hewlett Packard decided this technology called for new policies. Executives encouraged their employees to use company technology for their own use, with some restrictions (not for starting a business and not on company time). An employee keeping a personal budget on the spreadsheet would not wear out the spreadsheet, but this would provide a motivation for the employee to learn more about using spreadsheets. Later, Boeing recognized an

employee might need to take off a half day to sign papers on a new house, but by using the company fax, the employee could do some of this in less than an hour, enabling more work to be done. Executives there also changed their policies in this area as have many other businesses. Though I have not done a formal survey, informal inquiries have confirmed that there is little consistency across companies in dealing with this matter.

Recent WikiLeaks publication of embarrassing, and perhaps damaging, information exposing supposedly private diplomatic conversations brings to the forefront the challenging job of managing and protecting private information. Information theft used to require the transportation of large file cabinets filled to brimming with documents. Today an employee can carry many file cabinets full of documents out the door on a thumb drive buried in his or her pocket.

What technology has taken away, technology has given back in terms of tools for watching out over employee behavior. Technology can be used to track where an employee is and what he or she is doing on the computer.

In the mid 1990s, Xerox Parc (the research center for Xerox at the time) developed an early solution for tracking people. They developed a "smart badge" that employees wore. Wherever they went in the building, they could be tracked through a communications capability that had been installed throughout the building. Where is John? Entering his name in the computer would allow me to find he is in the conference room, the coffee area, or the bathroom. Efficient? Yes. But in their experiment they found that people would leave their badges on their desks. They didn't want to be tracked.

When I was at Boeing we had software that enabled the company to track every website a person visited from his or her computer. One individual tried to access porn sites from his office more than 1,500 times in one day, apparently not knowing that the company had blocked access to these sites. He was terminated for wasting company time.

Any business can set up software to track every keystroke from every employee computer throughout the day. And the law says that it is not necessary to let the employee know the company is doing this since the computer is company property. In the earlier management era, looking at people at work was enough to tell they were working. But today interchangeable windows and "boss buttons" (complete with fake official-looking spreadsheets) make it very difficult to tell from a distance what an employee is doing, so this tracking capability seems to offer the ideal solution.

The challenge with all of these tracking tools is what they do to the environment of trust. Is an employee, working on a creative task, as effective when it feels like the "electronic boss" is staring over his or her shoulder? Is his or her God-given dignity respected when every keystroke is recorded? According to the research of Robert Levering and his associates, the best places to work are ones that have a trusting environment (they are not necessarily the ones with the most vacation time or that allow employees to bring pets to work). Likewise, the most innovative companies give employees a great deal of freedom, since this seems to foster innovation. Consider what Google does today, or what 3M used to do in allowing time for their people to pursue whatever they like. Such tracking and monitoring is at odds with a free environment. Yet it is still necessary to identify and understand people who would abuse the freedom. Christian theology tells us that people are good *and* bad at the same time (much like technology, ironically), so they need freedom and accountability.

I believe the manager needs to get very good at assessing the value of the work that is done (next section) and the way in which a person affects the work environment. The nature of the work (a person answering the phone compared with a software developer who is creating something new) makes a big difference about the need for availability and time on task. This will dictate whether it is appropriate to use such monitoring tools. But when they are used, it is vital that management is clear that they will be used. Open communication is a must.

Allowing for more freedom in the workplace may offer other benefits to the organization. For example, consider technology experimentation. Facebook and Twitter are two of many products that suddenly appeared at level two of our model. With no obvious business application, this would seem to be an area that should be off-limits for the office. Surely these

are toys for personal use and a distraction from work. Or are they?

Bonnie Wurzbacher, senior vice president of Coca-Cola, looks at this differently:

[These tools affect us] in a big way. In some ways negatively and in some ways positively. First, negative ways: There are all kinds of rumors out there, things that aren't fact-based, that someone has just started to blog. We've had to figure out how to deal with getting the facts out there. We have also helped our own employees to understand the facts so that they feel confident about the company's behavior, actions, the ingredients in our products, and things like that.

On the positive side, it's an unbelievably effective marketing vehicle — so much more effective than TV is these days. We actually have a head of social media at the company and this person's job is to ensure that we are really leveraging and using the grassroots viral marketing that occurs through the use of those technologies. We are trying to use it effectively not only to share accurate information, but also to reach consumers in a way that we couldn't by more traditional methods.[5]

Few managers have the foresight to look at new products coming from technology (or even be aware of potentially useful ones) and pick the winners for the business. But creative people, tracking and experimenting with what is new, can discover new competitive offerings through this experimentation.

Assessing the Product of Work

Another big challenge is to adequately evaluate and manage work when it is not fully understood by management. This occurs in levels three and four of the proposed model. We will consider these separately (level four is addressed in the next section).

Level three is where the management of the technology infrastructure takes place. Here many of the decisions are made in managing technology, including the expenditure for technology, dealing with security, controlling the use of portable devices such as thumb drives and laptops. Demonstrating what many businesses think about technology, the chief technology officer often reports to the chief financial officer, suggesting that technology is primarily a cost that needs to be controlled.

Companies walk a fine line at level three. They want to control expenditures while at the same time making possible the ability for a company to sell over the Internet, communicate with suppliers, and manage internally. They want to make it easy for customers to connect with them and difficult for hackers to destroy them. The choices are often deeply technical and the details matter. I recently was asked to give a presentation at a company in Ireland, but was told they did not allow me to download the presentation from a thumb drive, company policy. So they asked me to email the presentation to them. Unfortunately, their fire wall never allowed my email to get through. They were very tight on the protection side, but so tight they couldn't take advantage of the technology in carrying out their business.

The technology experts working in the third layer are often people who move to a different drummer, and understanding what they can do and why they do it is a major management challenge. *Adventures of an IT Leader* is a very well written account that captures the essence of these tensions. The senior management often knows little about gigabytes, network protocols, and Web 2.0. Spending too little means lack of reliability and even the ability to do business. Spending too much has an impact on the bottom line. While at Boeing I was in a meeting with the CEO of our company and a leader from the technology industry, when the leader said to our CEO (likely drawing on an old advertising adage attributed to John Wannamaker), "You are probably spending twice as much as you need to spend on technology. The problem is, you don't know which half to cut."

Ironically, the leader of the infrastructure does the job best when all of this complexity is masked and the users are able to work seamlessly with the technology without becoming experts. But it can't be so easy that the difficulty of the work is not understood!

There are two main opportunities for managing the people in this part of the business. One is to create a council made up of impacted managers and technical people who can work together against the common objective for the company. It is vital that the technical people be a part of this, and that they are given a voice.

Second, in this uneven "marriage" between the business and the technical sides of the company, it is important that both learn a great deal about what the other does. On the business side, people need to know enough about technology to ask good questions. And the technology people need to understand the business at a deep enough level to create technology solutions that meet real needs, not that simply respond to requests. This collaboration is a vital part of people management in an age of technology, and it is easy to get it wrong.

Work in Business Transformation

Technology impacts a company not only at the Infrastructure level (level three) but also in the way companies define and deliver products (level four). Jack Welch, former CEO and chairman of GE, referred to this as the "digitization of everything." Technology enables the company to gain a temporary advantage over its competitors in the way it delivers value, or in the value contained in the products themselves. But because of the significant amount of technology being used, the same problem (as in level three), in a different form, confronts the manager: understanding the details of the product, what it can do, and the risks associated with it. I will draw on an article I wrote about this issue for *Ethix* in 2009.[6]

Two recent, highly visible examples show what might happen when management simply does not understand the nature of their products or the risks associated with them. The first is the creation, packaging, and sale of subprime loan derivatives, CDOs (collateralized debt obligations). The second involves the risks associated with deep-water drilling for oil. The first example was at the heart of the worldwide financial crisis, and the second played a significant role in the major oil spill from deep water well drilling in the Gulf of Mexico. There may have been some risk taking for short-term financial gain going on here as well, but there is strong evidence that management, in both cases, did not really understand its products or the people who created them.

In the economic arena, here are two quotes from Roger Lowenstein's book, *The End of Wall Street*, regarding executive understanding of the complex derivative issues:

> [At AIG] Joseph Cassano, the aggressive and volatile maestro of AIG's swaps unit … assured the brass that … AIG had insured only the highest-ranking "super senior" level CDOs.… Cassano frequently attended committee meetings of the directors, in whose company he was naturally charming and genteel. He emphasized to the board that, regardless of what was happening to the market value of CDOs, the instruments were safe, and would remain so barring a catastrophic recession. The directors, understanding little about CDOs except what Cassano told them, were reassured. (pp. 112, 113)

Robert Rubin, chairman of the executive group of Citigroup and former U.S. Secretary of the Treasury, "leaned with the odds. Unlike some senior execs, he understood what a CDO was, but not at the level of detail that might have aroused his concern. This half-knowledge was potentially lethal. He was enamored with the brainpower and mathematical elegance of academically trained financiers."

On the deep-water drilling question, I asked the former CEO of a large oil company for his insights into the cause and cure of the oil spill in the Gulf of Mexico. Here was his response: "I'm afraid this incident is way beyond my experience or understanding. The deep water and complex subsurface technology must make for huge challenges. The whole industry will be willing BP to find a speedy solution, and all of us will be praying that the slick dissipates without causing any lasting damage to marine environments or indeed the shoreline."

It might be easy to conclude, in both situations, that the technical people should have been better able to identify the risks. But there is evidence in both cases that they did understand the risks and their concerns simply were not heard or understood by management. There is also evidence that the technical people did not understand the context of the work they were doing. An analyst asked one of the people involved in creating mortgage-backed derivatives, "What would happen to your models if housing prices went down?"

The response was telling: "That can't happen." Every model has hidden assumptions, and identifying them is a critical part of the management task.

The frightening thing is that technology will take us further in the direction we have been headed, enabling the push for even shorter-term results, more new ways to make money from very complex situations, and an even greater gap between the capability of the people and the tools and the insight from those who use them.

What do managers do when they don't have the technology skills to understand the people they manage and make such decisions?

> Forming a technology council is a start. Even here, however, there are some significant pitfalls. In my observation, managers tend to gravitate toward technical people they can understand— and this often also means that they agree with them. An effective technology council will be made up of people with contrarian views, and who may not express those views in a very "politically correct" way. So I would suggest getting people on the council who are recommended by other technologists, rather than by management. Learning to work effectively with people who see the world differently than you do is the sign of a great leader. In this case we are not talking strictly about information technology people, but petroleum engineers (in the case of well drilling) and financial engineers (in the case of mortgage derivatives) as well. It is vital that these people are well informed of the business objectives and prepared to talk freely and openly about risks.[7]

These highly technical people are absolutely needed to compete in 21st-century business. But the management task is not for the faint of heart. And it is not adequate to simply let them do the technical part and management do the business part. These are tied together in such a way that the collaboration must be deep.

Technology's Impact on Society

Level five of our model suggests quite another way technology may present challenges in the way we manage people. Much has been written on the way technology affects society and the way business is conducted. For example, the drive to short-term thinking, 24/7 expectations, and expectation of being able to effectively multitask.[8]

Someone engaged in managing people is impacted in two direct ways. First, the environment for doing business is made more challenging. Second, there is a new kind of cultural gap that must be understood in this management task.

Technology has perpetuated a short-term business environment. When you receive an email, an instant message, or a call on your cell phone, somehow that connotes a more urgent response is needed. When reports are generated on a daily or weekly basis, rather than a quarterly or yearly basis, managers feel the pressure to respond more quickly.

For example, in 2006, commenting on the results of a survey of 400 CEOs, Jonathan Wellum notes that "80% said they would decrease spending on long-term things to meet short-term targets." And he added, "50% said they would delay new projects to achieve quarterly results even if it would lead to the long-term sacrificing of value creation."[9]

William Donaldson, former SEC chief, raised a related concern in his September 17, 2008, talk. "I believe the excessive focus by too many corporations on achieving short-term results, fanned by the practice of acceding to demands for regular guidance in forecasting such quarterly results—is certainly one of the root causes of some of the problems we face today."[10]

Efficiency through technology without careful insight can have disastrous consequences both within a company and beyond. This was a significant factor in both the mortgage derivative market and the deepwater drilling issues discussed earlier. And it affects older industries like manufacturing as well. When Toyota encountered the safety issue of acceleration of its Prius, and other quality problems that beset them, senior executives came to the following conclusion:

> Toyota Motor Corp. is extending the time it takes to develop new vehicles by about four weeks for more quality checks in the wake of its massive safety-related recalls, a top executive said Wednesday. Executive Vice President

Takeshi Uchiyamada said the company has learned a lot from its recalls of more than 8.5 million vehicles worldwide, including the need to slow the pace at which it develops new cars.[11]

Managing Digital Natives

Many younger people raised in a digital age assume they can effectively multitask. This includes texting while driving, but it also includes how work is carried out. Yet brain scientist John Medina argues (*Brain Rules*, 2009) that the human brain is incapable of doing two attention-rich tasks at the same time.[12]

"Google CEO Eric Schmidt points out that many aspects of modern technology have raised the bar and improved the quality of the young people hired at Google. However, he is also concerned that long form reading may be on the decline since media is often consumed in much smaller portions. This raises the important question of whether the Internet may be creating a generation with knowledge that is a mile wide but only an inch deep," according to an interview with Ravi Nagaranjan in February 2010.

Companies doing business globally now prepare managers for the cross-cultural encounters they must have as they interact with people around the world. It is equally important to prepare managers for the task of working with digital natives. I offer two suggestions here.

First, work with these people. Get to know them. Jack Welch, the former CEO at GE decided he had to get better at understanding technology. So he went into his organization and brought in a twenty-six-year-old "kid" to help him with technology. The kid became a mentor to Jack, he told us. They spent one day per month for a year working together, and it was at this point that GE embarked on its program to digitize everything. The book *Adventures of an IT Leader* mentioned earlier provides a good example of a leader who did just this in order to understand technology.

Second, businesses need leadership training to prepare their executives to work cross-culturally in this increasingly global world. And no less important, businesses need leadership training to prepare their people to work with digital natives, to manage work they don't understand, and to manage knowledge work that cannot be measured in widgets per hour. Some of the books I have mentioned could be a part of this training. This is new territory and will require a new approach.

Because of layer one in our model, I expect that twenty years from now the new generation of digital natives will again be foreign to today's people who are proficient in today's technology. The beat goes on.

Conclusions

Technology has fundamentally transformed business and the people in the business. To be effective in 21st-century business, managers must be conversant at some level with the technology. Technology affects the strategy, products, processes, thinking, and people of the business. At least for the near future, there will be no stable points in this transformation.

These issues raise important concerns about ethical leadership, because the changes take us to places we have not been before, to situations where we have no shared wisdom. And because of the technology intimidation factor, many managers conclude this is not something they can effectively deal with. This is wrong on two counts. First, it doesn't require an expert in technology to learn the right questions to ask. Second, it is important that a manager identifies key people who can bring the technological insight to the decision table.

There are great opportunities from the technology as well as great risks. Acting effectively with the technology, in communications and in business practices, is essential for any 21st-century manager.

Notes

[1] For transcriptions of these interviews, see http://www.ethix.org.
[2] I discussed this in more detail in "The Role of Technology in Building Virtual Teams," http://ethix.org/1999/12/01/the-role-of-technologies-in-building-virtual-teams, with a more recent update in "Twitter and Telecommuting," http://ethix.org/2009/08/01/twitter-and-telecommuting.
[3] Albert Erisman, "Pat Gelsinger: Faster Chips, More Opportunity?" *Ethix* 57, February 2008.
[4] See Marc Prensky, "Digital Native, Digital Immigrants," from *On the Horizon* (MCB University Press) 9, no. 5 (October 2001).
[5] Albert Erisman and Denise Daniels, "Bonnie Wurzbacher: Brining Meaning to Work," *Ethix* 67, October 2009.
[6] Albert Erisman, "Oil, Economics and Technology: The Surprising Connection between Two Disasters," *Ethix* 70, July 2010. http://ethix.org/2010/07/15/the-surprising-connection-between-two-disasters.
[7.] Ibid.

[8] Some books on this subject include *The Future of Success* by Robert Reich (2000), *Growing Up Digital* by Don Tapscott (1999), and *Dancing with Digital Natives* by Michelle Manafy and Heidi Gautschi (2011).
[9] Jonathan Wellum, "Managing Beyond Our Time," Comment, 2006. http://www.cardus.ca/comment/article/346/.
[10] William Donaldson, Keynote speech given at Committee for Economic Development Symposium, "Operating and Investing for the Long Term," New York, September 17, 2008. http://www.ced.org/news-events/corporate-governance/161-ced-co-hosts-best-practices-in-earnings-guidance-and-communications-symposium.
[11] "Toyota Adding More Time to New Vehicle Development," Associated Press, July 7, 2010. http://www.cleveland.com/business/index.ssf/2010/07/toyota_adding_more_time_to_new.html.
[12] John Medina, *Brain Rules* (Seattle: Pear Press, 2008).

Questions for Discussion and Reflection

1. How does Erisman think that the advances in technology have affected the task of management? Do you agree with him? Why or why not?
2. How does Erisman balance privacy with managing behavior in the workplace? Do you agree with his views on this?
3. How does Erisman view the impact of technology on the products of our work?

Cheryl Broetje: An Orchard with Fruit That Lasts

Albert M. Erisman and Kenman Wong

Ethix, November 1, 2005, 1–5.

Cheryl Broetje and her husband, Ralph, own and operate Broetje Orchards, which has operated since 1980 along the Snake River in the Southeastern part of Washington State. She and Ralph are the parents of nine children, ages 18–35, six of whom are East Indian by birth. They have six grandchildren.

Their goal is to use their business to serve the common good. As a result, Vista Hermosa was born to serve an immigrant community of approximately 650 Latinos who now live on their farm. It includes a preschool, an elementary school, a gym, chapel, grocery store, and coin-operated laundry through which a variety of social and educational opportunities are offered. Ten years ago, they started a residential program for struggling teen boys known as Jubilee Youth Ranch. About 50 boys are there currently.

Over the years Ms. Broetje has primarily served on the not-for-profit (or "community profit") side of the business. She founded the first of several not-for-profit faith-based organizations, The Center For Sharing, in 1986. Through the center, she largely lives out her passion for equipping people to live in ways that nurture a life-giving community between rich and poor, while serving marginalized people groups. Her work has allowed her to act in a role as midwife at the birthing of some 25 programs in the United States that serve among the poor and marginalized, such as housing, medical clinics, outreach and residential youth programs, and educational programs.

She has traveled to many places around the world in that role. The most recent extension of that work has occurred internationally. A servant-leadership house for young adults is nearing completion in the south of Mexico, and Ms. Broetje team-taught a five-week seminar in servant-leadership for clergy from Kenya, Uganda, and Tanzania during September 2005 in Nairobi, Kenya.

•   •   •

Albert M. Erisman: *Running an apple business sounds daunting to me. You face significant challenges from weather, international sales and competition, and a significant migrant workforce.*

Cheryl Broetje: My daughter, our general manager, told me recently that China is spending $1 a day for labor; we're spending $60 a day, per worker. Ten years ago, China was not a player in the apple market. Today they produce half of the world's apples.

In addition, China has a 30 percent tariff on apples coming in. Mexico has a 47 percent tariff on our apples going in. Free trade for the few who can play!

Erisman: *What do you regard as the most difficult things you do, day-to-day, in the apple business?*

Broetje: One is the issue of our employees. We estimate that upwards of half of them are here without legal documents. We require proper I.D., and they give us I.D., but we can't be detectives to determine which I.D. is real. When the government calls us or sends out those nice little papers saying please advise this person that something's not right with their card, we do our "due diligence," of course. We do everything that we're required to do by law.

The Agriculture Jobs Bill was just voted down, where our workers could have become legal in three years. Now we are concerned about [the Department of] Homeland Security. For any number of reasons, we could be forced out of business by the government's treatment of our employee group.

A few years ago it was the salmon issue. They were talking about pulling out all the dams on the

Snake River. A total of 13 orchards would cease to exist. We were so happy two or three years ago when there was a record salmon run, but that issue is far from over, also.

Getting Started

Kenman Wong: *How did you get into the orchard business? Is this where you were raised?*

Broetje: My husband, Ralph, and I met in traffic court when we were teenagers. He was charged with going too slow in a red corvette, and I was charged with going too fast in my parents' white Ford station wagon. We thought we might provide a little balance for each other! But he surprised me with his dream to run an orchard a few months after we were married.

We did not have college educations, and the only money we had came from selling his red corvette. But with the help of his father, we got a loan to buy a cherry orchard. Two weeks after signing papers on the orchard, early frost froze all of the buds on the trees. The next year we were rained out. The next year we were hit with an infestation of cherry flies.

We had no money to wait four years for a crop, but we trusted God. No one gave up on us, including the bank, our parents, or the former owner of the orchard. Finally we were able to get a crop, then another, and another. We paid off our debts and began to put money away. As we grew, we developed primarily in varieties of apples, and the cherry part of our orchards became a much more minor part.

Values for the Business

Wong: *How did you establish the set of values by which you run the orchards?*

Broetje: Early leaders in our lives acted out the values they believed. Values such as a commitment to serve others with a special eye to the vulnerable; empowerment of others; sharing of resources; mutual respect; and community.

We had started our lives together on the margin, so this helped us to respect and value others in this position. In the early days, our workforce was made up of white migrant workers who started in Texas, moved to California, and then came up the coast to Washington, following the harvest. Almost overnight this group stopped coming and was replaced by people with brown faces who spoke Spanish and were primarily young males.

This "special eye to the vulnerable" is very real in the agricultural business, and we quickly learned that these values must be a way that we operate. This business is hard work, and people who have other ways to earn money don't come. Any white person who comes out, we hire them, and we make a place for them. It amounts to two or three people a year.

We're big into service. If you're going to work here, you're going to serve, from the top of the organization to the bottom. And we are a community, not just a workplace. That can get a little messy sometimes.

Erisman: *How did these ideas develop?*

Broetje: We needed to learn more about our new workforce, so in 1982 our family took a Christmas trip of perspective to Mexico. There we witnessed our first glimpse of a reality unknown to us: Families living in garbage dumps; other families, hoping for a piece of land to call their own, were living in boxes the size of a washer or dryer just waiting; still other families were stacked in fragile adobe homes along hillsides everywhere. Our family was volunteering with an organization that works along the Mexican border. We arrived at a home just as a mother came out and said the baby next door had just died. She put a bowl of rice in our hands and asked us if we could please feed her child. We went in to find a young adult woman with no ears or eyes tied on a box waiting to eat.

My friend began feeding her, and I sat by her side putting my hand on her shoulder. Then this young woman began to feel my face. Soon she seemed to lose interest in the food, and instead, gave me a hug and then laid on my shoulder. This small incident changed my life. At that moment, a pink neon sign lit up in my mind's eye and began to blink the words of Jesus, "Whenever you feed someone who is overlooked or ignored, you do it to me."

After experiences like this, we came to believe that those showing up in our orchard were economic refugees. Yes, many were here without legal documents, but they were desperate to work toward a better future. In a statement made in his 1967 pastoral letter, Pope Paul VI said, "The human right to feed the family supersedes the right of a nation to establish borders and control entrance to and from that nation." The Mexican consul, Señor Medrazo, calls the Mexican workers in the United States heroes. Together they sent $16 billion home last year to support their families in Mexico, making this Mexico's number-one income source.

We came to believe that God was calling us not only to grow apples, but also to use that work as a context in which people who were being overlooked or ignored could grow as well.

In 1987, we built a warehouse, and Broetje Orchards became a grower, packer, and shipper organization. We hired 150 women to work in the warehouses, and we began hearing stories of the families of these immigrants. Children were left locked in apartments so their parents could work. Other kids were pulled out of school to take care of their younger siblings. There were serious health issues.

So first we built an on-site day care/preschool. One family started to ask us about housing. Their boy was being bitten by rats as he slept at night. In this country! We knew we had to do something more. Our people needed decent, affordable housing.

By 1990, our orchards were producing well, and we had $5.5 million in the bank. We had achieved the "American dream." But our employees were excluded from that. So we decided to build some housing next to the warehouse. We tried to find a financial partner, but nothing worked out. So we took all of our savings and built 100 two-, three-, and four-bedroom homes along with a gym, chapel, store, and laundry. The first residents held a contest and named the new community Vista Hermosa (beautiful view).

Of those first residents, about a third had kids with some prior gang involvement. We realized we would need to become social workers as well as apple growers or face the possibility of living next door to a new ghetto. Over the years, a number of programs have been birthed as a response to the needs of our people: an on-site bilingual library, a Christian elementary school, a residential program for at-risk teen boys (Jubilee Youth Ranch), after-school tutoring, college scholarships, ESL, parenting and job training, etc. We keep discovering new needs that, if not addressed, will become barriers to the health, stability, and development of our families.

Erisman: I understand you have about 900 permanent workers and 900 transient workers?

Broetje: Close. But "transient" is not a word we ever use.

Erisman: What is the right word?

Broetje: Well, "migrant" would be the legal description, but about 80 percent of our people come back to work for us every year. A thousand people work full time for us now, and we have about 125 families living on the farm permanently. You can only be classified as a migrant for four years. We, too, were migrants when we first moved to the orchard, because we had moved three times in less than four years. So the Broetjes were a migrant family. But after that, you lose your migrant status if you stay. So the people who live on our farm are not true migrants anymore. They are settlers.

Balancing the Work

Wong: And the ones who work full time, what do they do when you're not picking apples?

Broetje: That's where Ralph is brilliant. It fits with the product and market strategy that he has developed. We used to plant red apples and people bought them. Now, consumers want a certain taste, or certain packaging, or a cute little variation. It's just gone crazy. And if it's good today it doesn't mean it's going to be good next year. It's a global, consumer-driven industry, more and more now.

Ralph has a capacity to foresee what varieties might be popular. You can't just pull out trees every year and expect a yield, so you have to be thinking ahead. In doing this, he has a strategy to stagger the varieties so that we have the longest possible growing season that we can have. Cherries come on in July, and we're picking something straight through to when the snow flies in November. Now as soon as those apples are off, then they start immediately with pruning, and that takes months—we have close to a million trees out there! Early spring is our lowest time, but there's painting to be done, and new varieties to plant. With his strategies, we can keep people working year round with few exceptions.

Wong: How many employees do you have in social service, education, or administration?

Broetje: About 150 including teachers, social workers, store managers, and those in housing programs, etc.

Wong: Tell us about the evening program.

Broetje: When our first residents came, Eva Madrigal, SRH director, reported to us before very long that about a third of these kids had had some antisocial-behavior history. They had been uprooted from traditional communities, on the move, living in poverty, without a supportive community in place. Many come acting out and angry. They didn't ask to be brought here. They're socially ostracized and rejected, so they learn to play the game by the right rules, and they're still dead in the water if they are here undocumented. It fills them with rage.

And so creating a sense of belonging became an instant focus for the community in those early 1990s. In those early days of community-building, we had chapel every Saturday night. Then we would all go over to the gym and we would have refreshments or dinner and we'd play games or we'd share stories or do business there, as a community. Over time that has all evolved to resources like a weight room, computer lab, basketball teams, or fitness programs—you know, anything and everything that a few people express an interest in.

We also offer parenting programs, ESL, and other resources that will help them maintain and improve their spiritual, mental, emotional, physical health, and grow forward in ways that meet their interests and abilities within the limited time they have. Our families work hard and are tired at the end of the day.

Erisman: How do you deal with the cost issues?

Broetje: The day care costs around $25 a day for each child, but the most anybody pays is $7. We subsidize about two-thirds of the preschool income so that they can afford to put their children there. This is not primarily about baby-sitting anymore, but about preparing children so that they can enter into U.S. schools on par with other students.

Families who live in Vista Hermosa pay rent of about 40 to 50 percent of market value, based on their income. How to create livable wages is also a huge issue for us. Many employees earn about $7.50 per hour, and that's not much. So, we try to offset the gap with other in-kind goods and services. And we keep thinking about how to increase their assets.

We bring instructors in from the outside for the ESL class, and charge $10 for a year of instruction. Other basic services such as an open gym, computer lab, and college tutoring, are part of the grant program and we don't charge for those things. Summer day camp gives elementary kids a place to go all day, every day, for minimum fares. Here they receive academic tutoring, go on field trips, and take swimming lessons. All children of employees are eligible for scholarships to college.

How are we faithful to the people we serve and the community that we're a part of in light of the larger agricultural industry we are part of, and that in terms of global competition? That's our challenge!

Wong: Could you give us the total value of the subsidies for these programs?

Broetje: I don't know because we don't look at it like that. We are looking at people value, and we are doing what we can year to year. When we have a profitable year, we give away a large percent of our income anyway. We have chosen to answer the question, "How much is enough?" and the rest is given away.

Erisman: Do you have people who leave this picking business and "graduate" to other types of work?

Broetje: Yes, but we wish we had more. We are seeing more of this with the second generation. Most of the parents are working as hard as they can work to allow their children to be the beneficiaries. Their futures will be different. About 40 percent of the people who leave Vista Hermosa today are going on to become first-time home owners, and that's very exciting for us. Now they're building assets for themselves, and becoming good citizens in the communities to which they move, because they have practiced community here.

Technology and People

Erisman: *How does technology fit into running a business like yours?*

Broetje: We built the first packing line with that very question in mind. Our mission was to ask, "How can we best serve these people?" For us, the first step is all about creating steady jobs. Here again, Ralph gets the credit, because he really thought long and hard about that. We could have automated fully then and done away with a lot of the jobs.

But we asked a different question. What are the maximum amount of jobs we can make for human beings here — and still pump out enough product to be competitive? And like I say, we have a great team of people who are working with that every day. Our packing line is beautiful. But it was designed with the balance of remaining competitive and putting people to work. We try to grow apples, excellent apples ... so that we can help people grow.

Erisman: *What about the use of pesticides? How do you think about the environmental issues associated with farming?*

Broetje: We're proud to tell you we're 99.9 percent toxic-free, and have been for years. The public just needs to catch up with the times. You may find somebody out there that's still using illegal pesticides occasionally, but it isn't happening in our neck of the woods, and hasn't been for a long, long time.

Wong: *Where can we find your apples?*

Broetje: Costco, Albertson's, Safeway locally. It just depends on who's buying this week.

Wong: *Do they have your sticker on them?*

Broetje: They should have our label, "First Fruits," with a sticker showing little hands holding an apple. These are Trevor's hands, our son from Calcutta. Years ago when we needed a logo, we put an apple in his hands one day, and took a picture of him holding it when he was about 2 years old. Unfortunately, today more of the buyers are dictating the boxes we put the apples in. So you may not always see those hands.

Erisman: *It would be harder to run things the way you do if you had shareholders to be concerned about, wouldn't it?*

Broetje: Yes, it would. But most of the ideas for running a business while respecting people are clearly transferable to other businesses. By not having other shareholders, we have another problem. Ralph and I legally own all the assets of Broetje Orchards ourselves. That's a lot of power in the hands of two people.

In 1990, we built a small grocery store. We saw that many men in our community were being destroyed by alcohol. The resulting abuse was horrendous in families as well as the effects in the workplace. And so we built this store, and we said we will not sell alcohol or cigarettes in that store. The vendors called and told us how much money we would lose by not selling their products. But we were calling the shots. It has allowed us to hold to values that we happen to believe in, and we believe that our community is healthier and happier today. Today our true work is really about widening the understanding of and commitment to life-giving values that will sustain the community after we are gone.

Maintaining Accountability

Erisman: *So what keeps you accountable, because you have a lot of power, and a lot of money? I've seen other people who started off idealistically and they lose it. Probably an inch at a time. What do you do?*

Broetje: Well I don't have any fancy answers. I don't have a college degree and neither does Ralph. Although we are both voracious readers, the Bible has been our main value textbook. We find many stories there that give direction for wise leadership. And many were in agricultural settings so they apply literally!

We also have an open-door policy. Anybody can walk in and talk about the issues or decisions that affect them or their colleagues personally or corporately.

Erisman: *And it sounds like the crew meetings that your employees have also hold you accountable.*

Broetje: Oh, yes! In addition to our crew representative meetings, crew leaders gather every morning at 6 a.m. They share joys and concerns just like a faith community does … somebody's sick, somebody died yesterday, we need to raise money to ship the body home to Mexico or help with the family that has just been left with four kids to care for. It's extraordinary. This is also the place where they review the work schedule, share important information that affects the farm or our people, and generally check in with each other as they prepare to lead their teams for another day.

Many of them have little formal education; but they have so much integrity and heart and insight and will to serve. All I can tell you is that it is this spirit that results in trees that bear fruit … fruit that will last.

Questions for Discussion and Reflection

1. How do the Broetjes deal with employees who are in the country illegally? Do you agree with the way they handle this problem?
2. What do you think about the Broetjes providing housing and an on-site day care/preschool program? They consider this part of their obligation to their employees. Do you agree that it's an obligation of their company to provide these things?
3. How do you think their treatment of employees would be different if the company was publicly owned and had shareholders' interests to be concerned about?

The Ethics of Executive Pay: A Christian Viewpoint
Richard Higginson and David Clough
(Cambridge: Grove Books Limited, 2010).

Executive Remuneration: The Current Situation

The high level of executive remuneration is a subject that has attracted a great deal of public attention in recent years, especially since the global financial crisis in 2008 and the recession that has followed. The figures are striking, both in an absolute sense (how much money is being paid to senior executives) and a relative sense (how executives' pay compares with that of average workers).

In September 2009, the *Guardian*'s annual survey of directors' pay found that nearly a quarter of chief executives in the FTSE 100 Index of companies received financial packages of salary, bonuses and shares totalling more than £5m. Thirteen directors earned more than £10m and three more than £20m.[1] The highest earner was Bert Becht, chief executive of Reckitt Benckiser, with £36.76m. The average chief executive's package in the FTSE top 100 was £3.1m, a substantial increase—despite the recession—on the 2005 figure of £2.5m. How do such earnings compare with that of the average British worker? The average full-time employee who worked for a FTSE 100 company earned just over £26,000. This means that the pay differential between chief executives and average workers in such companies now stands at over 100 to 1. In 1970, the differential was approximately 10.1. Taking the FTSE as a whole (the top 250 companies), the 2009 figure is about 70.1.

These average differentials mask some major discrepancies between different companies. At Tesco, the total salary package of chief executive Sir Terry Leahy adds up to just over £9m. This compares with an average employee salary of about £12,000, a staggering differential ratio of 750.1. In contrast, a BBC programme about John Lewis—an equally successful retailer but one with a very different corporate structure and ethos—revealed that its chief executive, Andy Street, earns a mere £500,000 a year. The average wage is £11,000, but this is boosted by the fact that ordinary employees as well as directors benefit from bonuses when profits are high. John Lewis has actually set a limit on pay differential: the highest is only allowed to earn 75 times the lowest.[2] At the global money broker ICAP, the chief executive Michael Spencer has a total package of £6.73m, which makes him one of the highest earners. But the pay differential there is only 33.1, because the average salary per employee is just over £200,000. Other top payers where rewards are handsomely spread include the London Stock Exchange, the Man Group and 3i.

3i is a private equity investor which is also a plc. But many hedge funds, private equity firms and City investment banks are either privately owned or quoted in the USA rather than the UK. They therefore fall outside the *Guardian* data. It is no secret, however, that earnings in many of these private firms far outstrip those already cited in public listed companies. Marshall Wace, another of Europe's leading hedge funds, is said to pay $250m a year in commissions to individual brokers.[3] The investment bank Goldman Sachs, which is two-thirds owned by the public and a third owned privately by partners, paid 212 employees $3m in bonuses as recently as July 2009.[4]

Goldman Sachs is an American firm with a strong base in London. This leads to the observation that while the figures for UK executive remuneration (considered in both absolute and relative terms) give cause for concern, the comparative figures for US companies show much greater extremes. A typical chief executive in the top 200 US companies earned $8.85m in 2008. This is about 250 times the $37,500 pay of an average worker.[5]

Although UK pay packets and differentials are still markedly less than those in the USA, what has happened on the other side of the Atlantic has undoubtedly exerted a major influence on trends in the UK. The UK is reckoned to be the second most generous employer in the world when it comes to executive remuneration. Executive pay in France and Germany has also risen sharply during the last decade, but the pattern is less marked in some developed nations, notably those with a stronger ethos of social egalitarianism, such as Sweden.[6]

A Cause for Concern

Why are the high levels of executive remuneration attracting such attention? Why has it become a major cause for concern? It is possible to identify two waves of public objections to the trends described. The first wave was already rolling—fairly gently—prior to the global financial crisis. The second wave has gathered momentum since the crisis and is related to behaviour which is deemed to have provoked the crisis.

General Ethical Objections

The first wave of objections concerns the ethics of high pay in general. Huge wage packages and massive wage differentials are apt to be described as 'unfair.' The issue is seen as one of distributive justice.[7] Critics rarely dispute that senior executives should be paid more than other employees. They recognize that senior executives handle complex issues which carry a high degree of responsibility, require a high level of skill, and entail a considerable measure of risk (not least risk to reputation) should corporate fortunes experience a downturn. But critics of 'excessive' pay feel that current pay packages overvalue the contribution made by senior executives and undervalue the contribution made by employees at other levels in the organization. The success of a company depends on everyone from the highest position to the lowest fulfilling their duties, pulling their weight and providing excellent customer service. Each person — receptionist, accounts clerk, marketing manager — plays a vital role; each role brings its challenges and opportunities. In recent years, chief executives appear to be extracting gains bearing little relation to higher productivity and profitability. A wage structure that rewards certain individuals in excess of the contribution that they make, and values ordinary workers' contributions all too little, flies in the face of natural justice. It also contributes to inflation, as corporate costs rise and long-term shareholder value diminishes.

The counter-objection often made by those who defend high levels of executive pay is that, in the corporate world, justice is an abstract notion; the market determines how much chief executives should be paid. The laws of supply and demand come into play, and since executive talent is deemed to be thin on the ground — much slimmer than the pool of 'ordinary' labour, anyway — high salaries are necessary to attract the most talented staff. Economists tend to see this as an amoral process. If a company fails to pay a salary which is the going market rate, it will not get the executives it wants. Defenders of the *status quo* present that as a fact of life.

There is *some* truth in this argument. What individuals expect and demand is undoubtedly influenced by the salaries commanded by those of comparable ability and occupying similar positions. And we live in an increasingly mobile world where talent can be attracted from other countries and other business sectors. The market for executives, however, is far from the ideal competitive market. The non-executive directors who set the pay of executive directors tend to be drawn from the same circle of high-earning corporate executives, raising questions about their independence of judgment.

National Attitudes to Executive Packages

It is worth noting that the market varies a great deal from country to country, even between countries of comparable economic stature. It is difficult to avoid the conclusion that the market is not an objective force which operates in a quasi-universal way; rather, it is subtly yet substantially shaped by the culture in which companies operate. In some countries a huge salary is regarded as fair game if you can get it — though there is some evidence even in the USA of changing public attitudes. In other countries, like Sweden, it is regarded as greedy and socially divisive. The attitudes of *people* make themselves felt. There is something self-deceptive about sheltering behind the so-called truism that the market decides. Ultimately, most executive packages are decided by the remuneration sub-committees of boards of directors. They have real choices to make about how much they choose to pay their senior executives — just as the executives do about the packages they choose to accept.

In their fascinating book *The Seven Cultures of Capitalism*, Charles Hampden-Turner and Fons Trompenaars argued that capitalism is not one seamless robe but has countless variations, rooted in different national histories and cultures. Although the book was written in 1993, and globalization has led to some narrowing of the gap between these differences, their fundamental argument remains sound. They look specifically at the issue of executive pay, comparing salaries between countries and noting (even then) that 'top US salaries are astronomical by European and Asian standards.'[8] They explain this by a deep-seated individualism in American culture, and plot their selected countries on an individual-communitarian spectrum, showing how the more community-focused a society is, the less marked are the pay differentials that are tolerated.

In some countries, then, high levels of executive pay are seen as damaging society. The Prime Minister of Luxembourg, Jean-Claude Junker, described them as 'a social scourge,' since a rift is created between people by huge pay packets and massive differentials.[9] They affect national and corporate morale; they exacerbate social divisions. Those at the lower end of the wage spectrum feel demoralized and underappreciated. Those at the higher end become objects of envy and resentment. The negative social results of this are amply documented in Wilkinson and Pickett's *The Spirit Level*. They draw on around 200 different sets of data from reputable sources such as the United Nations, the World Bank and the World Health Organization. They show that on almost every index of quality of life, happiness or deprivation, there is a strong correlation between a country's level of economic inequality and its social outcomes. So countries with extreme inequality, like the UK and the USA, score poorly on indices such as mental health, obesity, crime and longevity, compared with more egalitarian countries such as Sweden and Japan. Countries which lie somewhere in between economically, like Australia and Germany, also occupy the middle ground socially.[10]

Personal Motivation

The alleged necessity of paying large salaries to attract the best people also raises major questions about personal motivation. The economists' view of a market which operates amorally makes at least three questionable assumptions: that people are motivated by self-interest; that self-interest is not a matter of morality; and that self-interest consists essentially in a calculation of financial benefits. Clearly, the lure of money is a strong motivating factor for many. But human beings are too varied, too interesting and too imbued with concern for other people for this view of *homo economicus* to be convincing as a universal description.

Senior executives might be motivated to work hard and serve their company well for a whole variety of reasons, including self-respect, job satisfaction, intellectual stimulus, innate creativity, leadership drive, joy in teamwork, a congenial working environment, meeting a challenge and a spur to excellence.

In the case of many highly-paid executives, their affluence is such that the presence or absence of, say, an additional half-million in their pay package is unlikely to make much difference to their lifestyle — or, for that matter, their work-rate. Many senior executives might agree with the former chief executive of Royal Dutch Shell, Jeroen van der Veer, who said: 'You have to realize: if I had been paid 50 per cent more, I would not have done it better. If I had been paid 50 per cent less, then I would not have done it worse.'[11]

Assessing motivation is also complicated by the fact that remuneration packages are precisely that — packages — and not to be measured in terms of sala-ries alone. As well as the basic salary, remuneration may consist of short-term bonuses, long-term incentive plans, share options, compensation arrangements and perks including anything from company cars and private executive jets to country club membership and insurance schemes. These extras can easily end up doubling or tripling a basic salary. Clearly, the level of take-home pay will also be affected by the amount of tax paid. That can vary greatly, both between countries and within countries, depending on the rate of taxation, the nature of the package and the advice taken from an executive's accountant. Such complexity has given rise to another objection — that there is often a lack of clarity about a package's total value and how it is arrived at. So executive remuneration is the subject of cries for greater transparency and fuller public disclosure. The more complicated the package, the more difficult it is for the outsider to ascertain the full value of what executives are being paid.

• • •

Theological Considerations

What should Christians make of all this? Are the concerns felt by the general public about executive remuneration something that we should share? In particular, what are the implications of the biblical teaching on justice and wealth for this issue?

Distributive Justice

The biblical writers talk about justice a great deal. The four words used for justice (two of them Hebrew — *tsedaqah* and *mishpat* — and two of them Greek — *dikaiosune* and *krisis*) occur over 1000 times. This is not always obvious from biblical translations, because these words are sometimes translated 'righteousness' and sometimes 'judgment,' but justice is the core meaning of each. 'Righteousness' expresses the concern for justice which looks to restore broken relationships and damaged community; 'judgment' the action which implements or puts into force God's decision for justice.

In their magisterial *Kingdom Ethics*, Glen Stassen and David Gushee pay particular attention to Isaiah, a book which has a great deal to say about justice, and show how several key passages are either applied to Jesus or by Jesus in the gospels.[18] These include:

- Isaiah 9.1–7—its language of light dawning in the darkness is taken up by Zechariah in relation to John the Baptist (Luke 1.67–79). Note the reference to the establishment of justice and righteousness in Isaiah 9.7.
- Isaiah 42.1–9—the first of the servant passages applied by Matthew to Jesus in Matt 12.15–21. The servant 'will bring forth justice to the nations' (Isaiah 42.1) and is determined to 'establish justice in the earth' (Isaiah 42.4).
- Isaiah 56.1–8—a remarkable vision of an open community in which outcasts and foreigners are welcome. Isaiah 56.7 is cited by Jesus when he cleansed the temple (Mark 11.17). He objects to the fact that the court intended to be reserved for the Gentiles had become a trading post.
- Isaiah 61—the opening verses of which were read by Jesus in the synagogue at Nazareth early in his ministry. He then caused consternation by saying, 'Today this Scripture has been fulfilled in your hearing' (Luke 4.16–30). Note the references in Isaiah 61 to 'oaks of righteousness' (v 3) and 'I the Lord love justice' (v 8).

It is notable that Jesus, in the course of his famous diatribe against the scribes and Pharisees, identifies justice among 'the weightier matters of the law' which he regards as core principles and feels they have neglected (Mt 23.23). Taken cumulatively, the biblical material on justice integrates the interrelated notions of impartiality, rendering of what is due, proportionality and normativity.[19]

These are all concepts relevant to the setting of wages. Impartiality implies treating people equally. Jesus' command to love one's enemy is actually modelled on God's egalitarian treatment of humanity: 'He makes the sun rise on the evil and the good, and sends rain on the righteous and the unrighteous' (Matt 5.45). The Torah commands impartiality in the administration of justice: 'You shall not be partial to the poor or defer to the great; with justice you shall judge your neighbour' (Lev 19.15). Some theologians talk about God's bias to the poor but that has no biblical support if held to mean absolving the poor from

responsibility for their misdeeds.[20] However, society's more recurrent temptation is a bias to the rich, as we see in the prophets' complaints about the administration of justice, and which James warns against in his advice to stewards ushering people to their places in church services (Jas 2.1–7).[21]

Within the context of a general equality of treatment, biblical writers identify different groups as warranting particular kinds of treatment. Plato's notion of *suum cuique*, 'rendering to each what is due,' is implicitly apparent.[22] Paul believed that husbands *owe* it to their wives, parents to their children and masters to their slaves to treat the other party in a particular way (Eph 5.21–6.9; Col 3.18–4.1). 'Similar treatment for similar cases' underlies the instructions of other biblical passages with regard to a wide range of groups, from widows on the one hand to strangers to the religious community on the other (see Deut 24.17–22 and 1 Tim 5.3–16). This enshrines the idea that there is a way of treating each type of person which accords them the dignity they deserve. In the Mosaic law, attention is given to the conditions under which day labourers were to be paid. Such labourers had probably lost their own land—hence the necessity to work for others—but still they are to be treated with respect. Leviticus 19.13 says, 'You shall not keep for yourself the wages of a labourer until morning,' an instruction which follows the core commandments 'Do not defraud' and 'Do not steal,' so perhaps late payment was seen as a form of one or both. Deuteronomy 24.14–15 makes a similar prohibition about delaying the payment of wages of labourers after sunset. Even worse than paying a labourer late is not paying him at all. Jeremiah 22.13 pronounces, 'Woe to him who builds his house by unrighteousness, and his upper rooms by injustice; who makes his neighbours work for nothing, and does not give them their wages.' This is a denunciation of Shallum, son of King Josiah; the prophets were clear that even monarchy should not expect people to work for nothing. In addition, justice requires proportionality between labour and reward. While the Bible contains an abundance of material on the principle of paying people and the conditions in which they should be paid, it offers less guidance on *how much* they should be paid. There is a paucity of material on pay differentials! However, there are passages where the extent of reward offered is linked to work well done — notably certain parables of Jesus, which we discuss later. Here we draw attention to a notable example of proportionality in making recompense in 1 Timothy 5.17, 'Let the elders who rule well be considered worthy of double honour, especially those who labour in preaching and teaching.' The interpretation of this has been debated. Is Paul saying that such elders should be paid twice as much as those who do not rule well or are not involved in preaching and teaching? That may be a crudely materialist understanding of Paul, but it is likely that his notion of honour includes financial reward, because v 18 continues, '. . . for the Scripture says, "You shall not muzzle an ox while it is treading out the grain," and "The labourer deserves to be paid."' So this text appears to provide implicit support to the practice of pay differentiation — though it is ironic that it occurs in the context of workers in the church, a sphere where today differentials are extremely small compared with those that prevail in commercial contexts.

There is one famous passage where labourers are all paid the same wage, irrespective of how many hours they have worked, Jesus' parable of the labourers in the vineyard (Matt 20.1–16). The landowner pays the usual daily wage, one denarius, to labourers who worked for nine hours, six hours, three hours or one hour. It is unlikely that Jesus was commending this as sensible commercial practice; rather, he is deliberately citing *unusual* practice to highlight God's grace in forgiving and accepting those who repent late in life. In other words, grace is a great equaliser; when it comes to salvation, we all depend on God's favour. Despite this, it is still common for many reading the parable to empathize with the complaint expressed by the labourers who worked all day, 'These last worked only one hour, and you have made them equal to us who have borne the burden of the day and the scorching heat' (Matt 20.12). The landowner replies, 'Friend, I am doing you no wrong; did you not agree with me for the usual daily wage?' (Matt 20.13). When Latin fathers like Jerome and Augustine come to comment on this parable, they are at pains to emphasize this. They both reject the claim of injustice because the vineyard owner was not paying less than the agreed sum; the labourers had entered freely into negotiation with him, and in their mutual dealings the owner stayed true to his word. This leads Jerome and Augustine to advocate free bargaining as a means to discerning a just wage.[23]

When the medieval scholastic theologians developed their concept of the just wage, they drew upon this tradition of patristic exegesis.[24] Overall, the scholastics were content to accept the just price as the market price, whatever was agreed by employers and labourers prior to work commencing. However, they recognized that this process might be distorted by fraud or coercion. A wage was considered unjust if one party had been deceived or forced into accepting terms against his will. The final ingredient in the biblical understanding of justice, normativity, expresses the truth that justice is ultimately grounded in the norm of God's moral law. It derives from the will and character of God. True justice is *God's* justice. The opening verses of Psalm 72 are a prayer that human justice (in this case the justice meted out by Israel's king) will be precisely that, asking that kings exercise God's justice, righteousness and concern for the poor (Ps 72.1–4).

•   •   •

The Agency Problem

In *The Walker Review of Corporate Governance*, it criticizes the way many banks and other financial institutions have operated recently. Sir David Walker feels that corporate executives have not sufficiently been held to account by non-executive directors and shareholders. Both need to engage more constructively with their investee companies, with the aim of supporting long-term improvement in performance. At present, shareholders often fail to exercise proper stewardship, creating a gap between the owners and managers of companies.[36] Christians should be well aware of this agency problem, because it mirrors a problem in God's relationship with humanity.

Patrick Gerard has pointed out that Jesus comments on the agency problem extensively — it features in no less than four of his parables.[37] In each, agents, who are variously described as servants, slaves, managers, stewards or tenants, are given responsibility by someone who stands in a master/owner relationship to them.

In the parable of the faithful and unfaithful servant (Lk 12.42–48, Mt 24.45–51), Jesus poses two possible scenarios. Interestingly, the servant is described both as a steward (*oikonomos*) in Luke 12.42, and as a slave (*doulos*) in 12.45; this reflects the dual nature of his relationship, in authority over other slaves and under authority to the one who employs and presumably owns him. This servant is put in charge of the house while the master is away. If the master returns and finds the house in good order, with the household having been fed at the proper time, the servant will be praised and promoted—given the extra responsibility of being put in charge of all the master's possessions. But if the master returns and finds that the servant has been maltreating others and gorging himself on food and drink, he will lose his position and be punished. The parable emphasizes trust (the master may be away for a long period of time—the second servant says, 'The master is delayed in coming'), responsibility and recompense, which may be either positive or negative depending on the agent's performance. In his comment at the end of the parable (12.48), Jesus makes clear that the greater the degree of trust shown, the higher the expectations—more is expected.

The better-known parable of the talents (Matt 25.14–30; Luke 19.11–27) echoes similar themes. Here, as Gerard points out, the master asks no questions about the behaviour of the servants, but judges them solely on the financial return they have made.[38] Three servants are allocated talents, to one five, to another two, and to a third one, 'to each according to his ability' (Matt 25.15). The master seems to have been perceptive in his assessment, because the first two servants—through the exercise of trade—both double their number of talents, whereas the third servant fails to do anything profitable, simply digging a hole to hide the number. When the master returns after 'a long time,' servants one and two are warmly praised in identical terms, 'Well done, good and trustworthy servant; you have been trustworthy in a few things. I will put you in charge of many things; enter into the joy of your master' (Matt 25.21, 23).

Servant three seeks to defend his lack of action on the grounds that his master was a harsh man but the master has no truck with this, scolding him, punishing him and reallocating the one talent he had to the most productive servant. Again we are given a sense of weighty responsibility which issues in very diverse outcomes depending on how it is handled.

We must be wary of reading more into these stories than Jesus intended—of seeking to draw too direct a comparison between a parabolic way of describing God's relationship with humanity and contemporary corporate governance. Yet there are certain details of the parables which are highly suggestive, notably:

- The servants are judged on their performance over a lengthy period of time—it is no superficial, short-term assessment.
- The judgment that issues is decisive—promotion in some cases, dismissal in others. Sustained long-term performance is rewarded, but there is no tolerance given to ongoing failure.
- The judgment covers both financial performance (in the Matthew 25 parable) and interpersonal behaviour (in the Luke 12 parable). Long-term, performance-related, decisive and relational—these are all criteria that have their place in the setting of executives' pay packages.

Interestingly, the FSA's report on remuneration policies argues that insufficient weight has been given to non-financial measures of performance alongside financial performance measures. They specify among the latter attitudes to risk and compliance. They say that a key element of effective risk management is the communication of the firm's values and objectives to employees, and a high degree of transparency about what is required of them if they are to benefit from variable remuneration awards. The report's principal message, however, is that the remuneration structures of senior employees and risk takers should be consistent with and promote effective risk management. Like the *Walker Review*, the FSA is keen to raise the awareness and involvement of both company boards and shareholders with regard to risk management. So a remuneration committee should 'be able to demonstrate that its decisions are consistent with a reasonable assessment of the firm's financial situation and future prospects';[39] and shareholders should 'reconsider the current practice, common in many firms, of accruing bonus pools ahead of any distribution of risk-adjusted returns to the providers of equity capital.'[40]

Conclusions

Both the *Walker Review* and the FSA Report appear to be moving in a sensible direction. They seek to reduce the repetition of corporate practice, recently prevalent in the financial services industry, where company directors pay themselves huge salaries and bonuses based far too much on short-term financial results which shield risk-laden strategies. They seek to encourage non-executive directors and institutional shareholders to take a more challenging and discerning role in a company's activities, holding executives to much closer account for their actions. If their recommendations pass into enforceable policy they may help to reduce some of the excessive pay packages detailed in our first section; but we should not underestimate the formidable vested interests that may stand in the way of those changes happening.

The question remains: what, from a Christian perspective, is an appropriate level of executive remuneration? It will be clear by now that this does not admit of an easy answer. What counts as excessive pay is a highly subjective opinion and a constantly moving target. The make-up of executives' pay packages is complex, so simply to judge by salary alone is inadequate. The packages which are within the capacity of church investors to influence, those relating to publicly-listed companies, are considerably lower than the pay meted out in some private companies, so there is a danger that seeking to restrict levels in one sphere could accentuate the gulf with another.

Nevertheless, we believe we have established solid grounds for believing that the levels of executive pay currently being paid in many FTSE 100 companies are a legitimate cause for concern. Biblical and theological considerations add weight to the cries that are being expressed by the general public. But they also point in some distinctive directions.

We offer four theological values from the preceding analysis to guide Christians' thinking in this area.

Concern for the Poor

Our survey of biblical material suggests the central concern of economic justice is adequate provision for those least well-off. This suggests that church investors should be as much concerned with helping the poor as restraining the rich—arguably, *more* concerned. Of course, the two may be connected. An astronomically high salary paid to a chief executive could affect the remuneration made to the lowest paid (though probably not by much); more likely, it may make the lowest-paid feel devalued and affect company morale. The substantive point is that we should be vigilant about the levels of pay at the bottom of an organization, not just the top.

Just Pay

Market arguments for unrestricted pay policies are weak even in their own terms; markets never operate in a vacuum, and cannot be relied on to set optimum salary levels. Biblical visions of justice suggest a just remuneration policy should be impartial, render to each what is due, proportionate to contribution and based on normative judgments of God's justice. This leads to the observation that the issue of pay differentials is more important than the levels of pay outright. Any salary in excess of £5m is apt to take the breath away, but it is even more disturbing to discover the huge difference in pay differentials between, for example, Tesco and John Lewis. Of course, corporate figures do not always lend themselves to straightforward comparison. Some business sectors by their nature employ a greater number of lower-skilled people. But even when such variables are taken into account, it does appear that some companies have a fairer pay salary than others—*ie* a structure which shows greater respect both for human beings' fundamental equality of status and the distinctive contribution made by every type of worker.

It is difficult to specify a precise maximum ratio of executive pay to those earning the lowest on the basis of Christian theology. Here one is aware of a tension between what we might consider the ideal and the reality of a particular culture in a fallen world. Several commentators (as varied as the banker John Pierpont Morgan and the Relationships Foundation) have suggested a 20:1 ratio.[41] While we have some sympathy for this as an aspirational figure, our guide for Christian investors was more modest in proposing an upper limit of 75:1 for companies that church bodies should invest in. We did so in recognition that change in this area is only likely to be achieved gradually and that for the Church Investors Group to adopt a much lower differential would lead to the churches disinvesting from a large number of FTSE companies, which in turn reduces the churches' capacity to influence those companies.

The fact that John Lewis operates according to a maximum ratio of 75:1 only came to light after the publication of our report—but the fact that they have admirable employee policies and excellent corporate morale encourages us to think our proposals are pointing in the right direction.

The Dangers of Wealth

Biblical texts are clear about how wealth can lead to greed and rejection of God's ways. Being paid a huge salary can actually be bad for individuals: it is likely to encourage selfishness, have a morally corrupting effect, and create an obstacle in individuals' relationships with God. Attracting candidates with inflated packages means that they are disproportionately likely to be focused on promoting their own financial interests rather than the long-term interests of the company and its shareholders. Those for whom remuneration is less significant are likely to serve the company better. Biblical warnings about the perils of wealth therefore apply to companies as well as individuals. Companies which seek to enhance their prestige by paying executives more than their rivals may succeed only in fuelling spiralling executive pay.

Good Stewardship

Stewardship of the resources of others is a significant biblical motif. Our survey confirms the importance of holding executives to account over their performance. We emphasize that this should be reasonably long-term (giving staff time to prove their worth), and that it should cover benefits to all stakeholders and not just financial value to shareholders. Performance-related pay is far from easy to work out equitably, but it is sound in principle. Bonuses have their place (properly handled) in a fair and competitive market. If substantial bonuses are to be paid, however, there is a case for lowering basic salaries. The corollary of paying extra for exceptional performance is that those who bear primary responsibility for culpable corporate failure should not be allowed to escape scot-free. Church investors ought to be asking hard questions of remuneration committees about 'golden parachutes' and other unduly comfortable severance arrangements. Claw-back mechanisms to recover generous remuneration which has proved to be misplaced should be considered. Pay packages also need to be made simpler and more transparent.

The recent financial crisis has highlighted the high-risk strategies undertaken by certain firms in the financial sector. Pay packages should not encourage risky behaviour which can lead to serious consequences, not just for the individual company but many other companies that are affected. Clearly, risk cannot be eliminated from business, nor would that be desirable. But the commercial climate in recent years has exaggerated the virtues of risk-taking to the neglect of the classical virtue of prudence. Pay packages which reward executives who pursue steady strategies aimed at gradual growth are to be commended.

Notes

1   These and the following figures are taken from a combination of articles from the *New Statesman* ('Executive pay not linked to performance, says survey,' 5 July 2010, http://goo.gl/uBKf) and *The Guardian* ('Pay gap widens between executives and their staff,' 16 September 2010, http://goo.gl/baeD).

2   M Pagano, 'Why John Lewis's Andy is streets ahead,' *The Independent*, 14 March 2010, http://goo.gl/YL6c.

3   http://en.wikipedia.org/wiki/Marshall_Wace.

4   'Tarp banks award billions in bonuses,' NWO Truth, 30 July 2009, http://nwotruth.com/?p=11354.

5   A Clark, 'Guardian pay survey: US executives enjoy solid pay rises despite crunch,' *The Guardian*, 12 September 2008, http://goo.gl/maI3.

6   D Gow, 'European anger at "scourge" of Anglo-American pay practices,' *The Guardian*, 13 September, 2008, {http://goo.gl/wLdu}; 'Swedish CEOs make peanuts in Euro study,' *The Local*, 15 September 2009, http://goo.gl/OygX.

7   See R W Kolb (ed), *The Ethics of Executive Compensation* (Oxford: Blackwell, 2006).

8 C Hampden-Turner and F Trompenaars, *The Seven Cultures of Capitalism* (London: Piatkus, 1993) p 57.

9 A Horin, 'Let's show those fat cats who's really the boss,' *The Wall Street Journal*, 16 August 2008, http://goo.gl/S7UC

10 R Wilkinson and K Pickett, *The Spirit Level: Why More Equal Societies Almost Always Do Better* (London: Allen Lane, 2009).

11 C Hoyos and M Steen, 'Shell chief calls for pay reforms,' *Financial Times*, 8 June 2009, http://goo.gl/X2dl Van der Veer received a salary of 10.3m euros in 2008.

• • • •

18 G H Stassen and D P Gushee, *Kingdom Ethics: Following Jesus in Contemporary Context* (Nottingham: IVP, 2003) chs 1 and 2.

19 As argued by E C Beisner in 'Justice and Poverty: Two Views Contrasted,' in H Schlossberg, V Samuel and R Sider (eds), *Christianity and Economics in the Post-Cold War Era: The Oxford Declaration and Beyond* (Grand Rapids: Eerdmans, 1994) pp 57–80. See also R Higginson, *Dilemmas* (London: Hodder and Stoughton, 1987) pp 172–177.

20 Notably David Sheppard, in his book of that name, *Bias to the Poor* (London: Hodder and Stoughton, 1983) and many Latin-American liberation theologians. Page 28.

21 See *eg* Is 5.23, which mentions 'those who acquit the guilty for a bribe, and deprive the innocent of their rights.'

22 Plato, *The Republic*, Book 1 (London: Penguin, 2007).

23 See E S Noell, 'Bargaining, Consent and the Just Wage in the Sources of Scholastic Economic Thought,' *Journal of the History of Economic Thought*, 20.4, 1998, p 476.

24 They wrote about this in conjunction with the just price; indeed, wages were often described as the price of labour. O Langholm, *The Legacy of Scholasticism in Economic Thought* (Cambridge University Press, 1998) is a leading authority.

• • • •

36 *Walker Review*, p 60.

37 See P Gerard, 'Executive Pay and Corporate Governance,' *Faith in Business Quarterly 11.2*, pp 23–8, along with his more detailed *Performance and Reward: Managing Executive Pay to Deliver Shareholder Value* (Leicester: Troubador Publishing, 2006).

38 'Executive Pay and Corporate Governance,' p 25.

39 *Reforming remuneration practices in financial services*, 4.12.

40 *op cit*, 1.24.

41 A Seager and J Finch, 'Pay gap widens between executives and their staff,' *The Guardian*, 16 September 2009 http://goo.gl/baeD; Jubilee Centre, 'Ethics of Executive Pay,' http://goo.gl/0rIN

Questions for Discussion and Reflection

1. What do you think of Higginson and Clough's view of executive compensation? Is it realistic in today's competitive business environment?
2. How does their concern for the poor relate to structuring executive compensation? Do you agree with them that concern for the poor should be a relevant consideration when determining executive pay?
3. Do you agree that there's a level of just pay that is not entirely market determined? Why or why not?

CASE STUDIES

Case 7.1: March Madness

The NCAA basketball tournament is an exciting time for basketball fans, particularly for those who cheer for schools that make deep runs into their bracket. It may not, however, be such an amusing time for employers as many workers stream games that occur during work hours directly to their workplace computers. In order to help viewers avoid getting caught by their supervisors, one streaming website even provides a "Boss Key" that turns the screen into a fake Excel spreadsheet when clicked. Employees could watch on their phones, but it would look more obvious. Some studies claim that billions of dollars in productivity could be lost during the first week of tournament games. Few companies do anything formal in terms of policy or technology to stop the problem, but it's clear that streaming video and personal uses of various forms of social media (i.e., Facebook) are becoming significant problems in the workplace.

Short of having supervisors physically walking around and inspecting what their workers are doing, employers can take several direct steps to prevent such a work distraction if they want the behavior curbed. They can restrict access to known streaming sites, block streaming video, or use software that records every website visited (and then give out punishment after the fact). Alternatively, they can set up televisions in a break room or provide other updates so that employees don't need to be fully engaged in watching games. Or, if they can use existing (or develop better) performance metrics to track employee productivity, they may not have to worry so much about how and when the work actually gets done, provided the quality of work (i.e., face-to-face interaction with a customer or client) doesn't get reduced.

Questions for Discussion

1. Assume you are a supervisor of a software development team and you suspected many of your employees were watching significant parts of games during normal working hours, how would you respond? Would walking around or using the technological tools violate employees' privacy, rob them of their dignity, or communicate mistrust in a damaging way?
2. How would you balance the need for productivity with respecting and trusting your employees?

Case 7.2: Paying the Next CEO

You are a board member of a large publicly traded company in the consumer electronics industry. For the past three years, you have served on the compensation committee (charged with determining executive pay). Just recently the CEO announced her retirement after a highly successful ten-year term. You are now representing the compensation committee on a task force to discuss the compensation range and package that will be offered to the next CEO. The task force is composed of yourself, a member of the board search committee, a representative of an outside executive search firm hired by your company, and a consultant from a renowned benefits and compensation advisory firm.

During the initial meeting, it becomes apparent that the other members of the task force basically want to continue past compensation policies for the CEO—a high "market-based" salary (probably around $10–$12 million per year) and incentive based stock options tied to "performance" as measured primarily by stock price. Using this formula, the recently retired

CEO often made $20–$25 million per year. "If we want someone good—and executives who are good are in high demand—we have to pay the going rate; that's simply how the game works," the compensation consultant says.

You are not so sure about continuing in this manner. You were once a staunch supporter of the policy advocated by the others on the task force but have begun to rethink your position amid public outcries about CEO pay. At a recent shareholders meeting, a highly vocal group began raising concerns that the CEO was paid far too much and that it was not only unfair, but bad for the long-term health of the company.

They accused the company of giving "rock star" treatment to the CEO and minimizing the contributions of other employees to the success of the company. To support their argument, they brought out charts that showed the rapidly widening gap between the CEO and the company's lowest paid workers (from 1:15 to 1:1000) during the past decade. They also showed that on a national basis, pay gaps are much larger in America when compared with other parts of the world. They questioned the impact of such a widening gap on overall morale and cohesion.

They also noted the possible abuses that incentive-based pay have contributed to in recent years (managing for short-term stock price gains versus building a company for long-term health). Moreover, they pointed out the "ridiculousness" of tying CEO pay to stock price, since many factors (including general economic conditions, Wall Street expectations, and the performance of many employees in the organization) may influence it. Finally, they noted that the "market-based" compensation model would only serve to attract someone who is "in it" primarily for the money, while they would hope a good company should be able to attract someone who is interested in leading an organization with "a sound sense of purpose."

Questions for Discussion

1. Which side will you take? Do you agree with the other members of the task force or with the shareholders who have raised concerns and want an alternative approach?
2. How might Christian ethics contribute to the discussion of executive pay? What considerations might it raise in this case?

Case 7.3: Spying or Managing?

Laura operates a small home-remodeling business based in Austin, Texas, that specializes in the installation of high-end custom countertops (granite, solid surfacing). She currently has five two-member crews (a foreman and an apprentice) that work at various (usually separate) job sites all through the city.

Most of her time is spent managing the operations and developing the business (meeting with architects, general contractors, and home owners and writing up competitive bids). Although her workers are paid hourly, they are given lots of freedom to complete their work free of her direct supervision. In most cases, she stops by individual job sites at the beginning and the end of the installations unless there is a problem and she is summoned to the site by the job foreman or another party (the general contractor, architect, or home owner).

One day during the late morning while meeting with an architect and a home owner to bid on a new job, she looks out the window and notices one of her company's trucks drive by. She thinks it odd and after the meeting checks her laptop to see if the worker (she didn't see who it was) was on the way to or back from a nearby jobsite. Much to her chagrin, the nearest current job site is over seven miles away. A few days later, she drives by a trendy part of town and sees one of her company trucks parked in a video game store parking lot.

Suspecting that her employees are running personal errands on company time, she decides to see what they are up to and issues new cell phones to every employee. Unbeknownst to them, the phones are all GPS equipped and she can monitor their whereabouts whenever the phones are turned on. In tracking their whereabouts, she notices legitimate work-related errands (to purchase additional tools or materials) but also sees that some of her workers are in locations (on company time and/or in company vehicles) that have nothing to do with the workday.

She soon calls a meeting and confronts those who committed offenses with the information she has on her hands. After picking their jaws up from the floor, most employees apologize. However, one long-term employee expresses disbelief in her lack of trust in him and his dismay that his privacy has been violated. "You could have just asked us what we were doing," he says. "Sure, I ran a few errands, and I'm sorry I didn't ask for permission first, but I also put in a lot of overtime, so some places I need to go are closed when I get off work. Have you ever had an issue with the quality and timeliness of my work? There was just no need for the James Bond act!"

Questions for Discussion

1. Is Laura's use of GPS technology in this manner a wise application of the tools at her disposal? Why or why not? Are there more intermediate steps she could have taken that might have avoided a direct confrontation with the employees? What might her "solution" do to trust and morale among her workers?
2. Is the employee right about his privacy being violated? Does he have a right to such expectations in the workplace? Why or why not?

COMMENTARY

Managing people is far from a value-neutral enterprise. Philosophical and theological viewpoints that may or may not be consistent with Christian (or other types of) values inform the theories behind the tools used to motivate and direct employees and measure their work. Conflicts are made more apparent when these theories (and the assumptions behind them) are developed into policies and practices.

As human development and well-being may exist in tension with economic competitiveness, challenging questions arise in the course of managing people. Can managers and/or organizations that seek to genuinely respect employees as people, prioritize their needs and development, and honor healthy work boundaries successfully compete in a fast-paced, rapidly changing 24/7 global marketplace?

Although Christian ethics cannot provide answers in the form of narrow prescriptions such as, "A chief executive's pay should absolutely never exceed twelve times that of the lowest paid employee," or "Every business must close on Sundays," it has much to offer in terms of paradigmatic-level guidance that can then be used to shape management theories, policies, and practices. While not comprehensive, the following are constructs from Christian ethics that are applicable to forming ethical standards with respect to managing people.

Given the amount of time and energy put into work and the sense of identity that is extracted from it, a key objective of management should be to create a place/context where vocation (service to God and neighbor) can be exercised. In addition to the need for purpose and meaning that Pollard insightfully illustrates, employees also need trust, respect, and challenge. As Beaton and Wagener point out, work that "enables people to perform at high standards, requires their full capacity and resources, and is socially responsible" is directly related to human flourishing. It is a leadership responsibility to incorporate these marks of "good work" into what employees do each day (and to permit and encourage employee input on these matters) if human capital is to be responsibly stewarded. Of course, a reciprocal relationship exists. Employees should do their best to add value, be worthy of the trust given them, and advance the objectives of the organization.

Justice is another central concept of Christian ethics that is applicable to management. With respect to justice, the Bible notes that God is particularly interested in the plight of vulnerable, oppressed, and voiceless people. Many commands, laws, and principles applied more broadly to economically poor people, widows, or orphans who lived in the broader society, but there is no reason to suggest that similar concepts cannot apply within an organization. How well an organization treats its lowest-level employees is a good test of its values, particularly its sense of justice. In many cases, low-level employees are practically voiceless and are seen as the most easily expendable (almost always the first to be cut during recessions). Given their need for income, they often lack negotiation power and must accept harsh working terms and conditions imposed by their employer. Rarely do these employees receive proper credit for their contributions, as is often reflected in large pay gaps.

In addition to moral reasons, a recent study also confirms the importance of low-level employees for practical, competitive reasons.[4] Justice must come in the form of actual policy changes. While the show *Undercover Boss* is a good concept, some of the "good deeds" done by CEOs who come to understand the plight of their workers come in the form of one-time favors rather than in any lasting changes. Broetje Orchards is an outstanding example of business leaders who have taken these values to heart and applied them throughout the way the organization is design and managed.

Christian ethics also informs the motivations behind why people are to be treated with respect and dignity — because they are valued by God, not because they are factors of production. In contrast, most management theories are based strictly on a financial model of the firm (or shareholder capitalism). Since the overriding objective of a firm is to maximize profit, employees will be treated accordingly. This doesn't mean, of course, that they will be treated poorly. There is clearly an enlightened self-interest-based motivation to treat employees well, because doing so will in some cases lead to higher profits ("We can get more out of them if they think we truly care about them"). However, outside of a "convergence zone," when there are tensions between what is best for the organization (as measured by profit) and what is best for an employee, capital will take priority every time under the finance model. Lower-level employees will be most impacted, as they are often seen as being more expendable and more easily replaceable; thus, the zone where financial and people interests converge will be small. Though there may be cases in which finance may legitimately win out, automatically prioritizing monetary gain over human well-being is not something that can be supported by Christian ethics. Pollard's understanding that profit is a means to the end goal of developing people is much more representative of Christian values than the other way around.

Christian ethics also offers perspective on human nature, which has bearing on practical matters such as the emphasis placed on material rewards and the amount of trust and accountability that is needed. Most Christian theological subtraditions agree that people have a "mixed" nature. That is, we are made in the image of God and are capable of good, but at the same

[4] Jody Heymann and Magda Barrera, *Profit at the Bottom of the Ladder: Creating Value by Investing in Your Work Force* (Boston: Harvard Business Press, 2010).

time, we are broken, so we have selfish tendencies and our intentions and motivations are rarely, if ever, pure.

As identified by a growing number of scholars, most management theories tend to assume the worst about human nature by reducing our motivations to economic self-seeking.[5] Other researchers believe that the emphasis on material rewards (coupled with a focus on individualism) of "mainstream management" may increase efficiency and productivity but harm other forms of human well-being (social, psychological, and ecological). These scholars advocate "multistream management" that is consistent with Christian ideas on human flourishing.[6]

Some organizations (as partially discussed by Pollard) reflect these different values and assumptions and operate in a much more people-centered way. Among human needs are professional growth and development, autonomy, and a sense of purpose/connection to making a contribution to something worthwhile. While beside the fact, these considerations may well produce a better long-term payoff in employee retention, recruitment, and development.[7]

Viewing human beings as having a mixed nature also means that trust and accountability are both realistic and necessary ingredients to operating an organization. Researchers at the Best Places to Work Institute have found that high-functioning organizations are characterized by high trust or at least a presumption of high trust. This makes good sense, but at some level employees also need accountability measures too, especially when trust has been broken.

Several exemplary Christian executives (Max DePree, Herman Miller; Don Flow, Flow Motors; Bill Pollard, ServiceMaster) have used similar concepts and have applied them to the management of their organizations. In some cases, their approach has been referred to as "covenantal management." In addition to the overt biblical language, "covenantal" can also be contrasted with more contractual frameworks for employee relations. Covenants have more room for unilateral duties, grace, and give-and-take than contracts, which specify more conditional duties. Marriage is a good metaphor for why a covenantal approach may be more appealing than a purely contractual one.

Let's take these values (human flourishing, vocation, justice, covenant) and see what type of guidance they may offer for specific issues like the distribution of material rewards. While driven in part by economics, pay practices reflect values. As noted by Higginson and Clough, "the market" is a representation of cultural values. In many organizations, executives are paid astronomical sums that are many times above what "regular" employees earn. Skilled executives are scarce, have to bear heavy leadership burdens,

[5] See, e.g., Fabrizio Ferraro, Jeffrey Pfeffer, and Robert I. Sutton, "Economics Language and Assumptions: How Theories Can Become Self-Fulfilling," *Academy of Management Review* 30 (2005): 8–24.

[6] Bruno Dyck and David Schroeder, "Management, Theology and Moral Points of View: Towards an Alternative to the Conventional Materialist-Individualist Ideal-Type of Management," *Journal of Management Studies* 42 (2005): 705–35. See also Dyck and Neubert, *Management*.

[7] See Amy Wrzesniewski et al., "Jobs, Careers, and Callings: People's Relations to Their Work," *Journal of Research in Personality* 31 (1997): 21–33; and Amy Wrzesniewski, "Finding Positive Meaning in Work," in *Positive Organizational Scholarship: Foundations of a New Discipline*, ed. Kim Cameron, Jane Dutton, and Robert Quinn (San Francisco: Barrett-Kohler, 2003).

and are responsible for many people and resources, so some degree of difference in pay is morally justifiable. The vast amount of the differences and the procedures used to determine them do, however, raise important questions. Do the gaps in pay fairly recognize the contributions of all employees? Or are executives receiving the "rock star" treatment at the expense of others? Is executive pay closely tied to overall organizational performance (multiple measures, especially since stock price is influenced by many factors)? Or is it more a result of cronyism? Is some compensation (i.e., the form of stock options) gained through a short-term gaming of the system or through real value creation for organizational stakeholders? Taking a step back, is "pay" used as the single motivating factor, thereby reducing employees to economically rational machines, or are broader purposes (i.e., service, development) emphasized to set work into a meaningful context?

Applying Christian ethics to pay philosophies and practices, nonmaterial, motivational factors (satisfaction from shared purpose, teamwork, personal development, etc.) should also be emphasized. Justice concerns should be expressed in how pay is actually distributed. Are the lowest status members of the organization fairly treated? Do they receive appropriate recognition for their work and opportunities for development? Consistent with these themes, some organizations limit executive pay to a set multiple of the lowest or average of other employees. Other organizations take deliberate measures to more evenly distribute bonuses in good times and to share in the burdens in difficult periods (through reduced pay and other measures of shared sacrifice).

Monitoring employees in order to measure their performance and/or compliance with company policies is not just a technological matter but a values matter that Christian ethics can inform as well. Rapid developments in technology allow for cheap and accurate data collection. Computer and/or GPS monitoring are widely used as are performance metrics such as call or customer volume, lines of computer code written, number of closed sales to appointments, etc.

Some performance measures are used simply because data *can* be collected. This may lead to the neglect of other behaviors that may be in reality more important to the organization but can't be easily measured. Other metrics (i.e., many sales commission systems) can encourage employees to game the system and/or compete in unhealthy ways with colleagues. Data can also be collected in ways that are intrusive, that strip employees of their dignity as people, and that communicate a lack of trust (as Erisman notes; possibly a self-fulfilling prophecy).

Justice is another concern that is manifested in electronic monitoring. Often lower-level employees are the ones who are most closely scrutinized.

While one could argue that these workers could quit if they don't like it, they are in a much more vulnerable position and must accept working conditions that are offered. When dealing with someone in a more vulnerable position, there is a fine line between negotiation and exploitation.

Sometimes monitoring employees is not a choice. Vicarious liability may make employing organizations responsible when an employee gets into a vehicular accident while in a company vehicle or if reported sexual harassment is not stopped. Contractual requirements (i.e., for security purposes) may also mandate the collection of some data. At other times, information is collected for a legitimate purpose (i.e., GPS tracking of delivery services, safety in public transportation), but in the absence of policies about when, under what conditions (i.e., just cause), and who reviews the information, the potential for abuse looms large. With the use of any technology, whether we "should" do so must be asked alongside of whether we "can." And the "should" must be informed by whether employees are treated in a way that reflects the fact that they are made in God's image.

Taking these concepts and applying them to job design looks much different than an efficiency-driven model. A well known, and still influential, illustration of the role and impact of values in management theory is scientific management, as developed by the likes of Fredrick Winslow Taylor. Under this approach, workers were assumed to be only interested in making money. Work tasks (then primarily in factories) were designed for maximum *efficiency*. Taylor thoroughly studied the movements of factory workers and reorganized their work (along the lines of choreography in some cases), resulting in the dramatic reduction of the number of workers (from 600 to 140) needed in an iron plant.[8]

The human costs were, however, like increased absenteeism, staggering, and the gains were only short term. Taylor ignored the uniquely human aspects of workers, failing to realize that they would not respond in machine-like fashion for very long. Taylor's theories were highly influential in the design of early factories (i.e., for Ford's Model T) and are still around today. Recently past and contemporary foci on "reengineering" and "lean and mean" efficiency performance metrics via technology are visible relics of the influence of scientific management.

Employees should also have a say in what they do and how they do it. Of course, getting enough done (efficiency) is a serious consideration, but the work should be designed to maximize what is uniquely human about it in terms of purpose, variety, creativity, and responsibility.

Of course, tasks need to be accomplished to keep an organization afloat, but people need more than money, and these needs are reflected in how jobs and specific tasks may be designed. Is work designed in such a way that it

[8] See Lee Hardy, *The Fabric of This World* (Grand Rapids: Eerdmans, 1990), 128–40, for a thoughtful description and critique of Taylor's philosophy and work.

honors the development of whole persons and helps them flourish (excellent, socially responsible, and engaging as summarized by Beaton and Wagener)?

Managers and the practices they use can influence people's lives for good or ill. Organizations (and their managers) that consider the deeper needs of employees for challenging, rewarding, and bounded work, and that operate fairly and justly will more likely create life-giving work experiences. In contrast, those that primarily emphasize material rewards, efficiency, and productivity or tacitly allow them to trump all other concerns, may well harm people and in the long run may undermine their ability to achieve what they intend.

EIGHT

Accounting and Finance

Introduction

The near collapse of the world's financial system in 2007–9 brought serious ethical issues in finance and accounting to the front pages of the world's newspapers again. The unprecedented government bailout of many of the largest banks and insurance companies in the world made headlines throughout the world's media and put government in the position of being a shareholder in some of them. The stock market lost roughly half its value in less than a year, and the retirement accounts of millions of individuals suffered such precipitous declines that many people who had planned on retiring now need to work indefinitely. All of this resulted in the worst economic slowdown since the Great Depression of the 1920s and '30s. Though it would not be accurate to describe this as a failure of global capitalism, it is clear that it was a failure of the global *financial* system. Wall Street firms justifiably received a great deal of the criticism, though the banks headquartered there share the blame with other financial institutions, such as mortgage companies and government-sponsored entities (GSEs) such as Fannie Mae and Freddie Mac, both of which were fully taken over by the federal government.

The causes of the global financial meltdown have been the subject of numerous books, but there seems to be consensus about some of the primary causes.[1] The roots of the crisis lie in the period of the late 1970s and '80s with the government's intensifying pressure on banks and mortgage companies to increase home ownership to historically disadvantaged communities. Combine that with unprecedented low interest rates throughout the late 1990s and early 2000s, due to the stock market crash in the late '90s and the 9/11 tragedy in 2001. This made it very cheap for virtually everyone to borrow money, and both individuals and institutions significantly increased their debt load. In addition, in 1999, the Clinton administration repealed the Glass-Steagall Act, which allowed investment banks on Wall Street to become commercial banks that accepted deposits.

To be more specific, the financial crisis began with the increasing issuance

[1] For one of the better analyses of the financial crisis, see Mark Zandi, *Financial Shock: Global Panic and Government Bailouts* (Upper Saddle River, N.J.: Pearson Education, 2009). See also Bethany McLean and Joe Nocera, *All the Devils Are Here: The Hidden History of the Financial Crisis* (New York: Portfolio, 2010).

of subprime mortgages—higher risk loans to more marginally qualified borrowers, which charged a higher interest rate to the borrower to compensate for the increased risk. These loans would be made by mortgage originators, who were paid a commission whenever they closed a loan. Those mortgages were then sold to financial intermediaries, such as banks, Wall Street, and Fannie Mae and Freddie Mac, who converted them to investment securities. The securities were then bundled in thousands, and pieces of those packages of mortgages were sold to investors around the world and often kept by the banks on their books as their investments too. These securities became increasingly complex instruments known as *derivatives*, and the ratings agencies, such as Moody's and Standard and Poor's, generally gave them AAA grade ratings. Investors looking for better returns and safer investments were eager to buy these mortgage-backed securities and their derivatives, since interest rates in the market were so low and the stock market had proven to be so volatile in the past decade.

The system that generated these mortgages soon became corrupted, and there were ethics failures at every point in the system. Mortgage originators began making adjustable rate loans to people who could not possibly repay them when they reset at the higher rates, usually in one to two years. The credit-worthiness of borrowers became increasingly irrelevant, as did the traditional documentation for their income. These subprime loans became known in the industry as "liar's loans" or NINJA loans—in which the acronym stood for "no income, no job, or assets." The mortgage originators didn't care much about the borrowers' ability to pay, since they were selling the loans to banks within a few months of closing the transactions. The banks (including Fannie Mae and Freddie Mac) who purchased the loans to convert them into securities assumed that even if some borrowers defaulted, the package of mortgages was so large that the defaults would be offset by the large number of them that were being paid on time. They assumed that housing prices would continue to rise, so that even if the default rate was greater, there was sufficient equity in the home to cover the mortgage balance. The ratings agencies thus rated them with the highest grade available. Investors couldn't get enough of them, and the mortgage companies couldn't close the loans fast enough to satisfy demand.

But then the unthinkable happened. Home owners began defaulting in alarming numbers, as the introductory low rate adjustable loans reset to higher interest rates. Further, housing prices actually began to fall, sharply in some areas, such as California, Arizona, and Nevada. That put many home owners "underwater" in their mortgages, which meant that they owed more than their home was worth. As the defaults continued, the securities that were based on these mortgages declined substantially in value, and the banks that were either attempting to sell them to investors or holding them on their own books now faced precipitous losses that threatened to send them into bankruptcy. In addition, insurance companies that had guaranteed these bonds against default were faced with a landslide of claims that they could not possibly pay out, sending companies such as AIG into potential bankruptcy. Many of the major banks were threatened with insolvency, and some of the leading investment banking firms either went bankrupt (Lehman Brothers) or were merged with other banks at essentially "fire sale" prices (Bear Stearns, Merrill Lynch). Many of these derivative securities that were generated by Wall Street and sold to investors were so complex that it was virtually impossible to know what they were worth. As a result of this mortgage meltdown, the banks had to hold on to as much of their capital as they could in order to cover potential losses, thereby causing the credit markets virtually to freeze. Banks quit lending money, and businesses that were dependent on these loans for their survival saw their financial lifeline disappear. This was the primary cause of the recession of 2007–9, and though the stock market has somewhat recovered and the banks are lending again, the shock waves that this sent through the world financial system nearly brought it to a collapse. The combination of *relaxed standards*, both for lending and for rating the mortgage-backed securities, the assumption of *perpetual value increase* in the housing market, and the *accepted complexity* of the derivatives and other investments all contributed to the near collapse of the financial system.

There were ethics failures at every stage in this system. Mortgage originators made loans to people they knew would default, but they didn't care because they would be paid regardless and the loans would be sold to someone else to service. Banks, including Wall Street and Freddie Mac and Fannie Mae, were "securitizing" these pools of mortgages (turning them into securities) and selling them to investors. They were reaping substantial fees for the process, and toward the end, they were dumping what they suspected were worthless securities onto unsuspecting investors. Wall Street was criticized for losing sight of its original mission of investment banking — making capital available to business — in favor of risky, highly leveraged trading of derivatives for its own in-house accounts. The ratings agencies routinely gave these securities AAA ratings, even though they were being paid by the banks that were issuing the securities. The ratings companies were making huge profits due to the volume of securitization and did not want to alienate the issuers who were paying them. It was "every man for himself" in this process, and government played a role too. The Securities and Exchange Commission (SEC) was criticized for its lax oversight, especially of the derivates, and congressional oversight of Fannie Mae and Freddie Mac was widely criticized as well. Shortsighted public policy contributed to an environment where greed flourished without many restraints and with catastrophic results.

[2] For one of the numerous accounts of the demise of Enron, see Bethany McLean and Peter Elkind, *The Smartest Guys in the Room: The Amazing Rise and Scandalous Fall of Enron* (New York: Portfolio, 2003).

[3] Cynthia Cooper, *Extraordinary Circumstances: The Journey of a Corporate Whistleblower* (Hoboken, N.J.: John Wiley and Sons, 2008).

[4] For more on the role of Arthur Andersen, see Barbary Ley Toffler with Jennifer Reingold, *Final Accounting: Ambition, Greed, and the Fall of Arthur Andersen* (New York: Broadway, 2003).

[5] John Byrne, "Restoring Trust in Corporate America," *Business Week*, June 24, 2002, 31–44. See also Joseph Nocera, "System Failure," *Fortune*, June 24, 2002, 62–74.

Since the late 1990s, accounting ethics has been prominently in the news as well, as a result of numerous high-profile accounting scandals. Perhaps the best known of these involved the collapse of Enron in 2001, as a result of fraudulent accounting that covered up years of losses.[2] You will read more about Enron in chapter 11, in which an interview with Sherron Watkins will highlight the organizational problems that led to the accounting problems. Other well-known accounting scandals, many of which resulted in company officials going to prison, include the phone company WorldCom,[3] cable TV giant Adelphia, Tyco, Sunbeam, Waste Management, health care giant Columbia/HCA, and Global Crossing. The accounting giant Arthur Andersen was implicated in some of these failed audits and suffered a substantial decline in the aftermath of its involvement with Enron.[4] These accounting failures shook the integrity of the profession, leading to the Sarbanes-Oxley Act in 2002, calling for greater transparency in financial reporting. *Business Week*'s cover story in the aftermath of Enron was about this erosion of trust in public accounting, capturing the fundamental ethical issues involved.[5]

The temptation to "cook the books" and make a company look like a better performer than it actually is has been around for some time. Agencies such as the SEC, which regulates the stock markets and the financial activity of publicly traded companies, and public accounting firms, which audit companies regularly, are both designed to assure the investing public that they can trust the financial statements that a company issues. Though the cases of clear fraud are the ones that make the headlines, they are the exception to the general rule.

Accounting standards are known by the acronym GAAP, or generally accepted accounting principles. These reflect the rules governing accounting practice, both in internal accounting and auditing. Sometimes new ways of doing business at times reflect a need to develop new principles or adapt existing ones. This was true in the past as companies did business on the Internet for the first time, or as health care companies wrestled with new ways of accounting for revenues, or as financial services firms accounted for increasingly complex products. A key dynamic in this process is that when the current interpretation of the rules is challenged by new ways of doing business, it usually takes some time for the accounting profession to react and carefully clarify how the standards should be applied or adapted to these new ways of conducting business. The final standards reflect an emerging consensus about the proper ways to account for particular transactions. The fact that "everyone is doing it" may actually be an indication of this new consensus rather than a rationalization for unethical behavior.

To understand the pressures on management and in particular on the company's financial officers, let's put a publicly traded company in a broader context. Think about four groups of individuals/institutions and how each group is involved in the process of investing and financial accountability. The first group is the *investing public*, which includes (1) individual investors, either through direct stock purchases or mutual funds; (2) institutional investors, such as pension fund managers and mutual fund managers; and (3) investment advisers, which include stockbrokers and financial planners. The second group is what we will call the *market makers*. It includes brokerage houses, banks, and stock analysts. This group of companies is what is commonly knows as "Wall Street," since most of the major market makers are located on Wall Street or close to it in New York City. Market makers are very influential on the direction of the stock market, and the opinions of stock analysts can move the market up or down depending on the opinions they issue. The third group is the *executive management* of publicly traded companies, which includes the top executives and is accountable to the board of directors. The board is ultimately responsible for the company's performance, though board members are traditionally distinct from the executive management. If the performance of management is not up to the investors' or analysts' expectations, then the investors can and often do sell the company's stock, sometimes sending its price downward and decreasing its market value. Thus the management feels great pressure to meet those expectations, which are passed along to the fourth and final group involved in this process, the *accountants and chief financial officers*, who are responsible for preparing the company's financial statements. They are guided by basic accounting conventions and by the generally accepted accounting principles, and have outside auditors who check the statements in order to assure the public that the statements are accurate and trustworthy.

To properly understand the "story" of the ethics of accounting and finance in the past few years, one needs to see it in the context of all four of these important parties. The role of accountants/CFOs and executive management is often the focus of ethics discussions in finance and accounting. The important side of this discussion is the pressure brought to bear on companies from the investing public and market makers to make a company's earnings appear as positive as possible, and to do so on a quarterly basis. It is this pressure that has driven many of the ethical dilemmas and cases of outright accounting fraud that have been in the business headlines in the past few years. You should recognize that the pressure on financial professionals comes not only from their CEOs and boards of directors, but the ultimate source of that pressure is the investing public and market makers who serve them.

The area of accounting/finance ethics is very broad, and it is easy to get caught up in the technicalities of specific accounting practices. In this chapter, our goal is to give you an overview of the various ethical issues that face accountants and financial professionals and some general principles for accounting with integrity. Some of the cases will put you in the place of the chief financial officer of a company facing ethical decisions on how to report your company's earnings in its financial statements. Others will put you in the position of the outside auditor, and you will wrestle with the ethical pressures that come with that position, where you are paid by the company you are auditing but also have a responsibility to the public. Another set of issues come more from the area of public policy for the financial professions and include areas such as insider trading, a long-term concern for the law.

The readings for this chapter will introduce you to the issues involved in accounting and finance. Ian Stewart, in his piece entitled "Accounting and Accountability: Double Entry, Double Nature, Double Identity," with a play on words for the double entry method of accounting, highlights the dual responsibilities of the accountant, particularly the auditor, both to the client and to the investing public, not to mention the conflict between the accountant's own integrity and his obligation to his company. He correctly describes accounting as an *interpretive art* that involves more than simply recording transactions (which is more the function of bookkeeping).

George Staubus, in his piece "Ethical Failures in Corporate Financial Reporting," expands Stewart's analysis and focuses it more specifically on accounting failures, both by corporate accountants and auditors. He particularly highlights the conflicting obligations of the auditor to the client who is paying his or her fees and to the investing public who is relying on the trustworthiness of the audit. He points out that calling the one paying for services the "client" is problematic since it subordinates the interests of the investing public to that of the client. He laments what he calls "auditor bias" toward the client at the expense of the investing public.

Moving into finance and out of accounting, John Terrill, in "The Moral Imperative of Investment Banking," looks at investment banking as a moral enterprise. This stands in sharp contrast to the public perception of Wall Street as a game that is rigged against the average investor, serving the interests of the banks, not the investing public or the business community. Terrill argues that the mission of investment banking is to make capital available to business and thereby insure that the business has the liquidity it needs to function. He sets his argument in the context of the recovery of Wall Street from the financial crisis, in part due to the bailouts from the federal government. This stands in contrast to the criticism of Wall Street that a disproportionate share of its revenues comes not from traditional investment banking but on trading for its own in-house accounts.[6]

[6] For more on this criticism, see Kevin Phillips, *Bad Money: Reckless Finance, Failed Politics, and the Global Crisis of American Capitalism* (New York: Viking, 2008), 29–68.

READINGS

Accounting and Accountability: Double Entry, Double Nature, Double Identity

I. C. Stewart

Crux 26, no. 2 (June 1990): 13–20.

Introduction

The basic activity of accounting is "giving an account." The primary function of the accountant is getting private or semiprivate information from the accounter (the managers) and abstracting it in a more public manner for whoever the accountees may be.[1] The accountees are no longer the owners and creditors, but nowadays the list includes suppliers, employees, investment advisors, business connections of various types, the government, and the public in general.[2] The problem of discerning the truth of this information flow from accountor to accountee gives rise to

The investigator says of the chairman of the Group, Mr. Donald Cormie, that he "deliberately permitted the companies to carry on while he took steps to disguise their true financial situation."[4] The investigator reported that the glossy 1985 annual review of the Principal Group contained a statement by the Chairman that the Group had made a profit of $607,000 in 1985, when the audited statements showed it suffered a $25.7 million loss. The $1.2 billion financial empire collapsed two years later in 1987. Meanwhile, a lot of people lost their life savings because of the misleading information put out by the Group.

Figure 1: The Accountability Relation

Accountor (Managers & their Accountants) ---- Auditors ----> Accountees (Shareholders, creditors, employees, suppliers, public, government)

the auditing profession. In terms of the accountability relation, the auditor comes between the accounter and the accountees to assure the integrity and the trustworthiness of the information.

The particular concern, of course, is that the accounters might engage in bluffing. By being given an intentionally deceptive message, accountees are unable to act in ways that they might act otherwise.[3] In his report on the collapse of the Principal Group, the Edmonton-based financial empire, the court-appointed investigator concluded that the company literature, designed to attract investors, clearly did not paint a true financial picture of the struggling empire.

This case highlights the elasticity of generally acceptable accounting principles. Although the accountant's judgment is more bounded nowadays than in the past, nevertheless, considerable discretion remains, enough for accounting practice to be described as an interpretive art. The purpose of the first section of this paper is to engage in a little accounting hermeneutics by considering the accountant as a producer of "text."[5] The emphasis is not on the double entry structure of accounts but on the interpretive act of making an account.

The second section of the paper examines the assumptions about human nature which underlie the interpretive act of making an account. The third section takes up the notion of accountability, and following William Schweiker's analysis, suggests that accountability enacts a doubleness crucial to our moral identity. In the final section, the paper outlines some of the implications for accounting practice of this construal of accountability.

Double Entry Languages

Accounting texts use three languages: English (in British Columbia), double entry, and mathematics. It is the last two which best characterize the work accountants do. Accounting practice is framed by an over-arching metaphor of numeracy. The columns of figures with their dual structure and mathematical accuracy create a presumption that the accountant's work is objective, that the accountant is representing reality "as is" through the use of numbers that are objective and value-free. The profit and loss, for example, is not thought of as a "mere" matter of interpretation, dependent on the accountant's perspective, values, or skill. The accountant is paid not merely to provide his/her point of view on the profit and loss status of the firm, but to state the objective facts of the matter.[6]

The truth is that the adequacy of accounts is no simple matter of their calculative accuracy, which can be determined independently of the concrete circumstances of the persons who make them. Accounting, as Don Lavoie points out, should be understood as a language; that is, a process of bidirectional and interpersonal communication.[7] Language, Lavoie states, "is not just talk, it is our way of seeing the real world."[8] So modern accounting is a way of writing the world. Gareth Morgan notes how the numerical view highlights those aspects of organizational reality that are quantifiable and built into the accounting framework (for example, flows of costs, revenues, and other values), but ignores those aspects of organizational reality that are not quantifiable in this way. Morgan illustrates this way: "Just as we might attempt to rate the quality of last night's dinner on a scale of 1–10, and in giving it a '9' capture that it was indeed a very good meal, the accountant's numerical form or representation provides a very 'thin' and limited char-

acterization. It leaves much of the quality and overall experience of the meal out of account. The metaphor 'it was a 9' remains silent on so many things."[9] So Morgan concludes by emphasizing that "accountants are always engaged in *interpreting* a complex reality, partially, and in a way that is heavily weighted in favor of what the accountant is *able* to measure and *chooses* to measure, through the particular schemes of accounting to be adopted."[10]

An Interpretive Art

What are some of the interpretive acts accountants make in drawing up accounts? The first involves the question of what items or events qualify for recognition on the financial statements. For example, in the balance sheet, the question of which assets or liabilities to include or exclude depends on how intangible, uncertain, unenforceable, unidentifiable, or nonseverable the item is that it ceases to be part of the organization.[11] For example, some New York banks now have what are described as "financial engineers" whose task it is to come up with new financial instruments to window dress the client's balance sheet.

Once a decision has been made to recognize certain items on the financial statements, the next step is to determine how these items are to be measured. A number of attributes could be chosen, such as historic cost, current cost, net realizable value, and present value. Answers to these recognition and measurement questions will define the size, health, structure, and performance — in other words — the reality of the organization.

Peter Miller and Ted O'Leary[12] have recently noted how the numerical view can also be allowed to shape the reality of the organization through the routine operation of the organization's *internal* accounting system, for example, people, students, patients, and work teams become profit centers generating revenues and expenses. Where financial considerations become a major issue, the data generated can exert a decisive influence on the accountant's reality construction.

Miller and O'Leary observe how by the use of standard costing and budgeting the accountant constructs a particular field of visibility. The accountant renders visible certain crucial aspects of the function of the enterprise. Standard costing enmeshed the factory worker within a calculus of efficiency and later moved on by means of the budget to do the same for executives. By surrounding individuals with norms and standards by which inefficiencies and wastes are rendered visible, a whole range of calculation programs and techniques come to dominate the life of the individual, and accounting becomes part of the network of power relations that are built into the very fabric of organizational life.[13]

So the accountant's role should not be seen as a merely technical one. The accountant is not an uncontested figure who reveals a pre-existing reality, a realm of fact, a realm of measurable efficiency.

Accounting is more like a photograph — it is taken from a particular vantage point, with a particular lens, at a particular time, for a particular purpose. In a sense, accountants do reflect reality, for example, cash at a bank corresponds to the number of monetary tokens held by the bank. But accounting is also constitutive, and people act on the basis of the picture which is painted.

It is important, however, to emphasize that there are often close affinities between the kinds of professional judgments which are made by accountants. Moreover, accounts are more than an expression of the subjective whims of various accountants. There are such things as generally acceptable accounting principles. The point to be emphasized in the present context is that accounts are not objectivistic in the sense of a pointer-reading science. To argue that accounting is like a barometer, or speedometer, for example, is to grossly misunderstand its nature.

It is the softness, then, of accounting numbers that is the reason why managers are so interested in them, for they can manipulate them where they may be motivated to do so.

Manager's Choice of Accounting Procedures

The most widely accepted explanatory theory of manager's choice of accounting procedures is based on the economics theory of the firm. This theory borrows on the property rights literature because of its emphasis on rights established by contract. Under this view, the firm is not a separate contract. Under this view, the firm is not a separate entity; rather it is composed of individuals who have contracted with the legal entity for certain property and it is these individuals who have objectives, namely, to maximize their utility. The firm is viewed as a team of self-interested individuals who recognize that their own welfare depends on the firm's success in competition with other firms. Each of the individuals comprising the firm contributes some input to the firm's productive process (raw materials, capital, managerial skills, labor). These individuals supply in expectation of earning a rate of return on their investment. Each recognizes that the other individuals will take action to maximize their utility so that conflicts of interest are bound to arise. To reduce these conflicts, the individuals write *contracts* that will specify each individual's specific rights in the firms' outputs under various contingencies, for example, specifying how the cash flows will be distributed in the event of bankruptcy.

Accounting is an integral part of these contracts, both in the drawing up of the terms of the contract and the monitoring of them. Contracts will not reduce the costs of conflict unless the firm can determine if the contract has been breached.

Empirical research[14] has shown that two financial contracts are particularly important in explaining managers' choice of accounting procedures. These are management compensation contracts and debt contracts.

Management compensation contracts are one means of aligning the managers' interests with the shareholders. Typically, managers are given a bonus, which is a function of their net income. In this situation managers obviously have strong incentives to prefer income-increasing accounting procedures. If managers controlled the calculation of net income, bonus plans would not exist for incentive purposes. To offset the manager's optimism, conservative accounting procedures are specified in the compensation contract.

Debt contracts usually contain a covenant that is designed to protect the debtholders from the managers using borrowed money for their own purposes and leaving them with a shell. Typically, the covenant specifies that the debt shall not exceed a certain proportion of total assets, or that net income shall cover interest on debt by a certain multiple. Again, managers running close to these restrictions have strong incentives to adopt income increasing accounting procedures. The reason for this is that infringement of debt covenants would entail costly renegotiation and possibly higher interest rates which would reduce net income and with it managers' bonus payments and the value of their share options.

Research has shown that there is one other key variable in manager's choice of accounting procedures, and that is political costs. The theory here builds on the economic theory of the political process in which the political process is viewed as a competition for wealth transfers. To the extent that a given firm is subject to potential wealth transfers in the political process (chiefly via taxes and regulations of various sorts), its managers are hypothesized to adopt accounting procedures that reduce the size of the transfer. For example, managers of the large oil companies use accounting procedures that reduce net income in order to defuse arguments that they are profiteering.

The empirical tests to which the theory of manager's choice of accounting procedures has been put show a very high degree of support for this sort of research.[15] It seems to be widely accepted today that managers, far from presenting a true and fair view of their corporations' operations and financial positions, choose those accounting procedures that will maximize their own self-interests. And the auditing profession, far from balancing the scales in favor of the public interest, appears to be sliding relentlessly into retailing representations in almost any way management might want. "Accountants," as John Nelson observes, "are rapidly becoming guns for hire with no code of honor to give their services adequate direction of justification."[16]

Sociobiology and Behavior Theory

This view from the accounting and economics literature that every agent is actuated only by self-interest is also consistent with sociobiology and behavior theory.[17] The modern incarnation of Darwin's evolutionary biology is known as sociobiology. The central dogma of evolutionary biology is that significant char-

acteristics are passed from parents to offspring in the genes. Not all organisms will be successful at surviving and reproducing, and thus not all genes will be equally likely to pass from one generation to the next. The genes that do survive will be the ones that make successful organisms. As a result, only genes that see to the successful pursuit of self-interest by organisms will survive. The implication of this line of thinking is that selfishness—the single-minded pursuit of genetic self-interest—is a biological fact of life, a natural necessity. What sociobiology has done is extend the concept of economic self-interest to domains of life that have been excluded by economists—domains including social relations within a group, relations between parents and offspring, and relations between mates. Human selfishness is clearly seen as a reflection of a natural law since it is of a piece with the selfishness of ants, birds, fish, and other living organisms.

In behavior theory (also cast in the shadow of Darwinism), organisms engage in essentially random activity. Some of that behavior has favorable consequences; it results in states of the environment that organisms want, that are reinforcing. The behavior that results in reinforcing consequences and only that behavior, continues to occur; other less successful behavior drops out. Because of this natural selection by reinforcement of behavior that works, the organisms that are seen have learned to do just the right thing to produce the outcomes they want or need. So just as the maximization of reproductive success drives the evolution of the species, the maximization of reinforcement or self-interest drives the development of individuals.

This picture of organisms as pursuers of reinforcement maximization fits nicely with the model of rational economic man. As Barry Schwartz concludes, "When we add these three disciplines together, they converge on a picture of self-interested, acquisitive human nature that is truly formidable."[18] The economist now says that people by their very natures are greedy economic men and women and can now turn in defense to sociobiology and behavior theory. The sociobiologist contends that birds and fish do not live in an artificially created free market society and yet they pursue self-interest also. The behavior theorist has evidence that human flexibility and diversity are themselves governed by principles of self-interest maximization.

In the sections that follow, the question of how one thinks with and yet gets beyond notions of rational agency centering on a self-realizing "I" are addressed.

Double Nature

It must be recognized at the outset that the deterministic, naturalistic approach is a necessary postulate of the scientific enquiry, and as John Macmurray[19] has noted, serves not merely to dictate its methodology, but also to isolate the aspect of personal behavior, which is amenable to the method. This is true of all the research outlined here from the accounting, economics, sociobiology and behavioral literature. "The method is to search for patterns of behavior which recur without change, and to formulate these in 'laws' of general application."[20] The result is an objective knowledge of other persons, knowledge that is *impersonal.*

It was Macmurray who showed that the *personal* is constituted by personal relatedness. The unit of the personal is not the "I" but the community of the YOU and I. This community is not merely a matter of fact (upon which all scientific knowledge is based), but it is also a matter of intention. Macmurray contrasts personal and impersonal knowledge in this way: "The one assumes and implies that men are free agents, responsible for their behavior, choosing their mode of action in the light of a distinction between right and wrong; the other that all human behavior follows determined patterns, and that the laws which we obey are, like those which govern all natural objects, discoverable by objective scientific methods of investigation. This duality of knowledge, personal and impersonal, is the concrete statement of the antinomy of freedom and determinism."[21]

This corresponds to the double element in man. On the one hand, man's creatureliness is emphasized in the deterministic, naturalistic view of man, and on the other hand, man's freedom is emphasized in man's agency as determinative.

As Macmurray concludes, "The question is not whether the personal conception of men as free agents or the scientific conception of man as a determined being is correct. Both are correct."[22] Macmurray goes on to explain that this is possible because they do not refer to the same field. Science is a deliberate attempt to improve and extend generalized knowledge of man. "Its field of reference is the genus *Homo sapiens*, that is to say, the class of existents which are identifiable by observation, as possessing the factual characteristics by which objects are assigned to this class."[23] The concept of the personal, by contrast, Macmurray argues, is not an exclusive concept. It is primarily the field in which we know one another as persons in relation. It includes the objective knowledge of one another we possess, but it does not take the scientific account as a complete account—as absolute and not relative—so that it entails the rejection of the personal conception, with the freedom it implies.[24] It is the attempt by accountants, economists, sociobiologists, and behaviorists to bring human existence under one sign only—that of nature—that must be objected to. It cannot be agreed that scientific research fixes human nature as always and only self-interested, permanently putting it outside the pale of argument. But while, on the one hand, Christians cannot accept a morality which regards sin as a given; neither, on the other hand, can they appeal to personal agency as the source of self-determination as though man's powers of rational, moral, and creative thought could bring his life to fulfillment. As V. A. Demant puts it, "The root of sin and non-fulfillment lies not in man's finitude, but in his disobedience to the laws of his being set by his creator."[25]

As Demant notes, each of these poles denies one aspect of man's double nature. History seems to swing from the perversions of one to exaggerations of the other. Secularism cannot find a point of unity behind the duality. There can only be a unity between freedom and dependency as it is recognized that Christian freedom, given by the Holy Spirit, must be accompanied by respect for the moral order which exists.

If economic forces are to be rendered morally responsible, the starting point must be to emphasize Macmurray's insights of the person as agent and personal existence constituted by the relation of persons. For if there is no moral agency, then as Francis and Arrington observe, "the whole question of accountability dissipates ... a subject who acts based on an involuntary inheritance from 'nature' cannot be accountable for those actions simply because she/he has no capacity to act otherwise."[26] And if this is true, mankind has become slaves to its own creations and the earth is subject to unending exploitation under the aegis of efficiency.[27]

Accountability

As Macmurray defines it, free agency is purposive action, and action is defined by intention.[28] Alasdair MacIntyre describes it this way: "To identify an occurrence as an action is ... to identify it under a type of description which enables us to see that occurrence as flowing intelligibly from a human agent's intentions, motives, passions and purposes. It is therefore to understand action as something for which someone is accountable, about which it is always appropriate to ask the agent for an intelligible account."[29] In a similar vein, William Schweiker has put it this way: "Giving an account is providing reasons for character and conduct, ones held to be understandable to others and thereby rendering life intelligible and meaningful."[30]

Schweiker argues that giving an account is crucial for moral life. "The ability to engage freely in purposive actions, to undergo, interpret and evaluate actions and relations, to make judgments of praise and blame, and to account for all of these activities is constitutive of the being of an agent.[31]

Double Identity

For it to be "appropriate to ask the agent for an intelligible account," to use MacIntyre's words, "there must be some norms, values, and beliefs that one shares in common with the agent—there must be some pre-understandings that warrant the attempt to place the agent in the position of responding to such a request."[32] This makes giving an account intrinsically a social act. To be accountable is first, as Macmurray put it, to be persons-in-relation or an individual-in-community.

As Schweiker has pointed out, this is why "when I say something about my life I do not simply instantiate the identity of the 'I.' On the contrary, there is enacted a pre-given relation to myself as an actor and to others. Not surprisingly, when this doubleness in identity is brought to light, by whatever means, it

can evoke a shock of self-recognition, understanding, a sense of pride, flat denial, shame or simple evasion about who we are and what we are doing."[33]

Schweiker argues that this otherness found in personal identity is also present in corporations. It inheres in the fiduciary relation between a company and the accountant. It is enacted when the accountant portrays relations relative to the larger community of accounters. Schweiker admits that persons and corporations are different and radically so, but he contends that the activity of accounting enacts a doubleness crucial to moral identity. This is because it evokes some awareness of pre-given relations to others, relations subject to claims about what is good and evil.[34]

Then secondly, Schweiker notes that because identity so engendered is deeply social, the motive of being accountable is never simple unadorned self-interest.[35] It entails a constitutive relation to others beyond simple contractual relations. This means that the reasons why people do things are infinitely complex. Humans are accountable to God, their church communities, their families, their environment, their colleagues, and so on. Action is defined by intention, and so the purpose of accountability is to reveal the agent's intentions, passions, motives, and purposes, not simply to presuppose the single motive of self-interest.

Finally, Schweiker argues that this construal of accountability says something about the limits of responsibility and its scope.[36] Schweiker suggests that agents are normally only accountable for actions they intended and/or undertook either directly or through the aid of others. However, he argues that the limits of accountability must be set within its scope. Insofar as giving an account is a rendering forth of the social and temporal structure of life, that scope is indeed considerable. It potentially opens onto an unlimited horizon of community. The structure of giving an account raises the questions: accountable to whom and whose needs are to count?

What Are the Implications for Accounting?

Schweiker draws attention to two sorts of conflicts faced by accountants and offers some guidance on adjudicating between them.[37] The first is a conflict of trusts or loyalties.[38] Insofar as the moral identity of a corporation is enacted through giving an account, then one norm of the accounting profession is that of integrity or truthfulness founded on trust. Hence the conflicts of loyalties that accountants have between their own moral integrity and the demands made on them by clients of the companies they work for. The dilemma for the accountant is to decide which relation of trust ought to override the other. Is the accountant the loyal agent of the corporation? For example, if management were to ask the accountant to change accounting procedures to achieve an increase in income, must the accountant oblige? Or, does the accountant have fiduciary obligation to render a truthful identity of that company and her- or himself.

Then giving an account not only understands moral identity around some norms but also addresses the question of what and whose goods the accountant serves. Clearly, the accountant serves the good of the agent (the accountor) and those others to whom the agent is responsible (the accountees). In other words, the self-interest of managers is always met and tested by other needs and good. This meeting, Schweiker argues, is "clarified through the activity of the accountant who, in the portrayal of an agent's identity, specifies that identity's interdependence with others, those to who one is then accountable."[39] Social responsibility, therefore, and concern for the common good must be part of the work of the accountant who takes on the burden of understanding his task as that of giving an account.

Just as there are conflicts of trusts so there are conflicts of goods. Which accountee's goods are to be pursued? For example, employees often sacrifice their health for corporations; corporations often sacrifice the common good to advance their own interests, for example, plant closures, pollution, and waste disposal. How then can the accountant adjudicate in these conflicts? If an accountable identity is constituted with others and open potentially to the whole horizon of time and community, Schweiker[40] argues that this implies:

1. consideration of the needs of others in the determination of courses of action since those others help to constitute an accountable identity;
2. in conflict situations, there is a presumption on behalf of the priority of the common good and

the needs of others. Thus private goods cannot override public goods.

Giving an account renders economic forces servants of larger human and environmental purposes without negating the singularity of their identities or motives. This is how the accounting profession can help marshal economic forces as powers for moral purposes. Yet it also means that the accountant cannot be made servile to corporate intentions and values because the accountant ultimately is the agent of a fiduciary relation through the scope of time and community. The accountant is then both an internal and external critic: *internal* because she/he is bound through a fiduciary relation to the corporation and its discourse: *external* because the accountant's perspective reaches beyond corporate intentions.

Epilogue

Schweiker's construal of accountability seems consistent with the emphasis found in biblical ethics on the need to prefer others' needs over one's own self-interests. But his notion needs to be radicalized further. Biblical ethicists would want to claim that as agents they live and act and have their being before God. Their decisions must be taken with a sense of accountability to God for the natural world and for one another, for the Christian life is a life in community. In this context, giving an account often takes the form of confession to God and to one another, as it did for Augustine who confessed his failure of trust and professed his thankfulness for God's faithfulness.

In summary, accounting is an interpretive art. Although the area for the exercise of professional judgment is somewhat more bounded than it used to be, managers and their accountants are free agents responsible for their choice of accounting procedures in righting the world. However, the scientific research agenda in accounting assumes that managers and their accountants follow a determined pattern, one dictated by their self-interests. Similar patterns of behavior have been observed by scientists working in the fields of economics, sociobiology, and behavior theory. The challenge presented by these research programs is that they do not have regard for the conception of man as a moral agent. As seen by the writers cited here, moral identity is constituted by the relation of persons. Insofar as the moral identity of a corporate agent is interpreted by the accountant in giving an account, accounting practice is determined by an internal ethic of truthfulness. This required the development of character sufficient to sustain accountants in this task. Insofar as an accountable identity is constituted with others (the larger community of accountees), social responsibility and concern for the common good must also be part of the work of an accountant. But more than this, the activity of all people, wherever they live and work, must be undertaken with a sense of accountability to God for the natural world, for one another, and for themselves.

Notes

1 C. T. Devine, *Essays in Accounting Theory,* Vol. V (Sarasota: American Accounting Association, 1985), 67.

2 Accounting Standards Steering Committee, *The Corporate Report* (London: Institute of Chartered Accountants in England and Wales, 1975).

3 J. C. Gaa, "User Primacy in Corporate Financial Reporting: A Social Contract Approach," *The Accounting Review* (July 1986), 443.

4 Reported in *The Vancouver Sun,* July 19, 1989, A1.

5 Useful introduction to accounting hermeneutics can be found in D. Lavoie, "The Accounting of Interpretations and the Interpretation of Accounts: The Communicative Function of 'The Language of Business,'" *Accounting, Organizations and Society,* Vol. 12, No. g (1987), 579–604.

6 Ibid., 580.

7 Ibid.

8 Ibid.

9 G. Morgan, "Accounting as Reality Construction: Towards a New Epistemology for Accounting Practice," *Accounting, Organizations and Society,* Vol.13, No. 5 (1988), 480.

10 Ibid., 480 (emphasis in original).

11 R. D. Hines, "Financial Accounting: In Communicating Reality We Construct Reality," *Accounting, Organizations and Society,* Vol. 13, No. 3 (1988), 251–61.

12 P. Miller and T. O'Leary, "Accounting and the Construction of the Governable Person," *Accounting, Organizations and Society,* Vol. 12, No. 3 (1987), 235–65.

13 Hoskin and Macve note that the origin of accounting as part of a disciplinary system of efficiency lies in the period 1810–1830 and emanates from the pedagogic arena. The authors contend that it was the invention of the academic mark, and its behavioral counterpart, the merit/demerit system, which provided a blueprint for rendering the individual worker (manager) a "calculable man." See K. W. Hoskin and R. H. Macve, "Accounting and the Examination; A Genealogy of Disciplinary Power," *Accounting, Organizations and Society,* Vol. 11, No. 2 (1986), 105–36; and by the same authors, "The Genesis of Accountability: The WestPoint Connections," *Accounting, Organizations and Society,* Vol. 13, No. 1 (1988), 37–73.

14 R. L. Watts, and J. L. Zimmerman, *Positive Accounting Theory* (Englewood Cliffs: Prentice-Hall, 1986).

15 Ibid.

16 J. Nelson, "Account and Acknowledge or Represent and Control? On Postmodern Politics and Economics of Collective Responsibility" (Unpublished manuscript, Department of Political Science, The University of Iowa, 1989), 6.

17 B. Schwartz, *The Battle for Human Nature* (New York: W. W. Norton & Company, 1986).

18 Ibid., 316.

19 J. Macmurray, *Persons in Relation* (London: Faber & Faber Limited, 1961), 39. I am grateful to Dr. Houston for referring me to this work.

20 Ibid.

21 Ibid., 30–31.

22 Ibid., 37.

23 Ibid., 38.

24 Ibid.

25 V. A. Demant, *Religion and the Decline of Capitalism* (London: Faber & Faber Limited, 1952), 114.

26 C. F. Arrington and J. R. Francis, "Accounting and The Labour of Text Production: Some Thoughts on the Hermeneutics of Paul Ricoeur" (Unpublished paper, Department of Accounting, The University of Iowa, 1989), 36.

27 W. Schweiker, "Accounting for Ourselves: Accounting and the Discourse of Ethics" (Unpublished paper, Divinity School, The University of Chicago, 1989), 1.

28 J. Macmurray, *Persons in Relation* (London: Faber & Faber Limited, 1961), 64.

29 A. MacIntyre, *After Virtue* (Notre Dame: University of Notre Dame Press, 1984), 209.

30 W. Schweiker, "Accounting for Ourselves: Accounting and the Discourse of Ethics" (Unpublished paper, Divinity School, The University of Chicago, 1989), 3.

31 Ibid., 3.

32 C. E. Arrington and J. R. Francis, "Accounting and the Labour of Text Production: Some Thoughts on the Hermeneutics of Paul Ricoeur" (Unpublished paper, Department of Accounting, The University of Iowa, 1989), 40.

33 Op. cit., 20. Thus there is an important linking between who one is and what one does, between one's character and one's conduct. Stanley Hauerwas argues that "Christian ethics is concerned more with who we are than what we do. This is not to suggest that our actions, decisions and choices are unimportant, but rather that the church has a stake in holding together our being and behaving in such a manner that our doing only can be a reflection of our character." *The Peaceable Kingdom* (Notre Dame: University of Notre Dame Press, 1983), 33–34. I am grateful to Dr. Houston for pointing me to Hauerwas's work.

34 Ibid., 20.

35 Ibid., 29.

36 Ibid., 30ff.

37 Ibid., 34ff.

38 L. Westra, "Whose Loyal Agent? Toward an Ethic of Accounting," *Journal of Business Ethics* (April 1986), 119–28.

39 Op. cit., 36.

40 Ibid., 38–39.

Questions for Discussion and Reflection

1. Stewart describes accounting as an "interpretive art." Do you agree with his assessment? Do you think seeing accounting this way opens the door to abuses?
2. What is the double identity problem, according to Stewart, and how does it apply to accounting?
3. Stewart suggests that there are two primary conflicts that accountants face—conflicts of trusts and conflicts of goods. What does he mean by each of these conflicts, and how does he suggest that these conflicts be resolved?

Ethical Failures in Corporate Financial Reporting

George J. Staubus

Journal of Business Ethics 57 (2005): 5–15.

Introduction

The focus of this essay is on ethical lapses that contribute to the failure of corporate accountants and auditors to fulfill their responsibilities for financial reporting to investors. In the context of the decentralized economies that are widely believed to serve the interests and aspirations of citizens of democracies in the 21st century, the role of investors (capitalists) is an important one. Success for absentee investors is critical to the continuing contribution of capital and capital markets to the welfare of those citizens. Information on enterprise success is a key link between suppliers of capital (household savers) and business enterprises employing that capital. When accountants (including auditors) fail to provide investors with reliable information that is relevant to their capital allocation decisions, investors and all citizens with stakes in the success of the economic system suffer.

Accounting failures are failures of individuals to perform their fiduciary duties, to fulfill their responsibilities, to behave ethically. Corporate accountants, financial officers, and top managers accept responsibility for reporting aspects of the financial affairs of the enterprise that investors can use in making their decisions, including evaluating the performance of management. Auditors accept responsibility for examining financial statements prepared by corporate personnel and attesting to their conformity with reporting standards. Accounting academics accept responsibility for contributing to the body of knowledge that can provide a basis for such financial reporting standards and for teaching that body of knowledge. Standards setters accept responsibility for the propriety of those standards as guides to financial reporting that can serve investors and society. Some members of all of those groups have failed to fulfill their responsibilities in recent years. A few of those failures have received so much attention that they have been recognized as scandals, often involving frauds; others appear as restatements of financial statements to correct reporting errors. A hypothesis of this paper is that many other failures are not recognized as frauds or restatements but nevertheless reduce the value of financial reports to their users. The purpose of this essay is to call attention to those failures, address the factors that underlie them, and suggest a few steps aimed at reducing their frequency in the future.

The dividing line between behavior that is acceptable and behavior that is unethical, or worse, is not always a bright one; different people see it in different places. We all recognize that individuals have responsibilities to themselves and their families—self-interest—that are not only legitimate but healthy. We have no desire to repeal the "law of self-preservation."

We all prefer higher incomes to lower incomes, and are expected to act accordingly—within limits. On the other hand, all of us are constrained in our behavior by ethical and legal bounds, but those constraints do not bind all of us equally. When in a critical mood, we may yearn for an old-fashioned sense of professional duty that for many has a religious context. Some believe (West, 2003) that members of a profession, in exchange for the prestige, independence, and incomes they are accorded, have responsibilities to serve clients, patients, and the public without always being concerned only with their own incomes. In this context, the question arises as to whether an auditor's primary responsibility is to the corporate management as client or to members of the investing public who rely on the financial reports.

A critical tone pervades this paper; I find much to criticize. My criticisms are aimed at features of the environment in which individuals act, rather than at individuals viewed as evil. Individuals willing to commit crimes will always be with us; I have no suggestions for making all humanity good. The few ideas I have for reducing the frequency of accounting failures involve changes in the institutional settings in which corporate accountants and managers, auditors, standards setters, and academics work.

Ethics Failures of Corporate Accountants and Managers

The ethics failures of a few corporate managers in recent years have received much publicity, but those few are newsworthy only because of the magnitude of their financial consequences; many others no doubt occur. Failures by management are mentioned first because corporate personnel have primary responsibility for financial reporting—more direct responsibility than that of auditors, academics, or accounting standards setters. They are the main perpetrators; others typically are only facilitators, or influencing parties.

Corporate accountants cannot be distinguished from corporate managers in this context. Personnel in financial management positions participate in management activities and in accounting decisions. Personnel in high corporate management positions participate in accounting decisions to the extent that

they influence those decisions. At the end of the day, the chief executive officer is the captain of the ship with the authority to determine the financial reporting and with responsibility for it, subject to the constraints imposed by external auditors. Financial reporting failures are failures by corporate managers. The motivations for managerial failures in the area of financial reporting are familiar. Whatever the form of the failure—outright fraud, earnings management, or honest bias—the corporate governance system with which I am familiar calls on management to report on its own performance, so the motivation to report financial information that makes management look good is built into the system. In the corporate governance system operating in large American corporations, it is common for top management to nominate individuals for membership on the board of directors, to control the proxy mechanism that assures the election of management's nominees, and, prior to 2002, to engage, work closely with, and dismiss the auditors, if they wish. When the management has the power to grant or take away valuable compensation and prestige enjoyed by friendly auditors and board members, those individuals are not fully independent of management. Instead, management controls them to some extent. Therefore, there is no independent control over management's reporting on its own performance, with the exception of the auditor's and management's fear of punitive sanctions if their failure is detected. That sets the stage for a significant probability of corporate reporting failures.

Strong motivation to succeed is a characteristic of managers that is not only natural and ethical but desirable from the standpoint of owners' interests. Substantially weakening it is not an objective. Uncontrolled power of top management, however, can yield undesirable results. Boards of directors and auditors have responsibility for such controls, but often fail to exercise it because of a lack of independence. The obvious public policy response is to require that nominations and elections of board members be controlled by shareholders with absolutely no involvement of management. Fortunately, substantial steps in these directions have been made in a few countries in the last two years, such as the Sarbanes-Oxley legislation and changes in the regulations of the Securities and Exchange Commission and the New York Stock Exchange in the U.S. and new rules established by the European Commission. But the principle of complete shareholder control has not been embraced.

Ethics Failures of Auditors

The starting point for a discussion of this subject must be recognition that auditors, in general, are not less ethical than other professionals and, in my experience, considerably more ethical than the typical member of several other professions. No remedy for the ethical failures of auditors that is based on the idea that the "bad apples" can be culled before they exhibit clearly unethical behavior will be successful. It is the corporate governance system in place in countries such as the U.S.A. that provides motivations for people with average ethical standards occasionally to fail. This assertion is supported in ensuing paragraphs by a description of the workings of that system in practice in the U.S. But first, I present a description of the system as the parties involved might see it at its best.

Participants' Views of the Current Governance/Auditing System

The views of three sets of participants are described here.

Managements' View

The Securities and Exchange Commission, an agency of the U.S. government, requires that companies whose securities are traded in a public market present "audited" periodic financial reports to the Commission and to the company's shareholders. Stock exchanges, such as the New York Stock Exchange, also require such reports. Company managers comply with those requirements by choosing an auditing firm to perform, for an agreed fee, an annual audit that culminates in an opinion stating whether or not the financial statements are presented fairly in accordance with generally accepted accounting principles (GAAP). Managers' criteria for choosing an auditing firm need not be disclosed. Their major concern is that the auditors render a favorable opinion that serves to lend credibility to their financial statements. Sec-

ondarily, managers feel responsible for minimizing the cost of the audit just as they seek to minimize other corporate costs. Managers work with members of the auditing team in the course of the audit and throughout the year to assist the auditors in understanding the company's operations and the reasoning underlying its accounting. The typical audited company engages the same auditing firm for many years, and auditors that work on the audit typically work on it for several consecutive years, often in roles with increasing responsibility; the typical "engagement partner" on an audit has had several years experience on that client's audits. This permits auditors to gain the understanding of the client's business that is conducive to an effective and economical audit. Considering that auditors occasionally encounter accounting procedures that they either do not understand or consider incorrect, the working relationship between audit and client personnel is critical to the resolution of any disputes in an amicable and proper manner. Without that relationship, the audit surely would be more costly, the work more unpleasant for both parties, and the risk of error perhaps greater. On the whole, the system works as well as could be expected, given the necessity for auditors to review the work of client personnel with a critical eye.

Auditors' View

Auditing is an extremely competitive profession now that auditors are permitted to engage in competitive bidding and low-ball pricing. The first consideration is that auditors have absolute independence from the client, so ownership of any stock interest or any other financial relationship between auditor personnel and the client company is forbidden. Because competition for initial engagements is so fierce, the economics of the auditing profession depend heavily on continuing relationships, preferably for many years, and on providing other, typically more profitable, services to audit clients. Those two factors also tend to improve the quality of the audit by enhancing the auditors' understanding of all aspects of the client's operations, such as personnel policies, research, manufacturing, distribution, and financial policies. Audit risk is higher on first-time engagements. Auditors' understanding and confidence in the client, which improves audit quality and contributes to economy, is further enhanced when alumni of the audit firm are serving in accounting and financial management capacities with the client. All-in-all, the closer the relationship with the client the better the service provided. As the retired auditor on my right at a recent professional dinner described his firm's relationship with a certain large client: "It was more like a marriage." While some of these practices are sometimes criticized as endangering independence, the fact is that there has never been a case in which an auditor's independence has been proven to have been impaired by them. Because independence is so critical to their reputations and financial success, auditors are always on their guard to avoid any behavior that could impair it.

Views of Investors

Audits and the auditor's certificate are vital parts of the information system on which investors with little direct contact with a company depend. Their role is to lend credibility to financial reports, thus permitting investors to depend on them with the confidence that is necessary if investors are to commit funds to the enterprise. Any concern that financial statements are misleading or actually fraudulent causes an immediate breakdown in that confidence. Audit failures are serious problems that investors cannot tolerate. Fortunately, they are rare; on the whole, the financial reporting system in America is as good as, or better than, that in any other country.

An Alternative View

The ethical challenges facing auditors in America cannot be understood without recognizing that a three-party arrangement is involved. Customarily, management hires, fires, and pays the auditor. Management's objectives are to meet the SEC requirement, to obtain and retain the confidence of investors, and to provide a favorable report on their own stewardship. The auditor's objectives are to earn a good income, which depends on pleasing and retaining the client and "cross-selling" non-audit services, and to avoid serious trouble, which requires following the rules and avoiding an audit failure. An investor's objec-

tive is to obtain information that is useful in making investment decisions. It is apparent that auditors are not paid for, and are not motivated to meet investors' objectives. The problem with this arrangement is illustrated by auditors' customary terminology: they refer to the enterprise being audited and/or its top management as the "client." But if the system is to serve the American economic system as described in the previous section of this paper, auditing must serve the investing public and treat it as the client. In fact, the auditing/governance system is not designed to provide that service.

Three-party economic arrangements always have a basic flaw that can only be overcome by a combination of stringent regulation and Herculean efforts by participants. In the more common economic relationship, one party provides a good and is paid for it by the second party who receives and enjoys the benefits of the good. This arrangement permits each party to compare his/her costs and benefits, thus maximizing the probability that he/she realizes a satisfactory cost/benefit relationship. In contrast, in a three-party relationship, A employs and compensates B to provide a good (credible information) to C. A does not benefit from the primary intended service, but takes some responsibility for the cost, which ultimately is borne by C. A also chooses the service provider. The service recipient (C) has no opportunity to compare cost and benefit. Consequently, no one matches the value of the information service against its cost. In simple terms, management uses owners' money to hire auditors to provide a stamp of approval on management's reports on its own performance to owners. There is no basis for expecting that such an arrangement will satisfactorily serve either society in general or the investing public in particular.

The auditor is in an awkward position. He makes his living by pleasing management, but his societal justification requires serving investors. The resulting strain should be expected to produce ethical lapses. The practice of a profession traditionally involves a professional person serving selected clients, patients, or other beneficiaries and being compensated by those who are served—a two-party arrangement. A lawyer represents his client. A doctor or dentist serves her patient. A clergyman ministers to his flock. Berenson has identified such an arrangement in a period when auditing was far more developed in Britain than in America and British auditors examined the books of American companies.

> These nineteenth-century accountants (...) were clear, clearer than they have ever been since, that they owed their allegiance to investors, not to management. The reason is simple: The United States depended on Britain for much of its capital, and many of the first American accountants were British, sent over by British banks and insurers who wanted to protect their investments. They were paid by, and answered to, their countrymen, not the American companies whose books they audited. (Berenson, 2003, p. 25)

That allegiance of auditors has been recognized by the high court in America.

> The U.S. Supreme Court, in a 1984 decision in U.S. vs. Arthur Young, confirmed the auditor's watchdog function when it wrote that the auditor's "ultimate allegiance" is to "a corporation's creditors and stockholders, as well as to the investing public." (Levitt, 2003, p. 118)

Unfortunately, practicing auditors do not see the investing public as their clients; corporate managers treat investors very much like other constituents; and, as noted in a subsequent section, even accounting regulators often are persuaded to accede to the wishes of corporate managers rather than to those of investors.

> Because they are not organized into a dues-paying group, ordinary investors are rarely, if ever, heard from and therefore don't flex their political muscle. They are the most undersupported and underrepresented constituency in the country. (Levitt, 2003, p. 244)

Three factors operating in the real world of auditing suggest that auditors typically do not have that "independence of mental attitude" that auditing standards require. First is the unlimited social intercourse between auditors and client personnel. Both sides are motivated to build and maintain friendly relationships, including engaging in leisure activities together

such as sporting events and other entertainments. They work together, even to the extent of auditors being assigned permanent office space on client premises, they drink and dine together, they attend each other's important family celebrations. One commonly hears: "Some of my best friends are auditors/clients." And they exchange gifts.

> It's quite the paradox: A contract officer from the U.S. Department of Defense can't take a free ham sandwich and a Coke from an engineer at a defense contractor. A regulator from the Environmental Protection Agency has to leave fifty cents on the table if he pours a cup of coffee while visiting a power plant. And even a corporate purchasing agent is rarely allowed to accept skybox seats from a supplier. Yet a partner of an accounting firm can fly a client CFO to the Olympics or to a center-court box at the U.S. Open tennis championships, put him up in a five-star hotel, and wine and dine him. These acts imply a friendship, a personal relationship or collaboration. But the relationship between a company and its external auditor is none of those things. Every action that has the potential to affect the auditor's obligation to the public must be avoided. It's not very much fun, but after having been so tainted by scandal, the auditor, like Caesar's wife, must be above suspicion. (Toffler, 2003, p. 251)

A second reason for lack of independence is the auditor's fear of losing the audit client. Some auditors feel that the worst thing that can happen to their career prospects is to lose a client. That means that the auditor will do almost anything to avoid the client's displeasure because of an accounting dispute. A consequence is that client personnel and auditors work together in resolving any such dispute in a manner that permits the client to achieve the management's performance reporting objective and permits the auditor to claim to be adhering to the letter of the relevant accounting rule. Service to the investing public is far removed from their minds in such circumstances.

Finally, non-audit services are critical to the financial success of an auditing firm that engages in fierce price competition on auditing engagements. Profitability of auditing is not required if non-audit services are immensely profitable. Consequently, the financial cost of losing a client often is measured by the firm's total billings to that client, not only auditing fees. That is why the dollar billings for non-audit services impair the auditor's independence more than the nature of the non-audit services. Of course, non-audit services that entail advocacy for a client are especially damaging to the independent attitude of audit firm personnel. Note that billings for non-audit services have continued to grow despite the expectation that recent scandals and restrictions on certain of those services would eat into the revenues of accounting firms (*Economist*, 2003).

The heart of the problem is that auditors have stronger incentives to please management than to serve the investing public, which can be disastrous for investors because of the conflict between their interests and those of management. Investors want unbiased information, but management is strongly motivated to render biased reports on its own performance. In the face of the behavior and circumstances outlined here, including the general perception among auditors that their client is the company being audited and its management, one is bound to conclude that only auditors and client personnel who continue to prosper under the present arrangement are able to honestly believe that auditors' bias is not a problem. A biased person is the last to recognize his bias.

Consequences of Auditor Bias

The management-auditor alliance has serious effects on the professionalism of auditors. If one views members of a profession as having "elevated occupational authority" (West, 2003, p. 40) to use their expertise in a specialized body of knowledge to serve members of the public, the auditors' behavior as described above casts doubt on their professionalism. One aspect is the emphasis on salesmanship in evaluating the performance of personnel in auditing firms. It is generally acknowledged that an increasingly important criterion for admission to one of the huge partnerships that perform the bulk of the industrial world's auditing is ability to bring in clients and to retain them. Weaknesses in technical expertise can be overcome by the practice of frequent inquiries of technical experts in the home office. Thus, "expertise in a specialized body of knowledge" is not as critical as marketing skills, raising the question of whether auditing is a profession or a more typical business.

Another characteristic behavior in the large, "independent" accounting/auditing firms is intense advocacy on behalf of clients. This includes siding with clients in opposing standards setters' proposals that are intended to improve financial reporting standards. Even more indicative of bias in favor of perceived clients is auditors' participation in national politics by lobbying legislators and regulators on behalf of clients and making financial contributions to the campaigns of candidates favored by clients.

> During the last presidential campaign, Arthur Andersen, through its PAC, contributed enough to George W. Bush's campaign to become one of his top five corporate contributors. Rival Ernst & Young was also in the top five. Between 1989 and 2002, Andersen contributed to the campaigns of 94 of 100 U.S. Senators and more than half of the members of the House of Representatives, according to the Center for Responsive Politics. The firm gave far more than Enron did, and the numbers for the rest of the Big 5 are equally outrageous. Such contributions imply the desire for access to government influence and, of course, the hope that politicians will adopt policies that work in their interest. If certified public accountants are to be independent and responsible to the public, they must remain absolutely clear of the political process in every way. (Toffler, 2003, p. 251)

To emphasize this point further, one may wonder what political issues have been so important to accountants directly—as opposed to in their roles as "advocates" for clients—that they would be willing to pay millions of dollars to gain influence with politicians. Note, also, that the largest contributions went to politicians who were known to "oppose accounting reforms" being pushed by the SEC and the Financial Accounting Standards Board—"reforms opposed by corporate managements and viewed by others as in the interests of investors."

The alignment of auditors' interests with those of client managements, as described above, has had an insidious effect on the professionalism of auditors in another way. The relationship between a professional person's authority, responsibility, and independence is seriously impaired. According to this view, CPAs in America have been granted exclusive authority to conduct audits of companies whose securities are publicly traded. Those audits are intended to serve the investing public by lending credibility to the financial statements as reliable compilations of information useful to investors.

Unfortunately, the bias of auditors has put such a strain on the system that a multitude of detailed rules has had to be promulgated by regulators in order to strengthen the resistance of auditors to managements' requests to depart from principles and to their own inclinations to help their management friends. Those "cookbooks" of accounting and auditing rules have gradually reduced auditors' dependence on their own professional judgment and have encouraged them to take refuge in rules as a substitute for accepting responsibility for such judgments. Putting together the pressure from their friends in management, the threat of malpractice liability and a natural willingness, if not desire, to find someone else to blame, it is not surprising that auditors take "flight from responsibility" (West, 2003, p. 171), seeking refuge in a morass of rules that they are forced to apply. That is a human response. It's not auditors' fault that auditing is now more a process of complying with a set of rules than it is applying truly professional judgment. Service to the investing public? What a quaint notion! Ethics lapses? Almost inevitable!

Another effect of the growth of the rules cookbooks has been the growth of the "standards avoidance" business. Auditors and client managers work together to exploit every loophole in finding ways that management can "tell its story" and still adhere to the letter of accounting rules. A comparison with the work of tax advisors in minimizing taxes shows great similarity. How many billable hours would auditors lose if they gave up that service to managements and worked for investors instead? Auditors' resistance to a change in the system is understandable.

Auditor Bias: Possible Mitigations

The uncomfortable position in which auditors are put by the present three-party arrangement offers temptations to behave unethically by favoring the interests of client managements over those of the investing public, thus compromising the integrity and effectiveness of the financial reporting system that is so important to those societies that depend on relatively free capital markets. The success of economic freedom in permitting people to achieve their goals is heavily dependent on the opportunity of all participants to compare their efforts (costs) with the resulting benefits to themselves. When that type of comparison by everyone involves a minimum of leakage as "externalities," the society benefits. Unfortunately, the three-party arrangement for auditing does not fit that description; auditors do not capture the benefits (or losses) they provide to society, so do not take them into their cost/benefit reckoning.

A better alignment of the interests of auditors and the investing public would be desirable—an arrangement that would permit auditors to feel the benefits to investors from informative financial reporting. Auditors need more contact with and understanding of investors' needs and less contact with and empathy for those of managers. Of course, auditors must work with client personnel, so complete lack of influence through those contacts is impossible. But a reduction of that influence might be achieved by: (a) prohibiting contact between the auditing firm and client management on matters pertaining to engaging, compensating, or dismissing the auditor; (b) prohibiting gifts in either direction between auditors and client personnel; (c) prohibiting auditors from participating in political activities by lobbying and making financial contributions to candidates (or, if constitutionally impossible, requiring disclosure of such activities); (d) prohibiting auditing firms from providing any other services to audit clients; (e) requiring that independent directors or a specialized committee of shareholders represent the latter in all contacts with auditors; (f) requiring rotation of audit firms on a moderate schedule such as every three years. Another desirable practice would be for audit committees to require, as part of the audit engagement, that auditors render a report on possible improvements in the client's financial reporting that could make the report more useful to investors. Such a requirement of auditors could help them keep service to investors in mind as they perform the audit. These reforms could be accomplished in America by the American Institute of Certified Public Accountants, the SEC, and the stock markets. Changes in the state corporation laws would be helpful, but because taxes and fees enjoyed by the state of incorporation are attractive to politicians, the temptation for states to compete in a "race for the bottom" can be expected to prevent such changes. (In America, promoters typically may choose the state in which to incorporate initially, and managements often switch to suit their own interests, for example, to a state with a pro-management anti-takeover law.)

If the proposals for changes listed above seem harsh, consider that the necessary physical proximity of auditors and client personnel is bound to engender some degree of friendship and understanding. Strong measures in other areas are required if the resulting bias is to be limited. Auditors might be willing to bear such constraints in exchange for the valuable franchise they hold. Another concern is the increased costs that the above-suggested reforms would impose on investors, primarily through audit fees. Those costs must be compared with the improvements they would produce in the information provided. Only investors are in a good position to make such cost/benefit comparisons, but the screams of client managers and auditors in response to reform proposals are likely to drown out the diffused interests of investors, so one should not bet on such reforms occurring soon.

Ethics Failures of Accounting Standards Setters

In the spirit of generous distribution of blame for financial reporting failures, the standards-setting establishment should not be neglected. In most countries, the responsibility for exercising some direction over financial reporting is divided among several institutions. In the U.S., these include the Securities and Exchange Commission, the Financial Accounting Standards Board, the American Institute of Certified Public Accountants, and the New York Stock Exchange. The remarks in this section shall be limited to the Financial Accounting Standards Board (FASB).

The seven members of the FASB have accepted a fiduciary responsibility to the general public by delegation from the SEC, which has the legal power to do everything the FASB does. To the extent that the Board has fallen short of its responsibilities to the public, it has failed in its responsibilities, so is subject to criticism for ethics failures. Three specific complaints are justified.

First, the Board and most observers not associated with a powerful special interest group recognize that investors (in the broad sense that includes all parties represented in an enterprise's ownership and suppliers of funds, commodities, and services on credit) are the primary group using enterprise financial reports. The importance of that user group is such that only "the general public" is likely to be mentioned in addition to investors when users are discussed.

Nevertheless, the charter of the FASB assigns major roles to other groups as providers of inputs to the standards-setting process. In practice, corporate management groups and their allies in the American Institute of CPAs and in the U.S. Congress exercise great influence — probably more than all other groups together. One might reasonably fault the Board for accepting and responding to that influence; its fiduciary duty is to give by far the greatest weight to the interests of investors. Note that the meddling by members of Congress is stimulated by the lobbying of corporate managements, not by investors, and, as noted in an earlier section of this paper, auditors do not feel the pain of investors to the extent that they do that of client managements. One might also observe that giving in to pressure from corporate managements sets a poor example for auditors.

The second complaint to be mentioned is that the Board has responded to management's and auditors' demand for "bright lines" between acceptable and unacceptable bending of accounting principles to achieve the reporting objectives of managers by promulgating standards consisting of detailed rules rather than principles. The serious adverse effects of too many rules have been documented brilliantly by West (2003). They include the development of a compliance-oriented culture in auditing firms and in corporate accounting departments, thus further reducing the already minor weight given to the interests of users of financial statements. Currently, the major national standards-setting bodies and the International Accounting Standards Board are cooperating in efforts to reverse the trend to cookbook accounting, but until the pressures from the powerful interests abate, the prospects are not favorable. However, a shift towards principles-based standards would appear to fit well with an investor-oriented style of auditing. In this context, the FASB's failure to carry its conceptual framework to its logical conclusion (regarding measurement preferences) was a blow against principles and a win for the special interests.

One more ethics failure by the FASB is significant. Its original charter set a goal of narrowing the areas of difference among alternative acceptable accounting practices. Examples of important areas of difference are accounting for inventories (stocks) and the depreciation of plant and equipment. In both cases, alternative vastly different practices are acceptable in a given set of circumstances. Failure to narrow those differences in its thirty-year life is a count against the FASB from the point of view of investors — the Board's proper primary beneficiaries.

Conclusion

The theme of this essay is that primary responsibility for financial reporting failures and deficiencies falls on corporate management and accounting personnel but that auditors, academic accountants, and members of standards-setting bodies must bear shares of the blame. All of those parties have fiduciary responsibilities, so failures to meet those responsibilities are ethics failures. The single most promising reform is disassociation of auditors from "client" management in favor of closer association with owners of the enterprise.

Decentralized economic systems' potential for service to society has been sabotaged by defects in systems of corporate governance that have given excessive power to those managers who, ideally, are the servants of the owners. When those managers control the "independent" auditors and the membership and activities of the board of directors, the system does not serve society to its full potential. The model of corporate governance in Britain's 1845 Companies Act — shareholders controlling both the board and the auditors, the board controlling hired managers — looks better. Until fundamental changes in corporate governance are made, we can expect more ethics failures in corporate financial reporting, more financial scandals, more rules to control the behavior of improperly motivated managers and auditors, and more hand-wringing about ethics failures.

References

Ball, R. and P. Brown: 1968, "An Empirical Evaluation of Accounting Income Numbers," *Journal of Accounting Research*, Autumn, 159–178.

Berenson, A.: 2003, *The Number* (Random House, New York). *Economist*: 2003, "Unresolved Conflicts," *Economist* 369 (8346), Oct 18, 14.

Levitt, A.: 2003, *Take on the Street* (Pantheon Books, New York).

Toffler, B.: 2003, *Final Accounting* (Broadway Books, New York). West, B.: 2003, *Professionalism and Accounting Rules* (Routledge, London and New York).

Questions for Discussion and Reflection

1. How does Staubus's "three-party arrangement" contribute to the ethical challenges faced by auditors?
2. What factors does Staubus suggest compromise auditor independence?
3. What is Staubus's criticism of the Financial Accounting Standards Board that sets accounting standards?

The Moral Imperative of Investment Banking

John Terrill

Cardus Comment, February 26, 2010, http://www.cardus.ca/comment/article/1523/ (accessed January 5, 2011).

A popular joke circulated just over a year ago:

What's the difference between a pigeon and an investment banker?
The pigeon can still make a deposit on a BMW.

In the last 18 months, times have certainly changed. Investment bankers are once again flush with cash. It is hard to understand today's extravagant bonuses, given the recent chaos and bailout of the industry. The venerable investment bank Bear Stearns collapsed, and its equal rival, Lehman Brothers, declared bankruptcy. A comatose Merrill Lynch sold itself to Bank of America, and Wells Fargo took over a faltering Wachovia. To deal with this mess and others like it, the U.S. Department of the Treasury formed the Troubled Asset Relief Program (TARP) to purchase or insure up to $700 billion in faltering assets.

Outrage at investment bankers, with their year-end bonuses and perceived arrogant manner, seems well deserved. Lloyd Blankfein, chairman and chief executive of Goldman Sachs, recently described himself to the *Times Online* as "just a banker doing God's work." Unsurprisingly, he was savaged by the public and the press for his comment. But Blankfein doesn't stand alone in his missteps. Other banking chiefs have been skewered for even more ludicrous actions. John Thain, former Merrill Lynch chief, was lambasted for buying an $87,000 area rug for his office while his company was self-destructing.

Stephen Green, chairman of HSBC, offered the following understated admission in a *Times Online* article: "The banking industry has not covered itself in glory, to say the least, in recent years." *Rolling Stone*, in an article last year entitled "Inside the Great American Bubble Machine," goes farther, describing Goldman, the most venerable of the investment banks, as "a great vampire squid wrapped around the face of humanity, relentlessly jamming its blood funnel into anything that smells like money." With sentiments like that, it is not surprising that *Bloomberg.com* recently reported on the uptick of Goldman Sachs executives filing for handgun permits for self-defense purposes.

But while the banking industry seems to lack wisdom, a rootedness in reality and a spirit of contrition for past mistakes, Lloyd Blankfein's basic assertion may be right. Investment banking can be God's work.

It's important to acknowledge that we can't blame the global recession entirely on investment banking or commercial banking. They contributed to it but are not the only reason we're in this mess. Jamie Dimon, chairman and CEO of JP Morgan Chase, outlined many of the underlying causes in his 2008 Letter to Shareholders. Banks contributed — certainly to the housing bubble — but there were glaring regulatory lapses, especially in the mortgage industry and with Fannie Mae and Freddie Mac. "Pro-cyclical" policies, such as loan loss reserving and mark-to-market accounting, according to Dimon, also played a role, as did the ensuing freeze of credit and financial markets. Consumers are culpable, too. Seduced by artificially low interest rates, they borrowed and consumed at unsustainable levels. In October 2008, credit card debt in the United States reached $1 trillion, a 25% increase in just five years, according to the Federal Reserve.

Furthermore, the work of investment bankers is complex and technical, and many of the products and services don't seem tangible, which, if you are like me, heightens your suspicion. In general, investment bankers help clients with capital: issuing stocks and bonds; trading securities; identifying and negotiating corporate mergers and acquisitions (M&A); and assisting with myriad other financial advisory services. They're like the circulatory system in a body, facilitating the flow of capital and other assets to entities that need it most and will put it to best use.

Aaron Westlund, director for Corporate Transactions at DaVita Inc., describes investment banking as "capital matchmaking." Mark Denton, a private banker with J.P. Morgan Chase & Co., agrees. He states that investment banking exists so "people with good ideas can find capital to grow a concept which benefits all of us." Lord Brian Griffiths, vice chairman of Goldman Sachs, takes this idea even farther in a recent interview in *Ethix*, suggesting that the profession contributes in material ways to the common good. "Consider what international banks have done through global capital markets to help China and India develop. It is phenomenal: Hundreds of millions of people have been taken out of dollar-a-day poverty. To me that is a social good and in part is the result of financial markets."

But with so much potential for creation of "social good," much of the industry seems to be seriously underperforming. Many leaders both within and outside of the profession suggest a moral crisis fed by years of misguided economic theory.

Contrary to popular economic thought, human beings are not mechanistic, perfectly rational creatures, and neither are the markets in which they act. George Akerlof and Robert Shiller explore this idea in their recent bestselling book, *Animal Spirits* (Princeton University Press, 2009). To create thriving economic systems, the authors contend, we cannot ignore the "animal spirits" that enliven people's emotions and behaviours.

Ken Costa, former vice chairman of UBS's investment bank, in delivering the 11th annual Wilberforce Address last June, concurs with the "non-rational" aspects of human behaviour but argues that "humans are more than just animals. We are moral and spiritual creatures, and if we fail to recognize that—either by pretending we are rational robots, or by pretending we are only animal spirits—we debase our humanity."

Pope Benedict XVI agrees, and in his recent encyclical *Caritas in Veritate*, he encourages business and government leaders to develop new frameworks that will diminish repetition of past mistakes: "Admittedly, the market can be a negative force, not because it is so by nature, but because a certain ideology can make it so. It must be remembered that the market does not exist in the pure state. It is shaped by the cultural configurations which define it and give it direction."

Tragically, economics is largely divorced from the moral and spiritual dimensions of life. But it shouldn't be. Prevailing economic theory needs to be challenged. When we divorce economics from moral imperatives, we relegate our work to base levels and diminish our commitment to serve our neighbour and contribute to human flourishing. *Caritas in Veritate* speaks directly to this important idea: "The conviction that the economy must be autonomous, that it must be shielded from influences of a moral character, has led many to abuse the economic process in a thoroughly destructive way."

Reform must come at many levels, especially at the place where the "heart" of the profession begins to change. Chi-Dooh "Skip" Li, founder of Seattle-based Ellis, Li & McKinstry PLLC, as well as Agros International, an NGO empowering land ownership for the economically impoverished around the world, made the following observation at a recent breakfast hosted by the School of Business and Economics at Seattle Pacific University. "Investment bankers have lacked a sense of reality, wisdom and shame.... If arrogance were a criminal offense, we'd see a lot of long-term jail sentences." Skip, reflecting on his own spiritual vulnerabilities, then spoke of the redemptive impact that authentic relationships, learning from failure and intentional proximity to the poor have made in his own professional journey.

Such habits are grounding, and engage the whole person. They check our impulses to elevate ourselves above others. For those who move in the halls of power, prestige, and wealth, developing sustained connections to some of the pain and injustice of the world is essential. Privilege, position, and capital are to be employed for the benefit of others. Living for selfish ambitions may result in short-term gains, but over the long haul it isolates us and diminishes our personhood. As Jesus taught, "Truly, truly, I say to you, unless a grain of wheat falls into the earth and dies, it remains alone; but if it dies, it bears much fruit" (John 12:24).

In carrying out the reconciling work that has been entrusted to us by God (2 Corinthians 5:18), Christians in the investment banking field—and all

Christians in business, for that matter — would be wise to exercise what Emmanuel Katongole and Chris Rice in *Reconciling All Things: A Christian Vision for Justice, Peace and Healing* refer to as the "discipline of lament." In the authors' words, "Lament is a cry directed to God ... of those who see the truth of the world's deep wounds and the cost of seeking peace. It is the prayer of those who are deeply disturbed by the way things are."

This habit doesn't come naturally or easily. Rice and Katongole, in examining the Scriptures, posit three ways to nurture it: pilgrimage, relocation, and public confession. *Pilgrimage* helps us "unlearn speed," slowing down long enough to "hear the crying" around us. *Relocation* helps us "unlearn distance," moving us to put ourselves in hard places, "tarrying long enough to be disturbed." And *confession* helps us "unlearn innocence," prompting in us responsibility and a commitment to realign ourselves to God's purposes. In the fast-paced world of banking and business, when we slow down long enough, get close enough, and regularly acknowledge our culpability in causing pain for others, we invite God's Spirit to do deeply constructive work in us and in the communities to which we belong.

Reform in investment banking is therefore dependent upon "soul" change. As individuals pursue what is good and right, personal, organizational, and industry-wide currents begin to change. Solid policies and practices, built on moral imperatives, create a virtuous cycle of healthy reform and mission.

J. Michael Bontrager, founder and managing principal of Chatham Financial, a highly respected interest rate and currency hedging advisory firm, emphasizes the importance of creating "life-giving" cultures. He sees the role of his company as "restoring a little corner of our world to a place that has more integrity and transparency, where relationships matter more and people are treated with respect without regard to their role or position."

Ken Costa offers an idea for corporate governance that also redirects the prevailing tide in the industry. "Let's invite teachers, voluntary sector executives, military personnel, academics, members of the medical profession, journalists, commentators and so-called 'outsiders' into our boardrooms. They will help us avoid some of the disastrous consequences of financial introspection."

John Steinbeck's classic novel *The Grapes of Wrath* chronicles the Joad family's journey West out of dust bowl devastation. This from its pages presents the challenge and opportunity before us today. "The bank is something more than men, I tell you. It's the monster. Men made it, but they can't control it." The moral and economic dimensions of the industry can be reunited. Re-integration can occur, but we need to stop pretending that markets and its participants are amoral.

Leaders in banking can shape who they are and what their industry becomes. Investment banking can be a shining example of God's work, and investment bankers can be God's stewards, allocating capital in ways that nourish and empower people, companies, communities, and entire countries.

Questions for Discussion and Reflection

1. What does Terrill see as the social good of investment banking?
2. How does Terrill attribute blame for the crisis in the financial system from 2007 – 9?
3. What is required, according to Terrill, for investment banking to function as it was intended?

CASE STUDIES

Case 8.1: Audit Adjustments

You are a CPA on the audit staff of a multinational public accounting firm. You are the senior auditor on an annual audit of a manufacturing company that is a small subsidiary of a larger company that is a significant client of your firm. In addition to a sizable fee for the annual audit, the parent company pays your firm additional fees each year for tax consultation and return preparation as well as other management consulting services. With this particular audit, as with many parent-subsidiary relationships, you are aware that there is a tremendous amount of pressure on the subsidiary company's management to reach certain projected sales goals for the year. Because of this, the climate at the subsidiary is tense as you begin your annual examination of the year-end financial statements.

During the course of the audit, you perform a sales cutoff test to ensure that all sales transactions at year-end were recorded in the proper period. Since title to the company's products passes when they are shipped to customers, shipments are required in order for a sale to be properly recorded. Accordingly, a standard audit procedure is to cross-reference sales recorded prior to year-end to related shipping records and to similarly trace information from shipping records to sales journals. The sales cutoff test revealed that numerous shipments made after the company's year-end were recorded as sales prior to year-end, which resulted in significantly higher revenue during the year you are auditing.

You are aware that as an independent auditor, you have a responsibility to your client and to those who might make decisions based on the company's financial statements, such as investors and lenders. When you inform the subsidiary's controller of the results of your sales cutoff test and that an adjustment to annual revenues and profits would likely be warranted, he takes the matter to the president of the subsidiary. During a follow-up meeting with the controller and president, the president attempts to get you to reconsider your proposed adjustment with the following arguments:

1. The amount of the adjustment you were proposing was not material to the parent company's financial statements.
2. All of the subsidiary's competitors did the same thing in recording shipments just after year-end as sales in the previous year.
3. It really didn't matter in the long run if sales were moved from the current year to the next year, since sales and profits for the next year would be greater.

At the end of the meeting, the president drops a not-so-subtle reminder that his company is a substantial client of your firm. You call the partner from your firm who is in charge of the audit for advice, and he tells you to "handle the situation on your own."

Questions for Discussion

1. Evaluate each of the three arguments made by the subsidiary president for not making the proposed adjustment to sales. Are there any merits to his arguments that are worth considering in making your decision?
2. Should the significance of the company as a client of your firm, in terms of the amount of fees paid to your firm each year, matter in making your decision?
3. What if, after considering all factors, you continue to feel that an adjustment to the company's financial statements is warranted, but after a closed door meeting with the client, the partner on the audit (your boss) decides to agree with the client and tells you not to make the adjustment. How should you react?

Case 8.2: The New Insiders

You are the vice president of research and development at TechCom, a company that manufactures high-speed devices for e-businesses, which the company hopes will revolutionize networking applications. The technology is both for established companies that augment traditional sales with Internet sales and companies that do business exclusively on the Web. TechCom recently went public, and its stock price has increased dramatically due to speculation that its technologies will soon be completed and gain widespread acceptance. You too are optimistic that the company's products will make a significant impact on networking applications, but to the extent that you understand the public markets and how companies like TechCom are valued at this stage in their life, you are less optimistic that the company is fairly valued, although the company has been careful to disclose the status and future of its various research and development activities to the public.

You are one of ten key executives who own stock in the company, and you have stock options to acquire additional shares at a price substantially below current market values. The fair market value of your shares held and shares you have an option to purchase is approximately 95 percent of your family's total net worth, including your home and all other investments, even after considering taxes that would have to be paid, simply because the value of the TechCom shares have increased so dramatically. Friends and family members have encouraged you to sell at least some of your shares in order to limit the risk associated with having such a large percentage of your net worth tied up in one investment. This is consistent with your natural instinct to diversify your investments. On the other hand, the company's founder and CEO, Jack Smith, who hired you for your position four years ago and who has been the driving force behind the company, has dropped some not-so-subtle hints to you and other company executives that he would be very disappointed in any of the company's executives who sold their shares, claiming that such a sale by a company insider, which would have to be reported to the public, would send the "wrong signal" to the markets that management lacked confidence in the company's future. He further claims that selling now would be foolish, because TechCom shares will be worth substantially more in the future.

Questions for Discussion

1. What factors would you consider in determining how much, if any, of your TechCom holdings you would sell, weighing the urgings of friends and family members to sell against the urgings of Jack Smith to hold your shares?
2. If you wouldn't sell any portion of your shares currently, when would you sell?

Additional Facts

After discussing the matter at length with your spouse over the weekend, you determine that you are going to sell a specific percentage of your shares on Monday morning after your weekly meeting with the TechCom research staff during which you are updated on research activities for the weekend. During the update meeting, however, you hear a report of significant technological problems, the discovery of which call into question the very viability of some of the company's key research programs. After the meeting, you call your stock broker as planned to sell TechCom shares, but based on the information you heard in the update meeting, you decide to triple the number of shares you instruct your broker to sell in comparison to the shares you and your spouse agreed to sell the previous day.

Questions for Discussion

3. Have you acted unethically in deciding to sell more shares than originally planned based on the information you discovered during the technical update meeting? Why or why not?

Additional Facts

The facts are the same as previously discussed, except that the report you receive during the Monday morning update meeting isn't of problems with the company's technologies, but rather that there have been significant technological discoveries such that it is now thought that the company's products will be even more revolutionary than previously thought. Once these breakthroughs become known to the public markets, TechCom's future will be even more highly regarded than it currently is. After the technical update meeting, you decide not to call your stock broker to sell the shares you and your spouse previously agreed to sell.

Questions for Discussion

4. Have you acted unethically in deciding not to sell the shares you had planned on selling before receiving the good news at the technical update meeting? Why or why not?

Case 8.3: Banking: Truth Telling or Compassion?

You work for a major bank that extends commercial lines of credit to auto, RV, and marine (boat) dealerships for the purpose of stocking their inventory to be sold on a retail basis. The inventory that is purchased by a dealer is financed through the credit line and serves as collateral to the loan. The loan is paid off immediately following the sale of the unit, allowing room on the credit line for additional orders. *A line of credit like this is the life-source of a dealership, for without it, business failure is almost certain.*

You manage and underwrite a portfolio of loans serving dealers primarily based in the Midwest. Your job is to evaluate both the risks and mitigating factors on each account and draft a write-up with a recommendation to continue, terminate, and/or adjust the terms of a credit line. The recommendation gets approved by at least two levels above you in the bank's corporate offices. It is common for you to come into contact with most dealers numerous times a month — sometimes on a daily basis.

Recently, a small RV dealership was due for a standard annual review in order to determine if credit would be continued or terminated. This dealer was one of the many RV dealerships severely affected by the economic recession in 2008 (as well as 2009 for many RV dealers).

The dealer had taken a loss in the previous year, which had weakened the balance sheet. In a conversation with the dealer, he revealed to you that he was using personal credit cards to help fund the business but had already significantly reduced the credit card balance in the last six months, when his credit bureau report showed he had racked up $60,000 in credit card debt to fund the business. Another two or three quarters of losses could very well put the dealer in an insolvent position, requiring the bank to pick up the inventory and potentially take a loss on the auction sale of the inventory.

Despite the recession, the dealer had been doing the right things to get back on the right track and had verbally reported that in the current year, numbers were doing much better. Numerous measures were taken by the dealer to cut costs, including laying off additional employees and reducing his personal salary to minimal levels. The most promising mitigating factor, however, was that the dealer had owned real estate property adjacent to the dealership that had been vacant for numerous years but was recently leased on a two-year contract that would bring him new $2000 monthly cash flow.

After evaluating all factors, you conclude that the dealer would make it through the difficult season and that the bank could be confident that no losses would occur. Furthermore, you believed the majority of higher management would agree, except for Amanda, who held the highest level of approval authority, and who would automatically elect to terminate the account simply because the owner used personal credit card debt to fund the business.

You are wondering whether to omit the information about the owner's credit card debt on your recommendation and write-up. It is standard practice to put down every detail and lay out all risks, yet you also know that Amanda is likely to lose all objectivity and rationality after learning the business was partly funded on credit card debt for a season. Both the bank's capital as well your job could be at risk if the bank took a loss. The owner had done everything the bank had asked him, and he had already seen recovery. Furthermore, a decision to close the credit line would likely force the dealership out of business.

Questions for Discussion

1. Is it ethically appropriate to omit the information about the owner's credit card debt on credit assessment for the sake of the dealer's survival as a business? Are the number of jobs potentially saved worth omitting the information?
2. How strong is your obligation to your employer when you don't agree with what will likely be their decision? How do you balance compassion for the dealer with your covenant obligation to your employer?

COMMENTARY

The world of accounting and finance is complex and has a variety of ethical issues that merit our reflection. The first of these has to do with the accountants and financial managers of a company. These people have to do with how a company represents itself in its financial statements, the traditional issues relating to accountants and chief financial officers. Under this heading we will discuss principles for accounting with integrity and isolate a handful of specific accounting techniques that raise ethical questions. We will further address the broader issue of the independence and objectivity of auditors. A second group of issues has to do not so much with a company's financial statements, but with broader questions about the integrity of the financial markets. These include the issues of insider trading and the role of investment banking.

Trust and Fiduciary Relationships

Accountants and financial managers are professionals with a high degree of technical expertise that the general public does not have. As such, that places them in a position to mislead their clients and others who are dependent on their information. This is not to say that the individual investor or bank loan officer has no responsibility to understand the risks of his or her investments or loans. The people who rely on the investor's or officer's reports and opinions are placing a high degree of trust in that person's expertise and integrity. Ethics is needed precisely because the financial services industry is built on trust. Even though there is widespread skepticism about Wall Street ethics and some consider Wall Street rigged against the small investor,[7] millions of transactions in the capital markets are handled smoothly, in part because trust is assumed between the parties. Without a high degree of trust, people would be unwilling to put their money at risk in various investments, though that is not to say that individuals are exempt from their responsibility to understand their investments. They certainly are not. This degree of trust is critical in broader circles too. For example, large institutional investors are unwilling to invest the capital at their disposal in countries that do not respect the rule of law, because they cannot trust that their investments will be handled properly. Further, they cannot trust that the best products will be the most competitive in the market when unethical practices such as bribery are customary.

Think about the necessity for ethics and integrity in the various parts of the financial services industry. When you invest your money with a financial adviser or stockbroker, you are trusting that he will invest your money properly, will give you reliable advice, and will look out for your best financial

[7] See this criticism, e.g., in Roger Lowenstein, *The End of Wall Street* (New York: Penguin, 2010).

interests. You trust that your adviser's opinion will not be colored by his own self-interest. Or consider when a banker is considering loaning money to a company and reads its financial statements. The banker trusts that the statements are truthful as they are presented. This is particularly true if the statements have been reviewed by an outside auditor. In these cases, the public who uses the financial statements to make decisions about loans or investments is trusting that when the auditors sign off on them, they are telling the truth about the company's fiscal condition and not concealing important information about the company. Without ethics, trust in the capital markets would be diminished and people would, as a result, be less willing to put their money at risk, thus depriving companies of badly needed investment capital. Again, that does not absolve the public from its responsibility to understand and exercise due diligence prior to making investment decisions.

The world of accounting and finance is an example of "fiduciary" relationships. What this means is that the accounting/financial professional has a special obligation to her clients, that is, to seek their best financial interests, even if it conflicts with her own self-interest. To put it another way, the self-interest of the professional is not to be placed ahead of advancing the interest of the client. The fiduciary is not to engage in practices that advance her interests to the detriment of the client. Physicians, lawyers, and mental health professionals also operate with fiduciary obligations that make ethics critical for these relationships of trust to function effectively.

It is widely accepted that the law is not sufficient to regulate all the aspects of trust necessary for the financial services industry to operate properly. The conventional wisdom in some business circles is that "if it's legal, then it's moral." In many cases, what this actually means is that a practice is acceptable as long as one does not get caught. We suggest that the law is the moral minimum, and with rare exceptions for civil disobedience, it is unethical to violate the law. However, ethics is certainly more involved than mere compliance with the law. Avoiding indictment is a worthy goal, but surely ethics requires more than that. No law can be crafted that would be specific enough to cover all the possible violations. In addition, the more specific the law, the more potential loopholes it contains. Human nature being what it is, it is inevitable that professionals in this area would search diligently for these loopholes and end up missing the spirit of the law, while perhaps being in compliance with the letter of the law.

Principles for Accounting with Integrity

Accounting with integrity is critical particularly for publicly traded companies, as investors rely on these published financial statements to make their

8 Mark Cheffers and Michael Pakaluk, *Understanding Accounting Ethics*, 2nd ed. (Sutton, Mass.: Allen David, 2007), 39. Italics not in original.

9 Ibid., 41–44.

10 The AICPA Code of Professional Conduct is available at www.aicpa.org/Research/ Standards/CodeofConduct/ Pages/default.aspx.

decisions. Accounting professors Mark Cheffers and Michael Pakaluk insist that "the task of accounting is to *provide the conditions of trust for a modern, market economy*."[8] They see accounting as a "watchdog for the marketplace," and thus, accounting professionals must be able to resist conflicts of interest and the temptations to compromise ethical and legal standards.[9] Since capital moves so rapidly in today's digital age, there is great quarterly pressure on public companies to "put their best foot forward" in their financial statements, or else face the possibility of a decline in their stock price.

The American Institute of Certified Public Accountants (AICPA), which sets standards and partners with the SEC to enforce them, has a code of professional conduct that governs internal accountants and external auditors.[10] GAAP principles are the specific guidelines for accounting for a wide variety of transactions. Underlying the AICPA rules and the GAAP standards are a handful of core ethical values. Keep in mind when reviewing these principles and working your way through the cases that it is easy to get bogged down in accounting details and miss the big picture. What follows are the overall ethical principles that govern accounting with integrity.

First, what the AICPA code of conduct is fundamentally about is the prevention of deception, based on the principles of truth telling and transparency. These moral principles are ultimately grounded in the ninth of the Ten Commandments, which prohibits bearing false witness. The original setting for this command was a trial, in which a witness was sworn to tell the truth. In many cases, someone's life depended on his or her veracity as a witness. Though CPAs are not generally in court as formal witnesses, their role as guardian of the company's financial statements with a responsibility to the public surely puts them in a similarly formal position and is analogous to the courtroom witness setting of the ninth commandment. The CFO of a publicly traded company or the CPA who audits them is duty bound to bear witness to the truth about the company's financial condition. Intentional misstatements are somewhat parallel to perjury on the witness stand. This general principle of truth telling is recognized as valid in virtually every culture, regardless of religious beliefs, and is clearly a part of virtually all moral traditions.

Thus, the financial professional is bound by the ethical norm of truth telling. This involves forthright and accurate financial accounting, following the norms of the generally accepted accounting principles. Cheffers and Pakaluk argue that the accountant must have "an inner orientation to the truth," suggesting that good accounting is more than the technical side of debits and credits and simply adhering to the rules.[11] Perhaps the best measure of the integrity of a company's financial statements comes from the perspective of the investor. A key question to ask in this regard is, "If the one preparing the

11 Cheffers and Pakaluk, *Understanding Accounting Ethics*, 41.

financial statements of the company were an investor, would he feel misled by the way in which the statements were prepared and the figures were presented?" Or to put the key question more bluntly, when considering how the financial statements are prepared, "is the intent to mislead investors about the company's financial health?" Or to put it another way, if you were an investor, would you be getting all the necessary information for understanding the company's performance during the period in question?[12] The same questions can apply to auditors. If the auditor was an investor, would she feel misled by the statements under review? Would she have all the critical information needed to accurately assess the company's performance? The investing public expects integrity and accuracy in financial statements and audits. There is no room for puffery or bluffing when it comes to financial disclosure. However, some of these issues of how to account for specific revenues and costs are difficult and involve legitimate gray areas in which professionals working in good faith can disagree. Generally it takes the accounting profession some time to wrestle with new challenges and new ways of doing business, and to carefully consider how the GAAP rules could be clarified.

[12] These were the suggestions of legendary investor Warren Buffett, encouraging corporate boards to force auditors to state their true opinions. Cited in "Put Bite into Audit Committees," *Fortune*, August 2, 1999, 90.

A second principle that underlies the AICPA code of ethics is to avoid conflicts of interest that could compromise one's objectivity and independence from the company one is analyzing.[13] One application of this principle is that auditors have for some time been prohibited from owning stock in companies they audit to avoid an obvious potential conflict of interest. Further potential conflict of interests include the auditor whose company has other, nonauditing business, such as consulting, with the client, which might tempt the auditor not to alienate a profitable consulting client. In fiduciary relationships that are dependent on trust, objectivity is critical. Fiduciary relationships, by definition, are to be uncolored by these kinds of potential conflicts. This is a crucial principle for integrity in the financial services and accounting areas.

[13] This is highlighted in the AICPA Code, Section 100, "Independence, Integrity and Objectivity."

A third principle that is not specifically included in the code of ethics but is of critical importance has to do with the defining of standards. Just because an accounting practice is the industry standard does not necessarily make it morally right. One should beware of what we call "industrial relativism," in which the specific industry is analogous to a culture that defines standards for itself. To be sure, GAAP and the AICPA code of ethics are generally accepted by the profession. But a particular and perhaps novel interpretation of GAAP is often justified with the observation that such a practice is common in the industry. That observation has no specific normative value. Just because it is an accepted practice, it does not follow that it should be so. For example, if it is accepted practice that earnings are smoothed out and some put into reserves to save for a poor performing quarter, that is irrelevant to the moral assessment of the practice. The question should be, "Is that a misleading practice?" not "Is everyone else doing it?" Duke University accounting professor Katherine Schipper suggests that there is a difference between what is acceptable and what is appropriate.[14] One hopes that auditors would uphold rigorous standards instead of allowing those who push the envelope to set the industry standard.[15] However, one should be aware that most of the changes to GAAP come *gradually* as the profession wrestles with new ways of doing business that do demand new ways of accounting. These new standards, or changes in the existing ones, usually are codified when they reflect a consensus in the profession about how to account for new types of transactions. It is true that just because everyone is doing something a certain way, that does not necessarily make it right, but that emerging consensus is precisely how GAAP gets updated.

Smoothing Earnings

A wide variety of accounting mechanisms can be used to make a company appear more profitable than it actually is. Most of these are not illegal and are broadly within the GAAP guidelines. But with increasing pressure on companies to meet earnings expectations, the need to manage a company's earnings carefully has increased. Many of these practices are widely used, particularly among new economy companies. They argue that they are not doing anything improper, but that new ways of doing business require new accounting rules or new interpretations of generally accepted principles.

One of the most common ways of managing a company's earnings is commonly called "smoothing" earnings. When companies report substantial fluctuations in earnings from quarter to quarter, it can be disastrous for the company's stock price and can cause catastrophic decreases in a company's market capitalization, that is, the total value of its investment capital. Smoothing is the practice of holding back a portion of the company's earnings in a given quarter and saving that portion "for a rainy day."[16] In other words, the company will not report all of its earnings in the quarter, typically a quarter in which it has done well, and save the reserve in the "cookie jar" for a quarter in which they fall short of expectations. The long-run picture on an annual basis is likely unchanged. That is, the annual earnings may be the same as if the earnings were not managed in this way. But from quarter to quarter, the company's earnings are being smoothed out in order to avoid damaging fluctuations. This too is a common practice in most Fortune 500 companies. It is not unusual for companies to be advised to treat their earnings in this way.[17] The long-run picture is not any different, since earnings are simply reallocated to different quarters. But in doing so, investors can be misled that the company is both cushioning poor quarters (some call it "dim-

[14] Cited in Richard Melcher, "Where Are the Accountants?" *Businessweek*, October 5, 1998, 146.

[15] Ibid., 146.

[16] The best-known case so far of the SEC prosecuting a company for managed earnings is the case of the chemical firm W. R. Grace, settled in 1998 with Grace admitting no wrongdoing. Cited in "SEC Files First Suit in Its Accounting Fraud Battle," *Los Angeles Times*, December 23, 1998, C3.

[17] One stock analyst suggested that companies should consider "hiding earnings for future use" and that "if you don't play the game, you're going to get hurt." Cited in Carol J. Loomis, "Lies, Damned Lies and Managed Earnings," *Fortune*, August 2, 1999, 92.

ming the signals") and underreporting positive ones. The counterargument is often that quarterly reporting requirements are themselves misleading, and the company's financial picture may be different over the long run; managing earnings is simply the most accurate way of presenting the company's long-term earnings. Further, the company could argue that it is acting to protect investors from stock price variations; thus, managing earnings is actually in the shareholder's interest.

Auditor Independence

CPAs who audit a company's financial statements have responsibilities to the client and to the public that they must carry out simultaneously. The client has hired them to perform the audit, or annual check of the accuracy of the company's books. But when the company is publicly traded, the auditors have another responsibility, to the investing public, to insure that the company's statements accurately represent its financial condition to the investors. In his reading in this chapter, Ian Stewart argues that this is the "double identity" problem that is at the heart of his view of accounting ethics, a conflict of trust. This puts the auditor in a potentially precarious position if the results of the audit reveal something negative about the company. There is an inherent conflict of interest that must be carefully managed. The client pays lucrative fees for the auditing service and can easily dismiss the auditor and hire another one if the results are not satisfactory to the company. George Staubus, in his article, insists that the close relationships between management and auditors is potentially very problematic. He argues that the tighter relationship should be between the auditor and the investors, reflecting the public component of auditing. The auditor must be aware of this potential problem and cannot compromise the accuracy of the audit for fear of losing the client's business for future audits. Cheffers and Pakaluk insist that this is a structural problem with public accounting, which creates a persistent conflict. They state plainly that "auditors are not paid by those whose interests they are supposed to represent (the investing public)."[18] Staubus suggests that even though the role of public accounting is to serve the public as its client, "the auditing/governance system is not designed to provide that service." We would suggest that even when one is paid by the interests he is supposed to represent, such as an internal accountant being paid by his company, that creates its own potential conflicts, since the accountant can be pressured by the potential loss of employment or transfer to less desirable areas of the company. The stakes can be high, for when audits are compromised by these conflicts and companies have to restate their earnings through revised financial statements, investor confidence is usually shaken and the stock price goes down, often dramatically, causing investors to lose substantial amounts

[18] Cheffers and Pakaluk, *Understanding Accounting Ethics*, 23–26. See also the discussion of this in Ronald F. Duska and Brenda Shay Duska, *Accounting Ethics* (Malden, Mass.: Blackwell, 2003): 79–87.

19 E.g., see the SEC allegations that Arthur Andersen helped Waste Management overstate its income in excess of $1 billion. Andersen paid $7 million in fines to settle the SEC's charges. In addition, Pricewaterhouse-Coopers paid $55 million to settle a class action lawsuit filed by shareholders in MicroStrategy. Cited in Marianne Lavelle, "Auditors Exposed! Cozy Deals Alleged!" *US News and World Report*, July 23, 2001, 40–42. For other examples, see Tony Tinker, *Paper Prophets: Fraudulent Accounting and Failed Audits* (New York: Beard, 2004).

20 Cited in Warren Buffett, "Put Bite into Audit Committees," 90.

of money.[19] This situation actually opens the auditors up to being sued by the investors to recover their losses.

The potential conflict of interests for auditors is complicated by another factor. Accounting firms generally provide a variety of other, nonauditing services to the companies they audit, including tax counsel, compensation systems, and financial information systems. The risk to the accounting firm is not just the loss of the auditing business but the loss of nonauditing lines of revenue if it is not retained. Many of the more formal consulting relationships have been severed and some accounting firms have spun off their consulting units in order to erect more of a wall between consulting and auditing. Auditing and nonaudit services will likely be mixed for the foreseeable future, bringing the potential for a conflict of interest that may not necessarily compromise audits but must be managed carefully.

The overall responsibility for insuring audit independence rests both with the accounting firm and the audit client itself. For example, the audit committee of the company board of directors needs to function as more than a rubber stamp of the audit but should exercise substantial oversight to insure that the report is not compromised by a conflict of interest. With the passing of the Sarbanes-Oxley Act in the aftermath of the Enron debacle, CEOs and board members are more accountable for the accuracy of the financial statements. Following the advice of Warren Buffet, the audit committee should ask the following questions of the auditors to help them manage the potential conflict of interest:[20]

1. If the auditor was an investor, would he or she have received the essential information accurately presented to understand the company's financial condition?
2. If the auditor was solely responsible for preparing the company's financial statements, would he or she have done anything differently?

Questions such as these are fundamentally ethical in nature and get at the principle of truth telling—that is, presenting an accurate view of the company's financial condition.

Integrity in the Financial Markets

Issues for accountants and CFOs, though timely and prominent in the news, do not exhaust the issues relating to integrity in the area of finance. Other issues exist that are not specifically related to accounting but are critical to the structure and integrity of the financial markets, namely, the stock markets and the investment banking industry, which are the vehicles through which companies raise the capital necessary to grow and thrive.

Insider Trading

While the concept sounds technically complex, the practice of "insider trading" is relatively simple to understand. With large amounts of money at stake, tidbits of private information about company activities become invaluable. All one has to do is find out about important developments shortly before they are made available to the public and either purchase or "sell short"[21] some shares of the company stock and a fortune can be made instantly. Other "insiders" have been more than willing to steal tips, sell them, tip off friends and relatives, and trade on them for their own profit. Insider trading received widespread public attention in the late 1980s through the illegal activities of Ivan Boesky and Michael Milken, and even more recently, well-known figures such as Martha Stewart have been accused of profiting from trading on insider information. Some of the most recent insider trading charges involve networking firms that connect hedge funds with experts who can provide critical information needed for their investment portfolio. The SEC has charged that some of these firms are actually buying insider information from strategically placed insiders and selling it to their clients.[22]

Insider trading is generally defined as using significant facts about a company that have not been made public in order to trade securities. Insider trading is illegal for two primary reasons. The first reason is that insider trading violates a company's property rights, of which confidential information is a prime example. As such, private information should be treated in the same manner as other corporate assets. Since the corporation "owns" the information, employees who trade on it or disseminate it without permission are engaging in theft of company property. However, if a company agrees to give permission to its employees to trade on such information, no theft of property occurs. And if this is announced to shareholders and the general public at large, it is indeed hard to imagine how anyone would be defrauded by such actions. Furthermore, many remote tippees and other "outsiders" have not purposefully or maliciously, or in some cases, even knowingly acquired insider information. Consequently, they have not stolen anyone's property, nor have they breached any fiduciary responsibilities to the corporation or its shareholders.

The second rationale is based on much broader goals of fairness and equity in the securities market. Insider trading is prohibited within this framework to ensure that all investors who trade on the securities market are playing on a "level playing field" in terms of access to information. From this perspective, it would seem wrong for anyone to trade on this type of information, regardless of how it is acquired. If the second rationale of fairness is consistently applied, it would seem that those trading on nonpublic information, no matter how they acquired it, should be held criminally liable

[21] "Selling short" refers to the practice of trading stocks by betting that the price will go down rather than up. The client borrows stock and repays the debt with stock that is sold at a lower price, thus making a profit.

[22] Stuart Pfeifer and Jessica Guynn, "Silicon Valley Firm at Center of Insider Trading Crackdown," *Los Angeles Times*, January 27, 2011, C1, 3.

for trading on the information, because doing so is "unfair." Thus, even if a grandmother overheard two executives in a train station and sold her shares in a company to avoid losing her retirement assets, she could be guilty of transgressing the line of fairness.

In addition, though fairness in terms of a level playing field is important, without which many investors would stay away from the market altogether, total fairness is an unrealistic aim. Some sophisticated investors will always find information that others will not. For example, many market professionals such as mutual fund managers and analysts constantly search for new information about companies as part of their responsibilities to shareholders. While they are not legally entitled to "inside" information such as an impending takeover or the date of new product releases that have not been made public, they have timely access to more accurate information than does the typical small investor. In many cases, market professionals and other large individual investors can have access to high-ranking officials of companies in which they are interested in investing. However, there is a difference between insider information and hard work, since insiders are privy to information that other resourceful investors or analysts are not, no matter how hard they work, short of bribing someone or stealing it another way.

But the line between insider information and good analysis may be less clear than one would like to think.[23] If fairness is really the goal, then it would seem that anyone trading on such information, no matter how they attained it, should be criminally liable. However, in related scenarios that we could all envision, it seems obvious that some remote tippees should not be criminally liable for their actions. While "unfair," it is hard to imagine that our fictitious grandmother who overhears two executives talking and trades on the information in order to avoid losses in her retirement portfolio has been malicious in her actions.

What makes insider trading laws difficult to enforce has to do with the distinction between acts of commission and omission. Imagine that you have a substantial number of shares of stock in your company, and in order to diversify your investment portfolio, you sell 5 percent of your shares each quarter and reinvest them. On the day that you are intending to sell some shares, you go to work and read a report from the research division that a potential new product has turned out to be a bust, and you expect the company's stock price to drop when that news reaches the public. You decide to sell 20 percent of your shares that day instead of the normal 5 percent. There is little doubt that under the law you are guilty of insider trading, and it probably would not be that difficult to detect your stock sale and link it to the bad news about the company's new product.

[23] John C. Coffee Jr., "Outsider Trading, That New Crime." *Wall Street Journal*, November 14, 1990.

But suppose that on that same day, you come to work with a reminder to yourself to sell 5 percent of your shares that day. But this time the news you hear from the research division is very positive about this new product. You are convinced that it will change the industry. Again, if you decided to buy additional shares based on this information, that would be an easily detectable case of insider trading. But suppose that you simply change your mind about selling your shares. That would also be insider trading under the law—an act of omission but based on clear insider information nonetheless. But apart from you telling someone about that decision, that instance of insider trading would be impossible to detect. Advocates of legalizing insider trading look at cases like this one and conclude that the current law prohibiting insider trading is difficult to apply consistently.

Some defenders of insider trading have argued that it is essentially a "victimless crime," and in fact, many outsiders will benefit from the moves of insiders.[24] Clearly though, we all can think of situations in which noninsiders can get hurt. For example, if insiders knew about an impeding negative legal judgment against a company and dumped their shares before the public announcements, investors who subsequently bought these shares would be financially hurt by the deals. Conversely, investors would be buying undervalued shares when trading on insider information that is considered good news for the company.

If, however, insider trading were made legal and all investors were made aware of this, it would be hard to imagine how anyone would then be defrauded in the cases like the preceding one, since all participants would then be privy to the rules. However, opponents of insider trading insist that there is a bigger picture than simply what happens between individual investors. They argue that permitting insider trading would erode the trust that is critical to confidence in the capital markets—a necessity for a vibrant economy.

It is hard to imagine that the many small investors whose finances make up a sizable portion of the total dollars invested would want to participate in transactions in which they could not acquire crucial information in order to be rational actors in the market. Buying stocks while knowing that others have critical information that you cannot acquire would be akin to buying a car without the ability to find information on its CARFAX—its repair record, fuel efficiency, or potential resale value. When only insiders or those who are tipped off by them are in possession of critical information, the whole basis for fair competition would be thwarted. Resembling places where bribery is the accepted custom, position and the ability to pay for information instead of fair competition would be the determinant factors for success. Specifically, profiting from investments would then have very little

[24] See, e.g., Robert McGee, "Applying Ethics to Insider Trading," *Journal of Business Ethics* 77, no. 2 (January 2008): 205–17; and John Allen Paulos, "Is Insider Trading So Bad?" *Forbes* 171, no. 10 (May 12, 2003): 50.

to do with research and analysis, traditional tools that even small investors can utilize. Since the legalized selling of information would allow tips to go to the highest bidder, success in the market would then be based on position in crucial organizations and the ability to pay large sums for information. Trust would eventually erode to the point where only a few investors would willingly place their money into the securities industry, a critical source of funds for corporate improvement and innovation.

In addition, significant fiduciary relationships may be jeopardized by allowing companies to permit insider trading among their employees. If insider trading were permitted, managers and executives would be placed in positions where conflicts of interest would only be magnified.[25]

In sum, while significant clarification should be made to insider trading laws, a good argument can be made that these activities should remain illegal. Permitting their practice would undermine the very foundations of trust that are central to a thriving, growing economy. Without trust in the basic fairness of the system, investors are not likely to place their funds in the market, thereby depriving companies of the capital they need for growth and competitiveness.

Investment Banking

Investment banking, often referred to synonymously with "Wall Street," has come under intense criticism for its role in the near collapse of the financial system in 2007–9.

As we discussed in the introduction to this chapter, Wall Street certainly played a role, but to put all the responsibility on the financial firms for the mortgage crisis disregards other institutions that deserve their share of criticism, such as the mortgage industry, individual home owners, institutional investors, and the government. Particularly with the repeal of the Glass-Steagall Act in the late 1990s that allowed investment banks to accept deposits (thus virtually eliminating the distinction between banks and investment banks), questions about the purpose of investment banking began to surface. The article in this chapter by John Terrill, "The Moral Imperative of Investment Banking," is a timely reminder about the real purpose of investment banking.

Terrill cites one investment banker who defines the purpose of investment banking when he says, "People with good ideas can find capital to grow a concept which benefits all of us." He compares it to the circulatory system in the body, "facilitating the flow of capital and other assets to entities that need it most and will put it to best use." Terrill cites Lord Brian Griffiths, who suggests that investment banking has been partially responsible for lifting hundreds of millions of the poor out of poverty around the world. Terrill

[25] Jennifer Moore, "What Is Really Unethical about Insider Trading?" *Journal of Business Ethics* (September 1990): 171–82.

suggests that when viewed in this way, investment banking can actually be God's work.

But it also seems clear that investment banking had lost its way in the first decade of the 2000s. The original mission of finance had given way to highly leveraged and risky trading of increasingly complex derivative securities that few investors understood and even fewer bank executives comprehended. Historian and commentator Kevin Phillips expresses concern about the growing prevalence of the financial sector in the economy, suggesting that that sector "got too big too carelessly and in way too much of a hurry."[26] Phillips and others argue that the traditional functions of investment banking had become something resembling a zero-sum game of betting and trading. He states, "Credit markets are being used less to facilitate economic activity and more to leverage bets on changes in asset prices."[27] He describes the result of changes in the political landscape as producing a financial sector that "was free to take on greater risk—and to maximize its growth and profitability through product innovation, massive borrowing and expanded leverage."[28] He suggests that this shift away from what Terrill would call the mission of investment banking and into trading was, in part, a cause of the crisis of the financial system in 2007–9.

Terrill brings a helpful perspective to finance today in restoring its role in facilitating the movement of capital into productive economic activity. Work in investment banking can indeed be a calling to God's work in the world and, as Terrill describes, "Investment bankers can be God's stewards, allocating capital in ways that nourish and empower people, companies, communities, and entire countries."

[26] Kevin Phillips, *Bad Money: Reckless Finance, Failed Politics, and the Global Crisis of American Capitalism* (New York: Penguin, 2008), 32.

[27] Ibid., 49.

[28] Ibid., 60.

Conclusion: Restoring Trust in the Financial Markets

Trust is essential for a functioning economic system, particularly the operation of the financial markets. When investors no longer trust in the rules of fair play in the markets, they will take their capital and invest it in areas in which they are assured of these standards. Investors must be able to trust a company's earnings reports, stock analysts' recommendations, auditors' affirmations, fiduciary responsibilities of investment bankers, and oversight of the board of directors if they are to restore confidence in the markets.

Ultimately, restoring trust is not a matter of extrinsic motivations, such as more regulations and stiffer penalties for noncompliance. These are important, but the SEC already has volumes of rules and guidelines. And more are coming. Rules alone are not adequate, because they cannot cover all the possibilities, and the law will always have loopholes. This area is a good example of why ethics is so important. Alexander Solzhenitsyn put it this way: "A society with no other scale but the legal one is not quite worthy of man.... The letter of the law is too cold and formal an atmosphere of moral mediocrity, paralyzing man's nobler impulses."[29] As you will see later in the book, this is why companies need programs in ethics rather than simply compliance. Ethics empowers our nobler impulses, and character is crucial to leadership. Trust is restored by character, not simply by obedience to rules and regulations. Increasingly the investing public is demanding that trust be restored, and corporate leadership is seeing that this is essential if the system is to function in a healthy way.

[29] Alexander Solzhenitsyn, commencement address, Harvard University, June 8, 1978, http://www.americanrhetoric.com/speeches/alexandersolzhenitsynharvard.htm.

NINE

Marketing and Advertising

Introduction

Marketing is commonly perceived to be one of the most highly controversial areas of business practice. Students who major in or emphasize marketing (or in one of its subdisciplines such as advertising), often find themselves on the defensive end of questions about morally appropriate professions to enter. The intensity of the conversations may well be even more pronounced on campuses of religiously affiliated schools. Some of our students, for example, report being asked, "How can someone who claims to be a good Christian go into a profession that promotes materialism and is (at best) about convincing people to buy things they really don't need?"

Undoubtedly, other professions (e.g., law, fashion design, and more recently, banking/Wall Street, come to mind) are the subjects of similar inquiries, but marketing likely ranks at or near the top in terms of the frequency and intensity in which these questions come to the surface. In addition to its role in promoting conspicuous consumption, some of the field's techniques, particularly those used in commercial advertising, are viewed as ethically unscrupulous. In sum, marketing is viewed negatively for its alleged deceptiveness, attempts to manipulative consumers, seemingly ever-expanding presence/ubiquity, and use of destructive messages.

The aim of this chapter is to examine the field of marketing in light of Christian ethics. How well do the imbedded values of marketing align with Christian ethics? Can marketing be practiced in a way that honors Christian values, particularly the concept of vocation (a place to serve God and others)? Can it be practiced in ways that are both economically viable and that advance human well-being by promoting healthy mutual relationships? What guidelines would Christian ethics offer for the practice of responsible marketing?

In the chapter's first essay, "Making Consumers," author Rodney Clapp uses a historical perspective to establish that consumers are not "born" as such. People do not naturally consume as a way of life. Rather, a brief journey back in time suggests that they had to be taught to do so, with early twentieth-century advertising serving as one of their primary instructors. Advertising, Clapp argues, continues today to create new needs and not merely respond to existing ones, all the while contributing to the ethos of consumption that has become our modern theology.

The second essay was written by Jean Kilbourne, a well-known author and speaker on college campuses who specializes in pointing out the damaging messages of advertising.[1] In "Jesus Is a Brand of Jeans," Kilbourne examines the content of commercial advertising and finds it filled with messages that are destructive to the human psyche and spirit. Advertising, she says, encourages us to use people and love objects, a direct reversal of how we ought to see and respond to the world around us.

The third essay, "Truth about Advertising," is a response to an address given by Kilbourne at Messiah College, where author David Hagenbuch serves as a marketing professor. In it he offers a refutation of some of Kilbourne's key criticisms and presents a case for how advertising may make more positive contributions to our lives.

"Marketing as a Christian Vocation" is the provocative title of the fourth essay (also written by David Hagenbuch). In the article, he seeks to refute the notion that marketing is an unsuitable vocation. Hagenbuch argues that marketing can be considered a "vocation" that contributes to reconciliation when done according to its "normative definition" (what it should be). Much of what critics argue is wrong with marketing, he contends, falls outside of the American Marketing Association's definition.

[1] Jean Kilbourne and Mary Pipher, *Can't Buy My Love: How Advertising Changes the Way We Think and Feel* (New York: Free Press, 2000); idem, *Deadly Persuasion: Why Women and Girls Must Fight the Addictive Power of Advertising* (New York: Free Press, 1999). See also Kilbourne's popular film series, Killing Us Softly (available at the Media Education Foundation, www.mediaed.org).

READINGS

Making Consumers

Rodney Clapp

From "Why the Devil Takes VISA: A Christian Response to the Triumph of Consumerism," *Christianity Today*, October 7, 1996.

It would be a gross distortion to act as if Protestantism alone invented and sustained consumer capitalism, though Protestantism's effects are significant if we are to understand the influence of consumerism on Christians. Still, it is crucial to note other historical factors essential to the birth and growth of consumerism. In terms of the push and pull of the everyday economy, historians are agreed that production-oriented capitalism moved on to become consumption-oriented capitalism because capitalism itself was so successful.

Until the twentieth century, most American homes were sites not only of consumption but of production. Even as late as 1850, six out of ten people worked on farms. They made most of their own tools; they built their homes and barns; they constructed their furniture; they wove and sewed their clothes; they grew crops and animals, producing food and drink; they chopped wood and made candles to provide heat and light. One nineteenth-century Massachusetts farmer, for instance, produced so much of what he needed at home that he never spent more than $10 a year.

The Industrial Revolution changed all that, very quickly. As the factory system and mass production came to dominance over the space of decades, it displaced home production by cheaply producing a host of commodities formerly made at home, driving out cottage industry and forcing millions into wage labor. From 1859 to 1899, the value of manufactured goods in the United States shot from $1.9 billion to $13 billion. Factories grew from 140,000 to 512,000.

Rather suddenly, this economic system could produce many more goods than the existing population, with its set habits and means, could afford and consume. For instance, when James Buchanan Duke procured merely two Bonsack cigarette machines, he could immediately produce 240,000 cigarettes a day—more than the entire U.S. market smoked. Such overproduction was the rule, not the exception, throughout the economy. From flour manufacturers to stovemakers, there was a widespread and acute recognition that the amount of goods available had far surpassed the number of buyers for those goods. Further, new products emerged for which markets needed to be developed. For instance, when Henry P. Crowell of Quaker Oats (benefactor of Moody Bible Institute, where a building is named after him) built an automated mill in 1882, most Americans ate meat and potatoes, not cereal, for breakfast.

There was, in short, a huge gap between production and consumption. How to close it? Industrial production's momentum had already built up, so cutting production was not feasible. Manufacturers decided instead to pump up consumption, to increase demand to meet supply. But they realized consumption was a way of life that had to be taught and learned. People had to move away from habits of strict thrift toward habits of ready spending. To be adequate consumers, they had to depart from a dependence on traditional skills, on production by families and artisans and local merchants. They had to learn to trust and rely on a multitude of products and services manufactured and promoted from far away by complete strangers.

By trial and error, manufacturers arrived at methods for reshaping people's economic habits. They instituted money-back guarantees and credit buying. They created brand names and mascots to give their mass-produced goods an appealing "personality." They introduced mail order and, as in the case of Sears, coached and reassured semiliterate customers to order by post ("Tell us what you want in your own way, written in any language, no matter whether good or poor writing, and the goods will promptly be sent to you"). And, of course, they advertised.

The Cultivation of Consumers

Many other factors were important in the rise of consumerism, but since advertising is the most insistent and undisguised face of advanced consumption, it merits special attention.

Until the late nineteenth century, advertising had been mainly informational. Advertising pages in eighteenth-century newspapers looked like the classifieds in today's papers. There were no pictures and, rather like news items, the ads simply did such things as announce when a shipment of rice would arrive from the Carolinas. But faced with a mass market and the crises of overproduction, manufacturers by the late nineteenth century initiated an advertising revolution. New advertising departed the realm of pure information, incorporating images and a host of persuasive tactics. It was, and remains, a primary tool in teaching people how to be consumers.

Early twentieth-century advertising, for instance, was used by Colgate to teach people who had never heard of toothpaste that they should brush their teeth daily. King Gillette, the inventor of the disposable razor, coaxed men to shave daily and to do it themselves, not see a barber. Thus his ads included shaving lessons, with leads such as "Note the Angle Stroke." Eastman Kodak advertising tutored the masses in making the portable camera their "family historian." Food manufacturers published cookbooks training housewives to cook with exact measures of (branded) products. Newly enabled by preservatives and far-flung distribution networks, Domino Gold Syrup sought in 1919 explicitly to "educate" people that syrup was not only for wintertime pancakes. Said the sales manager, "Our belief is that the entire year is syrup season and the people must be educated to believe this is a fact."

The effectiveness of advertising in selling any specific product remains debatable. What cannot be doubted is that early advertising successfully introduced an expansive array of products and services, playing a key role in the replacement of traditional home production by store-bought commodities. Furthermore, advertising and related media have served and still serve as important shapers of an ethos that has the good life attained through acquisition and consumption, and that would have its inhabitants constantly yearning for new products and new experiences.

Indeed, advertisers soon recognized that they must not simply cater to pre-existing needs, but create new needs. As Crowell of Quaker Oats noted, "[My aim in advertising] was to do educational and constructive work so as to awaken an interest in and create a demand for cereals where none existed." And as *The Thompson Red Book on Advertising* put it more generally in 1901, "Advertising aims to teach people that they have wants, which they did not recognize before, and where such wants can be best supplied." Consequently, one newspaper reader in 1897 said that not so long ago people "skipped [ads] unless some want compelled us to read, while now we read to find out what we really want."

Advertisers did not act alone in training consumers. Government began in the early twentieth century to solidify and boost the newly emerged strength of business corporations, capping this alliance with Herbert Hoover's expansion of the Department of Commerce in the 1920s. Schools quite self-consciously cooperated with corporations in molding young consumers.

One 1952 Whirlpool short-subject film, for instance, featured three teenage girls around a kitchen table, at work on a report about the emancipation of women. Did emancipation equal winning the vote? Assuming property and other legal rights? No, the girls decide, as the host rises from the table to attend a shiny washing machine. Real emancipation came with release from the drudgery of chores, with washing machines and dryers that liberated women from clotheslines and "dark basements." *Business Screen* magazine gave clear instruction for the film's use in its review: "Some good clean selling takes place during this half-hour.... The film will have special appeal to women's groups of all kinds and to home economics classes from teenage on up."

Consumers, in short, were made, not born.

The Deification of Dissatisfaction

Into the nineteenth century, then, advertising and consumption were oriented to raw information and basic needs. It was only in the late nineteenth and then the twentieth century, with the maturation of consumer capitalism, that a shift was made toward the cultivation of unbounded desire. We must appreciate this to realize that late modern consumption, consumption as we now know it, is not fundamentally about materialism or the consumption of physical goods. Affluence and consumer-oriented capitalism have moved us well beyond the undeniable efficiencies and benefits of refrigerators and indoor plumbing. Instead, in a fun-house world of ever-proliferating wants and exquisitely unsatisfied desire, consumption entails most profoundly the cultivation of pleasure, the pursuit of novelty, and the chasing after illusory experiences associated with material goods.

Sex appeal sells everything from toothpaste to automobiles. (Recently, a cancer-detection ad on the back of a Christian magazine headlined, "Before you read this, take your clothes off." Then, in fine print, it counseled how to do bodily self-examinations.) Often, cigarette and alcohol ads do not even depict their product being consumed, but instead prime us to associate them with robust cowboys and spectacular mountain vistas. By 1989, the American Association of Advertising Agencies explicitly stated that consumer perceptions "are a fundamental part of manufacturing the product—as much as size, shape, color, flavor, design, or raw materials."

In 1909, an advertising manager for Winton Motor Cars representing the old school had declared, "When a man buys an automobile he purchases a specific entity, made of so much iron, steel, brass, copper, leather, wood, and horsehair, put together in a specific form and manner.... Why attract his attention to the entity by something that is foreign thereto? Has the car itself not sufficient merit to attain that attention? Why suggest 'atmosphere,' which is something he cannot buy?"

But by 1925, "atmosphere" no longer seemed beyond the reach of the market. In that year advertising copywriter John Starr Hewitt wrote, "No one has ever in his life bought a mere piece of merchandise— per se. What he buys is the satisfaction of a physical need or the gratification of some dream about his life."

In the same year, Ernest Elmo Calkins, the cofounder of the Calkins and Holden ad agency, observed, "I have spent much of my life trying to teach the business man that beauty has a dollars-and-cents value, because I feel that only thus will it be produced in any quantity in a commercial age." Calkins recognized that, in his words, "Modernism offered the opportunity of expressing the inexpressible, of suggesting not so much the motor car as speed, not so much a gown as style, not so much a compact as beauty." All, of course, with a dollars-and-cents value attached.

Thus speed, style, beauty, sex, love, spirituality have all become for the modern consumer categories to be evoked and sampled at will by selecting from a vast array of products, services, and commodified experiences. Colin Campbell considers contemporary tourism a prime example. Tourism as an industry and a commodity depends for its survival on an insatiable yearning for "ever-new objects to gaze at." The same can be said for shopping, spectator sports, concert-going, movie-viewing, and other quintessential "consumer" activities. "Modern consumers will desire a novel rather than a familiar product because this enables them to believe that its acquisition and use will supply experiences they have not encountered to date in reality." Moreover, as those many now blissfully lost in cyberspace will attest, reality can be decidedly more inconvenient and less purely pleasurable than virtual reality.

In 1627, Francis Bacon's *New Atlantis* dreamed of a utopia in which technology could adjust growing seasons and create synthetic fruit tastier and better looking than natural fruit. In our culture, the *New Atlantis* has, after a fashion, come into being, and its plenty includes cosmetically enhanced fruit, artificial sweeteners, nonalcoholic beer, and fat-free junk food.

Yet, as Campbell reminds us, actual consumption is "likely to be a literally disillusioning experience, since real products cannot possibly supply the same quality of perfected pleasure as that which attends imaginatively enjoyed experiences." So we modern consumers are perpetually dissatisfied. Fulfillment and lasting satisfaction are forever just out of reach. And if we cannot escape completely to cyberspace, we reach for and grab again and again the product or commodified experience that provides temporary pleasure.

We are profoundly schooled and thousands of times daily reinforced—remember, the average American is exposed to more than three thousand sales messages daily—in an insatiability that is, as the theologian Miroslav Volf remarks, "unique to modernity." Insatiability itself is as old as humanity, or at least the fall of humanity. What is unique to modern consumerism is the idealization and constant encouragement of insatiability—the deification of dissatisfaction.

Economics and the consumerism it serves is, as the economist Robert Nelson candidly admits, "our modern theology." Modernity is that age that has believed in the future against the past, in limitless progress that would eliminate not just the practical but the moral and spiritual problems of humanity. Many of the major concerns and practices of classical Christianity were accordingly redefined along economic lines. Material scarcity and the resulting conflict over precious resources were seen as the sources of human sinfulness. So economic progress and the building of consumer societies has "represented the route of salvation to a new heaven on earth." Economic efficiency has for many replaced the providence of God.

Christian missionaries traveled to spread the gospel; economic theology has missionaries such as the

Peace Corps and international development agencies, delivering the good news of "economic progress, rational knowledge, and human redemption." Christianity saw the coming of Christ as history's supreme revelatory moment. Economic theology, or a theology of consumption, considers it to be the discoveries of modern science and technology. And twentieth-century religious wars are no longer fought between Roman Catholics and various Protestants, but "among men often inspired by Marxist, fascist, capitalist, and still other messages of economic salvation" (Robert Nelson).

The Importance of Character

"Whoever has the power to project a vision of the good life and make it prevail," the historian William Leach writes, "has the most decisive power of all. In its sheer quest to produce and sell goods cheaply in constantly growing volume and at higher profit levels, American business, after 1890, acquired such power and has kept it ever since."

Since consumer capitalism — today not just in America but around the world — so effectively promotes its version of the good life, and since consumers are made rather than born, a Christian response demands a consideration of character.

Every culture or way of life requires a certain kind of person — a "character" with fitting attitudes, skills, and motivations — to sustain and advance the good life as that culture knows it. Thus Sparta was concerned to shape its citizens in the character of the warrior; Aristotle hoped for a polity that would make aristocrats; and twentieth-century America charged its public schools with the task of instilling the American way of life in their students.

In the postwar boom days of 1955, retailing analyst Victor Lebow echoed his advertising predecessors, declaring, "Our enormously productive economy ...

demands that we make consumption our way of life, that we convert the buying and use of goods into rituals, that we seek our spiritual satisfaction, our ego satisfaction, in consumption.... We need things consumed, burned up, worn out, replaced, and discarded at an ever increasing rate."

Can there be any doubt that we now live in the world Lebow prophesied and desired? That shopping has become a conspicuous ritual profoundly indicative of our social ethic is facetiously but tellingly betrayed in such slogans as "I shop, therefore I am," and "They came, they saw, they did a little shopping," scrawled on the Berlin Wall shortly after East Germans were allowed to pass freely into West Germany.

Planned obsolescence, installment buying, and credit cards — all creations of this century — were key means to making consumption a way of life. Now, as with President Bush a few years ago, public officials dutifully appear on the evening news buying a pair of socks to inaugurate the Christmas season.

Our language is one significant indication that consumption is a way of life. We are encouraged to see and interpret more and more of our activities in terms of consumption. In the language of marketers, people who go to movies are not "audiences," but "consumers"; those who go to school are no longer "students," but "educational consumers." People who visit a physician are no longer "patients," those who go to church are no longer "worshipers," those who go to libraries and bookstores are no longer "readers," those who go to restaurants are no longer "diners." All are as frequently designated "consumers."

The church must examine and challenge consumerism at exactly this point. What sort of people does consumer capitalism want us to be? What are the key character traits of the consumer par excellence? And how do these stack up against the standards and aims of Christian character?

Questions for Discussion and Reflection

1. What do you think of Clapp's assessment of American consumer culture? Do you think he is correct, or has he overstated the case? Explain your answer.
2. Why do you think there is such a taboo on discussing what we do with our money?
3. Do you think it is necessary as a Christian to resist the consumer culture? If so, what would you suggest as some practical ways to get started?

Jesus Is a Brand of Jeans

Jean Kilbourne

New Internationalist 393 (September 2006): 1–9.

A recent ad for Thule car-rack systems features a child in the backseat of a car, seatbelt on. Next to the child, assorted sporting gear is carefully strapped into a child's car seat. The headline says: 'We Know What Matters to You.' In case one misses the point, further copy adds: 'Your gear is a priority.'

Another ad features an attractive young couple in bed. The man is on top of the woman, presumably making love to her. However, her face is completely covered by a magazine, open to a double-page photo of a car. The man is gazing passionately at the car. The copy reads, 'The ultimate attraction.'

These ads are meant to be funny. Taken individually, I suppose they might seem amusing or, at worst, tasteless. As someone who has studied ads for a long time, however, I see them as part of a pattern: just two of many ads that state or imply that products are more important than people. Ads have long promised us a better relationship via a product: *buy this and you will be loved.* But more recently they have gone beyond that proposition to promise us a relationship with the product itself: *buy this and it will love you.* The product is not so much the means to an end, as the end itself.

After all, it is easier to love a product than a person. Relationships with human beings are messy, unpredictable, sometimes dangerous. 'When was the last time you felt this comfortable in a relationship?' asks an ad for shoes. Our shoes never ask us to wash the dishes or tell us we're getting fat. Even more important, products don't betray us. "You can love it without getting your heart broken,' proclaims a car ad. One certainly can't say that about loving a human being, as love without vulnerability is impossible.

We are surrounded by hundreds, thousands of messages every day that link our deepest emotions to products, that objectify people and trivialize our most heartfelt moments and relationships. Every emotion is used to sell us something. Our wish to protect our children is leveraged to make us buy an expensive car. A long marriage simply provides the occasions for a diamond necklace. A painful reunion between a father and his estranged daughter is dramatized to sell us a phone system. Everything in the world—nature, animals, people—is just so much stuff to be consumed or to be used to sell us something.

The problem with advertising isn't that it creates artificial needs, but that it exploits our very real and human desires. Advertising promotes a bankrupt concept of *relationship.* Most of us yearn for committed relationships that will last. We are not stupid: we know that buying a certain brand of cereal won't bring us one inch closer to that goal. But we are surrounded by advertising that yokes our needs with products and promises us that *things* will deliver what in fact they never can. In the world of advertising, lovers are things and things are lovers.

It may be that there is no other way to depict relationships when the ultimate goal is to sell products. But this apparently bottomless consumerism not only depletes the world's resources, it also depletes our inner resources. It leads inevitably to narcissism and solipsism. It becomes difficult to imagine a way of relating that isn't objectifying and exploitative.

Tuned In

Most people feel that advertising is not something to take seriously. Other aspects of the media are serious— the violent films, the trashy talk shows, the bowdlerization of the news. But not advertising! Although much more attention has been paid to the cultural impact of advertising in recent years than ever before, just about everyone still feels personally exempt from its influence. What I hear more than anything else at my lectures is: 'I don't pay attention to ads ... I just tune them out ... they have no effect on me.' I hear this most from people wearing clothes emblazoned with logos. In truth, we are all influenced. There is no way to tune out this much information, especially when it is designed to break through the 'tuning out' process. As advertising critic Sut Jhally put it: 'To not be influenced by advertising would be to live outside of culture. No human being lives outside of culture.'

Much of advertising's power comes from this belief that it does not affect us. As Joseph Goebbels said: 'This is the secret of propaganda: those who are to be persuaded by it should be completely immersed in the ideas of the propaganda, without ever noticing that they are being immersed in it.' Because we think advertising is trivial, we are less on guard, less critical, than we might otherwise be. While we're laughing, sometimes sneering, the commercial does its work.

Taken individually, ads are silly, sometimes funny, certainly nothing to worry about. But cumulatively they create a climate of cynicism that is poisonous to relationships. Ad after ad portrays our real lives as dull and ordinary, commitment to human beings as something to be avoided. Because of the pervasiveness of this kind of message, we learn from childhood that it is far safer to make a commitment to a product than to a person, far easier to be loyal to a brand. Many end up feeling romantic about material objects yet deeply cynical about other human beings.

Unnatural Passions

We know by now that advertising often turns people into objects. Women's bodies—and men's bodies too these days—are dismembered, packaged and used to sell everything from chainsaws to chewing gun, champagne to shampoo. Self-image is deeply affected. The self-esteem of girls plummets as they reach adolescence partly because they cannot possibly escape the message that their bodies are objects, and imperfect objects at that. Boys learn that masculinity requires a kind of ruthlessness, even brutality.

Advertising encourages us not only to objectify each other but to feel passion for products rather than our partners. This is especially dangerous when the products are potentially addictive, because addicts do feel they are in a relationship with their substances. I once heard an alcoholic joke that Jack Daniels was her most constant lover. When I was a smoker, I felt that my cigarettes were my friends. Advertising reinforces these beliefs, so we are twice seduced—by the ads and the substances themselves.

The addict is the ideal consumer. Ten per cent of drinkers consume over sixty per cent of all the alcohol sold. Most of them are alcoholics or people in desperate trouble—but they are also the alcohol industry's very best customers. Advertisers spend enormous amounts of money on psychological research and understand addiction well. They use this knowledge to target children (because if you hook them early they are yours for life), to encourage all people to consume more, in spite of often dangerous consequences for all of us, and to create a climate of denial in which all kinds of addictions flourish. This they do with full intent, as we see so clearly in the 'secret documents' of the tobacco industry that have been made public in recent years.

The consumer culture encourages us not only to buy more but to seek our identity and fulfillment through what we buy, to express our individuality through our 'choices' of products. Advertising corrupts relationships and then offers us products, both as solace and as substitutes for the intimate human connection we all long for and need.

In the world of advertising, lovers grow cold, spouses grow old, children grow up and away—but possessions stay with us and never change. Seeking the outcomes of a healthy relationship through products cannot work. Sometimes it leads us into addiction. But at best the possessions can never deliver the promised goods. They can't make us happy or loved or less alone or safe. If we believe they can, we are doomed to disappointment. No matter how much we love them they will never love us back.

Some argue that advertising simply reflects societal values rather than affecting them. Far from being a passive mirror of society, however, advertising is a pervasive medium of influence and persuasion. Its influence is cumulative, often subtle and primarily unconscious. A former editor-in-chief of *Advertising Age*, the leading advertising publication in North America, once claimed: 'Only eight per cent of an ad's message is received by the conscious mind. The rest is worked and re-worked deep within, in the recesses of the brain.'

Advertising performs much the same function in industrial society as myth did in ancient societies. It is both a creator and perpetuator of the dominant values of the culture, the social norms by which most people govern their behavior. At the very least, advertising helps to create a climate in which certain values flourish and others are not reflected at all.

Advertising is not only our physical environment, it is increasingly our spiritual environment as well. By definition, however, it is only interested in materialistic values. When spiritual values show up in ads, it is only in order to sell us something. Eternity is a perfume by Calvin Klein. Infiniti is an automobile, and Hydra Zen a moisturizer. Jesus is a brand of jeans.

Sometimes the allusion is more subtle, as in the countless alcohol ads featuring the bottle surrounded by a halo of light. Indeed products such as jewelry shining in a store window are often displayed as if they were sacred objects. Advertising co-opts our sacred symbols in order to evoke an immediate emotional response. Media critic Neil Postman referred to this as 'cultural rape.'

It is commonplace to observe that consumerism has become the religion of our time (with advertising its holy text), but the criticism usually stops short of what is at the heart of the comparison. Both advertising and religion share a belief in transformation, but most religions believe that this requires sacrifice. In the world of advertising, enlightenment is achieved instantly by purchasing material goods. An ad for a watch says, 'It's not your handbag. It's not your neighborhood. It's not your boyfriend. It's your watch that tells most about who you are.' Of course, this cheapens authentic spirituality and transcendence. This junk food for the soul leaves us hungry, empty, malnourished.

Substitute Stories

Human beings used to be influenced primarily by the stories of our particular tribe or community, not by stories that are mass-produced and market-driven. As George Gerbner, one of the world's most respected researchers on the influence of the media, said: 'For the first time in human history, most of the stories about people, life and values are told not by parents, schools, churches, or others in the community who have something to tell, but by a group of distant conglomerates that have something to sell.'

Although it is virtually impossible to measure the influence of advertising on a culture, we can learn something by looking at cultures only recently exposed to it. In 1980 the Gwich'in tribe of Alaska got television, and therefore massive advertising, for the first time. Satellite dishes, video games and VCRs were not far behind. Before this, the Gwich'in lived much the way their ancestors had for generations. Within 10 years, the young members of the tribe were so drawn by television they no longer had time to learn ancient hunting methods, their parents' language or their oral history. Legends told around campfires could not compete with *Beverly Hills 90210*. Beaded moccasins gave way to Nike sneakers, and 'tundra tea' to Folgers instant coffee.

As multinational chains replace local character, we end up in a world in which everyone is Gapped and Starbucked. Shopping malls kill vibrant downtown centers locally and create a universe of uniformity internationally. We end up in a world ruled by, in John Maynard Keynes's phrase, the values of the casino. On this deeper level, rampant commercialism undermines our physical and psychological health, our environments and our civic life, and creates a toxic society.

Advertising creates a worldview that is based upon cynicism, dissatisfaction, and craving. Advertisers aren't evil. They are just doing their job, which is to sell a product; but the consequences, usually unintended, are often destructive. In the history of the world there has never been a propaganda effort to match that of advertising in the past 50 years. More thought, more effort, more money goes into advertising than has gone into any other campaign to change social consciousness. The story that advertising tells is that the way to be happy, to find satisfaction—and the path to political freedom, as well—is through the consumption of material objects. And the major motivating force for social change throughout the world today is this belief that happiness comes from the market.

Questions for Discussion and Reflection

1. What are the main criticisms of advertising that Kilbourne brings out? Do you agree with these criticisms?
2. She claims that advertising promotes the message that products are more important than people. Do you agree? Why or why not?
3. Do you believe that "advertising exploits our very real and human desires"? If so, do you believe that's a bad thing? Explain your answer.

Truth about Advertising: A Response to the Kilbourne Lecture

David J. Hagenbuch

Speech given at Messiah College, March 10, 2004.

I commend the School of the Humanities for bringing Dr. Jean Kilbourne, a nationally known lecturer, author, and consumer advocate, to our campus on March 10. Dr. Kilbourne aptly identified several important social concerns related to the negative influence of certain types of advertising. For example, some advertising portrays women in ways that treat them as objects. In addition, there is much more advertising than most of us would like for products such as cigarettes and alcohol. Also, ads for these specific products often do make blatantly false associations, e.g., healthy people smoke cigarettes.

It was unfortunate, however, that Dr. Kilbourne's portrayal of advertising was so one-sided. I cannot recall a single slide that served as a positive example of advertising, nor do I recollect a single mention of a redeeming aspect of the discipline. As a result, the not-so-subtle inference from the lecture was that all advertising is destructive to society. This interpretation of the lecture represents not only my own view but also those of others with whom I've spoken. In fact, one of the comments that compelled me to write this response came from an advisee and student of mine who, after attending the lecture, thought she should no longer be a marketing major.

Let me reiterate that Dr. Kilbourne did effectively and accurately identify several critical problems for which some advertisers must be held accountable. I also will add that I have spoken with other people who appreciated many aspects of Dr. Kilbourne's presentation. Ultimately, however, I feel that her lecture propagated an undeserved, negative stereotype of all advertising, which undermines possible reform. The balance of my response highlights specific concerns during her presentation.

In my classes, I have discussed several of the following methods that Dr. Kilbourne used, which researchers and lecturers generally try to avoid. First,

it's easy to find literature or other evidence to support almost any position, so one should strive for an objective portrayal and not selectively choose information. Some support for this criticism of the lecture was given above; more will follow. In addition, one should maintain clear separation between disparate issues, being careful not to mix them, which obscures arguments and misleads listeners. Throughout her lecture, Dr. Kilbourne repeatedly alternated between discussions of questionable advertising approaches (e.g., use of sexuality) and destructive products (e.g., beer). The methods that some advertisers use and the products that some ads portray represent two distinct issues. It's easy, however, to make the approach used to advertise a sweater appear questionable when that ad is showcased between an ad for Marlboros and another for Absolut Vodka. Finally, researchers are trained to be cautious about generalizing their findings. A sample should be representative if generalizations are to be made from it to the larger population. I have been a student of marketing (the broader discipline level). I also have worked in areas of advertising for about ten years. In addition, I am a consumer who, like most, encounters countless promotional messages each day. Despite this intentional and chance exposure to many advertisements, I recognized only a few of the ads Dr. Kilbourne shared. Her inference was that one could generalize from these few ads to all advertising. Anecdotal evidence, however, suggests that her sample ads are not representative of the entire population of advertising.

Beyond some dubious methods, however, the foremost criticism of Dr. Kilbourne's presentation stems from what might be considered biased content. I will focus on three inaccuracies. First, Dr. Kilbourne presented an uncharacteristically narrow view of advertising. Based upon the look of most of the ads (full-color, glossy) and her comments, it seemed that the vast majority of Dr. Kilbourne's ads were taken from national magazines, and most appeared to be those of for-profit companies. Admittedly, these types of ads are a significant portion of all advertising, yet according to any statistics that I have read, these types of ads are far from the majority of advertising. In keeping with this allegation of narrow focus, I do not believe Dr. Kilbourne offered a definition or meaningful description of the presentation's main construct—advertising (a formal identification of key terms is a good idea for any lecture).

Advertising is commonly considered to be any form of mass communication that is paid for by an identified sponsor. Advertising, therefore, encompasses regional and local promotions, as well as national ones; it includes a variety of media such as radio, television, newspapers, billboards and other signage, the Internet, brochures, flyers, and direct mail; and it is used by all types of organizations, including colleges, hospitals, government, social agencies, and churches. It is hard to imagine that advertising done in all of these forms and by all of these types of organizations is as categorically offensive as Dr. Kilbourne's presentation purported.

A second major flaw involved a misrepresentation of the marketing concept. Marketing is the process by which a seller encourages a buyer to participate in a mutually beneficial exchange of products, services, or ideas. The marketing concept refers to the seller's desire to satisfy the wants and needs of the buyer by strategically altering elements of the marketing mix, which are often labeled product, place, promotion, and price. The promotion variables involve ways in which the seller communicates with the buyer; advertising is one of those means of communication. Dr. Kilbourne misrepresented the marketing concept as she showed advertisements from trade publications that talked about delivering certain target markets to prospective advertisers. Certainly, some of the metaphors these ads used were in poor taste (e.g., forwarding a bag of eyeballs). On the other hand, one must question whether advertisements should be scrutinized for using some of the same benign humor and figures of speech that most of us use in our own daily communication. For instance, I've often heard people speak about acquiring a "headcount" for a luncheon or a meeting, but no one objects to this morbid-sounding talk. The industry expression "delivering a target market" may sound impersonal to those outside of marketing, but properly interpreted the phrase reflects a strategy that is consistent with the marketing concept and that is in the best interest of consumers. By identifying a specific group of people who are most likely to benefit from a firm's product (i.e., selecting a target market), and by tailoring the product and related elements to the unique needs of those individuals, the firm greatly improves the likelihood of meeting consumers' needs and of creating a win-win outcome.

Advertising that is well written and properly targeted, therefore, often receives a warm reception from consumers who are thankful for the information they receive, which allows them to purchase and benefit from products that they otherwise may not have been aware of—such is a true representation of the marketing concept. Personally, I am grateful that last year I saw a national television ad for a car that I otherwise would not have considered purchasing. I bought the car and have been very satisfied with it. I don't feel that I was manipulated, and I don't want my money back. I think the advertiser of the vehicle benefited; I know I did. My suspicion is that most consumers can identify many of their own such positive experiences with advertising.

Finally, Dr. Kilbourne purported that advertising is responsible for several social ills. As previously discussed, one first should be careful to distinguish certain types of harmful ads (ones that employ particular questionable tactics or those that promote specific destructive products) from the rest of advertising. Furthermore, in any research, one should be cautious about ascribing causality. Eating disorders represent a devastating social problem that we all would like to see eradicated. Do ads that show inordinately skinny models actually cause eating disorders, however? My instincts tell me that certain ads definitely cannot be helping the situation. At the same time, though, one should not overlook other influential factors, such as Americans' taste for high-calorie foods, aversion to regular exercise, and obsession with physical appearance. Although I am not willing to do so, one could tender a rather extreme argument that reverses the causal chain and contends that American's obsession with thinness leads advertisers, who want to meet consumers' needs and expectations, to choose emaciated models for their promotions.

Continuing this reasoning, many have argued that advertising is more a mirror of society's values than it is a molder of those values (e.g., Lantos, 1987; Pollay, 1986). It also may be fair to ask, why would advertisers want to conspire to create a society of gaunt consumers? If anything, one might speculate that such collusion would seek an opposite goal—to create a norm that favors larger consumers, who conceivably might demand more products and/or bigger ones. Again, let me say that I am not willing to absolve advertising of all responsibility related to eating disorders or to the other social problems that Dr. Kilbourne mentioned. I believe, however, that inaccurately or prematurely concluding that advertising is the principal cause of these problems may serve to discourage much needed research into other factors that are perhaps even more influential.

The advertising industry, like many fields, contains practices that cry out for reform. There is no question in my mind, however, that advertising as a whole serves many useful purposes both for the organizations that advertise and for the consumers who benefit from the products, services, and ideas that are advertised responsibly. There is nothing inherently wrong with paid-for mass communication. It is wrong, however, to forfeit objectivity and balance and to negatively stereotype an entire industry and group of people. Such a one-sided approach is likely to erect barriers to meaningful dialogue and estrange those in the advertising industry who have the power to turn recommended reforms into reality. I hope that certain advertising practices will be changed. I also hope that we will promote a balanced perception of advertising so that my advisee and other people of integrity will be encouraged to enter the field, not leave it, and in doing so, help bring about specific reforms where they are needed.

Questions for Discussion and Reflection

1. Do you think that Hagenbuch offers an effective critique of Kilbourne's view of advertising? Why or why not?
2. Do you agree with Hagenbuch that "advertising serves many useful purposes both for the organizations that advertise and for the consumers who benefit"? Explain your answer.

Marketing as a Christian Vocation: Called to Reconciliation

David J. Hagenbuch

Christian Scholar's Review, Vol. 48 (Fall 2002), 83–96.

In titling this paper "Marketing as a Christian Vocation," I was struck by the notion that for many other disciplines, a similar choice of words would be much less controversial. For instance, would people be as skeptical of an article entitled "Social Work as a Christian Calling" or "Nursing as a Christian Vocation"? This question is not meant to suggest that these disciplines are uninteresting or not conducive to Christian service. In fact, the implication is exactly the opposite: To a great extent, people seem to accept these and many other fields as ones in which people readily do work that is honoring to God. Marketing, however, enjoys few such positive associations.

Indeed, for some, to associate marketing with Christian vocation represents something between paradox and blasphemy, analogous to "Money Laundering as a Christian Calling," or "Pirating Software for Jesus." A teaching colleague of mine, for example, once bantered, "Your class is called Marketing Principles? Isn't that an oxymoron?" Also, during a sermon I heard a few years ago, the speaker remarked matter-of-factly, "Advertising is lying." Even in an introduction to a marketing textbook, a case study mentioned in passing that car salesmen are "the most untrustworthy people." These isolated comments are not particularly troubling; however, when considered along with numerous works that have documented negative perceptions of marketing,[1] the collective implications should be of concern to Christians in higher education. Marketing is a major at a large number of Christian colleges and universities, yet students often seem to be the recipients of a conflicting message that marketing is not an acceptable field in which to serve God.

The tragedy of this miscommunication is that our world greatly needs individuals to practice marketing in a way that is true to the discipline's theoretical foundation and is consistent with the central tenets of the Christian faith. The main purpose of this paper is to elucidate the foundational compatibility between Christianity and marketing, thus supporting the discipline's suitability as part of a Christian vocation. Unlike other works that have dealt with Christian responses to certain marketing-related ethical issues more superficially, this paper delves deeper into the core of both belief sets, those of marketing and of Christianity, by explicating two intimately related concepts, reconciliation and exchange. In doing so, the paper develops the following important linkage between Christian vocation and marketing: The main purpose of Christian vocation is reconciliation; reconciliation is related inextricably to exchange; exchange is the underlying social behavior that marketing directs; consequently, the proper practice of marketing facilitates mutually beneficial exchange, which fosters reconciliation and thereby supports Christian voca-

tion. In addition, this paper suggests practical ways in which Christians can help to reconcile marketing practice to both the discipline's normative theory and to appropriate societal expectations. Given this agenda, it is important to begin with a discussion of the paper's key terms: *vocation, reconciliation, marketing,* and *exchange.* I will now treat the first two concepts, vocation and reconciliation, and support how they are intimately related.

Reconciliation: The Main Purpose of Vocation

Much has been written about vocation, and while it is not my intention to review the breadth and depth of literature, I do feel the need to present my own understanding of the concept. Like many others, I see vocation as God's calling for all of one's life. Vocation derives from the Latin verb *vocare*, to call, and from a biblical perspective, that caller is God.[2] It is important to note that this calling applies to every area of one's life, as there is no distinction between sacred and secular.[3] An individual's vocation may include, for instance, his or her role as parent, spouse, sibling, deacon, scout leader, softball player, and choir member. As such, a vocation is a unique, individualized calling, often not discovered easily, that requires specific talents, offers true enjoyment, and accomplishes something of value.[4]

Of course, one's occupation is also part of one's vocation. Here my understanding of vocation is influenced by Lutheran theology, which suggests that almost any occupation may be part of a Christian calling.[5] All work has the potential to be of service to God.[6] Because the topic of this paper is "Marketing as a Christian Vocation," the occupational component of vocation is this paper's main focus.

It is important to note, however, that marketing is not practiced exclusively as an occupation; marketing may be part of any number of other vocational roles. Given the preceding description of vocation, one may conclude that every person's vocation is different; God's calling is always unique. Nevertheless, there is a sense that all Christian callings are united by a common purpose. Many see the unifying objective of vocation as loving God and one's neighbors.[7]

I agree wholeheartedly with this assertion, which is based soundly on Jesus' greatest commandments.[8] It is every Christian's calling to love God and to love others no matter what his or her specific vocation. I also offer, however, that the desired outcome of this love may be summarized aptly in a single concept: reconciliation. For me, the central purpose of vocation is reconciliation. The works of several Christian scholars as well as Scripture itself seem to support this belief that Christian vocation is fundamentally about living a life of reconciliation.

Most Christians are likely to agree that reconciliation is an essential, if not the most fundamental, component of the gospel,[9] but what makes reconciliation integral to vocation? The writings of various scholars help to illuminate the important connection. Henlee Barnette contends that because all Christians have themselves been reconciled through Christ, they are called to be agents of reconciliation; she adds, "God calls the Christian with a holy calling and for a definite purpose (Romans 8:28; 9–11; Ephesians 1:11; II Timothy 1:9). His aim for mankind is that of redemption and reconciliation."[10] Douglas Schuurman supports the importance of reconciliation to vocation by maintaining that "the purpose of God's call is for people of God to worship God and to participate in God's creative and redemptive purposes for the world."[11] Gary Badcock suggests that "the Christian calling refers to the reorientation of human life to God through repentance, faith, and obedience."[12] Furthermore, Robert Cushman adds that reconciliation is not restricted to private redemption but includes the restoration of social structures, suggesting that Christian vocation should be seen as "positive engagement with the living Christ in the reconciliation of the whole creation."[13]

The most compelling support for the inseparability of vocation and reconciliation, however, comes from Scripture. As 2 Corinthians 5:18–19 suggests, those who have been reconciled through Christ are called to practice reconciliation: "All this is from God, who reconciled us to himself through Christ and gave us the ministry of reconciliation: that God was reconciling the world to himself in Christ, not counting men's sins against them. And he has committed to us the message of reconciliation." Likewise, Colossians

1:18–20 speaks of Christ as the head of the church and the means through which all things are reconciled to God. It seems reasonable to conclude, then, that Christians, the members of Christ's body, are called to supportive roles in that reconciliation.

Although the preceding discussion has begun to reveal my understanding of reconciliation, it is appropriate to define this complex construct more completely. My use of the term in this paper stems primarily from the New Testament meanings of three related Greek verbs:[14] *diallasso*: to change; to renew friendship with one;[15] *katallasso*: to change; to exchange for an equivalent value; to return to favor those who are at variance; to adjust a difference;[16] and *apokatallasso*: to bring back to a former state of harmony.[17]

The writings of several Christian scholars help to elucidate the biblical term further. For instance, in keeping with the idea of returning to a former state of harmony, Badcock suggests, "Reconciliation in biblical terms means that we are no longer strangers or enemies [of God] but children and even friends."[18] In terms of a change or an exchange, Cristoph Schwöbel suggests that reconciliation involves exchanging wrath and enmity for love and peace.[19] In addition, although

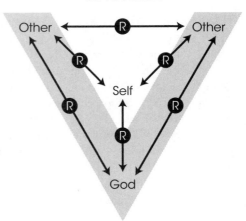

Figure 1: Model of Reconciliation as Vocation

V over all parameter for *vocation*

R *relationship* and potential path for reconciliation

reconciliation should occur first and foremost between an individual and God,[20] this reconciliation with the divine is tied closely to individuals reconciling with each other.[21]

Barnette affirms the preceding point and adds, "The ministry of reconciliation, however, is not limited to bringing men to God, but extends to the reconciliation of men with men. Moreover, all economic, social, and political ideologies are to be captured for Christ."[22] Reconciliation, therefore, is fundamentally about restoring, building, and maintaining strong relationships,[23] and as the model in Figure 1 illustrates, a Christian vocation understood in the broadest sense is one that supports reconciliation between oneself and God, oneself and others, others and God, and others and others.

I have shared my understanding of two of this paper's main constructs: vocation and reconciliation, arguing that the central purpose of vocation is reconciliation. The main question still remains, however: How can marketing be considered a Christian vocation? Furthermore, by defining vocation in terms of reconciliation, I suggest that marketing must be supportive of reconciliation if the discipline is to be considered a Christian vocation. A key transitional question, therefore, is: How does marketing support reconciliation? In order to address both of these questions, it is important to describe this paper's third and probably most controversial construct, marketing, as well as the social behavior that marketing is meant to facilitate, exchange.

Exchange: The Focus of Marketing

The American Marketing Association (AMA) describes marketing as "an organizational function and set of processes for creating, communicating, and delivering value to customers and for managing customer relationships in ways that benefit the organization and its stakeholders."[24] From this concise yet comprehensive definition of marketing, I would like to extract an implicit concept that many in the field have identified as the core focus of marketing — exchange.[25] Shelby Hunt confirms the centrality of exchange to marketing as he states, "The basic subject matter of marketing is the exchange relationship or

Figure 2: The Core Focus of Marketing

transaction ... marketing science is the behavioral science that seeks to explain exchange relationships."[26] Figure 2 provides a visual image of marketing's relationship to exchange.

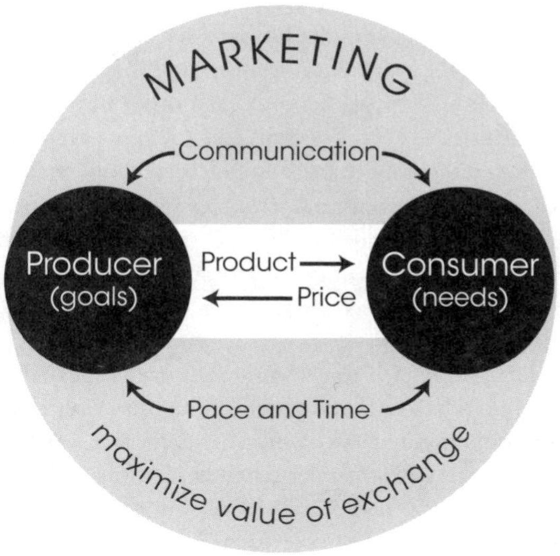

Marketing seeks to encourage exchange that benefits buyers and sellers equally. Unlike a zero-sum game in which one party must lose in order for the other to win, both parties improve their situations through the exchange.[27] This mutually beneficial exchange begins by sellers first identifying and embracing the needs of buyers[28] and then using that philosophy to guide choices related to: what is exchanged, where and when the exchange takes place, and how buyers and sellers share information related to the exchange. In doing so, marketing strives to maximize the value of the exchange, or the ratio of benefits received to costs incurred.[29] The central purpose of marketing, therefore, is to facilitate valuable, or mutually beneficial, exchange.

The next logical question, then, is: How does exchange, the central focus of marketing, support reconciliation? Exchange is a fundamental human behavior that involves two or more parties each receiving something of value by offering something of value in return. The parties participate in the transaction voluntarily because all expect to be better off as a result.[30]

God established exchange as part of the created order.[31] Even before the Fall, Adam and Eve offered their work and care for the Garden in exchange for its fruits. God also made humans with different talents and abilities, thereby necessitating that individuals and groups exchange with each other in order to lead productive lives. For example, 1 Kings 5 recounts how Solomon and Hiram, King of Tyre, cooperated in exchanging their nations' resources in order to build the Temple in Jerusalem. Likewise, the body of Christ, with its many different parts, serving a variety of complementary functions, seems to be an entity designed for exchange.[32]

Just as the need to exchange serves as a means for bringing individuals and groups into positive relationships, ongoing mutually beneficial exchange seems to be associated with the maintenance of strong interpersonal rapport. When parties are estranged, or not reconciled, they tend to avoid exchange. When spouses become alienated, they often fail to exchange words and affections. When nations become estranged, one of the first reactions is to curtail trade and diplomatic discourse. When buyers and sellers have disputes, products are seldom sold or purchased. "Confrontation demeans, destroys, and diminishes. Reconciliation results in growth, dignity, and mutual benefit to both parties."[33] In reconciled states there tends to be free-flowing, mutually beneficial exchange.

At a minimum, the phenomenon of exchange appears to be consistent with the concept of reconciliation. It also seems likely, based on the preceding examples, that exchange is a key ingredient of reconciliation and that reconciliation promotes exchange. Furthermore, one might even argue that reconciliation is exchange when one considers, as mentioned earlier, that the Greek New Testament meaning of reconciliation involves changing something relatively undesirable for something desirable, establishing a favorable state, and achieving value for all participants. So, by facilitating mutually beneficial exchange, marketing supports a God-given behavior that is consistent with, if not instrumental to, reconciliation. Presuming that the central purpose of vocation is reconciliation, the core of marketing appears uniquely suited to serve as part of a Christian calling. It is important to note that the preceding discussion describes what marketing

should be ideally. This paper's next section compares this normative description to actual marketing practice, both good and bad.

Reconciling Misconceptions of Marketing

Given the inherent consistency between marketing and Christian vocation, why do so many people still believe, as this paper's introduction has suggested, that the discipline fosters estrangement, not reconciliation? Unfortunately, such attitudes toward marketing are not entirely unfounded. The blame, however, does not rest with the fundamental tenets of the discipline but with the actions that some people and organizations take under the auspices of marketing. Every day, marketers facilitate a variety of exchanges that benefit buyers and sellers equally. For example, to a great extent, marketing is the reason why consumers don't have to drive to Battle Creek, MI to buy their breakfast cereal; a congregation is aware of its church's upcoming Worship Arts Weekend; bread costs $2.50 a loaf, not $5.00; and people can see well despite poor vision.

Regrettably, however, some sellers, under the guise of marketing, promote exchanges that favor themselves disproportionately. It is reasonable to conclude that these types of exchanges encourage dissonance rather than reconciliation. It is also important to note, however, that this category of actions does not reflect the core purpose of marketing accurately, as previously developed.

In order to address the discipline's apparent inconsistencies, it is helpful to distinguish inappropriate marketing practice from a proper conceptualization of the discipline. Such an aim is consistent with the work of Shelby Hunt, who differentiates positive marketing theory (actual observed marketing behavior) from normative knowledge of the discipline (what marketing strategy should be). Hunt further delineates two types of normative knowledge: rational normative, which is based on marketing's fundamental tenets, and ethical normative, which stems from moral principles.[34] The following section seeks to strengthen the argument further that marketing supports reconciliation and, therefore, can be part of a Christian vocation, by analyzing the positive and normative dimensions of three common marketing misconceptions in light of the preceding framework.

First Misconception: Marketing Theory Encourages Selling Things to People That They Do Not Need

One of the most common indictments of marketing theory is that it supports selling products to people that they do not need. Of course, at the root of this issue is the question of what constitutes a need. In the strictest sense, people need very few things to survive: air, water, food, clothing, shelter. The point, however, is not to argue that marketing is constrained by too narrow a definition of "need." One can concede that people need things beyond basic elements of survival; for example, people may need cars for transportation or need phones for communication, yet some products still seem to exceed the limits of what represents reasonable consumption. For instance, in a recent catalog, toy retailer F.A.O. Schwartz offered a $15,000 child-size Mercedes with rack-and-pinion steering and a $30,000 playhouse with bay windows.

Most people hear of these items and conclude quickly that there is no legitimate need for such products. I tend to agree with this judgment and add that ultimately such exchanges foster estrangement, not reconciliation. Although many kids would be thrilled to take ownership of a $30,000 playhouse, discord is likely to occur as parents rationalize the extreme gift as a reason for spending less time with their children, as envious friends become disenchanted with their own more modest toys, and as the young playhouse recipients develop a distorted view of money and possessions.

Likewise I will argue, however, that rational normative marketing knowledge also rejects the sale of such products. Although these exchanges may appear first to be mutually beneficial, they really are not. The probable outcomes described above and others like them (for example, children begin to lose interest in the playhouse after a few weeks) suggest that a family will never realize $30,000 worth of benefits from the purchase. The notion that the exchange is really not mutually beneficial should be reason enough to dissuade a marketer from promoting such a transaction,

even if actual marketing practice sometimes suggests otherwise. When practiced in a way that is consistent with its core tenets, marketing never seeks to sell things to consumers that they do not need but rather supports exchanges that produce real value for buyers and sellers. As such, marketing facilitates a virtually limitless number of valuable exchanges, helping to meet needs that vary from employment to entertainment, from food to friendship, and from education to esteem. As developed earlier, these exchanges themselves may play a role in reconciliation. Furthermore, having lower-level needs met may allow people to fulfill higher-level needs[35] and, perhaps, other forms of reconciliation.

Second Misconception: Marketing Theory Supports Deception in Order to Get People to Buy Products

A second common criticism of marketing theory is that it advocates using deception to persuade people to buy products. This criticism is perhaps levied most often at advertising, marketing's primary form of mass communication. First, it is important to understand that advertising is advocacy, and advertisers have a right to put their best foot forward, or to present their products in a favorable light.[36] Consumers are justified, however, in bemoaning television commercials that suggest an SUV can climb an unrealistically steep and treacherous hill or magazine ads whose models' glistening white teeth are due more to photo retouching than use of the advertised dental product. It is truly regrettable that there are instances of deception in some marketing promotion, for these types of practices certainly do not foster reconciliation. On the contrary, deceptive marketing communication is likely to stir resentment among buyers[37] who will terminate the exchange relationships when the deception is discovered. Unfortunately, such deception might also lead to estrangement in other relationships. For instance, family members may resent the purchaser for "wasting money," or consumers might grow to distrust marketers in general.

The practice of deceptive communication does not constitute the majority of positive marketing practice, however, nor does it represent normative marketing knowledge, the reasons for which are very similar to those outlined in the previous section. As inferred earlier, consumers who realize they have been deceived are unlikely to be satisfied with the exchange in question and, when possible, will try to avoid further association with that particular seller, and sometimes with that entire category of sellers. Deceptive communication is, therefore, antithetical to marketing's goals of facilitating mutually beneficial exchange and forging positive long-term relationships.

In contrast, when marketing communication is practiced with integrity, as it often is, buyers and sellers benefit and reconciliation is supported. For example, there are tens of thousands of ads that inform consumers realistically and accurately of potential exchanges such as ones involving sales of breakfast cereals, releases of newly published books, and meetings of single parent support groups.

Honest marketing communication, therefore, directly and indirectly supports positive relationships, or states of favor, among a variety of different parties. Such marketing facilitates exchange and reconciliation.

Third Misconception: Marketing Theory Suggests That a Given Product Should be Sold to Everyone

A third and final misunderstanding of marketing theory is that it encourages sellers to try to persuade all consumers to adopt their product offerings. It is true that sellers can potentially increase their own rewards by benefiting a greater number of buyers, and corporations often are under pressure to grow, which may mean expanding their markets and reaching more consumers. Unfortunately, there are instances of sellers trying to push their products outside a reasonable circle of consumers. For example, many people have received direct mail pieces that seemed entirely misdirected, such as a couple renting an apartment receives a mailing for new vinyl replacement windows, or a single, middle-age man receives a postcard announcing a sale at a teen girls' clothing store.

These examples seem rather benign, yet it would be difficult to argue that they support reconciliation, and other more intrusive promotions may actually provoke estrangement. For instance, the national Do-Not-Call List appears to reflect many consumers' disdain for the telemarketing of products that are often irrelevant to the consumers' needs. These types of examples do, unfortunately, represent actual marketing behavior to some extent. Such practices do not, however, represent the discipline's normative knowledge, or what marketing strategy should be.

In marketing, the quantity of prospective consumers should be secondary to the qualities of the consumers. The main reason that quality supersedes quantity is that not all buyers want or need the same things, and marketing is predicated upon creating beneficial exchanges, or meeting people's needs. In the aggregate, consumer demand tends to be divergent and heterogeneous,[38] which should lead a marketer to segment the whole market into smaller groups of more homogenous buyers who do have similar needs[39] and to target only that group of consumers whose needs the marketer is best suited to meet.[40] In addition, qualities of consumers are important because marketing theory values people and relationships,[41] a focus that encourages marketers to demonstrate care and compassion in their exchanges.

These market segmentation and target marketing strategies offer benefits both to buyers and sellers. First, by targeting a smaller and more homogenous group of consumers, organizations are able to satisfy those consumers' preferences more precisely and effectively.[42] Such need fulfillment is, of course, appealing to consumers. Second, organizations benefit by being able to make more efficient use of their limited resources, which enhances their profitability.[43] It is unreasonable for sellers to try to sell to all potential buyers, and it is impractical for firms to try to bring about a convergence of divergent consumer demand.[44]

When market segmentation and target marketing are employed, reconciliation is supported again. Consumers tend not to become disgruntled with marketers because consumers receive promotional messages for items in which they are interested. For example, a 30-year-old mother reading *Good Housekeeping* sees an ad for a vehicle with special child safety features, or a teenager listening to Christian radio hears an ad announcing the release of one of her favorite artist's new CDs. In such instances, marketing directly cultivates positive relationships between buyers and sellers. Furthermore, to the extent that marketing helps to fulfill some of consumers' basic needs, the discipline also enables people to move to higher-level need fulfillment, including that of other social needs.[45] Such marketing facilitates exchange and reconciliation.

Implications: The Roles of Christians in Reconciling Marketing

Having developed and supported the legitimacy of marketing's claim to Christian vocation, there remains the practical question of how the day-to-day practice of marketing can be reconciled both to the field's normative theory and to proper societal expectations of the discipline. More specifically, given this article's focus and the readership of *Christian Scholar's Review*, an even more relevant question considers the role that believers might play in redeeming, or reclaiming, the marketing function. There is, of course, no simple prescription for resolving the deep-rooted and long-standing tensions surrounding marketing. In order to move toward reconciliation, it is important that attitudes toward the discipline change for both marketers and consumers, given that exchange is a social phenomenon that involves two or more parties. To that end, the following paragraphs outline how three main groups of Christian stakeholders can encourage marketing's reconciliation.

Christian Higher Education

Perhaps the most obvious place to start with recommendations for change is within Christian colleges and universities, where a large number of future leaders in business and other fields develop long-lasting attitudes toward the discipline. Business faculty should take the lead, first in debunking the belief that marketing is simply advertising and selling, a notion that unnecessarily relegates the discipline to a narrow promotional role. Instead, Christian-business educators must help their own students, as well as students and faculty from other disciplines, learn about the true nature, or full scope, of marketing; that is, that marketing involves optimizing decisions related to products, distribution, pricing, and communication in order to best meet consumers' needs, thereby creating mutually beneficial exchange. Likewise, business faculty should help consumers across campus recognize and

appreciate how marketing activities make possible the products and services upon which everyone depends daily, for example, food, clothing, and transportation. This education must, of course, start in the classroom, but should then extend into other venues that reach more interdisciplinary audiences, such as public lectures, alternative chapels, seminars, panel discussions, collaborative research, and service projects.

The Church

As implied earlier, the Church is at times not an especially friendly environment for businesspeople, meaning that marketers, in particular, can be made to feel that their discipline undermines biblical teaching and Christian values. Some of this perceived conflict stems from the same narrow stereotyping of marketing described above, which can be addressed in similar ways. Beyond these measures, it is important for pastors and other Church leaders to affirm the legitimate and helpful roles of marketers and other Christian businesspeople within their congregations. This movement toward broader acceptance might begin by recognizing the precedent for "biblical businesspeople," for example, Job (a livestock magnate; Job 1:3), Lydia (a textile merchant; Acts 16:14), and Jesus (a carpenter/tradesman; Mark 6:3). Successful Christian businesspeople also should be encouraged to excel in the "grace of giving" (2 Corinthians 8:7), a spiritual gift that many possess, which can assist the Church's ministries greatly. In addition, the Church should appreciate the potential that marketers and other Christian businesspeople have to utilize their discipline-specific skills to further the Church's mission. For instance, many churches can use help in researching community needs, branding new programs, and promoting unique ministries.

Christians in Business/Marketing

The third group of stakeholders consists of Christian marketers themselves. The main way that these individuals can help to reconcile the discipline is by practicing it according to the normative theory described throughout this paper. Positive examples of mutually beneficial exchange will speak volumes more than any verbal defense of the discipline. In addition, it is helpful to reiterate one specific biblical guideline that lies at the heart of reconciliation—the Golden Rule: Treat others the way that you want to be treated, or as Jesus said, "Love your neighbor as yourself" (Mark 12:31). In following this one principle, Christian marketers will also uphold several other important mandates effectively, for instance, thinking long-term, considering all parties affected by one's actions, and putting people ahead of things. Ultimately, such a focus will produce the mutually beneficial exchange and reconciliation this entire paper has sought.

Concluding Thoughts

To summarize, I have argued that reconciliation is the central purpose of Christian vocation; therefore, an occupation or discipline must support reconciliation in order to be part of a Christian calling. Furthermore, I have attempted to establish that marketing, through its facilitation of mutually beneficial exchanges, is consistent with and supportive of reconciliation. Consequently, I have maintained that marketing can be part of a Christian vocation.

I would like to add that the discussion of whether marketing can be a Christian calling is vitally important not just for Christians who work or intend to work in marketing, but for everyone. The basis for this sweeping claim is that marketing involves and affects everyone. Although relatively few people practice marketing as an occupation, virtually everyone is a marketer of something. While individuals may not market products in the commercial sense, they do market their personal services and ideas. In addition, every living person participates in exchanges from a consumer's perspective.[46]

Furthermore, marketing has a tremendous impact on our world's social and economic structures. Many believe that business is the world's most dominant institution,[47] and marketing, which is at the heart of commerce, may be the quintessential business discipline. The power and influence of marketing is immense. Many of the world's largest corporations generate revenues of more than $200 billion a year and employ hundreds of thousands of people in the process of exchanging their products and services. While some might view this influence with dismay, a more enlightened perspective envisions the potential that marketing has to help overcome many societal woes.[48] When understood and practiced as part of a Christian vocation, marketing directs the God-given phenomenon of exchange rightly, affording a unique opportunity to support reconciliation in our world. Christian higher education should be a leader in encouraging individuals to practice marketing as part of their divine calling.

Notes

1 Kathleen Cholewka, "Survey Says: Some Sales Execs Are Liars," *Sales & Marketing Management* 153 (February 2001): 18; Richard N. Farmer, "Would You Want Your Son to Marry a Marketing Lady?" *Journal of Marketing* 41 (January 1977): 15–18; Ian Ryder, "Seven Key Challenges for Today's Communicators," *Strategic Communication Management* 7 (December 2002/January 2003): 20–23.

2 Gary D. Badcock, *The Way of Life* (Grand Rapids, MI: Eerdmans Publishing Co., 1998); Shirley J. Roels, "The Christian Calling to Business Life," *Theology Today* 60 (October 2003): 357–69; Leland Ryken, "Work as Stewardship," in *On Moral Business: Classical and Contemporary Resources for Ethics in Economic Life*, ed. Max L. Stackhouse, Dennis P. McCann, and Shirley J. Roels, with Preston N. Williams (Grand Rapids, MI: Eerdmans Publishing Co., 1995), 84–86.

3 Badcock, *The Way of Life*; Alexander Hill, *Just Business: Christian Ethics for the Marketplace* (Downers Grove, IL: InterVarsity Press, 1997); Arthur F. Holmes, *The Idea of a Christian College* (Grand Rapids, MI: Eerdmans Publishing Co., 1987).

4 Michael Novak, *Business as a Calling: Work and the Examined Life* (New York: The Free Press, 1996), 34–36.

5 Badcock, *The Way of Life*.

6 *Luther's Works: Volume 3, Lectures on Genesis Chapters 15–20*, ed. Jaroslav Pelikan (St. Louis, MO: Concordia Publishing House, 1961), 321; Robert A. Wauzzinski, "The Gospel, Business, and the State," in *Biblical Principles & Business: The Foundations*, ed. Richard C. Chewning (Colorado Springs, CO: NavPress, 1989), 203–22.

7 Badcock, *The Way of Life*; Douglas J. Schuurman, *Vocation: Discerning Our Callings in Life* (Grand Rapids, MI: Eerdmans Publishing Co., 2004).

8 Matthew 22:36–40.

9 James Denney, *The Christian Doctrine of Reconciliation* (New York: George H. Doran Company, 1918). Charles T. Matthewes, "The Academic Life as a Christian Vocation," *Journal of Religion* 79 (January 1999): 110–21.

10 Henlee H. Barnette, *Christian Calling and Vocation* (Grand Rapids, MI: Baker Book House, 1965), 20.

11 Schuurman, *Vocation*, 18.

12 Badcock, *The Way of Life*, 9.

13 Robert E. Cushman, *Faith Seeking Understanding: Essays Theological and Critical* (Durham, NC: Duke University Press, 1981), 225–26.

[14] James Strong, *Strong's Greek & Hebrew Dictionary* (Winterbourne, ON: Online Bible, 1993); William E. Vine, *Vine's Expository Dictionary of Old Testament and New Testament Words* (Nashville, TN: Thomas Nelson, Inc., 1940).

[15] Matthew 5:24.

[16] Romans 5:10–11; 1 Corinthians 7:11; 2 Corinthians 5:18–20; Colossians 1:21.

[17] Ephesians 1:10, 2:16; Colossians 1:20–21; Philippians 2:10.

[18] Badcock, *The Way of Life*, 30.

[19] Cristoph Schwöbel, "Reconciliation: From Biblical Observations to Dogmatic Reconstruction," in *The Theology of Reconciliation*, ed. Colin E. Gunton (London: T&T Clark Ltd., 2003), 16.

[20] Denney, *The Christian Doctrine of Reconciliation*.

[21] Matthewes, "The Academic Life as a Christian Vocation."

[22] Barnette, *Christian Calling and Vocation*, 20–21.

[23] Wayne T. Alderson and Nancy Alderson McDonnell, *Theory R Management* (Nashville, TN: Thomas Nelson, Inc., 1994); Colin E. Gunton, "Towards a Theology of Reconciliation," in *The Theology of Reconciliation*, ed. Colin E. Gunton (London: T&T Clark Ltd., 2003), 167–74.

[24] The American Marketing Association, "Marketing Definitions," (August 2004), http://www.marketingpower.com /content4620.php (accessed August 9, 2006).

[25] Wroe Alderson and Miles W. Martin, "Toward a Formal Theory of Transactions and Transvections," *Journal of Marketing Research* 2 (May 1965): 117–27; Richard P. Bagozzi, "Marketing as Exchange," *Journal of Marketing* 39 (October 1975): 32–39; Philip Kotler, "A Generic Concept of Marketing," *Journal of Marketing* 36 (April 1972): 46–54; Charles W. Lamb, Jr., Joseph F. Hair, Jr., and Carl D. McDaniel, *Marketing*, 7th ed. (Mason, OH: South-Western, 2004).

[26] Shelby D. Hunt, *Foundations of Marketing Theory: Toward a General Theory* (Armonk, NY: M. E. Sharpe, 2002), 132.

[27] George S. Day, *Strategic Market Planning: The Pursuit of Competitive Advantage* (St. Paul, MN: West Publishing Company, 1984).

[28] George S. Day, "The Capabilities of Market-Driven Organizations," *Journal of Marketing* 58 (October 1994): 37–52; Ajay K. Kohli and Bernard J. Jaworski, "Market Orientation: The Construct, Research Propositions, and Managerial Implications," *Journal of Marketing* 54 (April 1990): 1–18; Philip Kotler and Gary Armstrong, *Principles of Marketing*, 8th ed. (Upper Saddle River, NJ: Prentice-Hall, Inc., 1999); Philip Kotler and Sidney J. Levy, "Broadening the Concept of Marketing," *Journal of Marketing* 33 (January 1969): 10–15.

[29] Lamb, Hair, and McDaniel, *Marketing*, 7th ed.

[30] Philip Kotler, *Marketing Management: The Millennium Edition* (Upper Saddle River, NJ: Prentice-Hall, Inc., 2000).

[31] Roels, "The Christian Calling to Business Life," 359.

[32] 1 Corinthians 12:12–31.

[33] Alderson and McDonnell, *Theory R Management*, xv.

[34] Hunt, *Foundations of Marketing Theory: Toward a General Theory*.

[35] Abraham H. Maslow, "A Theory of Human Motivation," *Psychological Review* 50 (July 1943): 370–96.

[36] Edward D. Zinbarg, *Faith, Morals, and Money: What the World's Religions Tell Us about Ethics in the Marketplace* (New York: The Continuum International Publishing Group Inc., 2001).

[37] Schuurman, *Vocation*.

[38] Wendell R. Smith, "Product Differentiation and Market Segmentation as Alternative Marketing Strategies," *Journal of Marketing* 21 (July 1956): 3–8.

[39] Theodore Levitt, *The Marketing Imagination* (New York: The Free Press, 1986).

[40] Day, *Strategic Market Planning: The Pursuit of Competitive Advantage*.

[41] Martin Christopher, Adrian Payne, and David Ballantyne, *Relationship Marketing: Bringing Quality, Customer Service, and Marketing Together* (Oxford, England: Butterworth-Heinemann Ltd., 1993); Jonathan R. Copulsky and Michael J. Wolf, "Relationship Marketing: Positioning for the Future," *Journal of Business Strategy* 11 (July–August 1990): 16–20; Christian Grönroos, "Quo Vadis, Marketing? Toward a Relationship Marketing Paradigm," *Journal of Marketing Management* 10 (July 1994): 347–60; Michael D. Johnson and Fred Selnes, "Customer Portfolio Management: Toward a Dynamic Theory of Exchange Relationships," *Journal of Marketing* 68 (April 2004): 1–17.

[42] Smith, "Product Differentiation and Market Segmentation," 3–8.

[43] Yoram Wind, "Issues and Advances in Segmentation Research," *Journal of Marketing Research* 15 (August 1978): 317–37.

[44] Smith, "Product Differentiation and Market Segmentation," 3–8.

[45] Maslow, "A Theory of Human Motivation," 370–96.

[46] Kenneth S. Kantzer, "God Intends His Precepts to Transform Society," in *Biblical Principles & Business: The Foundations*, ed. Richard C. Chewning (Colorado Springs, CO: NavPress, 1989), 22–34.

[47] William H. Shaw and Vincent Barry, *Moral Issues in Business*, 10th ed. (Belmont, CA: Thomson Wadsworth, 2007); *On Moral Business: Classical and Contemporary Resources for Ethics in Economic Life*.

[48] Novak, *Business as a Calling*, 37; Roels, "The Christian Calling to Business Life," 357–69.

Questions for Discussion and Reflection

1. Do you think that marketing and a Christian vocation is a contradiction? Or do you believe that marketing can be an effective place of service for a Christian in the workplace? Explain your answer.

2. How does Hagenbuch integrate the notion of reconciliation with the practice of marketing and advertising? Do you agree with his view of this? Why or why not?

3. What do you think of the three misconceptions of marketing that Hagenbuch outlines? Do you agree that they are misconceptions? Or do they have more truth in them than Hagenbuch is willing to admit?

CASE STUDIES

Case 9.1: Diamonds Are Forever

One popular advertisement for engagement rings sponsored by the De Beers Diamond company poses the following question to men planning proposal: "Is two months' salary too much to spend?"

Many suitors take "two months' salary" as an unwritten rule of etiquette and as a measurement stick of how well they've faired in the jewelry aspect of courtship. However, "two-months" is not written in any well-known traditional books on wedding etiquette. It simply seems to be an extremely effective creation of the De Beers company, which controls a large share of the world diamond market.

While wedding rings were traditionally regarded as symbols of vows to lifelong commitment, they today symbolize wealth and, to some, how much the suitor loves his bride-to-be. Givers and receivers of the glimmering objects can be regularly comparing the caret weight, cost, and so on of their "symbols" with friends and family members.

This seems like a clear situation in which the diamond business has violated consumer autonomy by "creating" a new need through exploiting basic human needs to fit in and impress others. For some potential suitors, simply saying no in the face of social pressures to value his bride-to-be is difficult. Advertisers would probably respond that they are simply "fulfilling" latent human desires rather than creating them. Indeed, it appears that the "need" or desire to impress peers and the bride-to-be is already in existence.

Questions for Discussion

1. Is the prevalence of the belief of the "two months' salary rule" proof of the power of advertisers to create needs by exploiting human insecurity? Why or why not?
2. If so, does this unjustly violate the autonomy of consumers?

Case 9.2: Vanity Sells

Margaret began a retail business about a decade ago that specializes in making competitively priced customized wedding dresses. Customers loved her designs, and soon, through word of mouth alone, she had a very loyal but small customer base. At this point, however, her business was still struggling to make more than just a small profit.

Having also completed a few photography courses in college and getting lots of practice by taking photos of brides-to-be wearing her custom-made dresses for her portfolio, Margaret decided to try her hand at photographing weddings to increase her revenue. Over a few years, this too became a reliable source of income for her business.

But now, designing wedding dresses and doing wedding photography has Margaret spread way too thin. Her family life is feeling stressed, and she is often hurrying from one place to another, so she decides to try to make more economically efficient use of her time by attempting to focus her attention on fewer but higher-paying customers.

Over her years in business, Margaret has noticed that a couple of "tricks" usually make customers more amenable to higher dollar purchases (i.e., a more expensive dress design or ordering more photos). With respect to wedding gowns, Margaret has noticed that "vanity sizing" (telling a client that she is several sizes smaller than she really is) works to put clients in the mood to spend more money. On the photography side of her business, she has observed that clients will order a larger photo package if she takes the time to use software tools to make them appear thinner and younger.

Question for Discussion and Reflection

1. Knowing what she does, would Margaret cross any ethical lines by using appeals to "vanity" to sell more to her customers? Vanity sizing is a common practice among fashion merchandisers.
2. Can one reasonably argue that it is up to customers to protect themselves from such tactics?

Case 9.3: Who's Tricking Whom?

A provocative section on marketing appears in Malcolm Gladwell's book *Blink*. In this section of the book, he discusses the discoveries made by a pivotal figure in marketing named Louis Cheskin. In short, Cheskin discovered something called "sensation transference," which means that customers are apt to transfer their feelings about a product's packaging onto the product itself. For example, employees at the Cheskin Company discovered the importance of how taste perceptions are impacted by the shape of a bottle (wine) and the colors on a soda can (more lemon or lime flavor based on more yellow or green) though the products themselves are unchanged. Darrel Rhea, a principal at the Cheskin Company, notes that consumers associate ice cream that comes in a cylindrical container with better taste and are willing to pay a bit more for it. While this feels manipulative, Gladwell asks:

> If you double the size of the chips in chocolate chip ice cream and say on the package, "Now! Bigger Chocolate Chips!" and charge five or ten cents more, that seems honest and fair. But if you put your ice cream in a round

as opposed to a rectangular container and charge five or ten cents more, that seems like you're pulling the wool over people's eyes.

If you think about it, though, there really isn't any practical difference between those two things. We are willing to pay more for ice cream when it tastes better, and putting ice cream in a round container convinces us that it tastes better just as surely as making the chips bigger in chocolate chip ice cream does. Sure, we're conscious of one improvement and not conscious of the other, but why should that distinction matter? Why should an ice cream company be able to profit only from improvements that we are conscious of? You might say, "Well, they're going behind our back." But who is going behind our back? The ice cream company? Or our own unconscious?

Question for Discussion and Reflection

1. Is the use of sensation transference to market products (and charging more for them) fair? Is it manipulative or is it more akin to what Gladwell suggests—we are going behind our own backs?

Case 9.4: Reptilian Instincts and Purchase Decisions

Dr. Clotaire Rapaille, a former psychologist who once specialized in working with patients with autism, now serves as a consultant (through his company Archetype Discoveries) to large corporations, including many of the Fortune 500 and a purported half of the top 100. Procter & Gamble, Nestlé, Boeing, and General Motors are among the large, well-established companies that appear on Rapaille's client list. Rapaille's work, for which he is handsomely compensated, involves helping companies design and sell products that make an emotional connection to consumers through mining the depths of the human psyche to unlock cultural "codes." Marketing that is "on code" greatly improves the odds of a product being successful in the marketplace.

Rapaille's methods are unusual. He has a profound distrust in the tools of traditional marketing research because he doesn't believe that understanding consumer motivations can be accomplished by listening to what they say on the conscious level. To successfully decode the emotional motivators behind purchases, Rapaille conducts unusual focus groups that he calls "imprinting sessions." Groups of thirty participants are taken through a process in which they are eventually asked for associations that come from a deep unconscious level of the brain. Rapaille then uses these associations to develop a key to unlocking a culture's "code," which in turn is used to develop and market products. Believing that the key to understanding consumer behavior lies at the unconscious "imprint" or "reptilian" level of the brain where meaning and emotions lie,

Rapaille states, "My theory is very simple: The reptilian always wins. I don't care what you're going to tell me intellectually. I don't care. Give me the reptilian. Why? Because the reptilian always wins."[2] Rapaille, for example, helped marketers design their products and ad campaigns by uncovering the code for SUV ("domination") and the code for motherhood ("total paranoia.")

Using his focus group "discovery" process, Rapaille also helped Nestlé develop a market for coffee products in Japan, a traditionally tea-drinking country. As Rapaille himself tells it:

> They needed to give the product meaning in this culture. They needed to create an imprint for coffee for the Japanese. Armed with this information, Nestlé devised a new strategy. Rather than selling instant coffee to a country dedicated to tea, they created desserts for children infused with the flavor of coffee but without the caffeine. The younger generation embraced these desserts. Their first imprint of coffee was a very positive one, one they would carry throughout their lives. Through this, Nestlé gained a meaningful foothold in the Japanese market.... Understanding the process of imprinting—and how it related directly to Nestlé's marketing efforts—unlocked a door to the Japanese culture for them and turned around a floundering business venture.[3]

Rapaille also claims to have developed successful packaging for coffee (Folgers) and helped design the PT Cruiser and many other familiar products.

[2] Clotaire Rapaille, interview for "The Persuaders," PBS *Frontline*, November 2004, http://www.pbs.org/wgbh/pages/frontline/shows/persuaders/interviews/rapaille.html.

[3] Clotaire Rapaille, *The Culture Code* (New York: Random House, 2006), 9.

Questions for Discussion

1. Are Rapaille's attempts to bypass our conscious level of awareness to market products to us manipulative?
2. Does reducing consumers to their reptilian instincts honor their dignity or worth? Is it up to consumers to protect themselves?

COMMENTARY

Rapid advances in technology and global economic connections have allowed the visible presence of marketing to dramatically expand. With new tools at their disposal, many business leaders see unprecedented opportunities to expand the reach of their companies into new markets, while critics bemoan the prospect of increased intrusions into the physical, psychological, and spiritual dimensions of life.

For example, in addition to what may be deemed "traditional" (for people in older generations) media forms, advertisements have been directed to potential customers while they are surfing the Internet (banners and pop-ups), watching movies (paid product placements), refueling automobiles (video screens at gas pumps), and making use of public restrooms (billboards placed within view of toilets and lavatories). Some experts estimated that even prior to the advent of current technologies, Americans were exposed to three thousand advertising messages daily.[4]

Advertising has also extended its reach geographically and demographically. Ads promoting Western products are routinely seen in developing countries, contributing to cultural changes as they appear.[5] Furthermore, young children also find themselves the target audience of campaigns. Some advertisers see them as both having a strongly influential role in regular family purchase decisions, and as potential loyal long-term customers, especially if they can be "branded" at an early age.[6]

As noted by Clapp and Kilbourne, the values and practices of marketing, especially as manifested through advertising, raise many important questions about manipulation and the promotion of consumerism as a rival worldview or "theology." Add in concerns about deception, invasiveness, and ubiquity, and it is clear that marketing has to answer to a long list of ethical questions.

These types of criticisms need to be seriously considered, but as Hagenbuch points out, the story may not be so simple. Marketing is much more than advertising, and the latter even serves useful purposes in bringing people together in relationships of mutually beneficial exchange. Surely exchange is a more peaceful and more efficient way of distributing goods and services than through physical force or central government planning.

When its full spectrum of activities is considered, marketing seems to be a critical component of exchange in a market-based economy. In the absence of marketing, how else would producers know what to make (market research)? How would people know what products or services are available (advertising/promotion), even if what may be categorized as their "true needs" are far fewer than their "wants"? And how would either producers or consumers decide where to physically meet to make exchanges and what an efficient price might be (distribution, pricing)?

Marketing's role in exchange also works to create wealth by stimulating overall economic growth and development. While itself not the only (nor perhaps, most important) measure of human well-being, economic wealth is necessary to support social goods such as health, education, good governance, and other dimensions of a flourishing life.

In addition to its function, marketing is also sometimes defended as more of a benign reflection, rather than shaper, of cultural values. Seen in this

[4] In addition to traditional media sources such as television, billboards, print, and the Internet, consumers also see ads in the form of "brands" worn on clothing and placed on products.

[5] Critics allege that as citizens of developing countries rapidly buy into a materially based vision of the "good life," cultural conflict and economic and environmental damage will occur. For a well-articulated account of these and related criticisms, see David C. Korten, *When Corporations Rule the World* (Bloomfield, Conn.: Kumarian, 1995).

[6] John de Graaf and Vivia Boe, producers, *Affluenza* (KCTS Seattle and Oregon Public Broadcasting, 1997).

light, advertising is "information" packaged in a manner that is demanded by the consuming public. People respond to particular appeals because marketing truly reflects their often latent, but nevertheless real desires, and not because it has some mysterious power to manipulate. Consumers are willing participants who demand more than just the pure utility offered by products or services. Poetic descriptors, dreams, and fancy packaging are a part of the "mix" of what is purchased. In other words, marketing is in the business of giving us what we want. It seems as though marketing has to reflect cultural values to some degree, or its messages would be dismissed outright.

While marketing clearly serves a useful social function and at least partially reflects cultural values, the way it is done (its methods and techniques) is loaded with values and ethical implications that may or may not meet Christian standards. For example, as Kilbourne points out, some messages border on (and transgress) themes that are deceptive or destructive. An increasing number of branding strategies attempt to invade the spiritual realm, appealing to the need to belong and make meaning (needs once met by churches and other community and civic organizations).[7] Some market research techniques also feel manipulative, such as the ones used by Rapaille in mining our unconscious "reptilian instincts" in search of primal "codes" that help sell products.

In addition, Clapp notes that while *individual* ads have questionable amounts of influence, the aggregated message of advertising encourages a philosophy of shallow consumerism. As an ethos of "instant gratification" spreads into other areas of life, spiritual and moral values necessary to sustain meaningful relationships, such as family and community ties, can erode.

Hagenbuch insightfully argues that techniques that unfairly tilt the balance away from "mutually beneficial exchange" in favor of sellers go against the normative definition of marketing as developed by the American Marketing Association, "an organizational function and set of processes for creating, communicating and delivering value to customers and for managing customer relationships in ways that benefit the organization and its stakeholders."[8]

This is a very helpful starting point. However, a fair question to ask is whether marketing is predominantly practiced in ways that fall outside of its normative scope. Moreover, the definition leaves questions of "value" in the eye of the beholder. As it is stated, values are completely relative to individuals and have no grounding in transcendent values.

Hagenbuch is correct to assert that marketing can be a vocation—a place to serve God and neighbor, but (like all professions), only if it is practiced with the right motives and within appropriate ethical boundaries. Ethically responsible marketing surely suggests limits. Appealing to a deep-seated

[7] Douglas Atkin, an interview on "The Persuaders," *Frontline*, November 9, 2004, http://www.pbs.org/wgbh/pages/frontline/shows/persuaders/interviews/atkin.html. See also Naomi Klein, an interview on "The Persuaders," *Frontline*, November 9, 2004, http://www.pbs.org/wgbh/pages/frontline/shows/persuaders/interviews/klein.html.

[8] The American Marketing Association, "Marketing Definitions" (August 2004), http://www.marketingpower.com/AboutAMA/Pages/DefinitionofMarketing.aspx, accessed August 9, 2006.

[9] The "reasonable consumer"

or unconscious emotion such as insecurity, fear, or desire simply because it can be successfully targeted is morally deficient. Although marketing may not *create* insecurities or questionable social values, it sure can powerfully reinforce them. Thus, even if marketing primarily reflects cultural values, this does not mean that marketers are free from moral responsibilities to appeal to healthier parts of the human soul.

The need for ethical boundaries is even more apparent when attempting to sell products to vulnerable members of a target audience who do not meet a "reasonable consumer" standard.[9] For example, young children are becoming constant targets of a wide variety of marketing, including traditional broadcast media, packaging, and product placement. Most pernicious is the attempt to "brand" children at an early age in the attempt to create loyal long-term consumers.[10] These attempts work against the interests of parents and create family conflicts. Clearly, children cannot be expected to bear the responsibilities accorded to adult consumers in the marketplace. Thus, in almost all cases, children should be off-limits as targets of commercial messages.

Ethical considerations should also place limits on the physical reach of advertising. Commercial messages are now often seen in places once deemed off-limits. In addition to the new venues discussed in this chapter's introduction, school-age children now see advertising on *Channel One*, in hallways, and in the form of overtly branded "learning" materials provided by companies such as the maker of Tootsie Rolls.

In all likelihood, technology will continue to embolden and empower advertising. The mixing and matching of information found in powerful computer databases will allow advertisers to come ever closer to the once unimaginable goal of tailoring messages to *individual* consumers.

With the possibility for damaging effects on both our individual and collective identities, a Christian approach to marketing as a vocation (as it would be in any profession) is necessarily cautious and critical. The challenge is to appropriately manage the real tension inherent in preserving and enhancing the legitimate social contributions of advertising, while curbing its morally questionable elements. In addition to those offered by Hagenbuch, the following guidelines, while broad, can be used to engage in marketing in a morally responsible manner:

First, marketing should be open, honest, and transparent. One exemplary business we know (in the car sales business) endeavors to treat customers as valued friends. CEO Don Flow asks employees if they are proud of the way they treated customers that day to the extent that they could go home and tell their loved ones about it. To facilitate this belief in a practical way, lots of information is provided to the consumer to make the purchase as transparent

standard is widely used when trying to determine what a consumer should have known in legal disputes over advertising, particularly accusations of false and misleading campaigns.

[10] In the film *Affluenza*, cameras record a session of a conference called "Kid Power." The conference is not about empowering children, but about how to successfully market products and services to them. One presenter uses terms such as "branding them and owning them" in reference to kids.

as possible. The key question we should ask is whether or not we would be willing to trade places with the consumer.

While it is unfair to accuse most advertisements of deception, since most consumers can see through their claims, some campaigns can be misleading. Businesspeople who use advertising must be sensitive to claims or graphics that could mislead the audience.

Second, marketing appeals should be made to healthier parts of the human soul. Sexuality and insecurities such as social acceptance are part of our natural makeup. However, they should not be taken advantage of in order to make a sale. Healthy values such as true friendship and physical and social well-being are more appropriate means to reach an audience. In contrast, some campaigns clearly traverse the bounds of healthy persuasion. For example, many messages capitalize on insecurities about not fitting in. Others actively cultivate dissatisfaction through comparative statements about taste and/or status. More overtly, some campaigns attempt to appeal to raw sexual power. In many of the ads, the product itself is not the primary focus. Rather, provocatively dressed actors or models are used to grab attention and to lead the consumer to "associate" the product with sexual power or feelings. A disturbing aspect of these campaigns is that appeals to these parts of the psyche seem so unnecessary. There are countless examples of campaigns that instead rely on more appropriate expressions of creativity.

Third, marketers should be mindful of the vulnerable. The interpretative lenses of children, the elderly, new immigrants, and perhaps citizens of developing nations who have yet to develop the sophistication to see through messages we take for granted must be taken into consideration.

Fourth, marketing should be "broadcast" (and "narrow cast" in the case of customized database driven marketing) in the least invasive manner possible. To a large degree, a person's "space" and when it becomes violated is a culturally defined matter. Therefore, it is difficult to give set guidelines without being unduly and inappropriately legalistic. The more important point is that each culture has a point where "sacred" space may be violated. For sound moral (and business) reasons, advertisers would do well to respect these boundaries.

TEN

Environmental Stewardship

Introduction

Some years ago, executives of Herman Miller, Inc. (a market leader in high-end office furniture) faced a difficult decision. Over the years, the company (founded and led through the years by devout Christians) had acquired a stellar reputation for its pioneering environmental practices. Then executives were informed that the wood used in the company's signature product, the Eames chair, was contributing to the destruction of rain forests. A decision to use raw materials from another tree species would have been easy were it not for the fact that the wood in question gave the chair its distinctive "rosewood" finish. In fact, the suggestion to use a substitute source prompted one executive to state that the market for the chair would be destroyed. Further complicating the matter was the fact that the company was struggling financially at the time and could ill afford to risk the market position of its best-known product.[1]

The dilemma facing Herman Miller executives highlights the delicate relationship between business and the natural environment. In the course of sourcing, production, transportation, packaging, and many other routine operations, business both depends upon and impacts the natural environment. When partnered with human ingenuity, natural materials form the basis for life-enhancing products. Sand serves as the necessary material for silicon chips that serve as brains for our computing devices, wind has been harnessed to power buildings, and medicines have been made from compounds found in soil. However, as the recent Gulf oil spill involving BP (British Petroleum) so starkly reminds us, when things veer off course, unforeseen and lasting damage to nature and human well-being can be inflicted.

Along with the possibility of catastrophic damage come concerns about pollution and climate change caused by worldwide economic development and the business-promoted emulation of Western lifestyles across the globe.

[1] David Woodruff, "Herman Miller: How Green Is My Factory?" *Businessweek*, September 16, 1991.

It is not surprising then that environmental stewardship has become one of the most pressing and challenging ethical issues business leaders face. Environmental issues have become a primary concern under the broader umbrella of corporate social responsibility. Few credible large businesses operate today without trying to account for their environmental impact.

Beyond requirements set forth by law and perhaps economic demand from the marketplace for "green products," what level of responsibility does business have for the well-being of the natural environment? Should businesses proactively favor natural interests in its decisions? What if doing so could not be captured under the "win-win" category and were to come at a cost of lost market share and/or jobs? Wrapped into these issues are a growing number of strategic and pragmatic questions that must also be considered. For example, are there competitive advantages to "going green" (i.e., new lines of business, lower production or transportation costs, sustainable sources of raw materials)? By emphasizing green credentials, can environmentally conscious consumers or investors be attracted? Are enough consumers willing to pay premiums to cover any additional costs?

Beneath these questions are more fundamental philosophical and theological viewpoints about the relative value of nature that need to be addressed. These viewpoints, which often come in the form of unquestioned assumptions, form "the underlying rationales" by which environmental issues are addressed and deeply influence practical "on the ground" decisions. The first two articles in this chapter speak to these issues. The first essay, "Business and Environmental Ethics," by philosopher W. Michael Hoffman presents the case for one "underlying rationale" of the environment known as "biocentrism" and its implications for business. Developed in part as a reaction to environmental degradation, biocentrism has become a much more widely held position during the past several decades and has worked to inform business decisions and matters of public policy. In brief, biocentrism holds that nature has intrinsic value quite apart from any worth humans might take from or attribute to it. Upholding natural interests above or equal to human ones when a conflict occurs is one of the major practical implications of the view. Undoubtedly, there are strong implications for business decisions and practices.

The second article, "The Challenge of Biocentrism," by Thomas Sieger Derr is a critique of biocentrism. Derr, a self-described environmentalist, offers a philosophical and theological analysis of some of the key assumptions and policy implications of the biocentric framework, especially if taken to its extreme. Derr argues that the traditional Christian understanding of stewardship is a sufficient and more appropriate basis for the care of creation.

The third and fourth articles in this chapter address more practical issues related to environmental ethics and sustainability: establishing the "business case" and redesign of products. In the article "The Business of Climate Change: What's the Deal?" author Clive Mather makes a case for how large-scale environmental problems, specifically climate change, must be addressed: through shared responsibility and the establishment of a framework to unleash the power of business. Some readers may be surprised that someone with Mather's background (a Christian who recently retired as the CEO of Shell Canada after a long career in the petroleum/energy industry) takes such a strong stand on behalf of environmental sustainability.

"Remaking the Way We Make Things" is an overview and explanation of an emerging paradigm known as "cradle-to-cradle" design. The authors, a chemist and an architect, note that most attempts at environmental solutions are really after the fact, "end of pipe" fixes that only function in a reactionary manner to make things "less bad." In contrast, the cradle-to-cradle process "begins in the head of designers" and represents a thorough-going reimagination of the entire product life cycle. Though the authors are not writing from a Christian theological perspective, many of their ideas are thought-provoking and may be consistent with a stewardship framework for changing the way business interacts with the environment.

The last article, "Snack Chips and Lessons in Environmental Consciousness," by John Terrill describes some recent examples (including the effort by SunChips to introduce a new bag) that illustrate the difficulties in developing and successfully marketing environmentally friendly goods to finicky consumers. Terrill then suggests some possible ways to encourage consumer adoption of these products.

READINGS

Business and Environmental Ethics[1]

W. Michael Hoffman

Business Ethics Quarterly 1, no. 2 (1991): 169–84. Copyright © 1991.

Business has an ethical responsibility to the environment which goes beyond obeying environmental law.

The business ethics movement, from my perspective, is still on the march. And the environmental movement, after being somewhat silent for the past twenty years, has once again captured our attention — promising to be a major social force in the 1990s. Much will be written in the next few years trying to tie together these two movements. This is one such effort.

Concern over the environment is not new. Warnings came out of the 1960s in the form of burning rivers, dying lakes, and oil-fouled oceans. Radioactivity was found in our food, DDT in mother's milk, lead and mercury in our water. Every breath of air in the North American hemisphere was reported as contaminated. Some said these were truly warnings from Planet Earth of eco-catastrophe, unless we could find limits to our growth and changes in our lifestyle.

Over the past few years, Planet Earth began to speak to us even more loudly than before, and we began to listen more than before. The message was ominous, somewhat akin to God warning Noah. It spoke through droughts, heat waves, and forest fires, raising fears of global warming due to the buildup of carbon dioxide and other gases in the atmosphere. It warned us by raw sewage and medical wastes washing up on our beaches, and by devastating oil spills—one despoiling Prince William Sound and its wildlife to such an extent that it made us weep. It spoke to us through increased skin cancers and discoveries of holes in the ozone layer caused by our use of chlorofluorocarbons. It drove its message home through the rapid and dangerous cutting and burning of our primitive forests at the rate of one football field a second, leaving us even more vulnerable to greenhouse gases like carbon dioxide and eliminating scores of irreplaceable species daily. It rained down on us in the form of acid, defoliating our forests and poisoning our lakes and streams. Its warnings were found on barges roaming the seas for places to dump tons of toxic incinerator ash. And its message exploded in our faces at Chernobyl and Bhopal, reminding us of past warnings at Three Mile Island and Love Canal.

Senator Albert Gore said in 1988: "The fact that we face an ecological crisis without any precedent in historic times is no longer a matter of any dispute worthy of recognition."[2] The question, he continued, is not whether there is a problem, but how we will address it. This will be the focal point for a public policy debate which requires the full participation of two of its major players—business and government. The debate must clarify such fundamental questions as: (1) What obligation does business have to help with our environmental crisis? (2) What is the proper relationship between business and government, especially when faced with a social problem of the magnitude of the environment crisis? And (3) what rationale should be used for making and justifying decisions to protect the environment? Corporations, and society in general for that matter, have yet to answer these questions satisfactorily. In the first section of this paper, I will briefly address the first two questions. In the final two sections, I will say a few things about the third question.

I.

In a 1989 keynote address before the "Business, Ethics and the Environment" conference at the Center for Business Ethics, Norman Bowie offered some answers to the first two questions.

> Business does not have an obligation to protect the environment over and above what is required by law; however, it does have a moral obligation to avoid intervening in the political arena in order to defeat or weaken environmental legislation.[3]

I disagree with Bowie on both counts.

Bowie's first point is very Friedmanesque.[4] The social responsibility of business is to produce goods and services and to make profit for its shareholders while playing within the rules of the market game. These rules, including those to protect the environment, are set by the government and the courts. To do more than is required by these rules is, according to this position, unfair to business. In order to perform its proper function, every business must respond to the market and operate in the same arena as its competitors. As Bowie puts this:

> An injunction to assist in solving societal problems [including depletion of natural resources and pollution] makes impossible demands on a corporation because, at the practical level, it ignores the impact that such activities have on profit.[5]

If, as Bowie claims, consumers are not willing to respond to the cost and use of environmentally friendly products and actions, then it is not the responsibility of business to respond or correct such market failure.

Bowie's second point is a radical departure from this classical position in contending that business should not lobby against the government's process to set environmental regulations. To quote Bowie:

> Far too many corporations try to have their cake and eat it too. They argue that it is the job of government to correct for market failure and then they use their influence and money to defeat or water down regulations designed to conserve and protect the environment.[6]

Bowie only recommends this abstinence of corporate lobbying in the case of environmental regulations. He is particularly concerned that politicians, ever mindful of their reelection status, are already reluctant to pass environmental legislation which has huge immediate costs and in most cases very long-term benefits. This makes the obligations of business to refrain from opposing such legislation a justified special case.

I can understand why Bowie argues these points. He seems to be responding to two extreme approaches, both of which are inappropriate. Let me illustrate these extremes by the following two stories.

At the Center's First National Conference on Business Ethics, Harvard Business School professor George Cabot Lodge told of a friend who owned a paper company on the banks of a New England stream. On the first Earth Day in 1970, his friend was converted to the cause of environmental protection. He became determined to stop his company's pollution of the stream, and marched off to put his newfound religion into action. Later, Lodge learned his friend went broke, so he went to investigate. Radiating a kind of ethical purity, the friend told Lodge that he spent millions to stop the pollution and thus could no longer compete with other firms that did not follow his example. So the company went under, 500 people lost their jobs, and the stream remained polluted.

When Lodge asked why his friend hadn't sought help from the state or federal government for stricter standards for everyone, the man replied that was not the American way, that government should not interfere with business activity, and that private enterprise could do the job alone. In fact, he felt it was the social responsibility of business to solve environmental prob-

lems, so he was proud that he had set an example for others to follow.

The second story portrays another extreme. A few years ago, *Sixty Minutes* interviewed a manager of a chemical company that was discharging effluent into a river in upstate New York. At the time, the dumping was legal, though a bill to prevent it was pending in Congress. The manager remarked that he hoped the bill would pass, and that he certainly would support it as a responsible citizen. However, he also said he approved of his company's efforts to defeat the bill and of the firm's policy of dumping wastes in the meantime. After all, isn't the proper role of business to make as much profit as possible within the bounds of law? Making the laws—setting the rules of the game—is the role of government, not business. While wearing his business hat, the manager had a job to do, even if it meant doing something that he strongly opposed as a private citizen.

Both stories reveal incorrect answers to the questions posed earlier, the proof of which is found in the fact that neither the New England stream nor the New York river was made any cleaner. Bowie's points are intended to block these two extremes. But to avoid these extremes, as Bowie does, misses the real managerial and ethical failure of the stories. Although the paper company owner and the chemical company manager had radically different views of the ethical responsibilities of business, both saw business and government performing separate roles, and neither felt that business ought to cooperate with government to solve environmental problems.[7]

If the business ethics movement has led us anywhere in the past fifteen years, it is to the position that business has an ethical responsibility to become a more active partner in dealing with social concerns. Business must creatively find ways to become a part of solutions rather than being a part of problems. Corporations can and must develop a conscience, as Ken Goodpaster and others have argued—and this includes an environmental conscience.[8] Corporations should not isolate themselves from participation in solving our environmental problems, leaving it up to others to find the answers and to tell them what not to do.

Corporations have special knowledge, expertise, and resources which are invaluable in dealing with the environmental crisis. Society needs the ethical vision and cooperation of all its players to solve its most urgent problems, especially ones that involve the very survival of the planet itself. Business must work with government to find appropriate solutions. It should lobby for good environmental legislation and lobby against bad legislation, rather than isolating itself from the legislative process as Bowie suggests. It should not be ethically quixotic and try to go it alone, as our paper company owner tried to do, nor should it be ethically inauthentic and fight against what it believes to be environmentally sound policy, as our chemical company manager tried to do. Instead business must develop and demonstrate moral leadership.

There are examples of corporations demonstrating such leadership, even when this has been a risk to their self-interest. In the area of environmental moral leadership, one might cite DuPont's discontinuing its Freon products, a $750-million-a-year-business, because of their possible negative effects on the ozone layer, and Proctor and Gamble's manufacture of concentrated fabric softener and detergents which require less packaging. But some might argue, as Bowie does, that the real burden for environmental change lies with consumers, not with corporations. If we as consumers are willing to accept the harm done to the environment by favoring environmentally unfriendly products, corporations have no moral obligation to change so long as they obey environmental law. This is even more the case, so the argument goes, if corporations must take risks or sacrifice profits to do so.

This argument fails to recognize that we quite often act differently when we think of ourselves as *consumers* than when we think of ourselves as *citizens*. Mark Sagoff, concerned about our overreliance on economic solutions, clearly characterizes this dual nature of our decision making.[9] As consumers, we act more often than not for ourselves; as citizens, we take on a broader vision and do what is in the best interests of the community. I often shop for things I don't vote for. I might support recycling referendums but buy products in nonreturnable bottles. I am not proud of this, but I suspect this is more true of most of us than not. To stake our environmental future on our consumer willingness to pay is surely shortsighted, perhaps even disastrous.

I am not saying that we should not work to be ethically committed citizen consumers, and investors for that matter. I agree with Bowie that "consumers bear a far greater responsibility for preserving and protecting the environment than they have actually exercised,"[10] but activities which affect the environment should not be left up to what we, acting as consumers, are willing to tolerate or accept. To do this would be to use a market-based method of reasoning to decide on an issue which should be determined instead on the basis of our ethical responsibilities as a member of a social community.

Furthermore, consumers don't make the products, provide the services, or enact the legislation which can be either environmentally friendly or unfriendly. Grassroots boycotts and lobbying efforts are important, but we also need leadership and mutual cooperation from business and government in setting forth ethical environmental policy. Even Bowie admits that perhaps business has a responsibility to educate the public and promote environmentally responsible behavior. But I am suggesting that corporate moral leadership goes far beyond public educational campaigns. It requires moral vision, commitment, and courage, and involves risk and sacrifice. I think business is capable of such a challenge. Some are even engaging in such a challenge. Certainly the business ethics movement should do nothing short of encouraging such leadership. I feel morality demands such leadership.

II.

If business has an ethical responsibility to the environment which goes beyond obeying environmental law, what criterion should be used to guide and justify such action? Many corporations are making environmentally friendly decisions where they see there are profits to be made by doing so. They are wrapping themselves in green where they see a green bottom line as a consequence. This rationale is also being used as a strategy by environmentalists to encourage more businesses to become environmentally conscientious. In December 1989 the highly respected Worldwatch Institute published an article by one of its senior researchers entitled "Doing Well by Doing Good," which gives numerous examples of corporations improving their pocketbooks by improving the environment. It concludes by saying that "fortunately, businesses that work to preserve the environment can also make a buck."[11]

In a recent Public Broadcast Corporation documentary entitled "Profit the Earth," several efforts are depicted of what is called the "new environmentalism," which induces corporations to do things for the environment by appealing to their self-interest. The Environmental Defense Fund is shown encouraging agribusiness in Southern California to irrigate more efficiently and profit by selling the water saved to the city of Los Angeles. This in turn will help save Mono Lake. EDF is also shown lobbying for emissions trading that would allow utility companies which are under their emission allotments to sell their "pollution rights" to those companies which are over their allotments. This is for the purpose of reducing acid rain. Thus the frequent strategy of the new environmentalists is to get business to help solve environmental problems by finding profitable or virtually costless ways for them to participate. They feel that compromise, not confrontation, is the only way to save the earth. By using the tools of the free enterprise system, they are in search of win-win solutions, believing that such solutions are necessary to take us beyond what we have so far been able to achieve.

I am not opposed to these efforts; in most cases I think they should be encouraged. There is certainly nothing wrong with making money while protecting the environment, just as there is nothing wrong with feeling good about doing one's duty. But if business is adopting or being encouraged to adopt the view that good environmentalism is good business, then I think this poses a danger for the environmental ethics movement—a danger which has an analogy in the business ethics movement.

As we all know, the position that good ethics is good business is being used more and more by corporate executives to justify the building of ethics into their companies and by business ethics consultants to gain new clients. For example, the Business Roundtable's *Corporate Ethics* report states:

> The corporate community should continue to refine and renew efforts to improve performance and manage change effectively through programs in corporate ethics ... corporate ethics is a stra-

tegic key to survival and profitability in this era of fierce competitiveness in a global economy.[12]

And, for instance, the book *The Power of Ethical Management* by Kenneth Blanchard and Norman Vincent Peale states in big red letters on the cover jacket that "Integrity Pays! You Don't Have to Cheat to Win." The blurb on the inside cover promises that the book "gives hard-hitting, practical *ethical* strategies that build profits, productivity, and long-term success."[13] Whoever would have guessed that business ethics gets marketed as the newest cure for what ails corporate America?

Is the rationale that good ethics is good business a proper one for business ethics? I think not. One thing that the study of ethics has taught us over the past 2,500 years is that being ethical may on occasion require that we place the interests of others ahead of or at least on par with our own interests. And this implies that the ethical thing to do, the morally right thing to do, may not be in our own self-interest. What happens when the right thing is not the best thing for the business?

Although in most cases good ethics may be good business, it should not be advanced as the only or even the main reason for doing business ethically. When the crunch comes, when ethics conflicts with the firm's interest, any ethics program that has not already faced up to this possibility is doomed to fail because it will undercut the rationale of the program itself. We should promote business ethics, not because good ethics is good business, but because we are morally required to adopt the moral point of view in all our dealings—and business is no exception. In business, as in all other human endeavors, we must be prepared to pay the costs of ethical behavior.

There is similar danger in the environmental movement with corporations choosing or being wooed to be environmentally friendly on the grounds that it will be in their self-interest. There is the risk of participating in the movement for the wrong reasons. But what does it matter if business cooperates for reasons other than the right reasons, as long as it cooperates? It matters if business believes or is led to believe that it only has a duty to be environmentally conscientious in those cases where such actions either require no sacrifice or actually make a profit. And I am afraid this is exactly what is happening. I suppose it wouldn't matter if the environmental cooperation of business was only needed in those cases where it was also in business self-interest. But this is surely not the case, unless one begins to really reach and talk about that amorphous concept "long-term" self-interest. Moreover, long-term interests, I suspect, are not what corporations or the new environmentalists have in mind in using self-interest as a reason for environmental action.

I am not saying we should abandon attempts to entice corporations into being ethical, both environmentally and in other ways, by pointing out and providing opportunities where good ethics is good business. And there are many places where such attempts fit well in both the business and environmental ethics movements. But we must be careful not to cast this as the proper guidelines for business' ethical responsibility. Because when it is discovered that many ethical actions are not necessarily good for business, at least in the short-run, then the rationale based on self-interest will come up morally short, and both ethical movements will be seen as deceptive and shallow.

III.

What is the proper rationale for responsible business action toward the environment? A minimalist principle is to refrain from causing or prevent the causing of unwarranted harm, because failure to do so would violate certain moral rights not to be harmed. There is, of course, much debate over what harms are indeed unwarranted due to conflict of rights and questions about whether some harms are offset by certain benefits. Norm Bowie, for example, uses the harm principle but contends that business does not violate it as long as it obeys environmental law. Robert Frederick, on the other hand, convincingly argues that the harm principle morally requires business to find ways to prevent certain harm it causes even if such harm violates no environmental law.[14]

However, Frederick's analysis of the harm principle is largely cast in terms of harm caused to human beings and the violation of rights of human beings. Even when he hints at the possible moral obligation to protect the environment when no one is caused unwar-

ranted harm, he does so by suggesting that we look to what we, as human beings, value.[15] This is very much in keeping with a humanistic position of environmental ethics which claims that only human beings have rights or moral standing because only human beings have intrinsic value. We may have duties with regard to nonhuman things (penguins, trees, islands, etc.) but only if such duties are derivative from duties we have toward human beings. Nonhuman things are valuable only if valued by human beings.

Such a position is in contrast to a naturalistic view of environmental ethics which holds that natural things other than human beings are intrinsically valuable and have, therefore, moral standing. Some naturalistic environmentalists only include other sentient animals in the framework of being deserving of moral consideration; others include all things which are alive or which are an integral part of an ecosystem. This latter view is sometimes called a biocentric environmental ethic as opposed to the homocentric view which sees all moral claims in terms of human beings and their interests. Some characterize these two views as deep *versus* shallow ecology.

The literature on these two positions is vast and the debate is ongoing. The conflict between them goes to the heart of environmental ethics and is crucial to our making of environmental policy and to our perception of moral duties to the environment, including business. I strongly favor the biocentric view. And although this is not the place to try to adequately argue for it, let me unfurl its banner for just a moment.

A version of R. Routley's "last man" example[16] might go something like this: Suppose you were the last surviving human being and were soon to die from nuclear poisoning, as all other human and sentient animals have died before you. Suppose also that it is within your power to destroy all remaining life, or to make it simpler, the last tree which could continue to flourish and propagate if left alone. Furthermore you will not suffer if you do not destroy it. Would you do anything wrong by cutting it down? The deeper ecological view would say yes because you would be destroying something that has value in and of itself, thus making the world a poorer place.

It might be argued that the only reason we may find the tree valuable is because human beings generally find trees of value either practically or aesthetically, rather than the atoms or molecules they might turn into if changed from their present form. The issue is whether the tree has value only in its relation to human beings or whether it has a value deserving of moral consideration inherent in itself in its present form. The biocentric position holds that when we find something wrong with destroying the tree, as we should, we do so because we are responding to an intrinsic value in the natural object, not to a value we give to it. This is a view which argues against a humanistic environmental ethic and which urges us to channel our moral obligations accordingly.

Why should one believe that nonhuman living things or natural objects forming integral parts of ecosystems have intrinsic value? One can respond to this question by pointing out the serious weaknesses and problems of human chauvinism.[17] More complete responses lay out a framework of concepts and beliefs which provides a coherent picture of the biocentric view with human beings as a part of a more holistic value system. But the final answer to the question hinges on what criterion one decides to use for determining moral worth—rationality, sentience, or a deeper biocentric one. Why should we adopt the principle of attributing intrinsic value to all living beings, or even to all natural objects, rather than just to human beings? I suspect Arne Naess gives as good an answer as can be given.

> Faced with the ever returning question of "Why?," we have to stop somewhere. Here is a place where we well might stop. We shall admit that the value in itself is something shown in intuition. We attribute intrinsic value to ourselves and our nearest, and the validity of further identification can be contested, and is contested by many. The negation may, however, also be attacked through a series of "whys?" Ultimately, we are in the same human predicament of having to start somewhere, at least for the moment. We must stop somewhere and treat where we then stand as a foundation.[18]

In the final analysis, environmental biocentrism is adopted or not depending on whether it is seen to provide a deeper, richer, and more ethically compelling view of the nature of things.

If this deeper ecological position is correct, then it ought to be reflected in the environmental movement. Unfortunately, for the most part, I do not think this is being done, and there is a price to be paid for not doing so. Moreover, I fear that even those who are of the biocentric persuasion are using homocentric language and strategies to bring business and other major players into the movement because they do not think they will be successful otherwise. They are afraid, and undoubtedly for good reason, that the large part of society, including business, will not be moved by arguments regarding the intrinsic value and rights of natural things. It is difficult enough to get business to recognize and act on their responsibilities to human beings and things of human interest. Hence many environmentalists follow the counsel of Spinoza:

> It is necessary that while we are endeavoring to attain our purpose ... we are compelled ... to speak in a manner intelligible to the multitude.... For we can gain from the multitude no small advantages.[19]

I understand the temptation of environmentalists employing a homocentric strategy, just as I understand business ethicists using the rationale that good ethics is good business. Both want their important work to succeed. But just as with the good ethics is good business tack, there are dangers in being a closet ecocentrist. The ethicists in both cases fail to reveal the deeper moral base of their positions because it's a harder sell. Business ethics gets marketed in terms of self-interest, environmental ethics in terms of human interest.

A major concern in using the homocentric view to formulate policy and law is that nonhuman nature will not receive the moral consideration it deserves. It might be argued, however, that by appealing to the interests and rights of human beings, in most cases nature as a whole will be protected. That is, if we are concerned about a wilderness area, we can argue that its survival is important to future generations who will otherwise be deprived of contact with its unique wildlife. We can also argue that it is important to the aesthetic pleasure of certain individuals or that, if it is destroyed, other recreational areas will become overcrowded. In this way we stand a chance to save the wilderness area without having to refer to our moral obligations to respect the intrinsic value of the spotted owl or of the old-growth forest. This is simply being strategically savvy. To trot out our deeper ecological moral convictions runs the risk of our efforts being ignored, even ridiculed, by business leaders and policy makers. It also runs head-on against a barrage of counterarguments that human interests take precedence over nonhuman interests. In any event it will not be in the best interest of the wilderness area we are trying to protect. Furthermore, all of the above homocentric arguments happen to be true—people will suffer if the wilderness area is destroyed.

In most cases, what is in the best interests of human beings may also be in the best interests of the rest of nature. After all, we are in our present environmental crisis in large part because we have not been ecologically intelligent about what is in our own interest—just as business has encountered much trouble because it has failed to see its interest in being ethically sensitive. But if the environmental movement relies only on arguments based on human interests, then it perpetuates the danger of making environmental policy and law on the basis of our strong inclination to fulfill our immediate self-interests, on the basis of our consumer viewpoints, on the basis of our willingness to pay. There will always be a tendency to allow our short-term interests to eclipse our long-term interest and the long-term interest of humanity itself. Without some grounding in a deeper environmental ethic with obligations to nonhuman natural things, then the temptation to view our own interests in disastrously short-term ways is that much more encouraged. The biocentric view helps to block this temptation.

Furthermore, there are many cases where what is in human interest is not in the interest of other natural things. Examples range from killing leopards for stylish coats to destroying a forest to build a golf course. I am not convinced that homocentric arguments, even those based on long-term human interests, have much force in protecting the interests of such natural things. Attempts to make these interests coincide might be made, but the point is that from a homocentric point of view, the leopard and the forest have no morally relevant interests to consider. It is simply fortuitous if nonhuman natural interests coincided with human

interests, and are thereby valued and protected. Let us take an example from the work of Christopher Stone. Suppose a stream has been polluted by a business. From a homocentric point of view, which serves as the basis for our legal system, we can only correct the problem through finding some harm done to human beings who use the stream. Reparation for such harm might involve cessation of the pollution and restoration of the stream, but it is also possible that the business might settle with the people by paying them for their damages and continue to pollute the stream. Homocentrism provides no way for the stream to be made whole again unless it is in the interests of human beings to do so. In short it is possible for human beings to sell out the stream.[20]

I am not saying that human interests cannot take precedence over nonhuman interests when there are conflicts. For this we need to come up with criteria for deciding on interspecific conflicts of interests, just as we do for intraspecific conflicts of interest among human beings.[21] But this is a different problem from holding that nonhuman natural things have no interests or value deserving of moral consideration. There are times when causing harm to natural things is morally unjustifiable when there are no significant human interests involved and even when there are human interests involved. But only a deeper ecological ethic than homocentrism will allow us to defend this.

Finally, perhaps the greatest danger that biocentric environmentalists run in using homocentric strategies to further the movement is the loss of the very insight that grounded their ethical concern in the first place. This is nicely put by Lawrence Tribe:

> What the environmentalist may not perceive is that, by couching this claim in terms of human self-interest—by articulating environmental goals wholly in terms of human needs and preferences—he may be helping to legitimate a system of discourse which so structures human thought and feeling as to erode, over the long run, the very sense of obligation which provided the initial impetus for his own protective efforts.[22]

Business ethicists run a similar risk in couching their claims in terms of business self-interest.

The environmental movement must find ways to incorporate and protect the intrinsic value of animal and plant life and even other natural objects that are integral parts of ecosystems. This must be done without constantly reducing such values to human interests. This will, of course, be difficult, because our conceptual ideology and ethical persuasion is so dominantly homocentric: however, if we are committed to a deeper biocentric ethic, then it is vital that we try to find appropriate ways to promote it. Environmental impact statements should make explicit reference to nonhuman natural values. Legal rights for nonhuman natural things, along the lines of Christopher Stone's proposal, should be sought.[23] And naturalistic ethical guidelines, such as those suggested by Holmes Rolston, should be set forth for business to follow when its activities impact upon ecosystems.[24]

At the heart of the business ethics movement is its reaction to the mistaken belief that business only has responsibilities to a narrow set of its stakeholders, namely its stockholders. Crucial to the environmental ethics movement is its reaction to the mistaken belief that only human beings and human interests are deserving of our moral consideration. I suspect that the beginnings of both movements can be traced to these respective moral insights. Certainly the significance of both movements lies in their search for a broader and deeper moral perspective. If business and environmental ethicists begin to rely solely on promotional strategies of self-interest, such as good ethics is good business, and of human interest, such as homocentrism, then they face the danger of cutting off the very roots of their ethical efforts.

Notes

1 This paper was originally presented as the Presidential Address to the Society for Business Ethics, August 10, 1990, San Francisco, CA.

2 Albert Gore, "What Is Wrong with Us?" *Time* (January 2, 1989), 66.

3 Norman Bowie, "Morality, Money, and Motor Cars," *Business, Ethics, and the Environment: The Public Policy Debate*, edited by W. Michael Hoffman, Robert Frederick, and Edward S. Petry, Jr. (New York: Quorum Books, 1990), 89.

4 See Milton Friedman, "The Social Responsibility of Business Is to Increase Its Profits," *The New York Times Magazine* (September 13, 1970).

5 Bowie, 91.

6 Bowie, 94.

7 Robert Frederick, assistant director for the Center for Business Ethics, and I have developed and written these points together. Frederick has also provided me with invaluable assistance on other points in this paper.

8 Kenneth E. Goodpaster, "Can a Corporation Have an Environmental Conscience?," *The Corporation, Ethics, and the Environment*, edited by W. Michael Hoffman, Robert Frederick, and Edward S. Petry, Jr. (New York: Quorum Books, 1990).

9 Mark Sagoff, "At the Shrine of Our Lady of Fatima, or Why Political Questions Are Not All Economic," found in *Business Ethics: Readings and Cases in Corporate Morality*, 2nd edition, edited by W. Michael Hoffman and Jennifer Mills Moore (New York: McGraw Hill, 1990), 494–503.

10 Bowie, 94.

11 Cynthia Pollock Shea, "Doing Well by Doing Good," *World-Watch* (November/December 1989), 30.

12 *Corporate Ethics: A Prime Business Asset*, a report by the Business Roundtable, February 1988, 4.

13 Kenneth Blanchard and Norman Vincent Peale, *The Power of Ethical Management* (New York: William Morrow and Company, Inc., 1988).

14 Robert Frederick, "Individual Rights and Environmental Protection," presented at the Annual Society for Business Ethics Conference in San Francisco, August 10 and 11, 1990.

15 Frederick.

16 Richard Routley and Val Routley, "Human Chauvinism and Environmental Ethics," *Environmental Philosophy*, Monograph Series, No. 2, edited by Don Mannison, Michael McRobbie, and Richard Routley (Australian National University, 1980), 121ff.

17 See Paul W. Taylor, "The Ethics of Respect for Nature," found in *People, Penguins, and Plastic Trees: Basic Issues in Environmental Ethics*, edited by Donald Vandeveer and Christine Pierce (Belmont, CA: Wadsworth, 1986), 178–83. Also see R. and V. Routley, "Against the Inevitability of Human Chauvinism," found in *Ethics and the Problems of the 21st Century*, edited by K. E. Goodpaster and K. M. Sayre (Notre Dame: University of Notre Dame Press, 1979), 36–59.

18 Arne Naess, "Identification as a Source of Deep Ecological Attitudes," *Deep Ecology*, edited by Michael Tobias (San Marcos, CA: Avant Books, 1988), 266.

19 Benedict de Spinoza, "On the Improvement of the Understanding," found in *Philosophy of Benedict de Spinoza*, translated by R. H. M. Elwes (New York: Tudor Publishing Co., 1936), 5.

20 Christopher D. Stone, "Should Trees Have Standing?—Toward Legal Rights for Natural Objects," found in *People, Penguins, and Plastic Trees*, 86–87.

21 Stone, 83–96.

22 Lawrence H. Tribe, "Ways Not to Think about Plastic Trees: New Foundations for Environmental Law," found in *People, Penguins, and Plastic Trees*, 257.

23 Stone, 83–96.

24 Holmes Rolston III, *Environmental Ethics* (Philadelphia: Temple University Press, 1988), 301–13.

Questions for Discussion and Reflection

1. Do you agree with Hoffman's claim that the environment has value in and of itself? Why or why not?
2. Do you believe that a homocentric view of the environment reflects what Hoffman calls "human chauvinism"? Explain your answer.
3. Does Hoffman hold to the view that the environment should take precedence over human needs? How would you balance those competing interests?
4. Do you believe that animals have rights that should be protected? Plants? Nonliving things? On what basis?

The Challenge of Biocentrism

Thomas Sieger Derr

From *Creation at Risk?: Religion, Science, and Environmentalism*, ed. Michael Cromartie (Grand Rapids: Eerdmans, 1995), 85–104.

At first glance I might appear to be an unlikely person to be critical of the environmental movement in any way. A sometime countryman, I usually know where the wind is and what phase of the moon we're in. I take good care of my small woodland, and I love my dogs. My personal predilections carry over into public policy, too. I champion the goals of reducing the waste stream, improving air and water quality, preserving the forests, protecting wildlife. I think of environmentalism as in some form a necessary and inevitable movement.

But by current standards that does not make me much of an environmentalist, for I am profoundly unhappy with the direction of current environmental philosophy, and most especially because I am a Christian. My trouble stems partly from the determination of mainstream environmentalism to blame Christianity for whatever ecological trouble we are in. This is a piece of historical nonsense that apparently thrives on repetition, so that every time it appears in print more people feel free to quote the source as authoritative, and each reference has a further multiplier effect.

Although a canard of this sort cannot surely be traced to a single source, probably the closest we can come to its origin is an essay by the late, formidable medieval historian Lynn White, Jr., called "The Historical Roots of Our Ecologic Crisis," which appeared in *Science* in 1967 and has since enjoyed virtually eternal life in anthologies.[1] It is cited as evidence of the need for an alternative religion, as for example by George Sessions, premier philosopher of the currently popular "Deep Ecology" movement: "The environmental crisis [is] fundamentally a crisis of the West's anthropocentric philosophical and religious orientations and values."[2]

It is not so much that White himself blamed Christianity; he was far too careful a historian for that, and he wrote, moreover, as a Christian and an active churchman. But his essay was used by others to promote darker purposes.

To be sure, White gave them ammunition. He traced the modern technological exploitation of nature back through the ages to the famous "dominion" passage in Genesis 1:28, which gives humanity some form of supremacy over the rest of creation. Because, he argued, technology is now ecologically "out of control," it is fair to say that "Christianity bears a huge burden of guilt" for this result. We need to reject "the Christian axiom that nature has no reason for existence save to serve man." We must overcome our "orthodox Christian arrogance toward nature." White even gave his blessing to the counterculture's espousal of alternative religions: "More science and more technology are not going to get us out of the present ecologic crisis until we find a new religion, or rethink our old one.... The hippies ... show a sound instinct in their affinity for Zen Buddhism and Hinduism, which conceive the man-nature relationship as very nearly the mirror image of the Christian view."

Is Christianity really the ecological culprit? And did White really say that it is? The answer to both questions is no.

Many scholars have concluded that Christianity made an important contribution to the rise of science and technology in the West, but to make it the only cause would be too much. Yes, the doctrine of creation separates nature from God, makes it not itself divine, and suggests strongly that inquiry into its workings is a pious study of the mind of the Maker. That way of looking at the world surely abets the scientific and technological culture. But it is not a *sufficient* condition for the appearance of that culture, which did not arise in lands dominated by Eastern Christianity but only in the Latin West, and then only after a millennium. Nor is it a *necessary* condition, for science flourished without benefit of Christianity in China, ancient Greece, and the medieval Islamic world.

Neither can we say that it is chiefly Christian lands that are environmentally heedless. Ecological destruction like overgrazing and deforestation, sometimes enough to cause the fall of civilizations, has been committed by Egyptians, Persians, Romans, Aztecs, Indians, and even Buddhists. This probably comes as a surprise to no one except those gullible Westerners who romanticize other cultures of which they know very little. There is, for example, a noted Western ecologist who, despising his own civilization, extols "the Eastern and gentle Pacific cultures in which man lives (or lived) a leisurely life of harmony with nature."[3] That could only have been written by someone who knows nothing of the sorry, violent history of those peoples.

What, then, does produce the technological society? And what causes ecological pillage? As to technology, we may guess at primitive origins in simple artisanship and the domestication of animals; the natural human quest for labor-saving devices; trade and commerce with other societies where these developments are further advanced; or just the natural momentum of technological change, once started in however small a way. Other likely suspects include geography, climate, population growth, urbanism, and democracy. To this mix add the idea that the world is an intelligible order ruled by general principles, which we received from the ancient Greeks, mediated powerfully (as A. N. Whitehead asserted[4]) by the medieval insistence on the rationality of God; or perhaps the rise of purely *secular* philosophy celebrating human mastery over nature, as in Bacon, Descartes, and Leibniz. That is quite a list. Given this wealth of candidates, it would be impossible to sort out what the primary influences really are, and even White acknowledged that the causes are finally mysterious.

As for the causes of ecological harm, we may cite first the simple fact that there are more people on the earth than ever before, and their search for food and shelter frequently assaults the world around them. It is, notably, not only the factories of the developed nations, but the daily gathering and burning of wood for fuel by rural people in the Third World, along with the depredations of their domestic animals, that have damaged the world's soils and dirtied its air (which in the Third World is far more polluted than ours). Of course industrial development has caused ecological damage, but much of that is the result of ignorance and error, mistakes often quite correctable. Noisy voices in the environmental movement attribute the damage to corporate greed, and the more fanciful among them go searching for deeper roots in capitalist culture, which in turn they find spawned by Christian theology in some form. It is simpler and surely more accurate to say that human self-seeking is a constant in our natures that no culture, no matter what its religion, has managed to eliminate.

Lynn White really did not blame Christianity for our environmental difficulties. By "orthodox Christian arrogance toward nature" he did *not* mean, he said later, that arrogance toward nature is orthodox Christian doctrine, only that presumably orthodox Christians have been arrogant toward nature. By "the Christian axiom that nature has no reason for existence save to serve man," he meant, he claimed, that some Christians have *regarded* it as an axiom, not that it is a matter of true faith.[5] Qualifications like these really vitiate the apparent argument in his "Historical Roots" essay, which was that Christians were heedless of nature *because* they were Christians. But on reflection, after absorbing the storm, White retreated to saying only that Christians, like human beings everywhere, found it possible to misappropriate certain elements from their religious tradition to serve their selfish ends.

Having talked with White at some length about his essay, I believe that, although he may have been pleased at the notice it received, he was also disturbed at the way it was used. He was only half joking when he wrote me about the "theology of ecology," saying, "Of course I claim to be the founder!" But surely he would disown many of his offspring.

The Christian Approach to Nature

What is the *real* orthodox Christian attitude toward nature? It is, in a word, stewardship. We are trustees for that which does not belong to us. "The earth is the Lord's, and the fullness thereof; the world and they that dwell therein" (Ps. 24:1). The implications of this idea for environmentalism are profound and, I think, wholly positive. They have been spelled out in different ways by many writers, including Douglas John Hall in *The Steward*, Loren Wilkinson and his colleagues in *Earthkeeping in the Nineties*, and my own book of twenty years ago, *Ecology and Human Need*.[6]

The rough historical evidence suggests that this theoretical obligation has not been without its practical results. For example, some Christian lands in Europe have been farmed in an ecologically stable manner for centuries. Rene Dubos says flatly, "The Judeo-Christian peoples were probably the first to develop on a large scale a pervasive concern for land management and an ethic of nature."[7] Clarence Glacken, one of the most patient and exhaustive historians of these matters, concludes from his survey of the vast literature, "I am convinced that modern ecological theory ... owes its origin to the design argument," the idea so prominent in Christian theology of all ages that the complexity of the world is the work of a creator God.[8] Lynn White knew this, too. And in the past it has been common for even the ecological critics

of Christianity to say that the Christians' problem is only that they did not take their own doctrines seriously enough.

What is new in our world today is a rejection of this semi- or pseudo-irenic view and its replacement by a root-and-branch attack on the doctrine of stewardship itself by that increasingly powerful and pervasive school of environmental thought known as biocentrism, of course, and one must be careful not to overgeneralize. But it is fair to say of nearly all varieties that they find the idea of stewardship repulsively anthropocentric, implying as it plainly does that human beings are in charge of nature, meant to manage it for purposes that they alone are able to perceive. Stewardship, says Richard Sylvan (ex-Routley), means "Man as tyrant."[9] May we think of ourselves as the earth's gardeners? Bad metaphor: gardening is controlling the earth's fecundity in a way that nature, left to its own devices, would not do. Human design is wrongly imposed.

The problem is simply compounded by Christian theism, which places human beings at the apex of nature by design of the ultimate giver of life. Made, as we say, in the image of God, we give ourselves license to claim that our interests as a species take precedence over those of the rest of creation; stewardship of the creation means mainly that we should manage it so that it sustains us indefinitely. Nature is made for us, as we are made for God. Here, say the biocentrists, is the bitter harvest of anthropocentrism: human selfishness, parochialism, chauvinism, "speciesism" (the awful term Peter Singer uses of those who reject animal rights), moral naïveté, a profanation of nature, self-importance and pride carried to their extreme. Regarding humankind as of more inherent worth than other species is, says Paul Taylor, like regarding noblemen of more inherent worth than peasants. A claim to human superiority is "a deep-seated prejudice, ... a wholly arbitrary claim ... an irrational bias in our own favor."[10] Lynn White was right after all: it is simply arrogance.

Rights in Nature

What do the biocentrists propose instead? Their most fundamental proposition is that nature itself, the life process as a whole, is the primary locus of value. Within that process all species have value, intrinsic value, just because they *are*, because they would not *be* if they did not have an appropriate niche in the ecology of the whole. And if they have intrinsic value, we must say that they have rights of some sort, claims on us for appropriate treatment, an integrity of their own that is not available for our mere willful disposition.

Notice that the alleged rights of non-human entities do not depend on their possession of any attributes, like rationality or language or even sentience. That would be subtle anthropocentrism, say the biocentrists. It would make a semblance to human characteristics the test of value—a mistake made by many of the animal-rights advocates and one that separates them from the biocentrists. We must say instead that all entities have value simply in themselves. They have their own purposes, or "good," which they value, either consciously or unconsciously. Their value, and their consequent rights, depend solely on their essential need to be themselves, on their own "vital interests."[11]

This is, incidentally, the way a biocentrist would dispose of the animal-rights argument that human infants or mentally defective human beings may be surpassed by animals in certain qualities, such as intelligence or adaptability, and yet we would not (or most of us would not) deny human rights to these human beings; so why not give animals rights? The answer, says the biocentrist—and here, for once, I would agree—is that rights inhere in a class or species, and not in the possession of certain qualities that individuals in that species possess. My difference, as I will make plain in a moment, is that I would not extend rights below the human level.[12]

Intrinsic Value in Nature

Since the assertion that the natural world has rights we must honor begins with the claim that the natural world has intrinsic value, let us spend a moment on this prior claim. No one, to my knowledge, has worked harder or with greater care to establish this idea—that natural entities have value independent of human beings (or, for that matter, independent of God, whom he does not mention)—than Holmes Rolston.[13] If, as I will claim, even *his* most careful and

gracefully expressed formulations cannot stand, then one may suppose the biocentrists' foundations generally are weak.

To Rolston, the ability to support life is a natural good that the earth possesses without us, which means that the human experience of satisfaction is not necessary to have a "good." The earth is able to produce value without us. We recognize the presence of that objective value when we value our natural science, "for no study of a worthless thing can be intrinsically valuable."[14] Organisms are living beings and hence have a good for themselves, maintaining their own life; and this good is a value that can claim our respect. In fact, "the living individual ... is per se an intrinsic value."[15]

Rolston admits that the human participant supplies value to an object: "No value can in principle ... be altogether independent of a valuing consciousness.... If all consciousness were annihilated at a stroke, there would be no good or evil.... no right or wrong; only impassive phenomena would remain." However, "to say that something is valuable means that it is able to be valued, if and when human valuers come along, but it has this property whether or not humans ... ever arrive." The value is already in the thing, hence "intrinsic." Rolston does not like any account of value in natural things that depends on human psychology. He wants the value to emerge from nature directly, so that we can value the object "for what it is in itself." Value may increase with the attention of human beings, but it is present without them. Thus his theory is "biocentric."[16]

On the contrary, I argue that, with the important theistic exception noted below, we human beings *supply* the value, that nature is valuable because we find it so. There is no value without a valuer. Values are for someone or something. A thing can provide value to someone, and in that sense it possesses value, i.e., the capacity to provide value for someone. That is not the same as "intrinsic" value, which is value in and for the thing itself, whatever anyone makes of it. The mere fact that we value studying a particular thing does not make that thing intrinsically valuable; it makes it valuable *for us*. Someone may find it valuable for his peace of mind to finger worry beads, but that does not mean that we must accord those beads intrinsic value. Some elderly recluses have been known to save newspapers for years, valuing the accumulating mountain highly. But that does not make those old papers *intrinsically* valuable. Mosquitoes or bacteria may have a goal or drive for themselves in perpetuating their life; but that is quite different from having an *intrinsic* value that other, conscious beings are required to acknowledge.

The attempt of Rolston and other biocentrists—J. Baird Callicott, for example—to distinguish between human appreciation of nature's intrinsic value, and the value that human beings add to nature by appreciating it, strikes me as hairsplitting. It is much more compelling and credible to say simply that a natural object may generate value for us not by itself but only in conjunction with our situation. We supply the value; the object contributes its being. Value is not a term appropriate to it in isolation, by itself.

The Amorality of Nature

The discussion of value takes a different course if we are theists who accept the doctrine of creation as the foundation of our environmental philosophy, or theology. We may rightly say, as James Nash does, that all creatures must reflect their Maker in some way and that a presumption of value in their favor is not unreasonable.[17] This is not to say that natural entities have intrinsic value; their value still depends on the valuer. But here the valuer is other than human beings. God bestows the value, which still does not belong to the object as such.

This is a well-developed idea with impeccable Thomist credentials, yet it does not solve our ecological problem. If anything, it makes the problem more difficult. To say that "God saw everything that he had made, and behold, it was very good" establishes well our obligation to respect the natural world; it is the foundation of our stewardship duty, of course. But we still face, and in a peculiarly painful form (for it raises the ancient problem of theodicy), the observable amorality of nature and its frequent hostility to us. That nature is full of what we perceive as violence and ugliness is beyond dispute. It is the realm of the food chain, of brute struggle and painful death. Surprisingly, no one has put it more candidly and vividly than Rolston himself:

> Wildness is a gigantic food pyramid, and this sets value in a grim, deathbound jungle. Earth is a slaughterhouse, with life a miasma rising over the stench. Nothing is done for the benefit of another.... Blind and ever urgent exploitation is nature's driving theme.[18]

Worse yet, from our point of view, nature is frequently hostile to our human lives. From violent storm to volcanic eruption to drought to killer viruses, to say nothing of the cosmic possibilities that could end our lives in one great, sudden bang, the natural world is certainly not unambiguously our friend.

Can one read an ethic out of this natural behavior? Not likely, or at least not an ethic that any Christian could for a moment tolerate. It is not that nature is immoral, for to say that would be to read our human values into this world. But nature is certainly amoral, and we would not begin to derive our ethical standards from its actions. Nevertheless, the biocentrists, bound to locate value primarily in this amoral world, find something to cherish there, something that rises above the brutality of the food chain, something that relativizes the ugliness. Some choose the harmony that they profess to see behind the apparent chaos, the patterns that repeat themselves, the balances that are restored. Other biocentrists admire nature's vitality, fecundity, and regenerative power, its strength, endurance, and dynamism, even in the midst of its fury. New life emerges from rotting carcasses and burned forests. "Ugliness," says Rolston, "though present at time in particulars, is not the last word.... Over time nature will bring beauty out of this ugliness."[19]

But seeing it that way is a matter of choice. Harmony in an ecosystem is only apparent, superficial. There are emergent forces that triumph, species that disappear, balances that are permanently upset. To see harmony is to look selectively. Harmony, like beauty, is mostly in the eyes of the beholder. If it is natural power and regenerative strength that enthrall us, we can love the rapid reproduction of cancer cells or the terrible beauty of a tornado. We can love what kills us. Over time, nature means to destroy this world. The death of our sun might be beautiful if there were anyone to see it, I suppose, even though it would mark the end of planet Earth. We can appreciate the natural facts any way we choose. To say it once again: we supply the value.

But what shall we say to those theists who reply that surely God must value what he has made? Can we discern what God intends for the creation?

Faced with the puzzle of natural evil and the ancient lineage of the problem of theodicy, and bearing in mind the centuries of false prophets who have claimed to know God's will all too well, I think we must be very, very modest in answering this question. Given the centrality of the divine-human drama in Christian faith, given its proclamation of the redemptive event addressed to humankind, I am certainly willing to say—more than willing, in fact, insistent upon saying—that our focus must be on human life, and that our task with the earth is to sustain the conditions for human life for as far into the future as our wits and strength allow. But I am not willing to go much beyond that. I am not willing to guess at what the earth's good is, or, to put it better, to guess at what God intends for the earth, which by definition would be its good.

A Calculus of Rights

The biocentrists are much less modest. They do claim to know the good of nature. If I may turn the tables on them, I would say they are far more daring, even impudent, in their claims to know the purposes of nature (or of God with nature, if they are theists) than are traditional Christians. Building on their theory of intrinsic value in natural entities, the biocentrists tell us that there are severe limits on what we may do with the natural world. In search of a strong position that will have sufficient force to restrain human selfishness, many of them, though not all, adopt the language of rights. Nature has rights, and thus has claims against us, much as we human beings claim rights that other human beings may not transgress.

But at once they plunge us into a realm of competing rights. Whose rights take precedence? When may they be violated, and by whom? May we eat meat? experiment on animals in laboratories? spread agricultural pesticides? use antibiotics? dam rivers? May a cat kill a mouse? In order to solve these conflicts and save the whole concept from reduction to absurdity, its defenders propose an inequality of rights, or even a complete disjunction between our obligations to one another and to the natural world.

Constructing a calculus of variable rights for different levels of existence is no simple task, however. Nash, who calls himself a Christian biocentrist and who, for his theological care, deserves to be exempted from many of the faults of the larger movement, does it by using "value-creating" and "value-experiencing" as the criteria for relevant differences, with rights diminishing as we descend a scale established by the relative presence of these capacities. Thus he hopes to solve conflicts of rights by "appropriate adjustments for the different contexts."[20] Rolston similarly would have the rights of animals and other natural entities "fade over a descending phylogenic spectrum."[21] These systems give priority in rights to human beings, a lesser preference to creatures merely sentient, and still less to non-sentient entities.

More radical versions of rights in nature take a Schweitzer-like approach, avoiding all killing of "lesser" forms of life except under threat to our own lives, and then only with a profound sense of sorrow for this necessary evil. How many times have we heard it said in recent years, with wondering admiration, that American Indians, those supposed ecological paragons, apologized to their game before killing it? An Irish pacifist once told me, with appropriate sardonic tone, that political assassination in Ireland was so common it was considered a normal part of the political process rather than murder in the sense of violating the sixth commandment; "but," he added, "it is doubtful whether the victims appreciated the distinction." And so also the caribou, slain by an Indian arrow tipped with a profound apology.

Faced with these tangles, even the biocentrically inclined must be tempted to give up on rights language. Rolston verges on the cynical when he admits that rights may after all be merely "a cultural discovery, really a convention" that does not translate to ecosystems, but that it may be politically useful to use the term anyway. "It is sometimes convenient rhetorically but in principle unnecessary to use the concept of rights at all."[22] What matters is the power of the restraint, and the language may be adjusted as necessary.

Reining in Rights

With all due respect to the intellectual strength and agility of the biocentric arguments, I would slice through their Gordian tangles by limiting "rights" to intrahuman affairs. "Rights" is a political and social term in the first instance, applicable only to human society, often enshrined in a fundamental document like a constitution, or embedded in the common law. As a metaphysical term, the transcultural phrase "human rights" applies to that which belongs to human beings by their very nature, i.e., not by their citizenship. Theologically, we guarantee human rights neither by our nature nor by our citizenship but by the radical equality of the love of God, the concept of "alien dignity," a grace bestowed on us that does not belong to our nature as such. In none of these forms has nature participated in rights.

Biocentrists sometimes seek to redress what to them are these deficiencies in the history of ideas by what I will call the argument from extension. "Rights," they point out, originally applied only to male citizens; but just as rights were gradually extended to women, to slaves, and finally to all other human beings, so it is a logical extension of this political liberalism to extend rights now to nonhuman creatures and even to agglomerations like ecosystems. Or, if the forum is not politics but Christian ethics, one could argue that the command to love our neighbors must now apply to non-human "neighbors," our "co-siblings of creation,"[23] or that the justice we are obliged to dispense to the poor and oppressed must now be extended to oppressed nature, or even that the enemies we are asked to love may include nature in its most hostile modes.

Although I appreciate the generous spirit of this line of argument, I think it involves a serious category mistake. Non-humans cannot have the moral status that only human beings possess, by our very natures. It is not irrelevant that the command to love our neighbors, in its original context, does in fact *not* apply to non-humans. An "extension" amounts to a substantial misreading of the text. Our obligations to the natural world cannot be expressed this way.

Another use of the idea of extension, one that occurs in Nash and in a different way in Paul Santmire,[24] is to argue that ultimate redemption is meant not only for humankind but also for the natural world, indeed the whole cosmos. That would imply much about our treatment of nature, our companion in cosmic redemption. The Incarnation confers dignity not only on us but on the whole material world: the divine takes on not only human flesh but material being in general. Certain New Testament passages are suggestive here—Romans 8:18–25, Colossians 1:15–20, Revelation 21:1—and Eastern Orthodox theology has formally incorporated this notion.

This is a theological idea of considerable gravity, and it deserves to be taken seriously. Nevertheless the doctrine is only vaguely expressed and appears to faith as hope, a hope made legitimate by faith, but a hope without details. Indeed, if we are to be scientifically honest, it is a "hope against hope," given the secular geological wisdom about the death of planet Earth in fire and ice. The doctrine of eschatological renewal cannot tell us much about the care of nature beyond what we already know from our stewardship obligation, that we are to preserve this world as a habitat fit for humanity. The natural details of a redeemed environment are beyond our ken. Our trust in God for the eternal Presence beyond death does not require the preservation of these rocks and rills, these woods and templed hills. Again we find ourselves behind the veil of ignorance: we simply do not know nature's divine destiny.

In short, and in sum thus far, I believe it would be more consistent, more logical, and conceptually much simpler to insist that nature has neither intrinsic value nor rights. And I believe this is true whether we are secular philosophers or Christian theologians, whether we speak with the tongues of men or of angels.

Policy Consequences of Biocentrism

It is time now to ask what is practically at stake in this agreement. What are the policy consequences of the biocentrists' position, for which they seek the vocabulary of rights or other strong language? What is denied to us thereby that would be permitted from the viewpoint of Christian humanism?

Since the biocentrists will not allow us to use nature as we see fit for ourselves, but insist that it has rights or at least claims of its own against us, their general recipe is that it should be left alone wherever possible. There is of course disagreement about the details and the exceptions, but the presumption is in favor of a hands-off policy. That is the *prima facie* rule:

Let nature take its course. The burden of proof is on us to show why we should be allowed to impose our wills on natural processes.

Concretely this means we should take the necessary measures to protect existing species for their own sakes, not because they might offer something to us in the form of, say, aesthetic pleasure or possible future medicinal benefits. The Endangered Species Act should be vigorously defended and enforced; and its conflicts with human desires—the spotted owl vs. the timber industry, the snail darter vs. the Tennessee dam—should be settled in favor of the species threatened. The state will have to intervene to protect the species and the land, which means limitations on a landowner's use of his own property. After all, the wild animals and plants on the land should have their freedom, too.

Especially should we preserve and expand wild lands, the necessary larger habitats needed for these species, even though human beings may desire the land for other purposes, like farming. When it comes to such conflicts, mankind ought to lose. Arne Naess, founder of the Deep Ecology school (which is a form of biocentrism tending to argue the equal worth of all natural entities), says with astonishing frankness, "If [human] vital needs come in conflict with the vital needs of nonhumans, then humans should defer to the latter."[25]

We should also leave alone those injured wild creatures that we are tempted to save—the baby bird fallen from its nest, the wounded animal we come upon in the forest, the whale trapped by the ice. Intervention in the natural processes is wrong whether the motives are benevolent or not. The species is strengthened by the premature extinction of its weaker members. Respecting nature's integrity means not imposing our soft-hearted human morality upon it. We should let forest fires burn and have their way with the wild creatures.

We should not build monuments in the wild. No more Mount Rushmores, no Christ of the Andes, no railroads up Mount Washington, and probably no more wilderness roads or ski lifts.

We should suspend genetic engineering in agriculture and animal husbandry and not permit there anything we would not permit among human beings.

We should not take animal lives in teaching biology or medicine, and certainly not in testing cosmetics. Zoos and botanical gardens are suspect; better that the species there displayed should live in the wild. We should not keep pets. (There go my Springers.)

What about recreational hunting or fishing? Some biocentrists frown upon it as human interference with nature and unnecessary to our diet besides; but others would permit it as simply a form of predation, which is a fact of nature and not subject to our moral scrutiny. And by this same token there would be no moral obligation for us to become vegetarians. In fact, and rather awkwardly, even plants have a "good of their own" in the biocentric theory, which leads to some mental agility to sort out their permissible uses. It is all right to eat them, of course, for that is nature's way; but "frivolous" uses (Halloween pumpkins? Christmas trees?) are questionable. One suspects that even flower gardens would be a dubious activity, which may be why the biocentric literature rarely if ever mentions them.

Although we are in principle to leave nature alone, we are obligated to restore that which we have harmed. This form of intervention is acceptable because it is guided by the principle that pristine nature, before human impact, is somehow ideal. Here again the calculus of permissibility has to be rather finely tuned. It might be wrong to plant trees in a natural desert, for example, but obligatory to plant them if human activity had contributed substantially to creating that desert. Obviously this principle can be carried to extremes. Paul Shephard has seriously suggested that we in this country all move to the coasts and restore the land between to its pre-human condition, in which we would be permitted only as hunter-gatherers, like our most primitive ancestors. Few biocentrists would go anywhere near this far, but the principle is there. The argument is about the movable boundaries.

Stalking the Elusive Limits

My criticism of these limits begins with their vagueness and ambiguity, which is spiced with a generous dash of arbitrariness. Species, we are told, should be allowed to exist until the end of their natural "evolutionary time"; but how can we know when that time has arrived? We human beings should not take more than our "due" or occupy more than our "fair share" of land or exceed our "limits" in technological grasp; but these terms cannot even begin to be specified. What can be done with any creature turns on its degree of neural complexity, or some other hierarchical principle; but such distinctions will never be clear and are subject to a lot of pure arbitrariness. In the end I suspect that these measures are not in nature, but in ourselves. The lines are drawn according not to objective natural differences but to human preferences: human beings supply the values.

The matter of species disappearance is also confused. Leaving nature alone means allowing natural extinctions. Are we then to allow species to vanish, intervening only to save those threatened by human activity? (Yes, says Rolston. New life arises from the old when the demise is natural, but artificial extinction is "without issue."[26]) Or is it our responsibility to preserve as many species as possible, no matter what threatens them? Isn't domestication, far from being harmful interference with the wild, a useful way to preserve species? In defense of all of us dog owners, I note that many creatures have thrived because of the human presence—mice and rats, famously, and raccoons, and of course all species bred as pets or for agricultural utility.

The degree of simplicity of life is another matter of confusion. Some biocentrists would allow a fairly complex civilization. Others, like the bioregionalists, would turn their backs on the global economy and live in a locally sustainable way, even reverting to a simple agricultural economy. The movement as a whole can offer us very little real guidance about our permissible impact on the natural world. While it would allow us to feed and clothe and house ourselves, it would require of us some degree of self-limitation because of our exceptional talents, including particularly our talent for reproducing ourselves. But it is very difficult to tell what this directive might mean beyond the generalized complaint that we are too clever and thus exceed our space too readily. We have to pretend we are less, in effect, so that the other creatures may be more; but how and how much are quite unspecifiable.

The practical problems with the theory are many and are mainly intractable. They are also mostly unnecessary. Inevitably, once rights for non-human entities are proposed, the situation becomes impossibly complex. Absent this proposition, matters become much clearer, though solutions are seldom completely evident. We are still in for a process of experiment, of trial and error, mistake and correction. We have a lot to learn, mostly from science. But with a focus on human welfare we will have a reasonably clear idea how to use our knowledge; the complexities will be simpler, the conflicts easier to resolve.

Biocentric Fatalism: Many Must Die

There is one final, serious problem with biocentrism, and that is its fatalism. Biocentrists take their cues as to what *ought* to be from what *is*, and thus base their views of an acceptable future on what will happen if we let the natural world follow its own laws as far as possible. If an organism exists, the biocentrist presumes it has an important ecological niche and should be left alone. "Natural kinds are good kinds until proven otherwise."[27] If it is an ecological misfit, it will perish naturally anyway, and we should not regret its demise. Death may be bad for individuals, but it is good for the system.

Should this ecological "wisdom," if that is the word, be applied to *Homo sapiens*? Because the whole direction of biocentric thought is to answer this question affirmatively, and because the consequences are so fearsome for most people's sensitivities, it is hard to find candid replies. When they do come out, ordinary ethical opinion, unenlightened by this new environmental realism, is apt to be appalled. Should we curtail medicine so that more of us may die "naturally" and earlier? Yes. Should we refrain from feeding the hungry, so that population will not exceed its boundaries? Yes, said the "lifeboat school," and especially its helmsman Garrett Hardin, whose bluntness is plainly an embarrassment to the current generation of biocentrists. Or consider J. Baird Callicott's rendering of William Aiken's questions as direct statements: "Massive human diebacks would be good. It is our duty to cause them. It is our species duty, relative to the whole, to eliminate 90 percent of our numbers."[28]

Even Lynn White, that most humane and Christian man, walked up to the edge of this moral abyss. Human beings are crowding out earth's other species, our "comrades" on the planet, and a balance needs to be restored. How shall we do this? Shall individual human beings be sacrificed, in defiance of traditional Christian ethics, if some killing will save many species? White hesitated, he said, to "light candles before the saints requesting a new Black Death" to give us, like fourteenth-century Europe before us, a "tragic respite" from our ecological peril. Almost visibly he drew back from the fearful answer; and yet with only slight obliqueness he said it: Many must die.[29]

To be sure, and to be fair, many biocentrists recoil from the social implications of their theory. It is only the biocentric egalitarians, for whom all life is of equal value, who are driven to these fearful antihuman conclusions. For the others, their schema of hierarchical differentiation allows them to claim a different level of moral behavior among human beings, different from that between human beings and the natural world, and certainly different from natural amorality. Callicott insists that "humanitarian obligations in general come before environmental duties." Rolston calls it "monstrous" not to feed starving human beings, though he would let overpopulated wild herds die.

But the boundaries between nature and culture are blurred and repeatedly crossed, as the examples of White and Hardin show well enough. Callicott acknowledges that the conflicts are a "difficult and delicate question." Nash calls them "immensely complicated." Rolston says that ecological "fitness" means and implies different things in nature than it does for human beings, but (let the reader beware) the two meanings have similarity, too; they are "homologous" or "analogous." "This biological world that *is* also *ought* to be; we must argue from the natural to the moral.... So much the worse for those humanistic ethics no longer functioning in, nor suited to, their changing environment."[30] Apparently one can, in a way, import ethics from nature to culture.

And that is precisely the ethical problem. Without a secure anchor in humanism, Christian or otherwise, biocentrism risks great moral evils. At the extreme, it appears actually indifferent to human destiny. Paul Taylor says that as members of a biotic community we must be impartial toward all species, our own included: that in fact we are unnecessary to other species that would be helped by our extinction. Thomas

Berry is similarly minded: "The human species has, for some thousands of years, shown itself to be a pernicious presence in the world of the living on a unique and universal scale."[31] Since species must be allowed their "evolutionary time" and then die, and because this process is "good," the human species, too, must expect to perish; and from nature's point of view, that will be normal. If nature were capable of regret, there would be no regret for our passing. The ecosystem will survive as well or better without us at the top of the food chain. But since nature is amoral, we must say that our extinction is of no moral significance in nature.

Would God care? The whole direction of our faith says that God would indeed care, which suggests strongly that we should oppose biocentrism and not anticipate the demise of our species with equanimity. I admit that this is a conviction of faith. What God really is about I would not dare to say I knew.

Whether such modesty is becoming or not, it eludes the biocentrists, who seem to know more than I do about the ultimate principles that rule the universe. Here, for example, is Carol Christ:

> We are no more valuable to the life of the universe than a field [of flowers].... The divinity that shapes our ends is an impersonal process of life, death, and transformation.... The life force does not care more about human creativity and choice than it cares about the ability ... of moss to form on the side of a tree. The human species, like other species, might in time become extinct, dying so that other lives might live.[32]

Rolston is only moderately more hopeful: the evolutionary system is "not just a random walk" but "some kind of steady, if statistical heading." In the extinction of some species and the appearance of new ones "a hidden principle seems to be at work, organizing the cosmos in a coherent way." But that is scant comfort to human beings, who come very late to the story and are only "shortsighted and arrogant" if they think it was meant for them.[33] Rolston is quite fatalistic about our destiny: recognizing that there is nothing necessary or inevitable about our appearance on earth, we will simply have to accept the overall course of evolution as good, no matter where it eventually goes.[34]

James Gustafson, a justly celebrated ethicist, has written similarly that we should not count on humanity's being at the apex of creation nor consider that human good trumps the good of non-human nature. Our disappearance would not be bad "from a theocentric perspective," which acknowledges that "the source and power and order of all nature is not always beneficent in its outcomes for the diversity of life and for the well-being of humans as part of that." "The Divine ... [is] the ultimate source of all human good, but does not guarantee it." Such ruminations have led Nash to characterize Gustafson's "God" as "a nonconscious and nonmoral ordering power without intention, volition, or cognition.... This power sustains the universe, apparently unintentionally, but lacks the purposive, benevolent, or redemptive qualities to seek the good of individuals, the human species, otherkind, or the whole cosmos.... This perspective seems close to atheism or pantheism."[35]

The ecological ethic emerging from biocentric fatalism, such as it is, is simply to enjoy the earth's fecundity, to laugh and weep and celebrate all life, whether it is our life or not. "Humanity's highest possibility is to bear witness to and participate in the great process of life itself."[36] And so the biocentrist love affair with a mysterious Natural Process cultivates, inevitably, indifference to the human prospect.

It is, of course, a bit odd for biocentrists to view humanity as just another species serving out its evolutionary time, when with the same voice they must also acknowledge that we are a very special species, endowed with enormous power over the environment. We cannot renounce this power, either. It is ours to use for good or ill, and so they urge us to use it in a self-limiting way to preserve the rest of the environment and to care for the other creatures of the earth. Notice that the message is anthropocentric in spite of itself: our great power engenders our great responsibility. But that, of course, is precisely the Christian ethic of dominion and stewardship.

I do not know where the human story will end. But, as I think William Faulkner, that great literary icon of my college generation, said in accepting the Nobel Prize, "I decline to accept the end of man." I think that my efforts ought to be bent to perpetuating human life, and that that goal ought to be the overriding test of our ecological conduct. In arguing otherwise, large sections of the environmental movement are on the wrong track. In the name of its own humanistic faith, Christianity ought to criticize these environmentalists, rather than scramble to say, "Me, too." What is historic and traditional in our valuation of Creation is a perfectly sufficient guide to sound ecology.

Notes

1 Lynn White, Jr., "The Historical Roots of Our Ecologic Crisis," *Science*, 155 (March 10, 1967): 1203–7.

2 George Sessions, "Introduction" (to Part II, "Deep Ecology"), in Michael Zimmerman, ed. *Environmental Philosophy: From Animal Rights to Radical Ecology* (Englewood Cliffs, N.J.: Prentice Hall, 1993), 161.

3 Paul Ehrlich and Richard L. Harriman, *How to Be a Survivor* (New York: Ballantine, 1971), 129.

4 Alfred North Whitehead, *Science and the Modern World* (New York: Macmillan, 1950 [original 1925]).

5 Lynn White, "Continuing the Conversation," in Ian G. Barbour, ed., *Western Man and Environmental Ethics* (Reading, Mass.: Addison-Wesley, 1973). Also private conversations.

6 Douglas John Hall, *The Steward: A Biblical Symbol Come of Age* (Grand Rapids: Eerdmans, 1990). Loren Wilkinson et al., *Earthkeeping in the Nineties: Stewardship of Creation* (Grand Rapids: Eerdmans, 1991). Thomas Sieger Derr, *Ecology and Human Need* (Philadelphia: Westminster, 1973 and 1975).

7 Rene Dubos, *A God Within* (New York: Scribner, 1972), 161. See pp. 157–61 for his argument against White's thesis.

8 Clarence Glacken, *Traces on the Rhodian Shore: Nature and Culture in Western Thought from Ancient Times to the End of the Eighteenth Century* (Berkley: University of California, 1967), 423.

9 Richard Sylvan, "Is There a Need for a New, an Environmental Ethic?" in Zimmerman, *Environmental Philosophy*, 13–14.

10 Paul Taylor, "The Ethics of Respect for Nature," in Zimmerman, *Environmental Philosophy*, 78–80.

11 Biocentrists and animal-rights activists are further and seriously separated by the former's giving priority to species, and the latter's focus on saving individuals. A biocentrist, who is indifferent to suffering in the wild (just part of the natural ecosystem, which is good), would allow, even encourage, the death of weaker individuals so that the species as a whole may flourish. For this a leading animal-rights advocate, Tom Regan, has fastened upon biocentrism the charming sobriquet "eco-fascism" (*The Case for Animal Rights* [Berkeley: University of California, 1982], 262). But biocentrists reject this "humanitarian ethic" as misplaced in nature. It is not a true environmental ethic. Thus Mark Sagoff: "Mother Nature is so cruel to her children she makes Frank Perdue look like a saint" ("Animal Liberation and Environmental Ethics: Bad Marriage, Quick Divorce," in Zimmerman, *Environmental Philosophy*, 89–92).

[12] Not all biocentrists reject the argument from defective human beings, however. Kenneth Goodpaster uses it to deny that "moral considerability" should be restricted to humans because they are rational. He extends moral status beyond humans, and beyond animals, too, to all that is alive ("On Being Morally Considerable," in Zimmerman, *Environmental Philosophy*, 54, 56).

[13] Systematically in Holmes Rolston, *Environmental Ethics: Duties to and Values in the Natural World* (Philadelphia: Temple University Press, 1988).

[14] Ibid., 9.

[15] Ibid., 100.

[16] Ibid., 112–16.

[17] James A. Nash, *Loving Nature: Ecological Integrity and Christian Responsibility* (Nashville: Abingdon, 1991), 99. See also his essay "Biotic Rights and Human Ecological Responsibility," in *The Annual of the Society of Christian Ethics*, 1993, 137–62.

[18] Rolston, *Environmental Ethics*, 218.

[19] Ibid., 240–41.

[20] Nash, *Loving Nature*, 176, 181; "Biotic Rights," 150–51, 158–59. Nash would not award rights to abiotic entities, only organisms; and thus he rejects the term "rights of nature," though granting, like Rolston, that "the term remains rhetorically valuable" ("Biotic Rights," 148).

[21] Rolston, *Environmental Ethics*, 48.

[22] Ibid., 50–51.

[23] Larry Rasmussen's phrase, defending the extension of neighbor love even to inorganic nature; in Wesley Granberg-Michaelson, ed., *Tending the Garden: Essays on the Gospel and the Earth* (Grand Rapids: Eerdmans, 1987), 199. For an antitheological version of the extension argument, see J. Baird Callicott, following his hero, the much-cited Aldo Leopold, *In Defense of the Land Ethic* (Albany: State University of New York, 1989), 80–82.

[24] H. Paul Santmire, *The Travail of Nature: The Ambiguous Ecological Promise of Christian Theology* (Philadelphia: Fortress, 1985). Nash, *Loving Nature*, 124–33.

[25] Arne Naess, "The Deep Ecological Movement: Some Philosophical Aspects," in Zimmerman, *Environmental Philosophy*, 203. George Sessions is less severe but, as a "biocentric egalitarian," will give us no more than equality with nature: non-human entities have "equal inherent value or worth along with humans" ("Deep Ecology and Global Ecosystem Protection," in Zimmerman, *Environmental Philosophy*, 236).

[26] Rolston, *Environmental Ethics*, 155. That is not, strictly speaking, quite true. Nature has a way of restoring devastated land, whether it be laid waste by a volcano or an atomic bomb test.

Extinction of species on a grand scale is simply the way of nature, and always has been, since well before human life appeared.

[27] Rolston, *Environmental Ethics*, 103.

[28] Hardin's essay "The Tragedy of the Commons" (*Science*, December 13, 1968) is still routinely cited and anthologized, as are the conclusions he drew from it in another essay, "Living on a Lifeboat" (*Bioscience* 24, 1974). But harshest of all is *Exploring New Ethics for Survival: The Voyage of the Spaceship Beagle* (Baltimore: Penguin, 1973), which is virtually invisible today. The quotation from William Aiken is from his essay "Ethical Issues in Agriculture," in Tom Regan, ed., *Earthbound: New Introductory Essays in Environmental Ethics* (New York: Random House, 1984), 269; cited in Callicott, *In Defense of the Land Ethic*, 92. This is not Aiken's position, though Callicott's alterations make it appear to be so. Aiken says that these statements, which in his essay are questions, would be those of a position he calls "eco-holism," an extreme stance that he suggests may be ascribed to Paul Taylor among others, and which he rejects in favor of a more humanistic one. On page 272 he outlines a scale of comparative value much like Nash's, one that favors human beings.

[29] Lynn White, "The Future of Compassion," *The Ecumenical Review* 30, no. 2 (April 1978): 108.

[30] Rolston, *Environmental Ethics*, 329; Rolston, "Challenges in Environmental Ethics," in Zimmerman, *Environmental Philosophy*, 136; Nash, "Biotic Rights," 159; Callicott, *In Defense of the Land Ethic*, 93–94.

[31] Taylor, "Ethics of Respect for Nature," 71, 81. Berry, in Zimmerman, *Environmental Philosophy*, 174.

[32] Carol Christ, "Rethinking Theology and Nature," in Irene Diamond and Gloria Freman Orenstein, eds., *Reweaving the World: The Emergence of Ecofeminism* (San Francisco: Sierra Club, 1990), 68.

[33] Rolston, *Environmental Ethics*, 185–86, 195–98 (quoting in part P. C. W. Davies).

[34] Ibid., 344–45.

[35] James Gustafson, *A Sense of the Divine: The Natural Environment from a Theocentric Perspective* (Cleveland: Pilgrim Press, 1994), chaps. 1 and 3 in the unpaginated manuscript. Nash, *Loving Nature*, 233–34, n. 10, commenting on Gustafson's *Theocentric Ethics*, vol. 1 (Chicago: University of Chicago Press, 1981), 106, 183–84, 248–50, 270–73.

[36] Michael Zimmerman, "Deep Ecology and Ecofeminism: The Emerging Dialogue," in Diamond and Orenstein, *Reweaving the World*, 140. Zimmerman, like Naess and Sessions, is a "biocentric egalitarian"; thus: "Humanity is no more, but also no less, important than all other things on earth" (ibid.).

Questions for Discussion and Reflection

1. How does Derr's position on the environment differ from Hoffman's?
2. What are the elements of Derr's Christian approach to nature?
3. Do you agree with Derr that biocentrism leads to impractical and dangerous extremes? Why or why not?
4. Do you agree with Derr's claim that the environment has neither rights nor intrinsic value? Why or why not?

The Business of Climate Change: What's the Deal?

Clive Mather

Speech given at Business of Climate Change Conference II, Ottawa, Canada, October 30, 2007.

Current progress toward combating climate change is slow, patchy and ineffective. Only by harnessing the full force of business can we achieve effective global action. The technologies and other mechanisms exist, but for the time being the signals from the marketplace are too weak. The Albertan oil sands are a good example, with operators ready to do more, but facing daunting economics. International consensus would be a powerful enabler. More urgently national and regional legislation must establish a policy framework and a price of carbon, which will stimulate investment, innovation and competition. In parallel, improved information to consumers will help change buying habits and reinforce the business case. The profit motive will do the rest.

Concern about climate change is not new. Scientists had detected it almost 200 years ago, but it is only really in the last 20 years, since the Brundtland Report[1], that it has aroused broad interest with environmentalists, politicians, industrialists and consumers. Latterly the growth in interest has been exponential, focussing on the widespread evidence and potential consequences. Awareness of the increasing levels of GHG in the earth's atmosphere has generally been matched by acceptance that *homo sapiens* has been the root cause through population expansion and industrial activity. But it is an inconvenient truth that awareness and acceptance have not yet been matched by appropriate action—what specifically we need to do to stabilise and then reduce the CO_2 in the atmosphere? To be effective such action will have to be global, embrace all sectors of society and harness the power of new technologies. Which is why I for one am enthusiastic about the potential for commercial opportunities, because only business gets things done on that scale.

What drives business? It is the incentive to seize opportunity for commercial advantage. Companies compete through innovation, efficiency and scale to develop superior offers. And that's exactly what society needs to start tackling one of the biggest threats to its existence as we know it. It's not simply that the carbon levels in the atmosphere are high, but that they are going to grow inexorably for a long time commensurate with population growth and economic development, even if we start to act differently now. Ongoing scientific research will continue to enhance our understanding of the problem and the solutions, but time is not on our side. So we need to get started, accepting that the body of evidence is already compelling. The potential benefit of early action is immense, whilst it's hard to point to any potential downside.

But let's be clear, no matter how much business can achieve with innovation, technology and global reach, this is not just about business. The "deal", if we want it, is with all of us. We—you, me, big business, small business, governments, agencies and activists—we are all in this together. Governments must establish the policy frameworks; activists and academics must provide independent research and assurance; business must develop commercial products and consumers must change their habits. If we don't all respond in equal and timely fashion, we will all pay the price, whatever nature ultimately determines that should be. As author and naturalist Robert Pyle reminds us—"Nature bats last."[2]

Background

The impact of climate change—actual and predicted—is well reported. Sound research is available from many sources, of which the Intergovernmental Panel on Climate Change[3] is the most broadly based. I am persuaded by the environmental case for action and by Sir Nicholas Stern's economic analysis[4] that the cost of starting now will be so much less than later. But this is also about personal values. It seems to me that if we claim integrity as leaders, parents, or people of faith[5], then it's time we tackled both the symptoms and the causes of climate change. It is about human rights, as well as biodiversity and lifestyle.

Mankind's impact on the fragile ecosystems of our planet is not confined to greenhouse gases. The economic, social and environmental consequences of 6 rising to maybe 10 billion people goes way beyond climate change. Far from living off the interest, not the capital of nature[6], we are stretching mother earth's capacity to regenerate. Even if we make a credible and sustained reduction in carbon emissions, there remain other vital areas to be addressed — poverty, slavery, water, pollution, deforestation, AIDS and so on. But that's another deal altogether. The more focused the problem, the more likely something will be done. My bias is for action.

Climate change has become something of a cause célèbre on the international stage. Too many important nations have stepped back from Kyoto in its current form. For all its limitations, I applaud any international initiative that brings constructive engagement to this issue. If we wait until every country signs up to the same technical definitions and targets, we will wait too long.... The seas may literally boil or freeze over, depending on your view of how the stratosphere will behave. Above all we need leadership to look beyond immediate self-interest. The wider benefits for humanity may be obvious, but it's a tough sell with electorates who enjoy high standards of living. The ultimate irony is that everyone is in the same boat. The oceans, weather patterns and ecosystems know no national boundaries, so that as our environment adjusts to higher CO_2 levels, the impact will be felt everywhere.

International meetings regularly take place around the world. The G8+5 meeting in February and the Washington Climate Change Week in September were given prominence, but under the auspices of the Global Legislators Organisation for a Balanced Environment (Globe) and others, discussions are taking place all the time. But it is hard to get a meaningful deal and even harder with looming elections and the glare of the world's media. Clearly the solid support of the USA is fundamental to making the next big step and the active participation of China and India will then largely determine its long-term effectiveness. Canada and Europe can play a key role in achieving

these by demonstrating the business case. Exhortation and finger wagging achieve little and can be counterproductive. The way to get the attention and participation of the USA, China and India is by demonstrating successful business models. Self-interest is more compelling than social conscience. Successful nations will establish technology advantage, build export markets and increase influence in foreign policy.

The Individual Perspective

Climate change is a vast and complex subject, as evidenced by the ongoing debate within the scientific community as to the causes and effects. And whilst it is tempting to say that only the hard core now stoutly dispute the anthropogenic linkage, scientists on all sides will point to many unanswered questions and paradoxes. Hardly surprising therefore that for the rest of us it is easy to be confused about the role we play as citizens and consumers.

Photographs of melting glaciers and hungry polar bears deprived of their natural hunting grounds make powerful images, but understanding CO_2 emissions and how we tackle them takes time and effort. Making the link between electricity which produces no CO_2 at end use and an old fashioned coal fired power station which produces lots at source is not intuitive. More complicated still is hydrogen, which has been presented as a wonder fuel. It can be in Iceland which is blessed with abundant, super hot steam from natural fissures, but not if natural gas is needed to start the chain.

There are many traps for the unwary or excuses for inaction, if that's our personal inclination. Methane is a more damaging greenhouse gas (GHG) than CO_2 and flatulence of cattle is a primary cause of methane in the atmosphere, so does that mean we all have to become vegetarians? Sometimes cars are more fuel efficient per passenger than trains, so does that mean we should give up on public transport? Some household recycling creates significant environmental challenges, so does that mean we should stop recycling? Rhetorical these questions may be, but individuals and families lack consistent information as to how they should be responding.

A graphic picture of the smoking stack from a power station carried the caption "The polluter must pay". And of course they should and they will. But it's not just big bad business that pollutes — it's you and me. It's our lifestyle that the electricity serves and it's our pockets that must pay for something more efficient. This is not well understood, but it needs to be if we are to make a compelling case for action. Overcoming the resistance of ignorance, doubt and complacency will be hard. To date markets have been primarily responding to energy price signals rather than carbon ones. And in the affluent west even those signals have made little difference to consumer choices. This is why so many families in the developed world have traded away the greater fuel efficiency engineered by automakers and fuel companies in favour of size and power.

To shift individual behaviour and societal norms will require concerted action — information and explanation, encouragement and sanction. But above all we need commercial offerings that appeal direct to consumers' lifestyle and budgets. Compact Fluorescent Lights (CFL's) are a great example, offering convenience and cost advantage as well as significant carbon savings. But we need many more such examples all around home, work and transport so that being green is not just "cool", but cheap and practical as well. For that we need a stronger business case to attract resources and deliver results.

The Business Case

Climate change challenges the business community just as it does wider society. There are those who dispute the science and the need for action, but they are becoming fewer and even less who will say so publicly. There are those who sit on the fence. They probably represent the majority, avoiding any substantive commitment until the rewards are stronger. But many nevertheless wear green clothes, as TV commercials and supermarket aisles demonstrate. They presumably take the view that this is a low cost precaution against an uncertain future, but for the environmentally conscious consumer it is becoming ever harder to distinguish substance from packaging. And finally there are those taking substantive action, as yet modest in number, but growing as the business case emerges.

It is not rhetoric or reason that drives the business case, but hardnosed reality … making money. So it is

no surprise that almost every high energy usage business has been improving energy efficiency to reduce expensive energy bills. Investments in insulation, control systems and co-gen plants reduce CO_2 emissions but the driver has been attractive rates of return. To release the full power of business on climate change, we need to achieve the same economic stimulus across all industrial and commercial activity. What can do this?

1. Clear signals from the marketplace — systemic shifts in consumer or investor preferences. There is little evidence of such shifts in mass markets so far, although increasingly public and private contracts contain quite stringent environmental conditions.
2. Public policy — for example tax or tax relief which incentivises R&D, CO_2 reductions and capital investment in carbon neutral facilities. The EU Emissions Trading Scheme is the first major example but others are coming in Australia, Canada and the USA.
3. Reputational impact — the premium of positive publicity or the sanction of reputational laggard, enhanced if key competitors take a contrary position. Reputation has value. It impacts share price, sales and the ability to attract scarce resources to sustain your business. University campuses provide an acid test, but have no doubt that licences to explore, drill, construct and operate now increasingly reflect environmental reputation.

These are key drivers which will transform the business case and transfer mainstream resources to tackling CO_2 emissions. But let's be honest — overall the risk/reward equation is not yet compelling. Green is great at universities. Green is only slowly becoming important to consumers. And green has still to be proven with investors. There are more and more ethical funds now taking a position on climate change, but in the mainstream, analysts and fund managers are not convinced. My personal experience over the past 3 years may be summarised as "yes we are interested in what your company is doing regarding sustainable development and we note your initiatives, but do not expect any benefit in your share price, credit rating or market recommendation". In the jargon, climate change is still most definitely a "Hold".

The Albertan Oil Sands

Taking the long term view on climate change represents a short term challenge for CEO's, none more so than in the oil sands, where the scale of the resource, the engineering and the financial commitment set it apart from other sectors. The process of turning oil sands into much needed gasoline and diesel in N America releases lots of CO_2 into the atmosphere, from extraction, from upgrading and most (80%) from end use, such as transport and home heating. The issue is therefore how to harness this wonderful resource without aggravating climate change further. In principle this is no different to how we meet energy demand generally—whether from coal, gas or conventional oil—but the carbon characteristics and growth of production from the oil sands have attracted special focus.

There are those who believe that the development of the oil sands should be stopped—or at least industry should change course dramatically to focus on carbon reduction. These "Protagonists" hold that reserves of oil, gas, coal, oil shale or whatever should only be developed if it can be shown to represent a real reduction in CO_2 emissions. It's not impossible in the long term, but it is impractical in the medium term, given the world's appetite for energy and the lack of carbon neutral sources of supply. Wind, solar, biomass, wave power all have strong carbon credentials but even the most optimistic scenario suggests they will supply but a tiny fraction of the world's need in the next few decades.

"Protectionists" on the other hand support the continued development of the oil sands but under much more tightly described conditions. A new royalty structure, requirements to upgrade bitumen in Alberta, stringent water controls and other environmental constraints, infrastructure investment and so on are all proposed. Sound public regulation is necessary but I would argue to focus on carbon. History tells us that too many grandiose interventions have had unintended and painful consequences. The NEP in 1980 is a classic example in Canada, but every country has its own. The marketplace, rapidly so in our global economies, will assert itself and public policy objectives will be thwarted as investment dollars simply move elsewhere. Those who think Alberta has a right to investment and wealth, think again. Markets regulate more decisively than any government authority.

And thirdly it is the "Practitioners", the operators, investors, researchers, academics and others who have to wrestle with the day to day realities of managing this vast resource. The market is sending very strong price signals to increase production. At $50 bbl.WTI [barrel/West Texas Intermediate] the encouragement to develop the oil sands was clear ... let alone $60, $70 or $80. With construction capacity stretched to the limit, costs have risen to allocate the resources. So tough projects, spiralling costs, pressure from investors and now a Royalty Review, the pressure on CEO's in the oil sands is unremitting. However, in my experience, they genuinely want to do the right thing, whether operating standards, remediation, water management or carbon reduction. One company even made a commitment to manage its oil sands project, such that carbon emissions would be no greater than the alternative it displaced—that is to say imported crude oil.

What Are the Business Opportunities?

Energy efficiency and energy conservation offer a straightforward business case on the back of high energy costs. There are attractive returns for even substantial capital investments in plant or control equipment. This has been part of Shell Canada's continuous improvement for many years and will continue, driven by rising fuel prices and new technology.

The challenge with emissions trading is to move from a regulatory burden to a legitimate commercial opportunity. I understand the scepticism: the European Emissions Trading Scheme has not yet been a shining example, mainly because of over generous allowances in key sectors and key countries. And industry in Alberta is loathe to provide a free business for the market-makers out east. But trading in some form is part of any business and I am confident it will be so with carbon markets. It has the obvious merits of encouraging best practice and penalising inefficiency, but even more so it engages the financial community in Bay Street. That is vital if we are to tap into the full potential of what business can offer.

Renewable energy alternatives have not proved robust investments to date—good publicity, valuable experience but generally only marginal returns. The subsidisation of corn to ethanol has offered attractive returns, but without the environmental benefits. Cellulosic ethanol by comparison offers much stronger carbon credentials and I am involved with one of the leading companies in this area—Iogen Corporation in Ottawa. The short-term economics are not exciting, but with the right mix of fiscal incentives, it is on the verge of moving from pilot plant to commercial scale production. That will offer great CO_2 savings and a real fillip for Canadian technology.

Carbon capture on any scale—especially in a major existing manufacturing facility—requires massive capital to retro fit with expensive modern technology. Although a proven solution and well suited to Alberta's geology, sequestration also requires much capital to establish the infrastructure and injection facilities. For the oil sands it has an appealing logic, dealing directly with the carbon produced at source, but the economics are challenging. However, it is a vital opportunity for Canada to showcase an important technology to the world.

Given the energy needs of the oil sands—especially the in-situ bitumen which represents 80% of the total economic resource—nuclear generated electricity is emerging as a serious contender. The issue of spent fuel is a tough one and the local politics will be passionate, but the carbon benefit is obvious. New technology can produce finished product directly from the deep oil sands reservoirs, bypassing the need for expensive and carbon emitting upgrading, but has a huge appetite for direct energy. Watch this space.

Investment in innovation will also deliver, such as the growing carbon fibre business. Boeing's 787 Dreamliner and Airbus' A380 are current examples, but the automobile industry and civil engineering are not far behind. As markets expand, the capital intensity of production will fall, creating a virtuous circle that will make an increasing carbon impact.

What Would Accelerate These?

An international compact that embraced the major CO_2 emitters would send a powerful signal across the world and dramatically change the context for deci-sion makers in parliaments and board rooms around the world. It would stimulate national governments to review regulations, fiscal policy and subsidies. It would focus the business case and transform the prospects for investment and innovation.

Establish a realistic cost of carbon that would enable investment in R&D and plant to compete with alternatives that have obvious commercial application but no carbon benefit. It plays directly to the business case and must be the same for all sectors, all Provinces and all participants lest distortions negate the resulting market impact. It is not by accident that European car engines are more efficient than their N American counterparts—especially since the auto-makers are the same. Nor because Italians and French and Brits are inherently more carbon conscious than Canadians or Americans. Look at the infrastructure and look at the tax—on cars, on fuel, on emissions and engine efficiency.

Review subsidies to the North American farming industry for turning corn into ethanol. The environmental credentials are very poor and unwelcome, unintended consequences are beginning to show in many markets—the price of pasta in Italy for a start! Use the money to boost technology funds that will help accelerate new technology and develop commercial markets—whether carbon capture, sequestration, carbon fibre, geothermal energy, solar panels or renewable energy infrastructure.

Tackle the international aviation industry on CO_2 emissions. Kudos to Boeing and Airbus for making the next generation of jumbo jets more efficient in terms of weight and therefore fuel efficiency. This is a logical response to the price signals from jet fuel. However, there ought to be strong signals reflecting carbon emissions as well. Measures could be brought in by nation states for their domestic routes straight-away and a timetable set for regulation of international carriers.

Tighten regulations on new buildings, plants and equipment to ensure best practice on carbon emissions is built into all new investment at the design stage. Retrofitting existing homes, hospitals, offices, factories, cars, trucks, ships, heaters, coolers etc is difficult to do well and very expensive. It makes little economic sense. But we can make a huge difference from now on by applying what we already know.

And to back them all up target every household with practical information on the role they can play. (There are many examples, but "Green Tips"[7] is an excellent start.) By engaging families and individuals, demand will shift and with it the business case. And at schools and universities, let's mobilise young people whose awareness is high and who have most to gain. Their influence on older generations will be important reinforcement to government policies and commercial offerings.

"Deal or No Deal?"

I am confident that we have the means to tackle climate change if we choose to harness them — regulatory frameworks, technology and market forces. I am also realistic that it will probably happen later than it should or needs to. Unless we can strengthen the business case quickly, I fear it will take more compelling evidence of climate change and its harmful, widespread effects to persuade mankind that change is needed.

To achieve meaningful societal or global change will require leadership of an extraordinary kind to harness the power of science, tax, regulation, technology and personal interest. Coalitions of the willing will be necessary but by no means sufficient. However, help is at hand in the form of global markets.

They have proved their effectiveness in delivering rapid change in all continents — not all to everyone's taste of course — but impressive nonetheless. It is these key enablers that we need to target, responding to the stimuli of carrot and stick — incentives and sanctions, risks and rewards. Establish the right framework in enough key countries to establish critical momentum and let business do the rest. It will deliver the answers in the form of greater energy efficiency, and carbon avoidance, and carbon capture and many innovative mechanisms as yet unproven. That's what business does.

This is a big deal. The stakes are enormous, which is why countries, companies and consumers have been wary of taking early positions. Premature commitment to the wrong policy, or investment or technology could seriously weaken the national economy or the corporate cash flow or the family budget. For the most part, politicians have baulked at international protocols. Investors have generally stuck to the mainstream of capital projects, preferring to wait on major projects directed at carbon emissions. And families have not yet orientated their behaviours and purchases towards a greener agenda. But in all areas change is happening and the business case is growing stronger.

The business of climate change is becoming just that and not a moment too soon.

Notes

[1] G. Brundtland (ed.) *Our Common Future. Report by the World Commission on Environment and Development*. Oxford University Press. 1987.

[2] Attributed to Pyle, Robert M.

[3] Intergovernmental Panel on Climate Change. *Working Group 1 AR4 Report. Summary for Policymakers*. WMO and UNEP. 2007.

[4] Sir Nicholas Stern *Review on the Economics of Climate Change. Executive Summary*. HM Treasury. 2006.

[5] Nick Spencer and Robert White. *Christianity, Climate Change and Sustainable Living*. SPCK. 2007.

[6] Ronald Wright. *A Short History of Progress*. House of Anansi Press Inc. 2004.

[7] Gillian Deacon (comp.) *Green Tips. How to Save Money and the Planet*. Green Living Enterprises. 2006.

[8] The author wishes to make clear this article represents his own views.

About the Author

Clive Mather is the Chairman of Iogen Corporation, a Canadian biotech company that is the leading producer of cellulosic ethanol — a carbon neutral, renewable transport fuel from straw and grass. He is a member of the Premier's Council for Economic Strategy in Alberta and assists governments and NGO's on both sides of the Atlantic on energy and environmental issues. He is the Chairman of the Shell Pensions Trust Ltd. in the UK, managing assets of some $17bn. He is the Chairman of Tearfund, the international

Christian relief agency combating global poverty. In this role he is an ambassador for Tearfund around the world as well as chairing the Board.

Clive retired from Shell in 2007 after a career of 38 years which spanned all its major businesses, including assignments in Brunei, Gabon, North America, South Africa, the Netherlands and the UK. His last position was in Calgary as President and CEO of Shell Canada Limited, one of the largest publicly listed companies on the Toronto Stock Exchange, with operations across Canada. Under his leadership, the company embarked on a period of unprecedented growth in oil and gas exploration, and development of the Albertan oil sands. Leveraging Shell's resources and technology, he launched major new projects and strategic acquisitions. He took a high profile on environmental matters, presenting the business case for sustainable development and demonstrating best practice through operational performance. He was also a Director of Placer Dome Inc. and a Director of the C. D. Howe Institute.

Before this in 2001 he was appointed Chairman of Shell UK Ltd. and Head of Global Learning in Shell International. He was responsible for all Shell activities and reputation in the UK and for Shell's leadership development and learning globally.

An advocate of leadership for good and corporate social responsibility, he has held many public appointments in the UK, including Commissioner for the Equal Opportunities Commission, Chairman of the Government/Industry CSR Academy and Deputy Chairman of the Windsor Leadership Trust.

Clive was born in Warwickshire in 1947 and won scholarships to Warwick School and Lincoln College, Oxford. He is married with 3 children and a grandson. He lives with his wife Ann and their border collies in Guildford. He is a Companion of the Chartered Management Institute and Fellow of the Chartered Institute of Personnel and Development. He serves on various charitable Trusts but still finds time to enjoy sports—especially tennis and golf.

Questions for Discussion and Reflection

1. What do you think are the implications of Robert Pyle's statement that "nature bats last"?
2. What you think of Mather's view that climate change is not strictly a problem for business but is the result of our energy dependent lifestyles?
3. Do you agree with Mather that addressing climate change makes business sense? Why or why not? Or does it matter that it makes business sense? Defend your answer.

Remaking the Way We Make Things
William McDonough and Michael Braungart
Cradle to Cradle (New York: North Point Press, 2002).

The culture of innovation within the field of environmental technology and management is bringing forth significant change in the world of industry. From the growing influence of green chemistry and engineering to the emergence of environmental concerns in corporate research and development, one can see promising new initiatives in nearly every sphere of industrial activity.

Many of these developments, however, are limited by the "eco-efficient" framework in which they are applied. A widely adopted business paradigm, eco-efficiency is essentially a reductive agenda, its reforms rather narrowly aimed at minimizing the negative impacts of industry. New management tools based simply on efficiency, for example, may allow industry to use fewer resources, produce less waste and minimize toxic emissions, but they tend not to change the fundamental design of products or industrial production. In other words, efficient is not sufficient. As a result, even promising new technologies use energy and materials within a conventional cradle-to-grave system, diluting pollution and slowing the loss of natural resources without addressing the systemic design flaws that create waste and toxic products in the first place.

Global sourcing and lean production have standardized this state of affairs, with the result being a surfeit of products characterized by increasingly poor quality. On the Internet one can see an off-gassing diagram of a name-brand children's toy from the United States, which identifies more than thirty chemicals known to be mutagenic, desensitizing, or even suspected or known carcinogens.

The diagram (see at http://www.scribd.com/doc/37566076/C2C-Journal-of-Cleaner-Production-2007) illustrates that poor standards of quality result in everyday products that release hundreds of hazardous chemicals. Typically, these products, from electric shavers to carpets and upholsteries, are used indoors, where off-gassed chemicals accumulate. Energy efficient buildings, which are designed to require less heating and cooling, and thus less air circulation, can make things worse. A recent study in Germany, for example, found that air quality inside several highly rated energy efficient buildings in downtown Hamburg was nearly four times worse than on the dirty, car-clogged street.

The effects are hard to ignore. Where buildings with reduced air-exchange rates are common, so are health problems. In Germany, where tax credits support the construction of energy efficient buildings, allergies affect 42 percent of school age children between 6–7 years old, largely due to the poor quality of indoor air. This is what we would call chemical harassment. It is the result not of bad intentions, but of poor design.

A New Model for Industry

Cradle to Cradle Design offers a clear alternative, a framework in which the safe, regenerative productivity of nature provides models for wholly positive human designs. Working from this perspective, we do not aim to be less bad. Instead, our design assignment is to create a world of interdependent natural and human systems powered by the sun in which safe, healthful materials flow in regenerative cycles, elegantly and equitably deployed for the benefit of all.

Within this framework, every material is designed to provide a wide spectrum of renewable assets. After a useful life as a healthful product, cradle-to-cradle materials are designed to replenish the earth with safe, fecund matter or to supply high quality technical resources for the next generation of products. When materials and products are created specifically for use within these closed-loop cycles — the flow of biological materials through nature's nutrient cycles and the circulation of industrial materials from producer to customer to producer — businesses can realize both enormous short-term growth and enduring prosperity. As well, we can begin to redesign the very foundations of industry, creating systems that purify air, land, and water; use current solar income and generate no toxic waste; use only safe, healthful, regenerative materials; and whose benefits enhance all life.

This positive industrial agenda identifies a new definition of quality in product, process and facility design. From the cradle-to-cradle perspective, quality is embodied in designs that allow industry to enhance the well-being of nature and culture while generating economic value. Pursuing these positive aspirations at every level of commerce adds ecological intelligence, social equity, and cultural diversity to the conventional design criteria of cost, performance, and aesthetics. When these diverse criteria define good design, and when they are applied at every level of industry, productivity and profits are not at odds with environmental and social concerns. Indeed, as cradle-to-cradle design matures, we are increasingly able to design products and places that support life, that create ecological footprints to delight in rather than lament. This changes the entire context of the design process. Instead of asking, "How do I reduce the impact of my work?" and "How do I meet today's environmental standards?" we ask, "How might I increase my ecological footprint and enhance its positive effects? How might I grow prosperity and celebrate my community?

How might I create more habitat, more health, more clean water, more delight?"

The Cradle to Cradle Paradigm

Cradle to Cradle Design refocuses product development from a process aimed at limiting end-of-pipe liabilities to one geared to creating safe, healthful, high-quality products right from the start. In the world of industry it is creating a new conception of materials and material flows. Rather than seeing materials as a waste management problem in which interventions here and there slow their trip from cradle to grave, cradle-to-cradle thinking sees materials as nutrients and recognizes two safe metabolisms in which they flow.

In the biological metabolism, the nutrients that support life on earth—water, oxygen, nitrogen, carbon dioxide—flow perpetually through regenerative cycles of growth, decay, and rebirth. Rather than generating material liabilities, the biological metabolism accrues natural fecundity. Waste equals food. The technical metabolism can be designed to mirror natural nutrient cycles; it's a closed-loop system in which valuable, high-tech synthetics and mineral resources circulate in an endless cycle of production, recovery, and remanufacture. Ideally, the human systems that make up the technical metabolism are powered by the energy of the sun.

Biological Metabolism/Technical Metabolism

By specifying safe, healthful ingredients, industry can create and use materials within these cradle-to-cradle cycles. Materials designed as biological nutrients, such as detergents, packaging, or textiles for draperies, wall coverings and upholstery fabrics, can be designed to biodegrade safely and restore the soil after use, providing more positive effects, not fewer negative ones. Materials designed as technical nutrients, such as perpetually recyclable nylon fiber, can provide high-quality, high-tech ingredients for generation after generation of synthetic products—again a harvest of value.

Biological and technical nutrients have already entered the marketplace. The upholstery fabric Climatex Lifecycle® is a blend of pesticide-residue-free wool and organically grown ramie, dyed and processed entirely with nontoxic chemicals. All of its product and process inputs were defined and selected for their human and ecological safety within the biological metabolism. The result: the fabric trimmings are made into felt and used by garden clubs as mulch for growing fruits and vegetables, returning the textile's biological nutrients to the soil. The first product on the market designed as a biological nutrient, Climatex Lifecycle® has been followed by many others since its introduction in 1993.

Honeywell, meanwhile, is marketing a textile for the technical metabolism, a high-quality carpet yarn called Zeftron Savant®, which is made of perpetually recyclable nylon 6 fiber. Zeftron Savant® is designed to be reclaimed and repolymerized—taken back to its constituent resins—to become new material for new carpets. In fact, Honeywell can retrieve old, conventional nylon 6 and transform it into Zeftron Savant®, upcycling rather than downcycling an industrial material. The nylon is rematerialized, not dematerialized—a true cradle-to-cradle product.

Ideally, technical nutrients are designed as products of service, a key element of the cradle-to-cradle strategy. Products of service are durable goods—cars, computers, refrigerators, carpets—designed by their manufacturer to be taken back and used again. The product provides a service to the customer while the manufacturer maintains ownership of the product's material assets. At the end of a defined period of use, the manufacturer takes back the product and reuses its materials in another high-quality product. Material recovery systems such as these are the foundation of the technical metabolism. Widely practiced, the product-of-service concept can change the nature of production and consumption as human systems powered by renewable energy reuse valuable materials through many product life cycles.

The Practice of Cradle-to-Cradle Design

The Cradle-to-Cradle Design Framework incorporates nature's cyclical material model into all product and system design efforts through a process called Life

Cycle Development (LCD). While product development within this framework is not the same as life cycle assessment (LCA), "life cycle thinking" serves as an important structure for scientific inquiry and informs the process of cradle-to-cradle product design.

Life Cycle Development Process

LCD is a working, results oriented method for evaluating products and processes as they are being redesigned. While observing how a material or final product flows through any of its various life cycle stages (raw materials production, manufacturing, use, and recovery/reutilization) and identifying human and environmental health impacts at each stage, LCD phases out undesirable substances and replaces them with preferable ones. The redesign process occurs during—not after—environmental and human health assessment. This simultaneous work saves costs for manufacturers and users and allows manufacturers to maintain market presence and continue to generate revenue as they improve their products.

The LCD process is made up of three phases, which follow an initial identification of a product's proper metabolism. Defining each product as either a potential biological nutrient or a potential technical nutrient sets up two different sets of design criteria and informs all phases of product development. Biological nutrients will need to be compostable, for example, while the recovery of technical nutrients might require chemical recycling. All products, however, are assessed and developed through three phases:

- inventory of material flows
- impact assessment according to the life cycle of individual products
- optimization to produce a healthy, prosperous cradle-to-cradle life cycle.

These phases represent an iterative process that can be engaged at many levels. The process can start with an idea, as well as with a raw material (going into different products), a product (made of different raw materials), or a process.

Inventory

The first step in LCD is a material inventory designed to collect full information on every material used in

the manufacture of a product. Each material is then inventoried for its chemical constituents. The inventory process results in a complete listing of components by CAS (Chemical Abstract Service) number, name, function, and percent weight of the final material or product.

Impact Assessment

Assessing materials encourages product transparency and the conscious selection of ingredients that will have the most positive impact on human and ecological health. A material's impact on human and environmental health is assessed in five basic categories:

- Direct exposure covers the acute and chronic toxicological impacts on organisms that might be exposed to the materials, including carcinogenicity, endocrine disruption, irritation of skin and mucous membranes, and sensitization.
- The succession of generations includes potential impacts such as mutagenicity, reproductive and developmental toxicity, genetic engineering and persistence and biodegradation.
- Food chains are evaluated by bioaccumulation potential.
- Climactic relevance is evaluated based on global warming potential and ozone depletion potential.
- Value recovery assesses a material's potential as a biological or technical nutrient. To recover value and maintain materials in closed loop cycles, materials must be either returned safely to the soil or be perpetually recyclable. Evaluation of the value recovery potential of a material is based on the following considerations:

  Is it technically feasible to compost or recycle the material?

  Does a recycling or composting infrastructure exist for the material?

  What is the resulting quality of the recycled material or compost?

In addition, products must have a defined end-of-use strategy and be designed for disassembly so that recovery of materials is possible. Evaluating the recoverability of materials in a product is based on the following questions:

- What is the take back strategy for the product and its materials?
- Can dissimilar materials be easily separated?
- Can common or readily available disassembly tools be used?
- Can the material type be identified through markings, magnets, etc.?

Optimization

Once all materials have been assessed, those with the most positive human and environmental health characteristics and highest value recovery potential may be selected for inclusion in a redesigned product. Optimization is an iterative process. Complete optimization of a product or material may initially be impossible due to time or financial constraints, or lack of materials that meet the criteria for environmental and human health and value recovery. When all problematic inputs cannot be substituted, they can be prioritized for replacement and the manufacturing process can be redesigned to minimize exposure until a positive replacement is identified. Ultimately, the optimization phase is designed to yield positively defined products that enhance commercial productivity, social health, and ecological intelligence.

Getting Results: Cradle to Cradle Design at Work

The LCD process is the foundation for designing biological and technical nutrients. Examining some of the details of the design of a particular cradle-to-cradle product illustrates the process at work and begins to suggest how it can yield extraordinary value. Consider the technical nutrient carpet tile developed by Shaw Industries. Seeking a safe, beneficial product for its commercial customers, Shaw undertook a thorough scientific assessment of the material chemistry of its carpet fibers and backing. Dyes, pigments, finishes, auxiliaries—everything that goes into carpet—were examined according to the Cradle-to-Cradle LCD, and each ingredient was selected to meet its rigorous criteria. Out of this process has come the promise of a fully optimized carpet tile, a completely safe, perpetually recyclable, value generating product. And a highly

regarded product as well: Shaw's new design won the 2003 Presidential Green Chemistry Challenge Award.

Awards aside, Shaw's new product brings a much needed alternative to the commercial carpet market. Typically, carpet is made from two primary elements, a face fiber and a backing. Most face fiber today is nylon and most carpet backing is PVC. Commonly known as vinyl, PVC is a cheap, durable material widely used in building construction and a variety of consumer products, including toys, apparel, and sporting goods. The vinyl chloride monomer used to make PVC is a human carcinogen, and incineration of PVC can result in dioxin emissions. There are also concerns about the health effects of many additives commonly used in PVC, such as plasticizers, which off-gas chemicals known to be endocrine disrupters.

During conventional carpet recycling, nylon face fiber and PVC backing are recycled together, which yields a hybrid material of lesser value. In effect, the materials are not recycled at all but downcycled—and they're still on a one-way trip to the landfill or incinerator. There, the PVC content of the material makes recycled carpet hazardous waste.

Responding to widespread scientific and consumer concern about PVC, Shaw developed an alternative, a safe polyolefin-based backing system with all the performance benefits of PVC, which it guarantees it will take back and recycle into safe polyolefin backing.

The face fiber of Shaw's technical nutrient carpet tile also changes the game. It's made from nylon 6, which can be easily depolymerized into its monomer, caprolactam, and repolymerized repeatedly to make high quality nylon 6 carpet fiber. The main competing face fiber, nylon 6,6 is not easily depolymerized for recycling. Following protocols for value recovery, Shaw is developing an effective take-back and recycling strategy for all of its nylon 6 fiber.

In effect, Shaw's new carpet tile eliminates the concept of waste. The company now guarantees that all of its nylon 6 carpet fiber will be taken back and returned to nylon 6 carpet fiber, and its safe polyolefin backing taken back and returned to safe polyolefin backing. All the materials that go into the carpet will continually circulate in technical nutrient cycles. Raw material to raw material. Waste equals food. This cradle-to-cradle cycle, altogether different from eco-efficient recycling, suggests the benefits of a positive approach to managing material flows.

Other industries are also achieving significant results. Working with McDonough Braungart Design Chemistry (MBDC), the footwear manufacturer Nike is employing the Cradle-to-Cradle Framework to determine the chemical composition and environmental effects of the materials used to produce its line of athletic shoes. Focusing primarily on Nike's global footwear operations, the company's material assessment began with factory visits in China, where teams collected samples of rubber, leather, nylon, polyester, and foams, along with information on their chemical formulations.

In an ongoing partnership, when Nike and MBDC identify materials that meet or exceed the company's sustainable design criteria, those components are added to a growing palette of materials (a Positive List) that Nike will use in its products. These ingredients are designed to either be safely metabolized by nature's biological systems at the end of the product's useful life or be repeatedly recovered and reutilized in new products.

Nike's systematic effort to develop a positive materials palette has begun to produce tangible results, such as the phasing out of PVC. After two years of scientific review, Nike set its sites on the elimination of PVC from footwear and non-screenprint apparel. In Spring 2002, Nike highlighted two PVC-free products, Keystone Cleats and Swoosh Slides, as a way to begin a dialogue with customers about its PVC-free commitment.

Integrating Cradle-to-Cradle Design Strategies

Many companies begin adopting cradle-to-cradle principles by applying them to a single product. Ultimately, however, the strategy's effectiveness depends on its deep integration into the product development process. The furniture designer and manufacturer Herman Miller has gone a long way toward that end, developing an interdisciplinary Design for Environment (DFE) team that implements cradle-to-cradle material assessments, translates design goals throughout the company, measures environmental perfor-

mance, and engages its supply chain in implementing design criteria.

Working closely with MBDC and the German design consultancy EPEA, the DFE team built a chemical and material assessment methodology that could be effectively used by the firm's designers and engineers. Throughout the design process, the multifaceted assessment analyzes materials for their human health and toxicological effects, recyclabilty, recycled content and/or use of renewable resources, and product design for disassembly.

The DFE team includes a chemical engineer who incorporates findings from assessments into an evolving materials data base, and a purchasing agent who acts as a conduit and data source between the supply chain and Herman Miller's purchasing team. This strategy engages both groups as partners in implementing new design criteria, thereby ensuring the consistent procurement of safe materials. As one Herman Miller engineer has said, "Getting a handle on supply chain issues from an environmental standpoint has also helped us get a handle on the organization and prioritization of materials." Now, for example, Herman Miller can use the new database to record the volume and content of the raw materials it uses and distributes, figures it had not previously tracked.

Herman Miller put the DFE team to work on the design of its new task chair, a complement to its popular Aeron office chair. After assessing production processes, as well as 500 chemicals in 850 materials, and integrating those findings into the overall design process, Herman Miller unveiled the Mirra. Noting its pioneering design, *Metropolis* magazine suggested that the environmentally sound, high-performance Mirra might be "the next icon." Perhaps. What's certain is that the Mirra's combination of ergonomic, aesthetic, and environmental intelligence makes it not only extraordinarily comfortable and easy to adjust, but also a shining example of smart material and energy use.

Among other features, the Mirra is assembled using 100 percent wind power. Recycled content comprises more than 40 percent of its weight, and nearly 100 percent of its materials can be recycled, a strong step toward a cradle-to-cradle product. The elimination of PVC makes the chair environmentally safe, and its overall design makes it easy to disassemble. It is a bold move into 21st-century product design.

Managing Material Flows with Intelligent Materials Pooling

By defining product ingredients and engaging their respective supply chains, Shaw, Nike, and Herman Miller are all taking steps toward developing a safe, profitable technical metabolism. This is a critical step in the cradle-to-cradle strategy. Ultimately, the key to optimizing the assets of cradle-to-cradle materials lies in the intelligent management of regenerative material flows, just as in the world of energy the optimization of the strategy would lead us toward an effective use of renewable energy.

After eons of evolution, nature is well-equipped to effectively manage the material flows of the biological metabolism. We need to be sure that the materials we design as biological nutrients can safely biodegrade, and we need to set up recovery systems to be sure they are returned to the soil, but nature does not need our help to run its nutrient cycles. The technical metabolism, however, can only be managed by human design.

To safely and effectively manage the flows of polymers, rare metals, and high tech materials for industry, we have developed a nutrient management system for the technical metabolism, which we call Intelligent Materials Pooling (IMP). IMP is a collaborative approach to material flows management involving multiple companies working together to entirely eliminate hazardous materials. Partners in an IMP form a supportive business community, pooling information and purchasing power to generate material intelligence and profitable cradle-to-cradle material flows.

The evolution of an intelligent materials pool unfolds in four phases. The first is a community-building phase in which companies committed to cradle-to-cradle design discover shared values and complementary needs. A business network of willing partners emerges as each agrees to work together to phase out a common list of toxic chemicals.

Out of this shared commitment comes a community of companies with the market strength to engineer the phase-out and develop innovative alternative materials. The companies would share the list of materials targeted for elimination and develop a positive purchasing and procurement list of preferred intelligent chemicals.

The third phase involves defining material flows within the partnership. The partners would specify for and design with preferred materials. They would also establish defined use periods for products and services and individually set up take back programs. This phase establishes the infrastructure that supports the product of service concept, in which technical nutrients are designed to be returned to manufacturers for continual reuse. In effect, this transforms the partners into a material bank with renewable assets. Their "pool" of materials is not owned in common, but the partners' shared material specifications, their effectively managed technical metabolism, and their combined purchasing power allows them to profitably use positively defined, high quality materials.

The final phase of IMP is open-ended, as it involves the strengthening of the business partnership through ongoing support. This can involve such mutually beneficial activities as the creation of preferred business partner agreements, the sharing of information, the development of co-branding strategies, and support for the mechanisms of the newly created technical metabolism.

Finding willing partners in the competitive world of business might be hard to imagine, but it is hardly unprecedented. In the textile industry, innovative mills like Victor Innovatex and Rohner Textil, along with MBDC and Designtex, have profitably collaborated on the design and production of ecologically intelligent fabrics. In the textile and apparel industry at large, several companies have expressed deep interest in establishing a "polyester coalition." With the technology for truly recycling polyester in development, a polyester coalition could begin to close the loop on the flow of this widely used industrial material.

Design for the Triple Top Line

The various aspects of the Cradle-to-Cradle strategy, from Life Cycle Development to Intelligent Materials Pooling, together offer a framework for good design. While the protocols within the framework can be rigorous and exacting, they also create a space for enormous creativity. When a company decides to develop a biological or technical nutrient, for example, the chemical assessment of materials is just one step toward the complete rethinking of the design assignment. With a good scientific foundation and a positive, rather than reductive agenda, one can begin to ask some very interesting design questions.

The conventional design questions revolve around cost, aesthetics, and performance. Can we profit from it? Will the customer find it attractive? Will it work? Advocates of sustainable development have tried to expand those questions to include environmental and social concerns. While this "triple bottom line" approach has given companies a useful tool for balancing economic goals with a desire to "do better by the environment," the concept in practice often appears to center only on economic considerations, with social or ecological benefits considered as an afterthought. Businesses calculate their conventional economic profitability and add to that what they perceive to be the social benefits, with, perhaps, some reduction in environmental damage—lower emissions, fewer materials sent to the landfill, reduced materials in the product itself. These are important steps toward identifying problems, but ultimately they are strategies for managing negative effects.

What if this triad of concerns—economic growth, environmental health, and social equity—were addressed at the beginning of the design process as triple top line questions rather than used as an accounting tool at the end? That's where the magic begins. Instead of meeting the bottom line through a series of compromises between economy, ecology, and equity, designers can employ their dynamic interplay to generate revenue and value in all three sectors—triple top line growth. The goal is to create more positive effects not fewer negative ones. From this perspective, questions such as How can I create more habitat? How can I create jobs? become just as important as How much will it cost? Often, in fact, a project that begins with pronounced ecological or social concerns can turn out to be tremendously productive financially in ways that would never have been imagined if you'd started from a purely economic perspective.

The Fractal Triangle

Working with our clients, we have found that a visual tool, the fractal triangle, helps us apply triple top line thinking throughout the design process. Representing the ecology of human concerns, the fractal triangle shows how ecology, economy, and equity anchor a spectrum of value, and how, at any level of scrutiny, each design decision has an impact on all three. As we plan a product or system, we move around the fractal inquiring how a new design can generate value in each category.

In the pure Economy sector, we might ask, "Can I make my product at a profit?" As we see it, the goal of an effective company is to stay in business as it transforms. The Equity sector raises social questions: "Are we finding ways to honor all stakeholders, regardless of race, sex, nationality or religion?" Moving to the Ecology corner, the emphasis shifts to imagining ways in which humans can be tools for nature: "Do our designs create habitat or nourish the landscape?"

As we move around the triangle, questions expressing a complex interaction of concerns arise at the intersections of Ecology, Economy, and Equity. In the Economy/Equity sector, for example, we consider questions of profitability and fairness. "Are employees producing a promising product earning a living wage?" As we continue on to Equity/Economy, our focus shifts more toward fairness. Here we might ask: "Are men and women being paid the same for the same work?"

Often, we discover our most fruitful insights where the design process creates a kind of friction in the zones where values overlap. An ecologist might

Fractal Triangle

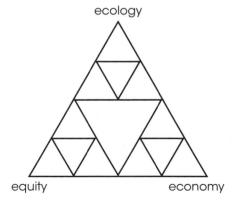

ecology

equity   economy

call these areas ecotones, which are the merging, fluid boundaries between natural communities notable for their rich diversity of species. In the fractal triangle, the ecotones are ripe with business opportunities.

Triple top line thinkers tap these opportunities not by trying to balance Ecology, Economy, and Equity, but by honoring the needs of all three. In an infinitely interconnected world, they see rich relationships rather than inherent conflicts. Their goal: to maximize value in all areas of the triangle through intelligent design. When designing a manufacturing facility, for example, they would ask: How can this project restore more landscape and purify more water? How much social interaction and joy can I create? How do I generate more safety and health? How much prosperity can I grow?

Questions such as these allow us to remake the way we make things. Today.

Getting Results: Generating Value in the Design Process

In projects already under way—indeed, already completed—triple top line thinking has sparked an explosion of creativity in our clients' decision-making. Consider, for example, the restoration of Ford Motor Company's Rouge River plant in Dearborn, Michigan. In May 1999, Ford decided to invest $2 billion over 20 years to transform the Rouge into an icon of 21st-century industry. As we approached the design process with Ford, many wondered if a blue chip company with a sharp focus on the bottom line could take a step toward something truly new and inspiring. Could inspiration and profits co-exist?

Well, yes. Using triple top line thinking and the Fractal Triangle, we explored with Ford's executives, engineers, and designers innovative ways of creating shareholder value. Rather than using economic metrics to try to reconcile apparent conflicts between environmental concerns and the bottom line, the company began to ask triple top line questions. Innovations would still need to be good for profits, but Ford's leaders began to examine how profits could be maximized by design decisions that also maximized social and ecological value.

Rather than trying to meet an environmental responsibility as efficiently as possible, Ford opted for a manufacturing facility that would create habitat, make oxygen, connect employees to their surroundings, and invite the return of native species. The result: a daylit factory with a 450,000 square-foot roof covered with growing plants—a living roof. In concert with porous paving and a series of constructed wetlands and swales, the living roof will absorb and filter stormwater runoff, making expensive technical controls, and even regulations, obsolete. All this with tremendous first cost savings, with the landscape thrown in for free. According to Ford, the natural stormwater system alone, compared to conventionally engineered water treatment systems, proved out a first cost saving of $5 million.

This is the power of positive, principled design.

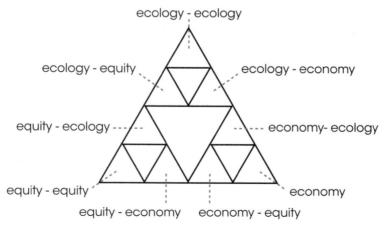

Fractal Callouts

Toward a Cradle-to-Cradle World

Designs that celebrate this diverse range of concerns bring about a process of industrial re-evolution. Our products and processes can be most deeply effective when they resonate with the living world. Inventive machines that use the mechanisms of nature instead of harsh chemicals, concrete, or steel are a step in the right direction, but they are still machines—still a way of using technology to harness nature to human purpose. New technologies do not themselves create industrial revolutions. Unless we change their context, they are simply hyper-efficient engines driving the steamship of the first Industrial Revolution to new extremes.

Natural systems take from the environment, but they also give something back. The cherry tree drops its blossoms and leaves while it cycles water and makes oxygen; the ant community redistributes nutrients through the soil. We can follow their cue to create a more inspiring engagement—a partnership—with nature.

Expressed in designs that resonate with and support natural systems, this new partnership can take us beyond sustainability—a minimum condition for survival—toward products and commercial enterprises that celebrate our relationship with the living earth.

We can create fabrics that feed the soil, giving us pleasure as garments and as sources of nourishment for our gardens.

We can build factories that inspire their inhabitants with sunlit spaces, fresh air, views of the outdoors, and cultural delights; factories which also create habitat and produce goods and services that re-circulate technical materials instead of dumping, burning, or burying them.

We can tap into natural flows of energy and nutrients, designing astonishingly productive systems that create oxygen, accrue energy, filter water, and provide healthy habitats for people and other living things. As we have seen, designs such as these are generators of economic value too. When the cradle-to-cradle principles that guide them are widely applied, at every level of industry, productivity and profits will no longer be at odds with the concerns of the commons. We will be celebrating the fecundity of the earth instead of perpetuating a way of thinking and making that eliminates it. We will be creating a world of abundance, equity, and health and be well on our way to an era of sustaining prosperity.

This is not a path one must travel alone. Green-Blue, a new non-profit organization established to encourage the widespread adoption of cradle-to-cradle thinking, is now providing the theoretical, technical, and information tools required to transform industry through intelligent design. Its mission is to make commercial activity an ecological and socially regenerative force, and its tools are designed to empower designers to participate in this transformation.

And so we invite you to join us in leaving behind design strategies that yield tragic consequences and taking up a strategy of hope, a strategy that allows us to create a world of interdependent natural and human systems powered by the sun in which safe, healthful materials flow in regenerative cycles, elegantly and equitably deployed for the benefit of all. Doing so is ultimately an act of love for the future, an act that allows us to take steps toward not simply loving our own children, but loving all of the children, of all species, for all time.

Questions for Discussion and Reflection

1. What do you think of the "cradle-to-cradle" life cycle design process as a new paradigm for sustainable industry? Do you think it's realistic? Why or why not?
2. To what degree do you think it's possible to "enhance the well-being of nature while generating economic value" at the same time? Defend your answer.
3. McDonough and Braungart give some examples of companies that are using the life cycle design process (Nike, Herman Miller, Shaw Industries). Do you think there are industries that are not compatible with life cycle design? Or is this a paradigm that should be followed by all industries?

Snack Chips and Lessons in Environmental Consciousness

John Terrill

Cardus Comment (January 28, 2011), http://www.cardus.ca/comment/article/2483/

I've been watching an interesting and instructive drama unfold these last several months involving, of all things, snack chips. The controversy swirled around Frito-Lay's new 100% compostable packaging for its SunChips®. Countless news outlets picked up the story, including Stephen Colbert, who spoofed the bag on the *Colbert Report.*

Here's what happened. Frito-Lay spent four years developing its new SunChips® biodegradable packaging, only to discontinue it this October after months of depressed sales and complaints that the bag was too noisy. Americans, it seems, enjoy their chips loud and crunchy but not their packaging, prompting Kate Sheppard of *Mother Jones* to quip: "Seriously? The company is bagging the bag because American couch potatoes can't hear their TVs over the sound of their chip sack?"

Admittedly, the SunChips® packaging is quite noisy. As reported in the *Wall Street Journal*, one consumer, a United States Air Force pilot, claimed that the bag was louder than his jet cockpit. His assertion may be justified. As reported later by the same publication, the packaging registered a whopping 95 decibels, more than a lawnmower or coffee grinder, and high enough that the European Union would require ear-protection in a workplace setting.

Acknowledging its earsplitting dilemma, Frito-Lay tried to assuage consumer complaints. The company placed creative in-store advertising appealing to the greater good: "Yes, the bag is loud, that's what change sounds like." Its altruistic efforts, though, fell on "deaf" American ears. In more environmentally-conscious Canada, as chronicled by *Fast Company*, Frito-Lay chose not to discontinue its packaging but, rather, to have some fun with the complaints by offering free earplugs with every bag of chips.

This story may seem comical, but the implications are serious. The old SunChips® bag takes 100 years to degrade; the new packaging, by contrast, fully decomposes in 14 weeks when put in an active compost pile. The choice of packaging clearly has long-term repercussions.

When it comes to environmental change, Americans are notoriously slow to respond. One need only point to the relative indifference of compact fluorescent bulbs, low-flush toilets, and low-flow shower heads in U.S. markets. Finding ways to help green products and packaging gain greater consumer acceptance is imperative for a sustainable future.

Accordingly, Frito-Lay is not the only consumer product company in recent months to venture into green packaging and product reformulations, only to see its efforts spurned by consumers. As reported by the *New York Times*, Proctor & Gamble recently changed its Cascade dish detergent line by reducing the amount of phosphates, which cause algae growth in lakes and rivers and deprive fish and plant life of oxygen. American consumers responded with irritation, complaining that the low-phosphate product didn't get their dishes clean.

GreenBiz.com recently ran another story on P&G, which also reformulated its Pampers Swaddlers and Cruisers diapers by making them 20% thinner, resulting in a 12% solid waste reduction for this product in landfills. Consumers eschewed these efforts in similar fashion, charging that the new diapers caused rashes. The Consumer Product Safety Commission is now investigating and class-action lawsuits have been filed by consumers. Maybe the diapers do have some problems, but are class-action lawsuits warranted? What's next? Suing Frito-Lay for noise pollution?

When searching for ways to change consumer response to eco-friendly products, three broad approaches seem to emerge. The first appeals to deeper aspirations and the belief that consumers want to align with companies that have an environment-friendly mission and a broad commitment to society. Some customers do make decisions based on such values, but the percentage of consumers in the U.S. who fall into this category is still small, albeit growing.

The second approach argues that eco-friendly products and packaging will only gain wide acceptance when they provide higher quality and lower cost than less environmentally-safe alternatives. Eric Felten in the *Wall Street Journal* makes this point by referring to history: "Market-friendly economists have long pointed to the introduction of kerosene, gas-lighting and then electric bulbs as putting an end to whale oil for lighting." It wasn't until there were cheaper and better product alternatives that whaling started to fall out of vogue. Similarly, Felten argues, pollution in rivers from 19th-century coal factories was only reduced when it was discovered that the discharge could be broken down into a purple dye and sold on the open market; coal-tar became too valuable to dump into water systems.

Stephanie Simon in a recent *Wall Street Journal* report, "The Secrets to Turning Consumers Green," advocates for the third approach, asserting that consumers change most readily when confronted by strong social forces, such as peer pressure and guilt. Case in point: the 2010 five-cent tax imposed in Washington, D.C., on disposable paper or plastic bags handed out by retailers. In the first two quarters of this year, as reported by the district's Office of Tax and Revenue, retail outlets that typically use 68 million disposable bags per quarter cut their number to 11 and 13 million, respectively. Some data indicates that it is not the marginal cost of the bag that changes consumer behavior but the social stigma of asking for one in public.

Studies in the U.S., Asia and Europe support such findings and affirm that appealing to social norms might be the most powerful force in changing environmental consciousness. Two oft-cited American academic studies from 2008 demonstrate this phenomenon. The first studied the effect of placards in hotel room bathrooms that encouraged guests to reuse their towels. One sign said "Help Save the Environment," while encouraging "Respect for Nature." The second sign read: "Join Your Fellow Guests in Helping Save the Environment" and further noted that almost 75% of all guests staying in the hotel participated in the program. The results were telling; the guests who viewed the second placard were 25% more likely to reuse their towels than their counterparts.

The second study involved public-service messages that were hung on middle-class neighborhood door knobs in San Marcos, California. The messages touted the environmental benefit of fan usage versus air conditioning and gave one of four reasons for choosing fans: (1) Households could save on average $54 per month; (2) Residents could prevent the release of 262 pounds of greenhouse gasses per month; (3) It was the socially responsible thing to do; and (4) 77% of their neighbors were already doing so. Meter readings demonstrated that the fourth message was by far the most effective in reducing energy consumption.

Care for the environment is fundamental to honoring God and taking seriously the biblical command to exercise dominion over creation through careful and responsible stewardship (Genesis 1:26–28). This passage is an important starting place for all Christians in forming and living out a theology of creation. But those in positions of business leadership and policy-making need to find ways to influence positive change in others.

Introducing change in a social context that has demonstrated openness is vital, a principle Frito-Lay may have missed. Additionally, appealing to a deeper sense of the common good, creating eco-friendly products that are of high quality and low cost, and utilizing social pressure are all strategies that can work. Some of these approaches may be more congruent with the ideals of scripture, but a case can be made for each given our theological realities this side of a restored, perfect world. Drawing on shared grace and the image of God stamped upon each human being, conversations about the greater good and service to others can take on deep significance. Similarly, while appeals to product attributes that make life easier and cost less may reinforce human self-interest, environment-friendly innovations and cost reductions do contribute to a flourishing society. Finally, an appeal to socially-approved behaviors draws on our hard-wired need to be in right relationship with others that dates back to our origins in the Garden of Eden and creation by a Triune, relational God.

John Terrill is director of the Center for Integrity in Business at Seattle Pacific University.

Questions for Discussion and Reflection

1. Terrill is very critical of consumers who complain about irritations with more environmentally friendly products? Do you agree with his criticism? Why or why not?
2. Which do you think will make a greater difference to consumers' adoption of environmentally sensitive goods—lower cost or peer pressure and guilt? Explain your answer.

CASE STUDIES

Case 10.1: A Tree or a Life?

Executives of a large pharmaceutical company acting as a private sector partner for the National Cancer Institute (NCI) want to bring to market a promising treatment for cancer, discovered by NCI scientists.[2] The company already has several existing products that arrest the growth of cancer cells, putting patients into remission and extending their lives. Each of these products produces side effects of varying duration and discomfort. Unfortunately, some cancers, such as ovarian, are very aggressive and are resistant to the chemotherapy agents available on the market.

While the recently discovered treatment has not yet received FDA (Federal Drug Administration) approval (a long and expensive process), early trials indicate that it is much more effective than existing treatments and produces fewer and less severe side effects. In addition to its medical promise, the drug also has the potential to be a huge profit maker for the company.

The problem lies in the fact that the substance for the treatment comes from the bark of the Pacific yew tree, a species that grows in the Pacific Northwest and has fallen victim to clear cutting, making them scarcer than they once were. Environmental groups are concerned that cutting down more of the trees will negatively impact sensitive ecosystems, habitat for other wildlife, and bio-diversity (prompting questions like, What other wonder cures/drugs might be destroyed if the forest is altered?)

Researchers and company executives have tried to come up with a way to sustainably harvest the trees to treat the 12,500 women (at the time) who die of ovarian cancer each year. However, the number of trees required (an esti-

[2] The company involved was Bristol-Myers (now known as Bristol-Myers Squibb), and the drug is known as Taxol. See Jordan Goodman and Vivien Walsh, *The Story of Taxol: Nature and Politics in Pursuit of an Anti-Cancer Drug* (Cambridge: Cambridge University Press, 2001).

mated three to six 100-year-old trees are needed to produce enough bark to treat one patient) and the fact that trees die once their bark is removed makes an easy solution unlikely.[3] New trees could be planted, but the species is slow-growing (often growing in the shade of conifers), reaching heights of twenty to thirty feet and a diameter of six to twelve inches.[4] The company has several efforts under way (and has funded several more at universities) to produce a synthetic version, but as of yet none are promising enough to take to market.[5]

Questions for Discussion

1. Provided the company can get U.S. Forest Service approval (many of the trees are on federal land) to cut down the necessary number of trees, should executives move forward with the development of the drug? How would you weigh/balance the lives of cancer patients with the natural interests involved?

2. Is this a case of people versus nature, or are long-term human interests involved too?

3. What difference might one's basis/worldview make in assessing this case? What might Christian ideas of stewardship contribute to it?

Case 10.2: Lion Meat

Amid controversy, enterprising restaurants try to capitalize on the public's interest in eating meat sourced from exotic animals. In the late 1990s, a high-end establishment in La Jolla, California, The Top O' the Cove, served lion meat as part of a sold-out annual black-tie extravaganza called Le Big Smoke Dinner. Patrons were charged $100 per plate for the exotic dish. Amid protests from People for the Ethical Treatment of Animals (PETA) and counter protestors who wore shirts reading "PETA People for the Eating of Tasty Animals," the restaurant's owner was not apologetic, telling a local newspaper, "The lion is farmed-raised in America; it's perfectly legal, and lots of restaurants serve it."[6]

More recently (in early 2011), Boca Tacos y Tequila, a Tex-Mex restaurant in Tuscon, Arizona, known for its exotic taco fillings (including alligator, python, elk, and turtle), offered lion meat tacos at a price of $8.75. The restaurant's owner, Bryan Mazon, told the *Arizona Daily Star* that it is perfectly legal to sell lion meat, according to the FDA, since it's not an endangered species. And, he said, "I'm doing the African lion to get my name out."[7]

According to Crawford Allen, regional director for TRAFFIC (the regional office of the largest international wildlife trade monitoring program), "Lions are not endangered. When bred in captivity, their meat is allowed to be traded. There are particular operations in the U.S. that are breeding lions, butchering them and selling them for meat." Provided those

[3] Sally Thane Christensen, "Is a Tree Worth a Life?" *Newsweek*, August 5, 1991. See also "Save a Tree or Save a Life," Stanford University News Service, September 30, 1991.

[4] Marshall Murray, "The Tree That Fights Cancer—Pacific Yew," *American Forests*, July–August 1991.

[5] In this case, a Florida State University–based researcher was able to develop a synthetic based on the needles, thus preserving the trees from being cut down. However, there may be future situations in which natural interests seem to be pitted against human ones, at least in the shorter term.

[6] "Carrot and Stick," *Vegetarian Times*, June 1997, 22.

[7] "Boca Gaining a Rep for Exotic Tacos, Plans Lion Meat Offering," *Arizona Daily Star*, January 22, 2011.

companies comply with international treaties, USDA standards, and other federal regulations, they can legally raise and butcher lions, Allan said.[8] Highlighting the controversial nature of this type of activity, Mazon decided to cancel the offering, after receiving violent threats.

Questions for Discussion

1. What are your thoughts about serving exotic meat such as lion for human consumption for the purposes of marketing and/or profit? Does it represent callousness toward creation?
2. Is eating (and serving) exotic meat permissible and/or necessary under a proper understanding of stewardship when there are so many other choices in a wealthy country like America? On the other hand, since the animals were bred for consumption, is it all that different than eating chicken or beef?

Case 10.3: Animal Testing for Cosmetics and Medicine

Animals are often used as live subjects to test the safety of many products made for human consumption. The cosmetic industry often uses animals to examine the safety of its products. In some tests, animals, such as rabbits, will have a substance placed into their eyes to test for toxicity and tissue damage. Opponents of such practices point to the suffering (and the eventual euthanization of many of the animals) as an inhumane and unethical practice. Peter Singer, for example, has argued that consideration of species should play no role in the calculation of pain and suffering in moral (utilitarian) considerations. Critics also point to flaws in animal testing and the availability of alternative methods. Some large cosmetic companies such as Avon and Mary Kay have already adopted humane testing methods. Many countries (e.g., the European Union) around the world have placed legal limits on the practice of using animals for testing cosmetics. There is no ban in the United States (as of yet), though the Federal Drug Administration (FDA) does *not* require animal testing for cosmetic safety.

Cosmetics may be easily dismissed as a consumer want; however, animals are also used to test pharmaceuticals and medical procedures, which are critical to sustaining human life. A recent controversy erupted (based on the filing of a complaint by the non-profit Physicians Committee for Responsible Medicine) over the use of ferrets by the University of Washington Medical School's neonatology department to train medical residents in the insertion of breathing tubes meant to prevent brain damage and/or to save the lives of premature babies.

According to a spokesperson for the school, available alternatives (plastic simulators) are inadequate in duplicating the very narrow airways of very low

[8] Russell Goldman, "Arizona Restaurant to Serve Lion Meat Tacos," *ABC News Travel*, January 22, 2011, http://abcnews.go.com/Travel/arizona-restaurant-boca-tacos-tequila-serve-lion-meat/story?id=12723838.

[9] Carol Ostrom, "Group Faults UW Use of Ferrets in Medical Training," *Seattle Times*, February 9, 2011.

birth weight (as little as one pound) babies. Moreover, according to the spokesperson, the animals are anesthetized, do not seem to suffer, are treated well, and do recover.[9]

While this particular case does not involve a direct commercial application (though there is a lot of money involved in medicine), animals have been used to test many other procedures and pharmaceuticals that have been brought to market by commercial enterprises. Many of these procedures and drugs have been successfully used to treat human health issues. In the absence of testing on animals, human subjects would likely need to be used instead. Critics of the practices point to suffering as well as flawed assumptions in using animals in the development of medical procedures for people.

Questions for Discussion

1. What are your thoughts on the ethics of animal testing? Is this something faithful stewardship would permit?
2. What difference might one's basis or worldview (i.e., biocentric, anthropocentric) make?
3. Would you draw a distinction between using animals for testing cosmetics versus testing for medical purposes? Why or why not?

Case 10.4: Buying Local

Rob is the majority owner of a small chain of supermarkets that operate in a large West Coast city.* The market has three locations, all in upscale urban communities. All of the stores are engaged in service endeavors and are viewed as hubs for community information and activities. In addition to fresh and cooked foods, the stores offer culinary classes and often open their meeting spaces for use by local groups. The stores also feature bustling coffee counters with stone fireplaces and attractive seating areas that are often full and buzzing with people in conversation.

A few years ago, Rob and his partners decided to enlarge the organic foods section of their stores and to carry more locally grown items. They were hoping to do more to protect the environment, encourage healthy eating, and meet the changing demands of their customers. After making the change, overall sales and profits rose. "Buy local" and healthy eating campaigns were gaining lots of traction at the time. One particularly helpful movement was the "100 mile diet," a movement that encourages people to eat only items grown within 100 miles of where they live. Doing so purportedly has significant benefits, among them: (1) support of local farmers and businesspeople; (2) monitoring of diet/health—knowing what goes into the food we eat and how it is produced; (3) improvement of environmental sustainability—reduced carbon footprint in using less fuel versus transporting food from faraway places.

Over time, Rob began to have doubts about whether distributing so many locally grown items was really the best way to go. While the items are profitable, he recently came across a newspaper report about farmers in the developing world who have seen their markets shrink as American consumers buy more locally grown foods. (For example, many grocery stores import grapes from Chile when local produce is not naturally in season.) A friend of Rob's (a local farmer) also mentioned to him that the greenhouses that have to be used to grow "off season" flowers and vegetables locally may produce carbon at a level that negates some or all of the benefits gained by not transporting goods from faraway sources.

Questions for Discussion

1. How should Rob and his partners proceed? How can they balance the shorter-term human interests with longer term ones?
2. How do they balance local human interests with global ones?

*These supermarkets are fictitious. Any resemblance to specific markets is coincidental.

Case 10.5: Green or Greenwashing?

A small business (thirty-five employees) in the highly competitive greeting card business is faced with a challenging issue. The company makes artistic, handmade greeting cards that are sold to local retail stores, who then sell them to consumers. The customer base of the retail stores is composed mainly of tourists and other affluent buyers looking for something more unique than what a local supermarket or discount store typically carries. The company markets the cards as environmentally friendly, usually with a note on the back indicating the cards are made from 100 percent recycled paper. The cards themselves also have a ruff-hewn quality to them that give a distinctive look and fingertip feel of being recycled and organic.

Business has been on a downward trend the past few years. Both the recession and increased competition have cut into market share. The owners of the business (a husband and wife) were recently approached by a representative of an organization that sells renewable energy credits (RECs). RECs are purchased by businesses to "offset" the carbon emissions they produce. The credits purportedly go toward renewable energy (i.e., plant trees and/or build wind turbines) and thus negate emissions produced.

The representative informs them that if they purchase enough of these credits, they can now additionally market their business with strong environmental claims along the lines of "carbon neutral" or "100% wind powered." Knowing the environmental views of most of their distributors and customers, the owners believe adding these monikers to their cards and other marketing materials would give them a small competitive advantage.

When they tell their employees that they intend to purchase these credits, one of their long-term staff members asks if the practice amounts to "greenwashing." "I know lots of other businesses make these claims," she states, "but aren't some of our customers going to picture wind turbines powering our production when in reality we are still on coal-generated electricity and haven't done anything to reduce our immediate and actual carbon footprint? In fact, given our promising sales this year and the longer distances we are shipping some products in new markets we have opened up abroad, I think we will actually increase our emissions by about 10 to 15 percent this year."

Questions for Discussion

1. Should the owners go ahead and purchase the offsets and make the claims? Would doing so without a simultaneous reduction in the company's environmental footprint be "greenwashing"?

2. Are RECs a legitimate means to achieve carbon neutrality, or are they a duplicitous way to make environmentally based claims? If indeed the credits do go toward renewable energy sources and carbon is being offset, aren't they a good way to secure funding to develop alternative energy sources? Moreover, don't they provide incentives to businesses to be greener, since they have to pay to offset increasing emissions?

COMMENTARY[10]

[10] Parts of this chapter's commentary have been previously published (with some modification) in Kenman Wong and Scott Rae, *Business for the Common Good: A Christian Vision for the Marketplace* (Downers Grove, Ill.: IVP Academic, 2011).

The BP Gulf Coast oil spill (2010) has served as a tragic reminder of the tenuous relationship between business and the environment. In providing products and services for consumers, businesses both depend upon and impact nature in numerous ways. The focus of the first two essays in this chapter is on establishing a proper philosophical/theological ethic of environmental responsibility. Two major viewpoints were identified (anthropocentrism, biocentrism) and critiqued, but can it be rightfully claimed that Christian ethics supports one over the other? In what follows, we attempt to answer this question through a faithful rendering of biblical teaching. We then address some of the more on-the-ground challenges of environmental considerations amid other competing interests that businesses face.

Before proceeding, however, it is worth noting that much of the contemporary discussion around environmental protection has become highly politicized, accompanied by the usual oversimplification, name calling, and caricature. It is easy to get caught up in the political debate, especially if we have something to immediately gain or lose, and to either overlook biblical teaching or to interpret it through our political ideologies. Thus, we must turn to the text itself and, as much as humanly possible, shed our presuppositions and/or cherished positions to attempt to give it a faithful reading in order to formulate a sound ethic for the environment.

Christian Ethics and the Environment

As noted by Thomas Derr, Christianity has sometimes been criticized for being the ideological cause of environmental degradation. In what was long considered conventional wisdom in environmental ethics, Lynn White Jr. published a 1967 article in which he held Christianity responsible for humankind's abuse of nature.[11] White accused Christianity of reducing the natural world to the status of a natural object, which could be controlled for the benefit of human beings, without regard for the harmful impact of this misuse. He further indicted Christianity for its role in the origin of modern science and technology, which gave humankind mastery over nature and the potential to exploit the environment while at the same time neglecting any responsibility for protecting the natural world. It is true that within the church there is a history of contributing to environmental problems, but whether the Bible actually justifies such action is an entirely different question (and as noted by Derr, White may have actually made that distinction himself).

Today it is becoming increasingly rare for any religious group to hold the view that White critiques. To be certain, some groups within the Christian tradition have come to environmental commitment more recently while others remain deeply suspicious due to political associations. However, one could make the case that religion has contributed positively to environmental concern by observing that spiritual traditions of all kinds, Christianity included, emphasize limits on materialism and consumption, and thus provide necessary checks on the kinds of economic growth that threaten nature.

From a biblical perspective, developing a Christian ethic of the environment begins at the beginning—in Genesis 1 wherein God is portrayed as the sovereign creator of all things. The natural world is good because it is *his* creation. As a result of this basis for creation having value, a theocentric view of the environment—neither anthropocentric (the environment exists solely for the benefit

[11] Lynn White Jr., "The Historical Roots of Our Ecological Crisis," *Science* 155 (March 10, 1967): 1203–7. This is echoed by the historian Arnold Toynbee, who linked monotheistic religion in general with environmental abuse. See his article "The Religious Background of the Present Environmental Crisis" in *Ecology and Religion in History*, ed. David and Eileen Spring (New York: Harper & Row, 1974). For a more detailed response to these criticisms, see Steven Bouma-Prediger, *For the Beauty of the Earth: A Christian Vision for Creation Care* (Grand Rapids: Baker Academic, 2001), 69–80.

[12] Further examples of biocentrism are found in the work of Paul Taylor, *Respect for Nature: A Theory of Environmental Ethics*, 25th annvy. ed. (Princeton: Princeton University Press, 2011). Biocentrism is often identified with a movement called "deep ecology," which maintains the intrinsic value of nonhuman organisms. See also Bill Devall and George Sessions, *Deep Ecology: Living as if Nature Mattered* (Salt Lake City: Peregrine, 1985); Alan Drengson and Bill Devall, eds., *The Ecology of Wisdom: Writings by Arne Naess* (Berkeley: Counterpoint, 2008); Frederic L. Bender, *The Culture of Extinction: Toward a Philosophy of Deep Ecology* (Amherst, N.Y.: Humanity, 2003). One of the primary criticisms of biocentrism is its inability to establish any kind of ranking of priority when the interests of human beings conflict with the interests of the natural world. That is, if all living things have biocentric equality, then it is difficult to resolve conflicts when competing interests collide. For further discussion of these critiques, see Bouma-Prediger, *For the Beauty of the Earth*, 129–32.

[13] Bouma-Prediger, *For the Beauty of the Earth*, 74.

[14] Calvin B. DeWitt, *Earthwise: A Biblical Response to Environmental Issues* (Grand Rapids: CRC Publications, 1994).

[15] It should be noted that in Psalm 104:20–22, the psalmist recognizes that part of the provision God makes for animals involves predators obtaining their food by killing and consuming their prey. It seems that animals were not restricted to being vegetarians any more than human beings were.

of human beings) nor biocentric (as advocated by Hoffman/all living things have value because they are living things) seems to be the most appropriate.[12]

Reading further in Genesis, human beings are given "dominion," with the responsibility akin to "junior partners" with God in extending his rule over creation. It is important to note that the notion of dominion has been terribly misapplied over centuries of church history, often serving as a justification for human beings to meet their own immediate needs and wants without regard for environmental impact. That is why it is critical to acknowledge that in Genesis *the call to exercise dominion over creation presumes stewardship for creation.* Though it is true that the term for dominion literally means "to rule over," in the overall context of the Bible, it is critical to note that ruling and serving always go together (Luke 22:24–27). This is reinforced by God's call to Adam and Eve to tend the garden, to serve and protect that over which they were given dominion (Gen. 2:15).[13] Such a role suggests that human beings will be held to account by God for their stewardship over creation. In *Earthwise: A Biblical Response to Environmental Issues,* Calvin DeWitt expands eloquently on this point:

> Genesis 2:15 conveys a marvelous teaching. Here, God expects Adam to serve the garden and to keep it. The Hebrew word for serve (*'abad*) is translated as till, dress or work in most recent translations of the Bible. Adam and his descendants are expected to meet the needs of the garden so that it will persist and flourish. But how on earth can we serve creation? Shouldn't creation serve us instead?
>
> God also expects us, as Adam's descendants, to keep the garden. This word "keep" is sometimes translated "tend, take care of, guard, look after." The Hebrew word on which these translations are based is the word *shamar.* And *shamar* indicates a loving, caring, sustaining type of keeping.[14]

Not only did God create, but *he also tends to and cares for his creation* in an ongoing way. In contrast to deism, the Bible portrays God as intimately involved with his world. Psalm 104 is a creation hymn that points out that the natural world is the home that he has provided for his creatures (Ps. 104:12, 17–18, 26; also Job 39:6). It is also clear that God uses creation to provide the daily sustenance for his creatures, human beings included. The psalmist puts it this way: "He waters the mountains from his upper chambers; the land is satisfied by the fruit of his work. He makes grass grow for the cattle, and plants for people to cultivate—bringing forth food from the earth" (Ps. 104:13–14). That is, the natural world is critical for God to house and feed his creatures, both animal and human.[15]

God's care for his creation is also evident from the Sabbath command requiring rest for animals (Ex. 20:8–11; Deut. 5:12–15) and penalties in the law for their mistreatment. In these commands, it is made clear that God expects human beings to emulate his care for creation and for his creatures. The command to keep the sabbatical year, thereby giving the land periodic rest, reinforces God's care for his creation and extends it to the land itself (Lev. 25:1–7). In fact, this command was considered so important that its repeated violation was a basis for the nation Israel being taken into exile (2 Chron. 36:20–21).

God's care for living things is also evident from an often-overlooked passage in the covenant he made with Noah following the flood. In Genesis 9, God actually makes the covenant not only with Noah and his family, but with all the living beings on earth. The covenant involved a promise never again to destroy the earth with a flood, and its significance in part has to do with how God's care for all living beings is reflected in his promise (vv. 9:8–16, summarized in v. 16 as "the everlasting covenant between God and *all living creatures of every kind* on the earth," emphasis added).

Creation can also be seen to have value because *the natural world will be redeemed when Christ returns*. God's plan of redemption includes more than simply individual human beings. It also includes a proper ordering of society (Isa. 42:1–4) and a renewal of the created order. Romans 8:19–21 makes this promise: "The creation waits in eager expectation for the children of God to be revealed. For the creation was subjected to frustration, not by its own choice, but by the will of the one who subjected it, in hope that the creation itself will be liberated from its bondage to decay and brought into the freedom and glory of the children of God." The text speaks of the natural world being freed from the curse of sin, and thus the object of God's renewing work. What this passage seems to make clear is that the present creation will not be destroyed at the return of Christ, but will be restored, analogous to a master painting that is in need of restoration to its original beauty and artistry. Thus, care for creation today is consistent with, and required by, the long-term plan of God for the natural world and is part of his plan for redeeming everything he created.

There have been some who, as a result of a misconstrued eschatology, have insisted that the created order will be destroyed at the return of Christ, and thus there need not be any concern with the environment. But such a view cannot be maintained from the Bible. In fact, in Romans 8, the renewal of creation is analogous to the renewal of the body for the believer (v. 23). One cannot argue that the future resurrection body justifies abuse/neglect of the body today. In the Bible, there is as much hope for the body as there is for the soul. In the same way, one cannot maintain that the future renewal of the creation justifies current abuse/neglect of the environment today.

People *vs.* the Environment?
Implications for Business

Sadly, environmental considerations have been primarily viewed by business as "externalities" to be borne by others or as constraints to be worked around. Given the content and scope of biblical teaching, a Christian ethic of the environment (and thereby human well-being) supports proactive care of nature, as stewardship implies. Today sincere efforts are being made to protect the environment. However, there has been so much public pressure (and perhaps "brand value") to "go green" that some companies are simply posturing ("greenwashing") by making cosmetic changes and/or outright false claims about their environmental credentials.[16]

Several implications can be drawn from the biblical instruction set out earlier. First, responsible use of the garden's resources is permissible to support the production of services and products that are driven by and result in the enhancement of human flourishing. However, consistent with broader biblical themes, particularly Genesis 2:15, the relationship is reciprocal. Business, too, must be an active partner in "serving" the garden.

Protecting the garden is the first step, but serving it goes further. "Tending" and "serving" the garden imply that movement beyond making things "less bad" and into the positive territory of making things whole again is necessary. Although conditions cannot be made perfect on earth, "serving the garden" implies that our ultimate objective must be to "make things right" or transform and restore them to harmony as much as possible. By comparison, as noted by McDonough and Braungart, most environmental efforts to date have been after the fact ("end of pipe") "solutions" aimed at slowing down the inevitable or minimizing harm (i.e., reducing "our footprint").

But how can this be accomplished? How can human interests be advanced while simultaneously protecting natural ones? Aren't they fundamentally at odds?

We believe it begins with three necessary (though still insufficient) shifts: (1) a reframing of the issues, (2) a paradigmatic shift in design (as argued by the likes of Braungart and McDonough), and (3) the bringing of business to the table (as noted by Mather).

First, a reframing is necessary away from the traditional posing of business and the environment in a direct standoff. For example, the dispute over Pacific Northwest forestland that has served as habitat for the endangered northern spotted owl was often posed as "owls vs. (logging) jobs." Likewise, domestic oil exploration and drilling is often framed in similar terms, "energy security vs. saving the planet."

[16] "Another Inconvenient Truth," *Businessweek*, March 26, 2007; "The Fuzzy Math of Eco-Accolades," *Businessweek*, October 29, 2007.

This construct is of course partially based in fact. Natural interests do sometimes collide with human ones, especially in (though not limited to) the more intermediate time horizon. Limited farmland creates a situation in which growing crops for corn-based fuels (ethanol) may serve to raise food prices. Likewise, "shop locally" initiatives (motivated in part to reduce carbon from long-distance transportation) may well hurt farmers, particularly those in the two-thirds/developing world who are dependent on export markets.

The connecting forces of globalization, however, seem to be rapidly contributing to additional and more nuanced ways to pose this relationship. Namely, there is a growing awareness of how integrally connected human interests are with natural ones and how they are intertwined *now* and not in some benign distant future. In his bestselling book, *Hot, Flat, and Crowded*, Thomas Friedman expands on these concerns and stresses the importance of why environmental issues and human well-being (on multiple dimensions) need to be seen in terms of mutual, shared interests:

> The world also has a problem: It is getting *hot, flat and crowded*. That is, global warming, the stunning rise of the middle classes all over the world, and rapid population growth have converged in a way that could make our planet dangerously unstable. In particular, the convergence of hot, flat and crowded is tightening energy supplies, intensifying the extinction of plants and animals, deepening energy poverty, strengthening petro-dictatorship and accelerating climate change.[17]

[17] Thomas L. Friedman, *Hot, Flat, and Crowded: Why We Need a Green Revolution—and How It Can Renew America* (New York: Farrar, Straus and Giroux, 2008), 5.

If Friedman is correct, the current pattern of global economic development destroys nature, harms human health, and contributes to geopolitical turmoil, directly harming people in the process. Moreover, the lives of economically impoverished people around the globe will be worsened as they compete for increasingly scarce resources needed to support basic living conditions. As Clive Mather notes, "It's about human rights as well as biodiversity and lifestyle."

Second, rethinking paradigms of economic growth is necessary; otherwise we may have to return to some sort of zero- or negative-growth mandate. Doing so, of course, might directly conflict with the importance God places on human well-being as slower economic growth likely lessens the opportunities for poor people to engage in economic activity and increase their resources. Solving this conundrum requires a paradigmatic shift in how economic activity fits into larger natural systems. In other words, we need "sustainable" growth that is more harmonious with nature rather than destructive of it. With modification, the recent movement toward a "triple bottom line" (economic, social, and environmental measures of success;

18 See, e.g., Andrew Savitz, with Karl Weber, *The Triple Bottom Line: How Today's Best-Run Companies Are Achieving Economic, Social and Environmental Success* (San Francisco: Jossey Bass, 2006).

sometimes referred to as "people, profits, and planet") offers a good starting point to envisioning the responsibilities of business.[18]

An even more robust way to rethink environmental care has been proposed by William McDonough and Michael Braungart in their groundbreaking book *Cradle to Cradle*. We saw a brief presentation of their ideas in their article "Remaking the Way We Make Things." They point out that manufacturing from the Industrial Revolution forward has been an unplanned, contrary-to-nature, linear, cradle-to-grave process that was not designed to be part of a larger system. Products are manufactured to be placed quickly into the hands of consumers and then thrown into landfills or incinerated when their "useful life" comes to an end. At best, some products are recycled (more accurately, "down-cycled"). For example, carpeting can be made from recycled soda bottles, but the process of "wrestling them" into forms they were never designed to take requires as much energy, creates as much waste, and may add more dangerous additives than starting from scratch.[19]

19 William McDonough and Michael Braungart, *Cradle to Cradle: Remaking the Way We Make Things* (New York: North Point Press, 2002), 4.

McDonough and Braungart call for a paradigm shift that moves beyond "sustainability" to a "partnership" that can enable "good growth" to occur. Instead of multiple bottom lines, they call for the environment to be one of the "top lines" that is used in business decisions and to shift to a "cradle-to-cradle" orientation that "begins in the designer's head instead of at the end of pipes."[20] As they state it:

20 Ibid., 153–54, 168.

> If humans are truly going to prosper, we will have to learn to imitate nature's highly effective cradle to cradle system of nutrient flow and metabolism, in which the very concept of waste does not exist. *To eliminate the concept of waste means to design things—products, packaging, and systems—from the very beginning on the understanding that waste does not exist....* Products can be composed of either materials that biodegrade and become food for *biological cycles*, or of technical materials that stay in closed loop *technical* cycles, in which they continuously circulate as valuable nutrients for industry.[21]

21 Ibid., 103–4.

Undoubtedly, these are very high (and likely unattainable) standards, as progressing through all of these steps is very expensive and some materials and reclamation methods do not yet exist. McDonough and Braungart, however, are realistic that incremental changes may only be possible at this point. And they note that if businesses are to be involved, the shift to "eco-effective" design has to make economic sense too. As noted in "Remaking the Way We Make Things," among the many corporate clients who have incorporated "cradle-to-cradle" design ideas is Herman Miller, the same company facing the dilemma described at the beginning of this chapter. With respect to the Eames chair situation (see page 392), the company stayed true to its values and took a great risk in switching to a more environmentally friendly wood.

Today the company takes even more comprehensive steps by practicing cradle-to-cradle design.[22] Executives at the company try to achieve holistic, integrated implementation of environmentally responsible concepts in its entire product development cycle. For example, with its Aeron and Mirra chairs, company personnel broke down the chemical composition of the designs, examined human health and environmental impacts, incorporated findings (and new materials) into design processes, and engaged its supply chain in acquiring better materials. Company products are now also being designed for eventual reclamation, so that "discarded" materials can be placed back into the product life cycle with minimal waste and ecological impact.[23]

The Business Case

The third shift involves establishing a better "business case" for going green. This will require the adoption of responsibility by everyone, from consumers to business leaders to governments, and it is necessary if the "full force of business can be harnessed." While Mather addresses the more specific issue of climate change in "The Business of Climate Change: What's the Deal?" the same can be said for most, if not all, environmental issues. To be clear, some business leaders do (and more should) have nonfinancial motivations (environmental concerns as another bottom line). However, the economic case that going green will benefit and/or, at a minimum, not harm the bottom line too greatly is a critical one to establish if significant changes are to occur. The point is not that the narrow interests of businesses need to be served; it's more that the hour is late and as such an important participant, a compelling argument must be made to invite business to the table. As Mather notes, "Only business gets things done on that scale," and "self-interest is more compelling than social conscience."

To a degree, a partial case exists already. Many businesses have been able to capitalize on green initiatives that fit within a strategic and profitable "win-win" framework. For example, the popular Toyota Prius sells at a substantial premium above similarly sized vehicles. Unless gas prices remain high and/or an owner drives many miles, the vehicle has a very long-term payback timetable, even after adding in a one-time tax credit some purchasers have received. So many Prius owners do in fact pay a "social" premium to own the vehicle. Some businesses have increased energy efficiency in facilities and have thereby lowered their operation costs. Others have turned by-products into new lines of business (i.e., used automobile and truck tires into

[22] Marc Gunther, *Faith and Fortune: The Quiet Revolution to Reform American Business* (New York: Crown Business, 2004), 170.

[23] William McDonough and Michael Braungart, "The Anatomy of Transformation: Herman Miller's Journey to Sustainability," *green@work*, March–April 2002.

playfield cushioning, used bicycle tires into handsome waterproof messenger bags, worn blue jeans into building insulation), and marketed environmentally friendly (i.e. organic) products at premium prices. Other large corporations are involved with environmental issues in order to sustain critical resources needed as inputs for their products. For example, McDonald's is active in clean oceans movements to insure the availability of Filet-O-Fish sandwiches.[24] Likewise, Starbucks is involved with climate-change issues over concern that global warming will reduce the amount of land available to grow coffee beans.[25]

Given these types of examples of win-win scenarios, some have claimed that environmental initiatives represent proven avenues to increase profit; "one can 'save the planet' and make money at the same time." As purportedly stated by one leader of the movement, "It's not just a free lunch, but one you are paid to eat."[26]

While the examples above illustrate some of the opportunities that exist, a more realistic and circumspect approach is necessary. As Mather points out with respect to climate change, although the "business case" is moving forward, it is not yet established. Terrill describes attempts, including the Frito-Lays SunChips bag and Proctor & Gamble's Cascade dishwashing detergent, that illustrate the fact that adopting sustainable practices may well involve significant costs and risks, especially in the nearer term, which may, in turn, impact shareholders negatively.

A number of challenges await organizations trying to become more environmentally sustainable. Even if the leaders of a business desire to be green in their production and distribution of goods, environmentally friendly input materials, recycling processes, and/or transportation options may not yet exist, may not be sufficiently available — or more to the point, may not be reasonably cost effective.

Marketplace pressures are also very real. Many environmentally sound practices may not reduce costs and actually may add nonrecoverable ones. From a competitive standpoint, a company that takes on additional costs (beyond what it can make up from environmentally conscious consumers) for the sake of environmental friendliness will find itself at a disadvantage if rivals do not follow suit. Management scholar Ian Maitland describes this challenge as akin to what might be described as "prisoner's dilemma" situations that occur in trying to solve "public goods" problems. While each firm may desire a cleaner environment, paying to do so may result in a disadvantage absent a mechanism to force competitors to make equal financial commitments.[27]

Some larger-scale initiatives (e.g., investments in alternative energy) require very long payback horizons, a privilege executives trying to make

[24] Marc Gunther, *Faith and Fortune: The Quiet Revolution to Reform American Business* (New York: Crown, 2004), 33.

[25] See "Tackling Climate Change," http://www.starbucks.com/responsibility/environment/climate-change.

[26] Ben Elgin, "Little Green Lies," *Businessweek*, October 29, 2007.

[27] Ian Maitland, "The Limits of Business Self-Regulation," *California Management Review* 27, no. 3 (Spring 1985): 132–47.

good on short-term shareholder expectations do not often enjoy. Moreover, these types of investments are very risky and only make economic sense if traditional nonrenewable energy prices remain elevated. As gasoline prices began dropping from their record highs, many biofuel businesses saw customers and investors flee.

Limited availability of capital adds a further challenge. Measuring how "well" capital is employed through ROI (return on investment) analysis can then create some significant tensions. Even in cases in which an environmentally friendly initiative can be shown to produce a positive return, it may be in direct competition with other potential uses of the same capital. As noted in the first case in this chapter, limited capital brings about some tricky tensions.[28]

Offering environmentally and financially sustainable products requires navigation of the tricky and sometimes narrow space between market leadership and current demand. Commenting on the high hurdle that products need to leap over, Joel Makower, executive editor of GreenBiz.com, is cited in *The Economist* as stating, "Most consumers will be happy to choose the greener product—provided it does not cost any more, comes from a trusted maker, requires no special effort to buy or use and is at least as good as the alternative."[29] While perhaps an overstatement, businesses leaders do take great risks for all of their stakeholders (including the environment). If they get too far ahead of what consumers demand, more damaging alternatives would be purchased in their place.

While these are indeed very realistic challenges, we are convinced that approaching business in a manner that is consistent with Christian ethics necessitates that environmental concerns serve as one of the "prisms" through which decisions are made. Avoiding risks by only providing customers with what they immediately want can become a convenient and easy excuse. It is also an irresponsible position, since short-term market interests would be the final forces in determining the fate of the environment (and consequently, human well-being). Such a stance also leads to an abdication of the necessary leadership role played by business and neglects the fact that businesses play a role in shaping consumer behavior. As consumers, we are often more short-sighted and narrowly interested in our product choices than we would like to admit. While business cannot be blamed entirely, most products are not designed and marketed with environmental suitability in mind. Moreover, consumer education and "social marketing" and other methods of appealing to social norms by business can modify end-user behavior to some degree. Henry Ford, founder of the Ford Motor Company, once remarked, "If I had asked my customers what they wanted, they would have said a faster horse."[30]

To be certain, biblical teaching on the environment (theocentric/

[28] Elgin, "Little Green Lies."

[29] "The Good Consumer," *Economist*, January 17, 2008.

[30] Cited in Tom Kelley, *The Ten Faces of Innovation* (New York: Currency/Doubleday, 2005); and Friedman, *Hot, Flat, and Crowded*, 241.

stewardship) provides a framework and boundaries, but some, perhaps many, decisions are judgment calls that rely on discernment and need to be worked out in partnership with rigorous scientific facts and in balance with other important obligations. Moreover, business is not solely responsible for the plight of nature. As Mather notes, we are all in this together.

As end users, consumers, particularly in affluent countries, must change their lifestyles in meaningful ways. Indeed, it is not just "big business" that pollutes. It is easy to complain about what businesses are or are not doing, while voting with our dollars for products and services that may be cheap and convenient in the short term but are destructive to the environment and to human health down the road. What consumers purchase functions as "market signals" to businesses and works to shape what ultimately gets produced and sold.

Good governmental policies are also needed. They require a long-term perspective and the right mix of incentives and direct regulations to establish a stronger "business case" to defeat the "prisoner's dilemmas" that prevent cooperative action.

Working to transform and restore the environment and our relationship with it to a more harmonious place is challenging. Applying ethical ideals (whether Christian or not) to a broken world almost always is. Proactive leadership in stewardship of the creation requires significantly more than just operating within the immediate win-win space. An authentic, committed effort requires courage, imagination, and dramatic shifts in thinking and acting.

ELEVEN

Organizational Integrity

Introduction

In the wake of recent scandals, it is not unusual for commentators to remark that ethical problems in business come down to flaws in personal character. For example, in the aftermath of the global financial system crisis, after a share of blame is given to lax regulation and shortsighted public policy, invariably the majority of the fault is said to lie with the failures of character, specifically greed.[1] Most discussions of business ethics end with a discussion of the principal issues and devote little if any attention to matters of individual moral character and development. However, ethics has to do with an organization's leadership, structures, and culture as well as an individual's character. That is, a company has moral responsibilities and exercises influence on its employees simply by virtue of being an organization with traditions, values, and reward systems. Organizations can either empower or discourage employees from following their moral convictions by a variety of both formal and informal mechanisms.

In this chapter, we examine the ways in which organizations can affect moral decision making, either for better or for worse. The important question raised in this chapter is how a company in its formal structure and informal practices can be a place that supports, rather than undermines, ethical behavior.

The readings in this chapter will assume that the behaviors mentioned as examples are clearly illegal or unethical, or both. They will view the organizational factors that either empowered or at least allowed these ethical failures to go unchecked. Business ethics professors Linda Trevino and Michael Brown take on some of the most common myths of business ethics (e.g., "It's easy to be ethical"; "It's just about bad apples"; "Ethics can be managed through formal programs") in the article "Managing to Be Ethical: Debunking Five Business Ethics Myths." They make the point that functioning in an organization adds levels of complexity for ethical decision making. They also outline several recommendations for effective ethics management.

[1] One of the many examples of this assessment is found in Bethany McLean and Joe Nocera, *All the Devils Are Here: The Hidden History of the Financial Crisis* (New York: Portfolio, 2010). There are also some very interesting assessments of character in Michael Lewis, *The Big Short: Inside the Doomsday Machine* (New York: W. W. Norton, 2010).

Perhaps the most helpful notion is that ethics requires leadership that creates a culture that is conducive to ethics. The second reading looks at the nature of organizational corruption from the perspective of social psychology. John Darley, in a very insightful piece, "The Cognitive and Social Psychology of Organizational Corruption," addresses questions such as how small scandals grow to such a large scale that they virtually insure that the participants get caught—what Darley calls "suicidally stupid." He further addresses the high frequency with which these scandals occur and questions why organizations staffed with basically morally good people find themselves involved in corrupt practices that are often frequently found out. The psychological component is important for understanding unethical behavior in organizations. Darley's article will help you understand why essentially good people find themselves caught up in organizational corruption. It serves as a helpful warning to anyone who thinks that "this will never happen to me." A third reading is an *Ethix* interview with former Enron vice president and whistle-blower, Sherron Watkins. In her interview, she describes the organizational structure that empowered the kinds of unethical accounting practices that ultimately led to Enron's demise. She tells the story of her courageous steps to alert the CEO of Enron at the time, Ken Lay, of the fraud that was being committed. She also gives some good advice to those who find themselves in ethically compromising positions and points out that the major lesson coming out of the Enron debacle is that capitalism requires morality and a long-term view of business, both of which, in her view, are breaking down.

READINGS

Managing to Be Ethical: Debunking Five Business Ethics Myths

Linda K. Trevino and Michael E. Brown

Academy of Management Executive 18, no. 2 (May 2004): 69–81.

The twenty-first century has brought corporate ethics scandals that have harmed millions of employees and investors, and sent shock waves throughout the business world. The scandals have produced "perp walks" and regulatory backlash, and business ethics is once again a hot topic. Academics and managers are asking:

What caused the recent rash of corporate wrongdoing, and what can we do, if anything, to prevent similar transgressions in the future? Perhaps because everyone has opinions about ethics and personal reactions to the scandals, a number of pat answers have circulated that perpetuate a mythology of business ethics management. In this article, we identify several of these myths and respond to them based on knowledge grounded in research and practice.

Myth 1: It's Easy to Be Ethical

A 2002 newspaper article was entitled "Corporate ethics is simple: If something stinks, don't do it." The article went on to suggest "the smell test" or "If you don't want to tell your mom what you're really doing … or read about it in the press, don't do it."[1] The obvious suggestion is that being ethical in business is easy if one wants to be ethical. A further implication is that if it's easy, it doesn't need to be managed. But that suggestion disregards the complexity surrounding ethical decision-making, especially in the context of business organizations.

Ethical Decisions Are Complex

First, ethical decisions aren't simple. They're complex by definition. As they have for centuries, philosophers argue about the best approaches to making the right ethical decision. Students of business ethics are taught to apply multiple normative frameworks to tough dilemmas where values conflict. These include consequentialist frameworks that consider the benefits and harms to society of a potential decision or action, deontological frameworks that emphasize the application of ethical principles such as justice and rights, and virtue ethics with its emphasis on the integrity of the moral actor, among other approaches.[2] But, in the most challenging ethical dilemma situations, the solutions provided by these approaches conflict with each other, and the decision maker is left with little clear guidance. For example, multinational businesses with manufacturing facilities in developing countries struggle with employment practice issues. Most Americans believe that it is harmful and contrary to their rights to employ children. But children routinely contribute to family income in many cultures. If corporations simply refuse to hire them or fire those who are working, these children may resort to begging or even more dangerous employment such as prostitution. Or they and their families may risk starvation. What if respecting the rights of children in such situations produces the greater harm? Such business

decisions are more complex than most media reports suggest, and deciding on the most ethical action is far from simple.

Moral Awareness Is Required

Second, the notion that "it's easy to be ethical" assumes that individuals automatically know that they are facing an ethical dilemma and that they should simply choose to do the right thing. But decision makers may not always recognize that they are facing a moral issue. Rarely do decisions come with waving red flags that say, "Hey, I'm an ethical issue. Think about me in moral terms!"[3]

Dennis Gioia was recall coordinator at Ford Motor Company in the early 1970s when the company decided not to recall the Pinto despite dangerous fires that were killing the occupants of vehicles involved in low-impact rear-end collisions. In his information-overloaded recall coordinator role, Gioia saw thousands of accident reports, and he followed a cognitive "script" that helped him decide which situations represented strong recall candidates and which did not. The incoming information about the Pinto fires did not penetrate a script designed to surface other issues, and it did not initially raise ethical concerns. He and his colleagues in the recall office didn't recognize the recall issue as an ethical issue. In other examples, students who download their favorite music from the Internet may not think about the ethical implications of "stealing" someone else's copyrighted work. Or, a worker asked to sign a document for her boss may not recognize this as a request to "forge" legal documents.

Researchers have begun to study this phenomenon, and they refer to it as moral awareness, ethical recognition, or ethical sensitivity. The idea is that moral judgment processes are not initiated unless the decision-maker recognizes the ethical nature of an issue. So, recognition of an issue as an "ethical" issue triggers the moral judgment process, and understanding this initial step is key to understanding ethical decision-making more generally.

T. M. Jones proposed that the moral intensity of an issue influences moral issue recognition,[4] and this relationship has been supported in research. Two dimensions of moral intensity—magnitude of consequences and social consensus—have been found in multiple studies to influence moral awareness.[5] An individual is more likely to identify an issue as an ethical issue to the extent that a particular decision or action is expected to produce harmful consequences and to the extent that relevant others in the social context view the issue as ethically problematic. Further, the use of moral language has been found to influence moral awareness.[6] For example, in the above cases, if the words "stealing" music (rather than downloading) or "forging" documents (rather than signing) were used, the individual would be more likely to think about these issues in ethical terms.

Ethical Decision-Making Is a Complex, Multistage Process

Moral awareness represents just the first stage in a complex, multiple-stage decision-making process[7] that moves from moral awareness to moral judgment (deciding that a specific action is morally justifiable), to moral motivation (the commitment or intention to take the moral action), and finally to moral character (persistence or follow-through to take the action despite challenges).

The second stage, moral judgment, has been studied within and outside the management literature.[8] Lawrence Kohlberg's well-known theory of cognitive moral development has guided most of the empirical research in this area for the past thirty years.[9] Kohlberg found that people develop from childhood to adulthood through a sequential and hierarchical series of cognitive stages that characterize the way they think about ethical dilemmas. Moral reasoning processes become more complex and sophisticated with development.

Higher stages rely upon cognitive operations that are not available to individuals at lower stages, and higher stages are thought to be "morally better" because they are consistent with philosophical theories of justice and rights. At the lowest levels, termed "preconventional," individuals decide what is right based upon punishment avoidance (at stage 1) and getting a fair deal for oneself in exchange relationships (at stage 2). Next, the conventional level of cognitive moral development includes stages 3 and 4. At stage 3, the individual is concerned with conforming to the expectations of significant others, and at stage 4 the per-

spective broadens to include society's rules and laws as a key influence in deciding what's right. Finally, at the highest "principled" level, stage 5, individuals' ethical decisions are guided by principles of justice and rights.

Perhaps most important for our purposes is the fact that most adults in industrialized societies are at the "conventional" level of cognitive moral development, and less than twenty per cent of adults ever reach the "principled" level where thinking is more autonomous and principle-based. In practical terms, this means that most adults are looking outside themselves for guidance in ethical dilemma situations, either to significant others in the relevant environment (e.g., peers, leaders) or to society's rules and laws. It also means that most people need to be led when it comes to ethics.

The Organizational Context Creates Additional Pressures and Complexity

Moral judgment focuses on *deciding* what's right—not necessarily *doing* what is right. Even when people make the right decision, they may find it difficult to follow through and do what is right because of pressures from the work environment. Research has found that principled individuals are more likely to behave in a manner consistent with their moral judgments, and they are more likely to resist pressures to behave unethically.[10] However, most people never reach the principled level. So, the notion that being ethical is simple also ignores the pressures of the organizational context that influences the relationship between moral judgment and action.

Consider the following ethical-dilemma situation. You find yourself in the parking lot, having just dented the car next to you. The ethical decision is relatively simple. It's about you and your behavior. No one else is really involved. You have harmed someone else's property, you're responsible, and you or your insurance company should pay for the repairs. It's pretty clear that you should leave a note identifying yourself and your insurance company. Certainly, there may be negative consequences if you leave that note. Your insurance rates may go up. But doing the right thing in this situation is fairly straightforward.

Contrast that to business-context situations. It is much harder to "just say no" to a boss who demands making the numbers at all costs. Or to go above the boss's head to someone in senior management with suspicions that "managing earnings" has somehow morphed into "cooking the books." Or to walk away from millions of dollars in business because of concerns about crossing an ethical line. Or to tell colleagues that the way they do business seems to have crossed that line. In these situations, the individual is operating within the context of the organization's authority structure and culture — and would likely be concerned about the consequences of disobeying a boss's order, walking away from millions of dollars in business, or blowing the whistle on a peer or superior. What would peers think? How would the leadership react? Would management retaliate? Is one's job at risk?

It may seem curious that people often worry about whether others will think of them as too ethical. But all of us recognize that "snitches" rarely fit in, on the playground or in life, and whistleblowers are frequently ostracized or worse.[11] The reasons for their ostracism are not fully understood, but they may have to do with humans' social nature and the importance of social group maintenance. Research suggests that people who take principled stands, such as those who are willing to report a peer for unethical behavior, are seen as highly ethical while, at the same time, they are thought to be highly unlikable.[12]

Nearly a third of respondents to the 2003 National Business Ethics Survey[13] said "their coworkers condone questionable ethics practices by showing respect for those who achieve success using them." Further, about forty per cent of respondents said that they would not report misconduct they observed because of fear of retaliation from management. Almost a third said they would not report misconduct because they feared retaliation from coworkers.

If you think this applies only to the playground or the factory floor, ask yourself why we haven't seen more CEOs proclaiming how appalled they are at the behavior of some of their peers after recent ethics scandals. Yes, we heard from a few retired CEOs. But very few active senior executives have spoken up. Why not? They're probably uncomfortable passing moral judgment on others or holding themselves up as somehow ethically better than their peers. So, social context is

important because people, including senior executives, look to others for approval of their thinking and behavior.

In sum, being ethical is not simple. Ethical decisions are ambiguous, and the ethical decision-making process involves multiple stages that are fraught with complications and contextual pressures. Individuals may not have the cognitive sophistication to make the right decision. And most people will be influenced by peers' and leaders' words and actions, and by concerns about the consequences of their behavior in the work environment.

Myth 2: Unethical Behavior in Business Is Simply the Result of "Bad Apples"

A recent headline was "How to Spot Bad Apples in the Corporate Bushel."[14] The bad-apple theory is pervasive in the media and has been around a long time. In the 1980s, during a segment of the *McNeil Lehrer Report* on PBS television, the host was interviewing guests about insider trading scandals. The CEO of a major investment firm and a business school dean agreed that the problems with insider trading resulted from bad apples. They said that educational institutions and businesses could do little except to find and discard those bad apples after the fact. So, the first reaction to ethical problems in organizations is generally to look for a culprit who can be punished and removed. The idea is that if we rid the organization of one or more bad apples, all will be well because the organization will have been cleansed of the perpetrator.

Certainly there are bad actors who will hurt others or feather their own nests at others' expense — and they do need to be identified and removed. But, as suggested above, most people are the product of the context they find themselves in. They tend to "look up and look around," and they do what others around them do or expect them to do.[15] They look outside themselves for guidance when thinking about what is right. What that means is that most unethical behavior in business is supported by the context in which it occurs — either through direct reinforcement of unethical behavior or through benign neglect.

An example of how much people are influenced by

those around them was in the newspaper in November 2002. Police in New Britain, Connecticut, confiscated a 50-ft. long pile of stolen items, the result of a scavenger hunt held by the "Canettes," New Britain high school's all-girl drill team. According to the Hartford Courant, police, parents, and school personnel were astonished that 42 normally law-abiding girls could steal so many items in a single evening. But the girls had a hard time believing that they had done anything wrong. One girl said: "I just thought it was a custom … kind of like a camaraderie thing, [and] if the seniors said it was OK and they were in charge, then it was OK!"

In another incident in May 2003, suburban Chicago high school girls engaged in an aggressive and brutal "hazing ritual" that landed five girls in the hospital.[16] We might say that these are teenagers, and that adults are different. But many of these teenagers are about to start jobs, and there are only a few years between these high school students and young people graduating from college.

Most adults are more like these teens than most of us think or would prefer. The influence of peers is powerful in both cases. When asked why they engaged in unethical conduct, employees will often say, "I had no choice," or "My boss told me to do it." Stanley Milgram's obedience-to-authority experiments, probably the most famous social psychology experiments ever conducted, support the notion that people obey authority figures even if that means harming another person.[17] Milgram, a Yale psychologist, conducted his obedience-to-authority experiments in the Hartford community on normal adults. These experiments demonstrated that nearly two-thirds of normal adults will harm another human being (give them alleged electric shocks of increasing intensity) if asked to do so by an authority figure as part of what was billed as a learning experiment.

Were these people bad apples? We don't think so. Most of them were not at all comfortable doing what they were being asked to do, and they expressed sincere concern for the victim's fate. But in the end most of them continued to harm the learner because the authority figure in a lab coat told them to do so.

How does this apply to work settings? Consider the junior member of an audit team who discovers something problematic when sampling a firm's financials and asks the senior person on the audit team for advice. When the leader suggests putting the problematic example back and picking another one, the young auditor is likely to do just that. The leader may add words such as the following: "You don't understand the big picture" or "Don't worry, this is my responsibility." In this auditing example, the harm being done is much less obvious than in the learning experiment and the junior auditor's responsibility even less clear, so the unethical conduct is probably easier to carry out and more likely to occur.

The bottom line here is that most people, including most adults, are followers when it comes to ethics. When asked or told to do something unethical, most will do so. This means that they must be led toward ethical behavior or be left to flounder.

Bad behavior doesn't always result from flawed individuals. Instead, it may result from a system that encourages or supports flawed behavior. A corollary of the bad-apples argument is that ethics can't be taught or even influenced in adults because adults are autonomous moral agents whose ethics are fully formed by the time they join work organizations, and they can't be changed.

This is simply not true. We know from many empirical studies[18] that the large majority of adults are not fully formed when it comes to ethics, and they are not autonomous moral agents. They look outside themselves for guidance in ethical dilemma situations, and they behave based to a large extent upon what those around them — leaders and peers — expect of them. So, we have to look at the very powerful signals that are being sent about what is expected. We also know that the development of moral reasoning continues into adulthood. Those who are challenged to wrestle with ethical dilemmas in their work will develop more sophisticated ways of thinking about such issues, and their behavior will change as a result.

Myth 3: Ethics Can Be Managed through Formal Ethics Codes and Programs

If people in organizations need ethical guidance and structural support, how can organizations best provide it? Most large organizations now have formal ethics or legal compliance programs. In 1991 the U.S. Sentencing Commission created sentencing guidelines for organizations convicted of federal crimes (see *www.ussc.gov* for information). The guidelines removed judicial discretion and required convicted organizations to pay restitution and substantial fines depending upon whether the organization turns itself in, cooperates with authorities, and whether it has established a legal compliance program that meets seven requirements for due diligence and effectiveness. These formal programs generally include the following key elements: written standards of conduct that are communicated and disseminated to all employees, ethics training, ethics advice lines and offices, and systems for anonymous reporting of misconduct. The Sarbanes-Oxley law, passed during the summer of 2002, requires corporations to set up an anonymous system for employees to report fraud and other unethical activities. Therefore, companies that did not previously have such reporting systems are busy establishing them.

Research suggests that formal ethics and legal compliance programs can have a positive impact. For example, the Ethics Resource Center's National Business Ethics Survey[19] revealed that in organizations with all four program elements (standards, training, advice lines, and reporting systems) there was a greater likelihood (78 per cent) that employees would report observed misconduct to management. The likelihood of reporting declined with fewer program elements. Only half as many people in organizations with no formal program said that they would report misconduct to management.

Yet, creating a formal program, by itself, does not guarantee effective ethics management. Recall that Enron had an ethics code, and the board voted to bypass its conflict-of-interest policy.[20] Not surprisingly, research suggests that actions speak louder than words. Employees must perceive that formal policies go beyond mere window dressing to represent the real ethical culture of the organization. For example, the National Business Ethics Survey reports that when executives and supervisors emphasize ethics, keep promises, and model ethical conduct, misconduct is much lower than when employees perceive that the

"ethics walk" is not consistent with the "ethics talk."[21] In another study[22] formal program characteristics were found to be relatively unimportant compared with more informal cultural characteristics such as messages from leadership at both the executive and supervisory levels. In addition, perceived ethics program follow-through was found to be essential.

Organizations demonstrate follow-through by working hard to detect rule violators, by following up on ethical concerns raised by employees, and by demonstrating consistency between ethics and compliance policies and actual organizational practices. Further, the perception that ethics is actually talked about in day-to-day organizational activities and incorporated into decision-making was found to be important.

So, for formal systems to influence behavior, they must be part of a larger, coordinated cultural system that supports ethical conduct every day. Ethical culture provides informal systems, along with formal systems, to support ethical conduct.[23] For example, the research cited above found that ethics-related outcomes (e.g., employee awareness of ethical issues, amount of observed misconduct, willingness to report misconduct) were much more positive to the extent that employees perceived that ethical conduct was rewarded and unethical conduct was punished in the organization. Further, a culture that demands unquestioning obedience to authority was found to be particularly harmful while a culture in which employees feel fairly treated was especially helpful.

The Fall of Arthur Andersen

Barbara Toffler's book *Final Accounting: Ambition, Greed, and the Fall of Arthur Andersen* (2003)[24] can help us understand this notion of ethical (or unethical) organizational culture. Andersen transformed over a number of years from having a solid ethical culture to having a strong unethical culture. The company's complete demise is a rather dramatic example of the potential results of such a transformation.

In the mid-1990s, Arthur Andersen did not have a formal ethics office, but it did have formal ethical standards and ethics training. Ironically, it also established a consulting group whose practice was aimed at helping other businesses manage their ethics. Barbara Toffler was hired to run that practice in 1995 after spending time on the Harvard Business School faculty and in her own ethics consulting business. After joining Andersen, Toffler learned quickly that the firm's own ethical culture was slipping badly, and she chronicles that slippage in her book.

The book opens with the following statement "The day Arthur Andersen loses the public's trust is the day we are out of business." Steve Samek, country managing partner, made that statement on a CD-ROM concerning the firm's Independence and Ethical Standards in 1999. It was reminiscent of the old Arthur Andersen. Andersen's traditional management approach had been a top-down, "one firm" concept. Arthur Andersen had built a strong ethical culture over the years where all of the pieces fit together into a seamless whole that supported ethical conduct. No matter where they were in the world, if customers were dealing with Andersen employees, they knew that they could count on the same high-quality work and the same integrity. Employees were trained in the "Andersen Way," and that way included strong ethics. Training at their St. Charles, Illinois, training facility was sacred. It created a cadre of professionals who spoke the same language and shared the same "Android" values.

Founders create culture, and Arthur Andersen was no exception. Toffler says that in the firm's early days, the messages from the top about ethical conduct were strong and clear. Andersen himself said, "My own mother told me, 'Think straight—talk straight.' This challenge will never fail anyone in a time of trial and temptation." "Think straight, talk straight" became a mantra for decades at Arthur Andersen. Partners said with pride that integrity mattered more than fees. And stories about the founder's ethics became part of the firm's lore. At the young age of 28, Andersen faced down a railway executive who demanded that his books be approved—or else. Andersen said, "There's not enough money in the city of Chicago to induce me to change that report." Andersen lost the business, but later the railway company filed for bankruptcy, and Arthur Andersen became known as a firm one could trust. In the 1930s Andersen talked about the special responsibility of accountants to the public and the importance of their independence of judgment and action. Arthur Andersen died in 1947 but was followed by leaders with similar convictions who ran the firm in

the 1950s and 1960s, and the ethical culture continued for many years. Pretty much through the 1980s, Andersen was considered a stable and prestigious place to work. People didn't expect to get rich—rather they wanted "a good career at a firm with a good reputation."

But, the ethical culture eventually began to unravel, and Toffler attributes much of this to the fact that the firm's profits increasingly came from management consulting rather than auditing. The leadership's earlier commitment to ethics came to be drowned out by the firm's increasing laser-like focus on revenues. Auditing and consulting are very different, and the cultural standards that worked so well in auditing didn't fit the needs of the consulting side of the business. But this mismatch was never addressed, and the resulting mixed signals helped precipitate a downward spiral into unethical practices. Serving the client began to be defined as keeping the client happy and getting return business. And tradition became translated into unquestioning obedience to the partner, no matter what one was asked to do. For example, managers and partners were expected to pad their prices. Reasonable estimates for consulting work were simply doubled or more as consultants were told to back into the numbers.

The training also began falling apart when it came to hiring experienced people from outside the firm—something that happened more and more as consulting took over. New employees had always been required to attend a three-day session designed to indoctrinate them into the culture of the firm, but new consultants were told not to forego lucrative client work to attend. So, Toffler never made it to the training, and many other consultants didn't either.

By the time Toffler arrived at Andersen, the firm still had a huge maroon ethics binder, but no one bothered to refer to it. Ethics was never talked about. And, she says, "when I brought up the subject of internal ethics, I was looked at as if I had teleported in from another world." The assumption, left over from the old days in auditing, was that "we're ethical people; we recruit people who are screened for good judgment and values. We don't need to worry about this stuff." But, as we all learned, their failure to worry about ethics led to the demise of the firm.

Could a formal ethics office have helped Arthur Andersen? Probably not, unless that office addressed the shift toward consulting, identified the unique ethical issues faced in the consulting side of the business, developed ethical guidelines for consulting, and so on. It is easy for formal ethics offices and their programs to be marginalized if they don't have the complete support of the organization's leadership and if they are inconsistent with the broader culture. In fact, Andersen still had ethics policies, and they still talked about ethics in formal documents. But the business had changed along with the culture that guided employee actions every day, while the approach to ethics management had not kept pace.

Myth 4: Ethical Leadership Is Mostly about Leader Integrity

In our discussion of Arthur Andersen, we suggested the importance of leadership. But what is executive ethical leadership? The mythology of ethical leadership focuses attention narrowly on individual character and qualities such as integrity, honesty, and fairness. The *Wall Street Journal* recently ran a story on its website entitled "Plain Talk: CEOs Need to Restore Character in Companies." It said, "The chief problem affecting corporate America right now is not the regulatory environment or snoozing board directors. It's character."[25] But as Arthur Andersen demonstrated, leaders must be more than individuals of high character. They must "lead" others to behave ethically.

Recent research has found that certain individual characteristics are necessary but not sufficient for effective ethical leadership. Such leadership at the executive level is a reputational phenomenon. In most large organizations, employees have few face-to-face interactions with senior executives. So, most of what they know about a leader is gleaned from afar. In order to develop a reputation for ethical leadership, an executive must be perceived as both a "moral person" and a "moral manager."[26]

Being perceived as a "moral person" is related to good character. It depends upon employee perceptions of the leader's traits, behaviors, and decision-making processes. Ethical leaders are thought to be honest and trustworthy. They show concern for people and are open to employee input. Ethical leaders build relationships that are characterized by trust, respect and support for their employees.

In terms of decision-making, ethical leaders are seen as fair. They take into account the ethical impact of their decisions, both short term and long term, on multiple stakeholders. They also make decisions based upon ethical values and decision rules, such as the golden rule.

But being perceived as a "moral person" is not enough. Being a "moral person" tells followers what the leader will do. It doesn't tell them what the leader expects *them* to do. Therefore, a reputation for ethical leadership also depends upon being perceived as a "moral manager," one who leads others on the ethical dimension, lets them know what is expected, and holds them accountable. Moral managers set ethical standards, communicate ethics messages, role model ethical conduct, and use rewards and punishments to guide ethical behavior in the organization.

Combining the "moral person" and "moral manager" dimensions creates a two-by-two matrix (see Figure 1). A leader who is strong on both dimensions is perceived to be an *ethical leader*. We can point to Arthur Andersen as an exemplar of ethical leadership. He was known as a strong ethical person who also clearly led his organization on ethics and values. People knew what they could expect of him, and they knew what he expected of them from an ethics perspective. Another example of ethical leadership is James Burke, CEO of Johnson & Johnson during the early 1980s Tylenol crisis (when Tylenol was laced with cyanide in the Chicago area). Burke handled that crisis masterfully, recalling all Tylenol at a huge financial cost to the firm.

But his ethical leadership had begun much earlier when he first took the CEO helm. He focused the organization's attention on the company's longstanding credo and its values. He demanded that senior executives either subscribe to the credo or remove it from the wall. He didn't want to run a hypocritical organization. He also launched the credo survey, an annual survey that asks employees how the company is doing relative to each of the credo values. Bill George, recently retired CEO of Medtronic, is a more current example of an ethical leader. In his book *Authentic Leadership*, George calls for responsible ethical leadership in corporate America while recounting his own struggles to stay true to the company's mission and to himself.[27]

A leader who is neither a moral person nor a

Figure 1: Executive Ethical Leadership Reputation Matrix*

	Moral Person	
	Weak	Strong
Strong	Hypocritical Leader Jim Bakker Michael Sears	EthicalLeader Arthur Andersen James Burke Bill George
Weak	Unethical Leader Al Dunlap Bernie Ebbers?	

Moral Manager (row label at left)

◄---Ethically Silent Leader---►
Sandy Well?

moral manager is an *unethical leader*. In our research, Al Dunlap was frequently identified as an unethical leader. Subject of a book entitled *Chainsaw*,[28] Dunlap was known as an expert turnaround manager. But while at Sunbeam, he also became known for "emotional abuse" of employees. As a result of his demands to make the numbers at all costs, employees felt pressure to use questionable accounting and sales techniques, and they did.

Dunlap also lied to Wall Street, assuring them that the firm would reach its financial projections. In the end, Dunlap could no longer cover up the sorry state of affairs, and he left a crippled company when the board fired him in 1998. In 2002, he paid a $500,000 fine for financial fraud and agreed never to serve as an officer or director of a public corporation. Unfortunately, there are many candidates for a more current example of unethical leadership: Dennis Kozlowski from Tyco, Bernie Ebbers from WorldCom, and Richard Scrushy from HealthSouth are just a few executive names attached to recent business scandals.

Leaders who communicate a strong ethics/values message (who are moral managers), but who are not perceived to be ethical themselves (they are not moral persons) can be thought of as *hypocritical lead-*

ers. Nothing makes people more cynical than a leader who talks incessantly about integrity, but then engages in unethical conduct himself and encourages others to do so, either explicitly or implicitly. Hypocritical leadership is all about ethical pretense. The problem is that by spotlighting integrity, the leader raises expectations and awareness of ethical issues. At the same time, employees realize that they can't trust the leader.

Jim Bakker, the founder of PTL Ministries, is our favorite example of a hypocritical leader. At its peak, his television ministry had 2000 employees and reached more than ten million homes. Bakker preached about doing the Lord's work while raising funds for his Heritage USA Christian theme park. The problem was that he sold more memberships than could ever be honored. He tapped millions of dollars donated by his followers to support PTL operating expenses, including huge salaries and bonuses for his family and high-ranking PTL officials. PTL filed for bankruptcy in 1987, and Bakker spent eight years in prison.[29]

Michael Sears, recently fired from Boeing for offering a job to an Air Force procurement specialist while she was overseeing negotiations with Boeing, represents a more recent example of a hypocritical

*Figure adapted with permission from Trevino, L. K., Hartman, L. P., Brown, M. 2000. "Moral Person and Moral Manager: How Executives Develop a Reputation for Ethical Leadership." *California Management Review* 42, no. 4: 128–42.

leader. Sears had played a significant role at the Boeing Leadership Center, which is known for its programs related to ethics. Also, shortly before his firing, Sears released advance copies of his book *Soaring Through Turbulence*, which included a section on maintaining high ethical standards.[30]

We call the final combination *ethically silent leadership*. It applies to executives who are neither strong ethical nor strong unethical leaders. They fall into what employees perceive to be an ethically neutral leadership zone. They may be ethical persons, but they don't provide leadership in the crucial area of ethics, and employees aren't sure where the leaders stand on ethics or if they care.

The ethically silent leader is not perceived to be unethical but is seen as focusing intently on the bottom line without setting complementary ethical goals. There is little or no ethics message coming from the top. But silence represents an important message. In the context of all the other messages being sent in a highly competitive business environment, employees are likely to interpret silence to mean that the top executive really doesn't care how business goals are met, only that they are met, so employees act on that message. Business leaders don't like to think that their employees perceive them as ethically silent. But given the current climate of cynicism, unless leaders make an effort to stand out and lead on ethics, they are likely to be viewed that way.

Sandy Weill, CEO of Citigroup, may fit the ethically silent leader category. The company has been playing defense with the media, responding to ugly headlines about ethics scandals, especially at its Smith Barney unit where stock analysts were accused of essentially "selling" their stock recommendations for banking business. Weill's management style is to hire competent people to run Citigroup's units and to let them do their jobs. That may work well for other aspects of the business, but ethics must be managed from the top and center of the organization. According to *Fortune* magazine, Weill has now "gotten religion," if a bit late. Weill has "told his board that he feels his most important job from now on is to be sure that Citigroup operates at the highest level of ethics and with the utmost integrity." New procedures and business standards are being developed at corporate

headquarters, and a new CEO was appointed at Smith Barney. However, *Fortune* also cites cynicism about this recent turnabout, noting that Weill is often "tone deaf" on ethical issues.[31] So, developing a reputation for ethical leadership requires more than strong personal character. Employees must be "led" from the top on ethics just as they must be led on quality, competitiveness, and a host of other expected behaviors. In order to be effective ethical leaders, executives must demonstrate that they are ethical themselves, they must make their expectations of others' ethical conduct explicit, and they must hold all of their followers accountable for ethical conduct every day.

Myth 5: People Are Less Ethical Than They Used to Be

In the opening to this article, we said that business ethics has once again become a hot topic. The media have bombarded us with information about ethics scandals, feeding the perception that morals are declining in business and in society more generally.

According to a poll released by the PR Newswire in summer 2002, sixty-eight per cent of those surveyed believe that senior corporate executives are less honest and trustworthy today than they were a decade ago.[32] But unethical conduct has been with us as long as human beings have been on the earth, and business ethics scandals are as old as business itself. The Talmud, a 1500-year-old text, includes about 2 million words and 613 direct commandments designed to guide Jewish conduct and culture. More than one hundred of these concern business and economics. Why? Because "transacting business, more than any other human activity, tests our moral mettle and reveals our character" and because "working, money, and commerce offer . . . the best opportunities to do good deeds such as . . . providing employment and building prosperity for our communities and the world."[33]

So, unethical behavior is nothing new. It's difficult to find solid empirical evidence of changes over time. But studies of student cheating have found that the percentage of college students who admit to cheating has not changed much during the last thirty years.[34] Some types of cheating have increased (e.g., test cheating, collaboration on individual assignments). Other types of cheating have declined (e.g., plagiarism, turning in another student's work). Certainly, given new technologies and learning approaches, students have discovered some clever new ways to cheat, and professors have their work cut out for them keeping up with the new methods. But the amount of overall cheating hasn't increased that much. Further, when employees were asked about their own work organizations, the 2003 National Business Ethics Survey found that employee perceptions of ethics are generally quite positive. Interestingly, key indicators have actually improved since the last survey conducted in 2000.[35]

Alan Greenspan said it well on July 16, 2002: "It is not that humans have become any more greedy than in generations past. It is that the avenues to express greed [have] grown so enormously." So, unethical behavior is nothing new, and people are probably not less ethical than they used to be. But the environment has become quite complex and is rapidly changing, providing all sorts of ethical challenges and opportunities to express greed. If ethical misconduct is an ongoing concern, then organizations must respond with lasting solutions that embed support for ethics into their cultures rather than short-term solutions that can easily be undone or dismissed as fads. The risk is that the current media focus on unethical conduct will result in "faddish" responses that offer overly simplistic solutions and that result inevitably in disillusionment and abandonment. Faddish solutions often result from external pressures to "do something" or at least look like you're doing something. The current focus on scandal certainly includes such pressures.[36] But the recognition that unethical conduct is a continuing organizational problem may help to convince managers that solutions should be designed that will outlast the current intense media focus.

What Executives Can Do: Guidelines for Effective Ethics Management

Building upon what we have learned, we offer guidelines for effective ethics management. The overarching goal should be to create a strong ethical culture supported by strong ethical leadership. Why culture? Because we've seen that being ethical is not simple, and

that people in organizations need ethical guidance and support for doing the right thing. Executive leaders must provide that structure and ethical guidance, and they can do that best by harnessing multiple formal and informal cultural systems.[37] People should respond positively to the kind of structure that aims to help them do the right thing. If management says, "We want you to do the right thing, the ethical thing, and we're going to try to create a culture that helps you to do that," employee response should be quite positive so long as employees believe that management is sincere and they observe consistency between words and actions.

First: Understand the Existing Ethical Culture

Leaders are responsible for transmitting culture in their organizations, and the ethical dimension of organizational culture is no exception. According to Schein, the most powerful mechanisms for embedding and reinforcing culture are: (1) what leaders pay attention to, measure, and control; (2) leader reactions to critical incidents and organizational crises; deliberate role modeling, teaching, and coaching by leaders; (3) criteria for allocation of rewards and status; and (4) criteria for recruitment, selection, promotion, retirement, and excommunication.[38]

If leaders wish to create a strong ethical culture, the first step is to understand the current state: What are the key cultural messages being sent about ethics? It's a rare executive who really understands the ethical culture in an organization. And the higher you go in the organization, the rosier the perception of the ethical culture is likely to be.[39] Why? Because information often gets stuck at lower organizational levels, and executives are often insulated from "bad news," especially if employees perceive that the organization "shoots the messenger." Executives need anonymous surveys, focus groups, and reporting lines, and people need to believe that the senior leaders really want to know, if they are to report honestly on the current state of the ethical culture.

In surveys, ask for employee perceptions of supervisory and executive leadership and the messages they send by their communications and behavior. And listen to what employees say. Ask employees whether they perceive that they are treated fairly, and whether the company acts as if it cares about them, its customers, and other stakeholders. Find out what messages the reward system is sending. Do employees believe that ethical "good guys" are rewarded and unethical "bad guys" are punished in the organization? What do employees think is required in order to succeed or to be fired? Follow the kinds of calls coming in to ethics telephone lines. Learn whether employees are asking questions and reporting problems. Use this information to identify needs for training and other interventions. In focus groups, find out who the organizational heroes are (is it the sales representative who steps on peers in order to get ahead or a manager who is known for the highest integrity?). Ask what stories veterans would tell a new hire about ethics in your organization.

Second: Communicate the Importance of Ethical Standards

Employees need clear and consistent messages that ethics is essential to the business model, not just a poster or a website. Most businesses send countless messages about competition and financial performance, and these easily drown out other messages. In order to compete with this constant drumbeat about the short-term bottom line, the messages about ethical conduct must be just as strong or stronger and as frequent. Simply telling people to do the right thing is not enough. They must be prepared for the types of issues that arise in their particular business and position, and they must know what to do when ethics and the bottom line appear to be in conflict. Executives should tie ethics to the long-term success of the business by providing examples from their own experience or the experiences of other successful employees. Make sure that messages coming from executive and supervisory leaders are clear and consistent. Train employees to recognize the kinds of ethical issues that are likely to arise in their work. Demand discussion of ethics and values as part of routine business decision-making. When making important decisions, ask, "Are we doing the 'right' (i.e., ethical) thing? Who could be hurt by this decision? How could this affect our relationships with stakeholders and our long-term reputation?" Share those deliberations with employees. Finally, be sure to let employees know about exemplary ethical conduct. For example, the famous story about Arthur Andersen

losing the railway business because he refused to alter the books was recounted over and over again in the firm and made it absolutely clear that "think straight, talk straight" actually meant something in the firm.

Third: Focus on the Reward System

The reward system may be the single most important way to deliver a message about what behaviors are expected. B. F. Skinner knew what he was talking about. People do what's rewarded, and they avoid doing what's punished.[40] Let's look at the positive side first—can we really reward ethical behavior? In the short term, we probably cannot. For the most part, ethical behavior is simply expected, and people don't expect or want to be rewarded for doing their jobs the right way.[41] But in the longer term, ethical behavior can be rewarded by promoting and compensating people who are not only good at what they do, but who have also developed a reputation with customers, peers, subordinates, and managers as being of the highest integrity. The best way to hold employees accountable for ethical conduct is to incorporate evaluation of it into 360 degree performance management systems and to make this evaluation an explicit part of compensation and promotion decisions. The idea is that the bottom line and ethical performance both count; unless individuals have both, they should not advance in the organization.

Also, exemplary behavior can be rewarded. At Lockheed Martin, at the annual Chairman's meeting, a "Chairman's Award" goes to an employee who exhibited exemplary ethical conduct in the previous year. All senior corporate leaders are expected to expend effort each year to find examples of exemplary ethical conduct in their own business units and make nominations. The award ceremony, attended by all 250 senior executives, is exactly the kind of "ritual" that helps to create an ethical culture. Stories are shared, they become part of the organization's lore, the potential impact growing as the stories accumulate over time.[42]

Perhaps even more important than rewarding ethical conduct is taking care not to reward unethical conduct. That's what began to happen at Arthur Andersen as generating revenue became the only rewarded behavior, and it didn't matter how you did it. For example, consultants were rewarded for making a project last by finding reasons (legitimate or not) to stay on. Toffler says, "Like the famous Roach Motel, consultants were taught to check in, but never check out."[43] So, clients were overcharged, consulting jobs were dragged out, and colleagues were "screwed" along the way because the rewards supported such unethical conduct.

And what about discipline? Unethical conduct should be disciplined swiftly and fairly when it occurs at any level in the organization. The higher the level of the person disciplined, the stronger the message that management takes ethics seriously. That's what is behind the "perp walks" we have observed in the media. The public wants to see that fraudulent conduct among America's executives will not be tolerated. Similarly, inside organizations, employees want to see misconduct disciplined, and disciplined harshly.[44] Overall, employees must perceive that good guys get ahead and bad guys don't — they get punished. But, remember, it's often not enough to punish or remove a bad guy or a bad apple. The system should be checked to see if the existing reward system or other messages contributed to the bad behavior.

Fourth: Promote Ethical Leadership throughout the Firm

Recall that being a "moral person" who is characterized by integrity and fairness, treats people well, and makes ethical decisions is important. But those elements deal only with the "ethical" part of ethical leadership. To be ethical leaders, executives have to think about the "leadership" part of the term. Providing ethical "leadership" means making ethical values visible — communicating about not just the bottom-line goals (the ends) but also the acceptable and unacceptable means of getting there (the means). Being an ethical leader also means asking very publicly how important decisions will affect multiple stakeholders — shareholders, employees, customers, society — and making transparent the struggles about how to balance competing interests. It means using the reward system to clearly communicate what is expected and what is accepted. That means rewarding ethical conduct and disciplining unethical conduct, even if the rule violator is a senior person or a top producer. Find a way to let employees know that the unethical conduct was taken seriously and the employee disciplined.

Ethical cultures and ethical leaders go hand in hand. Building an ethical culture can't be delegated. The CEO must be the Chief Ethics Officer of his or her organization.[45] Many CEOs may feel that they would rather pass on this challenge — that they don't really know how to do it — or they may prefer to believe that everyone in their organization is already ethical. But ethics is being "managed" in their organizations with or without their attention to it. Benign neglect of the ethical culture simply leads to employees reaching the conclusion, rightly or wrongly, that leaders don't care as much about ethics as they do about other things. Leaders develop a reputation in this arena. Chances are that if the leader hasn't thought much about this reputation or hasn't been very proactive about it, people in the organization will likely label him or her as an ethically neutral leader. That doesn't mean that the leader *is* ethically neutral or doesn't take ethics into account in decision-making. It does mean that people aren't sure where the leader stands on the frequent conflicts between ethics and the bottom line. Without explicit guidance, they assume that the bottom-line messages are the most important.

As we've said, senior executives are extremely important. They set the tone at the top and oversee the ethical culture. But from an everyday implementation perspective, front-line supervisors are equally important because of their daily interactions with their direct reports. An ethical culture ultimately depends upon how supervisors treat employees, customers, and other stakeholders, and how they make decisions. Do they treat everyone honestly, fairly, and with care? Do supervisors point out when their group is facing a decision with ethical overtones? Do they consider multiple stakeholder interests and the long-term reputation of the organization in decision-making? Do they hold themselves and their people accountable for ethical conduct? Or, do they focus only on short-term bottom-line results?

Ethics Isn't Easy

Unethical conduct in business has been with us as long as business transactions have occurred. People are not necessarily more unethical today, but gray areas abound along with many opportunities to cross into unethical territory. Much unethical conduct is the result not just of bad apples but of neglectful leadership and organizational cultures that send mixed messages about what is important and what is expected. It isn't easy to be ethical. Employees must recognize ethical issues in their work, develop the cognitive tools to make the right choices, and then be supported in those choices by the organizational environment. Executives must manage the ethical conduct of their employees as proactively as they manage any important behavior. And the complexity of the management system should match the complexity of the behavior being managed.

The best way to manage ethical conduct is by aligning the multiple formal and informal cultural systems in support of doing the right thing. Cultural messages about the importance of trust and long-term relationships with multiple stakeholders must get at least as much attention as messages about the short-term bottom line, and employees must be held accountable for ethical conduct through performance management and reward systems.

Notes

1 St. Anthony, N. Corporate ethics is simple: If something stinks, don't do it. *Star Tribune (Minneapolis-Saint Paul) Newspaper of the Twin Cities.* 28 June 2002.

2 For a simple overview of these theories, see Trevino, L. K., & Nelson, K. 2003. *Managing business ethics: Straight talk about how to do it right.* 3d ed. New York: Wiley.

3 Gioia, D. 1992. Pinto fires and personal ethics: A script analysis of missed opportunities. *Journal of Business Ethics*, 11(5,6): 379–389; Gioia, D. A. 2003. Personal reflections on the Pinto Fires case. In Trevino & Nelson.

4 Jones, T. M. 1991. Ethical decision making by individuals in organizations: An issue-contingent model. *Academy of Management Review*, 16: 366–395.

5 May, D. R., & Pauli, K. P. 2000. The role of moral intensity in ethical decision making: A review and investigation of moral recognition, evaluation, and intention. Manuscript presented at the meeting of the National Academy of Management, Toronto, August 2000.

6 Butterfield, K., Trevino, L. K., & Weaver, G. 2000. Moral awareness in business organizations: Influences of issue related and social context factors. *Human Relations*, 53(7): 981–1018.

7 Rest, M. 1986. *Moral development: Advances in research and theory.* New Jersey: Praeger.

8 Weber, J. 1990. Managers' moral reasoning: Assessing their responses to three moral dilemmas. *Human Relations*, 43: 687702; Weber, J., & Wasieleski, 2001. Investigating influences on managers' moral reasoning: The impact of context, personal, and organizational factors. *Business and Society*, 40(1): 79–111; Trevino, L. K. 1986. Ethical decision making in organizations: A person-situation interactionist model. *Academy of Management Review*, 11(3): 601–617; Trevino, L. K. 1992. Moral reasoning and business ethics. *Journal of Business Ethics*, 11:445–459.

9 Kohlberg, L. 1969. Stage and sequence: The cognitive developmental approach to socialization. In *Handbook of socialization theory and research.* D. A. Goslin, ed. Rand McNally, 347–380.

10 Thoma, S. J. 1994. Moral judgment and moral action. In J. Rest & D. Narvaez (ed.). *Moral development in the professions: Psychology and applied ethics.* Hillsdale, NJ: Eribaum: 199–211.

11 Miceli, M., & Near, J. 1992. *Blowing the whistle.* New York: Lexington Books.

12 Trevino, L. K., & Victor, B. 2004. Peer reporting of unethical behavior: A social context perspective. *Academy of Management Journal*, 353:38–64.

13 Ethics Resource Center. 2003. *National Business Ethics Survey: How employees view ethics in their organizations.* Washington, DC.

14 PR Newswire. How to spot bad apples in the corporate bushel. 13 January 2003. Ithaca, NY.

15 Trevino & Nelson; Jackall, R. 1988. *Moral mazes: The world of corporate managers.* New York: Oxford University Press.

16 Drill team benched after scavenger incident, Sleepover busted. *Hartford Courant*, 15 November 2002; Paulson, A. Hazing case highlights girl violence. *Christian Science Monitor*, 9 May 2003.

17 Milgram, S. 1974. *Obedience to authority: An experimental view.* New York: Harper & Row.

18 Rest, J. S. (Ed.). 1986. *Moral development: Advances in research and theory.* New York: Praeger. Rest, J. S., et al. 1999. *Postconventional moral thinking: A neo-Kohlbergian approach.* Mahwah, NJ: Eribaum.

19 Ethics Resource Center, 2003. op. cit.

20 Schmitt, R. B. Companies add ethics training: Will it work? *Wall Street Journal* (Eastern edition), 4 November 2002: Bl.

21 Ethics Resource Center, 2003. op. cit.

22 Trevino, L. K., et al. 1999. Managing ethics and legal compliance: What works and what hurts. *California Management Review*, 41(2): 131–151.

23 Trevino & Nelson.

24 Toffler, B. L., with J. Reingold. 2003. *Final accounting: Ambition, greed, and the fall of Arthur Andersen.* New York: Broadway Books. All of the following material on Toffler's experience at Arthur Andersen is from this source.

25 Kansas, D. Plain talk: CEOs need to restore character in companies. *WSJ.COM.* Dow Jones & Company, Inc., 7 July 2002.

26 Trevino, L. K., Hartman, L. P., & Brown, M. 2000. Moral person and moral manager: How executives develop a reputation for ethical leadership. *California Management Review*, 42 (4): 128–142; Trevino, L. K., Brown, M., & Pincus-Hartman. 2003. A qualitative investigation of perceived executive ethical leadership: Perceptions from inside and outside the executive suite. *Human Relations*, 56(1): 5–37.

27 George, B. 2003. *Authentic leadership: Rediscovering the secrets to creating lasting value.* San Francisco: Jossey-Bass.

28 Byrne, J. 1999. *Chainsaw: The notorious career of Al Dunlap in the era of profit-at-any-price.* New York: HarperBusiness.

29 Tidwell, G. 1993. Accounting for the PTL scandal. *Today's CPA.* July/August: 29–32.

30 Frieswick, K. Boeing. *CFO Magazine*, 1 January 2004. *www.cfo.com.*

31 Trevino & Nelson; Loomis, C. Whatever it takes. *Fortune*, 25 November 2002: 76.

32 PR Newswire. Big majority believes tough new laws needed to

[33] address corporate fraud: Modest majority at least somewhat confident that Bush will support such laws. 27 July 2002.

[33] Kahaner, L. 2003. *Values, prosperity and the Talmud. Business lessons from the ancient rabbis.* New York: Wiley.

[34] McCabe, D., & Trevino, L. K. 1996. What we know about cheating in college. *Change: The Magazine of Higher Learning.* January/February: 28–33; McCabe, D. L., Trevino, L. K., & Butterfield, K. 2001. Cheating in academic institutions: A decade of research. *Ethics and Behavior,* 11(3): 219–232.

[35] Ethics Resource Center, 2003. op cit.

[36] Abrahamson, E. 1991. Managerial fads and fashions. *Academy of Management Review,* 16: 586–612; Carson, 1999; Gibson, J. W., & Tesone, D. V. 2001. Management fads: Emergence, evolution, and implications for managers. *The Academy of Management Executive,* 15: 122–133.

[37] Trevino & Nelson, K.

[38] Schein, E. H. 1985. *Organizational culture and leadership.* San Francisco, CA: Jossey-Bass.

[39] Trevino, L. K., Weaver, G. A., & Brown, M. 2000. Lovely at the top. Paper presented at the Academy of Management meeting, Toronto, August.

[40] Skinner, B. F. 1972. *Beyond freedom and dignity.* New York: Bantam Books.

[41] Trevino, L. K., & Youngblood, S. A. 1990. Bad apples in bad barrels: A causal analysis of ethical decision-making behavior. *Journal of Applied Psychology,* 75: 376–385.

[42] Trevino & Nelson.

[43] Toffler, p. 123.

[44] Trevino, L. K. 1992. The social implications of punishment in organizations: A justice perspective. *Academy of Management Review,* 17: 647–676; Trevino, L. K., & Ball, G. A. 1992. The social implications of punishing unethical behavior: Observers' cognitive and affective reactions. *Journal of Management,* 18: 751–768.

[45] Trevino, Hartman, & Brown.

Questions for Discussion and Reflection

1. What are Trevino's five myths of business ethics? Do you agree that all of them are myths?
2. How does the organizational setting impact your ethical decisions, according to Trevino?
3. What is the inconsistency that Trevino points out at Arthur Andersen, highlighted in Barbary Ley Toffler's book to which Trevino refers?
4. What are the four types of ethical leaders that Trevino identifies?
5. What do you think of Trevino's suggestion to reward ethical behavior?

The Cognitive and Social Psychology of Organizational Corruption

John M. Darley

Brooklyn Law Review 70, no. 4 (2005): 1177–94.

I. Corporate Corruption: The Nature and Magnitude of the Problem

Seen in the clear light cast by hindsight, several related puzzlements emerge about the recent cases of corporate corruption. First, although such scandals may begin small, they often grow to huge and blatant proportions. Second, because of their blatant character, they seem suicidally stupid. They will eventually be detected, with the inevitable disgrace that this will bring about for participants. Third, in their later stages, they come to involve a number of people in the organization who are busily involved in committing complicit actions that forward the corruption. How all of this certainly unethical and generally stupid thought and behavior comes about is the problem that I will examine in this article. In sum, people seem more recruitable into corrupt practices than we would think.

Another puzzlement that has come to our attention is what seems to be the high frequency with which these problems occur. One social scientist, looking back over the past few decades, has produced a chapter on thirty-six different and major cases of what he calls corporate "crime and violence."[1] Over the past few years, many major U.S. corporations have been caught in acts of corruption of quite startling magnitude.

To emphasize the question that this raises, why are so many of these incidents taking place in organizations that we would have thought were staffed by morally good people who were also prudent enough to realize that corrupt practices are frequently detected? That is, these corrupt incidents so often seem to involve corrupt, rule-breaking actions by people whom we would have assumed were moral, prudential actors. One conventional answer that resolves the puzzlement is to retrospectively decide that the assumption that we made about the people in question, that they were moral and prudential actors, was wrong; more specifically, that they were persons searching for corrupt opportunities, and were blinded to the probabilities of detection by their greed. The reader will recognize this stance as a variant of the "few bad apples" theory that has been cited to explain recent acts of corporate corruption, such as the mutual fund scandals or the organizational corruption that led to the torture of Iraqi prisoners of war at Abu Ghraib.

I want to suggest that the bad apple theory is at best a factually incorrect reading of what has happened. In fact it is simply a useful fiction that enables those who hide behind it to avoid the more thorough-going implications of recent transgressions. Specifically, clinging to the myth enables us to avoid the realization that the world of corporate or governmental ethics requires more attention and more painful redesign than the minor housekeeping implied by the course of action involving the elimination of already discovered malefactors from a system that we assume is otherwise working perfectly. For those that hide behind the bad apple myth, the sole remedy is to be more careful at the recruiting and training end of the organizational world; perhaps checking the credentials of job candidates better, perhaps by the technological fix promised by the quest for the modern "lie detec-tor" that will ensnare the wrongdoer on the way to his wrongdoing.

In this article, I will attempt to answer two questions that come to the mind of a psychologist who thinks about organizational corruption. First, why are so many "initial corrupt acts" taken in organizations? The answer cannot be that it is simply already-corrupt people who take these actions. Part of the answer is that some of the people who launch these corruption-initiating acts do not scrutinize these contemplated acts from an ethical perspective. Strange as it may seem, they do not see them as unethical.

The second question then becomes "why is it so easy to recruit other members of the organization to take the actions that amplify, extend, and continue these initiating actions to produce more and more corrupt outcomes?" What causes the organization to turn itself into one that works together to produce full-blown ethical transgressions? To foreshadow what I will suggest, the answer to this second question is threefold. First, because these others often accept the implied definition that the first actions were ethical in nature, the distance between that first act and the next one that amplifies it are not easily recognizable. Second, these follow-on acts are perhaps seen as ethically grey and further are produced out of considerations of group loyalty and commitment. Third, when one is a committed member of an organization, social identity theory[2] points out that we experience an alteration in personality. We "become" the prototypic member of the group, and the cues around us are that the prototypic group members are engaging in the corrupt actions. Thus we do so also. Finally, it is a little noticed truth that our society offers alternate identities to citizens, and some of them allow for acting in ways that, from the perspective of another identity the person could assume, are unethical.

To arrive at a better explanation of the apparently "infectious explosion" of these acts of corporate and organizational corruption, we need to consider several sources of information. First, the narratives that have emerged from first party participants in episodes of corruption, second, a new perspective that is emerging from judgment and decision making research about how it is that human decisions are made, and third we must take a closer look at the choices faced by individuals in an organization as the corruption begins to impinge on them.

II. The Initiation of Corrupt Sequences

How does the first corrupt act, the one that starts the process in the wrong direction, come about? Let's look at the narratives first. Sometimes the stories of corruption are simple. The organizational leaders deliberately act to bring about corrupt or otherwise immoral actions by the organizations they lead. Thus, Film Recovery Systems, Inc. hired workers who could not read English so that they would not be able to read warnings on the containers of dangerous chemicals they were using in the deliberately dangerous processes of recovering silver from used photographic plates.[3]

Perhaps the easiest explanation for how the company is able to enlist the organizational members, in this case the foremen who gave the workers their orders, in carrying out the actual immoral actions is that the superiors who are determined to carry out corrupt practices simply recruit subordinates who will be willing to engage in corrupt practices.

But we should also consider some more disquieting narratives, which seem to suggest that the corrupt practices are somehow stumbled into, without exactly being intentional. This is a disturbing perspective, one that challenges the notion that corruption begins in corruption, that the source of corrupt acts is those individuals who are corrupt and extract corruption from their followers.

From this perspective, acts that start a chain of other actions that ultimately result in full-blown corrupt actions often have their origins in actions that are not themselves corrupt, or at least not perceived as so by the original actors. If this is so, then we lose the comfort of being able to deny that we ourselves would ever be enmeshed in corrupt acts. We deny the message given by the frequency with which we discover that the actors enmeshed in corrupt activities are anguished individuals, frequently individuals who saw very clearly that detection was, if not inevitable, at least highly likely. They simply could not see a way to escape from the meshes of the collective processes that were ongoing. In our conventional way of thinking about ourselves, we are confident that we would know in advance that to do some set of actions would

be morally wrong, and that this realization, occurring prior to the actions, would prevent us from taking them.

These comforting thoughts turn out to be not true. Instead, people habitually commit actions that are self-serving, or unduly favorable to the organizations in which they are situated. On careful examination by a non-biased individual, these actions would be judged to be morally dubious or morally just wrong. But they don't receive that scrutiny. These actions are often the ones that set in motion a cascade of further corrupt actions; that set up what we might think of as the tornado of corruption that gathers force and pulls in more of the organization's members. So let us call these initiating actions the generative actions of corruption.

An example of this is useful, and there is one that is often cited in the literature. The circumstances that bring it about are the constant and high pressures for a for-profit organization to show a steady rise in earnings in each successive reporting quarter. But what counts as "a sale" that can be counted as earnings in a particular quarter? There is often judgment required in answering this question. But if the sale can be counted in the present quarter, and it will move earnings to a higher level, then the temptation is to "recognize the revenue" in the present quarter.

The example involves the practice of tobacco companies at the end of the business quarter.

> Loading wasn't unique to Reynolds, every company did it to some extent. Just prior to its regular semiannual price hikes, Reynolds regularly offered huge volumes of cigarettes to its customers—customers and supermarket chains—at the old prices. Customers loved it because they could sell low-cost cigarettes at the new, higher prices. Reynolds loved it because it cleared away unwanted inventory, kept the factories humming, and, most important, produced large, artificial, end of the quarter profits.[4]

The problem with this was that the distributors were free to return the cigarettes to Reynolds a month or two into the new quarter, after they had served to create the fictitious "profits" at the end of the last quarter.

III. The Unfortunate Case of Automatic Intuitive Judgments

Earlier I said that some of these acts that initiated further corrupt practices were not decided upon in any very thoughtful way. This needs explication. Recently, psychologists have summarized[5] a good deal of research and thinking about decision processes as requiring us to make a distinction between several rather independent systems that inform us about the world. For some time, we have known that we need to distinguish the human perceptual system from the human reasoning system. The perceptual system presents us with what we "see." We know in fact from countless demonstrations that perception is in fact a decision process, in the sense that it involves a good deal of past learning, often confirms stereotypes and generally sees what we expect to be there. However, partially because perceptual processes are overlearned, partially because they are what we now call automatic, we are misled about the truth of our perceptions. What we "see" must be what is true, a stance that is generally called naïve realism. What we see is unproblematically true. On the other hand, when we engage the reasoning system, which we sometimes use to make decisions, we are aware that reasoning is in progress because that reasoning is controlled and effortful. It often involves deliberately engaging problem solving rules that we have learned before. Therefore it is often cued into action by the conscious recognition of "what kind of problem that it is."

It is Kahneman's recommendation[6] that it is worth distinguishing a third cognitive system that shares components of both of these other systems, and exists intermediate between them. This we will call the intuitive system. More will be said about it in a minute, but let me tell you the use I will make of it in this discussion of corporate corruption. Recent research demonstrates that it is often the case that the acts that can originate unethical chains of occurrences arise from the quick decisions that are products of the intuitive judgment system. As one consequence, these acts often are not subject to the scrutiny by the actor that we apply to action decisions that we know are the product of the more deliberative reasoning system.

Here is the cash value of this realization. It pinpoints the attributional mistake we make when we think people who commit unethical actions are characterologically unethical. We expect that all good people, and we ourselves, scrutinize acts that we are contemplating taking from an ethical perspective. Therefore we do not take unethical courses of action. We then reason that if an ethically wrong act is committed, a person who is morally corrupt has committed it — we have returned to the "bad apple" theory. The way to deal with corruption is to screen out individuals who are corrupt.

The disturbing message from those that study decision making is that these reassuring thoughts are untrue. Many of the actions that begin cycles of corruption are the products of the intuitive judgment system, which means that they are rapidly arrived at, less than consciously considered, and unintentional in their ethical dubiousness. Further, they are often the product of pressure to make fast decisions. And under this condition, they are not subject to the monitoring of the decision, which is done by the reasoning system. As Kahneman[7] comments, "The monitoring is normally quite lax and allows many intuitive judgments to be expressed, including some that are erroneous." The suggestion that emerges is that the "natural" intuitive decision is likely to be a self interested one.

To quote researchers on this topic:

> [S]elf-interest is automatic, viscerally compelling, and often unconscious. Understanding one's ethical and professional obligations to others, in contrast, often involves a more thoughtful process. The automatic nature of self-interest gives it a primal power to influence judgment and makes it difficult for people to understand its influence on their judgment, let alone eradicate its influence.[8]

This decision may be overridden by the more deliberate thinking of the reasoning system, but only if something triggers that system into action. Thus, in sum, corrupt actions are often committed by people who are not themselves corrupt.

A. Self-Interested Intuitive Judgments

Let us trace this out at the level of personal decision making. A doctor orders perhaps unnecessary tests for a patient from a testing laboratory in which he has a financial stake. He knows he did not make a self-interested decision because he knows that "he didn't even think" of his stake in the laboratory while he was making the decision. A human relations person hires a member of her ethnic group for a job for which there were many candidates, and is sure that the decision is a fair one because she "examined the credentials of all of the candidates with an open mind." An auditor examines the accounts of a corporation his firm is engaged to audit and is sure his judgments of the acceptability of various decisions that the corporation has taken are appropriate according to a fair reading of the auditing standards. But in all of these cases, it is possible that in fact these sorts of decisions are frequently biased by self-interest,[9] in-group favoritism,[10] egocentricism,[11] or conflicts of interest.

B. A Biased Intuition and Its Entrapping Consequences

A well-known example from corporate life is useful here. It is driven by the previously mentioned desire of the organization to produce smooth patterns of earnings across the quarterly reporting periods. It involves what becomes "improper revenue recognition." The problem it solves is enabling sales of product to be sufficiently concrete to be bookkeeped in the present quarter rather than the next one.

The famous organizational example involves the Kurzweil Applied Intelligence Company.[12] First, the CEO allowed salespersons to post sales that in fact came in a few days after the quarter closed. This seems a rather harmless practice, but it creates a slippery slope problem that is well described by Tenbrunsel and Messick.[13] By allowing the act, the CEO authoritatively stamped that act as ethically allowable. But if it is acceptable to "count" orders a little after the quarter closed, then why is it not ethical to count orders that came in a day or so after the late orders that were allowable?

Eventually, the company went so far down this path that they counted orders far into the next quarter as revenue, and then salespersons began forging customer signatures on orders that they thought would be forthcoming and counted those. And so on.

Notice two things that were happening. First, eventually a line was crossed from ethically grey actions to blatantly illegal ones; eventually when the auditors wrote to customers to verify sales contracts, bogus responses from "the customers" were also forged. And second, notice that the eventual fraudulent endpoint was a consequence of the first grey actions. Robbing sales from the next quarter to pad results for this quarter made it more likely that the next quarter would be short even more sales. Thus the company was in some very real sense committing itself to an increasingly morally wrong and desperate set of escalating acts. But that commitment was unlikely to be apparent to the actors who initially claimed a few sales from the beginning of the next quarter. The slippery slope was inevitable but unforeseen.

The moral is that an initial ethically grey act can later be seen as committing the corporation to further and further actions, and these later actions were more and more clearly across any ethically boundaries that could be imagined when the first steps were taken.

IV. Entrainment

I have given a brief sketch of psychologists' current thinking of the two rather different stances in which decisions get made. One way of drawing the implications of this for the present problem is to say that people are ethical, but only intermittently so. Whether we will be ethical depends on whether events in the past or the present trigger the reasoning system to generate a checking ethical perspective on courses of action that are generated from other more intuitive perspectives. This solves the problem of why it is that so many ethically bad actions are authored by individuals who are not themselves chronically unethical.

The next problem to solve is why these initial unethical actions so often seem to capture others in the organization, who build on, add to, and amplify the continuing chain of unethical actions. This past example of counting non-existent orders as revenue is one such example.

Let me give you a metaphor for what I want to suggest. Entrainment is a concept that comes from the early twentieth century that I want to borrow for an organizational process. Originally it referred to a perceptual phenomenon: an object is moving in one direction. As it passes other stationary objects, those objects themselves begin to move, and they move in the same direction as the original object. This seems to be a useful visual metaphor for the way that a corrupt act seems to affect an organization. Often it spreads in the following senses. More and more people commit similar acts, often ones "triggered" by the original acts, and those subsequent acts often grow more extreme in their wrongness. How this comes about is the next question to answer.

A. Imperceptible Differences

If an action is committed, and is not criticized, punished, or otherwise labeled as wrong, it becomes "the standard." It may not be criticized, even though many in the organization think that it is wrong, because their insecurity or their lower position in the organizational hierarchy makes them unwilling to say publicly what they really believe, which is that it is wrong. But when this happens, psychological research demonstrates an interesting process called "pluralistic ignorance."[14] Rather than realize that the other silent individuals are being silent for exactly the same reasons that he is, the individual tends to conclude that these others think that the act is an acceptably moral one and are keeping silent for that reason.[15] The individual then, is the deviant, and under this pressure, comes to think that the act is more normal and more ethical than he previously thought. It is now the standard for what is allowable in this organizational context.

But then, a slightly more unethical action becomes possible, and the then relevant question is the distance of this next possible act from the act that is now the standard. Tenbrunsel and Messick have a useful term for this, which is the "induction mechanism."[16] "This mechanism uses the past practices of an organization as a benchmark for evaluating new practices. If the past practices were ethical and acceptable, then practices that are similar and not too different are also acceptable."[17] In small steps, an organization moves from ethical actions to ones that are ethically grey to ones that are simply immoral.

It is possible that by progressing in these small steps, the organizational group never becomes aware of the moral wrongness of the procedures with which they end up. Recent business pages are full of reports of how insurance brokers got into the pattern of taking what were essentially kickbacks from insurance

firms to whom they brought clients. The stories of the final stages of this process seem so prototypically corrupt that it is hard to believe that the perpetrators could code them as anything but unethical, but that they did so is not yet clear. However, it is difficult to think that at least some of those involved did not at some point see the wrongness of their actions.

Here are some descriptions of the patterns of actions once the system was in full swing. Apparently charades were staged, in which some insurance providers were solicited to put in bids for insuring the broker's clients, but the bids were organized so that they would be higher than the bid of the provider who was to be the eventual winner of the insurance contract. The purpose of this was to provide "proof" to the client that the broker had solicited bids and was giving the contract to the lowest bidder, as was proper.

This is an interesting process, since it engages the high-bidding insurance providers in the charade, with the incentive that they someday will be allowed to be the "lowest bidder" and win a contract. One frequently sees mechanisms for recruiting other organizational units into a corrupt system, and here we have identified one.

These patterns, described as I have done, from the perspective of the final stages of the system, seem to so clearly be corrupt that it is hard to believe that they can be anything other than the consciously immoral acts of conspirators. However, if we think of a person being recruited into the system, it is possible that she would simply see it "as the way we do things around here." We will return to this theme later.

B. Loss Aversion

Recent psychological research has conclusively demonstrated that people will go to great lengths to avoid losses.[18] Several practices in corporate organizations have inadvertently guaranteed that that there will be "losses" to be averted. To illustrate this, we will return to our now familiar example of quarterly profits. The stock prices of American companies are significantly dependent on the company slightly increasing its earnings on a quarter-by-quarter basis. This apparently is taken as the sure sign of a steadily more profitable company, one that one should invest in. However, on reflection, there are many reasons why good companies would not produce that patterning of profit: seasonal sales profiles for one, high expenditures in one quarter for research and development costs is another. Companies are led to accounting practices that allow for "earnings management" to enable them to produce the preferred steady rise in earnings even when more standard accounting practices would produce variable quarter by quarter gains.

Suppose that you are in control of the accounting process in such a company and see that some perfectly justifiable expenses will bring you to earnings that fall just below those of the last quarter. And suppose that you correctly think that the "increased earnings every quarter" criterion is a stupid one. Yet you know that if you show reduced earnings in this quarter, the price of the company stock will drop, and research reports may comment about "disappointments at company X." If you are one of the company's executives that has a "pay for performance" plan, you realize that you may lose considerable sums of money, money that you had counted as already in your pockets. Would you stretch accounting rules to produce increased earnings? Perhaps not. But would you have been clever enough to "stash" some earnings from a previous highly profitable quarter that could now be pulled out of the "cookie jar"[19] to produce those earnings in this quarter? They were, after all, perfectly legitimate. Would you be morally wrong to ensure that your company was buffered from the ups and downs in stock prices caused by the essentially stupid focus on increases in quarter-by-quarter earnings?

Now recognize what is often the case, which is that the company CEO receives a good deal of added incentive pay if the corporation "makes its numbers" on a quarter-by-quarter basis. This means that there will be a good deal of pressure on the auditing group to make the audit output conform to the "steady growth in earnings" numbers. So the real question is not whether you yourself would independently produce numbers that you think it might be morally justified to produce, but whether you would resist pressures from corporate superiors to do so. And thinking about this as the CFO would, you should realize that there are a number of cases in which CFO's have been dead-ended or fired for refusing to go along with these directives from above.[20] Loss aversion might be less of

an abstract concept, and more a realistic fear of loss of job.

V. Group Loyalty and Commitment

We now see how an individual in an organization can impulsively take an action that is, from a perspective that was not apparent to the actor, wrong in the sense of being an action with morally flawed outcomes. Eventually, this action becomes known to other members of the organization. The question is how they react to it. We would hope that they would repudiate it, both because it is wrong and because it is likely to commit the organization to a bad course of action. However, there is one problem with people following this path. The action has already been taken. It is done. The pollutants have already been dumped into the river, or the quarter's profits have been overstated, or the member of my in-group has been hired. Often the consequences of these actions are irreversible. And even in those few occasions when the action consequences can somehow be reversed, it is still the case that there are likely to be records around that they were the actions initially taken by the organization.

Previously we considered the possibility that the performance of actions that from some outside perspective would be considered wrong might instead convince others within the organization that those actions were right in the context in which they were committed. They were, in other words, the way that my company does things. Now I want to consider another branch of the situation; the branch in which the other actors in the organization realize that the act is bad, either intrinsically bad or bad because of the consequences that will follow. Since the act has already been committed, the decision is not about making it disappear—that cannot be made to happen. The decision is between making others in the organization aware that bad actions have been taken and letting them continue, or abetting their continuation.

It is likely, for reasons of loyalty to the group, loyalty to the person who made the bad decision, and a feeling that the commitment to the course of action is irrevocable, that others in the group will allow or abet the continuation of the actions. This is particularly true when the actors who have become aware take actions that seem to temporize, and keep open the possibilities of later actions that halt the bad practices. These actually often allow the bad course of action to continue to develop, because if one does not intervene when one first becomes aware, it is very difficult to find an exact time when one should intervene later.

A famous example of this comes from the first person account of the fraud that the Goodrich Company backed into committing when they were pursuing a design for aircraft brakes that could not possibly work.[21] Briefly, an engineer had made calculational mistakes in designing a brake assembly for an airplane. The plans called for brake lining pads that were too small to provide the braking friction to stop the plane in the required distance. "The brake was too small. There simply was not enough surface area on the disk to stop the aircraft without generating the excessive heat that caused the linings to fail."[22]

From the point of view of our analysis, a critical incident then occurred. "New menaces appeared. An engineering team from LTV (the primary contractors) arrived at the plant to get a good look at the brake in action. Luckily, they stayed only a few days, and Goodrich engineers managed to cover the true situation without too much difficulty."[23] What I suggest is that the visit of outsiders caused the Goodrich personnel, although aware of the eventual guaranteed failure of the brake assembly, to rally to the support of their fellow engineers to conceal this critical fact. By doing so, many of them became complicit and caught up in perpetuating the fraud.

A different case, with the same ultimate consequence, occurs when the individual who first committed the bad action shifts perspective, and sees the potential bad consequences of the bad action that he launched. Here he needs to make sense of his own past actions. The true reason that the person committed the action is that he did not think at the time about the potential bad consequences of the action. From the intuitive perspective he adopted at the time of the decision, it was the right decision—or at least not the wrong one. This is the whole message of the previous excursion into the intuition-based decision system. However, one of psychology's more interesting discoveries is that people do not grant themselves this sort of charity. Instead, hindsight causes them to

think that it was a well-considered decision, made by the conscious, reasoning system. This retrospective perspective leads them to go into a sort of decision-hiding mode, in which they seek to deny their involvement in the decision, or to experience the dissonance they feel, and think of the reasons that the decision was the right one. To do the latter, they have to think about themselves in different ways.

A. Social Identity Considerations

A theory developed in the last two decades[24] has made and validated a very important point. When an individual is a member of a group, in the sense that she is committed to the purposes of the group and that a group has tasks to do, the task of the individual is to first become a prototypical member of that group, and then help the group as best she can in reaching its goals. Among other things, this may mean adopting the moral perspectives of the group.[25] And recall what we said earlier. Because of pluralistic ignorance, she may not be aware that others in the group consider the initial act an unethical one. The signal that silence conveys to her is the incorrect but persuasive message that the group regards the initiating act as a morally appropriate one. The task of the individual group member is to accept that decision and move the group forward. This may mean taking actions that conceal the prior transgressions, but these may also be the actions that continue the bad course of action. In the example from *Why Should My Conscience Bother Me?*[26] the loyalty-driven actions of the Goodrich workers in assuring the visiting team from the contractor that "everything is going along ok," contributed to the continuation of the doomed fraud.[27] The contractor then did not raise questions that could have headed off the final bad outcome.

B. Alternate Identities Are on Offer

The concept of identity can be made to do more work. There are identities in which it is part of the role enactment to adopt a different moral code from the one we usually espouse. The violence endemic in hockey and American football is an example. One inflicts violence on others in ways that would normally involve morally unacceptable acts. Of course, the allowable violence is constrained by rules, but there are two interesting things to note about that. Some acts of violence, like "late hits" in football and "slashing" in hockey are against the rules, but a second set of rules is in existence to assign penalties for those rule infractions, which in some sense brings the rule violations "within" a broader domain of "rule acceptable" actions. Second, as has been commented on by those who follow sports, team members often collectively adopt a "persona" that makes the goal of inflicting harm on the other side acceptable and even desired. "Let's get out there and knock them dead" is an injunction that brings violence within the somewhat ambiguous orbit of legitimacy in game settings. Other roles contain elements that legitimate morally dubious actions against others.

And all of us can give a reasonable performance in at least many of the roles. Let me give you an example of a situation in which a person who had detected corruption and is set to denounce it, is sent away instead with an offer of a role. If he accepts the role, he will embrace the deception and play his part in continuing and expanding it. He has entered the situation as an upstanding person of high moral rectitude, which too is a role. But how will he continue on when that role is challenged? Notice in this specific situation, considerable pressure exists to accept the new, deception-embracing role.

The dilemma arose for Michael Lewis, and is described in his book *Liar's Poker*,[28] in which he summarizes his experiences as a bond salesman in training with Salomon Brothers. An experienced trader had advised him that AT&T bonds would be good ones to sell to his customers, and he sold about three million dollars worth to one of his clients. The bonds rapidly dropped in value, harming the customer and harming the relationship of trust that Lewis had built with the customer. A more experienced salesman clued Lewis that the reason that these bonds were "good ones to sell" was that they were in Salomon Brothers' inventory, and the firm was quite sure that their value was going to decline. Thus they wanted to unload the bonds, and did so on unwary clients.

Lewis protested to the trader, arguing that they had quite badly harmed the client and behaved in a way that contradicted their high-flown ethics codes about duties to customers. "Look," he (the trader) said, losing his patience, "who do you work for, this guy or Salomon Brothers?" At this point, Lewis realized that the real practice of Salomon Brothers was to mistreat clients for the good of the firm. If he were to stay at Salomon Brothers, he would need to adopt the identity of "the jammer," a person who was willing to take these sorts of trust-violating actions. But the only other identity available to him at the moment of decision was that of a naïve fool, who did not know the ways that the real world worked. And he was surrounded, in the close confines of the trading floor, by many others who would certainly have contempt for a naïve fool and publicly express that contempt. These are the circumstances in which people adopt identities that enable them to act unethically toward certain groups of others.

VI. Conclusion

I have attempted to solve two puzzles. First, why so many acts that generate bad moral consequences are begun by people we would think are proper moral actors. The answer is that they are what most of us are, which is intermittent moral actors. They take a moral perspective if the reasoning system is engaged, but otherwise can be driven by quite intuitive and automatic thinking to "solve the immediate problem" which will often be done quite pragmatically.

The second problem might be called the "lemmings" problem. Why is it that other people in the organization so often seem to aid, abet, and advance the morally bad course of action? My answer here was more complicated, and involved a set of independent but generally correlated processes. Some of the processes lead to the prior corrupt act being perceived as ethically appropriate "within the organizational context." Others work by the engagement of a group loyalty or commitment, which causes people to work to conceal the prior corrupt actions from public view. This often entails further corrupt actions, either "covering up" the previous actions, or continuing them. It is sometimes the case that actors who previously were careful to act in moral ways, are now recruited into adopting a persona that goes along with, and even becomes an independent origin of corrupt practices.

Notes

[1] Russell Mokhiber, "Corporate Crime and Violence: Big Business, Power and the Abuse of the Public Trust" (1988).

[2] Michael A. Hogg and Elizabeth A. Hardie, "Prototypicality, Conformity and Depersonalized Attraction: A Self-Categorization Analysis of Group Cohesiveness," 3 *Brit. J. Social Psychol.* 41–56 (1992).

[3] A succinct account of this corporation and its misdeeds is given in Nancy Frank, "Murder in the Workplace," in *Corporate Violence*, Stuart L. Hills ed. (1987).

[4] Bryan Burrough and John Helyar, *Barbarians at the Gate: The Fall of RJR Nabisco* 58 (Harper Perennial ed., HarperCollins 1991) (1990).

[5] Daniel Kahneman, "A Perspective of Judgment and Choice: Mapping Bounded Rationality," 58 *Am. Psychol.* 697, 697–720 (2003).

[6] Id. at 697–99.

[7] Id. at 699.

[8] Don A. Moore and George Loewenstein, "Self-Interest, Automaticity and the Psychology of Conflict of Interest," 17 *Social Just. Res.* 189, 189–202 (2004).

[9] Id.

[10] Nilanjana Dasgupta, "Implicit Ingroup Favoritism, Outgroup Favoritism, and Their Behavioral Manifestations," 17 *Social Just. Res.* 143, 143–69 (2004). For a review of implicit ingroup favoritism research, see id. at 146–48.

[11] For a review of the work on egocentric ethics, see Nicholas Epley and Eugene Caruso, "Egocentric Ethics," 17 *Social Just. Res.* 171, 171–87 (2004).

[12] Mark Maremont, "Anatomy of a Fraud," *Bus. Week*, Sept. 16, 1996 at 90–94.

[13] Ann Tenbrunsel and David Messick, "Ethical Fading, the Role of Self-Deception in Unethical Behavior," 17 *Social Just. Res.* 223, 228–29 (2004).

[14] Deborah A. Prentice and Dale T. Miller, "Pluralistic Ignorance and Alcohol Use on Campus: Some Consequences of Misperceiving the Social Norm," 64 *J. Personality & Social Psychol.* 243, 243–56 (1993).

[15] Dale T. Miller & Cathy McFarland, "Pluralistic Ignorance: When Similarity Is Interpreted as Dissimilarity," 53 *J. Personality & Social Psychol.* 298, 298–305 (1987).

[16] Tenbrunsel and Messick, supra note 13, at 228.

[17] Id.

[18] See Daniel Kahneman et al., "Prospect Theory: An Analysis of Decision under Risk," 47 *Econometrica* 263, 263–91 (1979).

[19] Paul Munter, "SEC Sharply Criticized 'Earnings Management,'" *J. Corp. Acct. & Fin.* 31, 34 (1999).

[20] For a discussion of this, see Stephen Barr, "You're Fired," *CFO*, Apr. 1, 2000.

[21] Kermit Vandivier, "Why Should My Conscience Bother Me?" in *Corporate Violence*, Stuart L. Hills ed., 145–72 (1987).

[22] Id. at 148.

[23] Id. at 150.

[24] Dominic Abrams and Michael Hogg, *Social Identity Theory: Constructive and Critical Advances* (1990).

[25] Henri Tajfel, "Cognitive Aspects of Prejudice," 1 *J. Biosocial Sci.*, 173, 173–91 (1969).

[26] See Vandivier, supra note 21.

[27] See id.

[28] Michael Lewis, *Liar's Poker* (1989).

Questions for Discussion and Reflection

1. According to Darley, why do individuals initiate corrupt acts in organizations? Do you think it's possible for people to "stumble into" corrupt acts? Why or why not?
2. Why does Darley think that it is so easy to recruit others into corrupt actions?
3. What does Darley mean by the concept of "entrainment"? How do you think that relates to an environment that is conducive to ethical behavior?
4. According to Darley, how does group loyalty contribute to an environment conducive to fostering corruption? Do you agree?

Al Erisman: "Sherron Watkins: Did We Learn the Lessons from Enron?"
Ethix 53, June 2007

Sherron Watkins is the former vice president of Enron Corporation who alerted then-CEO Ken Lay in August 2001 to accounting irregularities within the company, warning him that Enron "might implode in a wave of accounting scandals." She has testified before Congressional committees from the House and Senate investigating Enron's demise. *Time* magazine named Sherron, along with two others, Coleen Rowley of the FBI and Cynthia Cooper of WorldCom, as their 2002 Persons of the Year, for being "people who did right just by doing their jobs rightly."

Now an independent speaker and consultant, she is co-author of *Power Failure: The Inside Story of the Collapse of Enron* (Doubleday, 2003).

Prior to joining Enron in 1993, Ms. Watkins worked for three years as the portfolio manager of MG Trade Finance Corp., a commodity lending boutique in New York, and for eight years in the auditing group of both the New York and Houston offices of Arthur Andersen.

Ms. Watkins is a certified public accountant. She holds a master's in professional accounting, as well as a B.B.A. in accounting and business honors from the University of Texas at Austin.

• • •

Ethix: *Was there a time when you really enjoyed your work at Enron?*

Sherron Watkins: Between 1993 and 1995, Enron's business was growing; the Jedi portfolio that I was working on in the finance area was a lot of fun. We were loaning money and investing in various oil and gas companies. It was exciting to see them have their dreams realized with our financing. And we were making money on the financing.

When did it start to change?

Watkins: The warning signs of fraud were there in 1996, and I now take those much more seriously than I did back then. In 1996, I simply protested, got nowhere, and switched divisions.

In 1996, the capital and trading division of Enron, run by Jeff Skilling, was on the wrong side of a gas trade and was facing a losing quarter. There were lots of meetings trying to figure out how the earnings shortfall was going to be filled. That is when "fair value" was created.

Enron was marking its commodity contracts to market, and that was fairly legitimate. With fair value accounting, they took this idea to a new level. They purchased a publicly traded company and took it private, with the intent of revamping it and taking it public again in five or six years. Just 27 days after the deal closed, Enron was raising its value by 50 percent. That flies in the face of generally accepted accounting principles. The fair-market value is what two arms length parties will pay for something. By saying this company is worth 50 percent more in just 27 days, they are claiming they hoodwinked the market somehow. This was an oil and gas development company that had drilled eight wells in those 27 days, seven of which were successful. The success was the reason given for the revaluation; however, the company's property development plan was all infill shallow drilling. These companies typically drill 100 wells in a year, and 80 percent of them are supposed to be successful, so this is no basis for raising the value. A widget maker cannot say it is worth more because they successfully produce the number of widgets they usually produce. I thought that was way over a line and protested to some Arthur Andersen partners I knew, and internal people, but did not get anywhere.

Then Andy Fastow (CFO) asked me to lie to one of our investors, and it was just a horribly uncomfortable situation. The fair-value accounting was happening within the Jedi portfolio, which I ran. I was not in the accounting department, but I did not want my name associated with that practice. So I moved to Enron International. The time period I worked at Enron International may have been the happiest at Enron. It ran like a normal company. Rebecca Mark and Joe Sutton, the two people running the division, were heavily involved in the details. They crunched numbers and routinely turned things down that did not have a completely rosy outlook.

But things went haywire in 1999 when Jeff Skilling decided to disband Enron International and pump up Broadband. So I would say the worst time was from Broadband on, basically 2000 to the end in late 2001.

A Personal Challenge

Did you think about quitting? Just walking away from it?

Watkins: Certainly I thought about quitting in 1996, but I had not yet made vice president. Back in those days nobody in Houston would have believed you would leave Enron. Enron was the cat's meow up until 2001. You do not get hired as a director and leave as a director. People would think you were being pushed out.

After I made vice president, my personal situation had changed. I had married and had a baby, and I wanted to have a second baby. When I transferred into Broadband after the demise of International, I became very disillusioned about the direction of Enron and had a personal crisis. Do I look for another job or do I try to have a second baby and then go? A successful maternity leave that doesn't hurt a career only happens when you are established long term at a company. So I was planning to have that second child and then leave. I never had the second baby.

Factors in the Enron Failure

What were the contributing factors in Enron's behavior?

Watkins: One of the major factors to the downfall of Enron was the performance ranking process. It was known as "rank and yank," and it was fairly brutal. Every six months your name was on a table with your peers. Early on in the '90s, they would rent a big conference room at a hotel, off site so you could not go back to your office. Literally, it started at 8 in the morning, and you would not be able to leave. Many times I was there until 2 in the (next) morning.

We reviewed all of the categories of people from admin to senior specialist to manager to director, and each category was rank ordered, initially with placards on the table. Someone would come by and say, "This &&&%#@ does not deserve to be up here. They did X, Y, Z to me, so they are down here." It resembled an Animal House fraternity selection process. Each employee's picture was up on the wall, projected electronically. They punched the button and looked at the bell curve, force-fitting people into groups from excellent to poor. There were only 5 or 10 percent of the people in the top category, 10 or 15 in the next, etc. Category four was a dangerous position, and category five meant you are going to be out of the company. People were always thinking, what have I done for Enron lately, what are people going to say about me on that table?

GE supposedly follows a similar process, but they value the right things. The things that put you at the top of the table have stayed in line with the company's core values. At Enron what put you at the top of the table were earnings. The means by which you generated those earnings did not matter, and that is where it started to come apart. Everyone was focused on the earnings they were generating.

So as these questionable deals were done, I witnessed smart people scratching their head but never understanding the problems. For example, they set up the Raptors structures, off balance-sheet companies funded with the promise of Enron stock. It was like a company not selling enough widgets, so they set up a company to buy the widgets and funded this new shell company with a promise of their own stock. The original company then sells the shell company widgets so that sales figures remain on target. The plan was that the shell company would then sell the widgets in the marketplace for cash; however, if the shell company is unable to sell the widgets out to third parties, then that shell company is able to access that pile of stock from the original company to raise cash and pay the amount owed for the widgets. Business and accounting does not work that way, but that was in effect what Enron was doing.

People would hear about the deals and not understand them. But they were under so much pressure for their own deal closings and earnings that they would say, "I know Arthur Andersen looked at this and they blessed it. I don't have time to focus on understanding it." Smart people stopped asking questions. They did not have time to get to the bottom of something that was bothering their gut, because they had to focus on that next deal. Some were concerned, such as the head of our Control and Risk Management, Rick Buy, and Vince Kaminski and some of his folks. In the end, they could not pursue it as far as they would like because of that "rank and yank" treadmill.

Blowing the Whistle

Can you talk a little bit about the process you went through that led you to decide to write the memo to Ken Lay? How did you evaluate that decision?

Watkins: Well, there was no process. Literally it was simply a reaction. I had gone back to work for Andy Fastow in the summer of 2001. I stumbled across these Raptors in the course of my work in July, and understood that they were capitalized with Enron stock. I started interviewing with Enron's competitors in earnest. I wanted out as soon as possible. I put my family plans on hold and just said I have to get out of here. I cannot work for a company that is committing such fraud.

I planned to meet with Jeff Skilling on my last day, when I had a contract with another company. But I will tell you, it was going to be tough to get up the courage to meet him because he really was kind of a ruthless "take no prisoners" type of guy. So I was even worried about it with the safety net of another job. But then he quit, which surprised everyone. The picture of the *Titanic* came quickly to mind. I was a crew member seeing the water come in, and Skilling's resignation was like the last partition breaking. It was the final piece of evidence that what I was seeing was really bad, and that he knew what was coming.

He quit on a Tuesday, and on Wednesday morning I typed an anonymous letter and sent it to Ken Lay, knowing that an all-employee meeting was coming up on Thursday. They had a process for looking at these things, and I just wanted to float it up there, so if he was really looking for the reason Jeff Skilling was leaving, maybe he would inquire about it. I went to the all-employee meeting, and Ken Lay was talking about our values: respect, integrity, communication, and excellence. He was the kinder, gentler face of Enron. He got this tremendous standing ovation when he announced that he was stepping back in as CEO. He said that our vision and values had slipped, that

we need to get back to our core values. And he said if anyone is truly troubled out there about anything that Enron is doing, please feel free to speak to Steve Kean, Cindy Olson (the head of human resources), or himself. But he didn't say anything about my memo.

I met with Cindy Olson that very afternoon. When I showed her the page I had sent to Ken Lay, she said, "Ken gravitates toward good news. He probably showed this to Rick Causey, the chief accounting officer, and to Andy, and they said there is no basis for concern. So he just threw it away. For him the issue is resolved. But he does better meeting people face to face. Would you be willing to meet with him?" I agreed to identify myself, and set up a meeting with him for the following week. That is about all there was to my thinking process.

What was your expectation for your meeting with Ken Lay?

Watkins: Unlike Jeff Skilling, who had abandoned ship, my view was that Ken Lay was an honorable, ethical man. I thought when I told him his ship had a fatal hole, he would check it out. If there was such a hole, he would try to save jobs and business lines, and he would form a crisis management team.

Ken Lay asked executives, as well as Vinson & Elkins, to relook at the plans to make sure we were unsinkable. But nobody went below deck to see if there was a hole. What I put in front of him was one basic question about the Raptor entities that owed Enron a lot of money. How were they going to fund the $500–700 million in losses? Was it from outside parties, from outside investors or creditors, or was it from Enron stock? If they are going to pay Enron back using Enron stock, I said, then we are done for.

If he had just tried to answer that question and truthfully engage another accounting firm about it, he would not have been able to escape the fact that Enron had committed accounting fraud. But he never looked at that question. He looked at whether I was bringing up anything new. He reassured me that the board knew about the Raptors, that Arthur Andersen had looked at the Raptors. It was bizarre. The CEO has to have pristine ethics, because if there is any erosion in values at the top, it gets magnified in the trenches.

I am often asked what I would do differently. The answer takes me back to 1996. The fair-value stuff I saw in 1996 was the beginning of the fraud, and I should have made an even bigger deal about it back then. But I also should have paid more careful attention to Ken Lay's reaction to me in 2001. If he was really looking into this, I would have had more meetings with Vinson & Elkins. I would have had a meeting with the general counsel at Enron, who never once called to meet with me.

Response from Others

Near the end, when it became apparent that you were making some waves, what was the reaction of your peers?

Watkins: Actually, not many people knew of my meeting with Ken Lay or that I was bringing up accounting fraud concerns until Congress leaked my memos to the press in January of 2002, well after the bankruptcy.

As I was planning to meet with Ken Lay in August of 2001, in that five-day period between the all-employee meeting and my scheduled appointment with Ken Lay, no one really knew what I was doing unless I told them, or made inquiries. During that five-day window of preparation work for me, certain employees in the finance, control and risk and accounting departments were very willing to feed me information. I think employees want to work for an ethical company. They saw things that bothered them and did not like it, so people were very willing to get me some spreadsheets, presentations, data, etc.

In hindsight, I also wish that some of my peers had gone with me to meet with Ken Lay. Jordan Mintz was an in-house lawyer who was very concerned about this. I did not know that he had already taken these things to another law firm, and they had said they are very problematic. I did not know that Vince Kaminski had protested these things. So if I had just Vince and Jordan with me, the outcome might have been different.

But the company went bankrupt and no one really knew about my role until Congress leaked my memos in mid January 2002. Within a couple of days the *New York Times* was printing the whole thing. I was inundated with a huge flood of support. People were concerned that the top executives would get away with it, and all the blame would go to Andy Fastow. It was not all Andy, but at this point, the executives had circled the wagons and said, "There is your crook; it is Andy Fastow."

Many employees knew that if their department had an earnings hole, the business heads went to Andy to fill it. Filling earnings holes with business done with your CFO and one of his funny structures made employees uncomfortable to say the least. The business unit heads, like all of us, were getting stock options that, over time, were quite lucrative. Many had done quite well for themselves. I believe over $1 billion of stock and stock options had been cashed out by Enron executives and board members within the last one–two years of the company's existence. If the whole mess could be blamed on Andy Fastow, the crooked CFO, then it was almost the perfect crime with Andy as the fall guy. They all could have gone home rich with $30 million to $100 million in the bank and Andy sitting in prison for life.

Advice

What advice would you give someone else in a position similar to yours?

Watkins: I tell college students, "If your values are being challenged, get out, because you cannot change an unethical corporation unless you are at the very top. Pay attention to rationalizations." The famous rationalization at Enron was, "What do we have accounting rules in this country for, if you do not use them?"

There is a story in *The Smartest Guys in the Room* that is perfect for describing how Enron was misusing accounting rules. They interviewed an accounting executive, unnamed, and he described how Enron rationalized nearly $15 billion off balance-sheet debt that had been recorded as asset sales rather than debt. The accounting rules are very specific for collateralized mortgage obligations for transferring risks, for rules when companies move assets into a special purpose vehicle and in effect sell the risk to a bank or an insurance company or an institution, and they are able to treat that as an asset sale. The analogy for Enron's use of these rules goes like this: Let's call the asset sale treatment a duck.

What Enron has is a dog, which is debt, but Enron wanted the duck treatment. So they looked through the accounting rules, which are very, very specific, and they describe what it takes to be a duck. You must have a white feathery back, orange webbed feet, and a yellow bill. So Enron takes its dog, glues white feathers all over its back, puts some orange plastic rubber feet on its little paws, straps a yellow bill to its nose and tells Arthur Andersen, "You tell me I do not have a duck. I meet all the conditions of a duck and I have a duck and I am going to treat this thing as a duck," and they are very forceful about it. They used rules in ways they were never meant to be used.

I counsel people, don't accept rules over principles. You know what the underlying principles are. If someone is in the unfortunate position where I was, I say don't go it alone. I should have found a few more people to go with me, because then they could not have dismissed me as one lone person.

What makes this country great is the system of checks and balances, and you need that system of checks and balances to work. You should not have to rely on individuals to have to jump in front of a train to stop something bad from happening. My warnings did not stop anything bad from happening. They were too little, too late. Enron is dead, Arthur Andersen is dead. Thousands of employees and shareholders are wiped out. The public accounting that Arthur Andersen should have been doing failed, the legal work that Vinson & Elkins was doing failed. The debt lending practices of the big banks failed.

It worries me that we are in this big climate of push back, where people are pushing against regulations, including the Sarbanes Oxley Act. Hank Paulson has a committee that includes John Thornton and others who are trying to limit the accountability and the liability of CEOs. We are repeating a pattern but we are not handling it correctly, and I really think we are at a crossroads, and we may choose the wrong path.

When I was a young auditor, all the worker safety and environmental regulations were put in place. Companies were really balking, saying that this is going to drive business overseas; we cannot compete if we have to live up to these environmental pollution standards or these worker-safety standards. But the country held firm. There was moral outrage that workers were losing their eyes or their limbs or their fingers or put in cancer-inducing situations. You can do business in a way that does not pollute the environment, and does not put workers in harm's way. We lived through those regulations and found a way, and our capitalist system works better for it.

Now they are pushing back on this accountability, and if you really look at the Sarbanes Oxley Act, it does nothing more than codify best practices. It does make it easier for CEOs to go to prison, but only for producing manipulated, misleading financial statements. They should not be doing that anyway. They should not even have a risk of doing that. It protects whistleblowers. It has independent directors meeting without management present. Things that were best practices, but the companies weren't doing them.

You don't need bulletproof internal controls; you need a zero-tolerance policy for ethically challenged employees. Internal controls should not prevent every fraud from happening, because that would be too costly and would not make sense. An internal-control system should be robust enough that it identifies ethically challenged employees so you can fire them. Unfortunately, leaders will fire an ethically challenged employee who is a dud. But if an ethically challenged employee is good with customers or generates a lot of earnings, they give that person a second chance. Citigroup is a prime example. They gave just a reprimand to those London traders who manipulated the Euro bond market. They did fire some folks over their Japanese private-banking snafu. But when you give ethically challenged employees a second chance, they just tend to go into a stealth mode and figure out an even sneakier way to get to their ends.

I worry that we do not have enough moral outrage about the accountability problems. It will be the country's downfall if we do not hold leaders accountable.

As I have read about the Enron case, Skilling, Fastow, and others seemed to be actively engaged in fraud, while Ken Lay kept trying to distance himself. He was not actively doing the wrong, but he was also not playing his leadership role. Is that accurate?

Watkins: Mostly. The story of the emperor's new clothing is an awfully good analogy to explain Ken Lay. In that fable, you have the swindlers, and I consider them to be Skilling and Fastow. But Ken Lay, the emperor, is focused on his appearance, very vain, always looking for the next set of fancy clothes and he does not pay attention to his kingdom at all. He was focused on the outward appearance of Enron, never involved in the details.

In that fable when the little boy says, "He is naked," the emperor does feel the chill in the air and realizes that if he had clothes, he would not feel so cold. But he holds his head up high and keeps marching down the parade ground, because what is he to do? He is the emperor. I think Ken Lay got stuck in a moment in time when he could have addressed the problem, or just kept marching. He chose to keep marching, but for him, that choice violated securities laws. His continuation down the parade route (so to speak), meant his continued touting of the Enron stock with statements like, "Now is a good time to buy Enron stock." Or, "We have the utmost faith in our CFO, Andy Fastow." Or "There are no accounting irregularities." All the statements he made turned out to be violations of security laws, because he was telling investors to stick with it or buy more.

What was it like to testify at the trials?

Watkins: The Congressional testimonies were very tough, high-pressure situations. In 2002, I testified for nearly five hours by myself in front of the House and for the same amount of time with Skilling in front of the Senate. Both situations were difficult, but I had thought it would be more so with Skilling sitting next to me in front of the Senate. But in the end, the senators were grilling him so

hard that I could just kind of sit back and watch. I also testified at Ken Lay's trial this past spring of 2006. That was an eerie experience. Ken Lay looked like he just found out his dog got run over by a car. He just looked sick to his stomach for the most part. But Skilling, who was also on trial with Lay ... I came to appreciate how hard it must be to be a Mafia witness, with the Don sitting there giving you that mean eye. It was unnerving. It is hard to be a witness because you are making eye contact with the person you are talking about.

What was your reaction to the news of Ken Lay's death?

Watkins: I was sad. It's very tragic. You wonder about all the pressures and whether that put him in an early grave. I was away on vacation, so I am glad I missed all the hoopla, but when I came back I was surprised at the outrage about it. People were really mad that he escaped justice. I kept wondering, "What do you mean escaped justice? He's dead." But a doctor who had been a victim of financial manipulations explained it to me. He said, "I just wanted to see Ken Lay in prison, I wanted to see that interview a decade later when some reporter went to the prison and interviewed him, because I wanted it to be a lesson for every CEO that they need to produce honest financial statements. Guys die all the time at 64; there is no lesson in that." That's a sad reaction.

What about lessons from Jeff Skilling?

Watkins: His prison sentence of 24 years is a long time. It will be a lesson. But at CEO conferences I have found that CEOs never see themselves as Skilling. They do relate to Ken Lay, but they never see themselves in Skilling's shoes. I have always thought a McKinsey consultant should never be CEO.

A lot of other companies have had similar types of scandals: Tyco, Andersen, ImClone. Have you talked with anyone involved with those organizations? Do you see similarities or differences between some of the other major corporate scandals and what happened to Enron?

Watkins: Enron represents a more systemic failure because it involved the bankers, the auditors, the lawyers, all of those hundreds of internal accountants, lawyers, finance professionals, and executives. Even Enron's board of directors waived the code of conduct twice. It involves universities touting Enron; Darden and Harvard did case studies on Enron as a model company. *Business Week*, *Fortune*, and *Forbes* all lauded the company. Wall Street analysts loved them. Most of the research analysts had Enron ranked a strong buy in October 2001, even after Skilling had left.

If you really looked at the financials, there were some glaring problems with Enron's cash flow, so glaring that the people should have seen them. When I was doing my book, I looked at Enron's press releases and then dissected the 10Qs. Skilling told the research analysts that Enron Energy Services had turned the corner. We had signed this contract and that contract, and business was looking great. But the 10Q would show all the income coming from just the pipelines or from other businesses. The 10Q did not match what he told them, but they had done their earnings reports and didn't pay attention.

Andersen was doing faulty audits for short-term gain. Vinson & Elkins were doing shoddy legal work. But it also took those banks loaning money to Enron, knowing it was debt on their books but revenues on Enron's. Citigroup and Chase both settled the Enron shareholder litigation for $2 billion apiece. When Enron declared bankruptcy, their long-term debt was $13 billion on its balance sheet. When they met with their creditors in December 2001, they announced the real long-term debt number of $38 billion. I would say at least $10 to $12 billion of the $25 billion of off balance-sheet debt was legitimate, debt that was tied to an international power plant or pipeline and had no recourse to Enron. But the other $12 to $15 billion was this funny stuff that CIBC did, that Citigroup did and Chase did, off balance-sheet debt that had claw-backs to Enron Corp.

WorldCom has the faulty research, where the Citigroup research analyst, Jack Grubman, was really pushing that stock. But for the most part, their fraud was six people from the CFO's office who moved a really big number from the income statement to the balance sheet. You have some faulty behavior from Arthur Andersen. When Cyn-

thia Cooper, in her role as internal auditor, first discovered problems, she called the Arthur Anderson partner on the WorldCom account about it, and he replied that he only talks to Scott Sullivan, the CFO of WorldCom. That is wrong. When your internal audit head says, "I think I have a problem," he should be meeting with her. So you have the faulty audit, but their board did the right stuff. She was able to go to the head of the audit committee, and they got rid of the bad seeds so to speak, and they did the right thing.

Tyco was asleep at the switchboard, so that has the board elements to it. The Adelphia board was not keeping a good rein on what the founders of the company were doing.

They can all be summed up by greed and arrogance and thinking you can get away with it. It is just that the Enron case covers it all. I had an MBA professor say, "We can make a whole semester course out of Enron. The others, we can just cover in a week or two."

Lessons Learned

What are the bigger lessons for corporations coming out of Enron?

Watkins: Capitalism requires morality and a long-term view. This has broadly broken down. For an Enron trader to be so predatory that they bankrupt their major customers in California and nearly bankrupt the state, seems to be shortsighted and stupid, because in the long run you don't have a good business when you have bankrupted your significant customers. But the money schemes and the pay schemes have gotten so far out of whack in this country that the long-term view is no longer important. If you can pump up the stock price, the energy traders could get $5 to $8 million dollar bonuses in one year. One of them is running his own multi-billion dollar hedge fund today. They didn't need to look out for Enron's long-term interests, because they can make enough to go home rich and start their own businesses.

What came out in *The Smartest Guys in the Room*, was what Andy Fastow was doing. If a banker was going to decline some business with

Enron, he would sweeten it with the promise of some investment banking business coming up. "If you can just do this one debt deal, you will move to the top on the list for the next IB deal." The bankers did not care about the long-term health of their banks, because they were making multimillion-dollar bonuses. They are now working for a hedge fund, living in the Hamptons. You do not have to have a career and work for two decades at a company to get legacy wealth anymore. You can do it pretty quickly and through funny stuff, which tears the fabric of the capitalist system apart. Even below the top tier there were problems. Several senior officials avoided indictments either by cutting deals in advance or simply by hiding in the shadows of other more prominent targets. These officials were not ethical; they were at the second tier of leadership and did the wrong thing. When the ethically challenged person, not just the outright crook, is promoted, it hurts the system.

The Future?

Are you hopeful, now that Enron has been put away, that everything is good for American business?

Watkins: Unfortunately, no. When the Enron story first broke in its full bloom around January 2002, E.J. Dionne from the *Washington Post* wrote an op-ed piece about Enron. He quoted James Madison, one of the founders of our country. Madison said that if men were angels, no government would be necessary, but men aren't angels, so we do need government. E.J. Dionne concluded that if capitalists were angels, we could deregulate everything, but obviously capitalists aren't angels.

We have had a paradigm shift and have lost some of the checks and balances of the system. I think shareholders and management used to be more connected. Up until the '80s, when I was still a public auditor, the companies I audited would get geared up for big shareholder meetings. 1,000 to 5,000 shareholders were going to show up, and there was always a sort of a buzz about one or two areas. They stayed honest because they knew of certain shareholders that read everything they ever produced, and these shareholders always got in

their face. In the '90s, everybody moved to mutual funds. No one invests in individual companies anymore. When your mutual fund isn't rising like your next-door neighbor's, you switch. The money managers know that, so they focus on the stock prices. Even the best of the best, like Vanguard, admit to rubber stamping nine out of 10 proxy statements. They get so many, they just go with management. We have lost a significant check and balance on management.

You can see that in the pay scale. In 1970, CEOs on average made 26 times more than the average worker. In 1980, it was 42 times. By 1990, it was 85 times. That is still somewhat reasonable, because in the '90s everyone moved to mutual funds and no one was really looking at proxy statements anymore but CEOs and benchmarking companies. By the year 2000, average CEO pay was 531 times above the average worker. No country in the world is even close. Great Britain is at 45. Canada is at 20. Brazil even is at 51. Japan is at 10.

Now the people like the National Association of Corporate Directors say that is a problem. The Blue Ribbon Commission at the Corporate Conference Board says that is a problem. Paul Volcker says we should do away with stock options and stock grants. CEOs should be just paid cash. The experts say this is a problem, yet nothing is happening. Pay just keeps going up. So I think it highlights that the board system in this country does not work; that we need a system that mirrors what the Europeans do, where the chairman is truly a separate role. It is never the retired CEO but a separate outside strong businessperson. Germany has an advisory board and a management board, and at least the advisory board gives backbone to the management board.

I often quote Michael Novak, who wrote *The Spirit of Democratic Capitalism*. He said that the capital system is a three-legged stool sitting on political freedom, economic freedom, and moral responsibility. Weakness in any one of the legs and the stool topples. The moral responsibility leg has had weaknesses in the past with child-labor abuse, workers' safety, and environmental pollution, and we now have laws that addressed those areas. I think it is because society had moral outrage about child labor, workers' safety, and environmental pollution.

This current problem is one of entitlement. Outrageous pay, where CEOs have put themselves first ahead of the organization, has not received the same kind of moral outrage. Unfortunately as a society, our first feeling is envy that the CEO has so much money. Then we are morally outraged. So we are not really getting behind any kind of movement, because we are still thinking, "One day I am going to be like that CEO." There is no one to point to the worker that died of cancer or lost a limb or that Lake Erie is on fire. But it is eroding the capitalist system. It is one of these things that we will look back at in a couple of decades and identify the point of no return, where we took the wrong path.

Future Leaders?

Are you hopeful about the next generation of leaders?

Watkins: Not right now. I sense from my interactions that they don't want the rules to change in the next decade, because they see the riches today's leaders have received, and they want them.

Questions for Discussion and Reflection

1. According to Watkins, what were some of the major factors that contributed to Enron's demise?
2. How did the "rank and yank" evaluation system contribute to the organizational corruption that Watkins describes?
3. Why do you think that Watkins didn't blow the whistle until the very end of her tenure at Enron?
4. What do you think of her advice, "If your values are being challenged, get out ..."?

CASE STUDIES

Case 11.1: Character and Executive Leadership

Mark Hurd was CEO of Hewlett Packard from 2005 to late 2010. He resigned unexpectedly after it was revealed that he falsified expense reports in order to hide a personal relationship with Jodie Fisher, who had worked with HP as a marketing consultant. Fisher accused Hurd of sexual harassment, of which he was cleared after an investigation by the HP board. Fisher denied having a sexual relationship with Hurd. However, they were frequent companions at CEO executive summit meetings at resort areas where HP executives met to connect with the company's top customers and woo potential ones. They regularly enjoyed long dinners together to wind down after a day of meetings. The board was reported to have terminated Hurd due to lapses in judgment that resulted from hiding the personal relationship with Fisher and falsifying the expense reports of company money spent on entertaining her. Hurd has promised to repay the expenses that were falsified.

Some suggested that HP overreacted. Larry Ellison, CEO of Oracle, called the decision to fire Hurd "the worst personnel decision since the Apple board fired Steve Jobs many years ago." Ellison later hired Hurd to be copresident of Oracle.

About the time Hurd was initially hired at HP, Boeing CEO Harry Stonecipher, who had come out of retirement to assume CEO duties, resigned after his affair with a female executive came to light. The woman did not report directly to Stonecipher, and the relationship was entirely consensual and had no impact on the woman's career path. Though the code of conduct does not specifically prohibit relationships within the company, the board said that the relationship had violated the section of the code that addressed hurting the reputation of the company. The board held that the affair reflected poorly on Stonecipher's judgment and "would impair his ability to lead the company going forward."

Sources

Sean Gregory, "Corporate Scandals: Why HP Had to Oust Mark Hurd," *TIME.com*, August 10, 2010, http://www.time.com/time/business/article/0,8599,2009617,00.html.

Chris Isidore, "Boeing CEO Out in Sex Scandal," *CNNMoney.com*, March 7, 2005, http://money.cnn.com/2005/03/07/news/fortune500/boeing_ceo/.

Questions for Discussion

1. What do you think is the connection between a person's character in private life and his or her ability to lead an organization?
2. Do you think the departure of Mark Hurd from HP was justified? Why or why not?
3. Is Harry Stonecipher's affair with a woman in the company enough of a reason to force his resignation? Defend your answer.

Case 11.2: Washington Mutual Mortgage Scandal

Washington Mutual, the largest American bank ever to fail, was found by a U.S. Senate investigation to have engaged in mortgage fraud. The Senate report concluded that WaMu created a "mortgage time bomb" by their involvement in subprime lending (to risky borrowers) and then selling off the fraudulent loans to investors in the form of risky mortgage-backed securities. The environment at the company was a mixture of high pressure from executives to close loans, enormous amounts of money to be made by doing so, and management turning a blind eye to fraud when it could have been stopped.

What began as Long Beach Mortgage Company (later bought out by WaMu), ended in bankruptcy, with foreclosure rates on its loans approaching 50 percent in some cities. Long Beach Mortgage was at one time one of the largest subprime lenders, and their story is similar to others in the industry, such as Ameriquest, Countrywide, and Argent Mortgage. A combination of lax lending practices and explicit management strategy to pursue the riskier subprime market led to the collapse of the subprime market and the bank itself. Exorbitant commissions and bonuses were paid to mortgage sales staff who met the demanding quotas each month. The salespeople were the heroes of the company and were rewarded very well. But the loan reviewers were among the lowest paid and were routinely ostracized by the top management. Among the practices that were commonplace at Long Beach Mortgage and later at WaMu were removing pages from files, forging documents, making up pay stubs and tax returns that document income, coaching brokers on how to forge documents, not requiring down payments or verification of income (the latter commonly called "liars loans"), giving kickbacks to loan reviewers to overlook questionable loans, making loans to people who had little ability to repay them, and often omitting critical information to borrowers about the terms of loans. Enormous pressure came from the top to close as many loans as possible, without regard to the credit-worthiness of the borrowers, since the bank would package the loans into securities for sale to investors. Management made the decision to go aggressively for the higher risk, subprime market, since it was more profitable than conventional mortgage loans. This shift, in addition to the money to be made in subprime, put significant pressure on the bank's mortgage origination staff to sell as many loans as they could.

Until it collapsed in 2008–9, WaMu made substantial profits on the loans, as Wall Street bought them in record numbers, paying huge fees to the bank for the service. It seemed as if the run would never end, until borrowers began to default in record numbers, thereby making the securities based on those loans drop in value. It turned out that the bank had kept many of the securities and the mortgages for themselves, since the interest rate was so high (given the riskiness of the borrowers), that when the defaults started in earnest, the bank was essentially insolvent.

Sources

David Heath, "At Top Subprime Mortgage Lender, Policies Were Invitation to Fraud," *Huffington Post*, December 21, 2009, http://huffpostfund.org/stories/2009/12/top-subprime-mortgage-lender-policies-were-invitation-fraud.

David Heath, "WaMu Executives Knew of Rampant Mortgage Fraud and Failed to Act," *Huffington Post*, April 12, 2010, http://www.huffingtonpost.com/2010/04/12/wamu-bank-executives-aware-rampant-fraud.

Jim Puzzanghera and E. Scott Reckard, "Washington Mutual Created 'Mortgage Time Bomb,' Senate Panel Says," *Los Angeles Times*, April 13, 2010, D1.

Questions for Discussion

1. You can read more about the WaMu failure at http://huffpostfund. org/stories/2009/12/top-subprime-mortgage-lender-policies-were-invitation-fraud. After reading this article, what do you think went wrong at WaMu that enabled the bank employees to engage in such widespread fraud? What do the articles by Trevino and Brown and Darley suggest about how such unethical behavior begins and is maintained in an organization?

2. What parallels do you see between WaMu and the environment at Enron that Sherron Watkins describes?

3. If you were the CEO of WaMu, what would you have done differently in order to either prevent or stop the fraud from occurring?

COMMENTARY

Organizations of all varieties have a greater stake than ever in developing and implementing policies that encourage ethical behavior within their ranks. In a climate of economic downturns, increased competition, and downsizing, temptations to cut ethical corners are greater than ever. The resulting damage caused by revelations of immoral behavior on the part of executives and employees can have a lasting impact on public trust and internal morale. In addition, companies can be punished and/or given leniency by the law, according to the steps that they have taken to either encourage or prevent misconduct on the part of its employees. As a result, companies are implementing policies that encourage ethical behavior in the workplace. It is now common for companies to have ethics and compliance offices and ethics executives to staff them. Many others pay consultants to provide ethics awareness and training sessions for their employees. Most companies have at least written ethics into their mission statements and have developed detailed corporate codes of conduct governing specific situations that employees may face in the course of their duties.

Despite the money being poured into these efforts, some critics loudly wonder whether ethics can truly be "taught" and fostered within the context of corporations.[2] To these critics, ethics is something that is learned in the family and is mostly a matter of personal character or integrity. Consequently, it is reasoned that in the absence of values in one's upbringing, it is too late to try and teach ethics to employees during a daylong or even a weeklong training session. However, Aristotle rightly reminds us that although

[2] See, e.g., Andrew Bartlett and David Preston, "Can Ethical Behavior Really Exist in Business?" *Journal of Business Ethics* 23 (2000): 199–209. See also Thomas R. Piper, Mary C. Gentile, and Sharon Daloz Parks, *Can Ethics Be Taught? Perspectives, Challenges, and Approaches at the Harvard Business School* (Cambridge, Mass.: Harvard Business School Press, 1993).

ethics starts with a good upbringing, they develop during the course of life through practical experience and critical reflection. Both Christian theology and contemporary social psychology affirm that we are fundamentally social beings. As a result, a person's moral development occurs in community. The first community in which it is shaped is the family, but other communities, including the workplace, make a difference in a person's character formation. Thus, while perhaps not quite affirming Lynn Sharp Paine's assertion that "ethics has everything to do with management," it seems clear that organizations can and do have a very real impact on the beliefs and behaviors of its members through both formal and informal mechanisms.[3] Fostering good ethics is not simply a matter of hiring morally upright people in the hope that their values will guide the organization's decisions. In many scandals, it is not "bad apples" in the form of rogue individuals or executives who explicitly set out to defraud the public, though that is often the explanation give to the public. Rather, it is usually a combination of organizational and environmental factors that play the biggest role in creating the "bad barrel" that leads to unethical actions. Trevino and Brown are correct in their insistence that corporate unethical behavior cannot be explained by the "bad apple" theory alone, and that most people "look up and look around" in the organization for ethical guidelines. Darley echoes this in his point that producing an environment conducive to ethics involves much more than simply screening out the bad apples.

In almost every well-publicized scandal in the business world, a group of well-educated and respected participants get caught in actions that seem to go beyond the bounds of how they would act as individuals. Coworkers, family members, neighbors, and fellow church congregants usually express shock and disbelief that the people they know as responsible employees, spouses, and citizens could actually commit illegal and immoral acts. How is it that otherwise good moral people in reputable organizations can get caught up in actions that would undoubtedly violate their individual consciences and also rationalize away their responsibility?

One possible explanation to this pressing question has to do with the nature and structure of organizations. For years, sociologists and psychologists have undertaken detailed studies of these entities and their effects on the beliefs and behaviors of their individual members. If they are accurate, their conclusions are startling, because they have found that individual members of groups will commit acts in violation of their own beliefs for the sake of obeying authority and going along with the group. Trevino and Brown suggest that "most people, including adults, are *followers* when it comes to ethics." They emphasize that the organization helps to form the person morally — that they are not entirely finished products when it comes

[3] Lynn Sharp Paine, "Managing for Organizational Integrity," *Harvard Business Review* 72, no. 2 (March–April 1994): 106.

to their ethics. Darley suggests that corrupt sequences are initiated as people "commit actions that are self-serving or unduly favorable to the organization in which they are situated." And the key point that Darley makes here is that these actions do not receive any scrutiny, but instead "set in motion a cascade of further corrupt actions." Darley calls these the "generative actions of corruption." Trevino and Brown further suggest that a myth of business ethics is that individuals always recognize the ethical issues that emerge (they most often do not), and that the language used to describe the issue can be a powerful part of the rationalization for unethical behavior. Management scholars Vikas Anand, Blake Ashforth, and Mahendra Joshi point out that there are a variety of "rationalization tactics" that allow what Darley calls the initiating stage of corruption to take root. These include denial of responsibility ("I had no choice"), denial of injury ("No one was harmed" or "Everyone is doing it"), denial of victim ("They deserved it"), and social weighting ("Others are worse than us").[4] One of the significant contributing factors to this organizational dynamic is known as "groupthink," which is defined as

> a mode of thinking that people engage in when they are deeply involved in a cohesive in-group, when the members striving for unanimity override their motivation to realistically appraise alternative courses of actions.... Group think refers to the deterioration of mental efficiency, reality testing, and moral judgment that results from in-group pressures.[5]

When groupthink occurs, the morality of a group decision or action goes unquestioned by the individuals within it. Darley describes how the original unethical action triggers a chain of other actions with his metaphor of "entrainment," which describes "a perceptual phenomenon": an object is moving in one direction. As it passes other stationary objects, those objects themselves begin to move, and they move in the same direction as the original object. Groupthink marginalizes anyone who is perceived as moving in the opposite direction.

Undoubtedly, these dynamics have a direct relevance for business ethics. Although we have focused mainly on ethical issues and decision making up until this point in this book, correct courses of action are not debated and undertaken in an organizational vacuum. Most business decisions and transactions are made within the context of organizational and group pressures. Consequently, most of us have or will face similar situations during careers in a variety of professions. As such, we must be aware of the effect of organizational pressures on the morals and actions of their individual members. The two following incidents are good examples of these dynamics at work:

WorldCom, the phone company that eventually merged with MCI, was guilty of the largest accounting fraud in U.S. history, reporting accounting

[4] Vikas Anand, Blake E. Ashforth, and Mahendra Joshi, "Business as Usual: The Acceptance and Perpetuation of Corruption in Organizations," *Academy of Management Executive* 18, no. 3 (November 2004): 9–23.

[5] Irving L. Janus, *Victims of Groupthink* (Boston: Houghton Mifflin, 1972), 9.

restatements to the total of $11 billion and having been fined $750 million. The SEC report cited the culture created by CEO Bernard Ebbers as a leading contributing factor to the fraudulent accounting practices. Specifically, within the organization there was a significant emphasis on teamwork and group cohesion, and given the pressures of a very competitive industry at the time, led to enormous pressure to maintain the company's earnings and stock price so that it could continue its aggressive growth. In addition, employees felt substantial pressure to avoid expressing opinions that would differ from the group consensus, thereby marginalizing any critics who might have stopped the trend toward fraud.[6] This is parallel to the Enron debacle, which Sherron Watkins describes in her reading in this chapter. She outlines a corporate culture in which people were penalized for deviating from the group consensus or for questioning the company's ways of doing business.

A second example comes from the space shuttle *Challenger* disaster. In the months leading up to the launch, executives at Morton Thiokol and NASA had ample evidence and warnings by several key engineers that O-ring failure would likely lead to an explosion shortly after ignition. The pressure to conduct the launch on schedule was enormous, and as a result, those who issued these warnings were not taken seriously and their opinions were dismissed. The *Challenger* exploded seventy-three seconds into flight, killing the seven astronauts on board.[7] Many companies have socialization processes, the goal of which is to inculcate employees with organizational values and orient them to the company's way of doing business. This socialization process continues more informally as the organization seeks to create loyalty and commitment on the part of the employee. Many of these informal practices of the corporate culture serve to reinforce specific behaviors through peer pressure, reward, and punishment. Those who play by the rules are clearly rewarded through praise, promotions, and pay increases. Non-team players are discouraged through threats of embarrassment, demotion, and the potential of being fired. Of course, loyalty and commitment are good things that companies are correct to encourage and that contribute to their ability to run smoothly. However, when these traits inhibit critical thinking and moral courage, they have moved from group cohesion to groupthink. Anand, Ashforth, and Joshi emphasize that employees can be socialized into corrupt practices by getting co-opted into unethical behavior incrementally. As Darley rightly points out, group cohesion can be the reason why unethical behavior, when detected, is not repudiated or the whistle is not blown on the parties responsible. Further, this emphasis on group cohesion, according to Darley, is what facilitates recruitment into corruption. When group cohesion is especially effective, the group can actually become something like a social cocoon, in which the employee compartmentalizes his or her life inside the

[6] M. M. Scharff, "Understanding WorldCom's Accounting Fraud: Did Groupthink Play a Role?" *Journal of Leadership and Organizational Studies* (Spring 2005).

[7] Gregory Moorhead et al., "Group Decision Fiascoes Continue: Space Shuttle Challenger and a Revised Groupthink Framework," *Human Relations* 44, no. 6 (June 1991): 539–50; Howard S. Schwartz, "On the Psychodynamics of Organizational Disaster: The Case of the Space Shuttle Challenger," *Columbia Journal of World Business* 22, no. 1 (Spring 1987): 59–67.

organization and plays by a different set of rules.[8] Sherron Watkins's description of the environment at Enron seems to at least partially fit this concept.

In addition to peer pressure, the deck is further stacked against ethics in organizations by the nature of hierarchical organizations.[9] The specialization of task and the division of labor that comes with bureaucratic structures prevents many employees from seeing the larger contexts and consequences of their actions. Those at lower levels are sometimes told that they don't have the big picture, and that it will be top management's responsibility if "anything happens." Thus, it is easier to "leave the driving" to others and to claim that they were "only following orders" than to assume responsibility.

The experience of Sherron Watkins and others at Enron is a good illustration of the institutional factors that can work against someone who desires to exercise moral courage. Competition in conjunction with groupthink and the demands of authority created enormous pressures on individuals to abandon conscience for the sake of the group's perceived well-being. Peer pressure and hierarchy further added to the deck-stacking effect. Watkins describes the "rank and yank" system of ranking employees annually, to decide not only bonuses, but who would have jobs in the next year. Enron employees were so cautious about doing anything that could affect their annual review before the "rank and yank" committee that they rarely took their reservations very far in the organization.

When it comes to building an organizational environment that is conducive to ethics, some of the *formal* mechanisms for accomplishing this include reporting relationships and incentive systems. Trevino and Brown rightly emphasize how important it is to know the existing ethical culture of the organization and communicate the standards and expectations clearly with formal codes of ethical behavior and regular education to further awareness. They further stress that the reward system of the organization can encourage ethical behavior or it can reward corruption.

The case of Sears Auto Centers is an example of this reward phenomenon.[10] As a result of numerous complaints and a statewide undercover operation, the state of California found that Sears was overcharging its customers by recommending unnecessary auto repair work—on an average of $235 per customer. In this situation, employees were inadvertently encouraged to commit fraud, because the only way for them to meet unrealistic sales goals established by higher management was to perform unnecessary "preventive" service. It certainly appears that no individual schemed to defraud the public. Rather, the reward system—unrealistically high quotas with threats of job loss, and commissions for what they sold in their roles as service advisers, directly contributed to a reward climate that was ripe for misconduct. Unethical behaviors will likely occur if they are rewarded.

[8] Anand, Ashforth and Joshi, "Business as Usual," 16.

[9] For more on this, see H. R. Smith and Archie B. Carroll, "Organizational Ethics: A Stacked Deck," *Journal of Business Ethics* 3, no. 2 (May 1984): 95–100.

[10] Cited in Paine, "Managing for Organizational Integrity," 107–8.

The reward system can also work in a positive direction. For example, beginning in the late 1990s, Conoco established the annual President's Award for Business Ethics. It is awarded to the employee who has exceeded the compliance expectations and who provides an "extraordinary example of leadership that demonstrates excellence in conduct" and is a "role model whose behavior embodies what Conoco stands for." Employees are nominated by peers, and a selection committee reviews the nominations and makes the final selection. The purpose of the award is to underscore Conoco's value of conducting business with the highest ethical standards.[11] Other formal mechanisms can also play a role in the shaping of culture through the development of creedal statements, the implementation of training programs, and the articulation of specific guidelines for employees. Efforts in these arenas will undeniably contribute to the infusing of ethics into the company climate. However, as Trevino and Brown emphasize, creeds and codes are insufficient if they are not enforced through formal mechanisms such as performance reviews and compensation- and promotion-related decisions. In fact, many critics have remarked that ethics codes and training programs are really no more than mere "window dressing" that serves as a useful public relations tool to ward off scrutiny and governmental interference. Indeed, many companies that are caught crossing ethical and legal lines have mission statements that claim ethics as a high priority. Thus, the developed creeds and codes must be lived as well as preached. If the stated values have no teeth to them, or if employees see executives betray them, some employees will swiftly catch on and likely revert to the behaviors that are, in fact, rewarded.

Moreover, a legalistic devotion to a codified compliance program is insufficient. Ethics must become a key part of strategic planning and objectives through the cultivation of integrity as the governing ethic. An ethic of integrity and trust that goes beyond mere legalistic compliance is a much better way of encouraging moral corporate climates. Compliance programs usually generate an environment where employees fear authority structures, and ethics is perceived as a top-down product created by management to catch employees and serve as liability protection.

In contrast, an "integrity strategy" encourages all employees to take ownership of ethics as a total corporate objective.[12] Managers at all levels and across functions need to be involved for a successful implementation of an integrity ethic. Involving managers at all levels in the discussion indeed serves to raise awareness and foster a sense of ownership of the objectives. We would add that even nonmanagerial employees must be involved in the dialogue. Environments of truly open two-way communications must be carefully cultivated if all employees are to be free to stand up to group and peer

[11] See the discussion of this award in O. C. Ferrell, John Fraedrich, and Linda Ferrell, *Business Ethics: Ethical Decision Making and Cases*, 6th ed. (New York: Houghton Mifflin, 2005): 377–95.

[12] See Paine, "Managing for Organizational Integrity," for more on the difference between compliance and ethics.

pressures. Phenomenon such as groupthink and blind obedience to authority can only be minimized by a climate that truly values a diversity of opinions. As Sears and other companies have found out, it is often employees at the lowest level of the hierarchy for whom ethical decisions are most pressing, since they are the ones in the trenches. Furthermore, many organizations are successful because they value innovative and creative thinking that challenges the group consensus. Thus, a climate where communication channels are open and feedback is welcome will likely contribute to both the financial and the ethical well-being of a company.

In addition to these formal mechanisms, informal ones further serve to shape behaviors. For example, every organization has a culture with its own stories, creeds, and norms for behavior that develops over a period of time. Narrative and stories can be powerful guides for action and socialization, because they communicate much about an organization's values. For example, the hero of a company tale may be one who possessed a moral voice and dared speak out against some unethical practice.

Usually, company management plays a significant role in developing the culture by telling these stories, developing creeds, and articulating and enforcing the company's values. If, however, company leadership does not articulate and model the values, a culture will evolve all on its own. Thus, the critical question is whether that culture will be one that fosters or actively discourages ethical behaviors on the part of employees. To have a better chance at the former, company leadership must be proactive in helping to shape the moral values of the corporate culture that develops. Although the saying "It starts at the top" now sounds like a well-worn cliché, company leadership, especially the CEO, is the critical values setter for the company, though as Trevino and Brown point out, that by itself is not adequate to insure an ethical culture. The leader's attitude toward ethics will often set the whole tone for the organization, both in what is said and what is modeled. Clearly when that which is modeled is somehow different than the message that is articulated verbally, that is an enormous setback for an ethical environment, since employees do what their superiors do, not what they say, when words and deeds conflict.

Conclusion

Companies can encourage moral corporate climates by the infusion of values through corporate culture and through the modeling of integrity on the part of executives who set the tone for the whole organization. However, talk of ethics in mission statements, creeds, and codes become empty if it is not seen as part of the long-term mission of the organization. Ethics must be rewarded through formal policies such as performance reviews and promotion decisions. Organizations must begin on the path to the creation of ethical climates by taking a long-term view and making ethics a key component of strategic planning. Only then will ethics filter downward and become a matter of day-to-day operating policy.

Our goal in this chapter has been to explain, and not excuse, the conditions for unethical behavior that occur in some organizations. If education can accomplish anything, it can raise our awareness about our tendencies to conform and can show us ways we can avoid these types of actions. Hopefully, being aware of our own propensities to go against our own moral convictions in the face of authoritarian and social pressures will be one step in the path of allowing us to stand for that which is morally right.

Credits

The authors are grateful to the publishers and copyright owners for permission to reprint the articles that appear in the Readings of this book.

Chapter 1

"Upgrading the Ethical Decision Making Model for Business," by David W. Gill, *Business and Professional Ethics Journal* 23.4 (Winter 2004): 135–51. Copyright © David W. Gill.

"The Bible in Culture and Ethics," by Bernard T. Adeney, in *Strange Virtues: Ethics in a Multicultural World* (Downers Grove, IL: InterVarsity Press, 1995), 79–105.

The Moral Context of Business, by Donald D. Schmeltekopf, Baylor School of Business, 2003. Copyright © Donald D. Schmeltekopf, 2003.

Chapter 2

"Is Business Bluffing Ethical?" by Albert Z. Carr. Reprinted by permission of *Harvard Business Review* (January-February 1968). Copyright © 1967 by the President and Fellows of Harvard College; all rights reserved.

"Why Be Honest if Honesty Doesn't Pay?" by Amar Bhide and Howard H. Stevenson. Reprinted by permission of *Harvard Business Review* (January-February 1990). Copyright © 1967 by the President and Fellows of Harvard College; all rights reserved.

"The Business of Business," by Dallas Willard, *Trinity Forum* (October 2006).

Chapter 3

"The Entrepreneurial Vocation," by Fr. Robert Sirico, *Journal of Markets and Morality* 3, no. 1 (Spring 2000): 1–21. Copyright © Center for Economic Personalism.

"Tough Business: In Deep, Swift Waters," by Steve Brinn, *Vocatio* 2, no. 2 (July 1999): 3–6. Copyright © 1999.

"Christ and Business," by Louke Van Wensveen Skier, *Journal of Business Ethics* 8 (1989): 883–88. Copyright © 1989, Kluwer Academic Publishers. Reprinted by permission of Kluwer Academic Publishers.

Chapter 4

"The Myth of CSR," by Deborah Doane, *Stanford Social Innovation Review* (Fall 2005). Copyright © 2005 by Leland Stanford Jr. University; all rights reserved.

"A Long-Term Perspective in a Short-Term World: A Conversation with Jim Sinegal," by Albert M. Erisman and David Gill, in *Ethix* (March/April 2003): 6–9, 16. Copyright © 2003.

"Rethinking the Social Responsibility of Business: A Reason Debate featuring Milton Friedman, John Mackey and TJ Rodgers," *Reason* (October 1, 2005). Copyright © 2005, Reason Magazine and Reason.com

Chapter 5

Globalization, Poverty and Economic Development: Insights from Centesimus Annus by Brian Griffiths (Grand Rapids, MI: Acton Institute, 2007). Copyright © 2007 Acton Institute.

"Globalization and the Poor: Reflections of a Christian Economist," by Bruce Wydick, *PRISM* 2007): 8–2, 15. This article originally appeared in the March-April 2007 issue of *PRISM* magazine (www.esa-online.org.PRISM).

"Corporate Social Responsibility in a Globalizing World: What's a Christian Executive to Do?" by Steven Rundle,in *Business and Professional Ethics Journal* 23:4 (2004): 171–83. Copyright © 2004, Business and Professional Ethics Journal.

Chapter 6

"Sweatshops," by Matt Zwolinski, in *Social Issues in America: An Encyclopedia*, vol. 7, ed. by Jim Ciment (Armonk, NY: ME Sharpe, 2006): 1640–48. Copyright © 2006 by ME Sharpe, Inc. Reprinted with permission.

"Ethical Theory and Bribery," by Bernard T. Adeney, in *Strange Virtues: Ethics in Multicultural World* (Downers Grove, IL: InterVarsity Press, 1995).

Fair Trade: Its Prospects as a Poverty Solution, by Victor V. Claar (Grand Rapids, MI: Acton Institute 2010). Copyright © 2010 Acton Institute.

"Moving the Fair Trade Agenda Forward by Paul Chandler," *Faith and Business Quarterly* 9:2 (2005): 25–30.

Chapter 7

"Mission as an Organizing Principle," by C. William Pollard, in *Leader to Leader* 16 (Spring 2000): 17–21. Copyright © 2000 by C. William Pollard. Reprinted with permission from *Leader to Leader*, a publication of the Leader to Leader Institute and Jossey-Bass.

Ethix Interview with Cheryl Brotje: An Orchard with Fruit that Lasts, by Al Erisman and Kenman Wong, in *Ethix* 44 (November 1, 2005): 1–5. Copyright © 2005.

"Building Healthy Organizations in Which People Can Flourish," by Richard Beaton and Linda Wagoner, in *Theology News and Notes* 57, no. 1 (Spring 2010): 1–4.

Albert M. Erisman, "Technology and the New Challenges of Management."

Chapter 8

"Accounting and Accountability: Double Entry, Double Nature, Double Identity," by Ian Stewart, *Crux* 26, 2 (June 1990): 13–20.

"Ethical Failures in Corporate Financial Reporting," by George J. Staubus, in *Journal of Business Ethics* 57 (2005): 5–15.

"The Moral Imperative of Investment Banking," by John Terrill, in *Cardus Comment*, February 26, 2010. This article originally appeared in *Comment* magazine, the opinion journal of CARDUS: www.cardus.ca/comment.